THE INDEX LIBRARY

ARCHDEACONRY OF SUDBURY PROBATE RECORDS

1354 — 1700

ISSUED BY
THE BRITISH RECORD SOCIETY

[96]

THE INDEX LIBRARY

INDEX OF THE PROBATE RECORDS

OF THE

COURT OF THE ARCHDEACON OF SUDBURY 1354 — 1700

Volume II

L - Z

Compiled by

M. E. GRIMWADE

Edited by

W. R. AND R. K. SERJEANT

Issued to Subscribers by

THE BRITISH RECORD SOCIETY

1984

Published by

The British Record Society, Limited

c/o Department of History, University of Keele, Keele, Staffordshire ST5 5BG

ISBN 0 901505 12 9 (Parts 1 and 2)
0 901505 14 5 (Part 2, L — Z)

This volume has been published with the aid of a grant from the British Academy and also generous financial assistance from Mr. John B. Threlfall of Madison, Wisconsin, which are most gratefully acknowledged.

Printed by Parchment (Oxford) Ltd., Oxford

CONTENTS

LIST OF ABBREVIATIONS

A	administration bond or act
als.	alias
bach.	bachelor
esq.	esquire
gent.	gentleman
husb.	husbandman
In.	inventory
jun.	junior
(N)	nuncupative will
R	Registered copy of will
sen.	senior
W	original will
wid.	widow(er)
yeo.	yeoman

Note: Where the date given in an entry is enclosed in brackets, this denotes that it is not the date of probate, but the date of the making of the will.

LACAS, George, husb., Elmswell, 1581. R2/38/264; W1/40/13
LACEBE, Christopher, Ellough, (1541). W1/51/67
LACFORD, John, Bury St. Edmunds, 1378. R2/1/38
LACFORTH, Richard, chaplain, Bury St. Edmunds, 1361. R2/1/13
LACK, Elizabeth, Stowlangtoft, 1610, (N). R2/47/191; W1/67/69
Frances, wid., Haverhill, 1699. R2/73/361; W1/153/21
Francis, Clare, 1690, (N). R2/71/314; W1/144/14; A5/6/133, A4/32/25
Henry, Clare, 1637. A5/4/53
John, Tuddenham, 1548. R2/21/462
LACY, Hugh, Walsham le Willows, 1529. R2/18/41
John, Lakenheath, 1528. R2/15/193
John, Sudbury, 1697. A5/7/3, A4/40/43
Mary, wid., Sudbury, 1698. A5/7/5 & 10
Nicholas, Naughton, 1523. R2/14/99
Richard, scrivener, Bury St. Edmunds, 1561. R2/8/372; W1/17/34
Rose, Edwardstone, 1568. A5/1/193
Thomas, yeo., Bury St. Edmunds, 1593. R2/42/343; W1/50/8
Thomas, the elder, gent., Walsham le Willows, 1574. R2/37/45; W1/33/16
Thomas, Walsham le Willows, 1647. A5/4/117
Walter, Hitcham, 1585. R2/39/359; W1/42/246a
William, Lakenheath, 1483. R2/11/302; W1/9/4
William, Lakenheath, (1508). R2/13/200
LADDE, John, tailor, Bury St. Edmunds, 1434. R2/1/207
Margaret, spinster, Bury St. Edmunds, 1450. R2/2/32
Thomas, Bury St. Edmunds, 1462. R2/2/28
LADEMAN, John, Little Whelnetham, 1547. R2/21/322; W1/10/150
William, yeo., Icklingham, 1673. R2/65/476; W1/125/113
LADYMAN, Clement, Little Whelnetham, 1537. R2/20/59; W1/4/47
Elisabeth, Bury St. Edmunds, 1556, (N). R2/8/293; W1/18/20
John, yeo., Little Whelnetham, 1625. R2/53/308; W1/81/93
Robert, Ashfield, 1630. A5/4/7
Susan, wid., Lidgate, 1630. R2/55/184; W1/86/203
Thomas, husb., Knettishall, 1674. R2/66/1; W1/126/126
Thomas, Little Whelnetham, 1469. R2/10/439
William, maltster, Icklingham, 1620. R2/52/45; W1/76/41
William, Little Whelnetham, (1553). R2/31/205
see also Ledeyman
LADYSMAN, John, sen., Great Finborough, 1440. R2/9/25
LAGDEN, Grace, als. Ewsden, Clare, 1678. A5/6/1, A4/15/1
William, gent., physician, Clare, 1686. R2/70/448; W1/140/60; In. 3/22/41
William, Denston, 1694. A5/6/170, A4/37/50
LAGGARD, John, Lavenham, 1439. R2/9/14
LAHAM, Elisabeth, wid., Mellis, 1540. R2/19/280; W1/36/39
LAIE, Ellen, Glemsford, 1573. A5/1/254
LAITHAM, Robert, Mellis, (1522). R2/15/41
LAKE, Robert, Bury St. Edmunds, 1466. R2/2/92
see also Lakke
LAKEIS, Edmund, Clare, 1661. In. 3/6/76; A5/5/15, A4/77/107
LAKERS, Edmund, cordwainer, Bradfield St. George, 1625. R2/53/310; W1/81/95
Henry, husb., Great Whelnetham, 1612. R2/48/231; W1/69/130; A5/3/118
William, Bradfield St. George, 1588. A5/2/112
LAKKE, Thomas, Snailwell, 1462. R2/10/373
LAKYNGHETH, Edward, Gislingham, 1405. R2/1/103
LAKYS, Richard, Culford, 1595. A5/2/204
LALLEFORD, John, Bury St. Edmunds, 1423. R2/1/164
Michael, shearman, Bury St. Edmunds, 1415. R2/1/136
LAMAN, John, husb., Bildeston, 1592. R2/42/216; W1/49/35
Thomas, Great Finborough, 1591. R2/42/43; W1/48/35
LAMB(E), Alice, wid., Bury St. Edmunds, 1534. R2/7/24
Ann, singlewoman, Stanningfield, 1664. A5/5/59, A4/2/60
Avis, wid., Ixworth, 1636. R2/57/14; W1/92/19
Barbara, wid., Thelnetham, 1634. R2/56/370; W1/90/145
Edmund, linen weaver, Redgrave, 1649. R2/60/255; W1/106/118
George, tailor, Thelnetham, 1660. R2/62/149; W1/112/193; In. 3/5/221
Henry, gent., Drinkstone, 1676. R2/66/394; W1/128/106; In. 3/19/132

LAMB(E) continued
Henry, Thorpe Morieux, 1672. A5/5/130, A4/9/29
John, husb., Buxhall, 1558. R2/27/223
John, Hartest, 1630. A5/4/3
Judith, wid., Haughley, 1599. R2/44/295; W1/57/92
Mildred, Fakenham, 1594. A5/2/195
Robert, Clare, 1526. R2/17/198; W1/24/35
Robert, Lakenheath, 1553. R2/23/113; W1/11/121
Robert, Redgrave, 1598. R2/44/149; W1/56/141
Robert, joiner, Westhorpe, 1559. R2/28/39; W1/22/40
Thomas, Stowmarket, 1694. A5/6/167, A4/37/7
Thomas, Wicken, 1563. R2/31/146; W1/26/28
Walter, Great Wratting, 1584. A5/2/58
Walter, Great Wratting, 1587. A5/2/86
William, Haughley, 1473. R2/10/547
William, carpenter, Haughley, 1593. R2/42/362; W1/50/30
see also Lodge als. Lambe
LAMBARD, Alice, Bury St. Edmunds, 1468. R2/2/113
Aneys, Bildeston, (1490). W1/24/54
John, Haverhill, 1520. R2/15/81
LAMBART, Annice, wid., Cowlinge, (1487). R2/11/412
LAMBERD, Henry, ploughwright, Lavenham, 1621, (N). R2/52/251; W1/77/37
James, tailor, Icklingham, 1627. R2/54/2; W1/83/5
Richard, Lavenham, 1453. R2/9/159
Richard, Whepstead, 1445. R2/9/92
Robert, tailor, Icklingham, 1674. R2/66/115; W1/126/6
LAMBERT, Alice, wid., Nayland, 1670. R2/65/2; W1/122/2; In. 3/15/15
Daniel, Hitcham, 1635. A5/4/38
John, Bures, 1638. A5/4/66
John, yeo., Combs, 1679. R2/67/473; W1/133/194
Mary, wid., Long Melford, 1667. R2/64/276; W1/119/140; In. 3/12/141
Richard, Combs, 1693. A5/6/161, A4/35/40
Robert, Buxhall, 1691. A5/6/140, A4/33/22
Robert, Kettlebaston, 1650. R2/61/342; W1/107/37; In. 3/3/49
Robert, Soham, 1669. In. 3/14/146; A5/5/99, A4/6/94
Thomas, husb., Soham, 1604. R2/45/346; W1/62/66a & b
Thomas, Thorndon, 1608. A5/3/53
William, cooper, Cavenham, 1683. R2/69/114; W1/137/90
William, Eye, 1586. A5/2/78
LAMBETT, James, tailor, Icklingham, 1662. In. 3/7/114; A5/5/32
LAMBIRD, Nathan, Lavenham, 1660. R2/62/107; W1/112/141; In. 3/5/143
LAMBLY, Anthony, Sudbury, 1636. A5/4/46
LAME, Thomas, Fordham, 1556. R2/25/65; W1/16/91
LAMKYN, John, Withersfield, 1520. R2/15/19
LAMLEY, Grace, wid., Sudbury, 1638. R2/57/326; W1/93/106
see also Lambly
LAMSEY, John, Glemsford, 1633. A5/4/27
LAMYE, John, Bildeston, 1548. R2/21/467
LAMYNGE, Richard, Bury St. Edmunds, 1506. R2/4/176
LANAM, John, the elder, Redlingfield, 1559. R2/28/236; W1/22/188
LANCASTER, Ann, wid., Newmarket, 1661. R2/62/272; W1/113/173; In. 3/6/237
Geoffrey, gent., Ousden, 1599. R2/44/273; W1/57/77
John, Clare, 1692. In. 3/24/43; A5/6/151, A4/34/37
Margaret, wid. of Matthew, gent., Bury St. Edmunds, 1662. R2/62/356; W1/114/79; In. 3/8/161
Matthew, gent., Bury St. Edmunds, 1634. R2/56/387; W1/90/166
Susanna, wid., Clare, 1693. R2/72/266; W1/147/153
Thomas, mercer, Bury St. Edmunds, 1675. R2/66/124; W1/127/1; In. 3/16/7
Thomas, Mildenhall, 1640. A5/4/85
Timothy, Newmarket, 1637. A5/4/50
see also Lancestre
LANCE, Edmund, servant, West Stow, 1601. R2/44/435; W1/59/35
Richard, Hopton, 1514. R2/12/88
LANCESTRE, Thomas, Ashley, 1517. R2/12/13
LANCKESTER, Henry, Clare, 1627. R2/54/57; W1/83/61

LAND, John, Wattisfield, 1695. R2/72/547; W1/149/103
John, Wyverstone, 1610. A5/3/101
Julia, wid., Wyverstone, 1615. R2/49/368; W1/72/135
LANDEMER, Ann, wid., Brome, 1611. R2/48/4; W1/68/21
see also Landimer
LANDER, Margaret, wid., Cavenham, 1636. A5/4/47
LANDIMER, William, cordwainer, Drinkstone, 1682. R2/68/454; W1/136/137; In. 3/21/71
LANDISDALE, John, the elder, clothier, Bury St. Edmunds, 1586. R2/40/48; W1/43/36
LANDMAN, William, labouring man, Buxhall, 1663. R2/63/53; W1/115/85
LANDSELL, Edward, cordwainer, Bury St. Edmunds, 1690. R2/71/332; W1/144/36
LANE, Edward, Newmarket, 1685. A5/6/96, A4/24/140 a & b
Henry, Badingham, 1675. R2/66/188; W1/127/63
Henry, Chippenham, 1675. In. 3/16/85
Isabel, West Stow, 1440. R2/9/9
James, bach., Kennett, 1679. A5/6/23, A4/16/83
John, Fordham, 1532. R2/19/116
John, Ixworth, 1442. R2/9/18
John, Nayland, 1454. R2/9/169
John, Nayland, 1471. R2/10/474
John, Soham, 1638. A5/4/61
John, Soham, 1671. A5/5/120, A4/8/5
John, fuller, Sudbury, 1557. R2/26/79; W1/20/46
Katherine, Rickinghall Superior, 1511. R2/13/201
Peter, Nayland, 1446. R2/9/83
Ralph, Bury St. Edmunds, 1471. R2/2/145
Richard, blacksmith, Soham, 1639. R2/58/70; W1/94/119
Robert, yeo., Thorndon, 1606. R2/46/40; W1/64/55
Simon, Pakenham, 1495. R2/13/75
Theophilus, husb., Finningham, 1636. R2/57/84; W1/92/101
Thomas, blacksmith, Soham, 1618. R2/51/104; W1/75/65
Walter, Stowmarket, 1554. A5/1/95
LANGAM, Thomas, labourer, Soham, 1569. R2/33/135
William, Great Finborough, 1628. R2/54/163; W1/84/37
LANGELYE, Henry, labourer, Lackford, 1573. R2/36/141; W1/32/36
LANGFORD, John, esq., bach., Fordham, 1661. In. 3/6/99; A5/5/16, A4/1/99
LANGHAM, Agnes, wid., Lakenheath, 1538. R2/20/111; W1/4/95
Alice, Snailwell, 1451. R2/9/126
Joan, Mildenhall, 1520. R2/15/69
John, chaplain, Bury St. Edmunds, 1417. R2/1/141
John, Lakenheath, 1538. R2/18/166
John, Mildenhall, 1476. R2/11/65
John, butcher, Stowmarket, 1691. R2/71/516; W1/145/75
Margaret, Bury St. Edmunds, 1430. R2/1/192
Marian, als. Jannings, Hitcham, 1607. R2/46/124; W1/97/46
Michael, cook, Boxted, 1625. R2/53/350; W1/81/130
Richard, bach., Stanstead, 1683. A5/6/71, A4/20/78
Richard, the elder, Stowmarket, 1615. R2/49/280; W1/72/65
Robert, Bury St. Edmunds, 1378. R2/1/38
Robert, weaver, Mildenhall, 1540. R2/19/273; W1/36/29
Thomas, Bury St. Edmunds, 1493. R2/2/200
Thomas, bach., weaver, Mildenhall, 1545. R2/19/556; W1/7/56
William, weaver, Bury St. Edmunds, 1508. R2/4/200
William, weaver, Bury St. Edmunds, 1509. R2/4/208
William, Mildenhall, 1532. R2/19/89
see also Langam
LANGLEY, George, weaver, Ashley, 1639. R2/58/101; W1/94/164
George, Ashley, 1679. A5/6/20, A4/94/53
George, Little Thurlow, 1638. R2/57/422; W1/93/254
James, Great Thurlow, 1599. R2/44/326; W1/57/106
Mary, Burgate, 1689. A5/6/130, A4/30/7
Richard, Ickworth, 1569. A5/1/207 & 208
Thomas, Poslingford, 1643. R2/59/62; W1/100/70
William, Ickworth, 1462. R2/10/343
William, yeo., Little Cornard, 1593. R2/42/347; W1/50/14
LANGLIE, Clemency, wid., Little Cornard, 1598. R2/44/157; W1/56/37a
see also Langeleye, Langly, Leyme als. Langley, Man als. Langley

LANGLOND, Isabel, Eye, 1453. R2/9/147
John, Eye, 1459. R2/9/264
LANGLY, Henry, cordwainer, Fornham All Saints, 1685. R2/70/177; W1/139/148
John, shoe maker, Chevington, 1678. In. 3/19/160; A5/6/8 & 10, A4/15/69 & 88
Zephaniah, Long Melford, 1662. In. 3/7/82
LANGMAN, see Jannings als. Langman
LANGTON, Richard, gent., Little Waldingfield, 1635. R2/56/460; W1/91/25
LANHAM, Bridget, Rickinghall, 1593. A5/2/185
Daniel, yeo., Rickinghall Inferior, 1680. In. 3/20/206; A5/6/41, A4/17/106
Elizabeth, Thrandeston, 1559. R2/28/405; W1/3/153
Geoffrey, Thrandeston, 1555. R2/24/212; W1/15/44
Henry, husb., Cowlinge, 1645, (N). R2/59/178; W1/102/7
Mary, wid., Eye, 1665. R2/63/314; W1/117/48
Mary, wid., Wortham, 1662. R2/62/358; W1/114/82; In. 3/7/112
Robert, linen weaver, Stowupland, 1628. R2/54/197; W1/84/71
Robert, yeo., Wortham, 1562. R2/31/100; W1/8/90
Robert, yeo., Wortham, 1593. R2/42/354; W1/50/22
Robert, yeo., Wortham, 1673. R2/65/443; W1/125/70
Stephen, yeo., Rickinghall Superior, 1649. R2/60/178; W1/106/24
Stephen, yeo., Wortham, 1608. R2/46/176; W1/65/35
Stephen, yeo., Wortham, 1670. R2/65/61; W1/122/74; In. 3/15/92
William, linen weaver, Wortham, 1640. W1/110/3
see also Lanam, Lanume
LANMAN, Anne, wid., Wetheringsett, 1521. R2/14/30, R2/17/9; W1/21/79
Jeffery, Hitcham, 1557. R2/26/270; W1/20/187
Joan, wid., Hitcham, 1561. R2/32/442; W1/19/78
John, the elder, yeo., Westhorpe, 1607. R2/46/139
Robert, als. Jannings, yeo., Cockfield, 1633. R2/56/263; W1/90/29
Robert, als. Jannings, the elder, husb., Hitcham, 1599. R2/44/235; W1/57/52
Robert, als. Janning, husb., Hitcham, 1612. R2/48/154; W1/69/36
Robert, Westhorpe, 1575. W1/95/15
William, als. Jannings, yeo., Hitcham, 1665. R2/63/326; W1/117/70
LANSDALLE, John, petty chapman, Bury St. Edmunds, 1598. R2/44/123; W1/56/114
LANSELL, John, Great Thurlow, 1520. R2/15/22
see also Landisdale, Landsell
LANUME, John, Eye, 1578. R2/37/371; W1/36/203
LAPPAGE, John, sen., yeo., Polstead, 1686. R2/70/504; W1/140/110; In. 3/22/16
Robert, yeo., Stoke by Nayland, 1613. R2/48/331; W1/70/115
LAPPIDGE, Edward, Polstead, 1697. A5/7/1, A4/40/19
LARCHE, John, Stanton, 1472. R2/10/535
Ralph, Stanton, 1460. R2/9/255
LARCK, Robert, Stanton, 1552. R2/31/58; W1/13/44
LARDENER, Edward, Bury St. Edmunds, 1447. R2/2/22
Roger, Bury St. Edmunds, 1429. R2/1/189
LARDYNER, William, Kennett, 1471. R2/10/499
see also Redell als. Lardener
LARENCE, Margaret, wid., Ixworth, 1615. R2/49/245; W1/72/31
LARETT, Thomas, Lidgate, 1588. R2/41/41; W1/45/35
LARGANT(E), Christopher, Barnham, 1628. R2/54/258; W1/84/116
Hugh, husb., Kirtling, 1632. R2/56/150; W1/89/51
John, yeo., Barnham, 1634. R2/56/352; W1/90/120
John, yeo., Downham, 1691. R2/71/473
Roger, West Stow, (1550). R2/21/110; W1/9/96
Thomas, Hargrave, 1566. R2/32/300
LARGE, Audrey, wid., Hundon, 1604. R2/45/356
John, Bury St. Edmunds, 1467. R2/2/110
John, labourer, Mildenhall, 1626. R2/53/467; W1/82/15
William, husb., Kedington, 1572. R2/36/2; W1/31/145
LARGEANT, Clemency, Downham, 1555. R2/24/165
John, Downham, 1560. A5/1/102
Simon, shepherd, Mildenhall, 1634. R2/56/406; W1/90/192
LARGEAWUT, John, Elveden, 1441. R2/9/20

LARGENT(E), Alice, als. Judde, Brandon, 1661. A5/5/21, A4/1/49
Edward, Fornham St. Genevieve, 1688. A5/6/117, A4/29/15
Elisabeth, als. Barton, Wickhambrook, 1651. A5/4/138
George, linen weaver, Downham, 1639. R2/58/38; W1/94/70
John, shepherd, Barnham, 1622, (N). R2/52/435; W1/78/56
John, sen., husb., Downham, 1591. R2/42/167; W1/48/79
John, weaver, Downham, 1612. R2/48/213; W1/69/109
John, Mildenhall, (1613). W1/111/77
John, Mildenhall, 1630. R2/55/116
Martin, labourer, Downham, 1638. R2/57/352; W1/93/142
Matthew, Elmsett, 1639. A5/4/70
Miles, Mildenhall, 1669. In. 3/14/90; A5/5/107, A4/7/62
Petronella, Brandon, 1607. A5/3/32
Richard, Wicken, 1669. In. 3/14/177; A5/5/110, A4/7/71
Robert, Kirtling, 1648. A5/4/120
Robert, Walsham le Willows, 1693. A5/6/163, A4/35/30
Robert, blacksmith, Wood Ditton, 1620. R2/52/113; W1/76/99
Thomas, Hargrave, 1595. A5/2/205
Thomasine, spinster, Barnham, 1660. R2/62/47; W1/112/57; In. 3/5/133
LARGIANT, Richard, shepherd, Fordham, 1633, (N). R2/56/277; W1/90/42
LARGIENT, Robert, labourer, Kirtling, 1595. R2/43/60; W1/53/47
LARGYANT, Thomas, Hargrave, 1547. R2/21/342; W1/10/159
see also Largant(e)
LARK(E), Agnes, wife of Thomas, Bury St. Edmunds, 1504. R2/4/164
Agnes, wid., Bury St. Edmunds, 1553. R2/8/67; W1/21/201
Andrew, Bury St. Edmunds, 1550. R2/4/6
John, Stanton, 1483. R2/11/286
Thomas, vintner, Bury St. Edmunds, 1500. R2/4/93
William, Bury St. Edmunds, 1552. R2/4/76; W1/21/209
see also Larck
LARKEN, John, Pakenham, 1611. R2/47/314; W1/68/9
LARKYN, Dorothy, wid., Wickhambrook, 1618. R2/51/235; W1/75/151
LARLIN, John, husb., Barnham, 1649, (N). R2/60/266; W1/106/132
Thomas, Elveden, 1628. R2/54/179; W1/84/55
LARLING, Richard, husb., Lackford, 1612. R2/48/160; W1/69/42
Robert, labourer, Barton Mills, 1660. In. 3/5/36; A5/5/1, A4/1/237
Samuel, shepherd, Downham, 1679. R2/67/251; W1/133/43
Thomas, labourer, Barnham, 1642. R2/58/316; W1/99/1
Thomas, Elveden, 1642. A5/4/94
William, Culford, 1635. A5/4/38
LARMOTH, John, yeo., Lackford, 1622. R2/52/361; W1/78/6
Mary, wid., Lackford, 1674. R2/66/23; W1/126/101; A5/5/164, A4/13/64
Thomas, gent., Lackford, 1666. R2/64/47; W1/118/48; In. 3/11/135
LARNER, John, herdsman, Little Downham, 1613. R2/48/270; W1/70/45
John, husb., Thrandeston, 1666. R2/64/159; W1/118/124; In. 3/12/56
Thomas, Timworth, 1557. R2/26/51; W1/20/30
LARNOR, Thomas, yeo., Little Saxham, 1622. R2/52/515; W1/78/116
William, husb., Rattlesden, 1511. R2/13/204
LARRANCE, John, als. Avis, singleman, Barnardiston, 1652. R2/61/597; W1/109/74; In. 3/4/77
LARRET(T), Samuel, yeo., Semer, 1694. R2/72/426; W1/148/161; A5/6/171, A4/37/57
Thomas, Waldingfield, 1638. A5/4/67
see also Larett
LARVER, James, Little Saxham, 1582. A5/2/38
John, Little Saxham, 1582. A5/2/44
LARWOOD, John, carpenter, Buxhall, 1680. In. 3/20/47
John, baker, Combs, 1666. In. 3/11/46; A5/5/73, A4/4/14
John, house carpenter, Great Finborough, 1680. R2/67/563; W1/134/45
Rebecca, wid., Combs, 1678. In. 3/19/87; A5/6/6, A4/15/51
LARYOT(T), Joan, wid., Assington, (1543). R2/19/378; W1/6/157
Thomas, Assington, 1477. R2/12/14
LAST, Agie, wid., Lakenheath, 1644. A5/4/104
Alice, wid., Stansfield, 1574. R2/37/37; W1/33/43
Edward, Chevington, 1631. A5/4/16
Edward, Chevington, 1666. In. 3/11/41; A5/5/72, A4/4/8
John, Haughley, 1681. A5/6/44, A4/18/13
John, gent., Haughley, 1682. R2/68/430; W1/136/119; In. 3/21/98
Mark, sen., butcher, Stradishall, 1637, (N). R2/57/122; W1/92/150
Mark, butcher, Stradishall, 1695. R2/72/540; W1/149/97

LAST continued
Mary, wife of John, Sudbury, 1680. R2/67/591; W1/134/67
Nicholas, Ampton, 1596. A5/2/220
Prudence, Lakenheath, 1636. A5/4/44
Richard, husb., Hundon, 1557. R2/26/200; W1/20/141
Robert, Pakenham, 1571. R2/35/91; W1/36/100
Robert, Sudbury, 1635. A5/4/38
Robert, Whepstead, 1647. In. 3/2/154; A5/4/118
Thomas, Burwell, 1697. A5/7/2, A4/40/23
Thomas, Glemsford, 1679. A5/6/15, A4/16/6
Thomas, Great Saxham, 1694. A5/6/174, A4/37/20
Thomas, the elder, husb., Lakenheath, 1619. R2/51/446; W1/132/113
Thomas, Lakenheath, 1644. A5/4/104
Thomas, Pakenham, 1593. R2/42/387; W1/50/53
William, Woolpit, 1627, (N). R2/54/19; W1/83/22
LATHAM, John, clothier, Great Waldingfield, 1598, (N). R2/44/73; W1/56/68
see also Laitham
LATHEBURY, William, husb., Soham, 1551. R2/23/80; W1/9/158, W1/11/36
LATHONER, see Howton als. Lathoner
LATTES, John, bach., Little Harleston, 1665. R2/63/332; W1/117/78
LAUDES, Joan, Wetherden, 1564. R2/32/130; W1/27/79
see also Lawdes
LAUFLINGE, Simon, Lavenham, 1635. A5/4/37
LAUGHLINE, Margaret, wid., Boxford, 1613. R2/48/245a; W1/70/16
LAUGHLYN, Simon, clothier, Boxford, 1597. R2/43/301; W1/55/70
see also Layghlen
LAUNCE, Edmund, Barnham, 1560. R2/29/165; W1/25/10
James, Barnham, 1561. A5/1/107
Peter, Barnham, 1476. R2/11/89
William, Barnham, 1560. A5/1/105
William, Barnham, 1570. R2/34/53; W1/30/49
see also Lawnce, Bovell als. Launce, Bovell als. Lawnce
LAUND(E), James, als. Pallant, yeo., Cowlinge, 1634. R2/56/373; W1/90/149
John, als. Pallante, Cotton, 1593. R2/42/448; W1/50/109
John, als. Pallaunte, husb., Thorndon, 1566. R2/32/288; W1/28/106
John, yeo., Thorndon, 1651. R2/61/498; W1/108/89
Richard, Hunston, 1572. A5/1/244
Robert, Bury St. Edmunds, 1606. A5/3/10
Robert, Thorndon, 1573. R2/36/122; W1/32/27
see also Lawnde
LAUNDER, Richard, bed weaver, Bury St. Edmunds, 1471. R2/2/144
LAURENCE, Christian, als. Strawe, wid., Glemsford, 1649. R2/60/198; W1/106/40
Hester, als. Goldsmith, Little Barton, 1682. A5/6/64, A4/19/105
John, als. Strawe, Glemsford, 1635. A5/4/42
Thomas, husb., Mildenhall, 1568. R2/33/62; W1/141/80
LAURET, Richard, husb., Assington, 1540. W1/36/43
LAUVERANNS, Margaret, Eye, 1452. R2/9/156
LAVENDER, William, yeo., Stoke by Nayland, 1636. R2/57/7; W1/92/9
William, Stoke by Nayland, 1585. A5/2/66
LAVENHAM, Margaret, wid., Sudbury, 1506. R2/13/169
Thomas, cutler, Sudbury, 1459. R2/9/258
LAVER, John, Acton, 1571. R2/35/61; W1/36/69
Thomas, husb., Acton, 1559. R2/28/49; W1/22/53
LAVEROK, Isabel, wid., Bury St. Edmunds, 1479. R2/2/275
Joan, Cockfield, 1459. R2/9/234
John, Bury St. Edmunds, 1459. R2/2/67
LAVOULD, John, blacksmith, Fornham St. Genevieve, 1651. R2/61/493; W1/108/84
LAW(E), Gamaliel, yeo., Little Wratting, 1675. R2/66/144; W1/127/19; In. 3/16/19
Henry, singleman, Dalham, 1637. R2/57/242; W1/192/297
Robert, West Rudham, 1534. W1/51/56
LAWDES, Thomas, Wetherden, 1564. R2/32/59
---, 1564. W1/27/7
LAWDHAM, Thomas, metalman, Shelland, 1616. R2/50/69; W1/73/80
LAWENDY, Edmund, Wicken, 1565. R2/32/202; W1/27/128
LAW(E)S, John, Redgrave, 1612. A5/3/116
Philip, miller, Fordham, 1617. R2/50/257; W1/74/56
Roger, the elder, Burwell, 1663. In. 3/8/80; A5/5/46

LAW(E)S continued
Stephen, (1570). W1/51/199
Thomas, tanner, Pakenham, 1612. R2/48/166; W1/69/46
Thomas, husb., Saham Toney, 1594. W1/51/135
William, Burgh, 1527. R2/17/254; W1/1/23
William, als. Bladsmyth, Bury St. Edmunds, 1517. R2/6/39
William, miller, Exning, 1617. R2/50/301; W1/74/91
William, Soham, 1475. R2/11/136
see also Lawse, Lawys
LAWMAN, Robert, butcher, Bildeston, 1553. R2/31/121; W1/13/86
LAWNCE, Edmund, husb., Barnham, 1572. R2/36/14; W1/31/121
Isabel, wid., Barnham, 1544. R2/19/471
John, Barnham, 1558. R2/27/450
LAWNDE, James, Wyverstone, 1572. R2/36/86; W1/31/48
John, singleman, Cotton, 1592. R2/42/306; W1/49/128
Robert, yeo., Cotton, 1590. R2/41/318; W1/47/4
Robert, Thorndon, 1545. A5/1/44
Thomas, bed weaver, Fornham St. Martin, (1497). R2/13/80
William, Bury St. Edmunds, 1507. R2/4/189
LAWNEY, John, Bury St. Edmunds, 1428. R2/1/186
LAWRANCE, Richard, Burwell, 1572. R2/36/69; W1/31/63
LAWRENCE, Ambrose, Bury St. Edmunds, 1577. R2/37/254
Ambrose, sen., bricklayer, mason, Bury St. Edmunds, 1668. R2/64/389; W1/120/111; In. 3/13/129
Alice, als. Smyth, wid., Ixworth, 1570. A5/1/223
Christopher, clothier, Bury St. Edmunds, 1611. R2/48/100; W1/68/118
George, tailor, Mildenhall, 1593. R2/42/394; W1/50/62
Henry, butcher, Bury St. Edmunds, 1639. R2/58/13; W1/94/24
John, minister, Exning, 1598. R2/44/107; W1/56/130
John, Great Livermere, 1598. R2/44/22; W1/56/15
John, als. Smyth, Ixworth, 1609. A5/3/71
John, Kentford, 1684. A5/6/75, A4/21/11
Katherine, wid., Soham, 1590. A5/2/136
Luke, blacksmith, Burwell, 1696. R2/73/25; W1/150/7
Margaret, wid., Bury St. Edmunds, 1602. R2/45/110; W1/60/22a & b
Richard, Assington, 1540. R2/19/277
Richard, als. Strawe, Glemsford, 1625, (N). R2/53/438; W1/81/202
Richard, als. Straw, clothier, Glemsford, 1700. R2/74/120; W1/154/116
Robert, shoe maker, Bury St. Edmunds, 1573. R2/36/208; W1/32/130
Samuel, yeo., Cockfield, 1677. In. 3/18/39; A5/5/168, A4/14/22
Thomas, als. Smyth, Rattlesden, 1562. A5/1/137
Thomas, als. Strawe, Stanstead, 1568. A5/1/202
William, Brandon, 1684. A5/6/77, A4/21/41
William, Chevington, 1611. A5/3/111
William, Eriswell, 1515. R2/12/115
see also Larence, Larrance, Laurence, Lorence, Avie als. Lawrence, Low als. Lawrence, Lowes als. Lawrence, Stanton als. Laurence
LAWRNER, Thomas, husb., Cavenham, 1612. R2/48/126; W1/69/3
LAWSALL, Richard, weaver, Clare, 1633, (N). R2/56/244; W1/90/6
LAWSE, Stephen, yeo., Gunton, 1574. W1/51/201a & b & 202
LAWSELL, George, Fordham, 1539. R2/19/305
John, wheelwright, Sudbury, 1602. R2/45/118; W1/60/35
Mary, wid., Sudbury, 1605, (N). R2/45/471; W1/63/121
LAWSON, Agnes, wid., Lawshall, 1588. R2/41/136; W1/46/141
John, tailor, Bury St. Edmunds, (1675). W1/312/5
Thomas, clerk, Bury St. Edmunds, 1639. A5/4/77
LAWTER, Samuel, cooper, Hepworth, 1695. R2/72/539; W1/149/96
LAWYS, John, bladesmith, Bury St. Edmunds, 1477. R2/2/232
LAXUM, Robert, Occold, (1697), (N). R2/73/144; W1/151/30; A5/7/3, A4/40/58
Susan, wid., Occold, 1698. A5/7/9
LAY(E), Alexander, Great Waldingfield, 1559. R2/28/407; W1/3/155
Ann, wid., Polstead, 1687. A5/6/110, A4/27/27
George, husb., Bures, 1603, (N). R2/45/139; W1/61/34
Henry, yeo., Bures, 1626. R2/53/460; W1/82/12
John, Bures, 1459. R2/9/237
John, Bures, 1526. R2/17/138; W1/21/135
John, Bures, 1564. R2/32/93; W1/27/41
John, Bures, 1585. R2/39/330; W1/42/263
John, yeo., Bures, 1623. R2/52/583; W1/79/36

LAY(E) continued
John, Edwardstone, (1534). R2/19/208
John, yeo., Ely, 1698. R2/73/223; W1/152/5
John, weaver, Hundon, 1623. R2/52/636; W1/79/69
Peter, Little Cornard, 1639. R2/58/15; W1/94/27
Richard, Assington, 1480. R2/12/7
Richard, husb., Bures, 1557. R2/26/314; W1/20/236
Robert, Bures, 1497. R2/13/42
Robert, carpenter, Lavenham, 1672. R2/65/341; W1/124/71
Robert, yeo., Layham, 1638. R2/57/360; W1/93/186b
Rose, Bures, 1571. R2/35/175; W1/38/162
Thomas, husb., Great Cornard, 1552. R2/31/28; W1/13/19
Thomas, husb., Little Cornard, 1593. R2/42/382; W1/50/48
William, Bures, (1536). R2/20/148, R2/22/98; W1/4/129, W1/10/3
William, yeo., Bures, 1619, (N). R2/51/390; W1/132/80a & b
see also Calf als. Lay
LAYER, Hugh, Great Cornard, 1608. A5/3/43
see also Layre
LAYGHLEN, Joan, wid., Boxford, 1540. R2/20/164; W1/4/140
LAYMAN, John, Hopton, 1603. R2/45/295; W1/61/102
John, wheelwright, Weston, 1640. R2/58/154; W1/96/60
Susan, wid., West Stow, 1629. R2/54/371; W1/85/69
Thomas, yeo., West Stow, 1638. R2/57/327; W1/93/107
William, carpenter, West Stow, 1608. R2/46/165; W1/65/18
William, West Stow, 1630. A5/4/5
LAYNERASS, Robert, Fordham, 1521. R2/15/128, R2/17/326
LAYRE, Stephen, yeo., Wickhambrook, 1585. R2/39/352; W1/42/250
LAYTE, Thomas, Bardwell, 1569. A5/1/210
LAYTON, John, yeo., Wicken, 1679. R2/67/372; W1/133/127
William, the elder, husb., Soham, 1649. R2/60/286; W1/106/158
LEA, John, Haverhill, 1594. A5/2/196
Lewis, Haverhill, 1619. R2/51/295; W1/132/21
see also Lee
LEACH, Ann, wid., Bury St. Edmunds, 1690. A5/6/136, A4/32/48
Ann, wid., Stansfield, 1671. A5/5/123, A4/86/33
Benjamin, Little Whelnetham, 1673. A5/5/139, A4/10/57
John, Little Waldingfield, 1632. A5/4/18
John, Sudbury, 1571. R2/35/97; W1/36/112
Joseph, Isleham, 1730. W11/7
Rose, singlewoman, Bury St. Edmunds, 1637, (N). R2/57/127; W1/92/157
Thomas, Milden, 1592. A5/2/165
Thomasine, wid., Mildenhall, 1682. In. 3/21/191; A5/6/60, A4/19/43
William, yeo., Alpheton, 1678. R2/67/171; W1/130/152; In. 3/19/213; A5/6/13, A4/93/111
William, Stansfield, 1663. In. 3/8/200
William, Tostock, 1598. R2/44/132; W1/56/105
LEADER, Abraham, shoe maker, Stradishall, 1648. R2/60/41; W1/105/51
Ann, Hopton, 1649. A5/4/131
John, tanner, Bury St. Edmunds, 1548. R2/8/36
John, wid., Bury St. Edmunds, 1579. R2/38/47; W1/39/32
Lydia, wid., Depden, 1619. R2/51/439; W1/132/109
Osmund, yeo., Hopton, 1648. R2/60/29; W1/105/42
William, husb., Higham, 1678. R2/67/173; W1/130/153; In. 3/19/214
see also Leder, Leeder
LEADES, Christopher, Bury St. Edmunds, 1559. R2/8/341; W1/17/78
LEAGET(T), Alice, wid., Icklingham, 1630. R2/55/162; W1/86/178
Robert, blacksmith, Bury St. Edmunds, 1623. R2/52/600; W1/79/51
LEAKE, John, Newmarket, 1579. A5/2/18
see also Leeke
LEAMAN, John, tailor, Stanstead, 1662. R2/62/426; W1/114/187; In. 3/7/246
LEAME, Margery, wid., Brandon, 1576. R2/37/180; W1/37/47
see also Leem, Leme
LEAMON, John, yeo., Layham, 1687. R2/70/378; W1/141/100; In. 3/23/15
LEAPER, Elizabeth, wid., Barrow, 1608. R2/46/189; W1/65/52 (and inventory)
LEARNER, Henry, husb., Cavenham, (1649). W1/110/21
Philip, sen., West Tofts, 1687. R2/70/569; W1/141/9
Thomas, husb., Downham, 1679. R2/67/274; W1/133/63
William, yeo., Downham, 1691. R2/71/493; W1/145/53
see also Lerner

LEASSE, John, labourer, Lackford, 1576. R2/37/194; W1/37/60;
In. 3/1/9
LEATE, James Oliver, Clare, 1661. In. 3/6/77
LEATHER, William, als. Stanton, yeo., Sudbury, 1585. R2/39/246;
W1/42/327
LEAVER, Henry, wheelwright, Wattisham, 1670. R2/65/96; W1/122/117;
In. 3/15/136
John, yeo., Hitcham, 1599. R2/44/195; W1/57/20
Thomas, Kersey, 1626, (N). R2/53/557; W1/82/81
William, Bury St. Edmunds, 1700. A5/7/16, A4/41/134
LEAVITT, George, shepherd, Elveden, 1698. R2/73/235; W1/152/16
LEAVOLD, Edmund, yeo., Redgrave, 1684. R2/69/359; W1/138/148
LEBOTE, Ralph, Little Saxham, 1452. R2/9/110
LECHE, Agnes, wid., Buxhall, 1548. R2/21/177 & 478
Agnes, Fordham, 1436. W1/24/155
Helen, Bury St. Edmunds, 1469. R2/2/127
John, cooper, Bury St. Edmunds, 1498. R2/4/74
John, Buxhall, (1493). R2/11/443
John, Buxhall, (1546). R2/21/642; W1/21/176
Laurence, barker, Stoke by Nayland, 1446. R2/9/66
Miles, Soham, 1541. R2/22/104; W1/10/26
Robert, Buxhall, 1538. R2/20/144
Robert, Stowmarket, 1471. R2/10/473
Thomas, Woodbridge, 1532. R2/19/93
Walter, Botesdale, 1447. R2/9/71
LEDDE, Richard, husb., Great Finborough, 1669. R2/64/526; W1/121/115;
In. 3/14/57
LEDER, Richard, Honington, 1570. R2/34/48; W1/30/44
Thomas, Barrow, 1662. In. 3/7/155; A5/5/35
LEDEYMAN, Francis, Flempton, 1684. A5/6/82, A4/21/88
LEE, Agnes, wid. of John, Assington, 1501. R2/13/124
Christopher, chaplain, Bury St. Edmunds, 1517. R2/6/41
Edmund, esq., Bury St. Edmunds, 1535. R2/7/32
Edmund, Great Saxham, 1522. R2/14/71
Elisabeth, wid., gentlewoman, Bury St. Edmunds, 1504. R2/4/155
Joan, wid., Haverhill, 1588. R2/41/111; W1/45/106
John, esq., Bury St. Edmunds, 1661. In. 3/6/113; A5/5/17, A4/1/88
John, Lavenham, 1697. A5/7/2, A4/40/28
John, sen., Stowmarket, 1469. R2/10/427
John, Stowmarket, 1592. A5/2/178
Josiah, Long Melford, 1672. A5/5/129, A4/9/18
Margaret, wid., Bacton, 1532. R2/19/117; W1/3/126
Matilda, wife of William, Shimpling, 1407. R2/1/116
Matthew, yeo., Long Melford, 1560. R2/29/49; W1/25/128
Roger, singleman, Boxford, 1686. A5/6/100, A4/26/84
Thomas, clothier, Long Melford, 1620. R2/52/52; W1/76/45
William, Haverhill, (1534). R2/18/129
William, Shimpling, 1404. R2/1/102
see also Lea, Legh, Leigh, Leye, Leyghe
LEECH, Henry, Bury St. Edmunds, 1663. In. 3/8/138; A5/5/47
John, Little Waldingfield, 1666. In. 3/11/151; A5/5/75, A4/4/40
John, Wortham, 1663. In. 3/8/92; A5/5/47
William, Stansfield, 1663. A5/5/51
see also Leach, Leche, Leich
LEEDER, Henry, parson, Whepstead, 1559. R2/28/326; W1/22/269
Rose, wid., Higham, 1680. R2/67/643; W1/134/108; In. 3/20/122
Sarah, wid., Stradishall, 1661. In. 3/6/78; A5/5/15, A4/1/106
Stephen, Barrow, 1664. In. 3/9/122; A5/5/60, A4/2/68
Thomas, Mildenhall, 1671. A5/5/122, A4/8/27
William, Wood Ditton, 1699. A5/7/13, A4/41/67
LEEDES, George, Tittleshall, 1578. W1/51/196
see also Leades
LEEKE, John, chaplain, Bury St. Edmunds, 1442. R2/1/263
John, Fakenham, 1637. R2/57/135; W1/92/166
Richard, labouring man, Stowlangtoft, 1605. R2/45/442; W1/63/85
see also Leake, Leke
LEEM, Thomas, sen., Brandon, 1472. R2/10/575
LEEMAN, John, blacksmith, Alpheton, 1610. R2/47/160; W1/67/40
Priscilla, wid., Alpheton, 1640. R2/58/207; W1/96/139
Roger, husb., Hundon, 1598. R2/44/84; W1/56/85
LEENGE, Stephen, Thurston, 1482. R2/11/277
LEES, Abraham, gardener, Lavenham, 1669. R2/64/530; W1/121/121;
In. 3/14/115

LEES continued
Edmund, parson, Stansfield, 1563, (N). R2/31/167, R2/32/51; W1/26/44 & 48
LEET(E), Ann, wid., Cheveley, 1682. R2/68/458; W1/136/138; In. 3/21/38
Clement, husb., Isleham, 1667. In. 9/20; A5/5/83, A4/12/4
George, yeo., Cowlinge, 1667. R2/64/259; W1/119/122; In. 3/12/128
George, Cowlinge, 1668. A5/5/94, A4/6/51
John, husb., Cowlinge, 1627. R2/54/108; W1/83/106
Roger, inn holder, Bury St. Edmunds, 1690. R2/71/355; W1/144/58
Thomas, yeo., Cowlinge, 1664. R2/63/230; W1/116/145; In. 3/9/207
Thomas, Gazeley, 1696. A5/6/184, A4/39/2
Thomas, Lidgate, 1699, (N). R2/73/433; W1/153/72; In. 3/26/3
William, Cowlinge, 1649. A5/4/126
see also Leate
LEFELD, Thomas, sen., Haverhill, 1474. R2/10/562
LEFE, Thomas, Bury St. Edmunds, 1536. R2/7/40
LEFF, John, Saxon Street, 1440. R2/9/26
LEFTEBEDE, Thomas, wid., wheelwright, Stowlangtoft, 1557. R2/26/14; W1/20/25
LEFTLEGGE, Margaret, wid., Stowlangtoft, 1557. R2/26/224; W1/20/119b
LEGATE, Edward, Mildenhall, 1669. In. 3/14/21; A5/5/103, A4/7/23
Elisabeth, wid., Bury St. Edmunds, 1680. R2/67/769; W1/134/201; In. 3/20/229
Elisabeth, wid., Icklingham, 1608. R2/46/184; W1/65/51
John, yeo., Icklingham, 1619. R2/51/404; W1/132/88
LEGAT(T), Alan, Hawstead, 1462. R2/10/317
Edmund, Bury St. Edmunds, 1523. R2/6/112
Giles, Fornham, 1541. R2/20/197
Robert, sen., baker, Bury St. Edmunds, 1465. R2/2/86
Robert, Hawstead, 1526. R2/17/207; W1/23/27
Robert, Icklingham, 1608. A5/3/42
Robert, Rattlesden, 1463. R2/10/337
William, tiler, Bury St. Edmunds, 1500. R2/4/100
LEGET(T), Alan, yeo., Hawstead, 1533. R2/18/212
Joan, wid., Stanton, 1595. R2/43/38; W1/53/30
Robert, Icklingham, 1534. R2/19/203
LEGGATE, John, yeo., Chevington, 1648. R2/60/45; W1/105/59
LEGGATT, William, sen., yeo., Thwaite, 1694. R2/72/376; W1/148/106
see also Leaget(t)
LEGGE, Henry, Bury St. Edmunds, 1407. R2/1/115
John, bed weaver, Bury St. Edmunds, 1452. R2/2/38
John, carpenter, Bury St. Edmunds, 1500. R2/4/107
LEGH, Joan, Sudbury, 1544. A5/1/107
LE GRICE, Charles, pewterer, Bury St. Edmunds, 1687. R2/70/343; W1/141/80
LEHMAN, John, Blofield, 1537. W1/51/22
LE HUNT, George, knight, Little Bradley, 1642. R2/58/327; W1/99/18
Richard, gent., Rushbrook, 1611. R2/48/74; W1/68/91; A5/3/113
LEICH, Robert, husb., Botesdale, 1640. R2/58/219; W1/96/158
LEIFCHILD, John, husb., Chippenham, 1599. R2/44/203; W1/57/25
Margaret, wid., Chippenham, 1679. A5/6/17, A4/16/19
Robert, Burwell, 1615. R2/49/235; W1/72/24
William, yeo., Burwell, 1668. R2/64/372; W1/120/89; In. 3/13/85
William, the elder, yeo., Chippenham, 1667. R2/64/196; W1/119/41; In. 3/12/60
LEIGH, Christopher, husb., Chedburgh, 1676. In. 3/17/141; A5/5/166, A4/13/89
Thomas, Burwell, 1639, (N). R2/58/57; W1/94/106
see also Lee
LEKE, Thomas, Burwell, 1591. R2/42/104; W1/48/126
LEMAN, John, Ixworth, 1491. R2/13/116
John, Wetheringsett, 1458. R2/9/240
Mary, spinster, Bury St. Edmunds, 1696. A5/6/187
LEME, Henry, Brandon, 1542. R2/22/1; W1/6/26
Thomas, Brandon, 1530. R2/19/54
LEMING, Ann, wid., Bury St. Edmunds, 1694. R2/72/169
Frances, spinster, Bury St. Edmunds, 1694. R2/72/377; W1/148/107; A5/6/187, A4/39/35
LEMMING, Mary, spinster, Bury St. Edmunds, 1687. A5/6/112, A4/27/54
LEMON, John, yeo., Alpheton, 1638. R2/57/274; W1/93/41
John, tailor, Lavenham, 1692. R2/72/108; W1/146/98

LENARDE, Thomas, husb., Yaxley, 1622. R2/52/514; W1/78/115
LENENEDE, John, als. Swayles, Mildenhall, 1621. W1/95/70
LENGE, Katherine, Thurston, 1482. R2/11/266
LENNARD, John, yeo., Ashley, 1698. R2/73/299; W1/152/70
LENNY, John, Brundall, 1528. W1/19/42
Robert, the elder, yeo., Occold, 1650, (N). R2/61/322; W1/107/16; In. 3/3/30
LENY, Robert, husb., Burgate, 1559. R2/28/145; W1/22/134
LENYS, Richard, Tostock, 1451. R2/9/104
Matilda, Tostock, 1452. R2/9/131
LEONARD, Henry, Yaxley, 1589. A5/2/121
see also Lenarde, Lennard
LEOPARR, Catherine, singlewoman, Bury St. Edmunds, 1661. W1/111/88
LEPENGWELL, Robert, Boxford, 1652. In. 3/4/39; A5/4/141
LEPPINGWELL, William, Lavenham, 1679. A5/6/22, A4/16/73
LERLYNG, William, Hopton, 1459. R2/9/241
LERNER, John, Lackford, 1550. R2/21/56; W1/51/267
LESCHE, Alexander, Bury St. Edmunds, 1380. R2/1/40
LESONNS, Katherine, wid., Bury St. Edmunds, 1558. W1/18/60
LESTER, George, linen weaver, Coney Weston, 1695. R2/72/513; W1/149/67
Nicholas, Bury St. Edmunds, 1370. R2/1/21
Richard, Bury St. Edmunds, 1367. R2/1/27
Richard, Fordham, 1527. R2/17/229, R2/18/5; W1/1/55
LE STRANGE, Hamon, Pakenham, 1660. In. 3/5/200
LE STRAUNGE, Eleanor, wife of John, Bury St. Edmunds, 1420. R2/1/149
LETCH, Abraham, Glemsford, 1693. A5/6/165, A4/35/11
John, Glemsford, 1674. A5/5/150, A4/11/65
John, Stoke by Nayland, 1635. A5/4/37
John, Sudbury, 1526. R2/17/195; W1/23/38
William, labourer, Stoke by Clare, 1687. R2/70/310; W1/141/54
LETTELE, Joan, singlewoman, Sudbury, 1615. R2/49/304; W1/72/84
LETTEN, George, husb., Thelnetham, 1580. R2/38/183; W1/39/119
John, husb., Thelnetham, 1568. R2/33/20; W1/29/29
LETTICE, John, Harleston, 1665. A5/5/68, A4/3/58
LEVAS, William, Thelnetham, 1446. R2/9/73
LEVELL, John, blacksmith, Fornham St. Genevieve, 1673. R2/65/392; W1/125/4
Thomas, Great Waldingfield, 1612, (N). W1/95/159
see also Levold(e)
LEVEN, Edmund, Great Wratting, 1671. R2/65/249; W1/123/126; A5/5/127, A4/8/69
see also Levinge, Levyn
LEVENS, John, clerk, Poslingford, 1584. R2/39/183; W1/27/48, W1/42/144
LEVENSON, John, als. Levesson, Bury St. Edmunds, 1467. R2/2/111
LEVENTHORP, John, Snailwell, 1444. R2/9/45
LEVER, Elisabeth, wid., Hitcham, 1557. R2/26/265; W1/20/181
Gregory, Hitcham, 1562. R2/31/40; W1/8/164
Henry, the elder, husb., Hitcham, (1539). R2/19/621, R2/20/216; W1/3/170
John, Hitcham, 1491. R2/13/101
John, Hitcham, 1555. R2/24/201; W1/15/34
John, Hopton, 1612. A5/3/115
Robert, Hitcham, 1554. R2/24/13; W1/14/13
Thomas, husb., Hitcham, 1604. R2/45/357; W1/62/82
see also Leaver
LEVERET, Richard, Wangford, 1608. R2/46/171; W1/65/27
LEVERICH, Agnes, wid., Redlingfield, 1565. R2/32/208; W1/27/131
Henry, Hitcham, 1609. R2/47/57; W1/66/64
Hugh, Rickinghall Superior, 1564. A5/1/154
John, Felsham, 1440. R2/9/33
John, Redlingfield, 1558. R2/27/583; W1/36/60
Richard, Woolpit, 1568. A5/1/207
Richard, Woolpit, 1569. A5/1/212
LEVERICKE, William, linen weaver, Hopton, 1634. R2/56/400; W1/90/183
LEVERIDGE, Sybil, Redlingfield, 1622. R2/52/351; W1/78/1
LEVERYCHE, John, singleman, Palgrave, 1559. R2/28/4
see also Lyverich, Coates als. Leveridge
LEVESSON, see Levenson als. Levesson

LEVET(T), Elisabeth, wid., Bury St. Edmunds, 1573. R2/36/226; W1/32/99
Elizabeth, wid., Exning, 1570. R2/34/59; W1/38/123
Humphrey, gent., Thelnetham, 1605. R2/45/416; W1/63/62
John, lime burner, Exning, 1568. R2/33/39; W1/29/48
John, lime burner, Exning, 1571. R2/35/124; W1/36/86
William, husb., Kedington, 1572. R2/65/335; W1/124/63
LEVINGE, Edward, Great Wratting, 1606. A5/3/10
Margaret, singlewoman, Bury St. Edmunds, 1618, (N). R2/51/155; W1/75/94
LEVITT, Sarah, wid., Sudbury, 1689. R2/71/273; W1/143/109
Stephen, Sudbury, 1687. A5/6/113, A4/27/68
William, Soham, 1640. A5/4/83
see also Leavitt, Levet(t), Levyt
LEVOLD(E), Edmund, tailor, Bury St. Edmunds, 1616. R2/50/177; W1/73/168
George, yeo., Fornham St. Genevieve, 1616. R2/50/48; W1/73/53
George, blacksmith, Nowton, 1690. R2/71/395; W1/144/99
Henry, tailor, Fornham St. Genevieve, 1619. R2/51/262; W1/132/6
John, Fornham St. Genevieve, 1639. A5/4/74
John, shearman, Rattlesden, 1602. R2/45/183; W1/60/110
John, yeo., Rattlesden, 1614. R2/49/21; W1/71/18
John, yeo., Rattlesden, 1640. R2/58/208; W1/96/141
John, yeo., Redgrave, 1677. R2/66/480; W1/129/60; In. 3/18/71
Robert, wood setter, Rattlesden, 1568. R2/33/11; W1/29/18
Robert, yeo., Redgrave, 1639. R2/58/25; W1/94/47
Thomas, tailor, Fornham All Saints, 1651. R2/61/456
see also Leavold, Lefeld, Levell
LEVYN, Thomas, singleman, Great Wratting, 1660. In. 3/5/196; A5/5/10, A4/1/152
LEVYT, Giles, Bury St. Edmunds, 1553. R2/8/56; W1/21/188 & 189
LEWE, John, Hopton, 1504. R2/12/37
LEWEN, see Powlter als. Lewen
LEWES, Ann, singlewoman, Clare, 1593. R2/42/384; W1/50/50
John, bowyer, Bury St. Edmunds, 1592. R2/42/244; W1/49/59
John, Depden, 1581, (N). R2/38/320; W1/40/61; In. 5/2/35
Margaret, wid., Palgrave, 1559. In. 2/28/381; W1/3/146
Matthew, Nayland, 1588. A5/2/102
Ralph, Bury St. Edmunds, 1479. R2/2/267
Thomas, Kedington, 1556. R2/25/130; W1/16/180
William, husb., Great Wratting, 1556. R2/25/95; W1/16/111
William, husb., Stoke, 1634. R2/56/397; W1/90/180
William, Wortham, 1601. R2/44/458; W1/59/73
LEWICE, Richard, husb., Needham, 1632. R2/56/188; W1/89/97
LEWIS, Elisabeth, spinster, Combs, 1690. R2/71/368; W1/144/75
John, Lakenheath, 1642. A5/4/95
William, husb., Lakenheath, 1690. R2/71/394; W1/144/98
see also Lewys
LEWKEN, Elisabeth, Kirtling, 1610. A5/3/106
LEWYN, Thomas, Stuston, 1474. R2/10/509
LEWYS, John, yeo., Wickhambrook, 1560. R2/29/2
LEYE, Richard, tailor, Clare, 1539. R2/19/298
LEY(E)S, Lucy, wid., Wickhambrook, formerly of Oldham, 1559. R2/28/395; W1/3/70
William, Exning, 1542. R2/22/64; W1/6/51
William, Exning, 1565. R2/32/218
LEYGHE, Gregory, Glemsford, 1559. R2/28/184; W1/22/164
LEYMAN, Henry, husb., Stowlangtoft, 1598. R2/44/30; W1/56/26
LEYME, Katherine, als. Langley, Ickworth, 1556. R2/25/63
Nicholas, Ickworth, 1556. R2/25/61; W1/16/69
LEYNDRAPER, Andrew, Bury St. Edmunds, 1366. R2/1/25
see also Lyndraper
LEYNGE, George, fuller, Bury St. Edmunds, 1450. R2/2/31
LEYR, George, mason, Bury St. Edmunds, 1452. R2/2/38
Margery, wid., Bury St. Edmunds, 1460. R2/2/65
William, mason, Bury St. Edmunds, 1444. R2/2/6
LEYSTON, Thomas, Lackford, 1476. R2/11/438
William, Wetheringsett, 1648. R2/60/27; W1/105/39
LICHFIELD, Henry, Little Saxham, 1625. R2/53/300; W1/81/86
Richard, Bury St. Edmunds, 1594. R2/42/588
LIFTCHILD, John, Chippenham, 1681. A5/6/47, A4/18/45
see also Leifchild

LIGBERT, William, husb., Rougham, 1626. R2/53/615; W1/82/144
LILES, John, yeo., Soham, 1690. R2/71/366; W1/144/72
LILLEY, Martha, wid. of Thomas, Wetherden, 1634. R2/56/315; W1/90/82
LILLIE, Dorothy, wid., Hartest, 1684. R2/69/245; W1/138/50
Joan, wid., Cotton, 1578. R2/37/376; W1/36/200
John, yeo., Westley, 1632. R2/56/157; W1/89/62
Nathaniel, husb., Stowlangtoft, 1680. R2/67/550; W1/134/33; In. 3/20/35
Thomas, husb., Eriswell, 1578. R2/37/340; W1/36/233
William, Horringer, 1573. A5/1/264
LILLY, Abigail, wid., Stowlangtoft, 1680. In. 3/20/256; A5/6/39, A4/17/84
Alice, wid., Langham, 1679. R2/67/338; W1/133/105
Barnaby, yeo., Pakenham, 1637. R2/57/206; W1/92/247
Benjamin, wheelwright, Hartest, 1666. R2/64/145; W1/118/113; In. 3/11/139
Benjamin, Lavenham, 1673. A5/5/136, A4/88/12
Gilbert, husb., Acton, 1588. R2/41/85; W1/45/81
Henry, labourer, Ixworth, 1686. R2/70/540; W1/140/145; In. 3/22/160
John, Burwell, 1693. A5/6/165, A4/35/10
John, husb., Hartest, 1690. R2/71/321; W1/144/24
John, blacksmith, Lavenham, 1616. R2/50/141; W1/73/145
John, the elder, Sudbury, 1639. R2/58/75; W1/94/127
John, Sudbury, 1668. A5/5/90, A4/6/6
John, labourer, Tuddenham, 1642, (N). R2/58/333; W1/99/26
Richard, blacksmith, Stoke by Nayland, 1680. R2/67/567; W1/134/47; In. 3/20/48
Richard, husb., Stowlangtoft, 1611. R2/48/79; W1/68/97
Thomas, Sapiston, 1685. A5/6/89, A4/105/32
Thomas, yeo., Stansfield, 1630. R2/55/154; W1/86/173
Thomas, yeo., Whepstead, 1571. R2/35/275; W1/38/25
Thomas, Whepstead, 1637. A5/4/48
William, Great Waldingfield, 1637. A5/4/54
William, Hawstead, 1684. A5/6/84, A4/21/111
William, yeo., Stansfield, 1700. R2/74/106; W1/154/108
William, the elder, clothier, Whepstead, 1693. R2/72/241; W1/147/131
see also Lyllie
LIMBER, Ann, wid., Hartest, 1675. R2/66/185; W1/127/57; In. 3/16/77
LIMER, Robert, Sudbury, 1665. A5/5/70, A4/3/77
LIMMAR, Robert, Hopton, 1696. A5/6/188, A4/39/45
LIMMER, John, innkeeper, Newton, 1649. R2/60/237; W1/106/92
Margery, wid., Hartest, 1675. R2/66/127; W1/127/4; In. 3/16/1
Richard, yeo., Hartest, 1674. R2/66/7; W1/126/116
Thomas, Hargrave, 1637. A5/4/52
Thomas, Sudbury, 1570. A5/1/232
William, yeo., Hargrave, 1678. R2/67/59; W1/130/46; In. 3/19/65
see also Lymer, Lymmer
LINCH, John, Polstead, 1631. A5/4/12
LINCOLN, Henry, say scourer, Sudbury, 1666. In. 3/12/136; A5/5/78, A4/4/76 & 77
James, Sudbury, 1688. A5/6/117, A4/29/3
Thomas, yeo., Walsham le Willows, 1647. R2/59/444; W1/104/74
see also Lyncoln
LINDFEILD, Gilbert, gent., Whatfield, 1692. R2/72/53; W1/146/50
LINDGE, Robert, yeo., Ashley, 1638. R2/57/276; W1/93/42
Robert, shepherd, Barnham, 1663. R2/63/70; W1/115/111; In. 3/8/145
Thomas, yeo., Herringswell, 1666. R2/64/146; In. 3/11/157
Thomas, husb., Herringswell, 1677. R2/66/517; W1/129/99; In. 3/18/125
Thomas, Herringswell, 1680. In. 3/20/204; A5/6/41, A4/17/105
William, bach., Herringswell, 1680. In. 3/20/203; A5/6/40, A4/17/101
William, yeo., Tuddenham, 1665. R2/63/344; W1/117/92; In. 3/10/108
see also Lyndge, Nindge als. Lyndge, Ninge als. Lindge
LINEING, John, labourer, Bury St. Edmunds, 1618. R2/51/48; W1/75/27
LING(E), Edmund, singleman, Haughley, 1664. A5/5/58, A4/2/62
Edward, Isleham, 1660. In. 9/2
Elisabeth, wid., Hepworth, 1631. R2/56/71; W1/87/104
Henry, yeo., Glemsford, 1610. R2/47/136; W1/67/18
Henry, Hargrave, 1586. A5/2/80
Joan, spinster, Haughley, 1664. A5/5/58, A4/2/63

LING(E) continued
John, shepherd, Barnham, 1667. In. 3/12/35; A5/5/83, A4/5/27
John, yeo., Freckenham, 1712. In. 10/43
John, yeo., Haughley, 1665. R2/63/379; W1/117/132; In. 3/10/163
John, Rattlesden, 1587. A5/2/89
John, husb., Yaxley, 1660. R2/62/81; W1/112/105; In. 3/5/110
Lambert, labourer, Risby, 1607. R2/46/116; W1/97/23
Lawrence, Stowmarket, 1566. A5/1/173
Lewis, singleman, Horningsheath, 1652. In. 3/4/10; A5/4/140
Mary, spinster, Bury St. Edmunds, 1700. A5/7/16, A4/41/110
Mary, wid., Fornham All Saints, 1661. R2/62/277; W1/113/184; In. 3/6/259
Peter, Bury St. Edmunds, 1685. A5/6/86, A4/24/2
Peter, Little Saxham, 1676. In. 3/17/6; A5/5/159, A4/13/9
Ralph, Thelnetham, 1566. A5/1/175
Robert, Lidgate, 1578. A5/2/10
Robert, Poslingford, 1621. R2/52/339; W1/77/117
Thomas, Freckenham, 1711. In. 10/42
Thomas, yeo., Hepworth, 1661. R2/62/209; W1/113/71; In. 3/6/131; A5/5/16, A4/1/100
William, singleman, Lakenheath, 1669. In. 3/14/108; A5/5/106, A4/7/49
William, yeo., Stowlangtoft, 1662. R2/62/392; W1/114/136; In. 3/7/169; A5/5/36
William, thatcher, Yaxley, 1680. In. 3/20/80; A5/6/35, A4/17/44
see also Leyng, Lyenge, Lyng(e)
LINGWOOD, Richard, bach., Tuddenham, 1683. A5/6/70, A4/20/66
Thomas, Bury St. Edmunds, 1677. In. 3/18/92; A5/5/171, A4/14/43
see also Lyngwood
LINKHORNE, John, say maker, Bury St. Edmunds, 1680. R2/67/577; W1/134/56; In. 3/20/76
John, alehouse keeper, Worlington, 1663, (N). R2/63/3; W1/115/4; In. 3/8/2
LINNETT, Thomas, husb., Little Cornard, 1647. In. 3/2/98; A5/4/118
see also Lynet, Lynnett
LINSDELL, John, yeo., Haverhill, 1700. In. 3/27/35; A5/7/13, A4/41/136
Thomas, yeo., Denston, 1675. R2/66/127; W1/127/5; In. 3/16/6
see also Lynsdell
LINTON, John, Wicken, 1596. R2/43/153; W1/54/30
see also Lynton
LINWOOD, William, carpenter, Cheveley, 1615. R2/49/501; W1/72/131
see also Lynwood
LIRKIN, John, sen., Hunston, 1691. R2/71/527; W1/145/84
LISTE, John, Soham, (1500). R2/13/119
LISTER, Edward, the elder, yeo., Alpheton, 1624. R2/53/42; W1/80/60
Elisabeth, wid., Wood Ditton, 1647. In. 3/2/150; A5/4/117
James, the elder, yeo., Alpheton, 1652. R2/61/600; W1/109/78
James, the elder, husb., Alpheton, 1679. R2/67/324; W1/133/96
Matthew, husb., Wood Ditton, 1642. R2/58/361; W1/99/61
Nicholas, husb., Stowlangtoft, 1618, (N). R2/51/193; W1/75/121
Roger, Bury St. Edmunds, 1428. R2/1/183
Thomas, yeo., Bury St. Edmunds, 1686. R2/70/530; W1/140/132
Thomas, Stanton, 1674. A5/5/147, A4/11/24
William, carpenter, Fordham, 1650. R2/61/403; W1/107/109
see also Lyster
LITCHFIELD, John, the elder, comber, Haverhill, 1661. R2/62/300; W1/113/218; In. 3/6/264
see also Lichfield
LITTLE, Ann, spinster, Sudbury, 1634. A5/4/31
Toby, say maker, Sudbury, 1616. R2/50/196; W1/73/184
see also Lettele, Lytell, Lytle, Lytyll
LITTLECHILD, Richard, blacksmith, Kirtling, 1681. R2/68/189; W1/135/138; A5/6/52, A4/96/108
William, bach., Kirtling, 1679. A5/6/29, A4/94/152
LITTLEPROUD, Robert, Bardwell, 1686. In. 3/22/62; A5/6/100, A4/26/76
LITTON, Joan, wid., Thelnetham, 1580. R2/38/185; W1/39/118
Paul, Rickinghall Superior, 1634. A5/4/34
LIVERMEERE, Mirabel, Little Thurlow, 1612. A5/3/117
LIVERMER, Peter, wicker worker, Great Thurlow, 1650. R2/61/393; W1/107/96; In. 3/3/107
Peter, Little Thurlow, 1612, (N). R2/48/198; W1/69/87

LIVERMORE, Daniel, clerk, Burwell, 1675. In. 3/16/79; A5/5/156, A4/12/39
John, Great Thurlow, 1693. R2/72/205; W1/147/96
Nicholas, Great Thurlow, 1660. A5/5/8, A4/1/174
Peter, yeo., Great Thurlow, 1662. R2/62/410; W1/114/161; In. 3/7/193
LLOYD, Jane, spinster, Fordham, 1669. A5/5/109, A4/7/58
Richard, surgeon, Norwich, (1524). W1/51/53
LOCAR, see Rydsdalle als. Locar, Loker
LOCK(E), Agnes, wid. of Richard, Wattisfield, 1568. R2/33/70; W1/29/91
Alice, wid., Wattisfield, 1532. R2/17/16; W1/21/72
Ann, wid., Hartest, 1643. R2/59/16; W1/100/24
Edmund, Hinderclay, 1606. R2/46/31; W1/64/40
Edmund, husb., Thelnetham, 1678. In. 3/19/100; A5/6/7, A4/15/58
Edward, the elder, yeo., Hinderclay, 1663. R2/63/75; W1/115/119; In. 3/8/155
Elisabeth, wid., Wattisfield, 1649. R2/60/273; W1/106/145
Frances, wid., Long Melford, 1629. R2/54/349; W1/85/53
John, the elder, yeo., Alpheton, 1621. R2/52/324; W1/77/105
John, Great Ashfield, 1685. A5/6/88, A4/24/18
John, Hinderclay, 1589. R2/41/182; W1/46/103
John, yeo., Lavenham, (1609). W1/95/123
John, Long Melford, 1632. A5/4/21
John, yeo., Nowton, 1695. R2/72/500; W1/149/53
John, Sudbury, 1671, (N). R2/65/278; W1/123/158; A5/5/129, A4/9/24
John, yeo., Thelnetham, 1666. R2/64/126; W1/118/96; In. 3/11/126
John, jun., Wattisfield, 1623. R2/52/664; W1/79/85
John, yeo., Westhorpe, 1664. R2/63/221; W1/116/133; In. 3/9/165
Nicholas, yeo., Wattisfield, 1628. R2/54/137; W1/84/8
Nicholas, potter, Whatfield, 1588. R2/41/28; W1/45/21
Richard, singleman, Long Melford, 1625. R2/53/284; W1/81/75
Richard, Wattisfield, 1568. A5/1/193
Robert, the elder, yeo., Hinderclay, 1626. R2/53/574; W1/82/100
Robert, singleman, Hunston, 1661. R2/62/239; W1/113/114; In. 3/6/168
Robert, yeo., Long Melford, 1647. R2/59/398; W1/104/25; In. 3/2/39
Susan, wid., Boxford, 1640. R2/58/203; W1/96/135
Thomas, yeo., Hartest, 1669. R2/64/422; W3/14/200
Thomas, Hopton, 1555. A5/1/98
Thomas, Stanton, 1558. R2/27/294
William, husb., Hopton, 1630. R2/55/109; W1/86/121
William, yeo., Long Melford, 1622. R2/52/431; W1/78/54
see also Lokke
LOCKES, Matthew, Boxford, 1638. A5/4/65
LOCKET(T), Robert, Bury St. Edmunds, 1562. A5/1/135
Robert, cordwainer, Gedding, 1679. R2/67/211; W1/133/19
Robert, glover, Thelnetham, 1599. R2/44/179; W1/57/9
LOCKINE, William, yeo., Little Cornard, 1644. R2/59/161; W1/101/88
LOCKWOOD, Alice, wid., Combs, 1638. R2/57/424; W1/93/257
Edmund, Combs, 1638. A5/4/64
Edward, yeo., Combs, 1604. R2/45/306; W1/62/3
Edward, Combs, 1610. A5/3/97
Edward, yeo., Mendlesham, 1614. R2/49/137; W1/71/93
Edward, yeo., Mendlesham, 1649. R2/60/274; W1/106/146
Francis, als. Baker, husb., Debenham, 1555. R2/24/230; W1/15/60
John, husb., Rattlesden, (1555). R2/24/247; W1/15/75
Leonard, Hitcham, 1559. R2/28/403
Magdalen, wid., Mendlesham, 1630. A5/4/1
Margery, wid., Combs, 1628. R2/54/161; W1/84/34
Martha, wife of William, Combs, 1634. R2/56/333; W1/90/97
Robert, sen., yeo., Combs, 1637. R2/57/168; W1/92/208
Robert, Eye, 1558. R2/27/461
Thomas, Brettenham, 1559. R2/28/369; W1/3/141
Thomas, yeo., Great Finborough, 1647. R2/59/414; W1/104/41; In. 3/2/49
Thomas, Mildenhall, 1628. W1/95/147
William, Combs, 1660. A5/5/10
see also Lokwod(e)
LODBROK, Andrew, Hinderclay, 1511. R2/12/81
LODGE, Elizabeth, als. Lambe, wife of Matthew, Layham, 1680. A5/6/39, A4/17/85

LOFHAM, Margaret, Bury St. Edmunds, 1370. R2/1/31
LOFTES, Daniel, Fordham, 1682. In. 3/21/198; A5/6/57, A4/19/11
LOKER, Agnes, wid., Long Melford, 1585. R2/39/263; W1/42/310
Henry, glover, Bures, 1631. R2/56/16; W1/87/20
see also Riddelsdale als. Loker, Rydsdalle als. Locar
LOKHODE, Robert, 1540. R2/20/206
LOKKE, Thomas, Wattisfield, 1537. R2/20/20
LOKWOD(E), Joan, wife of John, Sudbury, 1457. R2/9/185
Robert, Newmarket, 1521. R2/17/10; W1/21/78
LOKWOOD, Joan, als. Baker, wid., Debenham, 1555. R2/24/231; W1/15/61
John, als. Baker, the elder, yeo., Wetheringsett, 1555. R2/24/229; W1/15/59
LOKYER, John, clerk, Ixworth, 1675. In. 3/16/117; A5/5/156, A4/12/48
LOMAX, Joan, singlewoman, Eye, 1582. R2/38/358; W1/41/87
LOMELEY, Jane, wid., Lavenham, 1663. R2/63/58; W1/115/92; In. 3/8/112
John, sen., yeo., Lavenham, 1643. R2/59/20; W1/100/30
LOND(E), Jane, singlewoman, Thwaite, 1649. R2/60/243; W1/106/103
John, Clare, 1533. R2/19/146; W1/2/67
John, Hinderclay, 1529. R2/18/15
Richard, husb., Hopton, 1617. R2/50/280; W1/74/79
LONDON, Agnes, wid., Bures, 1593. R2/42/419; W1/50/81
Alice, Kedington, 1595. A5/2/211
Elisabeth, wid., Sudbury, 1615. R2/49/250; W1/72/35
Gregory, Kedington, 1590. A5/2/128
Isabel, wid., Fornham, 1526. R2/17/191; W1/23/42
James, Thompson, 1517. W1/51/58
Joan, wife of Robert, Eye, 1559. R2/28/6; W1/22/6
John, Barrow, 1470. R2/10/482
John, saddler, Sudbury, 1560. R2/29/137; W1/25/34
John, cordwainer, Sudbury, 1615. R2/49/217; W1/72/9
Julia, wid. of Robert, Thorndon, 1548. R2/73/483; W1/38/95
Margaret, wid., Thorndon, 1559. R2/28/186; W1/22/166
Robert, Freckenham, 1559. W8/5a & b
Robert, Thorndon, 1540. R2/19/275; W1/36/34
Rowland, Little Bradley, 1610. A5/3/96
Thomas, husb., Kedington, 1615, (N). R2/49/369; W1/72/137
Thomas, Worlington, 1576. R2/37/149; W1/37/17; In. 3/1/100
William, Thorndon, 1452. R2/9/156
William, husb., Thorndon, 1559. R2/28/187; W1/22/169
see also Lunden
LONDYSDALE, Robert, Bildeston, 1482. R2/11/259
LONG, Alice, Brandon, 1644. A5/4/105
Elisabeth, wid. of Robert, Foulden, 1666. R2/64/150; W1/118/117; In. 3/13/39
Harry, weaver, Bury St. Edmunds, 1497. R2/4/59
Helen, wid., Soham, 1597. R2/43/255; W1/55/33
Henry, clerk, Barrow, 1685. R2/70/222; W1/159/185
Isabel, wid., Culford, 1556. R2/25/78; W1/16/77
James, yeo., Alpheton, 1589. R2/41/216; W1/46/69
James, the elder, tailor, Great Barton, 1689. R2/71/233; W1/143/71; A5/6/130, A4/30/5
Joan, wid., Bury St. Edmunds, 1601. R2/44/341; W1/59/4
John, sen., Acton, 1441. R2/9/49
John, farrier, Acton, 1445. R2/9/88
John, Alpheton, 1575. R2/37/119; W1/34/62
John, the elder, brazier, Bury St. Edmunds, 1534. R2/7/19
John, clothier, Clare, 1563. R2/31/141; W1/26/21
John, Culford, 1542. R2/22/78; W1/6/18
John, miller, Hengrave, (1675), (N). R2/66/165; W1/127/41; In. 3/16/49
John, Soham, 1590. A5/2/140
John, Thurston, 1443. R2/9/55
Josias, yeo., Great Horningsheath, 1642. R2/58/355; W1/99/55
Katherine, Sapiston, 1590. A5/2/133
Margery, Wickham, 1455. R2/9/182
Richard, yeo., Clare, 1638. R2/57/346; W1/93/133
Richard, Stoke by Nayland, (1535). R2/18/130
Robert, Alpheton, 1562. A5/1/128
Robert, Alpheton, 1568. R2/33/26; W1/29/41
Robert, Assington, 1475. R2/11/131
Thomas, yeo., Brent Eleigh, 1589. R2/41/298; W1/46/14

LONG continued
Thomas, yeo., Culford, 1553. R2/23/95; W1/11/122
Thomas, Little Thurlow, 1530. R2/19/1
Thomas, yeo., Little Thurlow, 1604. R2/45/376
Thomas, painter, Rishangles, 1540. R2/19/587, R2/21/378; W1/5/51, W1/38/75
Thomas, Stoke by Nayland, 1540. R2/20/254; W1/4/193
William, yeo., Alpheton, 1554. R2/24/85; W1/14/66
William, yeo., Bacton, 1559. R2/28/35; W1/22/37
William, baker, Bury St. Edmunds, 1553. R2/8/61
William, brazier, Bury St. Edmunds, 1595. R2/43/111; W1/53/112
William, Pakenham, 1685. A5/6/93, A4/24/93
William, Soham, 1580. A5/2/24
William, Soham, 1593. A5/2/182
LONGENEY, Thomas, skinner, Bury St. Edmunds, 1423. R2/1/162
LONGES, John, Chippenham, 1554. A5/1/89
LONGLEY, Robert, husb., Stoke by Nayland, 1564. R2/32/102; W1/27/52
Thomas, husb., Polstead, 1548. R2/21/463; W1/38/32
Thomas, husb., Stoke by Nayland, 1557. R2/26/212; W1/20/151
William, Polstead, (1546). R2/21/652
William, husb., Polstead, (1546). R2/31/123
see also Lungley
LONGTOT, John, als. Standly, Chelsworth, 1650. A5/4/134
LONNE, John, Brandon, 1525. W1/5/35
LOODWILL, John, worstead weaver, Norwich, 1538. W1/51/49
LOONE, Margaret, Ingate, (1535). R2/19/215; W1/3/55
LOOTE, John, Assington, (1547). R2/21/335; W1/10/157
Richard, husb., Hawkedon, 1598, (N). R2/44/13; W1/56/13
Richard, Wickhambrook, 1548. R2/21/440
LOPHAM, Margaret, wid. of Thomas, Ixworth, 1529. R2/18/13
Robert, Mildenhall, 1607. A5/3/34
see also Lofham
LORD, Anthony, clothier, Bury St. Edmunds, 1608. R2/46/204; W1/65/82
Arnolphas, Burwell, 1493. R2/11/445
Edmund, husb., Bacton, 1595. R2/43/9; W1/53/12
Elisabeth, Wickhambrook, 1595. A5/2/215
Elisabeth, wid., Wickhambrook, 1684. R2/69/368; W1/138/158
Henry, yeo., Groton, 1555. R2/24/203; W1/15/37
Henry, Wicken, 1593. R2/42/391; W1/50/59
Jeffery, Norton, 1638. A5/4/63
John, Bury St. Edmunds, 1631. A5/4/12
John, husb., Finningham, 1664. R2/63/235; W1/116/155; In. 3/9/195
John, Milden, 1573. A5/1/256
John, Stanningfield, 1504. R2/13/150
John, Stanstead, 1559. R2/28/345
John, husb., Wetheringsett, 1540. R2/21/348; W1/38/91
Martha, spinster, Norton, 1627, (N). R2/54/118; W1/83/113
Maud, spinster, Bacton, 1618. R2/51/133; W1/75/82
Robert, yeo., Bury St. Edmunds, 1675. In. 3/16/98; A5/5/155, A4/12/32 & 33
Robert, labourer, Norton, (1588). R2/41/191; W1/46/95
Robert, Sudbury, 1608. A5/3/39
Robert, Wetherden, 1486. R2/11/363
Thomas, carpenter, Bacton, 1592. R2/42/251; W1/49/69
Thomas, carpenter, Finningham, 1642, (N). R2/58/354; W1/99/53
Thomas, Haughley, 1597. R2/43/259; W1/55/38
Thomas, yeo., Haughley, 1618. R2/51/156; W1/75/95
Thomas, husb., Norton, 1615, (N). W1/111/42
Thomas, husb., Ousden, 1679. R2/67/207; W1/133/15
Walter, Cockfield, 1457. R2/9/185
Walter, Wickhambrook, 1576. In. 3/1/71
William, Beyton, 1529. R2/18/19, R2/19/13
William, Depden, 1617, (N). R2/50/320; W1/74/106
William, carpenter, Finningham, 1607. R2/46/142
William, Finningham, 1661. In. 3/6/104; A5/5/16, A4/1/103
William, Lavenham, 1570. A5/1/202
William, Wicken, 1683. A5/6/70, A4/20/60
LORDYNG, Edward, Withersfield, 1481. R2/11/198
LORE, Katherine, wid., Cavenham, 1528. R2/15/211; W1/19/33b
LORENCE, John, als. Strawe, weaver, Glemsford, 1559. R2/28/151; W1/22/138

LORKEN, Thomas, clothier, Nayland, 1592. R2/42/257; W1/49/74
Thomas, husb., Freckenham, 1649. W8/13
Thomas, Wissington, 1580. R2/38/102; W1/39/175
LORKIN, Ann, wid., Hundon, 1668. In. 3/13/10; A5/5/91, A4/6/17 & 18
Henry, Hundon, 1667. A5/5/87, A4/5/65
James, Bures St. Mary, 1587, (N). R2/40/245; W1/44/86
Richard, Stanstead, 1567. A5/1/185
Robert, yeo., Cavendish, 1614. R2/49/58; W1/71/45
William, the elder, yeo., Little Cornard, 1692. R2/72/15; W1/146/15; In. 3/24/81
LORKYN, Abraham, Bures, 1689. A5/6/129, A4/30/14
Hugh, husb., Wissington, 1557. R2/26/96; W1/20/56
Jasper, Glemsford, 1649. A5/4/127
Joan, wid., Bures, 1650. In. 3/3/112; A5/4/137
John, als. Dystene, Long Melford, 1442. R2/9/59
Richard, Long Melford, 1522. R2/14/47
LOSSE, George, husb., Rougham, 1612. R2/48/248; W1/70/6
John, Buxhall, 1616. W1/95/78
LOTE, John, brewer, Bury St. Edmunds, 1448. R2/2/26
John, tiler, Bury St. Edmunds, 1476. R2/2/219
Rule, tiler, Bury St. Edmunds, 1475. R2/2/213
LOTKYN, Richard, als. Roper, Mildenhall, 1468. R2/10/415
see also Lottkyn
LOTT, Jeremiah, Clare, 1632. A5/4/17
Margaret, wid., Barton, 1554. R2/24/53; W1/14/41
LOTTEN, Robert, Sudbury, 1631. A5/4/16
LOTTKYN, John, Reading, 1476. R2/11/439
LOUDHAM, Thomas, Soham, 1601. R2/44/460; W1/59/74
LOUND(E), Agnes, wid., Bury St. Edmunds, 1464. R2/2/81
John, Bury St. Edmunds, 1411. R2/1/125
Richard, gent., Bury St. Edmunds, 1458. R2/2/61
William, Fornham All Saints, 1607. R2/46/123; W1/97/40
LOUNDS, Thomas, driver, Walsham le Willows, 1607. R2/46/137
LOVE, Henry, yeo., Palgrave, 1687. R2/70/281; W1/141/25
Robert, Newmarket, 1545. R2/19/494
Thomas, currier, Bury St. Edmunds, 1682. In. 3/21/127; A5/6/62, A4/19/80
LOVEDALL, Robert, Brandon, 1542. R2/22/28; W1/6/69
LOVEDAY, Edward, Little Thurlow, 1674. A5/5/147, A4/11/39
John, hosier, Bury St. Edmunds, 1480. R2/2/295
John, Bury St. Edmunds, 1690. A5/6/131, A4/32/1
John, Stoke by Clare, 1624, (N). W1/111/5
Leonard, tailor, Barnardiston, 1639. R2/58/7; W1/94/10
Margaret, wid., Great Thurlow, 1660. A5/5/9, A4/1/160
Miles, cordwainer, Lavenham, 1691. R2/71/522; W1/145/81
Nicholas, Wixoe, 1679. R2/67/502; W1/133/217
Peter, merchant, Bury St. Edmunds, 1463. R2/2/76
Richard, Great Bradley, 1507. R2/12/77
see also Lowffeday
LOVELL, Abraham, clothworker, Woolpit, 1677. R2/66/491; W1/129/71; In. 3/18/89
Edward, yeo., Long Melford, 1604. R2/45/328; W1/62/37
Robert, Woolpit, 1685. A5/6/96, A4/24/130
Thomas, comber, Great Waldingfield, 1612, (N). R2/48/243; W1/69/142; A5/3/115
Thomas, yeo., Mildenhall, 1680. R2/67/709; W1/134/157; In. 3/20/257
William, clothier, Woolpit, 1684. R2/69/327; W1/138/122
William, wool comber, Woolpit, 1689. R2/71/249; W1/143/89
William, Woolpit, 1695. A5/6/177, A4/38/22
see also Bradly als. Lovell
LOVELYCH(E), John, Bury St. Edmunds, 1398. R2/1/84
John, sen., Sudbury, 1474. R2/11/144
LOVENESSE, Benjamin, Great Saxham, 1632. A5/4/22
Philip, husb., Nedging, 1638. R2/57/391; W1/93/204
LOVERING, Jonathan, gent., Bures, 1690. R2/71/436, R2/72/195; W1/147/86, W1/144/142
LOVES, William, Soham, 1632. R2/56/160; W1/89/65
LOVETOP, William, Kersey, 1472. R2/10/571
LOVET(T), Henry, yeo., Hundon, 1640. R2/58/171; W1/96/88
John, Stoke by Nayland, 1641. A5/4/88
Robert, Brettenham, (1536). R2/18/87, R2/19/226

LOVET(T) continued
Thomas, yeo., Haverhill, 1673. R2/65/439; W1/125/67
Thomas, sen., yeo., Shropham, (1651). W1/110/30
LOVICKE, Elisabeth, wid., Hopton, 1637. R2/57/172; W1/92/212
John, Brandon, 1632. A5/4/20
LOW(E), Denise, Eye, 1538. R2/20/67; W1/4/61
Joan, Bury St. Edmunds, 1512. R2/5/12
Joan, Long Melford, 1622, (N). R2/52/356; W1/78/3
John, singleman, Wiston, 1680. R2/67/534; W1/134/17
Margaret, wid., Soham, 1584. A5/2/63
Richard, yeo., Wetherden, 1648. R2/60/119; W1/105/139
Sara, als. Lawrence, Shimpling, 1676. A5/5/165, A4/13/81
Thomas, Bacton, 1579. R2/38/11; W1/39/65
Thomas, yeo., Norton, 1631. R2/56/40; W1/87/57
William, Beyton, 1527. R2/12/144
see also Lowes
LOWDAY, Thomas, Barrow, 1525. W1/5/32
LOWDHAM, Alice, Soham, 1596. A5/2/219
Richard, yeo., Soham, 1621. R2/52/318; W1/77/97 a & b
William, Bury St. Edmunds, 1589. A5/2/126
see also Loudham
LOWEFORTH, Thomas, Sudbury, 1476. R2/11/50
LOWES, Helen, wid., Norton, 1639. R2/58/110; W1/94/183
Henry, husb., Hengrave, 1560. R2/32/440; W1/19/75
John, labourer, Soham, 1580. R2/38/228; W1/39/88
John, Soham, 1679. A5/6/28, A4/16/145
Nicholas, labourer, Soham, 1612. R2/48/186; W1/69/68
Robert, Coney Weston, 1527. R2/12/146
William, als. Lawrence, yeo., Shimpling, 1676, (N). R2/66/424; W1/128/136; In. 3/18/42; A5/5/165, A4/13/84
see also Low(e)
LOWFFEDAYE, Adam, herdman, Barrow, 1554. R2/24/88; W1/14/68
LOWNDE, Richard, Rede, 1541. R2/20/179
see also Lound(e), Lund
LOWNES, Robert, Wattisfield, 1633. A5/4/27
LOWTH, Robert, Bury St. Edmunds, 1448. R2/2/27
LOWTHER, Agnes, wid., Bury St. Edmunds, 1512. R2/5/10
LOWYN, Thomas, Wicken, 1455. R2/9/225
LOYS, William, Thurston, 1556. R2/25/45; W1/16/50
LUCAS, Antony, Nayland, 1533. R2/18/207
Benjamin, Bury St. Edmunds, 1694. A5/6/173, A4/37/91
Edward, Bury St. Edmunds, 1396. R2/1/82
Elisabeth, wid., Ixworth, 1694. R2/72/357; W1/148/82
Gibson, doctor of divinity, Horningsheath, (1696). R2/74/88; W1/154/91
John, haberdasher, Bury St. Edmunds, 1689. R2/71/189; W1/143/44
John, sen., yeo., Elmsett, 1582. R2/38/415; W1/41/20
John, Whatfield, 1596. A5/2/221
Joseph, tailor, Ixworth, 1671. R2/65/253; W1/123/132
Margaret, wife of Walter, Bury St. Edmunds, 1406. R2/1/106
Mary, wife of Richard, Ixworth, 1668. A5/5/93, A4/6/38
Matilda, wife of Robert, Bury St. Edmunds, 1394. R2/1/72
Matthew, Aldham, 1585. A5/2/71
Moses, joiner, Ixworth, 1660. R2/62/87; W1/112/114
Philip, Bury St. Edmunds, 1637. A5/4/49
Richard, tailor, Pakenham, 1689. R2/71/151; W1/143/11
Robert, Bury St. Edmunds, 1394. R2/1/69
Thomas, carpenter, Aldham, 1595. R2/43/64; W1/53/52
Thomas, Bury St. Edmunds, 1385. R2/1/45
Thomas, Great Horningsheath, 1595. A5/2/206
Thomas, Long Melford, 1677. In. 3/18/27; A5/5/167, A4/14/14
Thomas, carpenter, Pakenham, 1687. R2/70/278; W1/141/21
Walter, barker, Bury St. Edmunds, 1406. R2/1/106
William, Botesdale, 1583. A5/2/47
William, tailor, Ixworth, 1674. R2/66/39; W1/126/82
see also Scapy als. Lucas and Whiteing
LUCE, Elisabeth, Hundon, 1610. A5/3/81
Robert, shoe maker, Hundon, 1589. R2/41/164; W1/46/121
LUCK(E)Y, John, yeo., Bury St. Edmunds, 1608. R2/46/160; W1/65/6
Robert, Great Cornard, 1638. A5/4/63
Robert, Great Cornard, 1666. A5/5/80
Thomas, yeo., Acton, 1698. R2/73/260; W1/152/36
William, miller, Fornham St. Genevieve, 1615. R2/49/253; W1/72/38

LUCKIN, Mary, wid., Kennett, 1661, (N). R2/62/294; W1/113/208
see also Dearsley als. Lukyn
LUDBROCK, John, husb., Cockfield, 1576. R2/37/174; W1/37/39; In. 3/1/18
LUDBROKE, Margaret, wife of John, yeo., Stowmarket, 1591. R2/42/74; W1/48/62
Thomas, husb., Stanningfield, 1580. R2/38/220
LUDBROOKE, Joan, wid., Great Finborough, 1648. R2/60/21; W1/105/31
William, Great Finborough, 1639. A5/4/69
LUDBROUCK, John, Combs, 1571. R2/35/129; W1/36/84
see also Lodbrok
LUDKEN, Isabel, singlewoman, Mellis, 1627. R2/54/18; W1/83/21
LUDKINE, Richard, yeo., Great Wratting, 1596. R2/43/145; W1/54/23
LUDKYN, Edward, skinner, Norwich, 1594. W1/51/134
Katherine, wid., Bury St. Edmunds, 1605, (N). R2/45/445; W1/63/89; A5/3/2
Robert, tailor, Long Melford, 1550. R2/21/48; W1/10/191
LUDLOWE, Isabel, wid., Bury St. Edmunds, 1448. R2/2/26
LUDMAN, Robert, husb., Walsham le Willows, 1597. R2/43/332; W1/55/99
LUDPEK, Simon, labourer, Bury St. Edmunds, 1501. R2/4/111
LUFF(E), Ann, wid., Thelnetham, 1675. In. 3/16/42; A5/5/154, A4/12/19
Anthony, Thelnetham, 1669. In. 3/14/168; A5/5/109, A4/7/64
Elisabeth, wid., Finningham, 1682. R2/68/422; W1/136/113; In. 3/21/84
Elisabeth, wid., Wattisfield, 1679. R2/67/447; W1/133/175
John, husb., Finningham, 1678. R2/67/33; W1/130/32; In. 3/19/48
Richard, husb., Wattisfield, 1678. W1/130/169a; In. 3/19/180
LUFKYN, Richard, husb., Denham, 1591. R2/42/122; W1/48/115
Robert, yeo., Stowmarket, 1628. R2/54/136; W1/84/7
Thomas, Elmsett, 1638. A5/4/59
William, Groton, 1532. R2/19/113
LUGGARD, Philip, Kedington, 1639. A5/4/74
LUKE, John, Naughton, 1496. R2/13/77
LUKYN, see Dearsly als. Lukyn
LULLEMAN, John, Swainsthorpe, 1514. W1/51/68
LULLEY, William, Nayland, (1527). R2/17/251; W1/1/27
LULLY, Margery, wife of Robert, Brandon, 1527. W1/19/15
LUMBARD, Richard, Nayland, 1637. A5/4/54
LUMKYN, Ann, wid., Stanton, (1625). W1/111/70
Joan, wid., Ingham, 1561. R2/30/40; W1/28/226
John, Stanningfield, 1482. R2/11/256
Margaret, Mildenhall, 1560. R2/29/74; W1/25/92
Robert, Ingham, 1559. R2/28/411; W1/3/66 & 123
William, Bury St. Edmunds, 1591. A5/2/153
LUMLEY, Ann, wid., Lavenham, 1673. R2/65/476; W1/125/114
Isaac, linen draper, Lavenham, 1662. R2/62/315; W1/114/14; In. 3/7/5
James, yeo., Lavenham, 1678. In. 3/19/48; A5/6/3, A4/15/21
John, wool comber, Lavenham, 1695. R2/72/507; W1/149/59
Thomas, yeo., Lavenham, 1676. R2/66/409; W1/128/118; In. 3/17/157
see also Lomeley
LUMMAS, Anne, wid., Lavenham, 1589. R2/41/178; W1/46/107
William, carpenter, Lavenham, 1573. R2/36/193; W1/32/117
LUMMES, Richard, Lavenham, 1588, (N). R2/41/82; W1/45/77
LUMNIS, William, bricklayer, Bacton, 1689. R2/71/173; W1/143/31
LUMPKIN, Charles, yeo., Mildenhall, 1614. R2/49/16; W1/71/12
Richard, Fornham All Saints, 1608. A5/3/41
Robert, yeo., Weston, 1594. R2/42/556; W1/52/37
William, yeo., Stanton, 1629. R2/54/377; W1/85/75
LUMPKYN, Henry, husb., Coney Weston, 1574, (N). R2/37/39; W1/33/48
John, labourer, Hopton, 1641. R2/58/304; W1/98/96
John, yeo., Ingham, 1557. R2/26/334; W1/17/65 & 66
John, husb., Ingham, 1629. R2/54/414
John, yeo., Weston, 1612. R2/48/126; W1/69/4
Thomas, Mildenhall, 1542. W1/9/64
William, yeo., Hawstead, 1623. R2/52/602; W1/79/52
William, yeo., Rattlesden, 1569. R2/33/129; W1/28/196
see also Lumkyn
LUND, Robert, Hinderclay, (1545). R2/21/638; W1/28/120
LUNDEN, Joan, singlewoman, Worlington, 1626. R2/53/678; W1/82/199
LUNDON, Alice, Thorndon, 1457. R2/9/219

LUNGLEY, John, husb., Polstead, (1552). R2/31/105; W1/13/72
John, yeo., Polstead, 1600. R2/45/1 & 69; W1/58/1
LUNGLY, Robert, Bures, 1581. A5/2/37
Zephaniah, the elder, Long Melford, 1662. R2/62/340; W1/114/51
LUNLY, James, maltster, Stoke by Nayland, 1691. R2/71/464
LUNNEY, Margaret, Fordham, 1503. R2/12/27
LUNISE, Thomas, husb., Kersey, 1617. R2/50/356; W1/74/137
LUNNIS, Agnes, wid., Mildenhall, 1610. R2/47/242; W1/67/123
LUNT, John, Stoke by Nayland, 1451. R2/9/136
LURKIN, Samuel, Shropham, 1662. A5/5/35
LUSHER, Avis, wid., Euston, 1652. R2/61/566; W1/109/41
Francis, husb., Mildenhall, 1618. R2/51/78; W1/75/47
Francis, blacksmith, Pakenham, 1687. R2/70/307; W1/141/50
Robert, Coney Weston, 1557. R2/26/331; W1/20/252
Thomasine, wid., Mildenhall, 1626. R2/53/473; W1/82/21
LUSKINE, Robert, Groton, 1577. A5/2/6
LUSSKYNNE, William, Groton, 1563. A5/1/151
LUTKYN, Alice, wid., Stowlangtoft, 1470. R2/10/451
John, Rickinghall Superior, 1481. R2/11/211
LUTON, John, Lindsey, 1458. R2/9/193
LUTTE, Nicholas, Clare, 1606. A5/3/6
LUYNASS, Robert, Fordham, 1521. W1/14/117
LYCE, William, Debenham, 1557. R2/26/183; W1/20/147
LYDBEARDE, John, yeo., Culford, 1621. R2/52/256; W1/77/43
LYDEKYN, John, Bury St. Edmunds, 1413. R2/1/131
LYELS, Richard, husb., Soham, 1586. R2/40/63; W1/43/51
LYENGE, Joan, wid., Bury St. Edmunds, 1506. R2/4/182
Thomas, Culford, 1519. R2/15/114
William, dyer, Bury St. Edmunds, 1482. R2/2/328
LYES, John, Soham, 1590. A5/2/145
Richard, Long Melford, 1594. A5/2/197
Robert, yeo., Stoke by Nayland, 1589. R2/41/141; W1/46/136
LYGHTYLBURY, John, skinner, Bury St. Edmunds, 1478. R2/2/250
LYLE, John, Layham, 1531. R2/19/66
Martin, husb., Tostock, 1555. R2/24/137; W1/15/93
Thomas, Denston, 1552, (N). R2/23/204; W1/12/31
LYLES, Benjamin, yeo., Soham, 1664. R2/63/144; W1/116/34; In. 3/9/73
John, Burwell, (1545). R2/19/509; W1/7/28
John, yeo., Soham, 1626. R2/53/573; W1/82/99
Matthew, Soham, 1617. R2/50/338; W1/74/120
Richard, clerk, Soham, 1617. R2/50/258; W1/74/58
LYLLES, John, Soham, 1543. R2/22/7; W1/6/174
see also Liles, Lyels
LYLLIE, Lambert, Lidgate, 1562. A5/1/126
Thomas, als. Clemente, husb., Long Melford, 1531. R2/19/75
LYLLY, Beatrice, wid., Acton, 1599. R2/44/190; W1/57/18
Hugh, husb., Tostock, 1560. R2/29/151; W1/25/23
John, labouring man, Great Horningsheath, 1574. R2/37/25; W1/33/65
Margaret, wid., Soham, 1552. R2/31/36; W1/13/24
Robert, husb., Soham, 1552. R2/23/138; W1/11/103
Thomas, the elder, Eriswell, 1567. R2/32/421; W1/19/87
William, husb., Whepstead, 1597. R2/43/317; W1/55/84
LYLY(E), Ambrose, husb., Stowlangtoft, 1598. R2/44/123; W1/56/115
John, Soham, 1439. R2/9/3
John, Elmswell, 1477. R2/11/152
John, Wetherden, 1565. R2/32/229; W1/27/150
Thomas, the elder, Elmswell, 1548. R2/21/486; W1/38/42
LYMER, Thomas, cordwinder, Hargrave, 1679. R2/67/328; W1/133/98
LYMESY, Alice, wife of Richard, Bury St. Edmunds, 1444. R2/2/11
Richard, carpenter, Bury St. Edmunds, 1444. R2/2/11
LYMING, Edward, Kersey, 1566. R2/32/274; W1/28/121
LYMMER, John, yeo., Hargrave, 1620. R2/52/121; W1/76/106
John, Lavenham, 1538. R2/20/131; W1/4/111
John, musician, Stowmarket, 1595. R2/43/40; W1/53/33
Margaret, wid., Hargrave, 1622. R2/52/362; W1/78/7
Margaret, Stanstead, 1559. R2/28/300; W1/22/275
Thomas, ploughwright, Shimpling, 1599. R2/44/255; W1/57/65
William, yeo., Hargrave, 1614. R2/49/73; W1/71/57
LYMNAR, John, Stanstead, 1558. R2/27/574
LYMNOUR, Thomas, als. Lynne, Bury St. Edmunds, 1480. R2/2/298
LYNACRE, Thomas, glazier, Ixworth, 1642. R2/58/323; W1/99/13

LYNCH(E), Joan, Bures, 1610. A5/3/100
John, Bures, 1528. R2/15/191
John, Great Cornard, 1455. R2/9/228
Robert, yeo., Bures, 1601. R2/44/339; W1/59/6
Thomas, Bures, 1522. R2/14/45
William, the elder, clothier, Lavenham, 1550. R2/21/83; W1/9/150
see also Linch
LYNCOLN, John, Aspal, 1474. R2/10/591
John, Bury St. Edmunds, 1380. R2/1/39
LYNCON, Agnes, wid., Lakenheath, 1571. R2/35/305; W1/36/123
LYNDALL, Richard, als. Lyndeth, Great Horningsheath, 1637. W1/110/25
Richard, als. Lyndeth, gent., Great Horningsheath, 1639. R2/58/18; W1/94/32
LYNDESEY, Henry, Bury St. Edmunds, 1443. R2/2/4
John, Bury St. Edmunds, 1399. R2/1/88
see Lyndall als. Lyndeth
LYNDGE, Thomas, Kentford, 1570. R2/34/38; W1/30/35
LYNDRAPER, Isabel, Bury St. Edmunds, 1361. R2/1/16
see also Leyndraper
LYNES, Robert, husb., Rickinghall Superior, 1588. R2/41/103; W1/45/98
LYNG(E), Agnes, Chevington, 1610. A5/3/102
Bartholomew, Bury St. Edmunds, 1589. A5/2/127
Edward, tailor, Bury St. Edmunds, 1671. R2/65/215; W1/123/88
George, Fornham, 1470. R2/10/452
Humfrey, carpenter, Hepworth, 1623. R2/52/706; W1/79/121
John, husb., Barrow, 1650, (N). R2/61/399; W1/107/104
John, husb., Chevington, 1607. R2/46/144; W1/97/79
John, Hargrave, 1539. R2/19/298
John, labourer, Hundon, 1668. R2/64/343; W1/120/53; In. 3/13/150
John, Mildenhall, 1521. R2/15/121
John, Thrandeston, 1559. R2/28/119; W1/22/113
John, Whepstead, 1505. R2/13/168; W1/9/10
Katherine, Great Thornham, 1595. A5/2/206
Margaret, wid., Boxford, 1557. R2/26/53
Nicholas, yeo., Stowlangtoft, 1601. R2/44/353; W1/59/17
Peter, Risby, 1644. R2/59/101; W1/101/27
Robert, Chevington, 1564. R2/32/72; W1/27/23
Robert, Hinderclay, 1581. R2/38/337; W1/40/76
Robert, Sudbury, 1538. R2/18/169
Roger, fuller, Bury St. Edmunds, 1496. R2/4/52
Thomas, Chevington, 1534. R2/19/191
Thomas, Great Thornham, 1580. R2/38/105; W1/39/171
Thomas, Naughton, 1564. A5/1/158
William, Ickworth, 1579. A5/2/20
William, yeo., Lindsey, 1600. R2/45/66; W1/58/93
William, yeo., Rattlesden, 1549. R2/21/139; W1/9/78
---, 1451. R2/9/132
LYNGWOOD, Robert, shearman, Long Melford, 1605. R2/45/412; W1/63/55
LYNN(E), Avice, wid., Botesdale, 1560. A5/1/102
John, smith, Brandon, 1477. R2/11/185
John, Poslingford, 1475. W1/24/158
John, the elder, Redgrave, 1555. R2/24/243; W1/15/72
John, Stoke by Clare, 1540. R2/20/292; W1/4/220
Richard, smith, Brandon, (1548). R2/21/138; W1/9/75
Richard, Poslingford, 1440. R2/1/11
Robert, Brandon, 1580. A5/2/31
Robert, Burwell, 1451. R2/9/107
Thomas, armourer, Sudbury, 1553. R2/31/148; W1/13/98
see also Lymnour als. Lynne
LYNNETT, Elisabeth, wid., Little Cornard, 1650. In. 3/3/46; A5/4/134
William, Withersfield, 1632. A5/4/17
LYNSDELL, Frances, spinster, Burwell, 1697. R2/73/116; W1/151/7
LYNSTEDD, Elisabeth, wid., Potter Heigham, 1574. W1/51/242
LYNTON, William, tailor, Stoke by Clare, 1620. R2/52/118; W1/76/104
LYNWOOD, Alice, wid., Cheveley, 1616, (N). R2/50/125; W1/73/132
Edward, Stradishall, 1595. A5/2/210
John, carpenter, Cheveley, 1557. R2/26/178; W1/20/145
John, carpenter, Denham, 1551. R2/23/56; W1/11/37
William, Cheveley, 1610. R2/47/177; W1/67/54

LYON, James, Newmarket, 1630. A5/4/3
John, Little Waldingfield, 1522. R2/14/70, R2/17/17; W1/21/70
Thomas, husb., Hindringham, 1575. W1/51/204
William, pattern maker, Bury St. Edmunds, 1442. R2/1/258
LYSSE, Robert, Groton, 1480. R2/12/5
Walter, Edwardstone, 1440. R2/9/11
LYSTER, Agnes, Wattisham, 1565. A5/1/166
Alice, wid., Alpheton, 1683. R2/69/124; W1/137/100
Alice, wife of Roger, Bury St. Edmunds, 1438. R2/1/233
Christopher, thatcher, Fordham, 1669. R2/64/440; W1/121/25; In. 3/14/199
Elisabeth, wid., Norton, 1590, (N). R2/41/435; W1/47/115
Frances, wid., Fordham, 1693. R2/72/123
Gilbert, Bury St. Edmunds, 1411. R2/1/122
John, the elder, yeo., Fordham, 1693. R2/72/175
John, Hunston, 1562. R2/31/80; W1/8/106
John, Norton, 1581. A5/2/34
John, the elder, Pakenham, 1541. R2/21/580; W1/28/168
Marian, wid., Alpheton, 1634. R2/56/395; W1/90/175
Richard, Bury St. Edmunds, 1411. R2/1/124
Robert, Wattisham, 1565. A5/1/165
Samuel, wid., Soham, 1681. A5/6/51, A4/18/87
Thomas, Fordham, 1672. R2/65/307; W1/124/30
Thomas, labourer, Fordham, 1672. R2/65/365; W1/124/102
LYTELL, Thomas, butcher, Bury St. Edmunds, 1478. R2/2/253
LYTHER, Matthew, Stoke by Nayland, 1632. A5/4/18
Matthew, Stoke by Nayland, 1667. A5/5/84, A4/5/35
LYTHMAN, Thomas, Long Melford, 1454. R2/9/175
LYTLE, John, Great Finborough, 1545. A5/1/64
LYTTON, Richard, East Rudham, 1535. R2/14/147, R2/19/240
Robert, yeo., Thelnetham, 1620. R2/52/133; W1/76/118
Thomas, husb., Thelnetham, 1575. R2/37/74; W1/34/20
Thomas, the elder, Thelnetham, 1634. R2/56/428; W1/90/215
see also Litton
LYTYLL, Christine, Bures, 1478. R2/11/154
John, Dalham, 1477. R2/12/14
Richard, jun., butcher, Bures, 1445. R2/9/65
Richard, Stowmarket, 1458. R2/9/211
---, Sudbury, 1452. R2/9/110
LYVERICH, Richard, yeo., Redlingfield, 1599. R2/44/327; W1/57/111

M

MAAS, John, Bury St. Edmunds, 1513. R2/5/22
MABBESON, Isabel, als. Palmer, Barningham, 1481. R2/11/226
MABLYE, Richard, priest, Timworth, 1559. R2/28/407; W1/3/154
MACE, James, husb., Mildenhall, 1592. R2/42/249; W1/49/66
John, labourer, Mildenhall, 1601. R2/44/380; W1/59/40
see also Maas, Mase, Mayes
MACHAM, Barnaby, Cockfield, 1613. R2/48/309; W1/70/82
Elisabeth, wid., Mildenhall, 1643. R2/59/1; W1/100/2
William, Bury St. Edmunds, 1610. A5/3/92
see also Machem
MACHELL, Thomas, Bury St. Edmunds, 1500. R2/4/98
MACHEM, Margaret, wid., Cockfield, 1615. R2/49/267; W1/72/51
MACHEN, Thomas, Bury St. Edmunds, 1466. R2/2/90
MACHON, Isabel, Felsham, 1471. R2/10/490
John, Bury St. Edmunds, 1476. R2/4/227
Margery, Preston, 1498. R2/13/56
MACHROE, William, Risby, 1631. A5/4/13
MACHYN, Alice, wid., Little Saxham, 1575. R2/37/89; W1/34/10
William, the elder, Little Saxham, 1572, (N). R2/36/65; W1/31/76
MACKFARE, William, Soham, 1581. R2/38/302; W1/40/46
MACKWORTH, John, Soham, 1558. R2/27/560; W1/31/11
Thomas, Soham, 1525. R2/17/107; W1/21/103
see also Macworth, Makeworth
MACRO(E), Arthur, Chilton, 1673. A5/5/140, A4/10/62
Jane, wife of Roger, Lavenham, 1582, (N). R2/38/361; W1/41/82
John, Preston, 1590. A5/2/131
Margaret, singlewoman, Risby, 1635, (N). R2/56/462; W1/91/28
Robert, Snailwell, 1691. A5/6/140, A4/33/14
Roger, yeo., Long Melford, 1621. R2/52/279; W1/77/65

MACRO(E) continued
Susan, wid., Bury St. Edmunds, 1628, (N). R2/54/171; W1/84/46
Thomas, yeo., Bury St. Edmunds, 1620. R2/52/86; W1/76/71
Thomas, yeo., Great Saxham, 1700. R2/74/55; W1/154/53
William, baker, Bury St. Edmunds, 1661. In. 3/6/171; A5/5/20, A4/1/59
William, yeo., Great Whelnetham, 1614. R2/49/22; W1/71/19
William, yeo., Thurston, 1669. In. 3/14/81; A5/5/106, A4/7/48
MACROW(E), BarTholomew, Rougham, 1639. A5/4/71
John, smith, Hawstead, 1587. R2/40/244; W1/44/85
John, Soham, 1504. R2/13/148 & 150
John, husb., Tuddenham, 1683. R2/69/130; W1/137/106
Ralph, yeo., Great Whelnetham, 1569. R2/33/96; W1/19/122
Roger, yeo., Lavenham, 1581. R2/38/279; W1/40/26
Thomas, Lawshall, 1545. A5/1/33
William, yeo., Risby, 1663, (N). R2/63/118; W1/115/112; In. 3/8/130
see also Machroe, Makerowe, Makro(e), Maycrow
MACWORTH, Agnes, wid., Soham, 1560. R2/29/142; W1/25/30
Thomas, Soham, 1565. R2/32/219
MADDER, Frances, wid., Mildenhall, 1638. A5/4/59
Oliver, Mildenhall, 1635. A5/4/38
Thomas, yeo., Dalham, 1589. R2/41/172; W1/46/111
MADDIE, Richard, tailor, Bury St. Edmunds, 1637. R2/57/212; W1/92/253
MADDOX, Thomas, woollen draper, Mildenhall, 1673. R2/65/388; W1/125/1
MADDY, Thomas, Wicken, 1471. R2/10/477
see also Maddie
MADHAM, Andrew, Barnham, 1522. R2/15/57, R2/14/44
MADURE, John, Dalham, 1531. R2/19/65
MAFFYN, Nicholas, Great Waldingfield, 1590. A5/2/140
MAGER, Thomas, carpenter, Elmsett, 1598. R2/44/118; W1/56/119
MAGGYS, Agnes, wid., Bury St. Edmunds, 1449. R2/2/29
John, Bury St. Edmunds, 1434. R2/1/205
MAHEWE, John, Brockley, 1464. W1/24/156
Roger, tailor, Hawstead, 1588. R2/41/93; W1/45/89
MAIE, George, husb., Cavendish, 1577. R2/37/281
MAIER, Robert, husb., Ixworth, 1597. R2/43/225; W1/55/10
MAIHEW, James, yeo., Bradfield St. George, 1662. R2/62/376; W1/114/112; In. 3/7/150
MAISTER, John, Bury St. Edmunds, 1477. R2/2/241
John, Bury St. Edmunds, 1484. R2/2/198
John, yeo., Rickinghall Inferior, 1612. R2/48/163; W1/69/44
William, Stanton, 1592. A5/2/166
MAJOR, Ann, als. Hatfeild, wid. of Edward, Elmswell, 1682. R2/68/264; W1/136/6; In. 3/21/159; A5/6/47
John, Newmarket, 1688. In. 3/23/66; A5/6/120, A4/29/48
Lancelot, Polstead, 1600. R2/45/71; W1/58/101
Thomas, woollen draper, Redgrave, 1588. R2/41/52; W1/45/45
William, als. Hatfelde, husb., Elmswell, 1580. R2/38/179; W1/39/122
William, Newmarket, 1694. A5/6/169, A4/37/41
see also Mager, Hatfeild als. Major, Hatfelld als. Mager, Hatfield als. Major, Hatfild als. Major
MAKEING, Henry, sen., yeo., Preston, 1660. R2/62/106; W1/112/140; In. 3/5/169
MAKELL, John, Long Melford, 1464. R2/10/358
MAKEMERE, John, 1440. R2/9/27 (probate only)
MAKEN, Peter, husb., Rattlesden, 1650. R2/61/309; W1/107/4; In. 3/3/14
MAKEROWE, Adam, smith, Risby, 1565. R2/32/257
MAKEWORTH, John, the elder, Soham, 1476. R2/11/119
Thomas, sen., Soham, 1498. R2/13/84
MAKIN, George, yeo., Sudbury, 1647. R2/59/447; W1/104/77
Henry, weaver, Sudbury, 1652. R2/61/532; W1/109/16; In. 3/4/14
John, Rattlesden, 1631. R2/56/1; W1/87/2
Samuel, singleman, Rattlesden, 1687. R2/70/388; W1/141/112
William, yeo., Brettenham, 1692. In. 3/24/48; A5/6/149, A4/34/17
MAKING, George, Sudbury, 1674. A5/5/146, A4/11/28
Henry, labourer, Long Melford, 1639. R2/58/25; W1/54/46
Henry, the elder, Rattlesden, 1618. R2/51/136; W1/75/85
Henry, Rattlesden, 1674. A5/5/144, A4/11/3
John, Brettenham, 1561. A5/1/109

MAKING continued
Thomas, Long Melford, 1578. A5/2/7
see also Makeing, Maken, Makyn, Mayken
MAKRO(E), Thomas, yeo., Great Whelnetham, 1623. R2/52/680; W1/79/101
William, Soham, 1472. R2/10/568
MAKROWE, Roger, Lawshall, 1524. R2/17/72; W1/21/20
MAKYN, Christine, wid., Brettenham, 1561. R2/30/26; W1/28/218
Edward, clothier, Sudbury, 1640. R2/58/127; W1/96/10
Thomas, Eye, 1540. R2/19/589; W1/5/8
William, Ballingdon, 1610. R2/47/182; W1/67/59
William, Ballingdon, 1639. A5/4/72
William, Brettenham, 1648. A5/4/124
MAKYNG, Dennis, Hitcham, (1511). R2/13/201
MALCHER, Thomas, Great Waldingfield, 1459. R2/9/261
MALDEN, John, gent., Great Whelnetham, 1685. R2/70/40; W1/139/33
MALDIN(E), Thomas, Cockfield, 1606. A5/3/12
Thomas, carpenter, Soham, 1683. R2/69/54; W1/137/40
see also Maulden
MALETON, Edward, maltster, Sudbury, 1627. R2/54/35; W1/83/43
MALETT, Roger, Shelland, 1668. In. 3/13/140
MALKYN, Henry, Dalham, 1477. R2/12/14
MALKYNGYSSON, Robert, Bury St. Edmunds, 1445. R2/2/14
MALLABAR, Thomas, yeo., Mildenhall, 1676. R2/66/397; W1/128/109; In. 3/17/130
MALLEN, John, Stanningfield, 1559. R2/28/202; W1/39/92
William, rough mason, Stanningfield, 1559. R2/28/203; W1/39/93
MALLETT, Elisabeth, wid., Shelland, 1694. R2/72/367; W1/148/95
John, Stoke by Clare, 1632. R2/56/133; W1/89/22
John, Walshem le Willows, 1688. A5/6/122, A4/29/78a
see also Malett
MALLOUS, Ellis, yeo., Braiseworth, 1692. R2/72/73; W1/146/69
MALLOWES, Christopher, yeo., Hopton, 1669. In. 3/14/136; A5/5/109, A4/7/58
Elisabeth, wid., Wattisfield, 1667. A5/5/90, A4/5/89
John, gent., Bury St. Edmunds, 1637. A5/4/54 & 142
John, gent., Bury St. Edmunds, 1652. A5/4/142
John, yeo., Wattisfield, 1607. R2/46/103
John, Wattisfield, 1636. R2/57/99; W1/92/117
John, Wattisfield, 1645. A5/4/110
Rachael, wid., Wattisfield, 1637. R2/57/158; W1/92/198
Thomas, Eye, 1573. A5/1/232
MALMAN, Warren, Withersfield, 1640. A5/4/84
MALT, John, the elder, shepherd, Downham, 1624. R2/53/134; W1/80/128
John, shepherd, Downham, 1632. R2/56/170; W1/89/78
John, yeo., Lidgate, 1692. R2/72/55; W1/146/52; In. 3/24/58
Robert, Downham, 1630, (N). R2/55/59; W1/86/69
Thomas, Thelnetham, 1559. R2/28/263; W1/22/223
William, Fordham, (1543). R2/19/404; W1/6/102
see also Mault
MALTEWARD, Edward, Downham, 1602, (N). R2/45/130; W1/60/46
Thomas, yeo., Downham, 1602. R2/45/209; W1/60/148
MALTEWAYDE, William, yeo., Horningsheath, 1550. R2/21/153; W1/9/156
MALTIWARD, Samuel, yeo., Downham, 1621. R2/52/223; W1/77/18
MALTON, Thomas, yeo., Hartest, 1599. R2/44/251; W1/57/119
see also Maulton
MALTWARDE, Edmund, doctor of divinity, Rougham, 1556. R2/25/24; W1/16/24
MALTYWADE, John, Great Livermere, 1503. R2/13/129
Rose, wid., Bury St. Edmunds, 1496. R2/4/44
MALTYWARD, Anne, Bradfield, 1465. R2/10/392
Edmund, Barton, 1553. R2/31/167; W1/13/111
Henry, Downham, 1639. A5/4/70
John, mercer, Bury St. Edmunds, 1559. R2/8/353; W1/17/54
John, gent., Buxhall, 1699. In. 3/27/75; A5/7/13, A4/41/57
John, yeo., Rougham, 1597. R2/43/224; W1/55/9
Margery, wid. of William, Rougham, 1559. R2/28/30; W1/22/34
Richard, gent., Hunston, 1675. In. 3/16/141; A5/5/156, A4/12/47
Robert, yeo., Bury St. Edmunds, 1619. R2/51/421; W1/132/99
Stephen, Bury St. Edmunds, 1532. R2/7/7
Susan, Downham, 1631. A5/4/11
Theodosia, wid., Bury St. Edmunds, 1679. A5/6/18, A4/16/32
Thomas, wheelwright, Bury St. Edmunds, 1492. R2/4/3

MALTYWARD continued
William, Little Downham, 1629. R2/54/276; W1/85/2
William, yeo., Rougham, 1555. R2/24/205; W1/15/39
see also Malteward
MAMELL, Henry, mercer, Haverhill, 1583. R2/39/72; W1/42/38
MAMON, Henry, the elder, labourer, Great Wratting, 1621. R2/52/236; W1/77/28
Henry, husb., Great Wratting, 1626. R2/53/448; W1/82/5
MAMONT, John, Fornham All Saints, 1605. A5/3/1
MAMUNT, Henry, Elveden, 1641. R2/58/232; W1/98/3
MANBEE, Sarah, wid., Stowupland, 1695. R2/72/516; W1/149/69
MANBY, Henry, Eye, 1610. A5/3/105
John, Stowupland, 1676. In. 3/17/1; A5/5/159, A4/13/5
Richard, Wortham, 1699. R2/73/355; W1/153/14; In. 3/26/68
MANCE, Robert, Bury St. Edmunds, 1618. R2/51/81; W1/75/49
MANCER, Elizabeth, Shimpling, 1521. R2/14/17, R2/15/167
MANDALL, William, Lakenheath, 1684. A5/6/79, A4/21/61
MANDEFEILD, William, husb., Aldham, 1637. R2/57/125; W1/92/155
MANDVYLE, John, Stanton, 1400. W1/24/166
see also Maundevile
MANER, Thomas, Nowton, (1513). R2/15/5
William, Lakenheath, 1518. R2/15/7
MANERS, Thomas, Bury St. Edmunds, 1533. W1/2/60
MANESTRYE, John, weaver, Eye, 1554. R2/24/69; W1/20/53
MANFEILD, Henry, Drinkstone, 1680. A5/6/43, A4/17/128
George, weaver, Sudbury, 1625. R2/53/417
John, blacksmith, Combs, 1610. R2/47/266; W1/67/149
Lewis, Fordham, 1601. R2/44/412; W1/59/88
Matthew, wid., Sudbury, 1631. R2/56/62; W1/87/90
Roger, yeo., Stoke by Nayland, 1664. In. 3/9/38; A5/5/55, A4/2/19
Thomas, Norton, 1635. A5/4/41
William, yeo., Hundon, 1680. R2/67/717; W1/134/161; In. 3/20/184
MANFELD, William, Great Bradley, (1521). R2/14/112
William, carpenter, Thurston, 1571. R2/35/353; W1/36/139
MANFIELD, Edward, yeo., Hundon, 1694. R2/72/332; W1/148/67
John, bricklayer, Hundon, 1629. R2/54/334; W1/85/41
Roger, husb., Hundon, 1664. R2/63/132; W1/116/18
MANFILDE, Henry, carpenter, Thurston, 1615. R2/49/324; W1/72/102
see also Mandfeild, Manndfield, Maundfeilde, Mawndefelde
MANHODE, John, Alpheton, 1567. A5/1/187
Thomas, weaver, Bury St. Edmunds, 1511. R2/5/8
Thomas, the elder, clothmaker, Glemsford, 1557. R2/26/214; W1/20/129
MANHOODE, Thomas, yeo., Whelnetham, 1603. R2/45/237; W1/61/30
see also Manwood
MANING, Elisabeth, wid., Bury St. Edmunds, 1683. R2/69/41; W1/137/34; In. 3/21/4
John, the elder, cooper, Bury St. Edmunds, 1666. R2/64/35; W1/118/31
Richard, carpenter, Little Finborough, 1640. R2/58/186; W1/96/105
Robert, Soham, 1568. A5/1/206
Robert, yeo., Wickham Skeith, 1645. R2/59/186; W1/102/16
Thomas, Bury St. Edmunds, 1675. In. 3/16/122
Thomas, Rougham, 1675. A5/5/156, A4/12/45
William, the elder, yeo., Great Saxham, 1619. R2/51/464; W1/132/128
William, yeo., Rougham, 1678. R2/67/89; W1/130/72; In. 3/19/94
William, Whepstead, 1595. A5/2/207
MANISTRE, Edmund, tanner, Pakenham, 1682. R2/68/339; W1/136/56; In. 3/21/186
John, Chelsworth, 1684. A5/6/75, A4/21/19
John, tanner, Pakenham, 1693. R2/72/244; W1/147/133
see also Manestrye
MAN(N), Agnes, wid., Haughley, 1606. R2/46/106
Agnes, Lakenheath, 1615. R2/49/234; W1/72/23
Alice, wid., Mendlesham, 1578. R2/37/420; W1/36/153
Andrew, husb., Mildenhall, 1614. R2/49/77; W1/71/60
Ann, singlewoman, Bildeston, 1664. R2/63/176; W1/116/75
Anne, wid., Sudbury, 1598. R2/44/97; W1/56/136
Anne, wid., 1562. R2/31/60
Annice, Lakenheath, 1555. R2/24/147
Edmund, Wortham, 1650, (N). R2/61/323; W1/107/18; In. 3/3/31
Edward, yeo., Bildeston, 1665. R2/63/315; W1/117/50; In. 3/10/52

MAN(N) continued
Edward, yeo., Lakenheath, 1600. R2/45/5; W1/58/6
Elisabeth, wid., Bury St. Edmunds, 1616. R2/50/36; W1/73/37
Elisabeth, wid., Mildenhall, 1691. R2/71/448
Frances, als. Langley, wid., Lakenheath, 1683. A5/6/66, A4/20/12
George, singleman, Lakenheath, 1652. A5/4/140
Grace, wid., Mildenhall, 1595. R2/43/45; W1/53/36
Guy, Stanton, 1631. R2/56/71; W1/87/103; A5/4/14
Henry, yeo., Hawstead, 1560. R2/29/90; W1/25/75
Henry, tailor, Mildenhall, 1625. R2/53/409; W1/81/190
Henry, Stoke by Clare, 1628. R2/54/160; W1/84/33
Isabel, wid., Brettenham, (1460). R2/9/299
James, Bury St. Edmunds, 1664. A5/5/60, A4/2/72
James, yeo., Kersey, 1573. R2/36/206; W1/32/107
James, West Stow, 1630. A5/4/4
Jane, wid., Hepworth, 1640. R2/58/170; W1/96/87
Joan, wife of William, Clare, 1476. R2/11/51
Joan, Rattlesden, 1453. R2/9/161
Joan, wid. of Thomas, Troston, 1496. R2/13/77
Joan, wid., Troston, 1536. R2/19/238
John, Barnham, 1637. A5/4/54
John, Brettenham, 1458. R2/9/188
John, the elder, Brockford, 1512. R2/13/212
John, mercer, Bury St. Edmunds, 1607. R2/46/136
John, Bury St. Edmunds, 1685. A5/6/92, A4/24/76
John, yeo., Hepworth, 1639. R2/58/53; W1/94/98
John, Hunston, 1477. R2/11/82
John, Lakenheath, 1465. R2/10/385
John, Lakenheath, (1497). R2/13/83
John, Lakenheath, 1614. R2/49/162; W1/71/109
John, Lakenheath, 1631. R2/56/58; W1/87/84
John, Lavenham, 1561. R2/30/104; W1/28/256
John, the elder, singleman, Mendlesham, 1623. R2/52/650; W1/79/77
John, Mildenhall, 1547. R2/21/316; W1/10/129
John, the elder, Mildenhall, 1647. R2/59/409; W1/104/34; In. 3/2/2
John, yeo., Stanton, 1627. R2/54/77; W1/83/79
John, wid., Stanton, 1661. R2/62/256; W1/113/143; In. 3/6/238; A5/5/21, A4/1/52
John, Stowmarket, 1480. R2/11/216
John, carpenter, Sudbury, 1594. R2/42/519; W1/52/62
John, Thorpe Morieux, 1474. R2/10/550
John, Wetheringsett, 1521. R2/15/157
John, yeo., Wetheringsett, 1558. R2/27/568
Katherine, wife of John, sen., Kersey, 1450. R2/9/112
Margaret, singlewoman, Bury St. Edmunds, 1685, (N). R2/70/93; W1/139/84; A5/6/91, A4/24/64
Margaret, wid., Mildenhall, 1558. R2/27/494
Mary, wid., Mildenhall, 1571. A5/1/240
Matthew, husb., Lakenheath, 1595. R2/43/25; W1/53/22
Parnell, wid., Stanton, 1566. R2/32/306; W1/28/86
Rachel, singlewoman, Mendlesham, 1623. R2/52/550; W1/79/10
Reginald, husb., Timworth, 1613. R2/48/323; W1/70/100
Richard, fletcher, Bury St. Edmunds, 1557. R2/8/309; W1/18/35
Richard, yeo., Mendlesham, 1608. R2/46/175; W1/65/34
Richard, Mendlesham, 1620. R2/52/128; W1/76/112
Richard, Sudbury, 1583. R2/39/103; W1/42/14
Richard, husb., Wetheringsett, (1542). R2/22/46; W1/6/64
Robert, husb., Acton, 1551. R2/23/67; W1/11/38
Robert, carpenter, Brockford, 1561. R2/30/112; W1/28/280
Robert, carpenter, Clare, (1551). R2/31/29; W1/13/69
Robert, Finningham, 1680. In. 3/20/5; A5/6/31, A4/17/3
Robert, als. Pyper, Great Wratting, 1566. A5/1/179
Robert, Stanton, 1562. A5/1/136
Robert, yeo., Stowlangtoft, 1549. R2/21/564; W1/8/57
Robert, Troston, 1540. W1/5/36
Rose, singlewoman, Finningham, 1680. A5/6/32, A4/17/13
Sarah, spinster, Chevington, 1700. In. 3/27/16
Simon, husb., Stanton, 1624. R2/53/93; W1/80/106
Stephen, Stowlangtoft, 1460. R2/9/270
Susan, wid., West Stow, 1648. R2/60/62; W1/105/77
Thomas, Lakenheath, 1529. R2/15/51
Thomas, labourer, Lakenheath, 1572. R2/36/28; W1/31/28

MAN(N) continued
Thomas, husb., Lakenheath, 1619. R2/51/454; W1/132/118
Thomas, jun., Stanton, (1483). R2/11/384
Thomas, Stanton, 1486. R2/11/323
Thomas, Stanton, 1564. R2/32/134
Thomas, Thorndon, 1586. R2/40/87; W1/43/66
William, Clare, 1458. R2/9/194
William, Haughley, 1590. A5/2/137
William, the elder, Kersey, 1610. R2/47/204; W1/67/84
William, joiner, Kersey, 1634. R2/56/433; W1/90/218
William, yeo., Lakenheath, 1541. R2/22/107; W1/10/8
William, Lakenheath, 1546. R2/19/547; W1/7/49
William, Mildenhall, 1568. R2/33/66; W1/29/86
William, Thorpe Morieux, 1474. R2/10/550
William, Wetheringsett, 1457. R2/9/187
William, husb., Wicken, 1563. R2/32/17
---, Rattlesden, 1474. R2/10/583
see also Motown als. Man
MANNDFIELD, Edmund, carpenter, Stowmarket, 1567. R2/32/381; W1/3/97
MANNGERE, Thomas, Mendlesham, 1489. R2/11/407
MANNING, Annabel, wid., Denham, 1635. R2/56/479; W1/91/54
Anthony, yeo., Lidgate, 1679. R2/67/312; W1/133/91
Bridget, wid., Elmswell, 1661. A5/5/14, A4/1/120
Charles, Little Cornard, 1688. In. 3/23/12; A5/6/117, A4/29/12
Elisabeth, wid., Herringswell, 1682. A5/6/63, A4/19/98
Elisabeth, singlewoman, West Stow, 1679. R2/67/488; W1/133/204
Elisabeth, wid., Wood Ditton, 1663. In. 3/8/87; A5/5/46
George, the elder, tailor, Bury St. Edmunds, 1598. R2/44/165; W1/56/57
Henry, Bury St. Edmunds, 1670. A5/5/118
Henry, Bury St. Edmunds, 1691. A5/7/141, A4/33/32
Jacob, sen., yeo., Elmsett, 1691. R2/71/507; W1/145/67
James, Bury St. Edmunds, 1682. A5/6/57, A4/19/19
Jeremiah, yeo., Tuddenham, 1683. R2/69/35; W1/137/28
Joan, als. Ward, wid., Tuddenham, 1683. A5/6/69, A4/20/51
John, husb., Combs, 1621. R2/52/300; W1/77/81
John, Hawstead, 1644. A5/4/104
John, Lawshall, 1630. A5/4/2
John, cooper, Soham, 1686. R2/70/422; W1/140/44
John, sen., Westley, 1688. R2/71/81; W1/142/73
Joseph, Bradfield St. Clare, 1679. A5/6/22, A4/16/78
Lawrence, tanner, Sudbury, 1607. R2/46/107
Lydia, wid., Cockfield, 1690. A5/6/132, A4/32/12
Mary, wid., Elmsett, (1637). W1/110/4
Nathaniel, yeo., Little Saxham, 1692. R2/72/11; W1/146/10; In. 3/24/34
Prudence, Edwardstone, 1593. A5/2/179
Richard, gent., Cockfield, 1664. R2/63/246; W1/116/168; In. 3/9/242
Richard, Burwell, 1679. A5/6/21, A4/16/61
Richard, comber, Little Finborough, 1647. R2/59/439; W1/104/35; In. 3/2/162
Richard, Stradishall, 1695. A5/6/178, A4/38/25
Robert, locksmith, Diss, 1582. W1/95/26
Robert, ploughwright, Whepstead, 1617. R2/50/378; W1/74/161
Roger, yeo., Cockfield, 1634. R2/56/394; W1/90/174
Sara, Hawstead, 1660. A5/5/7
Sarah, wid., Rougham, 1668. A5/5/94, A4/6/47
Susan, singlewoman, Little Finborough, 1652. R2/61/583; W1/109/57; In. 3/4/57
Thomas, gent., Barton, 1685. R2/70/158; W1/139/134
Thomas, yeo., Cockfield, 1679. R2/67/348; W1/133/110
Thomas, Elmsett, 1575. W1/95/5
Thomas, house carpenter, Great Finborough, 1668. R2/64/341; W1/120/52; In. 3/13/154
Thomas, yeo., Great Saxham, 1611. R2/48/48; W1/68/70; A5/3/111
Thomas, Great Saxham, 1662. In. 3/7/57; A5/5/28
Thomas, bricklayer, Lawshall, 1660. R2/62/11; W1/112/10
Thomas, yeo., Rickinghall Superior, 1558. R2/27/247
Thomas, yeo., Saxon Street, 1663. R2/63/49; W1/115/80
Toby, Thurston, 1649. A5/4/129
William, Barrow, 1631. A5/4/11

MANNING continued
William, sen., webster, Great Saxham, 1699. R2/73/421; W1/153/63; In. 3/26/51
William, Herringswell, 1682. R2/68/363; W1/136/72; In. 3/21/115; A5/6/63, A4/19/97
William, Horningsheath, 1649. A5/4/128
William, Ickworth, 1699. In. 3/26/71; A5/7/13, A4/41/46
William, yeo., Isleham, 1614. R6/7
William, Naughton, 1631. A5/4/14
William, gent., Rougham, 1679. R2/67/486; W1/133/203
see also Maning, Mannyng, Manyng, Hayward als. Manning
MANNINGS, see Folkes als. Mannings
MANNOCK, John, gent., Fornham, 1538. R2/20/73; W1/4/69
John, gent., Fornham All Saints, 1611. R2/48/93; W1/68/112
Thomas, Fornham All Saints, 1608. A5/3/42
MANNOK, Robert, Stoke, 1504. W1/7/6
William, Stoke by Nayland, 1450. R2/9/117
see also Manoke
MANNYNG, Isabel, wife of William, Bardwell, 1499. R2/13/107
Joan, wid., Great Saxham, 1630. R2/55/178; W1/86/196
John, Badwell Ash, 1458. R2/9/209; W1/24/128
John, labourer, Bury St. Edmunds, 1515. R2/6/13
John, yeo., Hawstead, 1622. R2/52/489; W1/78/99
John, the elder, Little Finborough, 1600. R2/45/81; W1/58/115
John, Norton, 1449. R2/9/140
John, Semer, 1528. R2/15/236
John, singleman, Soham, 1589. R2/41/167; W1/46/118
John, Stowmarket, 1548. R2/21/407; W1/8/31
Nicholas, the elder, Little Finborough, 1588. R2/41/84; W1/45/79
Richard, yeo., Barningham, 1627. R2/54/73; W1/83/75
Richard, Little Whelnetham, 1490. R2/11/382
Richard, yeo., Timworth, 1556. R2/25/14; W1/16/13
Robert, husb., Aldham, 1557. R2/26/264; W1/20/179
Robert, Cotton, 1573. A5/1/259
Roger, Bury St. Edmunds, 1515. R2/6/57
Thomas, yeo., Beyton, 1631. R2/56/67; W1/87/99
Thomas, yeo., Great Barton, 1680. R2/67/687; W1/134/143; In. 3/20/160
Thomas, Lawshall, 1627. W1/111/7
Walter, Norton, 1447. R2/9/80
William, Bradfield Combust, 1445. R2/9/89
William, Brockley, (1549). R2/21/559; W1/8/60
William, Bury St. Edmunds, 1523. R2/6/111
William, husb., Layham, 1554. R2/24/1b; W1/14/1
William, Norton, 1474. R2/10/563
William, yeo., Redgrave, 1598. R2/44/126; W1/56/111
William, Whelnetham, 1503. R2/13/134
MANOKE, Ellen, als. Bredge, wid. of John, Stoke by Clare, 1564. R2/32/135; W1/27/85
MANSER, Henry, Gislingham, 1472. R2/10/463
Joan, wid., Gislingham, 1477. R2/11/85
John, yeo., Eye, 1625. R2/53/360; W1/81/138
see also Mancer
MANSFELD, John, yeo., Bildeston, 1528. R2/17/284
MANSFIELD, Ann, wid., Barnardiston, 1699. In. 3/26/30; A5/7/10, A4/41/3
MANSTER, Alice, als. Blosse, Eye, 1641. A5/4/93
MANTUA, John, Horningsheath, 1672. A5/5/128, A4/9/11
MANWARING, Henry, gent., Barton, 1686. R2/70/535; W1/140/140
MANWODE, Edmund, Great Cornard, 1576. R2/37/814; W1/37/74; In. 3/1/20
Isabel, wife of Robert, Shimpling, 1454. R2/9/173 & 229
Robert, Shimpling, 1454. W1/24/29
William, labourer, Sudbury, 1562. R2/31/8; W1/8/176
MANWOOD, John, husb., Alpheton, (1495). R2/13/74
Richard, Sudbury, 1593. A5/2/187
Thomas, Glemsford, 1592, (N). R2/42/3; W1/48/92
William, Sudbury, (1547). R2/21/469
William, labourer, Sudbury, 1562. R2/31/8
see also Manhood
MANYNG, Andrew, shoe maker, Thelnetham, 1610. R2/47/170; W1/67/47
Helen, Bardwell, 1460. R2/9/245

MANYNG continued
Joan, wid., Ixworth, 1556. R2/25/148; W1/16/163
Thomas, Brockley, 1556. R2/25/142; W1/16/170
Thomas, tailor, Bury St. Edmunds, 1536. R2/7/36
Thomas, Soham, 1573. R2/36/109; W1/32/9
William, the elder, carpenter, Whepstead, 1638. R2/57/161; W1/92/200
MAPLEHED, John, pewterer, Bury St. Edmunds, 1528. R2/6/147
Thomas, Bury St. Edmunds, 1561. R2/8/364; W1/17/43
MAPLES, Thomas, the elder, gardener, Sudbury, 1700. R2/74/45; W1/154/44
MARANT, Robert, Stowmarket, 1452. R2/9/156
MARCANTE, Margaret, wid. of John, Newmarket, 1571. R2/35/201
MARCAUNT, John, Ixworth, 1459. R2/9/234
MARCH(E), John, Eye, 1565. A5/1/170
Richard, chaplain, Bury St. Edmunds, 1412. R2/1/130
William, gent., Barrow, 1642. A5/4/96
MARCHALL, Agnes, Bury St. Edmunds, 1443. R2/2/3
Helen, Shimpling, 1588. A5/2/111
John, Bury St. Edmunds, 1432. R2/1/202
John, priest, Bury St. Edmunds, 1519. R2/6/68
John, currier, Bury St. Edmunds, 1523. R2/6/123
John, Great Thurlow, 1524. R2/41/104
John, priest, Lavenham, 1558. R2/27/300
John, husb., Long Melford, 1670. R2/65/61; W1/122/73; In. 3/15/103
Matilda, Stoke by Nayland, 1440. R2/9/28
Robert, Mildenhall, (1546). R2/21/219 & 653; W1/10/65
Robert, Sudbury, 1588. A5/2/104
Roger, Bury St. Edmunds, 1407. R2/1/117
MARCHANT, Elisabeth, Kersey, 1611. A5/3/111
George, Sudbury, 1588. A5/2/104
John, Boxford, 1647. In. 3/2/156; A5/4/117
John, labourer, Chelsworth, 1564. R2/32/132; W1/27/81
Mary, wid., Stoke by Nayland, 1652. R2/61/602; W1/109/79; In. 3/4/79
Peter, bricklayer, Lavenham, 1596. R2/43/184; W1/54/93
Richard, husb., Kersey, 1553. R2/31/98; W1/13/70
Robert, husb., Kersey, 1573. R2/36/126; W1/32/34
Robert, husb., Kersey, 1583. R2/39/33; W1/42/71
Robert, yeo., Kersey, 1625. R2/53/372; W1/81/152
Thomas, tallow chandler, Boxford, 1602. R2/45/180; W1/60/105
Thomas, husb., Chelsworth, 1567. R2/32/419; W1/19/88
William, mason, Lavenham, 1597. R2/43/373; W1/55/135
MARCHAUNT, John, the elder, Kersey, 1508. R2/13/190
Richard, Chelsworth, 1561. A5/1/124
Robert, Bradfield St. Clare, 1459. R2/9/210
Robert, yeo., Kersey, 1619. R2/51/311; W1/132/31
William, fuller, Bury St. Edmunds, 1449. R2/2/30a
MARCHAWNTE, Robert, Hitcham, 1476. R2/11/69
see also Marcante, Markant, Markhante, Markunt, Merchant, Merkant
MARCHELL, Henry, Cheveley, 1685, (N). R2/70/6; W1/139/7; A5/6/90, A4/24/43
MARCHES, Robert, Great Finborough, 1606. A5/3/12
MARCHOULE, John, clothier, Great Waldingfield, 1581. R2/38/310; W1/40/53
MARCOLL, William, Bury St. Edmunds, 1578. A5/2/13
MARDEN, William, chaplain, Bury St. Edmunds, 1406. R2/1/109
MARDON, William, Fordham, 1459. R2/9/259
MARGARAME, John, husb., Great Finborough, 1633. R2/56/250; W1/90/12
MARGERIE, John, Lavenham, 1560. A5/1/100
MARGERUM, William, yeo., Wyverstone, 1661. R2/62/241; W1/113/119; In. 3/6/156
see also Margarame, Marjeram
MARGERY, James, gent., Rougham, 1644. R2/59/78; W1/101/5
Margaret, wid., Walsham le Willows, 1605. A5/3/2
Ralph, Walsham le Willows, 1653. W1/110/31
Richard, Walsham le Willows, 1503. R2/13/142
Thomas, Haughley, 1563. R2/31/150; W1/26/30
Thomas, Walshem le Willows, 1536. R2/19/251
William, yeo., Wyverstone, 1590. R2/41/379; W1/47/73
William, yeo., Wyverstone, 1664. R2/63/152; W1/116/46; In. 3/9/67
see also Margerie

MARHAM, Ann, wid., Eriswell, 1685. A5/6/86, A4/24/3
Frances, wife of William, Mildenhall, 1642. W1/110/8
Grace, wid., Mildenhall, 1668. R2/64/392; W1/120/114; In. 3/13/91
Henry, the elder, yeo., Mildenhall, 1560. R2/29/71; W1/25/96
Henry, sen., yeo., Mildenhall, 1583. R2/39/103; W1/42/13a & b
James, Bury St. Edmunds, 1401. R2/1/89
Miles, shepherd, Eriswell, 1648. R2/60/134; W1/105/160
Miles, Eriswell, 1681. R2/68/16; W1/135/14
Robert, husb., Ludham, 1574. W1/51/243
Robert, Mildenhall, 1469. R2/10/429b
Simon, weaver, Bury St. Edmunds, 1520. R2/6/82
Thomas, yeo., Mildenhall, 1624. R2/53/169; W1/80/148
Thomas, the younger, Mildenhall, 1665. In. 3/10/45; A5/5/66, A4/3/30
Thomas, yeo., Mildenhall, 1669. R2/64/449; W1/121/37; In. 3/14/29
Walter, als. Wayte, Bury St. Edmunds, 1428. R2/1/181
William, shepherd, Eriswell, 1638. R2/57/358; W1/93/153
William, husb., Mildenhall, 1617. R2/50/260; W1/74/60
---, 1452. R2/9/109
see also Marram
MARION, Richard, Lavenham, (1526). R2/17/169
MARIOTT, Edmund, husb., Wetheringsett, 1610. R2/47/119; W1/67/4a & b
MARJERAM, John, Tostock, 1692. A5/6/146, A4/34/4
MARJEROM, Thomas, yeo., Drinkstone, 1699. R2/73/418; W1/153/60
MARKALL, Robert, parchment maker, Bury St. Edmunds, 1556, (N). R2/8/281; W1/18/10
Robert, Pakenham, 1694. A5/6/166, A4/35/2
MARKANT, Edward, gent., Semer, 1669. In. 3/14/207; A5/5/104, A4/7/32
MARKAUNT, Alice, wid. of John, Badwell, 1474. R2/10/521
Richard, Badwell, 1505. R2/13/156
William, Badwell, 1474. R2/11/22
MARKE, see Berrell als. Marke
MARKEDAY, John, Sudbury, 1495. W1/24/102
see also Merkeday
MARKHANTE, Thomas, Mildenhall, (1519). R2/15/23
MARK(E)S, Edmund, Bildeston, 1598. R2/44/52; W1/56/55
Elisabeth, Newton, 1561. A5/1/113
James, the elder, yeo., Old Newton, 1584. R2/39/167; W1/42/159
James, Wetherden, 1610. A5/3/81
John, yeo., Hawstead, 1617. R2/50/241; W1/74/39
John, husb., Ipswich, 1645. R2/59/207; W1/102/33
John, tailor, Old Newton, 1566. R2/32/312; W1/26/81
John, yeo., Stoke by Nayland, 1544. R2/21/585
Roger, husb., Langham, 1669. R2/64/429; W1/121/11; In. 3/13/168
Rose, Newton, 1528. R2/17/277
Thomas, husb., Langham, 1644. R2/59/135; W1/101/61
Thomas, Langham, 1693. A5/6/162, A4/35/34
Thomas, yeo., Old Newton, 1564. R2/32/68; W1/27/18
William, shoe maker, Combs, 1634. R2/56/404; W1/90/188
see also Markys, Aspolle als. Markes
MARKUNT, Alice, Badwell Ash, 1449. R2/9/141
MARKYS, John, Bury St. Edmunds, 1492. R2/4/5
John, Old Newton, 1458. R2/9/265
John, Stowmarket, 1496. W1/24/133
Richard, Old Newton, 1459. R2/9/237
Sakyn, Stowmarket, 1481. R2/11/274
MARLER, Thomas, weaver, Bury St. Edmunds, 1469. R2/2/121
MARLETON, Alderman, gent., Langham, 1671. R2/65/265; W1/123/145
John, butcher, Hartest, 1537. R2/20/26; W1/4/17
John, yeo., Hawkedon, 1647. R2/59/459; W1/104/91; In. 3/2/85
Margery, als. Coppyng, Wetherden, 1459. R2/9/264
Richard, yeo., Hawkedon, 1669. R2/64/571; W1/121/160; In. 3/14/173
Robert, butcher, Bury St. Edmunds, 1559. R2/8/348; W1/17/61
Robert, yeo., Hawkedon, 1687. R2/70/381; W1/141/104
Rose, Bardwell, 1452. R2/9/111
Thomas, husb., Hawkedon, 1651, (N). R2/61/430
William, the elder, butcher, Bury St. Edmunds, 1521. R2/6/83
William, gent., Langham, 1642. R2/58/346; W1/99/44, W1/110/32
MARLOW, John, Sutton Coldfield, 1510. R2/4/211
MARLTON, John, the elder, yeo., Langham, 1628. R2/54/163; W1/84/38
John, wheelwright, Wickhambrook, 1699. R2/73/402; W1/153/46; In. 3/26/53

MARLTON continued
Martha, singlewoman, Lawshall, 1677. R2/66/529; W1/129/110; In. 3/18/142
Thomas, carpenter, Hartest, 1692. In. 3/24/63; A5/6/151, A4/34/43
see also Marleton
MARRAM, Robert, husb., Mildenhall, 1562. R2/31/54; W1/8/123
Simon, husb., Mildenhall, 1587. R2/40/224; W1/44/71
MARRETT, Edmund, husb., Icklingham, 1647. R2/59/489; W1/104/125; In. 3/2/105
Ellis, Thorndon, 1595. A5/2/215
Sara, singlewoman, Mendlesham, 1620. R2/52/99; W1/76/86
MARRICK, Roger, say maker, Sudbury, 1616. R2/50/181
MARRIET, John, Old Newton, 1566. A5/1/172
MARRINER, Thomas, Ampton, 1626. R2/53/612
see also Marryner
MARRIOTT, Ann, wid., Rickinghall Superior, 1674. R2/66/83; W1/126/35
Robert, yeo., Brockford, 1683. R2/69/49; W1/137/38
Robert, butcher, Cotton, 1664. R2/63/248; W1/116/169; In. 3/9/219
William, linen weaver, Thorndon, (1675). R2/66/248; W1/127/117; In. 3/16/186
see also Mariot, Marrett, Marriet, Marryett, Marryott, Maryett, Meryott
MARROW, Edward, Bury St. Edmunds, 1668. A5/5/99, A4/6/102
Elisabeth, wid., Bury St. Edmunds, 1638, (N). R2/57/411; W1/93/231
Elisabeth, Bury St. Edmunds, 1668, (N). R2/64/388; W1/120/108; In. 3/13/99; A5/5/99, A4/6/104
John, Hundon, 1686. A5/6/103, A4/26/45
William, yeo., Lidgate, 1590. R2/41/332; W1/47/23
MARRYETT, William, Westhorpe, 1590, (N). R2/41/355; W1/47/49
MARRYNER, Agnes, singlewoman, Wickhambrook, 1588, (N). R2/41/86; W1/45/80
MARRYOTT, Alexander, yeo., Whepstead, 1584. R2/39/174; W1/42/153
Ann, singlewoman, Eye, 1615. R2/49/268; W1/72/52
MARSH, Ann, wid., Great Wratting, 1699. R2/73/472; W1/153/109; In. 3/26/10
Anthony, yeo., Elmswell, 1579. R2/38/63; W1/39/17
Edmund, bach., Elmswell, 1682. A5/6/61, A4/19/64
Elisabeth, Combs, 1621. R2/52/323; W1/77/103
Francis, Great Wratting, 1667. In. 3/12/192
Hannah, wid., Bures, 1693. R2/72/260; W1/147/145
Henry, Little Wratting, 1695. A5/6/177, A4/38/21
Jeremiah, singleman, Elmswell, 1698. A5/7/10
John, Brandon, 1683. A5/6/74, A4/20/113
John, yeo., Elmswell, 1645. R2/59/190; W1/102/21
John, yeo., Elmswell, 1661. R2/62/297; W1/113/215; In. 3/6/272
John, blacksmith, Eye, 1697. R2/73/143; W1/151/28
John, husb., Kedington, 1651. R2/61/486; W1/108/77
John, Soham, 1649. A5/4/126
Josias, yeo., Sapiston, 1697. R2/73/112; W1/151/3; A5/7/5, A4/40/81
Margaret, wid., Elmswell, 1564. R2/32/113; W1/27/67
Matthew, bach., Bury St. Edmunds, 1695. A5/6/177, A4/38/19
Matthew, Bury St. Edmunds, 1696. A5/6/190, A4/39/75
Nathaniel, husb., Ballingdon, 1668. R2/64/304; W1/120/6; In. 3/13/72
Robert, yeo., Wratting, 1689. R2/71/180; W1/143/37
Simon, Redgrave, 1608. R2/46/194; W1/65/61
Simon, knacker, Stoke by Clare, 1602. R2/45/191; W1/60/119
Sybil, singlewoman, Elmswell, 1685. R2/70/43; W1/139/35
Thomas, singleman, Elmswell, 1646. R2/59/305; W1/103/24
William, Elmswell, 1545. A5/1/119
William, yeo., Elmswell, 1685. R2/70/169; W1/139/140
William, the elder, yeo., Kirtling, 1638. R2/57/415; W1/93/239
MARSHALL, Alice, wid., Nowton, 1552. R2/23/217; W1/12/39
Bartholomew, husb., Santon Downham, 1669. R2/64/494; W1/121/89; In. 3/14/120
Catherine, wid., Isleham, 1621. R6/30
Edmund, Isleham, 1619. R6/18
Edward, singleman, Bury St. Edmunds, 1649. A5/4/132
Elisabeth, wid., Lavenham, 1679. R2/67/500; W1/133/216
Faith, wid., Long Melford, 1593, (N). R2/42/390; W1/50/69
George, knacker, Burwell, 1620. R2/52/37; W1/76/34
Henry, Soham, 1609. A5/3/65
John, miller, Boxted, 1585, (N). R2/39/283; W1/42/293
John, yeo., Gazeley, 1689. R2/71/219; W1/143/63

MARSHALL continued
John, petty chapman, Hundon, 1592. R2/42/217; W1/49/36
John, Shimpling, 1553. R2/21/663
John, labourer, Soham, 1576. R2/37/203; W1/37/66; In. 3/1/34
John, 1555. R2/24/236; W1/15/65
Magdalen, wid., Lavenham, 1663. In. 3/8/193; A5/5/51
Mary, wid., Bury St. Edmunds, 1673, (N). R2/65/473; W1/125/108; A5/5/143, A4/10/98
Nicholas, Isleham, 1636, (N). R6/77
Philip, Lavenham, 1594. A5/2/201
Robert, sen., butcher, Lavenham, 1666. R2/64/139; W1/118/105; In. 3/11/149
Robert, yeo., Naughton, 1663. R2/63/45; W1/115/71; In. 3/8/89
Robert, Shimpling, 1632. A5/4/18
Robert, 1578. A5/2/8
Rose, singlewoman, Little Waldingfield, 1664. R2/63/253; W1/116/177; In. 3/9/221
Susan, wife of Robert, sen., Assington, 1697. R2/73/200; W1/151/83
Thomas, Brandon, 1641, (N). R2/58/306; W1/98/103
Thomas, Brandon, 1664. In. 3/9/57; A5/5/57, A4/2/29
Thomas, Clare, 1639. R2/58/43; W1/94/78
Thomas, Fordham, 1529. R2/18/24
Thomas, carpenter, Fordham, 1670. R2/65/14; W1/122/18; In. 3/15/28
Thomas, Lavenham, 1580. A5/2/27
Thomas, yeo., Lidgate, 1606. R2/46/13; W1/64/16
Thomas, shearman, Sudbury, (1538). R2/18/192, R2/20/136; W1/4/116
Thomas, Sudbury, 1631. A5/4/13
William, butcher, Lavenham, (1672). W1/312/21
William, cloth worker, Stanstead, 1630. R2/55/178; W1/86/195
William, Stoke by Clare, 1557. R2/26/154; W1/20/92
see also Marchall, Marchell, Marchoule, Merchall, Mershall

MARSHAM, Thomas, Little Ashfield, (1487). R2/11/441
Thomas, husb., Mildenhall, 1587. R2/40/132; W1/44/13
Thomas, husb., Thwaite, 1558. R2/27/287
Thomas, yeo., Walsham le Willows, 1547. R2/21/315; W1/10/127
see also Masham

MARSTON, Mary, Bury St. Edmunds, 1694. A5/6/168, A4/37/25
Mary, wife of John, Bury St. Edmunds, 1698. A5/7/6

MARTEN, Agnes, wid., Layham, 1584. R2/39/191; W1/42/137
Alice, singlewoman, Walsham le Willows, 1569. A5/1/205
Archinwald, Honington, 1639. A5/4/74
Edward, Great Fakenham, 1567. A5/1/191
Henry, clothier, Bildeston, 1612. R2/48/193; W1/69/81
Jeffrey, shepherd, Elveden, 1558. R2/27/426
John, yeo., Cavendish, 1626. R2/53/488; W1/82/33
John, Exning, 1530. R2/19/28
John, Haverhill, 1556. R2/25/117; W1/16/128a
John, sen., Sudbury, 1550. R2/21/44; W1/10/175
John, Sudbury, 1556. R2/25/11; W1/16/9
John, labourer, Wood Ditton, 1570. R2/34/46; W1/30/42
Richard, Chelsworth, 1578. R2/37/323; W1/36/255
Richard, Mildenhall, 1683. R2/69/4; W1/137/5
Robert, Kersey, 1540. R2/21/350; W1/38/47
Robert, shoe maker, Soham, 1576. In. 3/1/75
Susan, singlewoman, Walsham le Willows, 1638, (N). R2/57/345; W1/93/131
Thomas, singleman, Culford, 1650. R2/61/362; W1/107/59; In. 3/3/72
Thomas, husb., Polstead, 1582. R2/38/387; W1/41/49
Thomas, Stradishall, 1538. R2/20/64; W1/4/56
Walter, Walsham le Willows, 1555. R2/24/253; W1/15/82

MARTEYN, John, husb., Sapiston, 1568. R2/66/71; W1/29/93

MARTHAM, Alice, wid., Rattlesden, 1480. R2/11/362
Edward, Woolpit, 1685. A5/6/97, A4/24/133
Thomas, Rattlesden, 1474. R2/10/509

MARTHUM, Edward, linen weaver, Woolpit, 1696. R2/73/75; W1/150/78

MARTIN, Alice, wid., Wixoe, 1661. R2/62/166; W1/113/16; In. 3/6/11
Barbara, Chelsworth, 1584. A5/2/54
Bridget, wid., Wickham Skeith, 1667. R2/64/241; W1/119/102
Christopher, Long Melford, 1593. A5/2/182
Edith, wife of Richard, Timworth, 1671. A5/5/126, A4/8/58
Edmund, yeo., Honington, 1564. R2/32/139; W1/27/88
Edward, yeo., Cockfield, (1647). W1/110/12

MARTIN continued
Edward, shepherd, Fornham St. Martin, 1620. R2/52/177; W1/76/158
Edward, Mildenhall, 1694. A5/6/174, A4/37/96
Elisabeth, spinster, Mildenhall, 1683. A5/6/68, A4/20/38
Henry, linen weaver, Honington, 1694. R2/72/391; W1/148/121
Hester, wid., Wickham Skeith, 1667. R2/64/239; W1/119/99; In. 3/12/124
James, woollen draper, Mellis, 1675. R2/66/164; W1/127/40
Joan, wid., Tuddenham, 1681. R2/68/227; W1/135/168
Joan, wid., Walsham le Willows, 1569. R2/33/139; W1/5/65; A5/1/217
John, cook, Barnham, 1630. R2/55/106; W1/86/116
John, Exning, 1548. R2/21/413; W1/8/30
John, Kersey, 1588. A5/2/109
John, yeo., Kersey, 1650. R2/61/342; W1/107/36; In. 3/3/50
John, gent., Mellis, 1699. R2/73/397; W1/153/43; In. 3/26/55
John, Polstead, 1651. R2/61/473; W1/108/61
John, husb., Wissington, 1667. R2/64/274; W1/119/138; In.½3/12/177
John, yeo., Wood Ditton, 1672. R2/65/299; W1/124/15
Leonard, husb., Layham, 1624, (N). R2/53/56; W1/80/79
Leonard, the elder, yeo., Layham, 1625. R2/53/351; W1/81/131
Margery, singlewoman, Bures, 1564. R2/32/109
Marian, als. Bettys, Ixworth, 1533. R2/19/184
Mary, wid., Rickinghall, 1672. R2/65/374; W1/124/117
Nicholas, yeo., Thrandeston, 1680. R2/67/578; W1/134/57; In. 3/20/60
Phineas, Bildeston, 1611. A5/3/114
Richard, yeo., Buxhall, 1634. R2/56/385; W1/90/164
Richard, yeo., Elmswell, 1676, (N). R2/66/337; W1/128/42; In. 3/17/44; A5/5/161, A4/13/26
Richard, Honington, 1641. A5/4/88
Richard, Long Melford, 1674. A5/5/147, A4/11/27
Richard, Sapiston, 1618. R2/51/240; W1/75/155
Robert, maltster, Bury St. Edmunds, 1636. R2/57/57; W1/92/67
Robert, yeo., Fornham St. Genevieve, 1692. R2/72/101; W1/146/92; In. 3/24/23
Robert, yeo., Hinderclay, 1682. R2/68/506; W1/136/172
Robert, Little Thurlow, 1694. A5/6/167, A4/37/13
Samuel, clothier, Bury St. Edmunds, 1662. R2/62/354; W1/114/75
Sara, wife of Richard, Brockley, 1661. A5/5/23, A4/1/32
Sarah, wid. of Robert, miller, Little Thurlow, 1699. R2/73/401; W1/153/45
Silvester, Honington, 1652. In. 3/4/49
Sylvester, gent., Honington, 1674. R2/66/66; W1/126/50
Thomas, yeo., Badwell Ash, 1700. R2/74/31; W1/154/30
Thomas, the elder, yeo., Combs, 1667. R2/64/205; W1/119/55; In. 3/12/68
Thomas, weaver, Great Cornard, 1681. R2/68/25; W1/135/23
Thomas, the elder, glover, Great Wratting, 1673. R2/65/434; W1/125/58
Thomas, yeo., Norton, 1680. R2/67/677; W1/134/134; In. 3/20/147
Thomas, cordwainer, Norton, 1688. R2/71/120; W1/142/107
Thomas, Sapiston, 1558. R2/27/293
Thomas, husb., Shimpling, 1557. R2/26/323; W1/20/230
William, clerk, Stanton, 1676. R2/66/373; W1/128/86; In. 3/17/108
William, Sudbury, 1573. A5/1/265
William, Wickham Skeith, 1661. In. 3/6/165; A5/5/19, A4/1/66

MARTYN, Agnes, Ashfield, 1471. R2/10/531
Agnes, Drinkstone, 1460. R2/9/252
Agnes, Livermere, 1442. W1/24/37
Alice, spinster, Clare, 1560. R2/29/5
Archinwald, the elder, yeo., Honington, 1608. R2/46/172; W1/65/31
Augustus, Semer, 1440. R2/9/27
Edmund, Lavenham, 1479. R2/11/149
Elisabeth, Layham, 1560. A5/1/100
Higham, gent., Great Thornham, 1690. R2/71/337; W1/144/41
James, Hartest, 1651. A5/4/139
Joan, wid., Bury St. Edmunds, 1627. R2/54/123; W1/83/122
Joan, wid., Weston, 1540. R2/20/251; W1/4/188
John, say weaver, Acton, 1649. R2/60/234; W1/106/88
John, Bures, 1650. In. 3/3/154; A5/4/135
John, Burgate, 1485. R2/11/339
John, tailor, Bury St. Edmunds, 1465. R2/11/86
John, tailor, Bury St. Edmunds, 1479. R2/2/285

MARTYN continued
John, Bury St. Edmunds, 1571. A5/1/235
John, the elder, coverlet weaver, Clare, 1528. W1/19/20
John, the elder, clothier, Clare, 1570. R2/34/58
John, Earl Stonham, (1521). R2/17/335
John, Great Livermere, 1475. R2/11/137
John, Honington, 1524. R2/17/79
John, Lakenheath, 1472. R2/10/515
John, husb., Layham, 1557. R2/26/296; W1/20/218
John, Mellis, 1662. In. 3/7/205; A5/5/38
John, Mildenhall, 1697. R2/73/154; W1/151/40
John, Rickinghall Inferior, 1585. R2/59/249; W1/42/324
John, Sapiston, 1630. A5/4/3
John, Soham, 1441. R2/9/37
John, yeo., Stoke by Nayland, 1662. In. 3/7/88; A5/5/29
John, thatcher, Stowlangtoft, 1579. R2/38/73; W1/39/10
John, Sudbury, 1446. R2/9/66
John, Troston, 1461. R2/9/286
John, Wangford, 1538. R2/20/69; W1/4/66
John, the elder, yeo., Wood Ditton, 1625. R2/53/309; W1/81/94
Margaret, Honington, 1464. R2/10/357
Margery, als. Odeham, wid., Bury St. Edmunds, 1516. R2/6/32
Robert, Bury St. Edmunds, 1642. A5/4/97
Robert, husb., Great Wratting, 1660. R2/62/139; W1/112/179; In. 3/5/218
Robert, Redgrave, (1546). R2/21/424; W1/8/2a
Robert, the elder, yeo., Wickhambrook, 1649. R2/60/287; W1/106/160
Roger, Drinkstone, 1453. R2/9/161
Silvester, Honington, 1652. A5/4/141
Simon, Wood Ditton, 1561. R2/30/88; W1/28/273
Thomas, barker, Bury St. Edmunds, 1411. R2/1/121
Thomas, maltster, Bury St. Edmunds, 1604. R2/45/326; W1/62/27
Thomas, husb., Layham, 1562. R2/31/27; W1/8/155
Thomas, Rickinghall Superior, 1562. A5/1/135
Thomas, yeo., Sapiston, 1626. R2/53/526; W1/82/58
Thomas, clerk, Stradishall, 1555. A5/1/99
Thomas, Withersfield, 1665. In. 3/10/65; A5/5/66, A4/3/32
Thomas, Wood Ditton, 1546. R2/21/254; W1/10/90
William, Chevington, 1411. R2/1/123
William, Rickinghall Superior, 1647. A5/4/118
William, Sudbury, 1497. R2/13/61
see also Marten, Brynce als. Martyn, Bryngse als. Martyn, Middleditch als. Jay and Martin, Thyng als. Martin

MARYAN, Charles, Lavenham, 1525. W1/23/63
see also Marion

MARYETT, John, Fornham, 1537. R2/20/19; W1/4/11
William, bladesmith, Bury St. Edmunds, 1480. R2/2/295 & 296

MARYOT, Robert, husb., Stoke Ash, 1550. R2/21/262; W1/10/19

MASCALL, Gabriel, Stansfield, 1665. A4/3/26
John, labourer, Great Thurlow, 1550. R2/21/133; W1/9/157b
John, miller, Stoke by Nayland, 1600. R2/45/45; W1/58/64
Margaret, Great Wratting, (1544). R2/21/597
Ralph, Hinderclay, 1574. W1/95/4
Robert, yeo., Hinderclay, 1652. R2/61/546; W1/109/26; In. 3/4/31
Thomas, leather dresser, Clare, 1665. R2/63/295; W1/117/25; In. 3/10/40

MASCHALL, John, chandler, Bury St. Edmunds, 1406. R2/1/109

MASCOLL, William, Cavendish, 1662, (N). R2/62/355; W1/114/76; In. 3/7/115; A5/5/32

MASE, Richard, Mildenhall, 1554. R2/24/91; W1/14/70
William, parchment maker, Bury St. Edmunds, 1520. R2/6/74
William, Chippenham, 1543. R2/19/361; W1/6/106

MASH, John, tailor, Soham, 1689. R2/71/207; W1/143/57
Robert, Barnardiston, 1700. A5/7/14, A4/41/74

MASHAM, Harry, husb., Badwell Ash, 1583. R2/39/81; W1/42/30
Joan, wid., Walsham le Willows, 1557. R2/26/293; W1/20/215
John, Ashfield, 1476. W1/24/36
John, husb., Badwell Ash, 1535. R2/18/132

MASKALL, Margaret, als. Rowghte, Bury St. Edmunds, 1570. A5/1/215
see also Mascall

MASKOLLFFE, Randolph, labourer, Wissington, (1555). R2/24/246; W1/15/73

MASLEN, John, Battisford, 1530. R2/18/63 & 69, R2/19/7
MASLYN, John, Stowmarket, 1571. A5/1/241
see also Mastline
MASON, Abigail, wid., Gazeley, 1687. R2/70/339; W1/141/78
Agnes, wid., Eye, 1486. R2/11/384
Alice, Ashley, 1630. A5/4/2
Alice, Bury St. Edmunds, 1386. R2/1/52
Alice, wid., Exning, 1635. R2/56/455; W1/91/16
Alice, singlewoman, Tostock, 1590. R2/41/399; W1/47/83
Alice, wid., Wickhambrook, 1556. W1/95/35
Ann, Chevington, 1636. A5/4/47
Anne, wid., Drinkstone, 1560. R2/32/441
Anthony, Wickhambrook, 1627. R2/54/1; W1/83/1
Barbara, prioress, Bury St. Edmunds, 1538. R2/7/50
Christopher, husb., Wattisfield, 1597. R2/43/243; W1/55/24
Edward, Burwell, 1684. A5/6/80, A4/21/64
Edward, yeo., Chippenham, 1669. R2/64/448; W1/121/34; In. 3/14/25
Edward, Exning, 1649. R2/60/295; W1/106/171
Edward, Exning, 1695. A5/6/176, A4/38/7
Edward, Gislingham, 1591. A5/2/147
Edward, tailor, Hessett, 1596, (N). R2/43/178 & 209; W1/54/62 a & b
Edward, jun., Rickinghall Inferior, 1464. R2/10/367
Elisabeth, wid., Exning, 1661. In. 3/6/292; A5/5/26, A4/1/5
Francis, yeo., Rickinghall Inferior, 1664. R2/63/237; W1/116/157; In. 3/9/189
George, labourer, Lackford, 1581. R2/38/322; W1/40/65
Gilbert, Bury St. Edmunds, 1413. R2/1/132
Harry, Exning, 1506. R2/13/181
Henry, yeo., Brome, 1622. R2/52/407; W1/78/40
Henry, Bury St. Edmunds, 1637. A5/4/56
Henry, Exning, 1469. R2/10/453
Henry, Exning, 1632. R2/56/210; W1/89/127
Hugh, husb., 1559. R2/28/321
James, yeo., Mildenhall, 1683. R2/69/37; W1/137/30
Joan, wid., Bury St. Edmunds, 1510. R2/54/1
Joan, wid., Bury St. Edmunds, 1540. R2/52/56; W1/21/178
Joan, wid., Combs, 1560. R2/29/42; W1/25/134
Joan, wid. of Thomas, Eye, 1540. R2/20/257
John, Beyton, 1596. R2/43/173; W1/54/86
John, yeo., Beyton, 1619. R2/51/346; W1/132/53
John, yeo., Beyton, 1660. R2/62/20; W1/112/22; In. 3/5/13
John, Bury St. Edmunds, 1566. A5/1/172
John, husb., Drinkstone, 1642. R2/59/330; W1/99/21
John, Exning, 1482. R2/11/265
John, Exning, 1482. R2/11/279
John, Exning, 1552. R2/23/218; W1/12/40
John, Eye, 1487. R2/13/11
John, Eye, 1529. R2/18/1
John, gent., Fordham, 1682. R2/68/355; W1/136/67; In. 3/21/168
John, inn holder, Redgrave, 1662. In. 3/7/198; A5/5/39
John, blacksmith, Stansfield, 1682. R2/68/331; W1/136/50
John, Stoke by Clare, 1477. R2/11/103
John, labourer, Tostock, (1440). W1/36/6
John, labourer, Tostock, 1540. R2/19/285
John, husb., Tostock, 1621. R2/52/277; W1/77/63
John, Wicken, 1631. A5/4/11
John, yeo., Wortham, 1666. R2/64/108; W1/118/80
Jude, yeo., Hopton, 1610. R2/47/121; W1/67/6
Katherine, wid., Felsham, 1700. R2/74/97; W1/154/99
Margaret, Bury St. Edmunds, 1422. R2/1/160
Margaret, singlewoman, Rattlesden, 1575, (N). R2/37/116; W1/34/54
Margaret, wid., Wickhambrook, 1617, (N). R2/50/261; W1/74/61
Margery, wid., Beyton, 1542. R2/56/9; W1/6/83
Marian, Bury St. Edmunds, 1513. R2/5/31 (admon. only)
Mary, wid., Redgrave, 1685. R2/70/44; W1/139/36
Nathaniel, yeo., Great Barton, 1664. R2/63/125; W1/116/9; In. 3/9/16
Ralph, Hartest, 1496. R2/13/35
Ralph, sawyer, Hitcham, 1549. R2/21/563; W1/8/58
Richard, maltster, Bury St. Edmunds, 1663. R2/63/71; W1/115/114
Richard, Eye, 1451. R2/9/106
Richard, husb., Stansfield, 1662. In. 3/7/165; A5/5/35
Richard, yeo., Wickhambrook, 1619. R2/51/434; W1/132/106

MASON continued
Robert, Burwell, 1639. A5/4/73
Robert, Eye, 1449. R2/9/95
Robert, Eye, 1561. A5/1/115
Robert, feather bed driver, Haughley, 1600. R2/45/23; W1/58/36
Robert, organ player, clerk, Mildenhall, 1559. R2/28/224; W1/22/192
Samuel, Soham, 1673. A5/5/142, A4/10/88
Simon, the elder, Bury St. Edmunds, 1612. R2/48/204; W1/69/96
Thomas, yeo., Beyton, 1595. R2/43/64; W1/52/51
Thomas, yeo., Beyton, 1630. R2/55/152; W1/86/170a & b
Thomas, Bury St. Edmunds, 1606. A5/3/7
Thomas, webster, Bury St. Edmunds, 1672. R2/65/348; W1/124/81
Thomas, Exning, 1589. A5/2/118
Thomas, sen., yeo., Exning, 1596. R2/43/176
Thomas, yeo., Exning, 1597. R2/43/259; W1/54/65, W1/55/37
Thomas, Eye, 1562. A5/1/138
Thomas, yeo., Fordham, 1661. R2/62/270; W1/113/171; In. 3/6/219
Thomas, Hartest, 1455. R2/9/227
Thomas, clothmaker, Lavenham, 1528. R2/15/230; W1/19/44
Thomas, bleacher, Market Weston, 1682. R2/68/328; In. 3/21/147
Thomas, bleacher, Stanningfield, 1682. W1/136/47
Thomas, clerk, Stanningfield, 1682. R2/68/431; W1/136/120; In. 3/21/100
Thomas, Sudbury, 1543. R2/19/396; W1/6/94
Thomas, inn holder, Sudbury, 1690. R2/71/345; W1/144/49
Thomas, yeo., Thelnetham, 1667. R2/64/200; W1/119/47
William, Bury St. Edmunds, 1370. R2/1/23
William, capper, Bury St. Edmunds, 1503. R2/4/128
William, Exning, 1695. A5/6/183, A4/38/87
William, labourer, Fordham, 1624, (N). R2/53/188; W1/80/161
William, Fornham St. Genevieve, 1649. A5/4/129
William, Hengrave, 1609. A5/3/72
William, Mildenhall, 1662. In. 3/8/203
William, Stowmarket, 1591. A5/2/157
William, Timworth, 1647. A5/4/116 & 119
William, yeo., Weeting, 1663. R2/63/116; W1/115/178
---, Stowmarket, 1606. A5/3/12
see also Masson, Mayson, Powle als. Mason, Prick als. Mason, Waltham als. Mason

MASSENGER, Rose, wid., Bury St. Edmunds, 1495. R2/4/40

MASSON, Ann, wid., Denston, 1560. W1/19/72

MASSY, Agnes, als. Nabyll, Bury St. Edmunds, 1516. R2/6/25

MAST(E), George, jun., Isleham, 1683. In. 9/61
George, yeo., Isleham, 1685. W7/102; In. 9/59
Mary, Isleham, 1672. In. 9/31; A12/8
Robert, yeo., Isleham, 1666. In. 9/19
Robert, sen., Isleham, 1667. W7/71
Robert, husb., Soham (1631). W1/95/65
Susan, wid., Isleham, 1676. In. 9/42

MASTER, Agnes, wid., Hinderclay, 1557. R2/26/121; W1/20/72
Robert, yeo., Hinderclay, 1615. R2/49/349; W1/72/121
Robert, Stanton, 1464. W1/24/49
see also Maister, Mastyr, Mayster

MASTLINE, John, Stowmarket, 1595. R2/43/104; W1/53/102

MASTYR, Adam, Stanton, 1496. R2/13/32

MATHE, John, maltster, Newmarket, 1644. R2/59/75; W1/101/1

MATHER, Agatha, wid., Dalham, 1620. R2/52/113; W1/76/98
Jane, spinster, Little Waldingfield, 1664. A5/5/62, A4/2/105
Lawrence, tailor, Ixworth, 1636. R2/57/54; W1/92/63
Roger, clothier, Little Waldingfield, 1664, (N). R2/63/260; W1/116/186; A5/5/63, A4/2/104

MATHEU, Robert, Mildenhall, 1590. R2/41/449; W1/47/99

MATHEW, Agnes, singlewoman, Bury St. Edmunds, 1582, (N). R2/38/387; W1/41/48
Agnes, wid., Stoke by Clare, 1616. R2/50/86; W1/73/94
Edmund, als. Rudland, yeo., Mendlesham, 1599. R2/44/170; W1/57/5
Elisabeth, wid., Isleham, 1625. R6/38
Elisabeth, wid., Newmarket, 1645. R2/59/228; W1/102/53
George, grocer, Great Livermere, 1661. In. 3/6/112; A5/5/17, A4/1/85
Henry, singleman, Newmarket, 1687. R2/70/356; W1/141/188
Jane, wid., Coney Weston, 1698. R2/73/254; W1/152/31
Jane, wid., Ixworth, 1643. R2/59/27; W1/100/37

MATHEW continued
Joan, Bury St. Edmunds, 1606. A5/3/17
John, als. Grover, Bury St. Edmunds, 1660. In. 3/5/89; A5/5/5, A4/1/208
John, husb., Glemsford, 1687, (N). R2/70/278; W1/141/20
John, yeo., Great Ashfield, 1698. R2/73/260; W1/152/37
John, miller, Icklingham, 1564. R2/32/109; W1/27/63
Margaret, wid., Great Ashfield, 1634. R2/56/379; W1/90/157
Richard, Bury St. Edmunds, 1619, (N). R2/51/266; W1/132/8
Richard, Stoke by Clare, 1644. A5/4/102
Robert, rector, Euston, 1682. R2/68/417; W1/136/111; In. 3/21/108
Robert, Ixworth, 1634. A5/4/32
Robert, Mildenhall, 1461. R2/9/293
Thomas, Great Ashfield, 1572, (N). R2/36/35; W1/31/128
Thomas, the elder, yeo., Great Ashfield, 1664. R2/63/234; W1/116/154; In. 3/9/193
Thomas, yeo., Newmarket, 1694. R2/72/404; W1/148/136
William, Bury St. Edmunds, 1495. R2/4/33
William, Buxhall, 1684. A5/6/85, A4/21/120
William, yeo., Ramsey, 1617. R2/50/347; W1/74/129
William, Stowupland, 1673. A5/5/137, A4/10/23
MATHEWMAN, John, the elder, Long Melford, 1598. R2/44/81; W1/56/70
MATHEWS, John, shoe maker, Bures, 1627, (N). R2/54/51; W1/83/56
MATHTHUE, Margaret, wid., Stoke by Clare, 1557. R2/26/316; W1/20/240
MATHUE, John, Wixoe, 1548. R2/21/430
Thomas, Hopton, 1546. R2/21/628; W1/28/133
MATHY, Joan, wid., Bury St. Edmunds, 1606. R2/46/90; W1/64/107
MATHYMAN, Edward, Lavenham, 1562. R2/31/43; W1/8/166
MATTHEW, George, Great Livermere, 1618. R2/51/236; W1/75/152
George, yeo., Stoke by Clare, 1687. R2/70/312; W1/141/56
John, yeo., Stoke by Clare, 1616. R2/50/19; W1/73/19
Richard, Isleham, 1697. In. 9/101; A12/15
William, yeo., Stoke by Clare, 1639. R2/58/77; W1/94/133
see also Matheu, Mathews, Sayer als. Mathew, Wicks als. Mathew
MAUDE, John, Hargrave, 1567. A5/1/185
MAUGHAN, Miles, Great Waldingfield, 1566. R2/32/330; W1/28/57
see also Mawen, Mawyn
MAULDEN, John, weaver, Bildeston, 1576, (N). R2/37/204; W1/37/67; In. 3/1/31
MAULDING, John, Fornham All Saints, 1678. In. 3/19/171; A5/6/11, A4/15/97
MAULINGE, William, Stanningfield, 1604. R2/45/307; W1/61/4
MAULL, Margaret, wid., Stoke by Nayland, 1586. R2/40/92
see also Mawle
MAULT, John, shepherd, Lidgate, 1663. R2/63/10; W1/115/18; In. 3/8/21
Richard, Icklingham, 1583. A5/2/50
MAULTON, Robert, yeo., Whepstead, 1660. R2/62/122; W1/112/164; In. 3/5/177
MAUNDELL, John, Newton, 1525. R2/17/97
MAUNDEVILE, Robert, Bury St. Edmunds, 1394. R2/1/67
MAUNDFEILDE, Richard, Stowmarket, 1566. A5/1/174
MAVESYN, John, Thrandeston, 1452. R2/9/111
MAWBOURN, Miles, Clare, 1593. A5/2/189
MAWDETT, Humphrey, gent., Old Newton, 1661. R2/62/214; W1/113/79; In. 3/6/85
Roger, Shelland, 1668. A5/5/91, A4/6/9
MAWDYON, William, Boxford, 1468. R2/10/409
MAWEN, William, Great Waldingfield, 1531, (N). R2/19/87
MAWLE, James, Nayland, 1608. A5/3/48
MAWLING, James, Eye, 1595. R2/43/55; W1/53/43
John, yeo., Great Whelnetham, 1600. R2/45/64; W1/58/89
John, yeo., Great Whelnetham, 1648. R2/60/61; W1/105/76
John, yeo., Great Whelnetham, 1650. R2/61/376; W1/107/77; In. 3/3/93
see also Maulinge
MAWNDEFELDE, Robert, Newton, 1538. R2/20/148; W1/4/130
MAWOR, William, Stanstead, 1557. R2/26/167; W1/20/96
MAWYN, Nicholas, Great Waldingfield, (1545). R2/19/531; W1/7/87
MAXWELL, William, yeo., Wetheringsett, 1660. R2/62/54; W1/112/66; In. 3/5/61

MAY, Augustus, Stanstead, 1590. A5/2/143
Edmund, husb., Lakenheath, 1559. R2/28/98; W1/22/96
George, singleman, Little Cornard, 1599. R2/44/183; W1/57/13
Henry, singleman, Bardwell, 1608. R2/46/192; W1/65/59
Henry, the elder, Wetherden, 1584. R2/39/138; W1/42/187
Henry, Wetherden, 1608. A5/3/46
Henry, yeo., Woolpit, 1570. R2/34/60
John, clothier, Badwell Ash, 1667. R2/64/173; W1/119/6; In. 3/12/16
John, Cavendish, 1588. A5/2/99
John, Mildenhall, 1682. In. 3/21/60; A5/6/60, A4/19/56
John, Stowlangtoft, 1640. A5/4/83
John, Wyverstone, 1582. R2/38/379; W1/41/58
Lewis, yeo., Wetherden, 1538. R2/20/74; W1/4/71 a & b (and inventory)
Margaret, Mildenhall, 1519. R2/14/12; W1/26/113b
Margaret, wid., Mildenhall, 1609, (N). R2/47/64; W1/66/73; A5/3/69
Margaret, wid., Stanningfield, 1558. R2/27/231
Margery, wid., Cavendish, 1589. R2/41/173; W1/46/110
Mary, wid., Badwell Ash, 1667. R2/64/231; W1/119/87; In. 3/12/87
Robert, Kersey, 1649. A5/4/131
Robert, husb., Mildenhall, 1636. R2/57/14; W1/92/27
Simon, husb., Buxhall, 1621. R2/52/272; W1/77/56
Stephen, Euston, 1443. R2/9/48
Thomas, Chevington, 1592. A5/2/168
Thomas, Fornham All Saints, 1695. A5/6/181, A4/38/61
Thomas, miller, Lavenham, 1595. R2/43/110; W1/53/111
Thomas, Mildenhall, 1621. W1/77/2
William, Bury St. Edmunds, 1699. A5/7/13, A4/41/53
William, yeo., Rickinghall Inferior, 1651. R2/61/507; W1/108/97
William, yeo., Westhorpe, 1603. R2/45/233; W1/61/27
see also Maie, Mey
MAYCROW, John, husb., Hawstead, 1557. R2/26/196
MAYDEGOODE, John, Great Bradley, 1444. R2/9/35
MAYEN, John, Sudbury, 1557. R2/26/217; W1/20/127
MAYER, Agnes, Great Thurlow, 1545. A5/1/60
Edward, yeo., Stoke by Nayland, 1557. R2/26/260; W1/20/176
Ellen, wid., Little Thurlow, 1682. R2/68/406; W1/136/101; In. 3/21/107
Elisabeth, wid., Long Melford, 1635. R2/56/524; W1/91/108
Henry, yeo., Barnardiston, 1570. R2/34/42; W1/30/39
Jeffery, yeo., Little Thurlow, 1684. R2/69/205; W1/138/18
Joan, wid., Mildenhall, 1556. R2/25/7; W1/16/5
Joan, Polstead, 1611. A5/3/113
John, carpenter, Dalham, 1670. R2/65/63; W1/122/76; In. 3/15/158
John, Great Thurlow, 1582. A5/2/39
John, the elder, yeo., Long Melford, 1578. R2/37/391; W1/36/181
Margery, wid., Great Thurlow, 1593. R2/42/353; W1/50/21
Mary, spinster, Cheveley, 1679. A5/6/17, A4/16/29
Mary, wid., Little Thurlow, 1685. R2/70/179; W1/139/150
Mary, wid., Walsham le Willows, 1688. R2/70/10; W1/142/7
Nicholas, glazier, Bury St. Edmunds, 1597. R2/43/247; W1/55/29
Reginald, Mildenhall, (1551). R2/23/70; W1/11/39
Thomas, husb., Great Wratting, 1603. R2/45/279; W1/61/85
Thomas, clerk, Ousden, 1696. R2/73/106; W1/150/122
William, glazier, Bury St. Edmunds, 1643. R2/59/14; W1/100/22
William, yeo., Denston, 1634. R2/56/407; W1/90/193
William, Little Bradley, 1677. In. 3/18/122; A5/5/173, A4/14/59
William, Soham, 1690. A5/6/133, A4/32/18
see also Maier, Mayor, Mayre
MAYES, Alice, Stanstead, 1610. A5/3/103
Ambrose, Bury St. Edmunds, 1636. A5/4/47
Edward, Great Cornard, 1669. In. 3/14/201; A5/5/102, A4/7/17
Elisabeth, wid., Bradfield St. George, 1647. A5/4/115
Elisabeth, singlewoman, Creeting All Saints, 1686. A5/6/99, A4/26/88
John, Bury St. Edmunds, 1636. A5/4/42
John, wheelwright, Hundon, 1609. R2/47/86; W1/66/101
Richard, Mildenhall, 1595. A5/2/209
Robert, esq., Bury St. Edmunds, 1667. A5/5/81, A4/5/7
Roger, Cockfield, 1666. R2/64/124; W1/118/94
Roger, wool comber, Walsham le Willows, 1668. In. 3/13/195; A5/5/91, A4/6/16
Thomas, labourer, Denston, 1564. R2/32/64

MAYES continued
William, Glemsford, 1641. A5/5/91
see also Mace
MAYEW, Edward, Rede, 1471. R2/10/537
Thomas, Shimpling, (1521). R2/15/97
William, Sapiston, 1524. R2/17/324b
MAYHEW, Alice, wid., Great Wratting, 1668. R2/64/361; W1/120/73
Alice, Horningsheath, 1610. A5/3/105
Anthony, Icklingham, 1630. A5/4/5
Edmund, smith, Cheveley, 1477. R2/11/105
Elisabeth, wid., Bury St. Edmunds, 1670, (N). R2/65/70; W1/122/83; In. 3/15/100; A5/5/115
Elisabeth, singlewoman, Hartest, 1629, R2/54/305; W1/85/22
Elisabeth, wid., Hunston, 1679. R2/67/457; W1/133/182
George, Bury St. Edmunds, 1563, (N). R2/8/383; W1/17/23
Grace, wid., Hartest, 1646. R2/59/349; W1/103/63
Joan, wid., Bury St. Edmunds, 1583, (N). R2/39/66; W1/42/44
Joan, Harleston, 1560, (N). R2/29/47; W1/25/131
John, Boxford, 1442. R2/9/38
John, Brockley, 1611. R2/48/7; W1/68/26; A5/3/110
John, baker, Bury St. Edmunds, 1443. R2/2/4
John, baker, Bury St. Edmunds, 1525. R2/6/123
John, als. Mayoe, Fornham St. Genevieve, 1594. A5/2/198
John, the elder, Whepstead, 1550. R2/73/120; W1/9/135
Joseph, Hunston, 1641. A5/4/88
Luke, ironmonger, Bury St. Edmunds, 1662. R2/62/408; W1/114/158
Luke, wid., Horningsheath, 1680. A5/6/41, A4/17/108
Luke, husb., Whepstead, 1626. R2/53/540; W1/82/68
Margaret, wife of John, Great Cornard, 1503. R2/13/139
Margery, wife of Simon, Bury St. Edmunds, 1435. R2/1/214
Martha, wid., Rede, 1629, (N). R2/54/303; W1/85/19
Miles, yeo., Worlingworth, 1649. R2/60/249; W1/106/110
Richard, cordwainer, Bury St. Edmunds, 1666. In. 3/12/152; A5/5/76, A4/4/44
Richard, Great Wratting, 1667. A5/5/88, A4/81/90
Richard, husb., Mildenhall, 1614, (N). W1/111/40
Robert, butcher, Great Waldingfield, 1694. R2/72/327; W1/148/58
Robert, the younger, yeo., Hawkedon, 1667. R2/64/198; W1/119/43; In. 3/12/32
Robert, tailor, Hawstead, 1644. R2/59/134; W1/101/60
Robert, Occold, 1483. R2/11/301; W1/9/5
Robert, tailor, Soham, 1660. R2/62/114; W1/112/151
Robert, yeo., Somerton, 1671. R2/65/163; W1/123/29
Robert, carpenter, Stanstead, 1603. R2/45/275; W1/61/78
Roger, Bury St. Edmunds, 1427. R2/1/174 & 175
Roger, Mildenhall, 1623. R2/52/615; W1/79/60, W1/95/74
Simon, Bury St. Edmunds, 1434. R2/1/204
Susan, spinster, Stansfield, 1647. R2/59/449; W1/104/80; In. 3/2/84
Thomas, Ickworth, 165-. W1/110/50
Thomas, grocer, Lavenham, 1696. R2/73/68; W1/150/87; In. 3/25/38
Thomas, husb., Whepstead, 1599. R2/44/328; W1/57/107
Ursula, wid. of Thomas, grocer, Lavenham, 1696. R2/75/11; W1/150/19
William, Bury St. Edmunds, 1528. R2/6/146
William, Hartest, 1575. R2/37/120; W1/34/63
William, tailor, Whepstead, 1536. R2/18/141
MAYHOO, John, Great Cornard, 1530. R2/19/19
Robert, Wickham Skeith, 1544. R2/21/608
William, carpenter, Great Livermere, 1615. R2/49/268; W1/72/53
MAYHOWE, John, husb., Whepstead, 1581. R2/38/330; W1/40/71
MAYHUE, Agnes, wid., Sapiston, 1560. A5/1/103
Austin, husb., Brockley, 1566. R2/32/363; W1/28/16
George, labourer, Great Horningsheath, 1595. R2/43/39; W1/53/31
Lucy, wid., Bury St. Edmunds, 1501. R2/4/113 (admon. only)
Thomas, fuller, Bury St. Edmunds, 1474. R2/2/194
William, the elder, weaver, Bury St. Edmunds, 1502. R2/4/121
see also Mahewe, Maihew, Mayowe
MAYKEN, Robert, husb., Buxhall, 1557. R2/26/213; W1/20/128
MAYKYN, Edmund, husb., Great Waldingfield, 1540. R2/19/609
William, husb., Acton, 1538. R2/20/134; W1/4/114
William, Alpheton, 1473. R2/11/17
MAYN, John, yeo., Rede, (1507). R2/13/196
see also Mayen, Meyn

MAYNARD, Elisabeth, Barrow, 1640, (N). R2/58/124; W1/96/4
John, yeo., Long Melford, 1639. R2/58/41; W1/94/73
John, blacksmith, Long Melford, 1689. R2/71/229; W1/143/68
John, husb., Rougham, 1640. R2/58/139; W1/96/34
William, 1625. R2/53/372; W1/81/151
MAYNER, Edmund, Culford, 1573. R2/36/228; W1/32/92
Edward, Great Thurlow, 1471. R2/10/504
Ellen, wid., Barrow, 1593. R2/42/476
Robert, Barrow, 1647, (N). R2/59/465; W1/104/99; In. 3/2/99
Rose, Tuddenham, 1481. R2/11/192
William, Groton, 1467. R2/10/403
MAYNOR, John, West Stow, 1589. W5/2/120
Nicholas, singleman, Culford, 1574, (N). R2/37/66; W1/33/10
MAYOE, see Mayhew als. Mayoe
MAYOR, Elisabeth, wid., Bradfield St. George, 1647. In. 3/2/158
George, yeo., Denston, 1624. R2/53/66; W1/80/88
John, husb., Chippenham, 1596. R2/43/179; W1/54/57
John, yeo., Walsham le Willows, 1684. R2/69/381; W1/138/166
Peter, Long Melford, 1638. A5/4/58 & 59
Robert, husb., Lakenheath, 1635. R2/56/499; W1/91/75
Robert, the elder, yeo., Worlington, 1690. R2/71/403; W1/144/108
William, apothecary, Bury St. Edmunds, 1693. R2/72/223; W1/147/113
MAYOUR, Henry, husb., Great Thurlow, 1555. R2/24/152; W1/15/1
MAYOWE, Henry, Ickworth, 1573. A5/1/264
John, Sapiston, 1560. R2/29/80; W1/25/87
MAYRE, John, Great Thurlow, 1537. R2/19/593, R2/20/30; W1/3/104
Richard, labourer, Great Thurlow, 1560. R2/29/101; W1/25/65
Robert, Little Bradley, 1540. R2/20/291; W1/4/219
Thomas, Eriswell, 1557. R2/26/210; W1/20/153
MAYSON, John, dyer, Bury St. Edmunds, 1536. R2/7/37
Miles, parson, Hengrave, 1569. R2/33/92
MAYSTER, Peter, Kedington, 1444. R2/9/45
MEAD, Isaac, husb., Great Bradley, 1670. In. 3/15/93; A5/5/114
MEADOW(S), Bridget, wid. of Thomas, yeo., Ipswich, 1650. R2/61/358; W1/107/55
Henry, yeo., Mendlesham, 1681. R2/68/61; W1/135/49
Joan, als. Sharpe, wife of John, Bury St. Edmunds, 1646. A5/4/112
John, gent., Bury St. Edmunds, 1669. R2/64/503; W1/121/96; In. 3/14/79
John, clerk, Bury St. Edmunds, 1697. R2/73/190; W1/151/75
John, yeo., Redgrave, 1646. R2/59/354; W1/103/69
John, carpenter, Rickinghall Inferior, 1683. R2/69/165; W1/137/131
Mary, Palgrave, 1663. A5/5/44
Robert, Brent Eleigh, 1590. A5/2/131 & 132
Thomas, blacksmith, Brent Eleigh, 1631. R2/56/102; W1/87/154
Thomas, grocer, Mildenhall, 1663, (N). R2/63/2; W1/115/2; In. 3/8/6
William, gent., Stoke by Nayland, 1694. R2/72/311; W1/148/39
see also Meddow, Medew, Medow(s)
MEAPOLE, John, husb., Burwell, 1567. R2/32/373; W1/3/21b
MEAPOWLE, Edward, shepherd, Nowton, 1633. R2/56/273; W1/90/38
MEARE, Thomas, rector, Stanstead, 1666. R2/64/140; W1/118/107
MEASANT, Caleb, yeo., Bures, 1665. In. 3/10/20; A5/5/65, A4/3/7
MEATCALFE, Robert, yeo., Denston, 1661. R2/62/266; W1/113/160; In. 3/6/208
MEDCALF, Grace, wid., Stansfield, 1627. R2/59/35; W1/83/44
Mirabel, wid., Sudbury, 1685. R2/70/83; W1/139/75; A5/6/91, A4/24/60
Philip, Bures, 1700. R2/74/62; W1/154/60
Robert, the younger, husb., Soham, 1552. R2/23/139; W1/11/104
Robert, husb., Soham, 1556. R2/25/128; W1/16/181
MEDDOW, Samuel, singleman, Stoke by Nayland, 1682. R2/68/485; W1/136/159
MEDELEY, Mary, wid., Fordham, 1673. R2/65/444; W1/125/71
MEDEW, Thomas, scrivener, Bury St. Edmunds, 1498. R2/4/65
MEDOW(S), Edmund, gent., Bury St. Edmunds, 1680. R2/67/518; W1/134/7
John, Eye, 1549. R2/21/507
Robert, the elder, carpenter, Brent Eleigh, 1638. R2/57/419; W1/93/248
Thomas, weaver, Nayland, 1594. R2/42/515; W1/52/67
Thomas, singleman, Westhorpe, 1651. A5/4/139
William, yeo., Pakenham, 1661. R2/62/169; W1/113/21; In. 3/6/30
William, husb., Thorndon, 1595. R2/43/87; W1/53/88

MEDULTON, Oliver, priest, Stansfield, 1538. R2/18/182
MEENE, Richard, tailor, Ixworth, 1630. R2/55/182; W1/66/200
MEGOWS, John, Lakenheath, 1685. In. 3/22/18
MEISTNER, John, say maker, Little Cornard, 1685. R2/70/113; W1/139/100
MEKYLWOOD, Henry, Wyverstone, 1496. R2/12/16
John, Stowmarket, 1462. R2/10/352
MELKESOP, John, Stoke by Clare, 1462. R2/9/291
MELLE, Thomas, Polstead, 1464. R2/10/358
William, Stoke by Nayland, 1471. R2/10/469
MELLER, Adam, Bury St. Edmunds, 1398. R2/1/84
Agnes, wid. of John, Barnardiston, 1558. R2/27/201
Agnes, Bury St. Edmunds, 1401. R2/1/93
Alexander, Bures, 1533. W1/2/30
Alice, wid., Norton, 1612. R2/48/192; W1/69/80; A5/3/118
John, Barningham, 1460. R2/9/251
John, Great Waldingfield, 1587. R2/40/249; W1/44/90
John, blacksmith, Norton, 1605. R2/45/446; W1/63/91
John, husb., Polstead, 1589. R2/41/199; W1/46/89
John, Stanstead, 1471. R2/10/459
John, als. Hyll, Walsham le Willows, 1484. R2/11/373
Richard, Glemsford, 1593. A5/2/187
Richard, weaver, Nayland, 1578. R2/37/401; W1/36/174
Robert, Hinderclay, 1458. R2/9/238
Robert, the elder, weaver, Long Melford, 1614. R2/49/60; W1/71/47
Robert, Naughton, 1471. R2/10/466 & 491
Robert, Stowmarket, 1690. R2/71/435; W1/144/141
Thomas, Glemsford, 1513. R2/13/207
Thomas, Withersfield, 1464. R2/10/345
William, the elder, husb., Great Bradley, 1609. R2/47/80; W1/66/95
William, yeo., Great Wratting, 1563. R2/31/120; W1/26/4 & 5
see also Barnard als. Meller, Mondessone als. Mellor
MELLEWARD, John, Bury St. Edmunds, 1452. R2/2/40
MELLIS, Robert, Hopton, 1571. R2/35/67; W1/36/64
MELLON, John, Stradishall, 1473. R2/10/580
Peter, Stradishall, 1485. R2/11/338
see also Melowne
MELLS, John, Cockfield, 1566. R2/32/277; W1/28/115
John, shearman, Cockfield, 1588. R2/41/99; W1/45/95
John, yeo., Mildenhall, 1662. R2/62/415; W1/114/172; In. 3/7/220
John, Nayland, 1595. R2/43/46; W1/53/37
Margaret, Nayland, 1667. In. 3/12/19
William, Chelsworth, 1598. R2/44/118; W1/56/43
MELLYNCKE, Joan, wid. of George, Ipswich, 1587. R2/40/288; W1/44/119
MELOWNE, Peter, Bury St. Edmunds, 1444. R2/2/11
MELSOM, William, husb., Depden, 1638. R2/57/421; W1/93/251
MELTON, Elisabeth, wid., Isleham, 1576. W7/43
John, clerk, Brome, 1558. R2/27/333
John, Fordham, 1521. R2/14/27
John, 1455. R2/9/176
Richard, labourer, Isleham, 1579. W7/45
Thomas, husb., Isleham, 1679. W7/92
William, Bury St. Edmunds, 1403. R2/1/98
William, Soham, 1460. R2/9/253
MELTUN, John, labourer, Aldham, 1591. R2/42/125; W1/48/112
MENDAM, John, gent., Mildenhall, 1595. R2/43/119; W1/53/123
Oliver, husb., Soham, 1629. R2/54/428; W1/85/109a
Stephen, Boxford, 1528. W1/19/53
MENDEHAM, John, Stowmarket, 1551. R2/23/93; W1/11/40
MENDHAM, George, Soham, 1649. A5/4/126
John, yeo., Burwell, 1661. R2/62/172; W1/113/25; In. 3/6/42; A4/1/147
Oliver, sen., Soham, 1607. R2/46/112; W1/97/14
Robert, tailor, Bury St. Edmunds, 1516. R2/6/29
MERCER, Alice, wife of John, Bury St. Edmunds, 1430. R2/1/196
Bartholomew, Bury St. Edmunds, 1426. R2/1/170
John, Bury St. Edmunds, 1430. R2/1/192
Walter, Bury St. Edmunds, 1378. R2/1/37
William, fuller, Bury St. Edmunds, 1414. R2/1/134
MERCHALL, William, Stoke by Nayland, 1564. R2/32/105; W1/27/57
MERCHANT, Bartholomew, yeo., Stoke by Nayland, 1637. R2/57/142; W1/92/178
Edward, rope maker, Groton, 1592. R2/42/224; W1/49/43
see also Marchant, Merkant

MERELL(S), John, the younger, Stanstead, (1524). R2/17/326
John, Wixoe, 1533. R2/19/137; W1/2/1
MERIELS, Michael, yeo., Stoke by Clare, 1583. R2/39/79; W1/42/31
Stephen, Sudbury, 1584. A5/2/63
MERILLS, Henry, farmer, Boxted, 1682. In. 3/21/137; A5/6/60, A4/19/47
MERITH, Richard, say weaver, Bury St. Edmunds, 1648. R2/60/83; W1/105/100
MERKANT, Robert, yeo., Newmarket, 1559. R2/28/104; W1/22/104
MERKEDAY, Joan, singlewoman, Bildeston, 1535. R2/19/210; W1/3/159
MERRELL(S), Alice, wid., Nayland, 1585. R2/39/333; W1/42/261
John, Clare, 1589. A5/2/120
John, weaver, Glemsford, 1584. R2/39/233; W1/42/98
Margery, wid., Edwardstone, 1595. A5/2/213
Margery, wid., Glemsford, 1595. R2/43/84; W1/53/79
William, Hepworth, 1595. A5/2/214
MERRILLS, Alice, spinster, Wixoe, 1667. R2/64/181; W1/119/18; In. 3/12/46
Edward, wool comber, Bury St. Edmunds, 1692. R2/72/111; W1/146/102; In. 3/24/33
Ralph, Glemsford, 1642. A5/4/95
Roger, Glemsford, 1694. A5/6/175, A4/37/106
Susan, Wixoe, 1652. A5/4/142
Thomas, gent., Bury St. Edmunds, 1689. R2/71/196; W1/143/47
William, the elder, yeo., Wixoe, 1619. R2/51/284; W1/132/19
see also Merell(s), Meryell, Murrell, Hible als. Merrells
MERRY, Richard, inn holder, Bury St. Edmunds, 1670. R2/65/128; W1/122/152
MERSHALL, John, husb., Nowton, 1552. R2/23/244; W1/12/54
MERVYNE, John, Layham, 1550. R2/21/45; W1/10/173
MERYELL, Agnes, Soham, 1471. R2/10/473
Joan, wid., Glemsford, 1506. R2/13/172
John, yeo., Nayland, 1573. R2/36/103; W1/32/1
John, Stanstead, 1480. R2/11/207
Richard, Long Melford, 1457. R2/9/220
MERYLES, John, Wixoe, 1575. R2/37/92; W1/34/17
MERYLLS, Dorothy, wid., Wixoe, 1591. R2/42/28; W1/48/18
MERYOTT, Thomas, Cheveley, 1545. R2/19/569; W1/7/67
MESENER, Alice, wid., Great Cornard, 1680. R2/67/538; W1/134/23; In. 3/20/21
MESENGAR, Leonard, Wicken, 1545. R2/19/513; W1/7/32
see also Massenger, Messager
MESHAM, John, Newmarket, 1523. R2/14/54
MESSAGER, John, goldsmith, Bury St. Edmunds, 1466. R2/2/92
MESSYNG, Margaret, Sudbury, 1520. R2/15/120, R2/17/313; W1/23/4
METCALFE, Augustin, labourer, Wickhambrook, 1588. R2/41/73; W1/45/61
George, bach., Bures, 1689. A5/6/127, A4/30/46
Jane, Denston, 1669. In. 3/14/8; A5/5/103, A4/7/28
Jane, singlewoman, Fornham St. Martin, 1591. R2/42/145; W1/48/98
John, husb., Stansfield, 1650. R2/61/374; W1/107/73; In. 3/3/114
Margaret, wid., Isleham, 1614. R6/4
Margaret, wid., Poslingford, 1686. In. 3/22/51; A5/6/98, A4/26/107
Robert, 1576. In. 3/1/12 & 121
Simon, Sudbury, 1562. R2/31/16; W1/8/145
William, yeo., Withersfield, 1601. R2/44/368; W1/59/33
see also Meatcalfe, Fison als. Metcalfe
METHEWOLD, John, Bury St. Edmunds, 1361. R2/1/10
Margaret, spinster, Bury St. Edmunds, 1469. R2/2/128
William, Bury St. Edmunds, 1417. R2/1/141
William, webster, Bury St. Edmunds, 1449. R2/2/30a
METSCHERPE, Thomas, Mendlesham, 1463. R2/10/318
METSHARP, Roger, Mendlesham, 1457. R2/9/191
METTEWYN(D), John, Wattisfield, 1458. R2/9/194
Katherine, Wattisfield, 1463. R2/9/308
William, Wattisfield, 1465. R2/10/383
METTON, John, vicar, Clare, 1562. R2/31/22; W1/8/148
MEY, Agnes, Lavenham, 1464. R2/10/345
Joan, wid., Bury St. Edmunds, 1496. R2/4/43
John, jun., Bury St. Edmunds, 1468. R2/2/121
John, the younger, weaver, Bury St. Edmunds, 1479. R2/2/274
John, Lavenham, 1443. R2/9/50
John, the elder, Mildenhall, 1556. R2/25/34; W1/16/36
John, yeo., Mildenhall, 1560. R2/29/152; W1/25/22

MEY continued
John, sen., Thornham, 1440. R2/9/11
Nicholas, warrener, Mildenhall, 1540. R2/19/279; W1/36/24
Richard, Mildenhall, 1547. R2/21/311; W1/10/137
Thomas, Stow, 1544. A5/1/20
Ursula, Stowmarket, 1537. R2/18/145, R2/19/594; W1/3/166
William, fuller, Bury St. Edmunds, 1394. R2/1/72
William, clothier, Bury St. Edmunds, 1538. R2/7/48
MEYN, John, Barnardiston, 1439. R2/9/5
MICHAELL, Thomas, husb., Mildenhall, 1612. W1/111/17
see also Mighell, Mitchell, Migely als. Michaell, Migely als. Mitchell
MICHELL, Anne, wid., Bury St. Edmunds, 1607. R2/46/145; W1/97/80
Henry, Bury St. Edmunds, (1557). R2/8/318; W1/18/48
Henry, gent., Gazeley, 1661, (N). R2/62/253; W1/113/138; In. 3/6/184; A5/5/21, A4/1/53
James, Brandon, 1664. A5/5/58, A4/2/52
Joan, wid., Gazeley, 1678. R2/67/85; W1/130/68; In. 3/19/92
John, Soham, 1686. In. 3/22/146; A5/6/106, A4/26/13
Thomas, Mildenhall, 1628. R2/54/182; W1/84/59
MICHYLL, John, chandler, Bury St. Edmunds, 1524. R2/6/119
MICKLEFELD, George, wheelwright, Hessett, 1678. R2/67/166; W1/130/147; In. 3/19/198
MICKLEFIELD, Martha, wid., Bradfield St. George, 1687. R2/70/363; W1/141/92
MIDDAY, John, butcher, Eye, (1609). W1/111/78
MIDDELDICH, John, cordwainer, Bury St. Edmunds, 1680. R2/67/759; W1/134/191; In. 3/20/211
Walter, Wood Ditton, 1584. A5/2/56
MIDDLEDICHE, Thomas, Great Bradley, 1625. R2/53/391; W1/81/169
MIDDLEDITCH, Ann, als. Jay and Martin, wid., Bury St. Edmunds, 1687. R2/70/349; W1/141/85
Clement, cordwainer, Kedington, 1686. In. 3/22/93; A5/6/102, A4/26/55
Daniel, cordwainer, Cheveley, 1661. R2/62/196; W1/113/57; In. 3/6/81
Giles, tailor, Glemsford, 1670. R2/65/59; W1/122/71; In. 3/15/100
Jasper, Bury St. Edmunds, 1689. A5/6/129, A4/30/21
John, the elder, Little Thurlow, 1640, (N). R2/58/194; W1/96/119
John, husb., Withersfield, 1671. R2/65/166; W1/123/31
Mary, spinster, Great Bradley, 1636. A5/4/42
Mary, spinster, Hundon, 1696. A5/6/186, A4/39/20
Mary, wid., Kedington, 1695. A5/6/181, A4/38/64
Mary, spinster, Palgrave, 1678. In. 3/19/133; A5/6/9, A4/15/73
Samuel, Great Wratting, 1700. A5/7/16, A4/41/122
Samuel, clerk, Long Melford, 1682. R2/68/443; W1/136/126
Susan, spinster, Great Bradley, 1636. A5/4/42
Thomas, labourer, Great Bradley, 1665. In. 3/10/15; A5/5/65
William, tailor, Great Bradley, 1612. R2/48/200
William, husb., Great Bradley, 1672. R2/65/304; W1/124/25; A5/5/130, A4/9/31
William, the elder, cordwainer, Lidgate, 1692. R2/72/31; W1/146/30
see also Midledich, Myddeldeche
MIDDLETON, Agnes, Shelland, 1628. R2/54/260; W1/84/118
John, Bury St. Edmunds, 1586. A5/2/77
John, Bury St. Edmunds, 1591. A5/2/146
John, clerk, Stradishall, 1682. R2/68/410; W1/136/104; A4/18/102
Mary, wid., Cavendish, 1692. A5/6/155, A4/35/94
Philip, yeo., Cotton, 1642. R2/58/394; W1/99/109
see also Medulton, Midleton, Myddeltone
MIDGELY, James, sen., shoe maker, Brandon, 1630. R2/55/167; W1/86/185
MIDLEDICH, Benjamin, cordwainer, Bury St. Edmunds, 1679. R2/67/290; W1/133/75
MIDLEDITCH, John, husb., Brockley, 1700. R2/74/95; W1/154/97
John, the elder, yeo., Great Wratting, 1683. R2/69/183; W1/137/142
Thomas, Stradishall, 1676. In. 3/17/120; A5/5/164, A4/13/65
William, Bury St. Edmunds, 1645. A5/4/107
MIDLEDYTCH, Benjamin, cordwainer, Bury St. Edmunds, 1647. R2/59/413; W1/104/39
MIDLETON, Richard, minister, Westley, 1594. R2/42/549; W1/52/44; A5/2/199
Thomas, yeo., Hitcham, 1638. R2/57/362; W1/93/158
MIDSON, Matthew, blacksmith, Clare, 1639. R2/58/95; W1/94/160

MIGELY, Ellen, als. Michaell, wid., Brandon, 1626. R2/53/661; W1/82/185
John, als. Mitchell, baker, Brandon, 1626, (N). R2/53/612; W1/82/139
MIGHELL, Robert, Bury St. Edmunds, 1594. A5/2/203
see also Myghell
MIHILL, Anne, wid., Bury St. Edmunds, 1621, (N). R2/52/326; W1/77/106
John, Mildenhall, 1680. In. 3/20/239; A5/6/15, A4/16/5
MILBIE, Katherine, Bury St. Edmunds, 1623. R2/52/603; W1/79/53
MILBORNE, Nathaniel, yeo., Groton, 1661. R2/62/304; W1/113/225
MILDENHALE, Isabel, wife of John, thatcher, Bury St. Edmunds, 1415. R2/1/135
John, webster, Bury St. Edmunds, 1430. R2/1/194
see also Myldenhale
MILEMAN, Edward, glover, Lavenham, 1682. In. 3/21/160; A5/6/60, A4/19/51
MILES, Amy, wid., Bury St. Edmunds, 1668. R2/64/316; W1/120/22; In. 3/13/191; A5/5/92, A4/6/28
Francis, sen., Hessett, 1680. R2/67/730; W1/134/171
Jeremy, the elder, yeo., Newmarket, 1650. R2/61/357; W1/107/54; In. 3/3/67
John, Kedington, 1620. R2/52/146; W1/76/129
John, Long Melford, 1606. R2/46/31; W1/64/39
Osmund, yeo., Redgrave, 1634. R2/56/409; W1/90/196
Robert, husb., Barrow, 1626, (N). R2/53/613; W1/82/142
Robert, gardener, Barrow, (1693). W1/312/34
Thomas, Long Melford, 1687. R2/70/338; W1/141/76
Thomas, Stoke by Clare, 1638. A5/4/66
see also Milys, Myeles, Myles, Mylys
MILESON, John, clerk, Norton, 1699. R2/73/381; W1/153/34
MILGATT, John, shoe maker, Bury St. Edmunds, 1531. R2/7/5
MILKSOPP, John, Sudbury, 1576. R2/37/175; W1/37/40; In. 3/1/66
see also Melkesop, Mylkesop, Mylsehopp
MILKYN, William, Cockfield, 1619. R2/51/465; W1/132/129
MILLER, Ann, Polstead, 1641. A5/4/87
Costin, labourer, Bury St. Edmunds, 1528. R2/6/156
Daniel, Brent Eleigh, 1638. R2/57/291; W1/93/63
Edmund, yeo., Great Thurlow, 1623. R2/52/692; W1/79/108
Edward, wid., Long Melford, 1649. A5/4/130
Elisabeth, Thurlow, 1610. A5/3/107
Francis, Haverhill, 1644. A5/4/101
George, labourer, Chelsworth, 1680. R2/67/595; W1/134/70; In. 3/20/74
George, yeo., Semer, 1634. R2/56/313; W1/90/80
Henry, Bures, 1642. A5/4/96
James, yeo., Great Thurlow, 1641. R2/58/252; W1/98/22; In. 5/4/92
John, inn holder, Ballingdon, 1666. In. 3/11/130; A5/5/77, A4/4/50
John, sen., Great Wratting, 1636. A5/4/43
John, gent., Isleham, 1631. R6/66
John, yeo., Ixworth, 1625. R2/53/399; W1/81/181
John, Lakenheath, 1585. R2/39/289; W1/42/288
John, yeo., Long Melford, 1629. R2/54/281; W1/85/4
John, Mendlesham, 1684. A5/6/79, A4/21/60
John, Wixoe, 1647, (N). R2/59/498; W1/104/137
Mary, Stowmarket, 1697. A5/7/3, A4/40/53
Philip, wid., yeo., Stowmarket, 1663. In. 3/9/89; A5/5/49
Richard, husb., Culford, 1638. R2/57/397; W1/93/213
Richard, husb., Ixworth Thorpe, 1625. R2/53/303; W1/81/88
Richard, butcher, Stanton, 1611. R2/48/114; W1/68/126
Robert, glazier, plumber, Brandon, 1688. In. 3/23/55; A5/6/121, A4/29/61
Robert, Polstead, 1639. A5/4/76
Stephen, yeo., Great Thurlow, 1604. R2/45/358; W1/62/85
Stephen, Great Wratting, 1611. A5/3/111
Thomas, Preston, 1631. A5/4/14
William, wool comber, Bury St. Edmunds, 1678. In. 3/19/169; A5/6/11, A4/15/94
William, yeo., Long Melford, 1639. R2/58/82; W1/94/142
see also Myller, Armenell als. Myller, Barnard als. Miller, Herdman als. Miller
MILLIGAN, James, Pakenham, 1696. A5/6/188
MILLINGTON, John, Little Thurlow, 1696. A5/6/188, A4/39/51
Prissana, Great Thurlow, 1661. In. 3/6/217; A5/5/18, A4/1/80

MILLS, Anthony, yeo., Cockfield, 1680. In. 3/20/215; A5/6/41, A4/17/113
Ann, wid., Long Melford, 1678. In. 3/19/18; A5/6/2, A4/15/10
Catherine, wid., Soham, 1670. In. 3/15/205; A5/5/120
Daniel, Bures, 1649. A5/4/127
Edward, clothier, Lavenham, 1636. R2/57/53; W1/92/61
Elisabeth, wid., Westhorpe, 1683. R2/69/18; W1/137/15
Elisabeth, wid., Wormegay, 1693. R2/72/225; W1/147/114
George, husb., Cockfield, 1630. R2/55/168; W1/86/186
Grace, singlewoman, Clare, 1618. R2/51/238; W1/75/153
Hugh, husb., Nayland, 1671. R2/65/233; W1/123/110
Isaac, yeo., Cockfield, 1630. R2/55/71; W1/86/82
John, the elder, yeo., Cockfield, 1624. R2/53/185; W1/80/158
John, tailor, Cockfield, 1665. R2/63/348; W1/117/98
John, tailor, Long Melford, 1638. R2/57/255; W1/93/16
John, tailor, Long Melford, 1677. In. 3/18/28; A5/5/167, A4/14/11
John, Stoke by Nayland, 1588. R2/41/5; W1/45/2
Margaret, wid., Wissington, 1667. R2/64/178; W1/119/12
Marmaduke, carpenter, Layham, 1581. R2/38/301; W1/40/43
Richard, Wissington, 1611. A5/3/112
Robert, Polstead, 1625. R2/53/240; W1/81/34
Robert, say weaver, Polstead, 1700. R2/74/57; W1/154/55; In. 3/27/42
Susan, wid., Bures, 1664. R2/63/241; W1/116/162; In. 3/9/235
Thomas, Bures, 1662. In. 3/7/153; A5/5/33
Thomas, yeo., Cockfield, 1672. R2/65/380; W1/124/124
Thomas, yeo., Cockfield, 1685. R2/70/59; W1/139/54
Thomas, yeo., Great Cornard, 1675. R2/66/133; W1/127/12; In. 3/16/4
Thomas, yeo., Mendlesham, 1699. R2/73/395; W1/153/42
Thomas, carpenter, Westhorpe, 1660. R2/62/30; W1/112/31
William, barber, Lavenham, 1684. R2/69/241; W1/138/46
William, carpenter, Westhorpe, 1679. R2/67/304; W1/133/87
see also Mylles, Haxall als. Milles
MILWARD, Elisabeth, wid., Bury St. Edmunds, 1606. R2/46/71; W1/64/79
see also Melleward
MILYS, Thomas, carpenter, Bury St. Edmunds, 1522. R2/6/91
MINES, Thomas, wid., Hopton, 1663. In. 3/8/11; A5/5/42
see also Minnes, Myn(e)s, Mynn(e)s
MINETT, Agnes, Freckenham, 1632. R6/70
Thomas, knacker, Freckenham, 1616. R6/15
MINOTT, Joan, wid., Lakenheath, 1635. R2/56/457; W1/91/20
see also Minnit, Mynett, Mynott
MINGIE, John, yeo., Palgrave, 1666. In. 3/11/3; A5/5/72, A4/4/2
MINNES, Henry, yeo., Shelland, 1614. R2/49/163; W1/71/110
Luke, singleman, Thurston, 1661. R2/62/288; W1/113/199; In. 3/6/254
see also Mines
MINNIT, John, collar maker, Wood Ditton, 1620. R2/52/105; W1/76/91
Richard, knacker, Freckenham, 1625. R6/42
MIRRELLS, John, the elder, yeo., Cockfield, 1612. R2/48/198; W1/69/88
John, yeo., Lawshall, 1680. R2/67/554; W1/134/37
see also Myrells
MIRTON, John, felt maker, Mellis, 1636, (N). R2/57/112; W1/92/134
Robert, Onehouse, 1484. W1/24/100
MISSLETON, Edward, cordwainer, Bury St. Edmunds, 1680. R2/67/696; W1/134/147; In. 3/20/166
MISSYNGE, Robert, tallow chandler, Sudbury, 1559. R2/28/49; W1/22/20
see also Messyng, Myssinge
MITCHELL, John, Little Waldingfield, 1683. A5/6/72, A4/20/92
Joseph, Brandon, 1672. A5/5/133, A4/9/61
Margaret, wid., Kersey, 1682. In. 3/21/105; A5/5/64, A4/19/104
Rebecca, wid., Lavenham, 1677. R2/66/493; W1/129/74
Richard, yeo., Alpheton, 1675. R2/66/193; W1/127/70; In. 3/16/88
Richard, yeo., Kersey, 1681. R2/68/22; W1/135/19
William, fellmonger, Kersey, 1686. In. 3/22/92; A5/6/102, A4/26/56
see also Michell, Mychell
MIXER, Joanna, wid., Groton, 1697. R2/73/189; W1/151/74
MODIE, John, Lidgate, 1560. R2/29/77; W1/25/90
MODY, Richard, Newton, 1468. R2/10/404
Robert, Finborough, 1453. R2/9/168
William, parson, Cockfield, 1568. R2/33/24
MOELEN, Machalen, wid., Norwich, 1594, (N). W1/51/147

MOLE, Mercy, singlewoman, Rattlesden, 1674. R2/66/24; W1/126/100; A5/5/151, A4/11/79
see also Moule
MOLENCE, Thomas, Bures, 1521. R2/15/132, R2/17/330
MOLHOWSE, Edward, Wattisfield, 1566. A5/1/171
John, Eye, 1583. A5/2/49
MOLINER, John, yeo., Wetheringsett, 1603. R2/45/287; W1/61/91
MOLL, William, Mendlesham, 1605. A5/3/2
MOLLANDE, Henry, Great Saxham, (1544). R2/21/1
MOLLENS, Bennett, Sudbury, 1526. R2/17/203; W1/23/30
MOLLOWES, William, linen weaver, Wickham Skeith, 1620. R2/52/14; W1/76/13
MOLOWS, Almorous, Wattisfield, 1461. R2/9/287
John, sen., Wattisfield, 1501. R2/13/121
Robert, husb., Ashfield, 1527. R2/17/251; W1/1/26
Thomas, yeo., Badwell, 1553. R2/31/164; W1/13/109
see also Molhouse
MONCK, Thomas, clerk, Bacton, 1617. R2/50/295; W1/74/86
MONDESSONE, Thomas, als. Mellor, Long Melford, 1457. R2/9/221
MONE, John, sen., miller, Fornham, 1457. R2/9/189
John, Newton, 1535. R2/18/223
Margery, Fornham, 1462. R2/9/342
Simon, Bury St. Edmunds, 1399. R2/1/94
see also Wykes als. Mone
MONEXE, John, Soham, 1539. R2/19/331
MONINGE(S), John, the elder, yeo., Badwell Ash, 1597. R2/43/235; W1/55/20
Margery, wife of John, yeo., Badwell Ash, 1598. R2/44/44; W1/56/39
Richard, Brettenham, 1564. A5/1/159
MONK, William, goldsmith, Bury St. Edmunds, 1475. R2/2/212
see also Monck
MONNINGE(S), Humfrey, Nedging, 1596. A5/2/218
Joan, wid., Stoke by Nayland, 1617. R2/50/357; W1/74/140
John, Sudbury, 1630. A5/4/6
MONNYNGE(S), Alice, wid., Nedging, 1587. R2/40/41; W1/44/22
Henry, Woolpit, 1468. R2/10/419
Richard, yeo., Stoke by Nayland, 1638. R2/57/430; W1/93/269
MONSEY, Edward, gent., Cotton, 1622. R2/52/451; W1/78/69
MONSON, Clement, carpenter, Lakenheath, 1638. R2/57/406; W1/93/225
John, jun., Long Melford, 1544. R2/21/607
see also Mondessone, Mounson, Munson
MONY, Elisabeth, wid., Sudbury, 1585. R2/39/385; W1/42/222
MONYNGE, William, blacksmith, Acton, 1588. R2/41/78; W1/45/68
MOODY, Ann, spinster, Bury St. Edmunds, 1694. R2/72/373; W1/148/102
Edmund, Gazeley, 1647. A5/4/118
William, sen., yeo., Isleham, 1699. In. 9/105
William, Isleham, 1701. A12/19
MOORE, Constance, Burwell, 1682. In. 3/21/109; A5/6/64, A4/19/101
Dorothy, singlewoman, Rattlesden, 1663. In. 3/8/201; A5/5/52
Edmund, yeo., Landwade, 1597. R2/43/310; W1/55/78
Elisabeth, spinster, Brettenham, 1696. R2/73/20; W1/150/11; In. 3/25/61
Elisabeth, Nowton, 1634. A5/4/34
Giles, Long Melford, 1668. In. 3/13/3; A5/5/92, A4/6/25
Isaac, yeo., Rattlesden, 1685. R2/70/18; W1/139/17
Joan, wid., Boxford, 1593. R2/42/364; W1/50/33
Joanna, wid., Whepstead, 1480. R2/11/206
John, yeo., Bures, 1625. R2/53/290; W1/81/80
John, Bury St. Edmunds, 1473. R2/2/172
John, yeo., Bury St. Edmunds, 1537. R2/7/41
John, say weaver, Bury St. Edmunds, 1670. R2/65/112; W1/122/34; In. 3/15/174; A5/5/117
John, yeo., Nettlestead, 1635. R2/56/459; W1/91/22
John, yeo., Onehouse, 1575. W1/95/6
John, the elder, yeo., Rattlesden, 1671, (N). R2/65/149; W1/123/8; A5/5/120, A4/8/6
John, Stanstead, 1440. R2/9/26
John, Stanstead, 1484. R2/11/340
John, Wickhambrook, 1682. In. 3/21/90; A5/6/63, A4/19/100
Laurence, Chippenham, 1679. A5/6/20, A4/16/51
Margaret, Rattlesden, 1563. A5/1/150
Michael, als. Barrell, yeo., Cavendish, 1624. R2/53/17; W1/80/25

MOORE continued
Nicholas, Ixworth, 1566. A5/1/173
Reginald, Boxford, 1588. R2/41/6; W1/45/4
Robert, Bildeston, 1611. A5/3/110
Robert, Long Melford, 1525. R2/17/135; W1/21/131
Robert, fuller, Long Melford, 1550. R2/21/51; W1/10/172
Robert, yeo., Thelnetham, 1569. R2/33/113
Robert, Withersfield, 1557, (N). R2/25/162; W1/16/153
Rose, wid., Withersfield, 1662. In. 3/7/16; A5/5/26
Samuel, weaver, Rattlesden, 1613. R2/48/245a; W1/70/17
Simon, Boxford, 1451. R2/9/126
Simon, Wickham Skeith, 1544. R2/19/467
Stephen, hoop maker, Rattlesden, 1660. In. 3/5/212; A5/5/8, A4/1/175
Stephen, jun., yeo., Rattlesden, 1687. R2/70/279; W1/141/22
Stephen, sen., yeo., Rattlesden, 1697. R2/73/166; W1/151/51
Thomas, tailor, Bury St. Edmunds, 1471. R2/2/164
Thomas, the elder, tanner, Bury St. Edmunds, 1608. R2/46/206; W1/65/91
Thomas, the elder, tanner, Bury St. Edmunds, 1624. R2/53/53; W1/80/76
Thomas, yeo., Bury St. Edmunds, 1674. R2/66/31; W1/126/90
Thomas, chaplain, Wetheringsett, 1473. R2/11/30
Walter, Rattlesden, 1526. R2/17/218; W1/23/9b
Walter, Stowmarket, 1458. R2/9/267
William, say weaver, Bury St. Edmunds, 1686. R2/70/520; W1/140/122
William, Great Cornard, 1471. R2/10/557
William, Long Melford, 1550. R2/21/151; W1/9/153
William, the elder, yeo., Rattlesden, 1669. R2/64/534; W1/121/126; In. 3/14/99
William, the younger, yeo., Rattlesden, 1675. R2/66/259; W1/127/127; In. 3/16/169
William, hosier, Sudbury, 1666. R2/64/3; W1/118/5; In. 3/11/14
see also Mawor, More, Mour
MOORECLARKE, John, Fornham St. Martin, 1573. A5/1/268
MOOTE, Agnes, Burwell, 1571. R2/35/56; W1/36/68
MOOTHAM, Anthony, tailor, Stoke by Clare, 1668. R2/64/336; W1/120/43; In. 3/13/46
Mary, wid., Buxhall, 1618. R2/51/32; W1/75/17
Thomas, husb., Brettenham, 1649. R2/60/201; W1/106/45
MORDBOICE, William, blacksmith, Hepworth, 1648. R2/60/55; W1/105/72
MORDEN, John, Exning, 1678. In. 3/19/5; A5/6/1, A4/15/4
Nicholas, Newmarket, 1611. A5/3/112
Roger, singleman, Burwell, 1638. R2/57/394; W1/93/210
see also Mordon, Moreden
MORDEW, Robert, Warham, 1536. W1/51/36
MORDON, Joan, Cheveley, 1481. R2/11/278
Phillippa, wid., Barton Mills, 1636. R2/57/33; W1/92/41
Thomas, Exning, 1569. A5/1/205
MORDOUN, Peter, Cheveley, 1478. R2/11/183
MORE, Agnes, wid., Withersfield, 1577. In. 3/1/10
Amy, wid., Great Thurlow, 1683. R2/69/40; W1/137/33
Christine, wid., Bury St. Edmunds, 1533. R2/7/15
Clement, tanner, Bury St. Edmunds, 1552. R2/8/53; W1/21/191
Edmund, cordwainer, Bury St. Edmunds, 1589. R2/41/251; W1/46/51
Elizabeth, wid., Bury St. Edmunds, 1548. R2/8/23
George, Pakenham, 1608. A5/3/40
Jasper, cordwainer, Boxford, 1626. R2/53/541; W1/82/69
John, sen., Bures, 1592. A5/2/164
John, Gislingham, (1493). R2/11/442
John, Haughley, 1453. R2/9/148
John, Lindsey, 1544. R2/19/488
Richard, Bury St. Edmunds, 1593. R2/42/430; W1/50/91
Richard, clerk, Icklingham, 1621. R2/52/336; W1/77/114
Richard, Onehouse, 1610. A5/3/92
Richard, gent., Stanstead, 1559. R2/28/373; W1/3/183
Thomas, Fornham, 1461. R2/9/276
Thomas, Hawstead, 1641, (N). R2/58/298; W1/98/86
Thomas, Lawshall, 1525. R2/17/95; W1/21/90
Thomas, yeo., Withersfield, 1621. R2/52/343; W1/77/121
Thomas, husb., Withersfield, 1662. R2/62/312; W1/114/9; In. 3/7/27
William, wheelwright, Bury St. Edmunds, 1469. R2/11/131

MORE continued
William, yeo., Bury St. Edmunds, 1533. R2/7/14
William, waterman, Lakenheath, 1559. R2/28/228; W1/22/182
William, clothier, Stowlangtoft, 1616. R2/50/101; W1/73/109
see also Moore
MOREDEN, William, Little Thurlow, 1607. A5/3/26
MORELL, John, Stoke by Nayland, 1485. R2/11/326
Robert, sen., Sudbury, 1484. R2/11/374
MORES, Stephen, Stoke by Clare, 1553. R2/31/98; W1/13/76
MOREWHYLL, Thomas, yeo., Mendlesham, 1554. R2/24/45; W1/14/37
MOREYS, Joan, wid. of Richard, Newmarket, 1513. R2/12/99
MORFE, Edmund, yeo., Hazlewood, 1574. W1/51/231
MORFEW, Thomas, Yaxley, 1640. R2/58/133; W1/96/23
MORGAN, John, Soham, 1681. A5/6/50, A4/18/77
MORGAYNE, Evans, husb., Knettishall, 1615. R2/49/376; W1/72/145
see also Andrewes als. Morgon, Carter als. Morgan
MORGRAVE, John, waterman, Lakenheath, 1589. R2/41/237; W1/46/55
MORICE, Dorothy, wife of Hugh, gent., Euston, 1698. R2/73/274; W1/152/52
William, Nayland, 1592. A5/2/170
MORIELL, John, the elder, skinner, Bury St. Edmunds, 1501. R2/4/112
John, Glemsford, 1479. R2/12/4
MORIS, Robert, yeo., Rickinghall, 1593. R2/42/414; W1/50/74
MORLE, Henry, Mildenhall, 1443. R2/9/40
John, saddler, Bury St. Edmunds, 1474. R2/2/192
John, saddler, Bury St. Edmunds, 1492. R2/2/200
John, sen., Mildenhall, 1471. R2/10/487
Richard, sen., Mildenhall, 1470. R2/10/426
MORLEY, Alice, wid., Barningham, 1694. R2/72/308; W1/148/36
Alice, Mildenhall, 1480. R2/11/201
Ann, spinster, Bury St. Edmunds, 1684. R2/69/343; W1/138/138
Annice, wid., Mildenhall, 1630. R2/55/12; W1/86/13
Christopher, husb., Lakenheath, 1680. R2/67/526; W1/134/11; In. 3/20/93; A5/6/31, A4/17/9
Edmund, the younger, husb., Lakenheath, 1672. R2/65/326; W1/124/51
Edmund, yeo., Lakenheath, 1675. R2/66/150; W1/127/22; In. 3/16/28
Edward, labourer, Exning, 1602. R2/45/114; W1/60/29
Elisabeth, wid., Bury St. Edmunds, 1670. R2/65/107; W1/122/128; In. 3/15/156
Ellen, wid., Exning, 1623. R2/52/667; W1/79/88
Henry, Mildenhall, 1549. R2/21/545; W1/8/70
Henry, Mildenhall, 1571. R2/35/155; W1/38/171
Henry, yeo., Mildenhall, 1626. R2/53/589; W1/82/118
Henry, the elder, yeo., Mildenhall, 1660. R2/62/69; W1/112/89; In. 3/5/105
Henry, Newmarket, 1683. R2/69/75
John, Barningham, 1693. A5/6/164, A4/35/21
John, singleman, Bury St. Edmunds, 1586. R2/40/42; W1/43/30
John, Euston, 1637. A5/4/55
John, labourer, Lakenheath, 1663. In. 3/8/157; A5/5/50
John, tailor, Lakenheath, 1671. R2/65/172; W1/123/41
John, Mildenhall, 1626. R2/53/532; W1/82/61
Richard, Mildenhall, 1522. R2/15/45
Richard, the elder, husb., Mildenhall, 1562. R2/31/85; W1/8/103
Richard, Mildenhall, 1573. R2/36/202; W1/32/119
Richard, Mildenhall, 1614. W1/95/154
Richard, Newmarket, 1683. W1/137/56
Robert, maltster, Brandon, 1664. R2/63/222; W1/116/135; In. 3/9/168
Robert, husb., Mildenhall, 1555. R2/24/252; W1/15/81
Samuel, Barrow, 1652. A5/4/142
Thomas, sen., Bury St. Edmunds, 1663, (N). R2/63/95; W1/115/145; In. 3/8/190; A5/5/53
Thomas, labourer, Lakenheath, 1631. R2/56/2; W1/87/4
Thomas, husb., Mildenhall, 1599. R2/44/289; W1/57/87
William, labourer, Bury St. Edmunds, 1622. R2/52/460; W1/78/74b
William, yeo., Cockfield, 1693. R2/72/263; W1/147/149b
William, husb., Lakenheath, 1647. R2/59/497; W1/104/135; In. 3/2/145
MORLIE, Andrew, Mildenhall, 1591. A5/2/157
Margaret, Mildenhall, 1592. A5/2/171

MORLY, Henry, Mildenhall, 1577. A5/2/2
Henry, yeo., Mildenhall, 1679. R2/67/322; W1/133/95
John, Bury St. Edmunds, 1586. A5/2/79
John, yeo., Cockfield, 1634. R2/56/354; W1/90/122
John, Lakenheath, 1686. R2/70/535; W1/140/139; In. 3/22/145
John, Mildenhall, 1576. R2/37/130; W1/37/1a; In. 3/1/120
William, yeo., Preston, 1679. R2/67/361; W1/133/118
see also Isaacson als. Morley
MOROWHYLL, Robert, Mendlesham, 1471. R2/10/489
MORPAS, Robert, Long Melford, 1640. A5/4/84
MORPHEW, John, singleman, Braiseworth, 1636. R2/57/22; W1/92/31
see also Morfew
MORRES, John, Rickinghall Superior, 1557. R2/26/244; W1/20/158
Ralph, Hundon, 1572. A5/1/252
MORRICE, Thomas, Hundon, 1581. A5/2/36
MORRIS, Agnes, wid., Lavenham, 1635. R2/56/477; W1/91/51
Alice, Gazeley, 1582. A5/2/39
Alice, wid., Hartest, 1594. R2/42/518; W1/52/63
Andrew, yeo., Redlingfield, 1700. In. 3/27/60
Caleb, tailor, Nayland, 1635. R2/56/498; W1/91/74
John, yeo., Hartest, 1592. R2/42/193; W1/49/17
John, Rickinghall Inferior, 1694. A5/6/172, A4/37/72
Margaret, wid., Stoke by Clare, 1623. R2/52/565; W1/79/24
Nicholas, blacksmith, Lakenheath, 1620. R2/52/27; W1/76/24
Ralph, Stowmarket, 1592. A5/2/175
Richard, Long Melford, 1671. A5/5/121, A4/86/15
Robert, yeo., Hinderclay, 1616. R2/50/22; W1/73/22
Rose, wid., Nayland, 1577. R2/37/265
Thomas, singleman, Rushbrook, 1696. R2/73/13; W1/150/17
William, Barton Mills, 1603. R2/45/291; W1/61/96
William, yeo., Redgrave, 1638. R2/57/287; W1/93/60
see also Mores, Moreys, Morice, Moris, Morys, Robson als. Morrys
MORS, Nicholas, als. Mos, Bury St. Edmunds, 1478. R2/2/260
MORSCHE, Isabel, Creeting, 1444. R2/9/54
MORSE, Edmund, yeo., Hazlewood, 1574. W1/51/231
John, wid., Hopton, 1679. A5/6/21, A4/16/67
Joseph, Palgrave, 1648. A5/4/122
Katherine, Stoke by Nayland, 1594. A5/2/200
Lionel, yeo., Flempton, 1587. R2/40/190
Lionel, Worlington, 1661. A5/5/17, A4/1/92
Mary, wid., Mildenhall, 1678. R2/67/70; W1/130/54
Robert, husb., Stoke by Nayland, 1552. R2/31/90; W1/13/64
MORSLIE, James, Eye, 1585. A5/2/77
MORSTLEY, Richard, weaver, Eye, 1612. R2/48/212; W1/69/108
MORTEMERE, John, Haverhill, 1454. R2/9/205
MORTIMER, John, linen weaver, Burgate, 1675. In. 3/16/78; A5/5/156, A4/12/38
John, Cotton, 1661. In. 3/6/214; A5/5/22, A4/1/42
see also Morttemere
MORTLACK(E), John, Haverhill, (1556). R2/24/263, R2/25/139
Lucy, wid., Little Barton, 1679. R2/67/386; W1/133/138
Michael, Gazeley, 1696. A5/6/187, A4/39/34
MORTLAKE, John, yeo., Newmarket, 1558. R2/27/3; W1/31/32
Richard, Haverhill, 1560. R2/29/72; W1/25/95
Robert, Worlington, 1575. R2/37/106; W1/34/46
Robert, blacksmith, Worlington, 1650. R2/61/386; W1/107/90; In. 3/3/103
Thomas, yeo., Haverhill, 1622. R2/52/387; W1/78/23
MORTLOCK(E), Ann, wid., Mildenhall, 1672. A5/5/133, A4/9/70
Edmund, inn holder, Brandon, 1630. R2/55/149; W1/86/167
Henry, singleman, Haverhill, 1572. R2/36/79; W1/31/55
Henry, Wood Ditton, 1686. R2/70/500; W1/140/105; In. 3/25/8
James, yeo., Mildenhall, 1608. R2/46/163; W1/65/15
James, Mildenhall, 1635. A5/4/40
John, Freckenham, 1713. In. 10/44
John, Little Barton, 1673. A5/5/136, A4/10/14
John, Wicken, 1667. In. 3/12/61; A5/5/84, A4/5/53
John, yeo., Worlington, 1620. R2/52/88; W1/76/73
Lewis, Mildenhall, 1670. In. 3/15/170; A5/5/116
Martha, Wood Ditton, 1695. A5/6/180, A4/38/52
Robert, tailor, Wicken, 1639. R2/58/72; W1/94/123
Samuel, yeo., Denham, 1682, (N). R2/68/461; W1/136/140; In. 3/21/69

MORTLOCK(E) continued
Samuel, Newmarket, 1687. R2/70/276; W1/141/18
Susan, wid., Newmarket, 1688. In. 3/23/68; A5/6/120, A4/29/50
Thomas, singleman, Haverhill, 1572. R2/36/66; W1/31/75
William, butcher, Lakenheath, 1689. R2/71/273; W1/143/110
MORTON, Catherine, wid., Wickham Skeith, 1649. A5/4/130
George, singleman, Wood Ditton, 1635, (N). R2/56/473; W1/91/45
Harry, Great Finborough, 1523. R2/17/317
Henry, Boxted, 1674. A5/5/147, A4/11/26
John, yeo., Occold, 1686. R2/70/575; W1/140/158; In. 3/22/80
Susan, wife of Edward, Great Saxham, 1682. R2/68/261; W1/136/3
MORTTEMERE, Richard, labourer, Soham, 1559. R2/28/98; W1/22/95
MORTYMER, John, Burgate, 1608. A5/3/54
Robert, rough mason, Mildenhall, 1539. R2/19/294
Rose, wid. of Robert, Mildenhall, 1540. R2/21/373; W1/38/77
MORWELL, James, Mendlesham, 1589. R2/41/294; W1/46/19
John, Tuddenham, 1595. A5/2/214
Margaret, wid., Mendlesham, 1571. R2/35/95; W1/36/98
Robert, husb., Mendlesham, 1593. R2/42/462; W1/50/115
MORWHOLL, Richard, Mendlesham, 1560. R2/29/65; W1/25/106
see also Morewhyll, Morowhyll
MORYELL, Clarissa, wife of John, Barrow, 1451. R2/9/107
Ellen, wid., Icklingham, 1521. R2/15/35
Joan, Burwell, 1458. R2/9/207
John, Hinderclay, 1477. R2/11/107
Nicholas, barker, Bury St. Edmunds, 1445. R2/2/16
Nicholas, mercer, Stanton, 1460. R2/9/275
Steven, Market Weston, 1491. R2/11/409; W1/51/190
MORYS, James, Stoke by Nayland, 1575, (N). R2/37/86; W1/34/6
MORYSBY, Ralph, Bury St. Edmunds, 1511. R2/5/6
MOSBYE, William, miller, Drinkstone, 1618. R2/51/74; W1/75/43
MOSELEY, Humphrey, esq., Ousden, 1663. R2/63/80; W1/115/130; In. 3/8/163
MOSS(E), Agnes, Stoke by Nayland, 1578. R2/37/406; W1/36/167
Alice, wife of John, skinner, Bury St. Edmunds, 1436. R2/1/226
Anne, wid., Stanton, 1602. R2/45/141; W1/60/62
Anthony, Dalham, 1639. A5/4/73
Dorothy, wid., Hinderclay, 1696. A5/6/188, A4/39/57
Elisabeth, Dalham, 1639. A5/4/68
James, linen weaver, Hinderclay, 1691. R2/71/490; W1/145/49
Jeffery, husb., Fornham All Saints, 1571. R2/35/171; W1/38/164; A5/1/242
John, Bury St. Edmunds, 1435. R2/1/216
John, clerk, Bury St. Edmunds, 1442. R2/1/260
John, Bury St. Edmunds, 1520. R2/6/75 (admon. only)
John, baker, Bury St. Edmunds, 1573. R2/36/198; W1/32/122
John, Dalham, 1556. R2/25/90; W1/16/117
John, husb., Dalham, 1562. R2/31/103; W1/8/196
John, bricklayer, Hawstead, 1672. R2/65/369; W1/124/109
John, Hunston, 1557. R2/26/230; W1/20/116
John, school master, Mendlesham, 1645. R2/59/239; W1/102/63
John, Sapiston, 1602. R2/45/199; W1/60/127
John, yeo., Stoke by Nayland, 1577. R2/37/295
John, yeo., Stoke by Nayland, 1667. In. 3/12/168; A5/5/89, A4/5/79
John, Tuddenham, 1489. R2/11/389
John, Wyverstone, 1557. R2/26/160; W1/20/106
Judith, wid., Hinderclay, 1637. R2/57/224; W1/92/269
Katherine, spinster, Bury St. Edmunds, 1679. R2/67/435; W1/133/166
Margaret, wid., Bury St. Edmunds, 1548. R2/8/254
Margaret, wid., Tuddenham, 1585. R2/39/298; W1/42/282
Mary, Hinderclay, 1695. A5/6/179, A4/38/44
Richard, Hinderclay, 1673. A5/5/144, A4/10/106
Richard, yeo., Hinderclay, 1680. R2/67/548; W1/134/32; In. 3/20/34
Richard, husb., Hunston, 1620, (N). R2/52/109; W1/76/95
Robert, Dalham, 1638. A5/4/60
Robert, yeo., Hinderclay, 1661. R2/62/187; W1/113/44; In. 3/6/60
Robert, husb., Stanton, 1595. R2/43/113; W1/53/114
Robert, singleman, Stoke by Nayland, 1602. R2/45/181; W1/63/106
Thomas, Bury St. Edmunds, 1531. R2/7/3
Thomas, Cavendish, 1689. A5/6/129, A4/30/17
Thomas, yeo., Whepstead, 1578. R2/37/390, W1/36/182

MOSS(E) continued
Walter, Dalham, 1558. R2/27/321
William, Fordham, 1631. A5/4/12
William, tailor, Fordham, 1667. R2/64/200; W1/119/46; In. 3/12/52
William, Hengrave, 1522. R2/14/57
William, yeo., Hinderclay, 1694. R2/72/427; W1/148/162
see also Mors als. Mos
MOSTE, Agnes, Whepstead, 1587. R2/40/235; W1/44/79
MOTHAM, Isaac, the elder, gent., Drinkstone, 1660. R2/62/50; W1/112/63; In. 3/5/51a
John, Buxhall, 1664. In. 3/9/107; A5/5/60, A4/2/65
see also Jeffery als. Motham
MOTHERSALL, Simon, Euston, 1612. R2/48/184; W1/69/66
MOTHERSOLL, John, the elder, blacksmith, Ixworth, 1680. R2/67/756; W1/134/190; In. 3/20/210
John, Ixworth, 1692. In. 3/24/10; A5/6/147, A4/33/95
MOTLES, John, singleman, Botesdale, 1680. R2/67/741; W1/134/179; In. 3/20/190
MOTOWN, Robert, als. Man, Gipping, 1485. R2/11/332
MOTT, Anne, singlewoman, Bury St. Edmunds, 1516. R2/6/26
Elias, husb., Great Waldingfield, 1621. R2/52/295; W1/77/76
Elisabeth, wid., Polstead, 1588. R2/41/49; W1/45/43
James, Acton, 1673, (N). R2/65/419
James, Barton Mills, 1572. A5/1/251
John, the elder, Burwell, 1552, (N). R2/23/188; W1/12/17
John, maltster, Burwell, 1639. R2/58/6; W1/94/7
John, carpenter, Bury St. Edmunds, 1661. R2/62/233; W1/113/103; In. 3/6/167
John, the elder, clothier, Bury St. Edmunds, 1679. R2/67/344; W1/133/107
John, Cowlinge, 1672. A5/5/131, A4/9/40
John, yeo., Dalham, 1575. In. 3/1/89
John, the elder, yeo., Dalham, 1576. R2/37/163
John, husb., Dalham, 1614. R2/49/60; W1/71/48
John, the elder, Fordham, 1529. W1/311/14
John, Haverhill, 1542. R2/22/6; W1/6/88
John, Polstead, 1587. A5/2/98 & 103
John, Soham, 1571. R2/35/139; W1/36/78
Marian, Chippenham, 1541. R2/19/316
Nicholas, Fordham, 1503. R2/12/73
Richard, Burwell, 1574. R2/37/42; W1/33/39
Richard, Old Newton, 1665. In. 3/10/123; A5/5/68, A4/3/57
Robert, Bury St. Edmunds, 1492. R2/4/3
Robert, Dalham, 1588. A5/2/100
Robert, yeo., Polstead, 1551. R2/23/10; W1/11/41
Sarah, singlewoman, Waldingfield, 1688. A5/6/119, A4/29/35
Stephen, draper, Bury St. Edmunds, 1423. R2/1/164
Thomas, Boxford, 1632. A5/4/17
Thomas, miller, Boxford, 1679. R2/67/498; W1/133/214
Thomas, clerk, Bures, 1681. A5/6/49, A4/18/65
Thomas, carpenter, Bury St. Edmunds, 1699. R2/73/463; W1/153/99; In. 3/26/6
Thomas, Dalham, 1533. R2/19/157; W1/2/92
Thomas, Dalham, 1607. A5/3/20
Thomas, Fordham, 1573. A5/1/257 & 258
Thomas, husb., Soham, 1558. R2/27/436
Thomas, Wickhambrook, 1464. R2/10/397
William, Fordham, 1484. R2/11/346
MOULE, Thomas, the elder, yeo., Rattlesden, 1683. R2/69/160; W1/137/128
see also Mole
MOULTON, James, labourer, Wortham, 1630. R2/55/41; W1/86/50
John, weaver, Redgrave, 1623. R2/52/558; W1/79/16
John, shoe maker, Thorndon, 1599. R2/44/296; W1/57/94
John, cordwainer, Thorndon, 1698. R2/73/329; W1/152/98
MOUNDEFORD, Alice, wid., Knettishall, 1682. A5/6/64, A4/19/119
Francis, gent., Bury St. Edmunds, 1614. R2/49/1; W1/71/2
Francis, the elder, esq., Knettishall, 1676. R2/66/351; W1/128/59; In. 3/17/64
George, Bury St. Edmunds, 1608. A5/3/44
Martin, Wyverstone, 1635. R2/56/505; W1/91/82

MOUNDES, Adam, Stanton, 1572. R2/36/46; W1/31/100
George, husb., Stanton, 1578. R2/37/382; W1/36/194
Robert, Stanton, 1565. R2/32/260; W1/27/163
MOUNDFORD, Henry, husb., Edwardstone, 1602. R2/45/187; W1/60/113
MOUNFORD, Elisabeth, wid., Milden, 1598. R2/44/240; W1/57/55
John, yeo., Milden, 1594. R2/42/499; W1/52/84
Robert, singleman, Hitcham, 1572. R2/36/24; W1/31/107
MOUNSON, Thomas, Long Melford, 1565. A5/1/163
MOUNT, John, Bury St. Edmunds, 1700. A5/7/16, A4/41/128
Margaret, wid., Bury St. Edmunds, 1684. R2/69/349; W1/138/43
Samuel, weaver, Bury St. Edmunds, 1682. In. 3/21/154; A5/6/61, A4/19/69
Thomas, sen., cordwainer, Bury St. Edmunds, 1680. R2/67/608; W1/134/80; In. 3/20/95
MOUNTAGUE, John, Newmarket, 1694. A5/6/167, A4/37/17
MOUNTECUTE, James, Edwardstone, 1631. R2/56/16; W1/87/21
MOUNTFORD, Stephen, yeo., Edwardstone, 1616. R2/50/5; W1/73/8
William, blacksmith, Chippenham, 1629. R2/54/427; W1/85/109b
see also Moundeford, Moundford, Mundford
MOUR, Robert, Onehouse, 1520. R2/15/99
MOWE, Richard, Bradfield, 1454. R2/9/176
William, Chelsworth, 1461. R2/9/297
MOWEARF, William, Alpheton, 1567. A5/1/182
MOWER, Joan, wid., Shimpling, 1579. R2/38/26; W1/39/53
John, thatcher, Bury St. Edmunds, 1528. R2/6/150
Peter, Shimpling, 1546. R2/21/247
Robert, Stoke by Clare, 1540. R2/20/288; W1/4/217
Thomas, Shimpling, 1503. R2/12/53
Thomas, Stanstead, 1532. R2/19/115; W1/3/110
see also Wright als. Mower
MOWRELL, Robert, yeo., Weston, 1570. R2/35/23; W1/38/137
MOWS, Alice, wid., Chelsworth, 1517. R2/12/98 & 99
Thomas, Mendlesham, 1558. R2/27/330
MOWTON, John, shoe maker, Thorndon, 1672. R2/65/316; W1/124/38
see also Motown
MOY(E), Daniel, Wetheringsett, 1679. A5/6/18, A4/16/41
John, Brockford, 1697. A5/7/1, A4/40/1
MOYES, Rebecca, wid., Great Finborough, 1666. R2/64/18; W1/118/18; In. 3/11/26
MOYSE, James, Finningham, 1662. In. 3/7/190; A5/5/37
John, Hopton, 1464. R2/10/365
John, yeo., Stowmarket, 1582. R2/38/395; W1/41/42b
Richard, Wetheringsett, 1609. A5/3/78
Thomas, yeo., Wetheringsett, 1676. R2/66/357; W1/128/66; In. 3/17/73
MOYSES, Richard, Haverhill, 1606. A5/3/7
MUDD, John, the elder, yeo., Chevington, 1648. R2/60/106; W1/105/128
John, yeo., Chevington, 1666. R2/64/91; W1/118/65; In. 3/11/84
Robert, Whatfield, 1553. R2/31/201; W1/13/63
Stephen, Great Barton, 1663. In. 3/8/217; A5/5/51
Stephen, Whatfield, 1561. R2/30/76
see also Trew als. Mudd
MULEE, Joseph, husb., West Stow, 1684. R2/69/360; W1/138/149; A5/6/76, A4/21/24
MULLEN, William, als. Onell, wheelwright, Soham, 1619. R2/51/474; W1/132/135
MULLENDER, John, husb., Mendlesham, 1694. R2/72/407; W1/148/141
MULLENER, Bridget, wid., Finningham, 1675. In. 3/16/63; A5/5/155, A4/12/28
John, tailor, Wickham Skeith, 1694. R2/72/288; W1/148/13
MULLENGER, Francis, sawyer, Stowupland, 1679. R2/67/494; W1/133/210
MULLEY, Caleb, Stowlangtoft, 1688. A5/6/120, A4/29/46
John, yeo., Culford, 1644. R2/59/167; W1/101/95
John, Mildenhall, 1573. R2/36/164; W1/32/70
Margaret, Bury St. Edmunds, 1618. W1/111/18
Robert, Pakenham, 1688. A5/6/121, A4/29/60
Robert, Stowlangtoft, 1688. A5/6/119, A4/29/36
see also Mulee, Mully
MULLIGAN, James, chapman, Bury St. Edmunds, 1699. R2/73/367; W1/153/26
MULLINER, Robert, Wetheringsett, 1698. A5/7/9
William, yeo., Thwaite, 1664. R2/63/237; W1/116/158; In. 3/9/245

MULLINER continued
  William, yeo., Wetheringsett, 1698. R2/73/233; W1/152/14
  see also Moliner, Mullener, Mullyner
MULLINS, Sarah, wid., Acton, 1689. R2/71/183; W1/143/40
MULLIS, James, inn holder, Acton, 1682. R2/68/363; W1/136/73; In. 3/21/48
  see also Mullys
MULLY, John, cloth weaver, Bury St. Edmunds, 1699. R2/73/471; W1/153/108
  John, miller, Sudbury, 1639. R2/58/14; W1/94/26
  Richard, yeo., Stanton, 1696. R2/73/104; W1/150/120
  Richard, yeo., Stowlangtoft, 1621. R2/52/262; W1/77/47
  Timothy, Culford, 1668. A5/5/97, A4/6/83
  William, yeo., Stowlangtoft, 1694. R2/72/351; W1/148/76
MULLYNER, Francis, cooper, Finningham, 1603. R2/45/287; W1/61/92
  Margaret, wid., Stowupland, 1630. R2/55/58; W1/86/68
MULLYS, John, Little Cornard, 1593. A5/2/186
MULTON, John, Little Thurlow, 1457. R2/9/220
  Katherine, Barnham, 1484. R2/11/310
MUMFORD, Edward, Assington, 1649. A5/4/132
  George, singleman, Groton, 1696. A5/6/185, A4/39/16
  George, Layham, 1697. A5/7/2, A4/40/38
  William, yeo., Stoke by Nayland, 1626. R2/53/600; W1/82/128
MUMFORTE, William, Polstead, 1465. R2/10/387
MUNDEFORD, John, yeo., Bury St. Edmunds, 1557. R2/8/298; W1/18/27
  John, Rishangles, 1451. R2/9/137
  Unity, Haughley, 1673. R2/65/486; W1/125/126
MUNDFORD, John, husb., Assington, 1605. R2/45/380; W1/63/5
  see also Mountford, Mumford, Munford
MUNDS, Agnes, wid., Stanton, 1661, (N). R2/62/181; W1/113/36; In. 3/6/50
  Elisabeth, wid., Bardwell, 1672. A5/5/128, A4/9/2
  George, husb., Great Fakenham, 1638. R2/57/427; W1/93/263
  John, husb., Bardwell, 1641. R2/58/311; W1/98/114
MUNDSON, Joan, Kirtling, 1472. R2/10/458
MUNDYE, Robert, Barney, (1594). W1/51/109
MUNES, John, Stanton, 1634. A5/4/33
  William, singleman, Burwell, 1694. R2/72/436; W1/148/168
MUNFORD, Henry, yeo., Milden, 1576. R2/37/214; W1/37/75; In. 3/1/21
  John, Chippenham, 1545. A5/1/62
  Martha, spinster, Edwardstone, 1625. R2/53/292; W1/81/81
  Robert, husb., Groton, 1694. R2/72/425; W1/148/160
  Simon, Hunston, 1533. R2/19/179; W1/2/27
MUNFURTHE, Robert, husb., Edwardstone, 1586. R2/40/8; W1/43/7
  see also Mundford
MUNING(S), Gregory, husb., Stoke by Nayland, 1611. R2/48/12; W1/68/30
  John, yeo., Mendlesham, 1605. R2/45/419; W1/63/66
  John, yeo., Mendlesham, 1652. R2/61/539; W1/109/21; In. 3/4/23
  John, yeo., Mendlesham, 1674. R2/66/41; W1/126/81
  William, tanner, Badwell Ash, 1637. R2/57/228; W1/92/277
MUNNES, Richard, labourer, Bures, 1634. R2/56/375; W1/90/151
MUNNING(S), Ann, wid. of John, yeo., Mendlesham, 1683. R2/69/55; W1/137/41; A5/6/67, A4/20/25
  Elisabeth, wife of Humphrey, clerk, Brettenham, 1631. R2/56/68; W1/87/100
  George, yeo., Cotton, 1639. R2/58/104; W1/94/171
  James, inn holder, Wetherden, 1668. In. 3/13/18; A5/5/93, A4/6/35
  John, gent., Badwell Ash, 1678. R2/67/56; W1/130/45; In. 3/19/62
  John, glover, Bury St. Edmunds, 1682. R2/68/274; W1/136/11
  John, yeo., Gipping, 1625. W1/81/185
  John, husb., Great Finborough, 1644. R2/59/83; W1/101/11
  John, yeo., Mendlesham, 1667. R2/64/240; W1/119/101; In. 3/12/98
  William, the elder, husb., Badwell Ash, 1603. R2/45/257; W1/61/60
  William, gent., Chevington, 1662. In. 3/7/175; A5/5/36
  William, clerk, Chedburgh, 1669. R2/64/578; W1/121/166; In. 3/14/160; A5/5/107, A4/7/58
  William, the elder, yeo., Semer, 1687. R2/70/307; W1/141/51
MUNNYNG(S), John, yeo., Badwell Ash, 1609. R2/47/46; W1/66/53
  John, yeo., Bury St. Edmunds, 1499. R2/4/88
  John, Norton, 1486. R2/11/356
  Nicholas, Tostock, 1476. R2/11/73

MUNNYNG(S) continued
Richard, Badwell, 1454. R2/9/175
Thomas, Bury St. Edmunds, 1539. R2/7/58
Thomas, Rattlesden, 1579. A5/2/14
see also Moninge(s), Monninge(s), Monynge, Muning(s), Munyng
MUNS, Adam, yeo., Stanton, 1632. R2/56/152; W1/89/52
Ann, als. Barnard, Stanton, 1638. A5/4/64
George, Sapiston, 1682. In. 3/21/150; A5/6/60, A4/19/57
John, maltster, Bardwell, 1692. In. 3/24/21; A5/6/148, A4/115/12
John, butcher, Burwell, 1677. In. 3/18/119; A5/5/172, A4/14/54
Matthew, Stanton, 1630, (N). W1/95/144
Thomas, Burwell, 1673. A5/5/142, A4/10/82
see also Munds, Munes, Munnes
MUNSON, Andrew, Long Melford, 1619. R2/51/369; W1/132/68
John, tailor, Lakenheath, 1601, (N). R2/44/355; W1/59/18
John, yeo., Wangford, 1678. R2/67/91; W1/130/73; A4/17/29
Marion, wid. of Robert, Lakenheath, 1601. R2/44/356; W1/59/21
Sarah, wid., Barningham, 1681. R2/68/239; W1/135/180
see also Monson
MUNTIQUE, Thomas, husb., Polstead, 1670. R2/65/75; W1/122/91
MUNYNG, Harry, husb., Brettenham, 1569. R2/33/119; W1/28/183
Thomas, Hunston, 1594. A5/2/199
Thomas, gent., Nedging, 1557. R2/26/45; W1/20/31
William, Norton, 1529. R2/18/34
William, Norton, 1549. R2/21/522; W1/8/3
MURDEN, Robert, yeo., Soham, 1591. R2/42/44; W1/48/36
MURDON, Agnes, wid. of John, Exning, 1567. R2/32/373
Elisabeth, wid. of Thomas, Exning, 1569. A5/1/210
MURDUN, John, yeo., Exning, 1558. R2/27/580
John, Newmarket, 1576. In. 3/1/35
MUREOCKE, John, Bury St. Edmunds, 1570. W1/10/218
MURIELL, Elisabeth, wid., Bardwell, 1637. A5/4/49
Helena, Thelnetham, 1578. A5/2/13
John, Barrow, 1451. R2/9/105
John, Hepworth, 1561. A5/1/106
Judith, wife of Francis, Bardwell, 1649. A5/4/133
Thomas, Walsham le Willows, 1641. A5/4/87
William, the elder, yeo., Oakley, 1672. R2/65/329; W1/124/55
MURRELL, George, husb., Weston, 1589. R2/41/245; W1/46/6
Jeffery, husb., Brandon, 1626. R2/53/580; W1/82/113
John, yeo., Wattisfield, 1649. R2/60/263; W1/106/125
John, husb., Wetheringsett, 1632. R2/56/203; W1/89/119
Joseph, basket maker, Oakley, 1661. In. 3/7/24; A5/5/22, A4/1/40
Margaret, als. Deye, wife of John, Sapiston, 1578. R2/37/407; W1/36/164
Richard, clothier, Glemsford, 1594. R2/42/501; W1/52/81
Thomasine, wid., Wetheringsett, 1634. R2/56/415; W1/90/199
William, yeo., Brockford, 1604. R2/45/317; W1/62/16
see also Moriell, Moryell, Mowrell, Muriell, Murriell, Muryell, Jordan als. Murriell
MURRELLS, George, Cockfield, 1666. In. 3/11/141; A5/5/76, A4/4/47
Richard, yeo., Hartest, 1683. R2/69/139; W1/137/112
see also Merrell(s)
MURRIELL, Francis, yeo., Weston, 1609. R2/47/40; W1/66/46
John, yeo., Weston, 1609. R2/47/90; W1/66/105
Margaret, wid., Redgrave, 1622. R2/52/396; W1/78/30
MURRILL, John, yeo., Lawshall, 1680. In. 3/20/41
MURTON, Agnes, wid., Haughley, 1606, (N). R2/46/70; W1/64/75
Audrey, wid., Barton, 1624. R2/53/93; W1/80/105
Catherine, wid., Ixworth, 1568. R2/33/157
Edmund, Buxhall, 1641. A5/4/87
Edmund, Haughley, 1546. W1/10/116
Edmund, Ixworth, 1558. R2/27/572
Edmund, husb., Ixworth, 1604. R2/45/320; W1/62/19
Elisabeth, wid., Occold, 1690. R2/71/344; W1/144/48
Joan, wid., Great Finborough, 1541. R2/21/575
John, yeo., Buxhall, 1617. R2/50/359; W1/74/143
John, Ixworth, 1533. R2/19/171
John, blacksmith, Walsham le Willows, 1648. R2/60/54; W1/105/71
Reginald, thatcher, Stanton, 1651. R2/61/486; W1/108/78
Robert, husb., Buxhall, 1578. R2/37/394; W1/36/180
Robert, Buxhall, 1605. R2/45/430; W1/63/74

MURTON continued
Thomas, Stanton, 1670. A5/5/116
William, Bildeston, 1594, A5/2/198
William, carpenter, 1616. R2/50/68; W1/73/79
see also Murton, Myrton
MURWYN, Thomas, card maker, Bury St. Edmunds, 1539. R2/7/54
MURYELL, Anne, wid., Stanton, 1614. R2/49/75; W1/71/58
Elisabeth, wid., Weston, 1539. R2/19/330
Isabel, wid., Walsham le Willows, 1497. R2/13/60
John, Hopton, 1446. R2/9/73
John, yeo., Hopton, 1645. R2/59/257; W1/102/75
John, Market Weston, 1560. R2/29/62; W1/25/111
Margery, wid., Hawstead, 1451. R2/9/136
Robert, Rattlesden, 1647. R2/59/500; W1/104/142; In. 3/2/164
Simon, singleman, Bardwell, (1519). R2/14/4
William, Hepworth, 1550. R2/21/169; W1/9/114
MUSCHAT, John, Drinkstone, 1458. R2/9/217
MUSGRAVE, John, Bury St. Edmunds, 1679. A5/6/16, A4/16/15
Robert, Lakenham, 1538, (N). W1/51/84
MUSK, Edmund, blacksmith, Honington, 1679. R2/67/289; W1/133/74
John, the elder, Wattisfield, 1669. In. 3/14/92; A5/5/108, A4/7/50
Nicholas, Honington, 1700. In. 3/27/56; A5/7/14, A4/41/89
MUSKET(T), Alice, wid., Coney Weston, 1697. R2/73/125; W1/151/14
Alice, Haughley, 1608. A5/3/44
Edward, yeo., Harleston, 1631. R2/56/31; W1/87/44
Elisabeth, wid., Drinkstone, 1578. R2/37/331; W1/36/244
George, Coney Weston, 1636. A5/4/42
Henry, Buxhall, 1539. R2/19/288
Henry, Haughley, 1468. R2/10/407
Henry, Haughley, 1590. A5/2/131
Henry, yeo., Haughley, 1638. R2/57/248; W1/93/9
Henry, yeo., Haughley, 1684. R2/69/283; W1/138/80
Henry, Stowmarket, 1635. A5/4/37
James, Brandon, 1610. A5/3/93
Joan, wid., Elmswell, 1647. R2/59/453; W1/104/85
John, husb., Harleston, 1558. R2/27/225
John, labourer, Harleston, 1660. R2/62/116; W1/112/155
John, Walsham le Willows, 1632. A5/4/19
Richard, gent., Bury St. Edmunds, 1628. R2/54/178; W1/84/54
Richard, Gipping, 1632. A5/4/22
Richard, yeo., Harleston, 1606. R2/46/57; W1/64/81
Richard, yeo., Haughley, 1616. R2/50/139; W1/73/144
Richard, Rattlesden, 1559. R2/28/265; W1/22/221
Robert, Haughley, 1646. A5/4/115
Thomas, Drinkstone, 1486. R2/11/375
William, yeo., Buxhall, 1629. R2/54/308; W1/85/24
William, yeo., Coney Weston, 1686. R2/70/429; W1/140/50; In. 3/22/88
William, husb., Drinkstone, 1568. R2/33/82; W1/29/1
William, the elder, husb., Drinkstone, 1603. R2/45/279; W1/61/83
William, yeo., Drinkstone, 1613. R2/48/256; W1/70/29
William, yeo., Elmswell, 1611. R2/48/30; W1/68/52
William, the elder, Haughley, 1544. R2/19/404 & 443; W1/6/97
William, yeo., Haughley, 1595. R2/43/60; W1/53/48
William, Sudbury, 1451. R2/9/134
Winifred, wid., Haughley, 1675. In. 3/16/151; A5/5/158; A4/12/69 & 70a
see also Muschat, Daynes als. Muskett
MUST, Edmund, labourer, Great Livermere, 1593. R2/42/405; W1/50/67
James, Sudbury, 1678. R2/67/17; W1/130/16; In. 3/19/21
John, Sudbury, 1526. R2/12/139, R2/17/170; W1/23/62
Thomas, say maker, Sudbury, 1671. R2/65/235; W1/123/114; A5/5/125, A4/8/54
MYCHELL, Joan, wife of Robert, Bury St. Edmunds, 1558. R2/8/337; W1/17/83
Joan, wid., Haverhill, 1523. R2/17/28; W1/21/58
John, Layham, 1533. R2/19/163; W1/2/89
Thomas, Exning, (1514). R2/13/217
William, Soham, 1567. R2/32/397; W1/3/35
MYCHILL, John, als. Barker, 1457. R2/9/187
MYDDELDECHE, Agnes, wid., Wood Ditton, 1573. R2/36/134; W1/32/18
MYDDELDYCHE, John, Cheveley, 1568. R2/33/40; W1/29/50

MYDDELTONE, William, coverlet weaver, Bury St. Edmunds, 1430. R2/1/195
MYELES, Andrew, tanner, Bildeston, 1576. R2/37/188; W1/37/55; In. 3/1/45
MYGHELL, Edmund, Barton Mills, 1572. R2/36/14; W1/31/122
MYHELL, John, Long Melford, 1609. A5/3/62
Margaret, wid., Mildenhall, 1592. R2/42/228; W1/49/47b
Richard, labourer, Lakenheath, 1584. R2/39/194; W1/42/132
Thomas, grocer, Norwich, 1594. W1/51/263
MYHILL, John, Mildenhall, 1648. A5/4/122
Thomas, Mildenhall, 1620. R2/52/131; W1/76/115
Thomas, Mildenhall, 1626. R2/53/446; W1/82/3
see also Mihill
MYLDE, Thomas, Clare, 1464. R2/10/354
MYLDENHALE, John, Bury St. Edmunds, 1361. R2/1/15
John, carver, Bury St. Edmunds, 1422. R2/1/160
John, Bury St. Edmunds, 1427. R2/1/176
MYLES, Ann, wid. of John, Sudbury, 1601. R2/45/363
Elisabeth, wid., Kedington, 1604. R2/45/371; W1/62/99
George, yeo., Bury St. Edmunds, 1588. R2/41/36; W1/45/29
Henry, Hengrave, 1590, (N). R2/41/356; W1/47/52; A5/2/135
Jermyn, Redgrave, 1558. R2/27/481
Joan, Redgrave, 1558. R2/27/480
John, carpenter, Brandon, 1557. R2/26/151; W1/20/102
John, Norwich, 1573, (N). W1/51/217
Joseph, miller, Bury St. Edmunds, 1662. R2/62/348; W1/114/67; In. 3/7/108
Nicholas, the elder, husb., Barnardiston, 1606. R2/46/64; W1/64/89
Richard, tailor, Soham, 1582. R2/38/426; W1/41/5
Robert, bladesmith, Redgrave, 1584. R2/39/189; W1/42/138
Robert, Thurston, 1559. R2/28/406; W1/3/67
see also Miles
MYLKESOP, John, husb., Great Cornard, 1552. R2/31/89; W1/13/60
MYLLER, Adam, Tostock, 1440. R1/24/175
Andrew, Bury St. Edmunds, 1527. R2/6/143
Edmund, Great Thurlow, 1535.
John, husb., Barnardiston, 1556. R2/25/39; W1/16/43
John, als. Wryght, clothier, Clare, 1540. R2/20/192; W1/4/155
John, wheelwright, Great Wratting, 1571. R2/35/96; W1/36/113
John, sen., Lakenheath, 1453. R2/9/161
John, Lakenheath, 1553. R2/31/13; W1/13/7
John, Walsham le Willows, 1577. R2/37/275
John, Wattisfield, (1477). R2/11/433
Margaret, Bury St. Edmunds, 1522. R2/6/101
Margaret, Withersfield, 1505. R2/13/161
Richard, als. Wright, Clare, 1544. R2/19/490
Robert, Flempton, 1546. R2/21/631; W1/28/129
Robert, husb., Hundon, 1565. R2/32/247
Robert, Norton, 1471. R2/10/466 & 491
Robert, husb., Stanstead, 1541. R2/21/573; W1/3/38
Roger, lime burner, Bury St. Edmunds, 1618. R2/51/17; W1/75/9
Roger, Stanstead, 1556. R2/25/41; W1/16/46
Susan, als. Barnard, wid., Stowmarket, 1637. W1/110/26
Thomas, als. Barnard, Great Bradley, 1567. R2/32/426; W1/19/80
Thomas, yeo., Great Wratting, 1556. R2/25/103; W1/16/99
Thomas, Mildenhall, 1458. R2/9/262
Thomas, Stanstead, 1557. R2/26/80; W1/20/47
William, yeo., Stanstead, 1614. R2/49/95; W1/71/72
MYLLERSON, Alice, wid., Sudbury, 1543. R2/19/367; W1/6/114
MYLLES, Ann, Sudbury, 1604. W1/62/90
George, Cockfield, 1609. A5/3/57
George, yeo., Cockfield, 1614. R2/49/43; W1/71/37
John, yeo., Wissington, 1577. R2/37/257
Thomas, tailor, Cavendish, 1579. R2/38/35; W1/39/33; A5/2/15
William, Stoke by Nayland, 1563. A5/1/142
MYLLYON, Nicholas, the elder, Haverhill, (1535). R2/18/130
MYLNE, Thomas, chaplain, Belchamp, 1370. R2/1/21
MYLNER, Margery, wid., Great Thurlow, 1557. R2/26/253; W1/20/167
William, Barrow, (1506). R2/13/176b
MYLON, John, Clare, 1473. R2/10/539
MYLSEHOPP, John, Stoke by Clare, 1494. R2/13/29
MYLYS, John, als. Plomer, 1483. R2/11/316
Robert, Stowmarket, 1500. R2/13/112

MYLYS continued
Thomas, Bury St. Edmunds, 1569. W1/10/213
Thomas, Little Waldingfield, (1521). R2/14/31
William, Bromeswell, 1529. R2/6/157
MYN(E)S, Agnes, Onehouse, 1601. R2/44/470; W1/59/80
John, Bury St. Edmunds, 1587. A5/2/98
MYNETT, Edward, 1626. R2/53/670; W1/82/194
Thomas, Wood Ditton, 1638. A5/4/61
MYNIT, Robert, husb., Ashley, 1631. R2/56/31; W1/87/43
MYNN(E)S, Henry, Onehouse, 1631. A5/4/15
Isabel, Harleston, 1578. A5/2/7
John, yeo., Chelsworth, 1685. R2/70/213; W1/139/181; In. 3/22/6
John, collar maker, Thrandeston, 1675. R2/66/176; W1/127/112; In. 3/16/64
William, Bardwell, 1562. R2/31/74; W1/8/190
MYNNYS, Richard, Harleston, 1559. R2/28/366; W1/3/105
Robert, Great Ashfield, 1469. R2/10/440
MYNOTT, John, gent., Stanton, 1679. A5/6/15, A4/16/1
William, the elder, Fordham, 1681. A5/6/44, A4/18/10
William, Knettishall, 1610. A5/3/95
MYNSTERCHAMBYR, William, gent., Shelland, 1563. R2/32/12; W1/26/73
MYNTER, Thomas, Wetheringsett, 1615, (N). R2/49/287; W1/72/67
MYNTON, Joan, Stowmarket, 1474. R2/10/522
John, glover, Bury St. Edmunds, 1456. R2/2/55
John, Mendlesham, 1446. R2/9/90
MYOT, John, Burwell, 1444. R2/9/45
MYRELLS, Nicholas, clothmaker, Sudbury, 1522. R2/14/120
MYRRELL, Alice, Thelnetham, 1558. R2/27/536
Thomas, butcher, Weston, 1570. R2/34/14; W1/30/13
MYRRELLS, Roger, baker, Stradishall, 1592. R2/42/193; W1/49/20
William, weaver, Stanstead, 1585. R2/39/253; W1/42/320
MYRRELTES, William, yeo., Nayland, 1554. R2/24/135
MYRTON, John, labourer, Stanton, 1599. R2/44/215; W1/57/37
Thomas, Haughley, 1533. R2/18/216, R2/19/173; W1/2/59
MYRTOON, John, Drinkstone, 1503. R2/13/135
MYSSINGE, Robert, Sudbury, 1563. A5/1/148
William, Sudbury, 1568. A5/1/202
MYTSON, Robert, Poslingford, 1611. R2/47/307; W1/68/3
William, husb., Walcott, 1594. W1/51/99

N

NABLE, Harry, eelmonger, Bury St. Edmunds, 1506. R2/4/183
see also Massy als. Nabyll
NALL, Edward, carpenter, Mildenhall, 1670. R2/65/96; W1/122/116; In. 3/15/143
NANSON, Christian, wid. of Thomas, Clare, 1551. R2/23/45; W1/11/42
Thomas, Clare, 1551, (N). R2/23/53; W1/11/43
NASEY, James, Mendlesham, 1673. A5/5/139, A4/10/48
Thomasine, wid., Mendlesham, 1685. A5/6/97, A4/24/131
NASH, Ann, wife of Henry, Mendlesham, 1665. In. 3/10/78
Dorothy, wid., Stoke by Clare, 1618. R2/51/48; W1/75/26
see also Barker als. Nash
NAYLER, Thomas, Whelnetham, 1587. A5/2/95
see also Philipp als. Nayler
NEALE, Alice, wid., Great Cornard, 1628. R2/54/228; W1/84/91
Edmund, Norton, 1635. A5/4/41
Henry, fishmonger, Bury St. Edmunds, 1601. R2/44/432; W1/59/105
Henry, Bury St. Edmunds, 1635. A5/4/41
Margaret, wife of Thomas, Eye, 1576. R2/37/226; W1/37/83; In. 3/1/13
Margaret, Thurston, 1566. A5/1/180
Richard, fishmonger, Bury St. Edmunds, 1604. R2/43/314; W1/62/13
Richard, Ixworth, 1573. A5/1/261
Robert, gent., Burgate, 1663. In. 3/8/103; A5/5/47
Robert, yeo., Wattisham, 1634, (N). R2/56/384; W1/90/163; A5/4/25
Susan, singlewoman, Cavendish, 1651. A5/4/138
Thomas, Boxford, 1561. A5/1/106
Thomas, Eye, 1641. A5/4/87
Thomas, Langham, 1644. A5/4/103
Thomas, say maker, Lavenham, 1671. R2/66/147; W1/123/4
William, the younger, Barnham, 1638, (N). R2/58/307; W1/93/80

NEALE continued
William, Barnham, 1640. R2/58/176; W1/96/94
William, Langham, 1610. A5/3/97
William, Lawshall, 1638. A5/4/64
see also Neele, Nele
NEATHERCOAT(E), John, yeo., Soham, (1676). W1/312/20
John, husb., Soham, 1693. R2/72/248; W1/147/138
Richard, Kennett, 1692. A5/6/146, A4/33/89
NEAVE, Ann, wid., Wattisham, 1679. A5/6/29, A4/16/146
Edmund, Lavenham, 1584. A5/2/61
Edmund, Long Melford, 1671. R2/66/201
Edward, the elder, clothier, Cavendish, 1616. R2/51/33; W1/73/32
Edward, Sudbury, 1700. A5/7/16, A4/40/133
George, Bradfield St. George, 1624. R2/54/184; W1/80/156
Helen, wid., Downham, 1630. R2/56/36; W1/86/40
Jeremy, yeo., Wattisham, 1647. R2/59/390; W1/104/16; In. 3/2/14
Thomas, yeo., Chelsworth, 1670. In. 3/15/3; A5/5/112
Walter, yeo., Woolpit, 1583. R2/39/24; W1/42/77
William, Wattisham, 1616. R2/50/194; W1/74/183
see also Neve, Neyve, Catour als. Neve
NECHE, Margaret, wid., Cowlinge, 1570. R2/34/21; W1/30/20
Thomas, clerk, Fornham, 1549. R2/21/5
NEDDINGE, James, Lavenham, 1580. A5/2/29
NEEDHAM, Elisabeth, Bacton, 1695. A5/6/179, A4/38/45
NEELE, John, Botesdale, 1504. R2/12/36
John, the elder, husb., Pakenham, 1554. R2/24/31; W1/14/28
Robert, labourer, Walsham le Willows, 1622. R2/52/393; W1/78/28
NEELL, Agnes, Fordham, 1484. R2/11/358
Alice, wid., Pakenham, 1554. R2/24/32; W1/14/29
Dionysius, Landwade, 1451. R2/9/133
John, Boxford, 1474. R2/11/25
Robert, yeo., Wattisfield, 1634. R2/57/357; W1/90/127
Roger, Long Melford, 1450. R2/9/117
Thomas, Fordham, 1476. R2/11/98
William, Fordham, 1471. R2/10/504
NEGUS, Alice, singlewoman, Poslingford, 1602. R2/45/102; W1/60/13
Henry, yeo., Lakenheath, 1680. In. 3/20/138; A5/6/37, A4/3/70
John, yeo., Lakenheath, 1686. R2/71/467; W1/140/78
John, clothier, Lavenham, 1686. R2/71/472; W1/140/83; In. 3/22/20
John, linen weaver, Thelnetham, 1684. R2/70/270; W1/138/68
Joseph, linen weaver, Market Weston, 1689. R2/72/280; W1/143/115
Mary, wid., Bury St. Edmunds, 1686. R2/71/415; W1/140/38; In. 3/22/76
Robert, Stanstead, 1616. R2/50/7; W1/73/9
Robert, linen weaver, Wattisfield, 1673. R2/65/408; W1/125/27
Thomas, the elder, clothier, Stanstead, 1631. R2/56/43; W1/87/61
William, yeo., Lakenheath, 1680. R2/67/528; W1/134/12
NEKETON, Richard, Bury St. Edmunds, 1401. R2/1/91
Robert, Stowmarket, 1481. R2/11/203
NELE, Alice, singlewoman, Norton, 1574. R2/37/29; W1/33/61
John, Langham, 1590. R2/41/342; W1/47/35
Peter, Buxhall, (1489). R2/11/383
Stephen, husb., Polstead, 1563. R2/32/11; W1/26/72
Thomas, the elder, Eye, 1568. R2/33/81
Thomas, Langham, (1543). R2/19/357; W1/6/139
NELL, Richard, Walsham le Willows, 1540. R2/21/360
NELSON, Ann, wid., Stowmarket, 1700. R2/74/129
George, minister, Edwardstone, 1650. R2/61/386; W1/107/89; In. 3/3/111
George, Horningsheath, 1692. A5/6/50, A4/34/31
George, Stanstead, 1667. In. 3/12/82; A5/5/85, A4/5/43
George, Stoke by Nayland, 1595, (N). R2/43/119; W1/53/122
John, the elder, butcher, Hartest, 1671. R2/65/153; W1/123/15
John, singleman, Hartest, 1675. R2/66/159; W1/127/33
NELYNGGE, John, als. Facon, Boxford, 1442. R2/9/49
NENGE, Alice, 1522. R2/14/75
NETHERCOAT(E), John, the elder, yeo., Soham, 1638. R2/57/322; W1/93/99
John, Soham, 1695. A5/6/182, A4/38/76
Richard, the elder, yeo., Soham, 1688. R2/71/68; W1/142/60; In. 3/23/31; A5/6/119, A4/29/38

NETHERCOAT(E) continued
Thomas, waterman, Burwell, 1682. R2/68/467; W1/136/145; In. 3/21/35
William, yeo., Soham, 1680. R2/67/700; W1/134/151; In. 3/20/170
NETHERCOTE, Andrew, labourer, Fordham, 1681. R2/68/11; W1/135/11
Joan, Soham, 1582. A5/2/41
John, the elder, husb., Soham, 1660. R2/62/67; W1/112/97; In. 3/5/81
John, sen., Soham, 1677. A5/5/167, A4/14/9
Margaret, wid., Soham, 1597. R2/43/365; W1/55/128
Thomas, the elder, thatcher, Soham, 1630. R2/55/94; W1/86/104
Thomas, yeo., Soham, 1661. R2/62/278; W1/113/185; In. 3/6/261
Thomas, the younger, yeo., Soham, 1663. R2/63/118; W1/115/183; In. 3/8/229
Winifred, Soham, 1676. A5/5/165, A4/91/86a
see also Neathercoat(e), Neythercote
NETHERSTREETE, Rebecca, wid., Clare, 1685. A5/6/89, A4/24/29
William, sen., yeo., Clare, 1638. R2/57/345; W1/93/132
William, Clare, 1668, (N). R2/64/389; W1/120/110; In. 3/13/167
NETHERSTRETT, Samuel, clothier, Clare, 1683. R2/69/26; W1/137/21; In. 3/21/18
NEUCE, Robert, gent., Dalham, 1633. A5/4/27
NEUSON, Anne, wid., Thorndon, 1618. R2/51/99; W1/75/62
NEVE, Joan, wid., Elveden, 1598. R2/44/118; W1/56/120
John, Bury St. Edmunds, 1377. R2/1/36
John, shepherd, Downham, 1652. R2/61/548; W1/109/29; In. 3/4/28
Thomas, Great Finborough, 1465. R2/10/394
Thomas, als. Boldinge, Icklingham All Saints, 1532. R2/19/111; W1/3/114 & 133
Thomas, Stansfield, 1480. R2/11/244
NEVELL, Anne, als. Smythe, Haughley, 1559, (N). R2/28/10; W1/22/12
NEVILL, Edward, Long Melford, 1671. A5/5/123, A4/8/30
Mary, wid., Sudbury, 1669. In. 3/14/149; A5/5/108, A4/7/48
NEWALL, Adam, Great Horningsheath, 1519. W1/26/122
NEWBERY, Abraham, Chedburgh, 1691. R2/71/495; W1/145/55
Ann, wid., Chedburgh, 1699. R2/73/439; W1/153/77; In. 3/26/35
NEWBOLT, John, clerk, Aldham, 1694. A5/6/167, A4/37/8
NEWCOME, Catherine, wid., Bardwell, 1638. A5/4/62
NEWDIGATE, Grizel, als. Hide, wid. of Sir Robert, Bury St. Edmunds, 1664. R2/63/178; W1/116/77
NEWEGATE, Robert, the elder, husb., Great Horningsheath, 1608. R2/46/215; W1/65/113
NEWELL, Robert, Hinderclay, 1694. In. 3/25/43; A5/6/175, A4/37/105
Samuel, Bury St. Edmunds, 1683. A5/6/68, A4/20/27
see also Newall, Newhall
NEWELOND, John, Bildeston, 1457. R2/9/221
NEWES, Arthur, Groton, 1593. A5/2/179
NEWGATE, John, maltster, Bury St. Edmunds, 1649. R2/60/250; W1/106/111
Philip, yeo., Great Horningsheath, 1636. R2/57/53; W1/92/62
William, Ickworth, 1530. R2/19/21
see also Newdigate
NEWHALL, Thomas, Little Horningsheath, 1476. R2/11/134
NEWHAM, Richard, Brockley, 1605. R2/45/398; W1/63/31
NEWHAWE, Adam, burgess, Bury St. Edmunds, 1496. R2/4/49
John, Horningsheath, 1464. R2/10/332
Margaret, wid., Bury St. Edmunds, 1519. R2/6/71
NEWMAN, Alice, wid., Woolpit, 1641. R2/58/309; W1/98/108
NEWMAN, Ann, singlewoman, Bury St. Edmunds, 1694. A5/6/173 & 174, A4/37/79 & 110
Bartholomew, yeo., Haughley, 1611. R2/48/21; W1/68/39
Beatrice, wid., Bury St. Edmunds, 1450. R2/2/32
Eden, wid., Haverhill, 1563. R2/32/48; W1/26/68
Edmund, Haughley, 1546. R2/21/193 & 616; W1/28/146
Edmund, Long Melford, 1668. In. 3/13/152; A5/5/96, A4/6/73
Edward, als. Turner, Cavendish, 1688, (N). R2/71/414; W1/144/116; A5/6/123, A4/29/87
Isaac, Long Melford, 1681. A5/6/43, A4/18/2
Joan, wid., Woolpit, 1478. R2/11/150
John, yeo., Boxford, 1651. R2/61/436
John, yeo., Boxford, 1676. R2/66/347; W1/128/53
John, Debenham, 1545. R2/19/491, R2/21/640; W1/21/181
John, Gillingham, 1582. W1/51/156

NEWMAN continued
John, Haughley, 1680. In. 3/20/228; A5/6/42, A4/17/121
John, Haverhill, 1577, (N). R2/37/265
John, Ixworth, 1503. R2/12/58 & 67
John, sen., Lavenham, 1464. R2/10/335
John, gent., Little Cornard, 1688. R2/70/38; W1/142/37
John, carpenter, Long Melford, 1600. R2/45/23; W1/58/34
John, Mendlesham, 1682. In. 3/21/87; A5/6/64, A4/19/106
John, Old Newton, 1504. R2/12/29
John, Pakenham, 1698. A537/8
John, yeo., Stanton, 1678. R2/67/82; W1/130/66; In. 3/19/140; A5/6/5, A4/15/34
John, baker, Sudbury, 1454. R2/9/170
John, baker, Sudbury, 1697. R2/73/204; W1/151/89
John, Woolpit, 1471. R2/10/492
Jonas, Little Thurlow, 1630. A5/4/2
Judith, Sudbury, 1699. In. 3/26/54
Katherine, wid., Haverhill, 1547. R2/21/282
Leonard, comber, Mellis, 1690. R2/71/400; W1/144/103
Margaret, wid., Bury St. Edmunds, 1506. R2/4/176
Margaret, wid., Nayland, 1637. R2/57/185; W1/92/222
Martha, Mellis, 1661. In. 3/6/152; A5/5/18, A4/1/83a & b
Martha, wid., Sudbury, 1616. R2/50/104; W1/73/112
Mary, singlewoman, Bury St. Edmunds, 1506. R2/4/187
Nicholas, Drinkstone, 1529. W1/311/2
Ralph, gent., Sapiston, 1677. R2/66/525; W1/129/107; In. 3/18/139
Rebecca, singlewoman, Bures, 1699. R2/73/388; W1/153/38
Richard, hermit, Bury St. Edmunds, 1517. R2/6/41
Robert, husb., Acton, 1544. R2/19/465
Robert, sen., husb., Acton, 1632. R2/56/186; W1/89/95
Robert, the elder, husb., Bildeston, 1557. R2/26/164; W1/20/98
Robert, Harleston, 1664. A5/5/62, A4/2/89
Robert, yeo., Haughley, 1645. R2/59/197; W1/102/27
Robert, yeo., Ixworth Thorpe, 1673. R2/65/418; W1/125/40
Robert, Sapiston, 1559. R2/28/339; W1/22/229
Robert, yeo., Sudbury, 1559. R2/28/50; W1/22/54
Roger, baker, Sudbury, 1494. R2/13/24
Sarah, spinster, Sudbury, 1685. R2/70/116; W1/139/104
Temperance, spinster, Acton, 1636. A5/4/44
Thomas, yeo., Acton, 1600. R2/45/59; W1/58/83
Thomas, draper, Bury St. Edmunds, 1535. R2/7/28
Thomas, yeo., Haughley, 1629. R2/54/372; W1/85/70
Thomas, gent., Little Cornard, 1680. R2/67/599; W1/134/74; In. 3/20/79
Thomas, Stowmarket, 1638. A5/4/67
Thomas, Sudbury, 1691. A5/6/141, A4/33/30
William, card maker, Bury St. Edmunds, 1443. R2/2/5
William, clothier, Clare, 1660. R2/62/111; W1/112/148; In. 3/5/170
William, Glemsford, 1634. A5/4/28
William, Haverhill, (1544). R2/21/619; W1/28/142
William, carpenter, Long Melford, 1602. R2/45/156; W1/60/77a & b
see also Nueman
NEWNUM, Richard, yeo., Woolpit, 1640. R2/58/159; W1/96/66
NEWPORT, George, Kedington, 1612. A5/3/115
Richard, Felsham, 1698. A5/7/8
Thomas, Kedington, 1526. R2/17/216; W1/23/15
NEWPOTT, Edward, singleman, Hawkedon, 1677. R2/66/433; W1/129/5; In. 3/18/3
Thomas, Bury St. Edmunds, 1690. A5/6/134, A4/32/30
Thomas, the elder, yeo., Stanningfield, 1684. R2/69/361; W1/108/151
NEWRES, John, sen., Bures, 1465. R2/10/417
NEWSON, Isaac, mercer, Bury St. Edmunds, 1698. R2/73/286; W1/152/59; In. 3/26/29
Samuel, clerk, Great Waldingfield, 1695. R2/72/552; W1/149/106
see also Neuson
NEWTON, Elisabeth, wid., Bures, 1662. R2/62/412; W1/114/166; In. 3/8/66
John, yeo., Boxford, 1640. R2/58/151; W1/96/57
John, cordwainer, Bury St. Edmunds, 1394. R2/1/64
John, servant, Lavenham, 1544. R2/19/455
John, yeo., Stanton, 1672. R2/65/378; W1/124/121
John, husb., Stowmarket, 1595. R2/43/66; W1/53/54

NEWTON continued
Joseph, wheelwright, Layham, 1697. R2/73/98; W1/150/112
Leonard, the elder, Barton, 1595. R2/43/77; W1/53/69
Leonard, yeo., Brandon, 1634. R2/56/355; W1/90/123
Margaret, wid., Gislingham, 1519. R2/14/1; W1/26/125
Margaret, wid., Isleham, 1660. A4/1/255
Nicholas, Stanton, 1664. In. 3/9/45; A5/5/56
Robert, Bures, 1644. A5/4/103
Samuel, Layham, 1698. A5/7/6
Thomas, Chelsworth, 1539. R2/19/296
Thomas, Stanton, 1591. A5/2/146
Thomas, yeo., Stanton, 1601. R2/44/474; W1/59/82
William, the elder, glover, Bildeston, 1583. R2/39/87; W1/42/24
William, glover, Bildeston, 1638. R2/57/342; W1/95/125
NEYTHERCOTE, Richard, Soham, 1582. R2/38/385; W1/41/53
NEYVE, William, Drinkstone, 1550. R2/21/60; W1/15/100
NICE, Edward, brick burner, Cockfield, 1672. R2/65/288; W1/124/5
Joan, Hepworth, 1693. R2/72/222; W1/147/111
William, Cockfield, 1672. A5/5/134, A4/9/73
NICHOLASSON, John, joiner, Bury St. Edmunds, 1597. R2/43/307; W1/55/75
NICHOLL(S), George, gardener, Bardwell, 1685. R2/70/181; W1/139/153
Henry, Clare, 1641. A5/4/92
John, Fornham St. Genevieve, 1660. R2/62/127; W1/112/170; In. 3/5/223
John, singleman, Rougham, 1686. R2/70/510; W1/140/115; In. 3/22/157; A4/27/35
Roger, Bury St. Edmunds, 1446. R2/2/19
Thomas, Cowlinge, 1688. In. 3/23/36; A5/6/118, A4/29/25
Thomas, the elder, yeo., Sapiston, 1587. R2/40/122; W1/44/4
Thomas, bricklayer, Sapiston, 1597. R2/43/279; W1/55/56
William, Eye, 1677. In. 3/18/78; A5/5/168, A4/14/21
William, Lavenham, 1685. A5/6/90, A4/24/52
see also Nicoll(s), Nycholl, Smyth als. Nycholl
NICHOLSEN, Ambrose, Long Melford, 1674. A5/5/149, A4/11/63
NICHOLSON, John, Bury St. Edmunds, (1576). W1/51/264
John, inn holder, Bury St. Edmunds, 1580. R2/38/114
John, Bury St. Edmunds, 1636. A5/4/43
NICKLESON, Matthew, Bury St. Edmunds, 1693. A5/6/158, A4/35/68
see also Nicholasson, Nicolasson, Nychalson
NICOLAS, William, Ixworth, 1477. R2/11/100
NICOLASSON, Mark, Bury St. Edmunds, 1585. A5/2/71 & 114a
NICOLL(S), Clement, Badwell Ash, 1634. A5/4/28
Geoffrey, Bury St. Edmunds, 1493. R2/4/22
John, Bury St. Edmunds, 1475. R2/1/210
John, Sapiston, 1572. A5/1/247
Walter, als. Clerk, Great Bradley, 1474. R2/10/520
NIEBLE, Thomas, 1449. R2/9/140
NIGHTINGALE, John, yeo., Ballingdon, 1663. R2/63/24; W1/115/40; In. 3/8/54
see also Nyghtingall, Nytingale
NINDGE, William, als. Lyndge, Herringswell, 1583. A5/2/50
NINGE, Faith, wid., Herringswell, 1628, (N). R2/54/143; W1/84/14
Thomas, als. Lindge, husb., Herringswell, 1677. R2/66/517; W1/129/99; In. 3/18/125
William, Woolpit, 1566. R2/32/357; W1/28/21
see also Nenge, Nyndge
NIPPE, John, husb., Wickham Skeith, 1566. R2/32/308; W1/28/84
NOBB(E)S, John, husb., West Creeting, 1561. R2/30/41; W1/28/228
Simon, husb., Dagworth, 1564. R2/32/137; W1/27/86
Ralph, bay maker, Glemsford, 1686. In. 3/22/15; A5/6/98, A4/26/110
NOBBYS, Nicholas, Stowmarket, 1553. R2/31/178; W1/13/118
NOBELL, Joan, wid., Thelnetham, 1565. R2/32/176
Richard, husb., Barrow, 1591. R2/42/149; W1/48/94
Richard, shearman, Icklingham, 1566. R2/32/346; W1/28/36
Walter, husb., Icklingham, 1567. R2/32/436; W1/19/113b
NOBILL, John, mercer, Bury St. Edmunds, 1445. R2/2/16
Richard, Westley, 1503. R2/12/60
NOBLE, Ann, wife of John, Great Livermere, 1559. R2/28/75; W1/22/78
Augustin, yeo., Sapiston, 1643. R2/59/45; W1/100/54
Elisabeth, wid., Great Livermere, 1665. R2/63/377; W1/117/128; In. 3/11/1

NOBLE continued
James, Cavendish, 1661. In. 3/6/58; A5/5/12, A4/1/129
James, Thelnetham, 1669. In. 3/14/82; A5/5/106, A4/7/53
John, yeo., Barrow, 1696. R2/73/61; W1/150/103
John, tailor, Bury St. Edmunds, 1679. R2/67/301; W1/133/83
John, Great Livermere, 1557. R2/26/23; W1/20/20
John, yeo., Great Livermere, 1685. R2/70/89; W1/139/80
John, Nayland, 1462. R2/10/352
John, yeo., Old Buckenham, 1611. R2/48/99; W1/68/117
John, Stanton, 1558. R2/27/295
Margaret, Icklingham, 1566. A5/1/179
Margery, wid., Great Livermere, 1546. R2/21/253; W1/10/92
Margery, Stanton, 1636. R2/57/78; W1/92/92
Nicholas, Hengrave, 1573. A5/1/256
Richard, Barnham, 1561. A5/1/107
Richard, Rougham, 1698. A5/7/5
Richard, yeo., Sapiston, 1602. R2/45/132; W1/60/51
Thomas, Barrow, 1684. A5/6/81, A4/21/82
Thomas, the younger, yeo., Stanton, 1619. R2/51/275; W1/132/14
Thomas, yeo., Stanton, 1630. R2/55/121; W1/86/135
Walter, Great Horningsheath, 1470. R2/10/447
William, clerk, Ampton, 1617. R2/50/213; W1/74/5
William, husb., Great Livermere, 1573. R2/36/146; W1/32/49
see also Nobell, Noboll
NOBLETT, Richard, Semer, 1584. A5/2/58
Robert, singleman, Walsham le Willows, 1639. A5/4/70
William, cordwainer, Bury St. Edmunds, 1645. R2/59/220; W1/102/44
NOBOLL, Thomas, Stanton, 1557. R2/26/225; W1/20/118
NOBYLL, Adam, Westley, 1458. R2/9/243; W1/24/88
Henry, Little Saxham, 1471. R2/10/467
Joan, Horningsheath, 1449. R2/9/96
John, Bury St. Edmunds, 1504. R2/4/160
NOCAR, Robert, Troston, 1522. R2/17/16; W1/21/71
NOCHE, Margaret, Bildeston, 1470. R2/10/446
NOCKARD, John, Flempton, 1504. W1/7/14
William, Flempton, 1520. R2/15/31
William, Flempton, 1593. R2/42/365; W1/50/34
NOCKER, Alice, wife of John, Flempton, 1560. R2/29/117; W1/25/52
see also Nocar, Nokord
NOCKWARD, Penelope, singlewoman, Brockley, 1696. R2/73/14; W1/150/16
NOELL, Thomas, Haverhill, 1448. R2/9/63
NOKES, Richard, Kersey, 1559. R2/28/380; W1/3/147
NOKORD, John, Flempton, 1559. R2/28/371; W1/3/94
NOLOTH, Robert, Thorndon, 1540. R2/29/280; W1/4/210
NONE, John, smith, Rattlesden, 1536. R2/18/137
John, yeo., Rishangles, 1540. R2/19/617; W1/5/26
John, yeo., Stanningfield, 1560. R2/29/125; W1/25/43
Margery, wid., Wissington, 1568. R2/33/32; W1/29/46
NONNE, Elisabeth, wid., Lawshall, 1688. R2/71/120; W1/142/108
George, Felsham, 1465. W1/24/101
Henry, singleman, Bury St. Edmunds, 1693. A5/6/154, A4/35/95
John, esq., Bury St. Edmunds, 1612. W1/111/86
John, yeo., Little Whelnetham, 1571. R2/35/309; W1/36/142
John, sen., Rougham, 1473. R2/10/516
John, Rougham, 1584. R2/39/197; W1/42/129
Margaret, spinster, Lawshall, 1687. R2/70/301; W1/141/44
Margaret, Wetheringsett, 1550. R2/21/30; W1/10/186
Robert, yeo., Bradfield St. George, 1592. R2/42/183; W1/49/4
Robert, Lackford, 1560. R2/29/66; W1/25/104
Robert, Rougham, 1554. R2/24/105; W1/14/79
Robert, clerk, Wetheringsett, 1573. R2/36/217; W1/32/152
Thomas, Bardwell, 1594. A5/2/202
Thomas, limer, Bury St. Edmunds, 1517. R2/6/40
Walter, maltster, Bury St. Edmunds, 1695. A5/6/182, A4/38/71
William, Pakenham, 1687. A5/6/114, A4/27/81
NOOKE(S), John, Kersey, 1518. R2/13/228
John, yeo., Surlingham, 1594. W1/51/139
Robert, Kersey, 1464. R2/10/356
NOOTE, William, Thurston, 1465. R2/10/390
NOOTH, Edith, wid. of Robert, yeo., Stoke by Nayland, 1649. R2/60/193; W1/106/36
Elisabeth, wid., Stoke by Nayland, 1632. R2/56/142; W1/89/37
John, the elder, husb., Polstead, 1639. R2/58/35; W1/94/64

NORBER, William, Cheveley, 1567. R2/32/381; W1/3/16
NORBERIE, Ellen, Cheveley, 1587. R2/40/139; W1/44/19
NORBERY, John, the elder, Cheveley, 1503. R2/12/27
John, Knettishall, 1592. A5/2/175
Robert, Kentford, 1560. R2/29/12; W1/25/171
Thomas, Cheveley, 1530. R2/19/32
NORBOROUGH, William, Fordham, 1693. A5/6/163, A4/35/28a
NORBOWR, William, Elveden, 1453. R2/9/161
NORCOP, Elisabeth, wid., Newmarket, 1686. In. 3/22/114; A5/6/104, A4/26/37
NORDEN, Michael, wid., Great Bradley, 1683. A5/6/71, A4/20/85
Susan, wid., Little Bradley, 1679. R2/67/319; W1/133/93
see also Anderson als. Norden
NOREYS, John, Brockford, 1472. R2/10/498
Robert, tailor, Bury St. Edmunds, 1437. R2/1/229
Thomas, Bury St. Edmunds, 1446. R2/2/20
William, Brockford, 1463. R2/9/308
William, Bury St. Edmunds, 1370. R2/1/32
NORFILDE, Joanna, Sudbury, 1587. A5/2/88
NORFOCKE, Grace, singlewoman, Glemsford, 1601. R2/44/356; W1/59/20
William, Burwell, 1576. R2/37/216; W1/37/78
NORFOKE, John, Soham, 1535. R2/18/135
NORFOLK, Ellen, wid., Soham, 1521. R2/14/19
Frances, wid., Soham, 1689. R2/71/199; W1/143/51
George, husb., Clare, 1586. R2/40/3; W1/43/2
George, Sudbury, 1632. A5/4/20
Grace, wid., Clare, 1630. R2/55/26; W1/86/31
Gregory, Clare, 1593. A5/2/181
Joan, als. Norman, wid. of Robert, Clare, 1565. R2/32/221
John, Clare, (1498). R2/13/95
John, als. Jankyn, bricklayer, Clare, 1559. R2/28/106; W1/22/105
John, Clare, 1577. In. 3/1/1
John, Soham, 1515. R2/12/116
John, the younger, Soham, 1516. W1/36/19
John, husb., Soham, 1558. R2/27/440 & 442
John, the elder, yeo., Soham, 1635. R2/56/540; W1/91/124
John, Soham, 1637. A5/4/49
John, singleman, Soham, 1639. A5/4/69
John, yeo., Soham, 1670. In. 3/15/95; A5/5/114
John, singleman, Soham, 1681. R2/68/38; W1/135/31
John, the elder, 1626. R2/53/472; W1/82/19
Richard, tanner, Clare, 1574. R2/37/45; W1/33/36
Robert, tanner, Clare, 1540. R2/19/273
Robert, yeo., Soham, 1620. R2/52/35; W1/76/32
Thomas, Soham, 1569. A5/1/212
William, husb., Clare, 1533. R2/19/145; W1/2/93
William, Clare, 1608. A5/3/48
---, 1455. R2/9/224
NORFOWK, William, the elder, Soham, 1522. R2/15/60
see also Norfocke, Northfolk
NORGETT, Thomas, Newmarket, 1670. R2/65/11; W1/122/15; In. 3/15/26
NORIDGE, Agnes, wid., Ashley, 1591. R2/42/95; W1/48/136
NORIGHE, Stephen, Ashley, 1583. R2/39/106; W1/42/11
NORIS, Edward, Palgrave, 1474. R2/10/509
NORMAN, Alice, wid., Soham, 1457. R2/9/184
Alice, wid., Wicken, 1675. R2/66/269; W1/127/136; In. 3/16/156
Bartholomew, cordwainer, Isleham, 1622. R6/31
Bridget, singlewoman, Bury St. Edmunds, 1662. R2/62/381; W1/114/119
Christopher, the elder, Fornham All Saints, 1679. R2/67/489; W1/133/206
Dorothy, singlewoman, Gipping, 1650. R2/61/359; W1/107/57; In. 3/3/75
Edward, yeo., Hengrave, 1582. R2/38/402; W1/41/36
Edward, Old Newton, 1643. A5/4/98
Elisabeth, wid., Cavenham, 1661, (N). R2/62/180; W1/113/34; In. 3/6/48; A5/5/13, A4/1/123
Elisabeth, Chevington, 1590. A5/2/131
Elisabeth, wid., Chippenham, 1592, (N). R2/42/300; W1/49/119
Elisabeth, wid., Isleham, 1569. W7/32
Ellen, wid., Isleham, (1692). W7/122; In. 9/87
Francis, miller, Fordham, 1700. R2/74/21; W1/154/19; In. 3/27/2
Francis, Isleham, 1685. In. 9/69

NORMAN continued
George, Eye, 1678. In. 3/19/228; A5/6/14, A4/15/126
George, carpenter, Wicken, 1672. R2/65/332; W1/124/58
Grace, Chippenham, 1648. A5/4/124
Henry, Burwell, 1561. A5/1/107
Henry, yeo., Culford, 1683. R2/69/128; W1/137/104
James, Chippenham, 1511. W1/9/169
James, carpenter, Isleham, 1649. W7/51
James, Isleham, 1685. W7/105; In. 9/54
Joan, wid., Chippenham, 1470. R2/10/449
John, Barrow, 1517. W1/9/51
John, Brome, 1587. R2/40/234; W1/44/76
John, tanner, Burwell, 1631. R2/56/107; W1/87/164
John, jun., chandler, Bury St. Edmunds, 1439. R2/1/238
John, ironmonger, Bury St. Edmunds, 1467. R2/2/113
John, Bury St. Edmunds, 1500. R2/4/101
John, shoe maker, Bury St. Edmunds, 1599. W1/95/132
John, shoe maker, Bury St. Edmunds, 1622. R2/52/528; W1/78/127
John, the elder, tailor, Bury St. Edmunds, 1625. R2/53/197
John, labourer, Chippenham, 1642. R2/58/390; W1/99/103
John, maltster, Chippenham, 1651. R2/61/428
John, Clare, 1595. A5/2/214
John, Icklingham All Saints, 1688. A5/6/124, A4/29/93
John, husb., Isleham, 1632. R6/68
John, singleman, Isleham, 1636. R6/69
John, Isleham, 1695. In. 9/92; A12/14
John, yeo., Lawshall, 1689. R2/71/268; W1/143/104
John, Little Finborough, 1460. R2/9/234
John, Occold, 1542. R2/22/8; W1/6/85
John, sen., Soham, 1443. R2/9/57
John, mercer, Soham, 1452. R2/9/146
John, Stansfield, 1462. R2/12/11
John, husb., Wicken, 1558. R2/27/21; W1/31/25
John, yeo., Wicken, 1679. R2/67/477; W1/133/198
John, yeo., Yaxley, 1589. R2/41/160; W1/46/123
Katherine, wid., Bury St. Edmunds, 1690. R2/71/385; W1/144/92
Leonard, Wicken, 1582. R2/38/400; W1/41/38
Margaret, Chevington, 1601. R2/44/373; W1/59/35
Margery, wid., Landwade, 1613. W1/111/6
Mary, Chevington, 1593. A5/2/190
Mary, wid., Fornham All Saints, 1690. R2/71/378; W1/144/85
Michael, husb., Burwell, 1679. R2/67/224; W1/133/33
Michael, labourer, Landwade, 1604. R2/45/325
Peter, clerk, Bury St. Edmunds, 1614. R2/49/92; W1/71/70
Richard, yeo., Eye, 1678. R2/67/31; W1/130/31; In. 3/19/42
Robert, miller, Cavenham, 1652. In. 3/4/81; A5/4/142
Robert, husb., Chippenham, 1577. R2/37/278
Robert, carpenter, Chippenham, 1616. R2/50/44; W1/73/48
Robert, tailor, Chippenham, 1661. In. 3/6/202; A5/5/20, A4/1/58
Robert, yeo., Eriswell, 1584. R2/39/195; W1/42/131
Robert, Flempton, 1681. A5/6/47, A4/18/51
Robert, husb., Freckenham, 1663. W8/17; In. 10/5
Robert, Gazeley, 1498. R2/13/105
Robert, yeo., Gazeley, 1634, (N). R2/56/379; W1/90/156
Robert, sen., Isleham, 1683. W7/99
Robert, jun., carpenter, Isleham, 1684. In. 9/64
Robert, Isleham, 1692. In. 9/82
Robert, labourer, Snailwell, 1616. R2/50/35; W1/73/36
Robert, Wicken, 1588. R2/41/21; W1/45/16
Robert, husb., Wicken, 1650. R2/61/368; W1/107/64; In. 3/3/85
Roger, carpenter, Isleham, 1651. W7/54
Roger, yeo., Mendlesham, 1660. R2/62/49; W1/112/61; In. 3/5/46; A5/5/3, A4/1/215
Samuel, Bury St. Edmunds, 1689. A5/6/130, A4/30/13
Samuel, the elder, Higham, 1633. R2/56/289; W1/77/32b
Simon, yeo., Chevington, 1625. R2/53/312; W1/81/96
Thomas, Bury St. Edmunds, 1698. A5/7/7
Thomas, Cavenham, 1534. R2/19/197
Thomas, Chevington, 1442. R2/9/16
Thomas, Chippenham, 1448. R2/9/97; W1/24/39
Thomas, Chippenham, 1462. R2/10/341
Thomas, Chippenham, 1632. A5/4/19

NORMAN continued
Thomas, weaver, Clare, 1539. R2/20/221; W1/4/165
Thomas, Flempton, 1649. A5/4/132
Thomas, labourer, Fordham, 1592. R2/42/187; W1/49/12
Thomas, labourer, Thelnetham, 1625. R2/53/320; W1/81/104
Thomas, yeo., Tuddenham, 1626. R2/53/578; W1/82/105
Thomas, yeo., Tuddenham, 1663. R2/63/113; W1/115/170; In. 3/8/206
Thomas, singleman, Wicken, 1693. R2/72/231; W1/147/120
Thomazine, Kirtling, 1581. A5/2/32
Tobias, yeo., Hopton, 1646. R2/59/294; W1/103/12
Toby, Mendlesham, 1607. A5/3/33
William, yeo., Barrow, 1499. R2/4/76
William, Bury St. Edmunds, 1564. W1/17/21
William, yeo., Chevington, 1587. R2/40/202; W1/44/60
William, Chippenham, 1549. W1/10/166a
William, husb., tailor, Chippenham, 1564. R2/32/105; W1/27/56
William, Chippenham, 1630. A5/4/8
William, Clare, (1520). R2/17/315
William, labourer, Freckenham, 1625. R6/39
William, Freckenham, 1707. In. 10/40
William, Kirtling, 1581. A5/2/32
William, Long Melford, 1535. R2/19/220; W1/3/49
William, Mendlesham, 1628, (N). R2/54/181; W1/84/57
William, Thurlow, 1440. R2/9/26; W1/24/177
William, Wicken, 1559. R2/28/375; W1/3/93
William, yeo., Yaxley, 1612. R2/48/236; W1/69/134
see also Norfolk als. Norman
NORMANTON, John, the elder, clothier, Bury St. Edmunds, 1638. R2/58/286; W1/93/59
John, woollen draper, Bury St. Edmunds, 1643. R2/59/43; W1/100/52
NORMEVILE, John, Weston, 1530. R2/19/43
NORREYS, Agnes, Bury St. Edmunds, 1396. R2/1/75
NORRIDGE, John, yeo., Ousden, 1617. R2/50/251; W1/74/49
Martin, clerk, Culford, 1683. R2/69/1; W1/137/1
Richard, yeo., Ashley, 1591. R2/42/49; W1/48/40
NORRIS, Edward, Bildeston, 1636. A5/4/47
John, gent., Bury St. Edmunds, 1689. R2/71/275; W1/143/111
John, Layham, 1640. A5/4/79
Robert, yeo., Thrandeston, 1680. R2/67/592; W1/134/69
NORRYS, Elisabeth, wid., Bury St. Edmunds, 1557. R2/8/314; W1/18/43
see also Noreys, Noris, Norreys, Browne als. Norris
NORS, Roger, butcher, Bury St. Edmunds, 1462. R2/2/73
Thomas, Downham, 1522. R2/15/45
NORTH, Dudley, Bury St. Edmunds, 1688. R2/71/28; W1/142/26
John, Bardwell, 1441. R2/9/13
Margaret, Bury St. Edmunds, 1430. R2/1/191
NORTHAGHE, Adam, Thorndon, 1443. R2/10/353
NORTHEN, Mary, wid., Stoke by Nayland, 1592. R2/42/242; W1/49/57
Walter, yeo., Gedding, 1673. R2/65/465; W1/125/101
NORTHFFE, John, Bury St. Edmunds, 1354. R2/1/2
NORTHFOLK, Edward, Soham, 1527. R2/17/261; W1/1/17
John, wright, Bury St. Edmunds, 1403. R2/1/97
NORTHUMBERLAND, Richard, harvest man, Wicken, 1647, (N). R2/59/480; W1/104/115
NORTLY, John, yeo., Elmsett, 1600. R2/45/28; W1/58/42
NORTON, Charles, Ashley, 1600. R2/45/34; W1/58/50
Elisabeth, wid., Gazeley, 1623. R2/52/591; W1/79/43
John, Carleton Forehoe, (1532). W1/51/27
John, Gazeley, 1593. A5/2/181
Leonard, Wood Ditton, 1676. R2/66/362; W1/128/72; In. 3/17/89
Robert, miller, Wood Ditton, 1688. R2/71/31; W1/142/28; A5/6/119, A4/29/32
Thomas, Bury St. Edmunds, 1427. R2/1/175
William, priest, Bury St. Edmunds, 1508. R2/4/202
NORWICH, Henry, Ashley, 1538. R2/18/184
Margaret, wid., Hundon, 1666. A5/5/73, A4/4/12
William, Bury St. Edmunds, 1361. W1/1/12
NORWITCH, John, yeo., Ashley, 1603. R2/45/294; W1/61/101a & b
see also Noridge, Norridge
NORWODE, Simon, Bury St. Edmunds, 1514. R2/6/9
NORWOLD, Joan, wid., Norton, 1522. R2/14/68
Matilda, Icklingham, 1457. R2/9/192

NORWOLD continued
Robert, Eriswell, 1475. R2/11/112
Thomas, Walsham le Willows, 1491. R2/13/104
William, Norton, 1506. W1/36/15
NOTE, John, Norton, 1444. R2/9/61
John, Thurston, 1446. R2/9/76
Thomas, Thurston, 1489. R2/11/417 & 424
Thomas, Thurston, 1492. R2/13/9
NOTEBEM, John, gent., Bury St. Edmunds, 1473. R2/2/177
NOTEWYN, Thomas, Burwell, 1475. R2/11/117
NOTH, Hugh, singleman, Stoke by Nayland, 1644. R2/59/161; W1/101/89
NOTLYE, Thomas, Onehouse, 1614. W1/111/73
NOTMAN, Martin, yeo., Haughley, 1570. R2/35/42; W1/38/145
NOTS, William, Langham, 1439. R2/9/1
NOTSON, John, Bury St. Edmunds, 1481. R2/2/304
NOTT, John, Lindsey, 1528. R2/15/192
John, Little Waldingfield, 1484. R2/11/372
John, the elder, Norton, 1554. R2/24/82; W1/14/62
John, West Stow, 1457. R2/9/205 (probate only)
Margery, wife of John, West Stow, 1457. R2/9/205 (probate only)
Robert, Groton, 1454. R2/9/169
Robert, Stanton, 1522. R2/17/315
Thomas, Groton, 1465. R2/10/387
see also Nutt
NOTYNGHAM, John, grocer, Bury St. Edmunds, 1439. R2/1/244
John, Bury St. Edmunds, 1503. R2/4/142
NOWCE, Henry, als. Tourner, Mildenhall, 1535. R2/19/219; W1/3/162
NUCE, Robert, tailor, Bury St. Edmunds, 1665. R2/63/325; W1/117/69; In. 3/10/106
NUDICK, James, Isleham, ----. W7/23
William, Mildenhall, 1617. R2/50/227
NUEMAN, Robert, Haughley, 1558. R2/27/400
NUMAN, Agnes, wid., Haughley, 1547. R2/21/307; W1/10/145
William, Norton, 1615, (N). W1/111/22
NUNINGE, John, yeo., Gipping, 1626. R2/53/682
NUNN, Abraham, tailor, Bury St. Edmunds, 1603. R2/45/260; W1/61/66; A5/3/10
Agnes, Badwell Ash, 1587. A5/2/92
Agnes, wid., Wortham, 1559. R2/28/196; W1/22/175
Ambrose, Fornham St. Martin, 1683. A5/6/67, A4/20/23
Amy, spinster, Hawstead, 1626. R2/53/499; W1/82/41
Ann, wid., Rougham, 1617. R2/50/350; W1/74/131 & 139
Anne, wid., Bury St. Edmunds, 1617. R2/50/357
Anthony, yeo., Chippenham, 1642. R2/58/377; W1/99/82
Christian, wid., Rougham, 1534. R2/18/73
Dorothy, wife of Henry, yeo., Whepstead, 1669. R2/64/494; W1/121/88
Edmund, yeo., Rattlesden, 1674. R2/66/75; W1/126/46
Edmund, yeo., Hawstead, 1667. R2/64/269; W1/119/132; In. 3/12/132
Edward, yeo., Bradfield, 1645. R2/59/194; W1/102/22
Elisabeth, wid., Felsham, 1670. R2/65/82; W1/122/101; In. 3/15/118
Elisabeth, wid., Rattlesden, 1686. R2/70/243; W1/140/14; In. 3/22/89
Elisabeth, Tostock, 1616. R2/50/92; W1/73/101
Elisabeth, singlewoman, Whepstead, 1682. A5/6/59, A4/19/33
Frances, wid., Whepstead, 1678. R2/67/51; W1/130/41
George, yeo., Felsham, 1559. R2/28/376; W1/3/145
George, Felsham, 1610. R2/47/239; W1/67/120
George, Hawstead, 1687. A5/6/109, A4/27/20
George, yeo., Lavenham, 1622. R2/52/477; W1/78/89
George, Rattlesden, 1526. R2/17/152; W1/21/144a
George, the elder, yeo., Rattlesden, 1629. R2/54/296; W1/85/14
George, husb., Stanton, 1605. R2/45/443; W1/63/87
Henry, yeo., Great Finborough, 1652. R2/61/526; W1/109/11; In. 3/4/1
Henry, wheelwright, Hartest, 1690. R2/71/319; W1/144/21
Henry, Whepstead, 1636. A5/4/43
Henry, the elder, glover, Wortham, 1668. R2/64/354; W1/120/66
Isabel, wid., Stowlangtoft, 1625, (N). R2/53/305; W1/81/90
Jane, Stanningfield, 1590. A5/2/135
Joan, Rougham, 1555. A5/1/96
Joan, wife of Henry, yeo., Soham, 1690. R2/71/375; W1/144/82
John, Bradfield St. George, 1560. R2/29/86; W1/25/79
John, Bradfield St. George, 1578. A5/2/13

NUNN continued
John, Bury St. Edmunds, 1673. A5/5/143, A4/10/94
John, Drinkstone, 1540. R2/20/247; W1/4/185
John, the elder, yeo., Drinkstone, 1587. R2/40/130; W1/44/12
John, the elder, husb., Drinkstone, 1627. R2/54/71; W1/83/74
John, yeo., Eye, 1607. R2/46/143
John, farmer, Eye, 1699. R2/73/362; W1/153/22; In. 3/26/67
John, Felsham, 1504. R2/13/154
John, husb., Hunston, 1637. R2/57/144; W1/92/179
John, pedder, Rattlesden, 1568. R2/33/81
John, sen., Rishangles, 1475. R2/11/110
John, jun., Rougham, 1459. R2/9/265
John, Rougham, 1668. In. 3/13/124; A5/5/101, A4/6/118
John, the younger, yeo., Stanningfield, 1650. R2/61/306; W1/107/1; In. 3/3/5
John, yeo., Stanningfield, 1650. R2/61/328; W1/107/25
John, Stanton, 1550. R2/21/163; W1/9/127
John, Stanton, 1555. A5/1/98
John, the elder, yeo., Thorndon, 1561. R2/30/91; W1/28/268
John, Troston, 1556. R2/25/131; W1/16/178
John, carpenter, Whepstead, 1558. R2/27/420
John, yeo., Whepstead, 1693. R2/72/168
John, Woolpit, 1535. R2/18/135
John, Wortham, 1668, (N). R2/64/363; W1/120/77; A5/5/97, A4/6/78
Joseph, woollen weaver, Bury St. Edmunds, 1612. R2/48/192; W1/69/79
Joseph, Sudbury, 1682. In. 3/21/77; A5/6/62, A4/19/73
Joseph, Sudbury, 1683. A5/6/70, A4/20/64
Joshua, Bury St. Edmunds, 1660. A5/5/4, A4/1/211
Leonard, Walsham le Willows, 1669. R2/64/430; W1/121/12; In. 3/13/127
Margaret, wid., Bardwell, 1603. R2/45/301; W1/61/110
Margaret, servant, Bury St. Edmunds, 1613. R2/48/282; W1/70/55
Margaret, wid., Hunston, 1661. R2/62/252; W1/113/136; In. 3/6/189
Margaret, wid., Thorndon, 1595. R2/43/58; W1/53/45
Margaret, wid., Wortham, 1612. R2/48/202; W1/69/92
Marion, Thorpe Morieux, 1474. R2/10/508
Martin, Felsham, 1628. R2/54/165; W1/84/41
Mary, wid., Bury St. Edmunds, 1629. R2/54/323; W1/85/33
Mary, wid., Bury St. Edmunds, 1692. R2/72/39; W1/146/36
Mary, wid., Drinkstone, 1683. R2/69/150; W1/137/122
Matthew, Rattlesden, 1584. A5/2/64
Nicholas, Hessett, 1447. R2/9/80
Philip, yeo., Lawshall, 1681. R2/68/234a; W1/135/175
Philip, yeo., Stanningfield, 1627. R2/54/112; W1/83/111
Philip, West Stow, 1679. A5/6/16, A4/16/14
Ralph, gent., Bury St. Edmunds, 1685. In. 3/22/144; A5/6/91, A4/24/61
Richard, Bury St. Edmunds, 1645. A5/4/110
Richard, husb., Hessett, 1578. R2/37/362; W1/36/214
Robert, yeo., Bradfield St. George, 1663. R2/63/43; W1/115/68; In. 3/8/71
Robert, yeo., Bury St. Edmunds, 1558. R2/8/331; W1/18/67
Robert, Drinkstone, 1606. A5/3/13
Robert, singleman, gent., Felsham, 1667. A5/5/82, A4/5/19
Robert, yeo., Hawstead, 1603. R2/45/272; W1/61/70
Robert, yeo., Hawstead, 1622. R2/52/392; W1/78/27
Robert, yeo., Hawstead, 1648. R2/60/64; W1/105/81
Robert, the elder, yeo., Hawstead, 1687. R2/70/565; W1/141/3
Robert, the younger, Hawstead, 1687. A5/6/109, A4/27/21
Robert, miller, Hopton, 1635. R2/56/511; W1/91/92
Robert, collar maker, Lawshall, 1609. R2/47/33; W1/66/38
Robert, knacker, Lawshall, 1643. R2/59/1; W1/100/3
Robert, Redgrave, 1616. R2/50/145; W1/58/148
Robert, singleman, Rougham, 1557. R2/26/220; W1/20/122
Robert, yeo., Stanningfield, 1672. R2/65/309; W1/124/32
Robert, maltster, Stoke by Nayland, 1664. In. 3/9/169; A5/5/61, A4/2/76
Robert, Thorndon, 1595. R2/43/54; W1/53/42
Robert, labourer, Wattisfield, 1635. R2/56/464; W1/91/32
Robert, the elder, yeo., Whepstead, 1624. R2/53/23; W1/80/33
Robert, yeo., Whepstead, 1660. R2/62/142; W1/112/185; In. 3/5/216
Robert, the elder, yeo., Whepstead, 1676. R2/66/301; W1/128/5; In. 3/17/36

NUNN continued
Robert, yeo., Whepstead, 1679. R2/67/408; W1/133/148; In. 3/20/26
Robert, yeo., Whepstead, 1680. R2/67/543; W1/134/27
Robert, Whepstead, 1692. A5/6/147, A4/34/1
Robert, yeo., Wickhambrook, 1669. R2/64/440; W1/121/24; In. 3/14/36
Robert, Wickham Skeith, 1573. R2/36/181; W1/32/95
Roger, yeo., Stanningfield, 1641. R2/58/287; W1/98/73
Rose, wid., 1573. R2/36/180; W1/32/89
Samuel, labourer, Wortham, 1671. R2/65/234; W1/123/111
Sarah, als. Chinnery, wid., Acton, 1683. A5/6/69, A4/20/56
Simon, the elder, labourer, Eye, 1676. In. 3/17/176; A5/5/166, A4/14/5
Thomas, priest, Bury St. Edmunds, 1518. R2/6/54
Thomas, wid., Buxhall, 1639. A5/4/68
Thomas, Culford, 1613. R2/48/267; W1/70/42
Thomas, Fornham St. Martin, 1518. R2/12/20
Thomas, yeo., Great Livermere, 1681. R2/68/33; W1/135/28
Thomas, clerk, Hessett, 1567. R2/32/410; W1/19/115a
Thomas, tailor, Hessett, 1602. R2/45/174; W1/60/98
Thomas, gent., Ingham, 1650. R2/61/396; W1/107/101
Thomas, labourer, Norton, 1666. In. 3/12/71; A5/5/75, A4/4/39
Thomas, labourer, Norton, 1667. R2/64/223; W1/119/75; In. 3/11/87
Thomas, Rougham, 1571. A5/1/234 & 237
Thomas, yeo., Rougham, 1605. R2/45/458; W1/63/105
Thomas, butcher, Stowlangtoft, 1615. R2/49/246; W1/72/32
Thomas, Westhorpe, 1696. In. 3/25/86; A5/6/190, A4/39/84
Thomas, yeo., Yaxley, 1628. R2/54/184; W1/84/61
Walter, maltster, Bury St. Edmunds, 1685. R2/70/55; W1/139/49
Walter, Hessett, 1494. R2/13/26
Walter, yeo., Stanningfield, 1646. R2/59/352; W1/103/66
Walter, the elder, Whepstead, 1576. R2/37/192; W1/37/59; In. 3/1/42
Walter, yeo., Whepstead, 1605. R2/45/413; W1/63/57
Walter, Whepstead, 1644. W1/110/18
Walter, yeo., Whepstead, 1644. R2/59/121; W1/101/49
Walter, yeo., Wortham, 1556. R2/25/51; W1/16/60
William, yeo., Bradfield St. George, 1674. R2/66/10; W1/126/111
William, Eye, 1592. A5/2/161
William, Hopton, 1648. A5/4/121
William, collar maker, Lawshall, 1671. R2/65/150; W1/123/9
William, Little Whelnetham, 1571. A5/1/234
William, yeo., Rattlesden, 1613. R2/48/267; W1/70/41
William, Rougham, 1496. R2/12/17
William, yeo., Stanton, 1624. R2/53/163; W1/80/144
William, Whepstead, 1683. A5/6/69, A4/20/48
William, husb., Wicken, 1563. W1/26/76
see also None

NUTMAN, Frances, spinster, Horningsheath, 1638. A5/4/59
Henry, husb., Timworth, 1626. R2/53/638; W1/82/163
Margaret, Bury St. Edmunds, 1577. A5/2/2
William, wheelwright, Stowlangtoft, 1596. R2/43/151; W1/54/28; A5/2/218

NUTT, Anthony, yeo., Stoke by Nayland, 1618. R2/51/154; W1/75/93
Cicely, wid., Redgrave, 1605. R2/45/389; W1/63/22
Edmund, the elder, yeo., Great Barton, 1607. R2/46/127
Edmund, yeo., Great Barton, 1615. R2/49/278; W1/72/63
Edmund, yeo., Great Barton, 1639. R2/58/111; W1/94/184
Francis, Great Barton, 1685. A5/6/91, A4/105/65
John, yeo., Great Barton, 1676. R2/66/376; W1/128/89; In. 3/17/119
John, husb., Norton, 1584. R2/39/217; W1/42/109
John, yeo., Rattlesden, 1696. R2/73/81; W1/150/73
John, husb., Thurston, 1562. R2/31/75; W1/8/108
John, yeo., Thurston, 1602. R2/45/96; W1/60/5
John, Thurston, 1647, (N). R2/59/454; W1/104/87
Robert, wid., Assington, 1664. A5/5/64, A4/2/111
Robert, Hartest, 1636. A5/4/46
Robert, Rushbrook, 1630. A5/4/8
Susan, wid., Great Barton, 1677. R2/66/508; W1/129/91; In. 3/18/115
Thomas, singleman, Tostock, 1560. R2/29/38; W1/25/137
William, Bardwell, 1680. In. 3/20/89; A5/6/36, A4/17/49
see also Note, Nott

NUTTALL, John, rector, Thorpe Morieux, 1638. R2/57/353; W1/93/144; A5/4/65
Margaret, Thelnetham, 1651. A5/4/138
Robert, husb., Thelnetham, 1651, (N). R2/61/423
Salmon, Pettistree, 1644. R2/59/104; W1/101/31
Thomas, parson, Gislingham, 1571. R2/35/325; W1/36/126
NUTTEN, Sarah, wid., Edwardstone, 1630. R2/55/5; W1/86/7
NUTTER, William, Kersey, 1571. A5/1/240
NUTTON, Edward, yeo., Boxford, 1651. R2/61/471
Elisabeth, wid., Kersey, 1651. R2/61/422
Sarah, singlewoman, Polstead, 1664. In. 3/9/187
see also Nutten
NYCHALSON, Lancelot, Haverhill, 1544. R2/21/604
NYCHOLL, Edward, Bury St. Edmunds, 1549. R2/8/4
NYCKOLLES, Francis, glover, Newton, 1593. R2/42/389; W1/50/56
NYCOLL(S), Alice, wid., Sapiston, 1594. R2/42/608; W1/52/88
John, smith, Bury St. Edmunds, 1434. R2/1/211
John, Hopton, 1507. R2/12/77
Roger, Chevington, 1450. R2/9/127
Thomas, Icklingham, 1555. R2/24/216; W1/15/46
Thomas, Stuston, 1542. R2/22/84; W1/6/22
William, husb., Bury St. Edmunds, 1504. R2/4/151
NYGHTE, Edmund, Gayton, 1535. W1/51/30
NYGHTINGALL, John, the younger, gelder, Kersey, 1558. R2/27/527
NYLDYLL, John, Lavenham, 1442. R2/9/59
NYNDGE, Lewis, yeo., Herringswell, 1633. R2/56/272; W1/90/37
William, Herringswell, 1584. A5/2/57
NYNGE, Margaret, wid., Herringswell, 1597. R2/43/346; W1/55/110
Thomas, yeo., Herringswell, 1624. R2/53/188; W1/80/162
NYTINGALE, Edmund, singleman, Troston, 1573. R2/36/140; W1/32/41
NYTYNGALLE, John, East Bradenham, 1550. R2/21/121; W1/9/94

O

OAKELY, Edward, bach., Sudbury, 1699. A5/7/12, A4/41/43
John, Lavenham, 1685. A5/6/93, A4/24/88
OAKLY, John, yeo., Long Melford, 1662. R2/62/346; W1/114/63; In. 3/7/78
see also Ockley, Ocley, Okelee, Okley
OAKWOD, Robert, Newmarket, 1521. R2/15/163
OARMES, John, labourer, Burwell, 1617. R2/50/264; W1/74/64
OATES, Elisabeth, Risby, 1673. A5/5/139, A4/10/51
OBTHORP, John, Bury St. Edmunds, 1426. R2/1/170
OCKEMAN, Jeremy, sen., husb., Kedington, 1660. R2/62/141; W1/112/183; In. 3/5/208
OCKERS, Rose, wid., Bury St. Edmunds, 1604. R2/45/314; W1/62/12
OCKLEY, John, maltster, Long Melford, (1705). W1/312/39
Stephen, woollen weaver, Groton, 1638, (N). R2/57/255; W1/93/17
Thomas, tailor, Wickhambrook, 1606. R2/46/38; W1/64/53
OCKLY, William, Great Waldingfield, 1612. R2/48/142; W1/69/26
OCLE, Andrew, Bury St. Edmunds, 1354. R2/1/2
Edmond, Bury St. Edmunds, 1436. R2/1/223
Peter, labourer, Great Thurlow, 1620. R2/52/95; W1/76/79
Robert, Westley, 1474. R2/11/28
William, Wickhambrook, 1578. A5/2/5
OCLEY, Edward, yeo., Little Cornard, 1686. R2/70/476; W1/140/88
ODAM, John, Bury St. Edmunds, 1469. R2/2/129
ODAR, Margery, wid., Bury St. Edmunds, 1569. W1/10/217
ODDER, see Berywell als. Odder
ODE, John, Soham, 1459. R2/9/269
Thomas, als. Osborne, Finningham, 1527. R2/17/222; W1/1/64
ODEHAM, Alice, als. Testwode, wife of John, draper, Bury St. Edmunds, 1452. R2/2/37
Margaret, wid. of John, Bury St. Edmunds, 1492. R2/4/8 & 9
Robert, tailor, Bury St. Edmunds, 1680. In. 3/20/142; A5/6/37, A4/17/64
see also Odam, Martyn als. Odeham
ODELYN, Agnes, wid., Wortham, 1563. R2/10/316
Edward, Wortham, 1452. R2/9/153
ODIE, Elisabeth, wid., Wetherden, 1579. R2/38/54; W1/39/22
ODYE, Benedict, yeo., Wetherden, 1564. R2/32/99; W1/27/50
OFEILD, Oliver, yeo., Barnardiston, 1628. R2/54/269; W1/84/124

OFFOODE, Bridget, wid., Redgrave, 1605. R2/45/404; W1/63/46
James, Wortham, 1577. A5/2/3
John, Stradishall, 1608. R2/46/181; W1/65/47
OFFORD, Augustin, Depden, 1676. In. 3/17/138; A5/5/165, A4/13/82
Charles, miller, Cowlinge, 1680. R2/67/620; W1/134/86; In. 3/20/96
Charles, Cowlinge, 1690. A5/6/133, A4/32/22
Mary, wid., Cavendish, 1678. R2/67/23; W1/130/21; In. 3/19/27
OFFOWARD, John, miller, Barrow, 1660. R2/62/119; W1/112/160; In. 3/5/161
OFFWOOD, Ann, wid., Gislingham, 1599. R2/44/248; W1/57/60
Bridget, spinster, Cockfield, 1700. R2/74/30; W1/154/29
Elisabeth, wid., Gislingham, 1641. R2/58/280; W1/98/64
James, bach., Westhorpe, 1686. In. 3/22/158; A5/6/105, A4/26/21
John, yeo., Gislingham, 1662. R2/62/313; W1/114/12; In. 3/7/99
John, singleman, Gislingham, 1686. A5/6/106, A4/26/11
Margaret, wid., Gislingham, 1673. R2/65/406; W1/125/24
Paul, Stoke Ash, 1604. R1/62/35
Robert, Gislingham, 1594. R2/42/577; W1/52/19
Robert, yeo., Naughton, 1619. R2/51/315; W1/132/33
Robert, Redgrave, 1604. R2/45/338; W1/62/53
Roger, grocer, Haughley, 1632. R2/56/214; W1/89/133
OFFWOOD, Ruben, Massingham, 1606. R2/46/98; W1/64/118
Stephen, yeo., Gislingham, 1683. R2/69/83; W1/137/63
Stephen, yeo., Gislingham, 1685. R2/70/123; W1/139/111; A5/6/93, A4/24/80
Stephen, yeo., Haughley, 1622. R2/52/452; W1/78/70
Stephen, Haughley, 1644. A5/4/102
Thomas, yeo., Gislingham, 1593. R2/42/434; W1/50/95; A5/2/179
Thomas, yeo., Gislingham, 1637. R2/57/72; W1/92/214
Thomas, yeo., Gislingham, 1663. R2/63/32; W1/115/52; In. 3/8/64
Thomas, yeo., Gislingham, 1698. R2/73/303; W1/152/74
Thomas, inn holder, Stowmarket, 1688. R2/71/27; W1/142/25
Walter, yeo., Gislingham, 1540. R2/20/114
William, labourer, Brent Eleigh, 1580. R2/38/222; W1/39/95
William, Little Livermere, 1647. A5/4/118
see also Offoode
OFHOO, Katherine, wid., Bury St. Edmunds, 1493. R2/4/24 & 31
OGER, Thomas, als. Harper, Icklingham, 1593. A5/2/191
OGRAM, Christopher, shepherd, Soham, 1676. In. 3/17/153; A5/5/165, A4/13/80
OGRUM, Christopher, the elder, yeo., Soham, 1649. R2/60/232; W1/106/86
Christopher, shepherd, Soham, 1666. R2/64/21; W1/118/21; In. 3/11/18
Joseph, yeo., Soham, 1692. R2/72/31; W1/146/29; In. 3/24/41
OKE, John, Wood Dalling, 1582. W1/51/163
OKELEE, Walter, Bury St. Edmunds, 1441. R2/1/252
William, Bury St. Edmunds, 1471. R2/2/154
OKELEY, Robert, tailor, Stowmarket, 1574. R2/37/17; W1/33/75
OKELY, Alice, wid. of Robert, Stowmarket, 1584. R2/39/179; W1/42/148
Joan, wid., Cockfield, 1637. A5/4/49
John, the elder, yeo., Long Melford, 1638. R2/57/285; W1/93/57
Martin, Little Saxham, 1674. A5/5/144, A4/89/5
OKEMAN, Thomas, shoe maker, Kedington, 1617. R2/50/273; W1/74/72
see also Ockeman
OKEY, Thomas, Soham, 1585. R2/39/361; W1/42/243
OKLEY, Peter, the elder, labourer, Great Thurlow, 1590. R2/41/444; W1/47/107
OKY, John, Mellis, 1452. R2/9/153
OLDALE, Ann, wife of Walter, Sudbury, 1461. R2/9/295
see also Oldhall
OLDEFEILDE, Thomas, cordwainer, Sudbury, 1594. R2/42/581; W1/52/13
OLDEFILDE, George, Kennett, 1587. A5/2/85
OLDEMAN, Richard, Hinderclay, 1542. R2/19/411, R2/22/6; W1/6/27
OLDFEILD, George, yeo., Kennett, 1616. R2/50/57; W1/73/68
William, maltster, Bury St. Edmunds, 1680. R2/67/569; W1/134/49; In. 3/20/59
OLDFIELD, George, blacksmith, Exning, 1616. R2/50/117; W1/73/123
see also Oldefeilde, Oulfyel
OLDHALL, Walter, Sudbury, 1472. R2/10/546
OLDLYN, Thomas, Fordham, 1539. W1/5/16
OLDMAN, John, Chippenham, 1462. R2/10/352

OLDMAINE, Edward, cordwainer, Bury St. Edmunds, 1691. R2/71/424; W1/144/127; A5/6/139, A4/33/6
Margaret, singlewoman, Bury St. Edmunds, 1649. R2/60/223; W1/106/74
OLDMAYNE, Timothy, Denham, 1637. A5/4/52
see also Oldeman
OLIFER, Ellen, Bures, 1631. A5/4/10
OLIFFE, John, yeo., Boxted, 1604. R2/45/332; W1/62/46
OLIVER, Anthony, jun., Eriswell, 1648. A5/4/123
Barnaby, Brandon, 1630. A5/4/8
Charles, gent., Bury St. Edmunds, 1649. R2/60/161; W1/106/4
James, Clare, 1661. A5/5/15, A4/1/108
John, gingerbread maker, Burwell, 1687. R2/70/285; W1/141/28
John, clerk, Knodishall, 1594. W1/51/252
William, upholsterer, Sudbury, 1665. R2/63/372; W1/117/123; In. 3/10/155
see also Olifer, Olliver, Olover, Olyver
OLLIE, George, husb., Long Melford, 1668. R2/64/370; W1/120/86; In. 3/13/113
OLLIFFE, Joseph, Sudbury, 1684. A5/6/82, A4/21/91
see also Oliffe, Olyfe, Olyve
OLLIVER, Christopher, labourer, Burwell, 1633. R2/56/274; W1/90/39
OLLY, George, sawyer, Whepstead, 1631, (N). R2/45/87; W1/87/131
see also Ollie
OLOVER, Richard, fishmonger, Bury St. Edmunds, 1562. W1/17/42
OLYAT, Thomas, Soham, 1503. R2/12/27
OLYFE, Joan, wid. of John, Glemsford, 1468. R2/10/405
John, weaver, Sudbury, 1567. R2/32/377; W1/3/173
OLYOTT, Alice, wid., Wangford, 1540. R2/19/588; W1/5/5
see also Olyatt
OLYVE, Agatha, wid., Bury St. Edmunds, 1458. R2/2/58
Blanche, Sudbury, 1595. A5/2/214
John, Haughley, 1451. R2/9/103
John, Mendlesham, 1439. R2/9/4
Thomas, saddler, Bury St. Edmunds, 1407. R2/1/117
William, Bury St. Edmunds, 1447. R2/2/22
William, sen., Cavendish, 1453. R2/9/160
William, Cavendish, 1501. R2/13/125
OLYVER, Margaret, als. Stone, wid., Bury St. Edmunds, 1577. R2/37/235 & 242
Robert, husb., Bures, 1616. R2/50/52; W1/73/61
Robert, als. Stonne, goldsmith, Bury St. Edmunds, 1571. R2/35/81; W1/36/105
William, Wangford, 1469. R2/10/402
William, Wangford, 1544. R2/19/438
OMFREY, John, sen., Combs, 1461. R2/9/284
OMPHERY, Anne, wid., Tuddenham, 1605. R2/45/392; W1/63/24
ONELL, see Mullen als. Onell
ONG(E), Adam, Barningham, 1439. R2/9/10 & 23
Ann, singlewoman, Bury St. Edmunds, 1630. A5/4/6
Christopher, Barningham, 1560. R2/29/111; W1/25/56
Christopher, yeo., Hawstead, 1670. R2/65/83; W1/122/103; In. 3/15/128
Edmund, jun., Hartest, 1700. A5/7/17, A4/41/157
Edmund, Lavenham, 1630. A5/4/2
Edmund, Sudbury, 1506. W1/36/14
Edward, butcher, Bury St. Edmunds, 1606. R2/46/37; W1/64/52
Edward, carpenter, Hartest, 1679. R2/67/252; W1/133/46
Grace, wid., Shimpling, 1697. R2/73/158; W1/151/44
James, Rickinghall Superior, 1637. R2/57/228; W1/92/276
John, tailor, Aldham, 1620. R2/52/124; W1/76/108
John, Badwell Ash, 1559. R2/28/310; W1/22/282
John, the elder, Bardwell, 1601. R2/45/94; W1/60/2
John, Barningham, 1558. R2/27/55; W1/21/162
John, reeder, Bury St. Edmunds, 1440. R2/1/247
John, Hartest, 1609. A5/3/63
John, Hepworth, 1504. R2/13/151
John, Hinderclay, 1609. A5/3/60
John, Stanton, 1507. R2/12/76
John, Stanton, 1567. A5/1/183
John, Thelnetham, 1540. R2/20/237; W1/4/175
John, Weston, 1482. R2/11/267

ONG(E) continued
Marion, wife of William, Norton, 1497. R2/13/68
Mary, wid., Bardwell, 1625. R2/53/316; W1/81/100
Robert, yeo., Barningham, 1628. R2/54/192; W1/84/67
Robert, wheelwright, Barningham, 1679, (N). R2/67/240; W1/133/9; A5/6/15, A4/16/4
Samuel, labourer, Bardwell, 1631. R2/56/27; W1/87/37; In. 5/4/28
Samuel, yeo., Bardwell, 1679. R2/67/234; W1/133/3
Thomas, labourer, Bardwell, 1642. R2/58/344; W1/99/42
Thomas, Bury St. Edmunds, 1431. R2/1/199
Thomas, Bury St. Edmunds, 1642. A5/4/98
Thomas, Hopton, (1543). R2/19/360; W1/6/142
William, yeo., Barningham, 1617. R2/50/262; W1/74/63
William, yeo., Barningham, 1630. R2/55/31; W1/86/36
William, bach., Coney Weston, 1681. A5/6/51, A4/18/95
William, Hepworth, 1538. R2/18/175
William, Stanstead, 1562. R2/31/65; W1/8/115
William, Wetherden, 1536. W1/51/38b
ONGOUR, William, Wetherden, 1555. R2/24/153; W1/15/2
ONION, William, Lidgate, 1668. In. 3/13/190; A5/5/100, A4/82/111
see also Onnion, Onyon
ONNAGE, Robert, Soham, 1598, (N). R2/44/150; W1/56/92
ONNION, Ralph, shepherd, Cavenham, 1626. R2/53/683; W1/81/186
ONSELL, William, labourer, Lakenheath, 1626. R2/53/487; W1/82/32
ONSLOWE, William, Norton, 1637. A5/4/51
ONYON, Ann, wid., Lidgate, 1688. R2/71/27; W1/142/24
ORAGE, Thomas, als. Worlidge, singleman, Lidgate, 1662. R2/63/28; W1/115/46; In. 3/8/44
ORAMS, Elizabeth, wid., Wicken, 1596. R2/43/138; W1/54/14
Reginald, husb., Wicken, 1595. R2/43/109; W1/53/109
Thomas, wid., Palgrave, 1679. A5/6/20, A4/16/50
ORANGE, Richard, als. Worlidge, wid., Lidgate, 1695. A5/6/179, A4/38/37
see also Orage
ORBELL, Ambrose, yeo., Denston, 1615. R2/49/315; W1/72/94
Ambrose, clothier, Denham, 1695. R2/72/570; W1/149/120
Anne, als. Smyth, wid., Clare, 1550. R2/21/166; W1/9/128
Henry, als. Smyth, Alpheton, 1565. R2/32/267; W1/27/159
John, clothier, Hartest, (1672). W1/312/3
John, bach., Hartest, 1683. A5/6/73, A4/20/108
John, yeo., Stansfield, 1580. R2/38/151; W1/39/136
John, yeo., Stansfield, 1619. R2/51/313; W1/132/32
John, Stansfield, 1676. A5/5/164, A4/13/70
John, Stansfield, 1677. In. 3/18/50
John, Wicken, 1516. R2/13/220
Ralph, als. Fuller, labourer, Acton, 1546. R2/21/180; W1/10/122
Richard, als. Smythe, Alpheton, 1563. R2/31/153; W1/26/34
Robert, als. Smythe, Clare, 1539. R2/20/220
ORBYLL, John, Stansfield, 1515. R2/13/218
ORDERS, Thomas, carpenter, Exning, 1623. R2/52/703; W1/79/117
Thomas, Exning, 1632. A5/4/18
William, Great Wratting, 1628. R2/54/294; W1/85/12
ORDERWCH, William, Hitcham, 1472. R2/10/499
ORDEWE, Thomas, scrivener, Bury St. Edmunds, 1500. R2/4/102
ORGER, Thomas, Mendlesham, 1454. R2/9/230
ORICE, John, yeo., Hitcham, 1695. R2/72/538; W1/149/94
ORIDGE, John, husb., Lakenheath, 1595, (N). R2/43/20; W1/53/15
ORLOW(E), Agnes, wife of John, bladesmith, Bury St. Edmunds, 1519. R2/6/64
John, bladesmith, Bury St. Edmunds, 1519. R2/6/60
ORME, John, miller, Lakenheath, 1584. R2/39/216; W1/42/111
ORMES, Agnes, wid., Burwell, 1619. R2/51/476; W1/132/137
James, Bury St. Edmunds, 1694. R5/6/165; W4/116/6
John, maltster, Bury St. Edmunds, 1623. R2/52/605; W1/79/54
John, Bury St. Edmunds, 1684. A5/6/78, A4/21/47
John, Yaxley, 1643. A5/4/99
Robert, Brandon, 1601. R2/44/380; W1/59/39
ORMYS, Nicholas, baker, Bildeston, 1539. R2/4/218; W1/4/164
see also Oarmes
ORNYSBY, Richard, fuller, Bury St. Edmunds, 1498. R2/4/67
ORRELL, Anne, Glemsford, 1615, (N). R2/49/370; W1/72/139
ORRIS, Stephen, 1607. R2/46/153; W1/98/99

ORSBY, John, Bury St. Edmunds, 1550. R2/8/14
see also Orysby, Osby, Ourysby, Owrsby
ORVICE, Edward, thatcher, Rattlesden, 1677. R2/66/499; W1/129/79; In. 3/18/98
ORVIS, Edward, thatcher, Stanton, 1684. R2/69/228; W1/138/33
Edward, thatcher, Stanton, 1693. R2/72/150
John, thatcher, Stanton, 1665. R2/63/331; W1/117/76; In. 3/10/111
ORWELL, Joan, Wicken, 1555. R2/24/219; W1/15/49
Michael, Wicken, 1556. R2/25/60; W1/16/70
Richard, herdsman, Ixworth, 1559. R2/28/383; W1/3/85
Robert, Wicken, 1549. R2/21/502; W1/28/152
Thomas, Aylsham, 1517. W1/51/60
William, Wicken, 1555. R2/24/166; W1/15/9
ORY, Elisabeth, singlewoman, Knettishall, 1635. R2/56/455; W1/91/17
ORYELL, Robert, Soham, 1558. R2/27/395
ORYSBY, William, weaver, Bury St. Edmunds, 1518. R2/6/51
OSBEE, Charles, blacksmith, Fordham, 1694. R2/72/298; W1/148/24
OSBERN(E), Agnes, Rickinghall Inferior, 1504. R2/12/29
Alice, wife of John, Bury St. Edmunds, 1420. R2/1/151
Geoffrey, Stow, 1458. R2/9/201
Henry, rector, Fornham St. Martin, 1442. R2/1/263
John, Bury St. Edmunds, 1354. R2/1/1
John, Bury St. Edmunds, 1413. R2/1/133
John, currier, Bury St. Edmunds, 1497. R2/4/59
John, Rickinghall Inferior, 1512. R2/13/220
Nicholas, currier, Bury St. Edmunds, 1463. R2/2/78
William, Cotton, 1463. R2/9/308
OSBOND, Richard, yeo., Wickhambrook, 1676. R2/66/410; W1/128/120; In. 3/17/158
OSBONE, John, yeo., Cockfield, 1660. R2/62/150; W1/112/197; In. 3/5/184
OSBORNE, Alice, wid., Bury St. Edmunds, 1627. R2/54/53; W1/83/59a
Alice, wid., Rickinghall Inferior, 1578. R2/37/361; W1/36/215
Ann, wid., Finningham, 1540. R2/20/272
Christian, wid., Wattisfield, 1679. R2/67/238; W1/133/8
Edmund, yeo., Diss, 1668. R2/64/382; W1/120/101
Edmund, husb., Great Thornham, 1636. R2/57/110; W1/92/130
Edmund, Harleston, 1668. A5/5/98, A4/82/89
Edmund, Haughley, 1696. A5/6/189, A4/39/59
Edmund, labourer, Shelland, 1594, (N). R2/42/575; W1/52/22
Elisabeth, wid., Wattisfield, 1629. R2/54/337; W1/85/46
Francis, Wattisfield, 1608, (N). R2/46/217; W1/65/117
George, Elmswell, 1690. A5/6/139, A4/33/8
George, Stanton, 1596. R2/41/443; W1/47/108
George, the elder, pewterer, Sudbury, 1605. R2/45/390; W1/63/20
George, pewterer, Sudbury, 1638. R2/57/373; W1/93/176
George, yeo., Wetherden, 1683. R2/69/105; W1/137/81
James, Bury St. Edmunds, 1642. A5/4/97
Joan, wid., Sudbury, 1623. R2/52/676; W1/79/95
John, yeo., Finningham, 1642. R2/58/400; W1/99/117
John, Haverhill, 1640. A5/4/86
John, labourer, Norton, 1606. R2/46/58; W1/64/82
John, Norton, 1667. In. 3/12/160; A5/5/85, A4/5/47
John, wid., Norton, 1685. A5/6/94, A4/24/95
John, yeo., Old Newton, 1643. R2/59/23; W1/100/33
John, yeo., Old Newton, 1679. R2/67/438; W1/133/168
John, yeo., Shelland, 1639. R2/58/107; W1/94/177
John, Stowmarket, 1660. In. 3/5/131; A5/5/6, A4/1/189
John, yeo., Thrandeston, 1691. R2/71/465
John, gent., Wattisfield, 1619. R2/51/334; W1/132/47
John, gent., Wattisfield, 1651. R2/61/442
John, chairmaker, Wickhambrook, 1648. R2/60/7; W1/105/11
Josias, Elmsett, 1638. R2/57/438; W1/93/279
Katherine, Chilton, 1589. A5/2/114b
Margaret, wid., Bildeston, 1637, (N). R2/57/239; W1/92/294
Margaret, wid., Combs, 1692. A5/6/150, A4/34/26
Margaret, wid., Stowmarket, 1652. A3/4/11, A5/4/141
Mary, Clare, 1665, (N). R2/63/378; W1/117/131; In. 3/10/161; A5/5/70
Nicholas, yeo., Bildeston, 1652. R2/61/585; W1/109/58; In. 3/4/65
Nicholas, Chelsworth, 1634. A5/4/31
Nicholas, yeo., Stoke by Clare, 1677. R2/66/433; W1/129/6; In. 3/18/1

OSBORNE continued
Richard, Stowmarket, 1551. R2/23/104; W1/11/44
Richard, clothier, Stowmarket, 1586. R2/40/239; W1/44/80
Richard, clothier, Stowmarket, 1623. R2/52/586; W1/79/38
Richard, Stowmarket, 1679. R2/67/291; W1/133/77
Richard, Sudbury, 1641. R2/58/305; W1/98/101
Richard, Wickhambrook, 1697. A5/6/191, A4/39/87
Robert, sen., Bildeston, 1669. In. 3/14/185; A5/5/104, A4/7/31
Robert, yeo., Great Cornard, 1682. R2/68/289; W1/136/22; In. 3/21/11
Robert, Great Wratting, 1678. In. 3/19/131; A5/6/9, A4/15/72
Robert, husb., Mellis, 1562. R2/31/99; W1/8/91
Susan, wid., Haughley, 1686. A5/6/105, A4/26/26
Susan, als. Bryde, Wickhambrook, 1671. A5/5/121, A4/86/18
Thomas, yeo., Bury St. Edmunds, 1587. R2/40/134; W1/44/14
Thomas, Edwardstone, 1679. A5/6/25, A4/16/102
Thomas, yeo., Little Harleston, 1681. R2/68/105; W1/135/79
Thomas, yeo., Norton, 1602. R2/45/117; W1/60/34
Thomas, Wattisfield, 1671. A5/5/122, A4/8/19
William, yeo., Badwell Ash, 1640. R2/58/183; W1/96/102
William, Bury St. Edmunds, 1591. A5/2/148
William, Layham, 1679. A5/6/27, A4/16/129
William, yeo., Walsham le Willows, 1610, (N). R2/47/140; W1/67/24
OSBOURNE, Elizabeth, wid., Bury St. Edmunds, 1610. R2/47/267; W1/67/150
John, Bures, 1638. A5/4/57
Robert, Sudbury, 1555. R2/24/215; W1/15/45
OSBURNE, Agnes, wid., Bury St. Edmunds, 1587, (N). R2/40/214; W1/44/66
Edward, husb., Assington, 1685. R2/70/107; W1/139/94
John, goldsmith, Sudbury, 1532. R2/19/112
Robert, husb., Stanton, 1664, (N). R2/63/129; W1/116/13; In. 3/9/50; A5/5/56, A4/2/27
Thomas, yeo., Cavendish, 1661. R2/62/278; W1/113/186; In. 3/6/260
William, yeo., Westhorpe, 1642. R2/58/351; W1/99/51
see also Hosbern, Hynes als. Osborne, Ode als. Osborne
OSBY, Amy, wid., Bury St. Edmunds, 1558. R2/8/341; W1/17/80
OSLER, Edmund, yeo., Woolpit, 1609. R2/47/4; W1/66/4
Thomas, husb., Soham, 1689. R2/71/188; W1/143/43
OSMOND, Elisabeth, wid., Nedging, 1679. R2/67/209; W1/133/18
Henry, Walsham le Willows, 1585. A5/2/64
John, husb., Assington, 1470. R2/10/457; W1/24/138 & 178
John, Polstead, 1477. R2/11/82
Margery, wid. of John, sen., Polstead, 1478. R2/11/162
Robert, the elder, mercer, Bildeston, 1531. R2/19/64
Robert, yeo., Nedging, 1663. R2/63/90; W1/115/140; In. 3/8/173
OSMUND, Agnes, wid., Bildeston, 1640. R2/58/174; W1/96/92
Henry, yeo., Nedging, 1638. R2/57/304; W1/93/78
Joan, wid., Bildeston, 1572. R2/36/33; W1/31/129
John, tailor, Bildeston, 1527. R2/17/222; W1/1/17
OSTELAR, Robert, husb., Rougham, 1551. R2/23/65; W1/11/45
OSTELER, John, Bury St. Edmunds, 1417. R2/1/148
Peter, carpenter, Hundon, 1626. R2/53/609; W1/82/135
Roger, Shelland, 1439. R2/9/3
OSTLER, Abraham, tailor, Bury St. Edmunds, 1614. R2/49/20; W1/71/17
Alice, wid., Rede, 1589. R2/41/296; W1/46/16
Augustine, carpenter, Bury St. Edmunds, 1578. R2/37/417; W1/36/155
George, Felsham, (1530). R2/19/42
George, husb., Rede, 1580. R2/38/159; W1/39/132
Joan, wid., Felsham, 1533. R2/19/176; W1/2/54
Peter, carpenter, Hundon, 1647. R2/59/448; W1/104/78; In. 3/2/79
Ralph, tailor, Great Thurlow, 1624. R2/53/56; W1/80/80
Robert, husb., Bures, 1628. R2/54/163; W1/86/39
Robert, carpenter, Hundon, 1662. In. 3/7/67
Robert, Little Cornard, 1585. R2/39/259; W1/42/315
Robert, blacksmith, Stansfield, 1581. R2/38/271; W1/40/21
Robert, blacksmith, Stansfield, 1581, (N). R2/38/320; W1/40/62
Thomas, Little Thurlow, 1642. A5/4/92 & 94
see also Hostler, Osler, Ostelar
OTELEY, Alice, wid., Kentford, 1605. R2/45/394; W1/63/33

OTLEY, William, the elder, yeo., Dalham, 1679. R2/67/270; W1/133/59
William, the elder, yeo., Lidgate, 1566. R2/32/332; W1/28/55
William, weaver, Lidgate, 1610. R2/47/263; W1/67/145
OTLYE, John, Kirtling, 1595. A5/2/217
OTTELE, Agnes, wid., Bury St. Edmunds, 1504. R2/4/156
John, Little Saxham, 1443. R2/9/46
William, Little Saxham, 1483. R2/11/282
OTTELEY, John, Kirtling, 1544. R2/21/603
OTTLEE, Ralph, Bury St. Edmunds, 1500. R2/4/94
OTTLEY, Margaret, wife of Harry, Bardwell, 1503. R2/13/133
William, husb., Ashley, 1692. R2/72/2; W1/146/2; In. 3/24/102
William, wid., Dalham, 1678. A5/6/11, A4/15/93
William, Little Saxham, 1439. R2/9/5
OTTRINGTON, Peter, shoe maker, Sudbury, 1563. R2/37/136; W1/26/17
OTTWELL, John, Bury St. Edmunds, 1609. A5/3/74
Thomas, Stradishall, 1670, (N). R2/65/40; W1/122/45; In. 3/15/60; A5/5/113
OULAY, John, chaplain, Brundish, 1355. R2/1/4
OULDIS, Alexander, gent., Hoxne, 1665. In. 3/10/178
OULFYEL, William, Kennett, 1612. R2/48/183; W1/69/64
OUNDSWORTH, William, cordwainer, Eye, 1683. R2/69/99; W1/137/76
see also Ownsworth
OURYSBY, John, jun., woolman, Bury St. Edmunds, 1448. R2/2/25
OUTLAW, George, Stowmarket, 1636. A5/4/46
Thomas, Bury St. Edmunds, 1690. A4/32/31
Thomas, inn holder, Bury St. Edmunds, 1699. R2/73/407; W1/153/50
OVERALL, Giles, parson, Aldham, (1543). R2/19/358; W1/6/153
OVEREND, John, yeo., Whepstead, 1620. R2/52/65; W1/76/53
Thomasine, wid., Bury St. Edmunds, 1604. R2/45/348; W1/62/69
OVEREY, John, skinner, Kentford, 1477. R2/11/104
Thomas, Ingham, 1480. R2/11/205
OVERSOTH, Thomas, Bury St. Edmunds, 1535. R2/7/27
OVERSOUTH, William, Westley, 1443. R2/9/41
OVERSTALL, Thomas, husb., Kersey, (1668). R2/66/120
OVERTON, Joan, Bury St. Edmunds, 1413. R2/1/133
Petronella, wife of Richard, Bury St. Edmunds, 1380. R2/1/40
Richard, spicer, Bury St. Edmunds, 1370. R2/1/29
OVYRMEDOW, Nicholas, Soham, 1460. W1/24/62
OWEN, Nathaniel, bach., Little Thurlow, 1683. A5/6/72, A4/20/97
William, the elder, brazier, Newmarket, 1693. R2/72/188; W1/147/77
OWERS, Charles, yeo., Wickhambrook, 1638. R2/57/353; W1/93/143
John, husb., Fordham, 1646. R2/59/360; W1/103/74
John, Fordham, 1694. A5/6/168, A4/37/31
John, the elder, yeo., Wickhambrook, 1610. R2/47/123; W1/67/9
John, Wickhambrook, 1673. A5/5/142, A4/88/84
Margaret, Long Melford, 1536. R2/19/260
Richard, husb., Wickhambrook, 1559. R2/28/408; W1/3/4
Richard, Wickhambrook, 1648. A5/4/123
Robert, singleman, Lawshall, 1650. R2/61/379; W1/107/80; In. 3/3/99
Robert, Risby, 1696. A5/6/185, A4/39/7
William, Newmarket, 1632. A5/4/21
William, Wood Ditton, 1668. In. 3/13/100; A5/5/100, A4/6/106
OWEY, John, brazier, Bury St. Edmunds, 1475. R2/2/211
OWLES, Thomas, gent., Risby, 1642. R2/58/319; W1/99/7
OWNG, Catherine, Market Weston, 1520. R2/15/81
OWNSWORTH, John, cordwainer, Eye, 1669. In. 3/14/164; A5/5/108, A4/7/55
OWRHEY, Letitia, als. Hervy, Icklingham, 1475. R2/11/116
OWRSBY, Thomas, sen., weaver, Bury St. Edmunds, 1537. R2/7/43
OWSBIE, George, Homersfield, 1594. W1/51/251
OXAR, Thomas, als. Farrowe, husb., Woolpit, 1665. R2/63/318; W1/117/57; In. 3/10/8
OXBOROUGH, Edward, gent., Bury St. Edmunds, 1699. R2/73/359; W1/153/18
Samuel, grocer, Bury St. Edmunds, 1698. R2/73/301; W1/152/72
OXBOROWE, George, butcher, Sudbury, 1624. R2/53/62; W1/80/84
John, gent., Sudbury, (1544). R2/19/440, R2/21/592
OXBORROWE, Alexander, maltster, Bury St. Edmunds, 1650. R2/61/338; W1/107/34; In. 3/3/47
OXE, John, husb., Bury St. Edmunds, 1632. R2/56/121; W1/89/8
John, yeo., Drinkstone, 1669. R2/64/443; W1/121/29; In. 3/14/4

OXE continued
Robert, yeo., Hunston, 1645. R2/59/265; W1/102/80
Thomas, maltster, Bury St. Edmunds, 1633, (N). R2/56/266; W1/90/30
OXFORD, John, barber, Bury St. Edmunds, (1557). R2/8/318; W1/18/49
Richard, husb., Wattisfield, 1696. R2/73/71; W1/150/84
Simon, Bury St. Edmunds, 1558. R2/8/346; W1/17/67
OXFURD, James, Long Melford, 1695. R2/72/523; W1/149/77

P

PACHARELL, John, Hartest, (1528). W1/19/31
PACHETT, Robert, Mildenhall, 1488. R2/11/410
PACK, Thomas, Occold, 1557. R2/26/244; W1/20/160
William, Sudbury, 1694. A5/6/174, A4/37/95
see also Pake, Pakke
PACKARD, Elisabeth, wid., Mendlesham, 1681. A5/6/47, A4/18/50
George, cooper, Stowupland, 1664. R2/63/224; W1/116/138; In. 3/9/182
John, yeo., Mendlesham, 1661. R2/62/157; W1/113/1; In. 3/6/21
John, bach., Mendlesham, 1681. A5/6/47, A4/18/48 & 49
Nicholas, Mendlesham, 1621. R2/52/346; W1/77/125
Thomas, cooper, Stowmarket, 1680. R2/67/623; W1/134/89; In. 3/20/100
Mary, singlewoman, Stowupland, 1667. In. 3/12/167; A5/5/88, A4/5/73
PACKERD, Mary, wid., Stowmarket, 1663. R2/63/57; W1/115/88; In. 3/8/104
see also Pakard
PADGE, Alexander, baker, Sudbury, 1602. R2/45/119; W1/60/37
Thomas, miller, Soham, 1591. R2/42/168; W1/48/78
PADLEY, Thomas, labourer, Whatfield, 1583. R2/39/86; W1/42/25
PADNALE, John, Stowmarket, 1476. R2/11/75
PADNALL, Thomas, cooper, Stanton, 1669. R2/64/478; W1/121/70; In. 3/14/103
see also Cotton als. Padnall
PADYLL, William, Snailwell, 1482. R2/11/267
PAFOOTT, Ames, Isleham, 1560. W7/21
PAGE, Abigail, wid., Bury St. Edmunds, 1669. R2/64/457; W1/121/46; In. 3/14/53
Agnes, wid., Brandon, 1569. A5/1/211
Agnes, wid., Pakenham, 1589. R2/41/262; W1/46/44
Agnes, wid., Sudbury, 1603. R2/45/277; W1/61/81
Alice, spinster, Ickworth, 1473. R2/10/548
Alice, wid., Thurston, 1695. A5/6/178, A4/38/28
Ann, spinster, Felsham, 1694. R2/72/309; W1/148/37
Ann, wid. of Philip, Pakenham, 1679. R2/67/418; W1/133/155
Anne, wid., Icklingham, 1633. R2/56/305; W1/90/72
Ben, Haverhill, 1663. In. 3/8/185; A5/5/51
Edmund, ash burner, Stowmarket, 1561. R2/30/25; W1/28/217
Edmund, als. Baxter, gent., Sudbury, 1585. R2/40/7; W1/43/6
Edmund, Walsham le Willows, 1503. R2/12/65
Edward, woollen draper, Bury St. Edmunds, 1663. In. 3/8/77
Edward, gent., Westley, (1553). R2/37/100; W1/13/71
Elisabeth, wid., Hawstead, 1645. R2/59/189; W1/102/19
Geoffrey, husb., Barton Mills, 1596. R2/43/187; W1/54/87
George, Bury St. Edmunds, 1648, (N). R2/60/135; W1/105/161
George, singleman, Langham, 1665. R2/63/314; W1/117/47
George, yeo., Walsham le Willows, 1619. R2/51/466; W1/132/130
Gregory, yeo., Hinderclay, 1629. R2/54/302; W1/85/17
Helen, wid., Icklingham, 1636. R2/57/28; W1/92/37
Henry, Bury St. Edmunds, 1482. R2/2/332
Henry, weaver, Bury St. Edmunds, 1692. R2/72/24; W1/146/23
Henry, yeo., Palgrave, 1643. R2/59/17; W1/100/26
Henry, sen., Walsham le Willows, 1696. A5/6/189, A4/39/62
Isabel, wid., Fornham St. Martin, 1474. R2/11/24
James, inn holder, Bury St. Edmunds, 1685. R2/70/152; W1/139/130
James, husb., Lakenheath, 1606. R2/46/53; W1/64/69
James, Rattlesden, 1562. A5/1/123
Joan, wid., Burgate, 1568. R2/33/12; W1/29/19; A5/1/200
Joan, wid., Hunston, 1582. R2/38/362; W1/41/81
John, thatcher, Brandon, 1674. R2/66/77; W1/126/44
John, weaver, Brockford, 1558. R2/27/342
John, Bury St. Edmunds, 1367. R2/1/20

PAGE continued
John, Bury St. Edmunds, 1405. R2/1/107
John, sen., butcher, Bury St. Edmunds, 1442. R2/1/265
John, locksmith, Bury St. Edmunds, 1479. R2/2/275
John, chaplain, Bury St. Edmunds, 1499. R2/4/77
John, scrivener, Bury St. Edmunds, 1509. R2/4/210
John, the elder, Bury St. Edmunds, 1526. R2/7/59
John, webster, Glemsford, 1685. R2/70/12; W1/139/13
John, husb., Hinderclay, 1578. R2/37/363; W1/36/212
John, cordwainer, Hopton, 1681. R2/68/48; W1/135/41
John, Hunston, 1568. R2/33/65; W1/29/84
John, Hunston, 1649. A5/4/130 & 137
John, Icklingham, 1545. R2/19/566; W1/7/64
John, Ickworth, 1473. R2/10/548
John, Ingham, 1676. In. 3/17/3; A5/5/159, A4/13/6
John, Ixworth, 1452. R2/9/100
John, goldsmith, Ixworth, 1539. R2/19/332
John, clerk, Ixworth, 1674. R2/66/79; W1/126/40
John, victualler, Ixworth, 1696. R2/73/83; W1/150/69; In. 3/25/46
John, singleman, Langham, 1639. R2/58/67; W1/94/115; A5/4/76
John, Mildenhall, 1558. R2/27/19; W1/31/27
John, Rougham, 1593. A5/2/189
John, Stanstead, 1462. R2/10/312
John, husb., Stowupland, 1674. R2/67/100; W1/126/17
John, Thurston, 1524. R2/12/135
John, yeo., Thurston, 1584. R2/39/188; W1/42/139
John, Thurston, 1694. A5/6/173, A4/37/81
John, Thurston, 1695. A5/6/178, A4/38/29
John, the elder, yeo., Walsham le Willows, 1606. R2/46/7; W1/64/9
John, Walsham le Willows, 1640. A5/4/83
John, gent., Walsham le Willows, 1667. R2/64/290; W1/119/154; In. 3/14/135
John, the younger, cordwainer, Wattisfield, 1672. R2/65/311; W1/124/34
John, the elder, gent., Westley, 1535. R2/19/209; W1/3/181
John, gent., Westley, (1546). R2/21/648; W1/9/71
John, Wetherden, 1487. R2/11/386
John, Withersfield, 1541. R2/21/1; W1/10/37
John, Worlington, 1472. R2/10/507
John, Wortham, 1473. R2/11/26
John, yeo., Wortham, 1557. R2/26/278; W1/20/198
John, 1540. W1/51/65
Joseph, labourer, Hawstead, (1675). W1/312/2
Joseph, Stowmarket, 1672. A5/5/134, A4/9/76
Katherine, wid., Bury St. Edmunds, 1454. R2/2/46
Katherine, Rickinghall Superior, 1478. R2/11/173
Katherine, Stowmarket, 1483. R2/11/290
Katherine, Woolpit, 1606. R2/46/2; W1/64/3; In. 5/3/5
Lawrence, Rattlesden, 1632. R2/56/204; W1/89/122
Margaret, wid., Bury St. Edmunds, 1611. A5/3/110
Margaret, Kirtling, 1472. R2/10/507
Margaret, wid., Thurston, 1558. R2/27/563; W1/31/15
Margery, wid., Bury St. Edmunds, 1540. R2/8/4
Margery, wid., Cowlinge, 1616. R2/50/67; W1/73/77
Marian, wid., Walsham le Willows, 1559. R2/28/209; W1/22/206
Mary, wid., Bury St. Edmunds, 1620. R2/52/11; W1/76/10
Mary, wid., Walsham le Willows, 1626, (N). R2/53/605; W1/82/131
Mary, Walsham le Willows, 1640. A5/4/79
Mary, wid., Wetherden, 1684. R2/69/360; W1/138/150
Michael, glover, Haverhill, 1619. R2/51/367; W1/132/66
Paul, yeo., Ixworth Thorpe, 1632. R2/56/205; W1/89/123
Phillip, yeo., Pakenham, 1583. W1/40/44
Phillip, yeo., Pakenham, 1678. R2/67/124; W1/130/109; In. 3/19/153
Phillip, yeo., Thurston, 1601. R2/44/405; W1/59/62
Phillip, yeo., Thurston, (1676). W1/312/19
Phillippa, wid., Long Melford, 1592. R2/42/321; W1/49/141
Prudence, wid., Hunston, 1676. R2/66/312; W1/128/14; In. 3/17/8
Richard, Bury St. Edmunds, 1478. R2/2/254
Richard, Bury St. Edmunds, 1562. A5/1/135
Richard, glover, Haverhill, 1619. R2/51/388; W1/132/79
Richard, husb., Icklingham, 1558. R2/27/559; W1/31/9 & 10
Richard, Walsham le Willows, 1478. R2/11/151

PAGE continued
Richard, husb., Walsham le Willows, 1557. R2/26/308; W1/20/254
Richard, yeo., Walsham le Willows, 1639. R2/58/37; W1/94/67
Richard, Withersfield, 1560. A5/1/100
Robert, locksmith, Bury St. Edmunds, 1465. R2/2/88
Robert, yeo., Bury St. Edmunds, 1574. R2/37/3; W1/33/92
Robert, yeo., Cawston, 1594. W1/51/114
Robert, yeo., Gazeley, 1620. R2/52/55; W1/76/46
Robert, Great Bradley, 1592. R2/42/245; W1/49/60
Robert, Great Saxham, 1470. R2/10/483
Robert, Hundon, 1568, (N). R2/33/23; W1/29/36
Robert, yeo., Hunston, 1600. R2/45/8; W1/58/12
Robert, Hunston, 1649. A5/4/130 & 137
Robert, Langham, 1638. A5/4/62
Robert, Stowmarket, 1495. R2/13/20
Roger, Bury St. Edmunds, 1499. R2/4/87
Roger, Wicken, 1651. R2/61/473; W1/108/62
Simon, yeo., Eriswell, (1550). R2/21/130; W1/9/90 & 110
Sybil, wid., Walsham le Willows, 1640. R2/58/227; W1/96/173
Thomas, blacksmith, Brandon, 1600. R2/45/78; W1/58/111
Thomas, Bury St. Edmunds, 1437. R2/1/227
Thomas, Gasthorpe, 1578, (N). R2/37/368; W1/36/208
Thomas, husb., Groton, 1626. R2/53/563; W1/82/90
Thomas, yeo., Hawstead, 1637. R2/57/146; W1/92/182
Thomas, Hunston, 1556. R2/25/116; W1/16/129
Thomas, yeo., Hunston, 1623. R2/52/598; W1/79/49
Thomas, yeo., Hunston, 1648. R2/60/91; W1/105/112
Thomas, jun., Hunston, 1649. A5/4/130 & 137
Thomas, Hunston, 1664. In. 3/9/135; A5/5/60, A4/2/66
Thomas, yeo., Icklingham, 1624. R2/53/19; W1/80/29
Thomas, Ickworth, 1472. R2/10/542
Thomas, gent., Long Melford, 1686. R2/70/248; W1/140/19
Thomas, husb., Ousden, 1605. R2/45/391; W1/63/19
Thomas, yeo., Pakenham, 1596. R2/43/132; W1/54/10
Thomas, yeo., Palgrave, 1698. R2/75/224; W1/152/6
Thomas, Thorpe Morieux, 1611. A5/3/114
Thomas, Thurston, 1546. R2/21/636; W1/28/124
Thomas, yeo., Thurston, 1681. R2/68/75; W1/135/59
Thomas, the elder, Walsham le Willows, 1618. R2/51/115; W1/75/72
Thomas, weaver, Wicken, 1640. R2/58/163; W1/96/75
Thomas, yeo., Wicken, 1686. R2/70/234; W1/140/3; In. 3/22/101
Walter, Eye, 1462. R2/10/362
Walter, Ickworth, 1440. R2/9/26
Walter, Lavenham, 1469. R2/10/455
William, carpenter, Brandon, 1626. R2/53/580; W1/82/112
William, linen weaver, Bury St. Edmunds, 1697. R2/73/127; W1/151/17
William, tailor, Great Ashfield, 1607. R2/46/149; W1/97/92
William, carpenter, Great Horningsheath, 1562. R2/31/4; W1/8/133
William, shepherd, Icklingham, 1612. R2/48/208; W1/69/100
William, yeo., Ingham, 1637. R2/57/145; W1/92/181
William, Risby, 1506. W1/36/18
William, Soham, 1533. W1/2/53
William, yeo., Thurston, 1573. R2/36/204; W1/32/106
William, yeo., Walsham le Willows, 1542. R2/22/53; W1/6/29 & 61
William, tailor, Walsham le Willows, 1624. R2/53/24; W1/80/34
William, the elder, yeo., Walsham le Willows, 1628. R2/54/132; W1/84/3
PAINE, Abraham, yeo., Glemsford, 1686. In. 3/22/24; A5/6/99, A4/26/97
Ambrose, wool comber, Lawshall, 1686. R2/70/243; W1/140/13
Ann, wid., Lavenham, 1646. R2/59/291; W1/103/6
Ann, Lavenham, 1695. A5/6/180, A4/38/55
Anthony, gent., Bury St. Edmunds, 1607. R2/46/104
Christian, wid., Glemsford, 1692. In. 3/24/64
Clement, singleman, Great Fakenham, 1676. W1/312/12
Edward, Bury St. Edmunds, 1686. A4/26/1
Edward, husb., Ickworth, 1649. R2/60/221; W1/106/70
Elisabeth, Felsham, 1681. A5/6/54, A4/18/124
Elisabeth, singlewoman, Ingham, 1660. R2/62/68; W1/112/87; A5/5/6, A4/1/198
Gabriel, Clare, 1683. A5/6/67, A4/20/22
George, yeo., Stanstead, 1665. In. 3/10/113; A5/5/66, A4/3/21

PAINE continued
  Giles, Lawshall, 1533. W1/2/57
  Hester, wid., Long Melford, 1637. A5/4/50
  John, weaver, Great Cornard, 1685. R2/70/33; W1/139/29
  John, Thelnetham, 1663. In. 3/8/8; A5/5/42
  Margaret, Barrow, 1675. R2/66/203; W1/127/78; In. 3/16/107
  Margaret, Lackford, 1684. A5/6/83, A4/21/98
  Richard, Groton, 1638, (N). R2/57/379; W1/93/184
  Richard, Hartest, 1667. In. 3/12/140; A5/5/89, A4/5/80
  Richard, jun., Lavenham, 1688. A5/6/124, A4/29/97
  Richard, yeo., Little Waldingfield, 1619. R2/51/270; W1/132/12
  Richard, Stanstead, 1681. A5/6/47, A4/18/47
  Robert, clothworker, Boxford, 1665. In. 3/11/2; A5/5/71, A4/9/82
  Robert, Brettenham, 1684. A5/6/77, A4/21/35
  Samuel, Brent Eleigh, 1672. A5/5/131, A4/9/49
  Stephen, Kedington, 1684. A5/6/77, A4/21/34
  Thomas, Bury St. Edmunds, 1634. A5/4/33
  Thomas, baker, Bury St. Edmunds, 1680. In. 3/20/252; A5/6/36, A4/17/51
  Thomas, Cockfield, 1624. R2/53/165; W1/80/145
  William, Bures, 1661. In. 3/6/128; A5/5/16, A4/1/93
  William, Fornham All Saints, 1678. In. 3/19/165; A5/6/11, A4/15/91
  William, blacksmith, Lakenheath, 1699. R2/73/413; W1/153/55; In. 3/26/5
  William, clothier, Lavenham, 1673. R2/65/451; W1/125/81
  William, Little Livermere, 1680. In. 3/20/12; A5/6/31, A4/17/8
  William, Saxham, 1546. R2/21/649
  William, Stanstead, 1568. In. 3/23/22; A5/6/118, A4/29/23
  William, Thelnetham, 1565. A5/1/161
  see also Payne
PAINTER, Daniel, maltster, Sudbury, 1694. R2/72/395; W1/148/125; A5/6/170, A4/37/49
  Daniel, Sudbury, 1697. A5/6/4, A4/40/59
  Nicholas, Bury St. Edmunds, 1695. A5/6/178, A4/38/27
  see also Paynter, Peyntor
PAKARD, John, Bury St. Edmunds, 1389. R2/1/57
PAKE, John, Occold, 1540. R2/19/602
PAKENHAM, John, Cockfield, 1452. R2/9/129
  Richard, Bury St. Edmunds, 1384. R2/1/48
  Thomas, Bacton, 1564. R2/32/120; W1/27/72
  Thomas, Ixworth, 1504. R2/12/70
PAKKE, Robert, Walsham le Willows, 1477. R2/11/49
  William, Eye, 1459. R2/9/269
PALE, John, cook, Pakenham, 1664. R2/63/205; W1/116/112; In. 3/9/141
PALEYSER, John, Culford, 1445. R2/9/64
PALFREMAN, William, parson, Worlington, (1544). R2/21/604
PALFREY, Agnes, Pakenham, 1593. A5/2/193
  John, yeo., Pakenham, 1624. R2/53/29; W1/80/39
  Margaret, wid., Pakenham, 1685. R2/70/189; W1/139/158; A5/6/95, A4/24/111b
  see also Palfrie, Palphry
PALFREYMAN, Richard, Bury St. Edmunds, 1519. R2/6/61
  see also Palfreman
PALFRIE, Nicholas, yeo., Pakenham, 1622. R2/52/356; W1/78/4
PALGRAVE, Geoffrey, carpenter, Brockford, 1638. R2/57/393; W1/93/208
  Geoffrey, husb., Wetheringsett, 1540. R2/21/383; W1/38/74
  John, husb., Wetheringsett, 1551. R2/23/34; W1/11/46
  Olive, als. Porter, wife of William, Stoke by Nayland, 1479. R2/12/3
  Robert, Langham, 1563. A5/1/143
  Theophilus, yeo., Mendlesham, 1621. R2/52/329; W1/77/110
  Thomas, Wetheringsett, 1551. R2/23/25; W1/11/47
  Thomas, Wetheringsett, 1602. R2/45/192; W1/60/120
  William, Newmarket, 1452. R2/9/110
  see also Pelgrave
PALLANT, see Laund als. Pallant, Laund als. Pallaunte
PALLYNGTON, Thomas, Mildenhall, 1559. R2/28/96; W1/22/93
PALMER, Abraham, labourer, Burwell, 1682. R2/68/310; W1/136/36; In. 3/21/169
  Ann, wid., Burwell, 1683. R2/69/88; W1/137/66; A5/6/69, A4/20/44
  Catherine, wid., Lakenheath, 1666. In. 3/11/103; A5/5/79, A4/4/81
  Clement, husb., Soham, 1667. R2/64/251; W1/119/114; In. 3/12/190

PALMER continued
Edmund, Combs, 1578. R2/37/356; W1/36/219
Edmund, yeo., Combs, 1614. R2/49/34; W1/71/28
Edmund, Lakenheath, 1666. A5/5/79, A4/4/82
Edmund, singleman, Lakenheath, 1667. R2/64/180; W1/119/16; In. 3/12/2
Elisabeth, wid., Burwell, 1692. R2/72/22; W1/146/20
Elisabeth, wid., Lakenheath, 1688. R2/71/132; W1/142/120
Elisabeth, wid., Soham, 1686. R2/70/533; W1/140/137; In. 3/22/123
Ellen, Burwell, 1694. R2/72/383; W1/148/111
George, the elder, Burwell, 1661. In. 3/6/65; A5/5/14, A4/1/116
George, the elder, Burwell, 1684. A5/6/80, A4/21/68
George, Rattlesden, 1581. A5/2/31
Henry, Elmswell, 1449. R2/9/99
Henry, gent., Norwich, 1594. W1/51/126
Isabel, Bury St. Edmunds, 1428. R2/1/184
Joan, Burwell, 1592. R2/42/193; W1/49/18
Joan, wid., Combs, 1585, (N). R2/39/374; W1/42/234
John, Bury St. Edmunds, 1428. R2/1/186
John, tailor, Bury St. Edmunds, 1435. R2/1/214
John, fishmonger, Bury St. Edmunds, 1583. R2/39/121; W1/42/1
John, husb., Combs, 1546. R2/21/197; W1/10/115
John, Great Finborough, 1604. R2/45/309; W1/62/9
John, Icklingham, 1527. W1/19/13
John, Kersey, 1636. A5/4/43
John, Lakenheath, 1687. A5/6/115, A4/27/94
John, Soham, 1451. R2/9/106
John, Soham, 1524. R2/12/130
John, Soham, 1648. A5/4/125
John, wool comber, Soham, 1668. R2/64/310; W1/120/16; In. 3/13/32
John, the younger, Stoke by Nayland, 1670. A5/5/110, A4/7/69
John, sen., Wickhambrook, 1448. W1/24/130
Katherine, wid., Fordham, 1558. R2/27/300
Margaret, Sudbury, 1606. A5/3/11
Mary, wid., Stoke by Nayland, 1676. R2/66/324; W1/128/29; In. 3/17/28
Michael, Kersey, 1671. A5/5/120, A4/8/7
Nicholas, yeo., Great Witchingham, 1594. W1/51/136b
Nicholas, draper, Nayland, 1684. R2/69/424; W1/138/202
Richard, Bury St. Edmunds, 1357. R2/1/6b
Richard, Bury St. Edmunds, 1474. R2/2/186
Richard, Elmswell, 1547. R2/21/330; W1/10/153
Richard, yeo., Lavenham, 1667. R2/64/227; W1/119/78; In. 3/12/92
Richard, als. Bryant, tailor, Stoke by Clare, 1639. R2/58/41; W1/94/75
Robert, Braiseworth, 1635. A5/4/35
Robert, Burwell, 1693. A5/6/160, A4/35/49
Robert, Colveston, 1538. W1/51/7
Robert, Finningham, 1668. In. 3/13/112; A5/5/97, A4/12/79
Robert, Finningham, 1679. A5/6/28, A4/16/143
Robert, Ixworth, 1488. R2/11/396
Robert, inn holder, Ixworth, 1582. R2/38/360; W1/41/84
Robert, singleman, Stoke by Nayland, 1665. R2/63/358; W1/117/109; In. 3/10/145
Robert, Stowmarket, 1670. In. 3/15/125; A5/5/114
Stephen, yeo., Burwell, 1666. R2/64/155; W1/118/121; In. 3/11/121
Susan, wid., Burwell, 1681. R2/68/148; W1/135/112
Thomas, husb., Burwell, 1544. R2/19/475
Thomas, Burwell, (1618). W1/95/146
Thomas, Burwell, 1647. R2/59/479; W1/104/113
Thomas, husb., Burwell, 1675. R2/66/214; W1/127/90; In. 3/16/114
Thomas, dyer, Bury St. Edmunds, 1497. R2/4/62 (admon. only)
Thomas, Lakenheath, 1666. A5/5/77, A4/4/51
Thomas, Layham, 1443. R2/9/36
Thomas, yeo., Palgrave, 1695. R2/72/300; W1/148/27
Thomas, Polstead, 1642. A5/4/95
Thomas, Rattlesden, 1558. R2/27/18
Thomas, Stoke by Clare, (1532). R2/18/64
Thomas, Stowmarket, 1666. In. 3/11/116
Thomas, yeo., Wattisham, 1553. R2/23/136; W1/11/124
William, Burwell, (1507). W1/9/13

PALMER continued
William, husb., Burwell, 1555. R2/24/248; W1/15/76
William, Burwell, 1563. R2/32/30; W1/26/90
William, Burwell, 1681. R2/68/101; W1/135/76
William, vintner, Bury St. Edmunds, 1680. R2/67/638; W1/134/102; In. 3/20/262
William, yeo., Lakenheath, 1697. R2/73/130; W1/151/18
William, gardener, Landwade, 1638, (N). R2/57/392; W1/93/205
William, collar maker, Soham, 1592. R2/42/289; W1/49/105
William, husb., Soham, 1650. R2/61/369; W1/107/65; In. 3/3/86
William, husb., Soham, 1675. R2/66/212; W1/127/88; In. 3/16/112
William, yeo., Soham, 1698. R2/73/221; W1/152/4; A5/7/10
William, tailor, Sudbury, 1603. R2/45/239; W1/61/35
William, Wordwell, 1457. R2/9/213
see also Pamer, Paulmer, Pawmer, Mabbeson als. Palmer
PALPHRY, James, Pakenham, 1681. A5/6/43, A4/18/4
PALSY, Robert, webster, Hartest, 1639. R2/58/111; W1/94/185
PALTON, Nicholas, Mildenhall, 1556. R2/25/106; W1/59/143; A5/1/63
PALTROPE, Thomas, the younger, Mildenhall, 1559. R2/28/71; W1/22/73
PAMAN, Agnes, wid., Bury St. Edmunds, 1570. W1/10/222
Agnes, Chevington, 1582. R2/38/414; W1/41/21
Dorothy, wid., Denham, 1640. R2/58/150; W1/96/56
Edmund, Chevington, 1580. R2/38/112; W1/39/164
Elisabeth, wid., Lidgate, 1602. R2/45/204; W1/60/134
George, husb., Chevington, 1622. R2/52/475; W1/78/87
Giles, yeo., Chevington, 1640. R2/58/134; W1/96/27
Harry, Chevington, 1514. R2/12/218
Henry, the elder, yeo., Chevington, 1539. R2/19/309
Henry, yeo., Chevington, 1558. R2/27/1
Henry, Chevington, 1579. A5/2/16
Henry, yeo., Chevington, 1613. R2/48/247a; W1/70/20
Henry, the elder, yeo., Wickhambrook, 1647. R2/59/398; W1/104/24; In. 3/2/29
John, Barton Mills, 1576. R2/37/171; W1/37/35; In. 3/1/93
John, husb., Bury St. Edmunds, 1562. R2/8/375; W1/17/30
John, Chevington, 1573. R2/36/180; W1/32/90
John, jun., Great Saxham, 1483. R2/11/285
John, yeo., Lidgate, 1627. R2/54/74; W1/83/77
John, the elder, yeo., Tuddenham, 1558. R2/27/169
Katherine, wid., Chevington, 1552. R2/23/101; W1/11/105
Margaret, wid., Chevington, 1572. R2/36/16; W1/31/120
Marian, wife of William, Chevington, 1578. A5/2/6
Martin, yeo., Chevington, 1616. R2/50/97; W1/73/106
Parnell, wid., Chevington, 1584. R2/39/136; W1/42/192
Reginald, the elder, Chevington, 1521. R2/14/41
Reginald, husb., Chevington, 1548. R2/21/457; W1/38/34
Richard, Great Saxham, 1478. R2/11/153
Robert, sen., Chevington, 1475. R2/11/92
Robert, Chevington, 1524. R2/14/101
Robert, the elder, Chevington, 1559. R2/28/12; W1/22/14 & 15
Robert, yeo., Cockfield, 1647. R2/59/397; W1/104/23; In. 3/2/33
Robert, Whepstead, 1562. A5/1/128
Rose, wid., Chevington, 1603. R2/45/227; W1/61/19
Simon, Lackford, 1685. R2/70/20; W1/139/20
Thomas, Great Livermere, 1561. R2/30/65; W1/28/237
Thomas, Nedging, 1595. A5/2/208
William, Chevington, 1522. R2/14/47
William, the elder, Chevington, 1527. R2/17/244; W1/1/38
William, yeo., Chevington, 1557. R2/26/208; W1/20/156
William, yeo., Chevington, 1662. R2/62/350; W1/114/69; In. 3/7/100
William, Tuddenham, 1562. A5/1/130
see also Payman
PAMANT, Ann, wid., Hunston, 1678. In. 3/19/119
Ann, wid., Ixworth, 1661. R2/62/229; W1/113/99; A5/5/19, A4/1/71
Frances, wid., Ixworth, 1666. In. 3/13/34; A5/5/73, A4/4/16
Henry, Fordham, 1694. A5/6/169, A4/37/36
Katherine, wid., Tuddenham, 1623. R2/52/543; W1/79/6
Leonard, Wickhambrook, 1640. A5/4/84
Mary, Chevington, 1595. A5/2/216
William, Dalham, 1558. R2/27/161
PAMENT, Agnes, wid., Little Thurlow, 1584. R2/39/207; W1/42/120

PAMENT continued
Ann, wid., Norton, 1678. R2/67/109; W1/130/93
James, wid., Soham, 1677. In. 3/18/147; A5/5/173, A4/14/61
James, Tuddenham, 1612. R2/48/213; W1/69/111
Richard, Norton, 1677. In. 3/18/86; A5/5/171, A4/14/42
Thomas, yeo., Soham, 1676. R2/66/399; W1/128/112; In. 3/17/148
William, yeo., Soham, 1677. R2/66/510; W1/129/93; In. 3/18/118
PAMER, Gabriel, shoe maker, Ousden, 1664. R2/63/159; W1/116/54
Jane, wid., Combs, 1560. R2/29/145; W1/25/27
PAMERTON, Samuel, Thorpe Morieux, 1583. A5/2/47
PAMIS, Richard, Isleham, 1685. In. 9/67
PAMMANT, Edward, sen., yeo., Isleham, 1701. In. 9/106; A12/18
PAMMENT, Audrey, wid., Westhorpe, 1647. R2/59/395; W1/104/21; In. 3/2/34
Robert, Kennett, 1695. R2/72/487; W1/149/44
William, yeo., Norton, 1677. In. 3/18/79; A5/5/170, A4/14/39
PAMONT, Christian, wid., Little Saxham, 1539. R2/19/314
see also Pamant
PAMPLIN, Gilbert, bricklayer, Soham, 1624, (N). W1/95/72
John, collar maker, Soham, 1663. R2/63/75; W1/115/120; In. 3/8/159
PANE, Stephen, yeo., Burwell, 1663. R2/63/50; W1/115/81; In. 3/8/95
PANELL, Edmund, singleman, Hawstead, 1564. R2/32/134; W1/27/83
John, Long Melford, 1480. R2/12/6
PANIERMAKER, Ralph, Bury St. Edmunds, 1396. R2/1/76
PANNELL, Daniel, singleman, Sudbury, 1663, (N). R2/63/11; W1/115/20; In. 3/8/42; A5/5/43
Elisabeth, wid., Sudbury, 1691. R2/71/501; W1/145/63; A5/6/143, A4/33/58
John, Bury St. Edmunds, 1695. A5/6/184, A4/38/93
John, yeo., Denston, 1605. R2/45/470; W1/63/118
John, the younger, say maker, Sudbury, 1649, (N). R2/60/270; W1/106/138
John, say maker, Sudbury, 1680. R2/67/673; W1/134/132; A5/6/38, A4/17/71
John, Sudbury, 1693. A5/6/164, A4/35/20
Oliver, Sudbury, 1693. A5/6/164, A4/35/19
Thomas, Little Thurlow, 1648. A5/4/120
Thomas, say maker, Sudbury, 1682. R2/68/298; W1/136/29; In. 3/21/156
see also Panell
PANTRELL, John, weaver, Bury St. Edmunds, 1465. R2/2/86
PANTRIE, William, sexton, Pulham St. Mary, 1582. W1/51/167
PAPE, Henry, vicar, Wickhambrook, 1561. R2/30/90; W1/28/276
PAPP, Walter, Glemsford, 1450. R2/9/123
PAPPES, William, weaver, Boxford, 1594. R2/42/576; W1/52/21
PARBE, Richard, Stoke, 1573. R2/36/209; W1/32/134
PARBYE, Thomas, husb., Stoke by Clare, 1592. R2/42/305; W1/49/126
PARCEVALL, John, Eriswell, 1546. R2/21/266; W1/10/87
PARCIFER, Henry, Wortham, 1696. In. 3/25/14; A5/6/185, A4/39/9
PARCIVALL, Philip, Mildenhall, 1634. A5/4/27
PARCYVALE, Nicholas, Bury St. Edmunds, 1507. R2/4/193
PARES, Emily, wid., Nayland, 1588. R2/41/47; W1/45/41
PAREYS, Thomas, Soham, 1431. R2/13/114
PARFAIE, John, Newmarket, 1570. A5/1/216
PARFERIE, John, husb., Hepworth, 1619. R2/51/256; W1/132/3
PARFEY, Edward, Little Cornard, 1670. A5/5/113
Katherine, wid. of John, Bury St. Edmunds, 1518. R2/6/55
PARFREY, Reginald, husb., Hepworth, 1635. R2/56/471; W1/91/39
Thomas, the elder, Thelnetham, 1588. R2/41/108; W1/45/105
PARFYE, John, the younger, yeo., Great Waldingfield, 1671. R2/65/151; W1/123/11
see also Parphe
PARHAM, John, Eye, 1465. R2/10/361
Walter, Bury St. Edmunds, 1419. R2/1/152
PARIS, Thomas, wire drawer, Nayland, 1583. R2/39/54; W1/42/54
PARISH, Alice, wid., Combs, 1616. R2/50/34; W1/73/34
Henry, wheelwright, Combs, 1608. R2/46/161; W1/65/9
James, wheelwright, Combs, 1660. R2/62/96; W1/112/130; In. 3/5/152
Joseph, Sudbury, 1693. A5/6/164, A4/35/14
Peter, yeo., wheelwright, West Stow, 1699. R2/73/454; W1/153/92; In. 3/26/24
William, Colchester, 1640. A5/4/81
see also Parrish

PARK(E), Agnes, Bury St. Edmunds, 1452. R2/2/35
Geoffrey, shoe maker, Bury St. Edmunds, 1499. R2/4/80 (admon. only)
George, Palgrave, 1626, (N). R2/58/480; W1/82/25
John, Bury St. Edmunds, 1503. R2/4/135
John, gent., Kersey, 1661. In. 3/6/240; A5/5/18, A4/1/81
Joseph, gent., Kersey, 1679. A5/6/17, A4/16/30
Robert, yeo., Acton, 1593. R2/42/443; W1/50/105
Robert, Great Cornard, 1686. In. 3/22/91; A5/6/102, A4/26/57
Thomas, singleman, Kettlebaston, 1665. In. 3/10/168; A5/5/70, A4/3/78
Walter, Bury St. Edmunds, (1556). R2/8/285; W1/18/14
William, mercer, Bury St. Edmunds, 1556. R2/8/296; W1/18/26
PARKAR, Thomas, Clare, 1552. R2/25/199; W1/12/26
PARKEN, John, als. Wolman, husb., Lackford, 1558. R2/27/379
Martha, wid., Weston, 1606. R2/46/26; W1/64/31
Robert, labourer, Weston, 1580. R2/38/110; W1/39/166
Thomas, Barningham, 1604. R2/45/364
PARKER, Agnes, Bury St. Edmunds, 1448. R2/2/25
Alice, wid., Bury St. Edmunds, 1550. R2/8/261
Amy, wid., Bury St. Edmunds, 1608. R2/46/200; W1/65/74
Amy, Bury St. Edmunds, 1638. A5/4/58
Andrew, inn holder, Bury St. Edmunds, 1689. R2/71/174; W1/143/33
Andrew, butcher, Cotton, 1596. R2/43/125; W1/54/1
Andrew, the elder, yeo., Cotton, 1672. R2/65/285; W1/124/1
Andrew, Haughley, 1545. R2/19/518; W1/7/97
Ann, wid., Denston, 1661. R2/62/239; W1/113/113; In. 3/6/135
Ann, Haughley, 1686. A5/6/98, A4/26/111
Anne, wid., Haughley, 1627. R2/54/62; W1/83/67
Anne, wid., Lidgate, 1671. R2/65/235; W1/123/112
Augustine, the elder, gent., Stanton, 1634. R2/56/407; W1/90/195 a & b
Avice, wid., Bury St. Edmunds, 1564. R2/8/388; W1/17/16
Edmund, yeo., Little Saxham, 1661. R2/62/166; W1/113/17; In. 3/6/20
Elisabeth, wid., Bury St. Edmunds, 1672. A5/5/128, A4/9/4
Elisabeth, wid., Culford, 1634. R2/56/337; W1/90/104
Elisabeth, wid., Norton, 1687. R2/70/394; W1/141/117
Francis, Nayland, 1590. A5/2/129
George, weaver, Bacton, 1634. R2/56/392; W1/90/171 a & b
George, husb., Burwell, 1661. In. 3/6/195; A5/5/21, A4/1/55
George, yeo., Thelnetham, 1613. R2/48/242a; W1/70/13
George, gent., Wattisfield, 1626. R2/53/564; W1/82/91
Harry, Hawstead, 1503. R2/13/130
Henry, Bury St. Edmunds, 1637. A5/4/54
Henry, Bury St. Edmunds, 1638. A5/4/60
Henry, Semer, 1462. R2/9/289
Henry, Wickhambrook, 1663. In. 3/8/79; A5/5/44
James, yeo., Badwell Ash, 1573. R2/36/185; W1/32/108
James, gent., Eriswell, 1686. R2/70/532; W1/140/134; In. 3/23/39
James, tailor, Hundon, 1662. R2/62/320; W1/114/19; In. 3/7/30
James, yeo., Nowton, 1671. R2/65/190; W1/123/59
James, Thelnetham, 1554. R2/24/17; W1/14/17
Joan, wid. of William, Great Waldingfield, 1507. R2/13/182
Joan, wife of John, Shimpling, (1488). R2/11/228
John, the elder, yeo., Ashley, 1669. R2/64/565; W1/121/155; In. 3/14/142
John, Ashley, 1679. A5/6/19, A4/16/46
John, Barnardiston, 1484. R2/11/324
John, Barnardiston, 1509. R2/15/1
John, cook, Bury St. Edmunds, 1515. R2/6/16
John, woollen draper, Bury St. Edmunds, 1600. R2/45/56; W1/58/78
John, Chilton, 1646. R2/59/355; W1/103/73
John, Eye, 1569. A5/1/210
John, singleman, Hengrave, 1614. R2/49/100; W1/71/75
John, reed maker, Hinderclay, 1689. R2/71/284; W1/143/118
John, singleman, Hundon, 1589. R2/41/165; W1/46/120
John, yeo., Ixworth, 1601. R2/44/518; W1/55/140
John, Newton, 1536. R2/18/86
John, Norton, 1588. A5/2/100
John, Nowton, 1644. A5/4/104
John, yeo., Preston, 1578. R2/37/366; W1/36/209
John, Semer, 1515. R2/12/93

PARKER continued
John, Shimpling, 1476. R2/11/64
John, yeo., Stanton, 1575. R2/37/97; W1/34/70
John, Thelnetham, 1550. R2/21/111; W1/9/138
John, Thelnetham, 1601. R2/44/436; W1/59/109
John, Thelnetham, 1635. A5/4/42
John, Timworth, 1578. A5/2/7
John, Walsham le Willows, 1537. R2/20/5; W1/4/3
John, yeo., Wattisfield, 1643. R2/59/19; W1/100/29
Katherine, Walsham le Willows, 1540. R2/19/284
Margaret, wid. of Thomas, carrier, Clare, 1629. R2/54/504; W1/85/95
Margaret, wid., Denston, 1625. R2/53/263; W1/81/52
Margaret, wid., Whepstead, 1664, (N). R2/63/123; W1/116/4; A5/5/56, A4/2/25
Margery, Stoke by Clare, 1630, (N). R2/55/111; W1/86/124
Marion, wid., Bury St. Edmunds, 1518. R2/6/50
Martha, wid. of Tobias, Lawshall, 1679. R2/67/349; W1/133/111
Mary, wid., Barton Mills, 1616. R2/50/55; W1/73/65
Mary, wid., Exning, 1649. R2/60/170; W1/106/17
Nicholas, mason, Great Thurlow, 1629. R2/54/426; W1/85/108
Nicholas, Walsham le Willows, 1557. R2/26/137; W1/20/85
Peter, yeo., Old Newton, (1586). R2/40/238; W1/44/77
Philip, yeo., Denston, 1619. R2/51/417; W1/132/97
Philip, Stowmarket, 1699. A5/7/10, A4/41/4
Richard, Bury St. Edmunds, 1356. R2/1/6a
Richard, Bury St. Edmunds, 1479. R2/2/287
Richard, cooper, Cotton, 1671, (N). R2/65/217; W1/123/90
Richard, yeo., Hawstead, 1641. R2/58/237; W1/98/9
Richard, Hepworth, 1631. A5/4/13
Richard, Nayland, 1699. A5/7/13, A4/41/48
Richard, gent., Walsham le Willows, 1691. R2/71/558 & 563; W1/145/110
Richard, Whepstead, 1590. A5/2/139
Richard, yeo., Wickhambrook, 1627. R2/54/4; W1/83/6
Robert, wright, Bury St. Edmunds, 1440. R2/1/246
Robert, button maker, Bury St. Edmunds, 1669. In. 3/14/114; A5/5/107, A4/7/65
Robert, Hawstead, 1494. R2/13/72
Robert, Lidgate, 1441. R2/9/21; W1/24/151 & 176
Robert, inn holder, Stowmarket, 1664, (N). In. 3/9/58; A5/5/56, A4/2/38
Robert, Whepstead, 1605. A5/3/1
Robert, linen weaver, Wickham Skeith, 1679. R2/67/480; W1/133/200
Samuel, wid., Woolpit, 1697. A5/7/5, A4/40/75
Simon, baker, Bury St. Edmunds, 1611. R2/48/22; W1/68/41; A5/3/111
Thomas, Ashley, 1562. R2/31/91; W1/8/98
Thomas, Ashley cum Silverley, 1532. R2/19/121; W1/3/124
Thomas, husb., Barton Mills, 1614, (N). R2/49/70; W1/71/53
Thomas, Bildeston, 1533. R2/19/158; W1/2/91
Thomas, yeo., Brockley, 1682. R2/68/492; W1/136/163; In. 3/21/3
Thomas, smith, Bury St. Edmunds, 1420. R2/1/153
Thomas, Bury St. Edmunds, 1493. R2/4/16
Thomas, rough mason, Bury St. Edmunds, 1547. R2/8/41
Thomas, yeo., Clare, 1619. R2/51/490; W1/132/145
Thomas, blacksmith, Culford, 1625. R2/53/204; W1/81/7
Thomas, blacksmith, Culford, 1627. R2/54/122; W1/83/120
Thomas, Denston, 1643. A5/4/99
Thomas, Exning, 1640, (N). R2/58/169; W1/96/82
Thomas, yeo., Hawstead, 1612. R2/48/138; W1/69/20
Thomas, Hinderclay, 1640. A5/4/85
Thomas, yeo., Honington, 1665. R2/63/316; W1/117/51; In. 3/10/49
Thomas, yeo., Hundon, 1585. R2/39/382; W1/42/225
Thomas, the elder, cooper, Ixworth, 1668. R2/64/377; W1/120/94; In. 3/13/92
Thomas, cooper, Ixworth, 1691. R2/71/463
Thomas, haberdasher, Lavenham, 1563. R2/32/42; W1/26/102
Thomas, husb., Lawshall, 1612. R2/48/183; W1/69/63
Thomas, husb., Nowton, 1571. R2/35/291; W1/36/120
Thomas, yeo., Nowton, 1614. R2/49/51; W1/71/42
Thomas, Rougham, 1696. A5/6/190, A4/39/73
Thomas, yeo., oatmeal maker, Stowmarket, 1667. R2/64/217; W1/119/69; In. 3/12/73

PARKER continued
Thomas, Thelnetham, 1580. R2/38/214; W1/39/100
Thomas, Thorpe Morieux, 1453. R2/9/160
Thomas, gent., Walsham le Willows, 1632. R2/56/154; W1/89/58
Thomas, Wetherden, 1559. R2/28/8; W1/22/9
Tobias, yeo., Lawshall, 1677. R2/66/489; W1/129/68; In. 3/18/84
Walter, labourer, Mildenhall, 1588. R2/41/34
William, husb., Barnardiston, 1632. R2/56/119; W1/89/5
William, husb., Great Livermere, 1567. R2/32/412; W1/3/176
William, yeo., Haughley, 1592. R2/42/302; W1/49/122
William, yeo., Haughley, 1622. R2/52/495; W1/78/102
William, yeo., Haughley, 1670. R2/65/37; W1/122/42; In. 3/15/61
William, labourer, Icklingham, 1573. R2/36/104; W1/32/3
William, Ixworth, 1539. R2/19/302
William, Ixworth, 1639. A5/4/69
William, Ixworth, 1666. A5/5/78
William, singleman, Lavenham, 1634. R2/56/390; W1/90/168
William, Lawshall, 1681. A5/6/53, A4/96/113
William, Lidgate, 1535. R2/18/129
William, yeo., Pakenham, 1670. R2/65/47; W1/122/54; In. 3/15/74
William, labourer, Soham, 1558. R2/27/35; W1/31/33
William, husb., Walsham le Willows, 1560. R2/29/20
William, Withersfield, 1590. A5/2/131
see also Parkar, Perker, Cook als. Parker, Shylborne als. Parker
PARKES, John, Great Bradley, 1681. A5/6/51, A4/19/86
PARKIN, Joan, Hopton, 1632. R2/56/164; W1/89/71
John, yeo., Burwell, 1594. R2/42/555; W1/52/38
John, Bury St. Edmunds, 1650. In. 3/3/88; A5/4/136
John, yeo., Honington, 1662. R2/62/366; W1/114/97; In. 3/7/123
John, the elder, carpenter, Market Weston, 1686. In. 3/22/111
John, the elder, yeo., Market Weston, 1686. R2/70/419; W1/140/43; In. 3/22/82
Richard, Burwell, 1558. R2/27/31; W1/31/17
Richard, husb., Great Barton, 1661. R2/62/241; W1/113/118; In. 3/7/62
Robert, Bury St. Edmunds, 1670. In. 3/15/144; A5/5/116
Simon, Elveden, 1603. R2/45/227
Simon, Hepworth, 1585. A5/2/74
Thomas, Barningham, 1558. R2/27/59; W1/21/161
Thomas, als. Wolman, rector, Eriswell, 1566. A5/1/174
Thomas, husb., Great Whelnetham, 1616, (N). R2/50/99; W1/73/107
Thomas, linen weaver, Thelnetham, 1678. R2/67/48; W1/130/39; In. 3/19/54
Thomas, Weston, 1581. A5/2/36
Thomas, husb., Weston, 1591. R2/42/129; W1/48/108
Thomas, the younger, thatcher, Weston, 1650. R2/61/350; W1/107/46; In. 3/3/63
William, Dalham, 1622. R2/52/445; W1/78/64
PARKING, John, Dalham, 1617. R2/50/250; W1/74/47
William, vicar, Burwell, 1565. R2/32/215
see also Parken, Parkyn, Bogas als. Parkyn, Heigham als. Parkin
PARKINGTON, John, Combs, 1694. A5/6/166, A4/37/2
Martha, Combs, 1639. A5/4/69
PARKINS, Beatrice, als. Stanton, wife of Ezekial, Fordham, 1649. R2/60/285; W1/106/157
Katherine, wid., Sudbury, 1613. R2/48/327; W1/70/109
Lawrence, Nowton, 1680. In. 3/20/241; A5/6/33, A4/17/22
PARKYN, Ann, Redgrave, 1692. A5/6/149, A4/34/21
Bartholomew, Thelnetham, 1563. R2/31/145; W1/26/25
Bartholomew, Weston, 1635. R2/56/537; W1/91/119
Joanna, wid., Barningham, 1481. R2/11/218
John, sen., Barningham, 1460. R2/9/259
John, Downham, 1564. A5/1/156
John, Great Livermere, 1440. R2/9/33
John, Lackford, 1516. R2/13/223
John, als. Wullman, Newmarket, 1543. R2/19/368; W1/6/108
John, yeo., Weston, 1616. R2/50/70; W1/73/81
Laurence, Coney Weston, 1641. A5/4/89
Margery, wid., Lackford, 1551. R2/23/46; W1/11/48
Nicholas, Downham, 1563. A5/1/143
Robert, tailor, Honington, 1616. R2/50/67; W1/73/78
Robert, the elder, Weston, 1570. R2/35/21; W1/38/138

PARKYN continued
Rose, wid., Thelnetham, 1564. R2/32/58; W1/27/4
Thomas, Burwell, 1536. R2/19/230
Thomas, Burwell, 1556. R2/25/125; W1/16/184
Thomas, maltster, Bury St. Edmunds, 1571. R2/35/281; W1/36/116
Thomas, als. Wulman, Lackford, 1550. R2/19/498; W1/7/25
Thomas, the elder, Weston, 1527. W1/311/19
Thomas, Weston, 1571. A5/1/233
Thomas, weaver, Weston, 1577. R2/37/294
Thomas, Weston, 1685. A5/6/95, A4/105/112
Timothy, Mildenhall, 1595. A5/2/215
PARLE, John, Bildeston, 1455. R2/9/226
John, barker, Lavenham, 1446. R2/9/87; W1/24/106
Robert, Lavenham, 1493. R2/11/444
PARMAN, Charles, the elder, yeo., Wickhambrook, 1667. R2/64/292; W1/119/156; In. 3/12/181
Edmund, yeo., Higham, 1675. In. 3/16/135; A5/5/157, A4/12/61
Edmund, butcher, Stradishall, 1549. R2/21/551; W1/8/67
Edmund, butcher, Stradishall, 1589. R2/41/299; W1/46/12
Edward, Wickhambrook, 1558. R2/27/529
Elisabeth, wid., Polstead, 1573. R2/36/210; W1/32/135
John, yeo., Gazeley, 1596. R2/43/204; W1/54/68
John, Gazeley, 1690. A5/6/131, A4/32/2
John, sen., yeo., Higham, 1669. R2/64/559; W1/121/147; In. 3/14/134
John, yeo., Wickhambrook, 1576. R2/37/143; W1/37/13; In. 3/1/107
Mary, wid., Gazeley, 1676, (N). R2/66/358; W1/128/67; In. 3/17/76; A5/5/162, A4/13/45
Richard, husb., Cowlinge, 1602. R2/45/209; W1/60/149
Robert, yeo., Gazeley, 1681. R2/68/201; W1/135/148
Robert, Wickhambrook, 1463. R2/10/590
Thomas, husb., Lakenheath, 1560. R2/29/173; W1/25/1
Thomasine, wid., Cowlinge, 1604. R2/45/337; W1/62/51
William, tailor, Polstead, 1572. R2/36/38; W1/31/109
see also Parmen, Perman
PARMATER, Isabel, wid., Clare, 1557. R2/26/158; W1/20/88
William, Clare, 1554. R2/24/98; W1/14/76
PARMEFOY, Judith, wid., Stoke by Nayland, 1644. R2/59/159; W1/101/85
see also Parmifoy, Parnafy, Permephaye
PARMEKER, John, Great Finborough, (1422). R2/9/308
PARMEN, Robert, yeo., Gazeley, 1626. R2/53/519; W1/82/54
PARMENTER, Agnes, wid., Bury St. Edmunds, 1456. R2/2/53
Joan, Worlington, 1525. R2/17/134; W1/21/129
John, Barningham, 1569. A5/1/207
John, Bury St. Edmunds, 1434. A2/1/210
John, the elder, husb., Great Wratting, 1661. R2/62/160; W1/113/8; In. 3/5/215
John, sen., yeo., Long Melford, 1684. R2/69/225; W1/138/31; In. 3/22/154; A5/6/81
John, Sapiston, 1505. R2/12/44
John, Westhorpe, 1414. R2/1/134
Joseph, Brent Eleigh, 1693. A5/6/164, A4/35/15
Margaret, wid., Stansfield, 1650, (N). R2/61/350; W1/107/44; In. 3/3/142
Richard, weaver, Bury St. Edmunds, 1462. R2/2/74
Robert, weaver, Bury St. Edmunds, 1493. R2/4/21
Robert, yeo., Clare, 1668. In. 3/13/157; A5/5/96, A4/6/75
Rose, wid., Bury St. Edmunds, 1495. R2/4/37
Samuel, singleman, Wickhambrook, 1679. A5/6/22, A4/16/70
Thomas, Bury St. Edmunds, 1461. R2/2/70
Thomas, Bury St. Edmunds, 1469. R2/2/123
Thomas, yeo., Edwardstone, 1650. In. 3/3/8; A5/4/133
Ursula, wid., Stansfield, 1619. R2/51/406; W1/132/89
William, barker, Bury St. Edmunds, 1434. R2/1/211
William, barker, Bury St. Edmunds, 1458. R2/2/62
William, Mildenhall, 1477. R2/11/129
William, husb., Stansfield, 1650, (N). R2/61/350; W1/107/45; In. 3/3/141
PARMETER, James, Flempton, 1556. R2/25/68; W1/16/87
John, Flempton, 1586. A5/2/78
Joseph, yeo., Brent Eleigh, 1678. In. 3/19/104
William, Hitcham, 1439. R2/9/4
see also Parmater, Parminter, Permenter, Permeter

PARMIFOY, John, Stoke by Nayland, 1636. A5/4/47
John, Stoke by Nayland, 1637. A5/4/48
PARMINTER, Juliana, wid., Denston, 1637. R2/57/219; W1/92/264
PARMITER, Stephen, Acton, 1692. A5/6/153; A4/115/54
PARNAFY, Richard, weaver, Hartest, 1644. R2/59/160; W1/101/87
PARNELL, Agnes, wid., Bures, 1593, (N). R2/42/441; W1/50/103
PARPHE, John, Great Wratting, 1554. A5/1/93
PARR, Francis, Icklingham, 1639. R2/58/115; W1/94/193
Henry, labourer, Icklingham, 1660. R2/62/32; W1/112/34; In. 3/5/32
Henry, Icklingham, 1674. A5/5/149, A4/89/57
Henry, Tuddenham, 1674. R2/66/38; W1/126/85
Richard, husb., Icklingham, 1616. R2/50/57; W1/73/67
PARRIS, Andrew, inn holder, Nayland, 1611. R2/48/36; W1/68/58
Thomas, labourer, Lidgate, 1648. R2/60/115; W1/105/136
Thomas, weaver, Lidgate, 1665. In. 3/10/84; A5/5/67
see also Pares, Paris, Parys
PARRISH, James, wheelwright, Combs, 1683. R2/69/47; W1/137/36
Robert, wheelwright, Stowmarket, 1638. R2/57/318; W1/93/96
Thomas, Lidgate, 1666. A4/4/37
see also Parish
PARSANE, William, Finningham, 1541. W1/38/80
PARSELY, Ambrose, Wattisfield, 1693. A5/6/165, A4/35/12
Dorcas, Wattisfield, 1693. A5/6/164, A4/35/13
PARS(E)Y, Robert, Cavendish, 1551. R2/23/46; W1/11/49
William, Acton, 1688. A5/6/121, A4/29/62
PARSL(E)Y, Elisabeth, spinster, Sudbury, 1691. R2/71/535; W1/145/92
Thomas, Bacton, 1676. In. 3/17/48; A5/5/161, A4/13/20
Thomas, joiner, Stowlangtoft, 1612. R2/48/197; W1/69/86
see also Parsely
PARSON, Charles, singleman, Bardwell, 1664. R2/63/172; W1/116/68; In. 3/9/93
John, yeo., Great Livermere, 1549. R2/21/555; W1/8/64
John, carpenter, Great Livermere, 1556. R2/25/18; W1/16/17
John, Rougham, 1556. R2/25/98; W1/16/17 & 104
Marah, wid., Freckenham, 1678. W8/28
Margaret, Hengrave, 1569. W1/5/1
Marian, wid., Tuddenham, 1632, (N). R2/56/173; W1/89/81
Martin, Tuddenham, 1631. A5/4/10
Peter, weaver, Boxford, 1602. R2/45/120; W1/60/38
Philippa, wid., Boxford, 1605. R2/45/392; W1/63/34
Richard, farmer, Mildenhall, 1699. In. 3/26/69; A5/7/11, A4/41/18
Robert, Lavenham, 1478. R2/11/174
Thomas, husb., Barton Mills, (1615). W1/95/98
William, Eriswell, 1641. A5/4/88
William, Wicken, 1531. R2/18/62, R2/19/64
William, Wicken, 1573. A5/1/262
see also Person
PARSONS, Abraham, Poslingford, 1661. R2/62/224; W1/113/92; In. 3/6/114
Jonas, yeo., Poslingford, 1648. R2/60/84; W1/105/101
Mary, wid., Cavendish, 1680. In. 3/20/115; A5/6/37, A4/17/59
Peter, say maker, Stoke by Nayland, 1695. R2/72/556; W1/149/111
Robert, yeo., Redgrave, 1595. R2/43/33; W1/53/29
Thomas, yeo., Poslingford, 1666. R2/64/33; W1/118/29; In. 3/11/24
PARTE, Samuel, Rattlesden, 1677. R2/66/439; W1/129/12; In. 3/18/8
PARTINGTON, Elisabeth, singlewoman, Combs, 1629. R2/54/375; W1/85/73
PARTINTON, James, wid., yeo., Combs, 1665. In. 3/10/10; A5/5/66, A4/3/19
PARTYNTON, Richard, Cockfield, 1578, (N). R2/37/353; W1/36/222
see also Pertington
PARTRICH, Isabel, wid., Tuddenham, 1571. R2/35/131; W1/36/82
John, the elder, Icklingham, 1600. R2/45/21; W1/58/29
Richard, yeo., Bromeswell, 1610. R2/47/212; W1/67/90
Robert, yeo., Acton, 1525. R2/17/115; W1/21/113 & 114
Thomas, Stowmarket, 1566. A5/1/178
William, the elder, husb., Great Whelnetham, 1586. R2/40/86; W1/43/67
PARTRICK, Avery, clerk, Bures, 1563. A5/1/150

PARTRIDGE, Amy, wid., Polstead, 1681. R2/68/211; W1/135/155
George, yeo., Felsham, 1700. R2/74/28; W1/154/27; In. 3/27/6
George, Polstead, 1671. A5/5/123, A4/8/35
Henry, Great Whelnetham, 1688. A5/6/123, A4/29/82
John, yeo., Stoke by Nayland, 1697. R2/73/199; W1/151/82
Richard, yeo., Herringswell, 1687. R2/70/568; W1/141/7; In. 3/23/58
Robert, Great Livermere, 1688. A5/6/123, A4/29/83
Robert, Isleham, 1560. W7/17
Robert, gelder, yeo., Isleham, 1622. R6/27
Roger, wid., Bury St. Edmunds, 1682. A5/6/62, A4/19/77
Thomas, clothier, Long Melford, 1631. R2/56/64; W1/87/94
Thomas, Wickham Skeith, 1627. R2/54/44; W1/83/50
William, sen., Isleham, 1674. In. 9/38
William, yeo., Isleham, 1675. W7/85
PARTRIGE, John, Isleham, 1563. W7/27
Robert, Isleham, 1574. W7/39
Robert, husb., Wicken, 1569. R2/33/136; W1/5/67
PARTRYCH(E), George, Lavenham, 1543. R2/19/403; W1/6/98
Isabel, wid., Acton, 1545. R2/19/572; W1/7/91
Nicholas, yeo., Creeting All Saints, 1574. R2/37/57; W1/33/22
Thomas, the elder, Tuddenham, 1547. R2/21/285; W1/38/66
Thomas, the elder, Tuddenham, 1558. R2/27/358
PARTRYTCHE, Henry, gent., Carbrooke, 1534. W1/51/191
see also Patridge, Patteridge, Pattridge, Pertrych, Petrych
PARY, John, als. Rynglonde, Fornham St. Martin, 1526. R2/15/50
PARYS, William, painter, Great Wratting, 1556. R2/25/88; W1/16/121
PASCALL, Thomas, yeo., Creeting All Saints, 1663. R2/63/76; W1/115/122; In. 3/8/166
PASHELER, Robert, Wickham Skeith, 1636. R2/57/46; W1/92/56
PASHELEY, Robert, weaver, Palgrave, 1572. R2/36/5; W1/31/69
PASK(E), Alice, wid., Wickhambrook, 1568, (N). R2/33/21; W1/29/31
Clement, Dalham, 1620. R2/52/60; W1/76/49
Edward, singleman, Wixoe, 1638, (N). R2/57/438; W1/93/280
Elisabeth, singlewoman, Sudbury, 1641. A5/4/91
George, the elder, yeo., Wickhambrook, 1585. R2/40/25; W1/43/19
John, husb., Boxted, 1633, (N). R2/56/242; W1/90/1
John, yeo., Long Melford, 1684. R2/69/340; W1/138/136
John, the elder, yeo., Stansfield, 1638. R2/57/346; W1/93/134
John, Stradishall, 1577. R2/37/312
John, tanner, Wickhambrook, 1538. R2/20/143 (and inventory); W1/4/123
John, husb., Wickhambrook, 1610. R2/47/138; W1/67/20
John, Wickhambrook, 1675. In. 3/16/142; A5/5/158, A4/12/62
Joshua, Stradishall, 1661. In. 3/6/12; A5/5/11, A4/1/144
Richard, husb., Wickhambrook, 1610. R2/47/159; W1/67/39
Robert, Denston, 1648. A5/4/123
Roger, yeo., Wickhambrook, 1612. R2/48/182; W1/69/62
Sarah, wid., Denston, 1679. R2/67/422; W1/133/158
Thomas, Cheveley, 1583. A5/2/46
Thomas, husb., Hundon, 1640. R2/58/145; W1/96/46
William, husb., Great Bradley, 1663, (N). R2/63/117; W1/115/181; In. 3/8/228
William, yeo., Wickhambrook, 1634. R2/56/353; W1/90/121
PASKFEILD, George, inn holder, Fornham St. Martin, 1622. R2/52/391; W1/78/26
PASLEY, Robert, gent., Hundon, 1633. R2/56/261; W1/90/28a
PASSEVALL, Margaret, Wangford, 1567. A5/1/225
PASSEVELL, Margaret, Wangford, 1570. A5/1/217
PASSHELL, John, Gazeley, 1481. R2/11/273
PASSON, Elisabeth, wid., Isleham, (1692). W7/124; In. 9/93
PASSWATER, John, yeo., Eriswell, 1570. R2/34/26; W1/30/25; A5/1/222
John, yeo., Eriswell, 1610. R2/47/230; W1/67/110
John, Fornham, 1650. In. 3/3/104
PASWATER, John, yeo., Fornham All Saints, 1646. R2/59/307; W1/103/28
Manser, singleman, Eriswell, 1617. R2/50/346; W1/74/128
PATCH, Joan, wid., Isleham, 1620. R6/22
PATE, Katherine, wid., Soham, 1545. R2/19/538; W1/7/43
Robert, Soham, 1545. R2/21/200; W1/10/45
Thomas, Soham, 1503. R2/13/133

PATE continued
Thomas, Soham, 1533. W1/2/31
see also Payte, Peyte
PATELE, Isabel, Finningham, 1357. R2/1/6b
PATERNOSTER, Robert, weaver, Sudbury, 1525. R2/17/102; W1/21/97
Simon, Creeting, 1609. A5/3/27
PATIE, Alice, Bildeston, 1563. A5/1/148
PATLE, Margaret, Bardwell, 1594. A5/2/202
PATMER, Edward, maltster, Cavendish, 1639. R2/58/75; W1/94/128
PATON, John, Drinkstone, 1463. R2/10/338
Rose, wid., Preston, 1520. R2/15/76, R2/17/313; W1/23/6
Thomas, the elder, Elmsett, 1526. R2/17/145; W1/21/139
see also Patton, Payton, Clerk als. Paton
PATRICK, Anne, wid., Bury St. Edmunds, 1620, (N). R2/52/159; W1/76/144
John, husb., Ampton, 1687. R2/70/401; W1/141/125
John, miller, Badwell Ash, 1642. R2/58/335; W1/99/29
John, Badwell Ash, 1682. A5/6/60, A4/19/48
John, Badwell Ash, 1691. A5/6/139, A4/33/7
John, yeo., Whelnetham, 1683. R2/69/3; W1/137/3
Margaret, spinster, Great Whelnetham, 1633. R2/56/283; W1/90/48
Richard, Ballingdon, 1562. A5/1/127
Stephen, yeo., blacksmith, Cockfield, 1660. R2/62/72; W1/112/92; In. 3/5/107
Stephen, Cockfield, 1667. A5/5/85, A4/5/48
Ursula, Bury St. Edmunds, 1692. A5/6/149, A4/34/24
see also Patterick, Pattryck
PATRIDGE, John, yeo., Stoke by Nayland, 1686. R2/70/552; W1/140/155; In. 3/22/162; A5/6/107, A4/26/7
Robert, husb., Great Livermere, 1674. R2/66/30; W1/126/92
PATRYCHE, William, smith, Fornham St. Martin, 1566. R2/32/349; W1/28/31
PATT, John, Burwell, 1537. R2/18/163
William, Soham, 1525. R2/17/127; W1/5/30, W1/21/127
PATTELL, Arthur, Badwell Ash, 1579. R2/38/59; W1/39/20
Francis, husb., Barrow, 1631. R2/56/87; W1/87/132
John, yeo., Badwell Ash, 1590. R2/41/346; W1/47/38
John, husb., Cotton, 1634. R2/56/335; W1/90/99
Matthew, grocer, Long Melford, 1700. R2/74/118; W1/154/114b
Thomas, husb., Mendlesham, 1630. R2/55/119; W1/86/133a & b; A5/4/62
William, Walsham le Willows, 1567. A5/1/187
PATTEN, Anthony, Bures, 1646. A5/4/114
Elizabeth, wid., Coney Weston, 1596. R2/43/161; W1/54/42
John, husb., Wissington, 1605. R2/45/470; W1/63/119
Robert, husb., Wissington, 1583. R2/39/61; W1/42/47
Rose, wid., Nayland, 1585. R2/39/247; W1/42/326
Thomas, yeo., Coney Weston, 1588. R2/41/75; W1/45/65
PATTENT, Robert, Wiston, 1583. A5/2/48
PATTERICK, William, yeo., Great Whelnetham, 1626. R2/53/556; W1/82/80
PATTERIDGE, Alice, Stoke by Nayland, 1635. A5/4/40
John, husb., Great Whelnetham, 1624, (N). R2/53/44; W1/80/64
PATTISON, John, Bury St. Edmunds, 1638. A5/4/63
PATTLE, Abraham, Whepstead, 1694. A5/6/171, A4/37/56
Alice, wid., Woolpit, 1571. R2/35/285; W1/36/253
Ann, Whepstead, 1637. A5/4/55
Edmund, Wetheringsett, 1631, (N). W1/95/140
Gabriel, Bacton, 1665. In. 3/10/159; A5/5/70, A4/3/71
Hugh, yeo., Whepstead, 1629. R2/54/395; W1/85/89
Jasper, Bury St. Edmunds, 1636, (N). R2/57/62; W1/92/71
Margaret, Barrow, 1632. A5/4/17
Margaret, wid., Thwaite, 1633, (N). R2/56/311; W1/90/78
Robert, yeo., Whepstead, 1695. R2/72/471; W1/149/27
Thomas, woollen weaver, Bury St. Edmunds, 1641. R2/58/266; W1/98/43
Thomas, yeo., Combs, 1638. R2/57/309; W1/93/84
see also Patele, Patle, Pattell, Patyll
PATTON, Daniel, Denston, 1684. R2/69/339; W1/138/135; A5/6/76, A4/21/21
Thomas, Elmsett, 1562. A5/1/123

PATTRIDGE, Ann, als. Hankyn, Stoke by Nayland, 1637. A5/4/53
John, sen., say weaver, Long Melford, 1692. R2/72/97; W1/146/89; In. 3/24/18
PATTRYCK, Robert, parson, Great Fakenham, 1559. R2/28/43; W1/22/45
PATY, Robert, Eye, 1522. R2/15/42
PATYLL, William, Badwell, 1460. R2/9/305
PATYNMAKER, John, Bury St. Edmunds, 1436. R2/1/221
PAULMER, Henry, tailor, Bildeston, 1572. R2/36/16; W1/31/118
PAULSON, John, Lavenham, 1680. In. 3/20/65; A5/6/34, A4/17/36
PAUSEY, John, Brockley, 1683. A5/6/68, A4/20/43
John, cartwright, Stanstead, 1546. R2/21/204; W1/10/113
PAUSIE, Christian, singlewoman, Hartest, 1679. R2/67/265; W1/133/55
William, yeo., Shimpling, 1609. R2/47/9; W1/66/8
PAVES, Mary, Gazeley, 1666. In. 3/11/68; A5/5/74, A4/4/19
PAVIS, John, husb., Chevington, 1662. R2/62/326; W1/114/31; In. 3/7/45
Martha, wid., Barrow, 1662. R2/62/414; W1/114/169; In. 3/7/222
Richard, the elder, labourer, Chevington, 1622. R2/52/499; W1/78/103
PAVYS, Agnes, wid., Stowmarket, 1573. A5/1/267
Joan, als. Day, spinster, Edwardstone, 1616. R2/50/172; W1/73/165
John, Soham, 1464. R2/10/369
William, weaver, Bildeston, 1580. R2/38/230; W1/39/86
see also Daye als. Pavis
PAWFLEN, John, tanner, Stoke by Clare, 1605. R2/45/396; W1/63/35
PAWLIN, John, Wattisham, 1687. A5/6/110, A4/27/36
PAWMENT, Richard, carpenter, Fordham, 1596. R2/43/167; W1/54/48
PAWMER, Thomas, 1544. R2/19/437
PAWNPAYN, Thomas, Kentford, 1447. R2/2/24
PAWSEY, Alice, wife of Joseph, carpenter, Stradishall, 1699. R2/73/469; W1/153/106
Dorothy, wid., Shimpling, 1684. R2/69/246; W1/138/51
Edward, clothier, Hartest, 1674. R2/66/53; W1/126/66
George, clothier, Stanstead, 1690. R2/71/352; W1/144/56
Isaac, Great Livermere, 1687. A5/6/115, A4/27/90, A4/30/53
Isaac, Great Livermere, 1688. A5/6/116 & 117, A4/29/2 & 4
John, Brent Eleigh, 1546. R2/21/242; W1/10/96a
John, yeo., Great Livermere, 1685. R2/70/4; W1/139/5
John, Hartest, 1558. R2/27/534
John, yeo., Hundon, 1700. R2/74/53; W1/154/51
John, Long Melford, 1651. A5/4/139
John, the elder, yeo., Shimpling, 1661. R2/62/269; W1/113/168
John, Stanstead, 1638. A5/4/59
John, yeo., Stradishall, 1700. In. 3/27/20
Randall, yeo., Hartest, 1642. R2/58/326; W1/99/16
Roger, yeo., Shimpling, 1669. R2/64/557; In. 3/14/137
Susan, wid., Great Livermere, 1688. R2/71/75; W1/142/66
Thomas, yeo., Hartest, 1632. R2/56/201; W1/89/115
Thomas, yeo., Shimpling, 1636. R2/57/83; W1/92/100
William, yeo., Glemsford, 1609. R2/47/26; W1/66/28
William, Lawshall, 1664. In. 3/9/163; A5/5/62, A4/2/93
William, weaver, Stanstead, 1636. R2/57/100; W1/92/118
PAWSIE, John, yeo., Shimpling, 1613. R2/48/272; W1/70/48
PAWSYE, William, yeo., Stanstead, 1604. R2/45/323; W1/62/21
see also Pausey
PAXMAN, Edward, Burwell, 1477. R2/11/106
Thomas, Burwell, 1457. R2/9/187
Thomas, Burwell, 1474. R2/10/520
Thomas, yeo., Lawshall, 1605. R2/45/397; W1/63/28
William, Burwell, 1449. R2/9/143
William, Burwell, 1617. R2/50/374; W1/74/155
William, Exning, 1504. W1/7/12
William, Fordham, 1545. R2/19/535; W1/7/42
PAXTON, John, chaplain, Bury St. Edmunds, 1402. R2/1/100
PAYCHE, Thomas, Soham, 1477. R2/11/86
PAYELLE, William, Norwich, 1594. W1/51/120
PAYEN, Edgar, Bury St. Edmunds, 1686. In. 3/22/161

PAYFOITE, John, husb., Fordham, 1558. R2/27/395
PAYFOOTE, Isaac, Wicken, 1637. A5/4/52
John, husb., Fordham, 1612. R2/48/239; W1/69/138
Robert, yeo., Wicken, 1625. R2/53/277; W1/81/64
Thomas, Wicken, 1571. A5/1/237
Thomas, clothier, Wicken, 1637. R2/57/210; W1/92/250
PAYFOT, Margaret, Landwade, (1539). R2/20/188; W1/4/152 & 153
Robert, Wicken, 1644. R2/59/114; W1/101/39
William, Freckenham, 1560. W8/6
PAYKEN, John, Nayland, 1553. R2/23/142; W1/11/123
PAYMAN, John, the elder, Chevington, 1522. R2/14/63
John, Tuddenham, 1546. R2/21/610
Ralph, Great Livermere, 1572. R2/36/92; W1/31/49
PAYMONTE, John, Little Bradley, 1570. A5/1/218
PAYNE, Abraham, Brandon, 1568, (N). R2/33/22; W1/29/34
Agnes, Bury St. Edmunds, 1470. R2/2/135
Agnes, wid. of John, Nayland, 1526. R2/17/158
Ambrose, gent., Bury St. Edmunds, 1699. R2/73/423; W1/153/65
Ambrose, carpenter, Glemsford, 1688. R2/71/133; W1/142/121; In. 3/23/86
Ann, wid., Lavenham, 1645. A5/4/111
Ann, wid., Stowmarket, 1633. A5/4/26
Benjamin, yeo., Burwell, 1631. R2/56/33; W1/87/46
Cecily, wid., Hopton, 1491. R2/11/453
Clement, Great Fakenham, 1676. A5/5/160, A4/13/14
Edmund, yeo., Combs, 1581. R2/38/326; W1/40/69
Edmund, Euston, 1544. R2/21/609
Edmund, husb., Thelnetham, 1581. R2/38/259; W1/40/9
Edward, grocer, Bury St. Edmunds, 1667. R2/64/215; W1/119/68
Edward, yeo., Great Horningsheath, 1616. R2/50/117; W1/73/124
Elisabeth, wid., Bury St. Edmunds, 1647, (N). R2/59/500; W1/104/40
Elisabeth, wid., Worlington, 1630. R2/55/35; W1/86/39
Emma, wid., Stowmarket, 1566. R2/32/364; W1/28/15
Geoffrey, Wortham, 1455. R2/9/181
George, the elder, clothier, Bury St. Edmunds, 1648. R2/60/15; W1/105/20
Giles, Bury St. Edmunds, 1585. A5/2/65
Grace, wid., Stanstead, 1681. R2/68/62; W1/135/51
Henry, miller, Kirtling, 1688. R2/71/74; W1/142/65; In. 3/23/41
Henry, Wattisham, 1612. A5/3/115
Henry, gent., Worlington, 1639. A5/4/72
Isaac, barber, Long Melford, 1665. R2/63/294; W1/117/23; In. 3/10/14
James, yeo., Mellis, 1691. R2/71/559; W1/145/111b
James, the elder, weaver, Stowmarket, 1582. R2/38/463; W1/41/35
Jeffery, Little Livermere, 1549. R2/21/3; W1/10/169
Joan, wid. of John, Wissington, 1527. R2/17/247; W1/1/34
John, Barrow, 1651. A5/4/139
John, clothier, Boxted, 1600. R2/45/24; W1/58/38
John, glover, Bury St. Edmunds, (1431). R2/1/203
John, spooner, Bury St. Edmunds, (1432). R2/1/200
John, gent., Bury St. Edmunds, 1477. R2/2/239
John, Bury St. Edmunds, 1513. R2/5/25
John, butcher, Bury St. Edmunds, 1587. R2/40/149; W1/44/32
John, butcher, Bury St. Edmunds, 1647, (N). R2/59/498; W1/104/136
John, baker, Bury St. Edmunds, 1652, (N). R2/61/602; W1/109/81; In. 3/4/7
John, Lawshall, 1676, (N). R2/66/373; W1/128/85
John, the elder, yeo., Little Waldingfield, 1687. R2/70/305; W1/141/49; A5/6/113, A4/27/72
John, als. Barker, yeo., Polstead, 1595. R2/43/5; W1/53/4
John, Rickinghall Inferior, 1484. R2/11/292
John, clothier, Bury St. Edmunds, 1690. R2/71/404; W1/144/109
John, apothecary, Bury St. Edmunds, 1699. R2/73/461; W1/153/97; In. 3/26/31
John, Cockfield, 1651. A5/4/140
John, Euston, 1550. R2/21/159; W1/9/87
John, yeo., Lawshall, 1609. R2/47/72; W1/66/84
John, clothier, Lawshall, 1646. R2/59/320; W1/103/39

PAYNE continued
John, gent., Stoke by Nayland, 1597. R2/43/374; W1/55/136
John, Thelnetham, 1519. R2/15/135
John, the younger, Thelnetham, 1519. R2/15/135
John, Wortham, 1448. R2/9/94
John, 1457. W1/24/99
Margaret, wid., Cockfield, 1662, (N). R2/62/356; W1/114/78; In. 3/7/230; A5/5/32
Margaret, wid., Combs, 1594. R2/42/497; W1/52/85
Margery, wife of John, Haverhill, 1442. R2/9/39
Margery, Wortham, 1455. R2/9/228
Mary, wid., Fornham All Saints, 1684. R2/69/234; W1/138/40
Mary, wid., Glemsford, 1642. R2/58/379; W1/99/85
Mary, wid., Long Melford, 1683. R2/69/103; W1/137/79
Matthew, Long Melford, 1630. A5/4/5
Reginald, fuller, Bury St. Edmunds, 1411. R2/1/124
Richard, clothier, Boxted, 1575. R2/37/102; W1/34/42; In. 3/1/46
Robert, Brandon, 1638. A5/4/66
Robert, Bury St. Edmunds, 1569. A5/1/213
Robert, yeo., Glemsford, 1564. R2/32/395; W1/3/33
Robert, Lawshall, 1646. A5/4/112
Robert, yeo., Polstead, 1647. R2/59/450; W1/104/82; In. 3/2/87
Robert, Sudbury, 1460. R2/9/306
Robert, Thelnetham, 1461. R2/9/306
Robert, Thelnetham, 1519. R2/15/135
Robert, husb., Thelnetham, 1624. R2/53/73; W1/80/95
Roger, labourer, Kirtling, 1663, (N). R2/63/117; W1/115/180; In. 3/8/224; A5/5/54
Roger, husb., Long Melford, 1584. R2/39/156; W1/42/166
Samuel, the elder, yeo., Little Waldingfield, 1669. R2/64/491; W1/121/86; In. 3/14/127
Simon, Brome, 1565. R2/32/237
Thomas, Bardwell, 1503. R2/12/56
Thomas, labourer, Bildeston, 1557. R2/26/97; W1/20/57
Thomas, yeo., Boxted, 1544. R2/19/484
Thomas, clothier, Boxted, 1676. R2/66/400; W1/128/113; In. 3/17/146
Thomas, baker, Bury St. Edmunds, 1684. R2/69/243; W1/138/48
Thomas, Clare, 1610. A5/3/94
Thomas, yeo., Clare, 1636. R2/57/93; W1/92/110
Thomas, cooper, Cockfield, 1682. R2/68/289; W1/136/21
Thomas, yeo., Creeting St. Peter, 1609. R2/47/6; W1/66/6
Thomas, husb., Downham, 1596. R2/43/197; W1/54/78
Thomas, Great Barton, 1693. A5/6/160, A4/35/52
Thomas, Hengrave, 1643, (N). R2/59/61; W1/100/68
Thomas, clothier, Long Melford, 1620, (N). R2/52/168; W1/76/151
Thomas, scrivener, Sudbury, 1554. R2/24/95
Thomas, cordwainer, Thelnetham, 1639. R2/24/52; W1/94/95
Thomas, yeo., Whatfield, 1662. R2/62/403; W1/114/150; A5/5/38
Thomas, als. Barker, tailor, Whatfield, 1700. R2/74/79; W1/154/82; In. 3/27/11
Walter, Cavenham, 1680. In. 3/20/208; A5/6/41, A4/17/107
Walter, Swaffham, (1534). W1/51/78
William, bed weaver, Bury St. Edmunds, 1481. R2/2/324
William, butcher, Bury St. Edmunds, 1638, (N). R2/57/324; W1/93/104
William, husb., Glemsford, 1603. R2/45/275; W1/61/77
William, Great Cornard, 1649. A5/4/131
William, husb., Groton, 1640. R2/58/209; W1/96/143
William, Layham, 1518. R2/12/102
William, Little Waldingfield, 1632. A5/4/21
William, Sudbury, 1460. R2/9/306
William, gent., Worlington, 1617. R2/50/258; W1/74/57
see also Paine, Pane, Payen, Peyne, Denney als. Payne

PAYNTER, John, husb., Thrandeston, 1589. R2/41/149; W1/46/131
Richard, Stowmarket, 1610. A5/3/108
Susan, wid., Stowmarket, 1633. R2/56/284; W1/90/49
Thomas, Stowmarket, 1621. R2/52/216; W1/77/15
William, priest, Bardwell, 1560. R2/29/1; W1/25/67

PAYNTOUR, John, husb., Burwell, 1440. R2/9/28
PAYTE, Agnes, Stradishall, 1545. R2/19/530; W1/7/110
  Thomasine, wid., Sudbury, 1639. R2/58/109; W1/94/181
PAYTON, Adam, yeo., Bury St. Edmunds, 1590. R2/41/408; W1/47/88
  John, singleman, Thurston, 1635. R2/56/475; W1/91/48
  Jonathan, Drinkstone, 1693. A5/6/154, A4/35/96
  Ralph, Fornham St. Martin, 1582. A5/2/43
  Robert, Whepstead, 1583. A5/2/48
  Thomas, wid., Thurston, 1566. R2/32/315; W1/28/75
  Thomas, yeo., Thurston, 1640. R2/58/131; W1/96/20
  William, Risby, 1556. R2/25/58; W1/16/72
  William, husb., Thurston, 1569. R2/33/121; W1/28/186
  see also Paton, Peyton
PEACH, Alexander, labourer, Lawshall, 1597. R2/43/270; W1/55/47
  Alice, wid., Bury St. Edmunds, 1559. W1/17/76
  Alice, wid., Lawshall, 1637. A5/4/48
  George, Bures, 1639. A5/4/72
  Joan, singlewoman, Lawshall, 1673. R2/65/396; W1/125/10
  Mary, spinster, Lawshall, 1637. A5/4/56
  Richard, Bures, 1643. A5/4/100
  Richard, yeo., Haughley, 1627. R2/54/62; W1/83/68
  Richard, Lawshall, 1598. A5/2/201
  Roger, Lawshall, 1624, (N). R2/53/32; W1/80/44
  William, 1630. R2/55/26; W1/86/30
  see also Peche, Petch, Barrett als. Peach, Peachey als. Peach,
  Pechy als. Peach
PEACHELL, Roger, Bury St. Edmunds, 1649. A5/4/130
PEACHEY, Ann, Mildenhall, 1650. A5/4/133
  Ann, wid., Soham, 1647. R2/59/483; W1/104/117; In. 3/2/121
  Edmund, yeo., Mildenhall, 1660. R2/62/25; W1/112/25
  Francis, Mildenhall, 1629, (N). R2/54/429; W1/85/110
  Henry, yeo., Mildenhall, 1645. R2/59/175; W1/102/4
  James, yeo., Mildenhall, 1647. R2/59/486; W1/104/121;
  In. 3/2/113
  John, Bury St. Edmunds, 1645. A5/4/108
  John, the elder, woollen draper, Mildenhall, 1624. R2/53/161;
  W1/80/143
  John, yeo., Mildenhall, 1647. R2/59/432; W1/104/62;
  In. 3/2/69
  John, carpenter, Mildenhall, 1660. R2/62/110; W1/112/145;
  In. 3/5/173
  John, Mildenhall, 1668. In. 3/13/63
  John, yeo., Mildenhall, 1669. R2/64/547; W1/121/136;
  In. 3/14/126
  John, Mildenhall, 1679. A5/6/22, A4/16/72
  Mark, Soham, 1649. A5/4/126
  Mary, wid., Eriswell, 1686. A5/6/100, A4/26/87
  Mary, wife of Robert, Mildenhall, 1651. R2/61/464
  Mary, wid., Mildenhall, 1684. R2/69/402; W1/138/183
  Mary, wid., Soham, 1685. R2/70/171; W1/139/142
  Matthew, husb., Mildenhall, 1668. In. 3/13/172; A5/5/98,
  A4/6/86
  Nathaniel, Chippenham, 1684. A5/6/81, A4/21/75
  Nicholas, the elder, yeo., Mildenhall, 1664. R2/63/150;
  W1/116/42; In. 3/9/105
  Nicholas, shepherd, Mildenhall, 1667. R2/64/285; W1/119/149;
  In. 3/12/171
  Peter, Mildenhall, 1683. A5/6/67, A4/20/18
  Richard, grocer, singleman, Burwell, 1692. R2/72/13; W1/146/12,
  In. 3/24/73
  Richard, yeo., Mildenhall, 1642. R2/58/364; W1/99/65
  Richard, Mildenhall, 1649. A5/4/131
  Richard, Soham, 1662. In. 3/7/23; A5/5/26
  Richard, yeo., Soham, 1689. R2/71/149; W1/143/8
  Robert, als. Peach, yeo., Lawshall, 1649. R2/60/171; W1/106/18
  Robert, singleman, Mildenhall, 1684. R2/69/422; W1/138/200;
  A5/6/192
  Robert, husb., Mildenhall, 1684. R2/69/428; W1/138/206
  Robert, yeo., Tuddenham, 1695. R2/72/498; W1/149/51
  Thomas, Burwell, 1673. A5/5/139, A4/10/49
  Thomas, yeo., Mildenhall, 1672. R2/65/346; W1/124/78
  William, shepherd, Mildenhall, 1631. R2/56/25; W1/87/33
  William, Mildenhall, 1649. A5/4/128

PEACHIE, Alice, wid., Soham, 1581. R2/38/240
Richard, the elder, yeo., Mildenhall, 1603. R2/45/248; W1/61/47
PEACHY, Ann, wid., Mildenhall, 1640. A5/4/81
Edward, Burwell, 1700. In. 3/27/51; A5/7/15, A4/41/125
Geoffrey, yeo., Bures, 1633, (N). W1/111/45
Henry, Lawshall, 1671. A5/5/122, A4/86/21
Joan, wid., Mildenhall, 1668. A5/5/95, A4/6/58
John, Soham, 1640. A5/4/83
John, Soham, 1668. In. 3/13/68; A5/5/94, A4/6/50
Jonathan, gent., Mildenhall, 1673, (N). R2/65/437; W1/125/63
Richard, tanner, Kennett, 1700. In. 3/27/71; A5/7/14, A4/41/85
Richard, Mildenhall, 1660. A5/5/3, A4/1/221
William, Mildenhall, 1691. A5/6/141, A4/33/39
see also Pechee, Pechey, Petchee
PEACK, John, husb., Fordham, 1618. W1/95/121
PEACOCK(E), Ann, wid., Ixworth, 1695. R2/72/538; W1/149/95
Edward, linen weaver, Mildenhall, 1636. R2/57/29; W1/92/38
George, husb., Ixworth, 1639. R2/58/44; W1/94/80
Henry, Bury St. Edmunds, 1611. A5/3/114
Joan, wid., Lavenham, 1660. R2/62/15; W1/112/13; In. 3/5/9
John, Ixworth, 1639. A5/4/71
John, clothier, Lavenham, 1690. R2/71/429; W1/144/133
John, husb., Rougham, 1609. R2/47/14; W1/66/13
Nicholas, Great Waldingfield, 1593. R2/42/378; W1/50/43
Richard, fellmonger, Lavenham, 1689. R2/72/162; W1/143/23
Thomas, Barton Mills, 1671. A5/5/127
Thomas, Ixworth, 1687. In. 3/23/11; A5/6/109, A4/27/17
Thomas, Mildenhall, 1672. A5/5/134, A4/9/79
William, labourer, yeo., Barton Mills, 1670. R2/65/43; W1/122/50; In. 3/15/65
William, Mildenhall, 1593. A5/2/186
William, yeo., Pakenham, 1680. R2/67/603; W1/134/75; In. 3/20/81
PEACOKE, John, yeo., Ixworth, 1675. R2/66/167; W1/127/43; In. 3/16/48
see also Pecock(e)
PEAD, John, Hengrave, 1650. In. 3/3/116
Mary, wid., Bury St. Edmunds, 1617. R2/50/237; W1/74/32
Thomas, gent., Bury St. Edmunds, 1614, (N). R2/49/160; W1/71/107
PEAKE, Alexander, yeo., Timworth, 1611. R2/48/72; W1/68/89
Barbara, wid., Nowton, 1679. A5/6/28, A4/16/139
Edmund, husb., Icklingham, 1678. R2/68/121; W1/130/105; In. 3/19/144
George, maltster, Nowton, 1674. R2/67/8; W1/126/114
John, husb., Fordham, 1661. R2/62/302; W1/113/222; In. 3/6/221; A5/5/20
John, yeo., Great Thornham, 1682. R2/68/433; W1/136/121; In. 3/21/93
John, labourer, Little Livermere, 1668. R2/64/370; W1/120/85; In. 3/13/137
John, singleman, Mellis, 1624. R2/53/32; W1/80/45
John, the younger, bach., gent., Stowmarket, 1688. In. 3/23/120; A5/6/122, A4/29/68
John, Stowmarket, 1690. R2/71/305; W1/144/5
John, husb., Wicken, 1684. R2/69/211; W1/138/22
Lucy, wid., Fordham, 1633. R2/56/295; W1/90/58
Mary, wid., Cotton, 1648. R2/60/80; W1/105/96
Nicholas, Mellis, 1573. R2/36/120; W1/32/29
Philip, say maker, Sudbury, 1668. R2/64/314; W1/120/20; In. 3/13/35
Richard, yeo., Cotton, 1639. R2/58/114; W1/94/190
Richard, yeo., Fordham, 1632. R2/56/170; W1/89/79 a & b
Richard, Fordham, 1677. In. 3/18/104; A5/5/172, A4/14/50
Richard, yeo., Palgrave, 1609. R2/47/91; W1/66/107; A5/3/78
Richard, Stoke Ash, 1626. R2/53/567; W1/82/93
Richard, yeo., Troston, 1674. R2/66/18; W1/126/104
Robert, gent., Weston, 1637. A5/4/48
Robert, Weston, 1673. A5/5/137, A4/88/21
Roger, tailor, Bury St. Edmunds, 1686. R2/70/441; W1/140/56; In. 3/22/21

PEAKE continued
Thomas, Fordham, 1694. A5/6/175, A4/37/102
Thomas, fellmonger, Market Weston, 1681. R2/68/154; W1/135/117
Thomas, husb., Mellis, 1581. R2/38/297; W1/40/40
Thomas, yeo., Thwaite, 1581. R2/38/282; W1/40/28
Thomas, clerk, Westhorpe, 1659. W1/110/54
Thomas, Weston, 1681. A5/6/50, A4/96/85
see also Peack, Peeck, Peike, Pek(e)
PEARCE, Anthony, blacksmith, Hopton, 1663. R2/63/37; W1/115/59; In. 3/8/56
see also Pearse, Peers, Perse, Pyers
PEARE, Simon, Lavenham, 1577. R2/37/287
PEARLE, Abigail, wid., Rattlesden, 1688. R2/71/106; W1/142/97; In. 3/23/87
Edmund, yeo., Great Livermere, 1678. A5/6/5, A4/15/38
Francis, yeo., Rattlesden, 1640. R2/58/188; W1/96/109
George, husb., Thorndon, 1624. R2/53/3; W1/80/4
George, husb., Thorndon, 1638. R2/57/392; W1/93/206
John, Braiseworth, 1648. A5/4/123
John, sen., yeo., Rattlesden, 1685. R2/70/104; W1/139/93
Prudence, wid., Old Newton, 1684. R2/69/417; W1/138/196
Thomas, tanner, Buxhall, 1649. R2/60/212; W1/106/58
Thomas, Rattlesden, 1566. A5/1/178
Thomas, yeo., Rattlesden, 1688. R2/71/117; W1/142/105; In. 3/23/115
see also Perle
PEARSE, Joan, Bury St. Edmunds, 1591. A5/2/159
Thomas, linen weaver, Hopton, 1615. R2/49/306; W1/72/85
PEARSON, John, husb., Mildenhall, 1638. R2/57/378; W1/93/182
Richard, Isleham, 1652. A4/1/2
William, ploughwright, Barrow, 1614. R2/49/168; W1/71/114
William, maltster, Bildeston, 1616. R2/50/161; W1/73/157
William, weaver, Boxford, 1605, (N). R2/45/401; W1/63/39
see also Peerson, Peirson, Pereson, Person
PEART, Christopher, clerk, Ingham, 1647. R2/59/455; W1/104/88; In. 3/2/90
Elisabeth, wid., Rattlesden, 1681, (N). R2/68/233; W1/135/173
PEASE, Robert, yeo., Thwaite, 1667. R2/64/289; W1/119/152; In. 3/12/172
Thomas, Sudbury, 1583. A5/2/45
PECAS, Agnes, Brandon, 1471. R2/10/460
PECE, Margaret, wid., Sudbury, 1543. R2/19/386 & 408; W1/6/101 & 129
PECHE, Agnes, wid., Buxhall, (1546). W1/38/100
Agnes, wid., Soham, 1506. R2/12/75
Alice, wid., Soham, 1520. R2/15/83, R2/17/310; W1/39/76
Anne, wid., Lawshall, 1564. R2/32/87; W1/27/34
Anthony, husb., Icklingham, 1627, (N). R2/54/109; W1/83/107
Cicely, wid., Soham, 1535. R2/18/134
John, labourer, Lawshall, 1559. R2/28/403; W1/3/151
John, the elder, Mildenhall, 1560. R2/29/104; W1/25/62
Margaret, wid., Mildenhall, 1548. R2/21/420; W1/8/15
Margaret, wid., Soham, 1545. R2/19/536; W1/7/122
Richard, husb., Mildenhall, 1562. R2/31/108; W1/8/200
Robert, Mildenhall, 1552. R2/23/214; W1/12/38
Robert, the elder, Mildenhall, 1556. R2/25/100; W1/16/101
Robert, the elder, Mildenhall, 1557. R2/26/70
Rose, Soham, 1530. R2/19/33
Samuel, yeo., Haverhill, 1668. R2/64/352; W1/120/64; A5/5/97, A4/6/77
Thomas, the elder, Haverhill, 1595. R2/43/76; W1/53/67
Thomas, Soham, 1523. R2/17/32; W1/21/53
Thomas, Soham, 1525. R2/17/87; W1/21/3
William, Mildenhall, 1545. R2/19/557; W1/7/80
William, husb., Mildenhall, 1573. R2/36/141; W1/32/47
William, Soham, 1488. R2/11/400
William, Soham, 1543. R2/19/378; W1/6/123
PECHEE, William, Mildenhall, 1516. R2/12/118
PECHES, Eleanor, wid. of John, Kirtling, 1578. R2/36/211; W1/32/137
PECHEY, Ann, singlewoman, Soham, 1648. R2/60/62; W1/105/78
Ann, wid., Soham, 1670. R2/65/128; W1/122/153

PECHEY continued
Christian, wid., Mildenhall, 1578. R2/37/389; W1/36/187
James, labourer, Mildenhall, 1679. R2/67/459; W1/133/184
John, Haverhill, 1546. R2/21/228; W1/10/101
John, husb., Isleham, 1576. W7/41
John, Mildenhall, 1685. A5/6/92, A4/24/78
John, Soham, (1503). R2/12/73
John, yeo., Soham, 1616. R2/50/15; W1/73/16
John, the elder, yeo., Soham, 1617. R2/50/270; W1/74/69
John, yeo., Soham, 1684. R2/69/295; W1/138/89
John, labourer, Soham, 1689. R2/71/163; W1/143/13
Richard, the younger, husb., Mildenhall, 1595. R2/43/102; W1/53/100
Richard, Mildenhall, 1680. In. 3/20/248; A5/6/36, A4/17/50
Richard, gent., Soham, 1693. R2/72/178
Richard, gent., Soham, 1696. R2/73/18; W1/150/12
Robert, Bury St. Edmunds, 1611. A5/3/110
Robert, yeo., Soham, 1663. R2/63/69; W1/115/110; In. 3/8/140
Walter, husb., Soham, 1682. R2/68/281; W1/136/14; In. 3/21/199
Walter, yeo., Soham, 1696. R2/73/15; W1/150/15; In. 3/25/60
William, yeo., Mildenhall, 1624. R2/53/168; W1/80/147
William, husb., Mildenhall, 1682. In. 3/21/45b
William, gent., Soham, 1687. R2/70/319; W1/141/63

PECHIE, Alice, Mildenhall, 1568. A5/1/200
Edmund, yeo., Soham, 1614. W1/95/115
Elisabeth, Soham, 1591. A5/2/150
Geoffrey, Bures, 1634, (N). R2/56/356; W1/90/125
John, the younger, yeo., Soham, 1608. R2/46/196; W1/65/67
John, singleman, Soham, 1622. R2/52/386; W1/78/22
Margaret, wife of John, Soham, 1584. A5/2/57
Margery, wid., Mildenhall, 1558. R2/27/497
Matthew, yeo., Soham, 1624. R2/53/16; W1/80/24 a & b
Richard, yeo., Mildenhall, 1623. R2/52/720; W1/79/133
Richard, sen., yeo., Soham, 1625. R2/53/211; W1/81/13
Robert, husb., Soham, 1619. R2/51/449; W1/132/115
Thomas, Mildenhall, 1638. R2/57/267; W1/93/30
Thomas, yeo., Soham, 1608. R2/46/165
William, yeo., Soham, 1614. R2/49/79; W1/71/62

PECHY, Edmund, als. Peach, yeo., Lawshall, 1624. R2/53/114; W1/80/117
Edmund, husb., Soham, 1553. R2/31/161; W1/13/107
Ellen, wid., Soham, 1501. R2/13/119
John, labouring man, Soham, 1586. W1/43/50
Robert, Soham, 1480. R2/11/224
Robert, the elder, Soham, 1555. R2/24/217; W1/15/48
Thomas, husb., Soham, 1557. R2/26/261; W1/20/177
Thomas, husb., Soham, 1564. R2/32/125; W1/27/76
William, Soham, 1503. R2/12/71
William, the elder, Mildenhall, 1559. R2/28/146; W1/22/135
William, Soham, 1529. R2/18/25; W1/311/15
William, Soham, 1595. A5/2/212

PECK, Bridget, spinster, Snailwell, 1691. R2/71/451
Elisabeth, wid., Fornham All Saints, 1679. R2/67/482; W1/133/201; A5/6/29, A4/16/156
John, wid., Thwaite, 1623. R2/52/644; W1/79/72
Joan, wid., Walsham le Willows, 1608. A5/3/43
John, physician, chirurgeon, Bury St. Edmunds, 1604. R2/45/350; W1/62/72
John, yeo., Creeting All Saints, 1663. In. 3/8/168; A5/5/51
John, yeo., Fornham All Saints, 1667. R2/64/229; W1/119/82; In. 3/12/100
John, yeo., Ingham, 1600. R2/45/17; W1/58/24
John, husb., Ingham, 1612. R2/48/204; W1/69/95
John, yeo., Mildenhall, 1690. R2/71/347; W1/144/51
John, butcher, Stanton, 1694. R2/72/289; W1/148/14
John, Stoke Ash, 1671. R2/65/220; W1/123/95
John, the elder, tailor, Walsham le Willows, 1610. R2/47/276; W1/67/161
Joseph, wid., Hepworth, 1681. R2/68/123; W1/135/94; A4/18/67
Martin, singleman, Timworth, 1575. R2/37/89; W1/34/13

PECK continued
Richard, weaver, Bury St. Edmunds, 1440. R2/1/250
Richard, Fornham St. Genevieve, 1571. R2/35/163; W1/38/168
Simon, carpenter, Cheveley, 1676. In. 3/17/163; A5/5/166, A4/13/95
Simon, Stanton, 1632. A5/4/18
Simon, Walsham le Willows, 1605, (N). R2/45/400; W1/63/37
Susan, wid., Ingham, 1627. R2/54/127; W1/83/126
Thomas, wid., Cheveley, 1678. In. 3/19/205; A5/6/13, A4/15/110
Thomas, Hargrave, 1603. R2/45/277; W1/61/82
Thomas, Stowmarket, 1686. A5/6/103, A4/26/42
Thomas, husb., Timworth, 1558. R2/27/519
William, carpenter, Cheveley, 1696. In. 3/25/9; A5/6/185, A4/39/13
William, Gislingham, 1587. A5/2/87
see also Pec, Pek(e)
PECKOVER, Thomas, yeo., Boxford, 1693. R2/72/249; W1/147/139; A5/6/156, A4/35/79
PECOCK(E), Alice, wid., Brent Eleigh, 1569. R2/33/127; W1/28/194
John, Herringswell, 1561. A5/1/117
John, carpenter, Pakenham, 1566. R2/32/316; W1/27/74
William, Pakenham, 1545. R2/19/526; W1/7/38
PECOK(E), Edmund, husb., Little Wratting, 1536. R2/18/141
John, Bury St. Edmunds, 1441. R2/1/252
John, Worlington, 1576. In. 3/1/41
Richard, Pakenham, 1576. R2/37/139; W1/37/10; In. 3/1/114
Richard, yeo., Pakenham, 1632. R2/56/140; W1/89/32
Thomas, Pakenham, 1575. R2/37/79; W1/34/26
Walter, Pakenham, 1533. W1/2/33
PEDDER, Alice, wife of Robert, Ixworth, 1465. R2/10/378
Edward, inn holder, Bury St. Edmunds, 1695. R2/72/479; W1/149/36
William, Stoke by Clare, 1461. R2/10/341
PEDER, John, Elmsett, 1668. In. 3/13/186; A5/5/101, A4/6/119
see also Hamond als. Pedder
PEDYWADE, John, Great Waldingfield, 1526. R2/17/214; W1/23/18
PEECK, William, yeo., Fornham, 1576. R2/37/183; W1/37/50; In. 3/1/54
PEEK(E), Joan, Lavenham, (1473). R2/11/9
John, Stoke by Nayland, 1590, (N). R2/41/323; W1/47/12
Nicholas, husb., Weston, 1595. R2/43/72; W1/53/60
Thomas, Lawshall, 1451. R2/9/126
Thomas, sen., Lawshall, 1471. R2/10/485
PEELE, Robert, Hartest, 1573. R2/36/192; W1/32/116
Robert, Mildenhall, 1610. A5/3/93
PEERS, Philip, Sudbury, 1465. R2/10/393
William, als. Reder, Bury St. Edmunds, 1478. R2/2/258
PEERSON, Agnes, wid. of Robert, Fordham, 1544. R2/19/453, R2/21/183; W1/10/39
Alice, wid., Badwell Ash, 1564. R2/32/113; W1/27/66
Richard, Isleham, 1572. W7/35
Robert, Fordham, 1540. R2/20/154
Rose, wid., Thelnetham, 1616. R2/50/138; W1/73/142
William, Holme, 1582. W1/51/158
PEETTE, Robert, sen., Wattisfield, 1580. R2/38/190; W1/39/115
PEGAS, Christian, Brandon, 1440. R2/9/26
William, Lakenheath, 1479. W1/24/27
PEGAYS, William, sen., Brandon, 1474. R2/11/357
see also Pecas, Pygas
PEGG, Elisabeth, Wattisham, 1649. A5/4/126
Henry, Semer, 1679. A5/6/25
Mary, Gazeley, 1699. R2/73/358; W1/153/17
Nicholas, yeo., Naughton, 1644. R2/59/149; W1/101/74
William, Boxford, 1698. A5/7/8
William, singleman, Whatfield, 1644. R2/59/85; W1/101/15
see also Roper als. Pegg
PEIKE, John, weaver, Sudbury, 1592. R2/42/271; W1/49/90
PEIRSON, Elisabeth, wid., Little Saxham, 1631, (N). R2/56/23; W1/87/29
James, weaver, Thelnetham, 1623. R2/52/684; W1/79/103
John, Thelnetham, 1649. A5/4/128

PEIRSON continued
John, Thelnetham, 1666. In. 3/11/101; A5/5/78, A4/4/78
Mary, wid., Freckenham, 1678. In. 10/21
Richard, Thelnetham, 1648. A5/4/121
Robert, labourer, Ixworth, 1674. R2/66/83; W1/126/36
Robert, linen weaver, Weston, 1646. R2/59/341; W1/103/55
William, Hinderclay, 1648. A5/4/123
William, husb., Wangford, 1631. R2/56/110; W1/87/169
PEK(E), John, Rickinghall Superior, 1536. R2/17/110
John, Stowmarket, 1439. R2/9/3
Richard, husb., Ingham, 1628. R2/54/234; W1/84/96
William, turner, Gislingham, 1562. R2/31/112; W1/8/198
William, Rickinghall Superior, 1585. R2/39/242; W1/42/331
William, husb., Stoke Ash, 1556. R2/24/108; W1/16/142
---, Palgrave, 1550. W1/9/121
PEKERELL, John, Thurston, 1461. R2/9/293
Robert, Stowmarket, 1524. R2/16/322
Roger, Thurston, 1461. R2/9/296
Thomas, Rickinghall Superior, (1458). R2/9/240
PEKHAR, William, Bury St. Edmunds, 1449. R2/2/27
PEKYRELL, John, Wetherden, 1439. R2/9/5
PELGRAVE, John, Hepworth, 1587. A5/2/88
PELL, Martha, wid., Langham, 1700. A5/7/16
Thomas, Kedington, 1594. R2/42/586; W1/52/8
PELLICAN, Margaret, wid., Sudbury, 1526. R2/17/147; W1/21/140
PELLYCAN, John, Sudbury, 1444. R2/9/52
Rose, wid., Sudbury, 1489. R2/11/379
PELLYNG, John, Chelsworth, 1567. A5/1/188
PELTYR, John, Clare, 1462. R2/10/313
PEMAN, Henry, Lidgate, 1581. R2/38/271; W1/40/20
PENDLETON, Elisabeth, wid., Stowmarket, 1681. A5/6/49, A4/18/71
PENEY, William, Great Fakenham, 1565. R2/32/151; W1/27/93
PENNALL, John, Stanton, 1681. A5/6/48, A4/18/62 a & b
Rose, als. Windart, wid., Bardwell, 1682. In. 3/21/2
see also Pennyall, Penold, Penyall
PENNIE, Simon, yeo., Hinderclay, 1670. R2/65/31; W1/122/36; In. 3/15/59
PENNING, John, yeo., Thrandeston, 1619. R2/51/350; W1/132/54
Katherine, wid., Edwardstone, 1614. R2/49/109; W1/71/80
Robert, yeo., cooper, Palgrave, 1660. In. 3/5/155; A5/5/6, A4/1/194
Sabian, cooper, Palgrave, 1648. R2/60/24; W1/105/35
William, gent., Eye, 1651. R2/61/457
see also Pennyng
PENNOCK, John, Stoke by Nayland, 1632. A5/4/20
see also Penock
PENNY, Agnes, wid., Thelnetham, 1562. A5/1/136
Alice, wid., Lakenheath, 1617. R2/50/362; W1/74/146
Elisabeth, wid., Eye, 1626. R2/53/582; W1/82/110
Humphrey, husb., Thelnetham, 1625. R2/53/279; W1/81/67
Jane, wid., Hinderclay, 1640. R2/58/205; W1/96/137
John, Brandon, 1574. W1/95/3
John, joiner, Eye, 1660. In. 3/5/33; A5/5/3, A4/1/224
John, Hinderclay, 1579. A5/2/17
Mark, weaver, Lakenheath, 1615. R2/49/341; W1/72/112
Richard, labourer, Lakenheath, 1590. R2/41/352; W1/47/45
Roger, Thrandeston, 1668, (N). R2/64/381; W1/120/99; In. 3/13/111
Simon, husb., Hinderclay, 1589. R2/41/277; W1/46/31
see also Peney, Pennie, Peny
PENNYALL, John, Stanton, 1542. R2/22/24; W1/6/74
John, Stanton, 1546. R2/21/650
Robert, Stanton, 1525. R2/17/130; W1/21/126
PENNYNG, John, yeo., Thrandeston, 1583. R2/39/64; W1/42/45
Nicholas, Great Thornham, 1543. R2/19/347; W1/6/156
Robert, gent., Eye, 1636. R2/57/44; W1/92/55
Robert, gent., Eye, 1676. R2/66/416; W1/128/128; In. 3/17/173
PENOCK, Christopher, yeo., Assington, 1580. R2/38/175; W1/39/124
PENOLD, John, yeo., Stanton, 1651. R2/61/421
PENTEN, Thomas, Stowmarket, 1612. A5/3/116
PENTENEY, Ralph, als. Sporyer, Ixworth, 1462. R2/10/375
PENTLOE, George, Sudbury, 1672. A5/5/131, A4/9/46

PENTNEY, John, cordwainer, Icklingham, 1671. R2/65/182; W1/123/53
Robert, tailor, Bury St. Edmunds, 1617. R2/50/366; W1/74/150
see also Penteney
PENY, George, Hinderclay, 1562. R2/31/33; W1/8/185
Thomas, Weston, 1557. R2/26/254; W1/20/170a
William, husb., Hinderclay, 1552. R2/23/176
PENYALL, Isaac, Stanton, 1621. R2/52/322; W1/77/102 a & b
John, Flempton, 1533. W1/2/26
John, Stanton, 1573. R2/36/196; W1/32/125
PENYNGTON, John, baker, Bures, 1477. R2/11/83
PEPER, John, Norwich, (1517). W1/51/57
Robert, sen., Eye, 1451. R2/9/106
Thomas, Rickinghall, 1562. R2/31/47; W1/8/128
William, Isleham, 1560. W7/19
PEPPER, Ann, Isleham, 1626. R6/44
Edward, Little Waldingfield, 1678. In. 3/18/126; A5/5/173, A4/14/60
Elisabeth, wid., Lavenham, 1630. R2/55/181; W1/86/199
John, Burwell, 1569. A5/1/211
John, Landwade, 1640. R2/58/130; W1/96/17
John, yeo., Lavenham, 1625. R2/53/203; W1/81/6
John, Occold, 1558. R2/27/346
Nicholas, als. Pyper, yeo., Bury St. Edmunds, 1627. R2/54/86; W1/83/87
Philip, clothier, Bury St. Edmunds, 1668. In. 3/13/141; A5/5/97, A4/6/82
Robert, Snailwell, 1683. A5/6/66, A4/20/9
Simon, Wood Ditton, 1626. R2/53/561; W1/82/86
PEPYR, John, Haughley, 1541. R2/21/582
Sara, Palgrave, 1449. R2/9/95
Thomas, Bury St. Edmunds, 1517. R2/6/65
PERCEY, Joan, wife of Robert, Wetheringsett, 1521. R2/15/161, R2/17/328
PERCYVALE, Robert, Newmarket, (1471). R2/11/141
PERCYVALL, Margaret, wid., Nowton, 1560. R2/32/440; W1/19/76
Robert, Eriswell, 1566. R2/32/302; W1/28/93
see also Parcevall, Parcivall, Passevall, Persevall
PERESON, John, ploughwright, Barrow, 1591. R2/42/107; W1/48/124
William, yeo., Hinderclay, 1601. R2/44/466; W1/59/78
PERFEE, Annice, Burwell, 1562. R2/31/1; W1/8/132
Thomas, husb., Burwell, 1562. R2/31/51; W1/8/126
PERFREY, Benedict, Pakenham, 1564. R2/32/103
PERKEN, Simon, Hopton, 1463. R2/10/316
Stephen, Hopton, 1528. R2/15/225; W1/19/27
PERKER, Agnes, wid., Nowton, 1572. R2/36/47; W1/31/92
George, Great Cornard, 1588, (N). R2/41/14; W1/45/11a
Mary, wid., Badwell Ash, 1609. R2/47/82; W1/66/99
PERKIN, John, carpenter, Market Weston, 1686. R2/70/232; W1/140/2
Lettice, wid., Bury St. Edmunds, 1662. A5/5/39
Thomas, Eriswell, 1559. R2/28/325; W1/22/273
see also Perken, Perkyn
PERKINS, Elisabeth, Downham, 1610. A5/3/100
PERKINSON, William, Great Bradley, 1578. R2/37/385; W1/36/190
William, yeo., Great Bradley, 1625. R2/53/327; W1/81/110
PERKYN, Alice, wid., Hopton, 1528. R2/15/226
Edmund, West Stow, 1494. R2/13/25
John, sen., Barningham, 1457. R2/9/195
John, Ingham, 1483. R2/11/296
John, Stanton, 1504. R2/12/33
Juliana, wid., Hepworth, 1545. R2/19/498; W1/7/94
Margaret, wid., Weston, 1537. R2/20/83; W1/4/81
Margaret, wid. of John, Stanton, 1520. R2/15/103
Margery, Culford, 1460. R2/9/298
Robert, yeo., Weston, 1596. R2/43/185; W1/54/90
Simon, Hopton, 1471. R2/10/489
Simon, husb., Norton, 1528. R2/15/233; W1/19/28
Thomas, physician, Bury St. Edmunds, 1630. R2/55/129; W1/86/145
Thomas, the elder, Weston, 1529. R2/18/24
Thomas, Weston, 1540. R2/20/186; W1/4/151
William, Barningham, (1475). R2/11/91

PERKYN continued
William, yeo., Dalham, 1639, (N). R2/58/50; W1/94/92
William, Landwade, 1479. R2/11/184
William, West Stow, 1485. R2/11/343
---, 1526. R2/12/142
PERLE, John, merchant man, Clare, 1548. R2/21/441; W1/38/103
John, Lavenham, 1458. R2/9/215
Robert, weaver, Lavenham, 1562, (N). R2/31/13; W1/8/177; A5/1/127
PERMAN, Agnes, wid., Timworth, 1560. R2/29/168; W1/25/6
Isabel, wid., Stradishall, 1494. R2/13/115
John, the elder, Wickhambrook, 1602. R2/45/115; W1/60/31
Robert, Wickhambrook, 1463. R2/10/339 & 590
William, Stradishall, 1528. R2/15/190
see also Parman
PERMENTER, Richard, als. Cowper, Gazeley, (1542). R2/22/79
PERMEPHAYE, Roger, als. Deye, Edwardstone, 1562. A5/1/122
PERMETER, John, Eye, 1542. R2/22/59 & 72; W1/6/55
PERPHE, John, Great Wratting, 1555. R2/24/198; W1/15/32
PERPONTE, Margaret, Westhorpe, 1439. R2/9/1
PERPOUNT, John, sen., Denston, 1453. R2/9/149
PERRY, George, yeo., Stradishall, 1622, (N). R2/52/527; W1/78/125
John, Bury St. Edmunds, 1693. A5/6/161, A4/35/41
John, Clare, 1680. In. 3/20/196; A5/6/40, A4/17/99
John, Icklingham, 1690. A5/6/135, A4/32/39
John, yeo., Mildenhall, 1662. R2/62/308; W1/114/3
John, Nayland, 1601. R2/44/352; W1/59/16
Martin, yeo., Withersfield, 1663. R2/63/85; W1/115/134; In. 3/8/148
Mary, wid., Great Bradley, 1649, (N). R2/60/279; W1/106/151
Thomas, yeo., Barningham, 1678. R2/67/161; W1/130/144; In. 3/19/197
William, yeo., Great Bradley, 1645. R2/59/220; W1/102/45
see also Pery(e), Pyrye
PERRYMAN, Abraham, Bury St. Edmunds, 1689. A5/6/128, A4/30/31
William, husb., Bures, 1608. R2/46/161; W1/65/7
see also Peryman
PERRYN, John, cooper, Bury St. Edmunds, 1647. R2/59/425; W1/104/54; In. 3/2/58
see also Pyryn
PERSAY, John, draper, Bury St. Edmunds, 1509. R2/4/214
John, Newmarket, 1569. R2/33/139
PERSE, Alice, wid., Barrow, 1601, (N). R2/44/425; W1/59/100
Habakuk, Hopton, 1639. A5/4/68
John, yeo., Bradfield St. Clare, 1596. R2/43/154; W1/54/32
Thomas, carpenter, Soham, 1572. R2/36/15; W1/31/119
Robert, chaplain, Bury St. Edmunds, 1407. R2/1/116
PERSEVALL, John, shepherd, Eriswell, 1597. R2/43/273; W1/55/50
PERSIFEILD, Robert, Mildenhall, 1631. A5/4/11
PERSON, Alice, Bury St. Edmunds, 1396. R2/1/80
Bartholomew, Wattisfield, 1592. R2/42/264; W1/49/82
James, tailor, Barrow, 1639. R2/58/100; W1/94/163
Joan, wid. of John, Great Livermere, 1555. R2/24/204; W1/15/38
John, Rougham, 1475. R2/11/138
John, linen weaver, Thelnetham, 1660. R2/62/96; W1/112/129; In. 3/5/150; A5/5/78
Margaret, Wicken, 1521. R2/15/150
Richard, Ampton, 1471. R2/10/484
Richard, Burwell, 1528. R2/15/213; W1/19/21
Richard, Great Livermere, 1558. R2/27/73
Robert, singleman, Euston, 1597, (N). R2/43/312; W1/55/80
Robert, labourer, Walsham le Willows, 1598. R2/44/54; W1/56/41
Robert, yeo., Wangford, 1629. R2/54/391; W1/85/84
Thomas, Fordham, (1496). R2/13/119
William, yeo., Thelnetham, 1641. R2/58/269; W1/98/50
---, 1538. W1/51/46
see also Parson, Pirson
PERSY, Roger, yeo., Hessett, 1673. R2/65/413; W1/125/36
PERTINGTON, Robert, Combs, 1618. R2/51/186; W1/75/116
PERTRYCH, John, Fordham, 1477. R2/11/130
William, Acton, 1483. R2/11/293

PERY(E), Joan, wid., Great Saxham, 1627. R2/54/8; W1/83/9
Joan, singlewoman, Hartest, 1601. R2/44/358; W1/59/23
John, Barningham, 1602, (N). R2/45/116 & 191; W1/60/32 & 117
John, husb., Burwell, 1546. R2/21/267; W1/10/86
John, Great Whelnetham, 1462. R2/10/326
John, Haverhill, 1455. R2/9/228
John, Kersey, 1453. R2/9/150
Robert, Kersey, 1455. R2/9/223
Thomas, Great Saxham, 1605. A5/3/3
William, Burwell, 1529. W1/311/13
PERYMAN, John, Bures, 1557. R2/26/302; W1/20/225
Juliana, wid., Bures, 1578. R2/37/411; W1/36/160
Margery, wid., Bures, 1567. R2/32/407; W1/19/106
Walter, Bury St. Edmunds, 1440. R2/1/249
William, yeo., Assington, 1600. R2/45/43; W1/58/62
William, Bures, 1564. R2/32/71; W1/27/22
PESTALL, Mary, wid., Wicken, 1696. R2/73/44; W1/150/46
PESTELL, Laurence, Wicken, 1669. R2/64/487; W1/121/81; In. 3/14/68
Lawrence, Wicken, 1689. A5/6/129, A4/111/19
PESTLE, Laurence, Wicken, 1700. A5/7/15, A4/41/96
PESYE, John, husb., Great Finborough, 1584. R2/39/148; W1/42/176
PETCH, Edmund, Flempton, 1687. A5/6/114, A4/27/80
John, Mildenhall, 1485. W1/24/167
John, thatcher, Mildenhall, 1687. R2/70/405; W1/141/127
Margaret, wid., Haverhill, 1596. R2/43/214; W1/54/54
Margaret, wid., Lakenheath, 1693. R2/72/149
Robert, Tuddenham, 1700. In. 3/27/23; A5/7/14, A4/41/105
PETCHEE, Thomas, husb., Mildenhall, 1592. R2/42/199; W1/49/25
PETCHEY, Dorothy, wid., Bury St. Edmunds, 1651. R2/61/441
John, Bury St. Edmunds, 1689. A5/6/130, A4/30/6
Lawrence, Mildenhall, 1663. A5/5/46
Margaret, wid., Bury St. Edmunds, 1685. R2/70/225; W1/139/187; A5/6/97, A4/24/137
William, husb., Soham, 1573. R2/36/144; W1/32/44
William, yeo., Soham, 1642. R2/58/383; W1/99/92
PETCHIE, Richard, Mildenhall, 1626, (N). R2/53/664; W1/82/188
William, the elder, husb., Soham, 1614. R2/49/155; W1/71/104
PETCHY, Ann, Bury St. Edmunds, 1637. A5/4/49
Henry, cordwainer, Bury St. Edmunds, 1685. R2/70/224; W1/139/186; A5/6/97, A4/24/136
Luke, Bury St. Edmunds, 1630. A5/4/7
Matthew, Soham, 1632. A5/4/21
Peter, Mildenhall, 1594. A5/2/202
Richard, Mildenhall, 1540. R2/19/271; W1/36/28
Robert, Soham, 1523. R2/17/317
PETER(S), Bridget, wid., Sudbury, 1686. R2/70/517; W1/140/120; In. 3/22/141
Henry, 1629, (N). R2/54/357; W1/85/57
see also Petre, Wood als. Peters
PETERSGYLL, Agnes, wid., Bury St. Edmunds, 1567. W1/10/204
PETEWADE, Thomas, the elder, Glemsford, 1557. R2/26/315; W1/20/242
PETHYATON, Henry, Sudbury, 1442. R2/9/16
PETIVER, Thomas, Long Melford, 1539. R2/19/313
see also Petyver
PETIWAT(T), John, Glemsford, 1496. R2/13/77
John, clothier, Glemsford, 1600. R2/45/34; W1/58/51
PETLOWE, Edmund, Assington, 1635. A5/4/39
Susan, Assington, 1637. A5/4/48
PETRE, Margaret, wid., Stanningfield, 1697. R2/73/216; W1/151/103
PETRYCH, Katherine, Acton, 1443. R2/9/56; W1/24/11
PETT, Benjamin, yeo., Wattisfield, 1662, (N). R2/62/431; W1/114/197; A5/5/40, A4/3/38
Benjamin, cooper, Wattisfield, 1665. R2/63/302; W1/117/31; In. 5/5/66
Bridget, wid. of Benjamin, Wattisfield, 1663, (N). R2/63/37; W1/115/57; A5/5/45
Edmund, Wattisfield, 1632. A5/4/23
Henry, Woolpit, 1558. R2/27/28

PETT continued
Leonard, miller, Rickinghall Superior, 1602. R2/45/179; W1/60/103
Robert, yeo., Wattisfield, 1598. R2/44/61; W1/56/67
Robert, linen weaver, Wattisfield, 1637. R2/57/148; W1/92/185
Robert, Wattisfield, 1649. A5/4/130
Samuel, the elder, yeo., Hepworth, 1660. R2/62/104; W1/112/136
Thomas, linen weaver, Wattisfield, 1643. R2/59/28; W1/100/39
William, weaver, Wattisfield, 1643. R2/59/35; W1/100/45
---, Wattisfield, 1455. W1/24/112
see also Pytt
PETTAUGH, John, Stanton, 1650. A5/4/136
PETTAWE, Henry, Eye, 1554, (N). R2/24/125; W1/14/98
PETTET, Andrew, Ixworth, 1666. R2/64/2; W1/118/3; In. 3/11/8; A5/5/72, A4/4/1
John, yeo., Pakenham, 1592. R2/42/310
Robert, glazier, Bury St. Edmunds, 1681. R2/68/204; W1/135/150; In. 3/21/231
William, say weaver, Clare, 1663. R2/63/39; W1/115/61; In. 3/8/74
PETTEWARD, Henry, Timworth, 1649. R2/60/295; W1/106/170
see also Pedywade, Petewade, Petiwat(t), Pettiwate, Petywade
PETTIT(T), Alice, Great Wratting, 1587. A5/2/90
Ambrose, singleman, Wickhambrook, 1678. R2/67/114; W1/130/98; In. 3/19/127
Bartholomew, husb., Pakenham, 1628. R2/54/217; W1/84/81
Christopher, Sudbury, 1671. A5/5/123, A4/8/76
Christopher, Sudbury, 1698. A5/7/5
Edmund, Ashley, 1681. A5/6/46, A4/18/37
Giles, yeo., Fordham, 1635. R2/56/503; W1/91/80
Giles, yeo., Withersfield, 1619. R2/51/456; W1/132/121
James, Mildenhall, 1699. In. 3/27/44; A5/7/13, A4/41/51
John, Bury St. Edmunds, 1650. In. 3/3/74; A5/4/135
John, Buxhall, 1699. R2/73/447; W1/153/86
John, Great Barton, 1640. A5/4/81
John, Great Thurlow, 1667. A5/5/85
Margaret, wid., Milden, 1648. A5/4/123
Robert, blacksmith, Withersfield, 1683. R2/69/143; W1/137/117
Susan, Sudbury, 1681. A5/6/52, A4/18/109
Walter, yeo., Kirtling, 1662. In. 3/7/185; A5/5/37
William, Chevington, 1583. A5/2/50
see also Pettet, Pettyt(t), Petyt(t)
PETTIWATE, Margaret, Stradishall, 1632. R2/56/203; W1/89/117
William, yeo., Depden, 1652. R2/61/552; W1/109/33; In. 3/4/40
PETTNAT, Agnes, wid., Ousden, 1644. R2/59/142; W1/101/66
Ambrose, Ousden, 1642. R2/58/339; W1/99/34
PETTYKIN, William, Haughley, 1641. A5/4/87
see also Petyken
PETTYS, John, Bury St. Edmunds, 1471. R2/11/142
Roger, Bury St. Edmunds, 1434. R2/1/213
PETTYT(T), James, yeo., Creeting All Saints, 1620. R2/52/158; W1/76/143
John, husb., Ixworth, 1612, (N). R2/48/211; W1/69/103
Richard, yeo., Wratting, 1586. R2/40/102; W1/43/79
Thomas, husb., Cowlinge, 1604. R2/45/338; W1/62/52
William, Glemsford, 1610. A5/3/85
PETYKEN, Andrew, husb., Great Waldingfield, 1589. R2/41/274; W1/46/35
PETYT(T), George, Bury St. Edmunds, 1558. R2/8/333; W1/17/89
Giles, husb., Withersfield, 1560. R2/29/157; W1/25/16
John, Brandon, 1470. R2/10/425
William, the elder, Cowlinge, 1596. R2/43/187; W1/54/88
PETYTH, John, Withersfield, 1537. R2/19/260 & 578, R2/20/1 & 52; W1/3/165
Richard, Pakenham, (1506). R2/13/193
PETYVER, Joan, wid., Long Melford, 1550. R2/21/171; W1/9/112
PETYWADE, John, the younger, Glemsford, 1525. R2/17/101; W1/21/96
PETYWATE, John, Glemsford, 1471. R2/10/474
Robert, yeo., Chedburgh, 1616. R2/50/136; W1/73/140

PETYWAT(T), Austin, butcher, Sudbury, 1587. R2/40/112; W1/43/89
John, sen., Glemsford, 1479. R2/12/4
John, clothmaker, Glemsford, 1530. R2/19/8
PEVANS, John, Wetheringsett, 1585. A5/2/71
PEYKOT, John, Withersfield, 1452. R2/9/110
PEYNE, John, Ditton, 1477. R2/11/57
PEYNTOR, Margaret, wid. of John, Burwell, 1493. W1/24/8
PEYNTOUR, John, Burwell, 1482. R2/11/265
PEYTE, John, Hundon, 1504. R2/12/37
Richard, Hundon, (1535). R2/18/128
PEYTON, Alice, wid., Great Bradley, 1626. R2/53/594
Elisabeth, wid. of Francis, Bury St. Edmunds, 1537. R2/7/44
Francis, esq., Bury St. Edmunds, 1529. R2/6/159
Joan, wid., Bury St. Edmunds, 1595. R2/43/56; W1/53/44
John, Woolpit, 1482. R2/11/279
Reginald, gardener, Soham, 1585, (N). R2/39/316; W1/42/205
Robert, Bury St. Edmunds, 1442. R2/1/265
Thomas, gent., Bury St. Edmunds, 1439. R2/1/240
William, Little Saxham, 1487. R2/11/367
see also Payton
PHALMAN, Harry, Sudbury, 1447. W1/24/72
PHELIPE, John, Long Melford, 1474. R2/10/567
PHELYPP, Rose, Long Melford, (1498). R2/13/86
PHILIPP(S), Eleanor, wid., Soham, 1558. R2/27/372
Peter, Bury St. Edmunds, 1697. A5/6/191, A4/39/97
Thomas, als. Nayler, Bury St. Edmunds, 1431. R2/1/198
PHILLIPS, Elisabeth, wid., Great Cornard, 1640. R2/58/226; W1/96/170
John, Fornham, 1581. A5/2/34
Mary, Cavendish, 1638, (N). R2/57/284; W1/93/54
Mary, Fornham All Saints, 1670. A5/5/112
Reginald, carpenter, Brome, 1681. R2/68/226; W1/135/167
Richard, gent., Fornham All Saints, 1675. R2/66/132; W1/127/10; In. 3/16/24
William, gent., Kedington, 1695. R2/72/442; W1/149/2
William, Newmarket, 1652. R2/61/609; W1/109/88; In. 3/4/33
see also Felip, Fillippes, Phelipe, Phillop, Phylypp
PHILLIPSON, Anne, wid., Hartest, 1553. R2/21/662
John, the elder, yeo., Hartest, 1546. R2/21/656
John, yeo., Hartest, 1558. R2/27/517
Susan, wid., Ashen, 1694. R2/72/395; W1/148/127
Thomasine, Hartest, 1570. R2/34/30; W1/30/27; A5/1/223
PHILLOP, John, husb., Wangford, 1539. R2/19/304
PHILPOT, John, Bury St. Edmunds, 1462. R2/2/73
PHYLYPP, Nicholas, West Stow, 1506. R2/13/172
PHYNBOW, Michael, shoe maker, Walsham le Willows, 1578. R2/37/379; W1/36/197
PICHERE, Mebor, wid., Kentford, 1454. R2/9/205
PICHES, Rebecca, wid., Stoke by Nayland, 1662. R2/62/373; W1/114/106; In. 3/7/117
PICKARAM, John, husb., Great Thurlow, 1621. R2/52/248; W1/77/34
PICKARD, Richard, Burwell, 1590. R2/41/338; W1/47/30
PICKERAM, John, singleman, Rougham, 1683. R2/69/125; W1/137/101
see also Pickaram, Pickerum, Pickram
PICKERELL, John, Bury St. Edmunds, 1631. A5/4/11
John, Bury St. Edmunds, 1638. A5/4/57
John, Stowmarket, 1580. R2/38/155; W1/39/134
John, yeo., Thurston, 1613. R2/48/265; W1/70/40
Margaret, als. Bollocke, wid., Bury St. Edmunds, 1578. R2/37/381; W1/36/195
Margaret, wid., Bury St. Edmunds, 1638. A5/4/57
see also Pekerell, Pekyrell, Pyckrell, Pykerell, Pykrell
PICKERING, Roger, als. Kente, Stoke by Clare, 1592. R2/42/250; W1/49/68
William, clerk, Denham, 1660. R2/62/56; W1/112/69; In. 3/5/65
PICKERUM, Thomas, Pakenham, 1674, (N). R2/66/26; W1/126/99
William, yeo., Pakenham, 1688. R2/71/23; W1/142/19
PICKES, John, yeo., Newmarket, 1618. R2/51/126
PICKIS, Richard, gent., Newmarket, 1636. R2/57/64; W1/92/75 a & b
PICKLIN, Robert, Brandon, 1601. R2/44/498; W1/59/123
PICKLING, John, yeo., Bury St. Edmunds, 1690. R2/71/343; W1/144/47

PICKOVER, John, Great Wratting, 1589. A5/2/125
John, Kedington, 1590. A5/2/132
John, Kedington, 1591. A5/2/152
PICKRAM, Thomas, husb., Pakenham, 1685. R2/70/68; W1/139/60
PICROFT, Richard, husb., Exning, 1650, (N). R2/61/404; W1/107/110; In. 3/3/121
PIDGEON, Henry, gent., Bury St. Edmunds, 1667. A5/5/83, A4/5/33
PIGEON, Nicholas, Fornham All Saints, 1575, (N). R2/37/101; W1/34/41
PIGOTT, Elnathan, gent., Bury St. Edmunds, 1675. A5/5/158, A4/12/66 & 67
see also Pycot
PIKE, John, clerk, Bury St. Edmunds, 1473. R2/2/180
William, Barnham, 1623. R2/52/706; W1/79/120
William, Bury St. Edmunds, 1467. R2/2/107
see also Pyke
PIKEBON, John, Bury St. Edmunds, 1398. R2/1/87
PILBAROW, John, yeo., Buxhall, 1639. R2/58/27; W1/94/49
PILBOROUGH, John, Great Finborough, 1630. A5/4/2
Nicholas, the elder, Hitcham, 1622. R2/52/517; W1/78/117
Ralph, yeo., Rattlesden, 1686. R2/70/460; W1/140/75; In. 3/22/54
Stephen, Brockley, 1641. R2/58/250; W1/98/20
PILBOROW, Edward, yeo., Great Barton, 1698. R2/73/322; W1/152/89
John, Woolpit, 1685. A5/6/90, A4/24/44
Rachel, wid., Great Barton, 1664, (N). R2/63/158; W1/116/52; In. 3/9/64; A5/5/57, A4/2/40
Richard, yeo., Rattlesden, 1664. In. 3/9/8; A5/5/56, A4/2/22
William, yeo., Shelland, 1623. R2/52/689; W1/79/112
PILBROW, John, Bures, 1685. R2/70/64
Stephen, victualler, Ixworth, 1683. R2/69/154; W1/137/125
see also Pylbarow
PILGRAM, Ann, wid., Bury St. Edmunds, 1666. A5/5/78, A4/12/79
PILGROME, Alice, wid., Stoke by Clare, 1581. R2/38/331; W1/40/72
PIMAN, John, thatcher, Haughley, 1684. R2/69/409; W1/138/189
PIMPERNELL, John, butcher, Norton, 1590, (N). R2/41/443; W1/47/109
see also Pympernel
PINBORROUGH, Anne, wid., Eye, 1672. A5/5/130, A4/9/35
PINCHBACK, John, Sudbury, 1636. A5/4/44
Reginald, clothier, Nayland, 1612. R2/48/222; W1/69/122
Thomas, Assington, 1583. A5/2/51
PINCHBECK, Anne, wid., Poslingford, 1534. R2/19/199
John, draper, Lavenham, 1648. R2/60/35; W1/105/45
John, Nayland, 1588. A5/2/104
Martha, wid., Nayland, 1594. R2/42/509; W1/52/77
Richard, Nayland, 1580. R2/38/174; W1/39/125
see also Pynchbeck
PINDAR, Paul, clerk, Barnardiston, 1677. R2/66/452; W1/129/28
PINDER, John, Stradishall, 1652. In. 3/4/78; A5/4/142
see also Pyndar
PINNER, William, husb., Knettishall, 1680. R2/67/556; W1/134/39; In. 3/20/40
see also Pynner
PINSON, William, Thorndon, 1640. A5/4/84
PIPER, Edward, husb., Hundon, 1627. R2/54/85; W1/83/85
John, Fordham, 1563. R2/31/152; W1/26/33
John, als. Wainflett, Groton, 1645. R2/59/276; W1/102/92
John, Hundon, 1694. A5/6/171, A4/37/64
Mark, Kedington, 1698. A5/7/6
Michael, Great Cornard, 1694. A5/6/171, A4/37/62
William, Fordham, 1599. R2/44/180; W1/57/10
see also Pyper, Brygtheve als. Pyper, Man als. Pyper, Pepper als. Pyper, Waneflet als. Piper, Waynfleet als. Pyper
PIRSON, James, linen weaver, Thelnetham, 1616. R2/50/45; W1/73/50
Richard, Brettenham, 1625. R2/53/231; W1/81/28
Richard, the elder, linen weaver, Thelnetham, 1630. R2/55/139; W1/86/155
PISSEY, John, wool comber, Little Finborough, 1664. W1/312/24
John, Finborough, 1680. W1/312/25

PISSY, Thomas, Hessett, 1689. R2/71/170; W1/143/28
PISTOR, Alexander, rector, Bradfield St. George, 1680. R2/67/586; W1/134/63; In. 3/20/71
PITCHER, Thomas, Rickinghall Superior, 1590. A5/2/137
see also Pytcher
PITCHES, Agnes, wid., Hawkedon, 1626. R2/53/542; W1/82/70
Ann, wid., Ashley, 1636. A5/4/47
Edward, yeo., Lidgate, 1661. R2/62/274; W1/113/178; In. 3/6/242
Giles, yeo., Kirtling, 1634, (N). R2/56/403; W1/90/186
James, the elder, yeo., Kirtling, 1626. R2/53/603; W1/82/129
Jeremy, the elder, Westley, 1683. A5/6/72, A4/20/98
John, yeo., Barnardiston, 1636. R2/57/38; W1/92/47
John, yeo., Hundon, 1681. R2/68/180; W1/135/132
John, Newmarket, 1647. A5/4/117
Nicholas, Ashley, 1631. A5/4/11
Richard, yeo., Stoke by Clare, 1609. R2/47/16; W1/66/17
Thomas, alehouse keeper, Newmarket, (1675), (N). R2/66/253; W1/127/124; In. 3/16/154
William, Rede, 1634. A5/4/30
see also Peches, Piches, Pyches, Pytches
PITTMAN, Richard, Stowmarket, 1565. R2/32/234; W1/27/146
see also Pytman
PITTOCK, Nicholas, Kersey, 1699. A5/7/12, A4/41/39
see also Pyttock
PITTS, Elisabeth, wid., Great Saxham, 1644. A5/4/102
George, Wicken, 1678. In. 3/19/209; A5/6/12, A4/15/104
Simon, yeo., Great Saxham, 1641. R2/58/241; W1/98/11
PLACE, Andrew, Mildenhall, 1560. R2/29/70; W1/25/98
Ellen, wid. of Henry, Mildenhall, 1619. R2/51/487; W1/132/143
George, Mildenhall, 1480. R2/11/205
George, the elder, Mildenhall, 1549. R2/21/530; W1/8/77
Henry, yeo., Mildenhall, 1608. R2/46/171; W1/65/28
Henry, yeo., Mildenhall, 1642. R2/58/393; W1/99/107
John, Lavenham, 1441. R2/9/24
John, Mildenhall, 1527. R2/17/259; W1/1/20
John, Mildenhall, 1550. R2/21/21; W1/10/178
John, yeo., Mildenhall, 1618. R2/51/174; W1/75/107
John, baker, Sudbury, 1678. R2/67/13; W1/130/13; In. 3/19/13
Margaret, wid., Mildenhall, 1571. R2/35/153
Nicholas, Bury St. Edmunds, 1644. A5/4/103
Nicholas, wool man, Bury St. Edmunds, 1697. R2/73/157; W1/151/42; A5/7/3, A4/40/41
Richard, husb., Mildenhall, 1516. R2/13/221
Robert, singleman, Mildenhall, 1555. R2/24/183; W1/15/18
Rose, wid. of Robert, Mildenhall, 1441. R2/9/22
Simon, sen., Mildenhall, 1554. R2/24/111; W1/14/84
Stephen, shepherd, Mildenhall, 1679. R2/67/302; W1/133/85
Thomas, Mildenhall, 1457. R2/9/191
Thomas, husb., Mildenhall, 1560. R2/29/70; W1/25/97
Thomas, yeo., Mildenhall, 1648. R2/61/76; W1/105/93
Thomas, the elder, yeo., Mildenhall, 1686. R2/70/534; W1/140/138; In. 3/22/135
William, priest, master of the hospital of St. John, Bury St. Edmunds, 1504. R2/4/158
William, Bury St. Edmunds, 1700. A5/7/14, A4/41/90
William, husb., Mildenhall, 1555. R2/24/251; W1/15/80
William, yeo., Mildenhall, 1608. R2/46/195; W1/65/66
PLACES, James, Mildenhall, 1694. R2/72/369; W1/148/99
PLAFORTH, Katherine, wid., Fordham, 1522. R2/15/45
PLAIFORD, Joseph, bach., Troston, 1682. A5/6/58, A4/19/28
PLAMPEN, Henry, Nayland, 1600. R2/45/24; W1/58/37
Henry, the elder, tailor, Nayland, 1671. R2/65/213; W1/123/85
Reginald, yeo., Nayland, 1608. R2/46/167; W1/65/21
Robert, weaver, Stoke by Nayland, 1544. R2/19/470
PLAMPEYN, Thomas, Nayland, (1496). R2/13/35
PLAMPIN, Dorcas, the elder, spinster, Shimpling, 1686. R2/70/523; W1/140/126; In. 3/22/120
Frances, spinster, Shimpling, 1682. R2/68/368; W1/136/76; In. 3/21/148
John, Elmsett, 1588. A5/2/101
John, Lavenham, 1588. A5/2/105a

PLAMPIN continued
John, cordwainer, Nayland, 1640. R2/58/126; W1/96/9
John, the elder, gent., Shimpling, 1663. R2/63/67; W1/115/108; In. 3/8/118
John, Shimpling, 1670. In. 3/15/119; A5/5/115
Margaret, wid., Nayland, 1605. R2/45/418; W1/63/63
Peter, thatcher, Nayland, 1628. R2/54/266; W1/84/121
Robert, Lindsey, 1673. A5/5/137, A4/10/28
Robert, yeo., Long Melford, 1646. R2/59/300; W1/103/19
Robert, gent., Shimpling, 1679. R2/67/474; W1/133/195
Thomas, Stoke by Nayland, 1680. A5/6/38, A4/17/71
Thomas, Wiston, 1636. A5/4/44
Thomas, jun., yeo., Wiston, 1642. R2/58/234; W1/99/15
William, gent., Felsham, 1698. R2/73/307; W1/152/76
William, singleman, Stoke, 1626. R2/53/614; W1/82/143
William, husb., Stoke by Nayland, 1618. R2/51/159; W1/75/97
William, tailor, Stoke by Nayland, 1635. R2/56/477; W1/91/52
William, Wiston, 1607. R2/46/132; W1/97/58; A5/3/27
PLAMPION, Joanna, wid., Polstead, 1642. R2/58/339; W1/99/35
Thomas, yeo., Newton, 1639. R2/58/38; W1/94/71
PLAMPYN, Priscilla, spinster, Shimpling, 1692. R2/72/45; W1/146/41; In. 3/24/98
Robert, yeo., Great Cornard, 1675. R2/66/125; W1/127/2; In. 3/16/8
Robert, yeo., Lindsey, 1668. R2/64/398; W1/120/121; In. 3/13/189
Robert, yeo., Preston, 1600. R2/45/60; W1/58/84
Thomas, Great Cornard, 1543. R2/19/381; W1/6/126
see also Planpyne, Plompen
PLANDON, John, the younger, gent., Barton Mills, 1540. R2/20/244; W1/4/183
John, Bury St. Edmunds, 1493. R2/4/16
John, husb., Bury St. Edmunds, 1512. R2/5/14
John, weaver, Bury St. Edmunds, 1559. R2/8/350; W1/17/59
John, yeo., Eriswell, 1549. R2/21/535; W1/8/75
John, Lavenham, (1488). R2/11/396
Richard, Long Melford, (1481). R2/11/356
Thomas, Poslingford, 1527. R2/17/220; W1/1/65
PLANE, Margaret, Bury St. Edmunds, 1442. R2/1/262
see also Playne
PLANPYNE, William, husb., Weston, 1560. R2/29/18; W1/25/162
PLANT, John, Great Finborough, 1450. R2/9/115
Ralph, Layham, 1523. R2/14/85
PLANTYN, Ann, Walsham le Willows, 1584. A5/2/59
William, Walsham le Willows, 1584. A5/2/59
PLATT, Christopher, Bury St. Edmunds, 1594. A5/2/202
PLAYFERE, John, clerk, Depden, 1632. R2/56/152; W1/89/20
PLAYFOR, John, Drinkstone, 1610. A5/3/90
PLAYFORD, Agnes, Troston, 1472. R2/10/581
Anne, wid., Walsham le Willows, 1643. R2/59/5; W1/100/7
John, Mildenhall, 1468. R2/10/404
John, Mildenhall, 1474. R2/10/566
John, Oxborough, 1594. W1/51/107
Thomas, Mildenhall, 1482. R2/11/252
William, Walsham le Willows, 1638. A5/4/63
see also Plaiford
PLAYFORTH, John, Hepworth, 1561. A5/1/107
John, Wattisfield, 1567. A5/1/187
Robert, Ingham, 1558. R2/27/447
see also Plaforth
PLAYNE, Richard, Wicken, 1569. R2/33/116; W1/28/181
William, gent., Preston, 1632. A5/4/22
PLAYSTOWE, William, physician, Lavenham, 1651. R2/61/446
PLEASANCE, Ambrose, Glemsford, 1699. A5/7/13, A4/41/62
Amy, wid., Brandon, 1662. In. 3/7/189; A5/5/37
Anthony, Exning, 1642. R2/58/336; W1/99/32
Clement, gent., Herringswell, 1619. R2/51/458; W1/132/222
Edmund, yeo., Acton, 1627. R2/54/21; W1/83/27
George, yeo., Barrow, 1632. R2/56/143; W1/89/38
George, Hargrave, 1678. A5/6/7, A4/15/52
Grizel, wid., Brandon, 1622. R2/52/458; W1/78/73 & 74a
Henry, husb., Hartest, 1605. R2/45/428; W1/63/72

PLEASANCE continued
Henry, Sudbury, 1687. A5/6/109, A4/27/15
John, husb., Barrow, 1615. R2/49/320; W1/72/98
John, Great Saxham, 1685. A5/6/89, A4/24/34
Margaret, wife of Richard, parson, Hargrave, 1634. R2/56/403; W1/90/187
Mary, wid., Wicken, 1635. R2/56/474; W1/91/47
Richard, parson, Hargrave, 1638. R2/57/319; W1/93/97
Richard, yeo., Icklingham All Saints, 1682. R2/68/429; W1/136/118; In. 3/21/111
Robert, bach., Barningham, 1698, (N). R2/73/269; W1/152/45; A5/7/7
Robert, Bury St. Edmunds, 1642. A5/4/97
Thomas, Wicken, 1633. A5/4/26
William, gent., Brandon, 1673. R2/65/481; W1/125/121
William, Glemsford, 1648. A5/4/124
PLEASANT, Charles, the elder, yeo., Exning, 1662. R2/62/327; W1/114/34; In. 3/7/53
Robert, Kennett, 1667. In. 3/12/64b; A5/5/81, A4/5/8
PLEASAUNCE, George, Barrow, 1566. A5/1/177
Margery, wid., Barrow, 1587. R2/40/288; W1/44/120
Thomas, yeo., Exning, 1584. R2/39/152; W1/42/170
William, the elder, gent., Brandon, 1640. R2/58/197; W1/96/125
see also Plesance
PLEDGAR, Thomas, Poslingford, 1691. A5/6/144, A4/33/62
PLEDGEARD, Thomas, yeo., Hundon, 1626. R2/53/533; W1/82/63
PLEDGER, Thomas, yeo., Poslingford, 1700. R2/74/38; W1/154/38
Thomas, say weaver, Sudbury, 1685. R2/70/36; W1/139/31
William, the elder, inn holder, Hundon, 1700. R2/74/3; W1/154/3; In. 3/27/39
PLESANCE, Edmund, husb., Hargrave, 1625. R2/53/345; W1/81/124
George, Little Saxham, 1618. R2/51/134; W1/75/83
Thomas, Barrow, 1541. R2/19/399
PLESANTS, Ann, als. Roote, wid., Wicken, 1667. In. 3/13/138
PLESAUNCE, Margaret, wid., Barrow, 1520. R2/15/99
PLESAUNS, Robert, sen., Barrow, 1559. R2/28/275; W1/22/212
PLESSANCE, Edmund, Risby, 1686. R2/70/262; W1/140/29; In. 3/22/70
James, yeo., Little Saxham, 1685. R2/70/201; W1/139/169
PLOME, Marion, wid., Langham, 1589. R2/41/159 & 228; W1/46/61 & 124
PLOMER, Edward, Bury St. Edmunds, 1674. R2/66/31; W1/126/91
Edward, carpenter, Whepstead, 1638. R2/57/367; W1/93/167
John, Bury St. Edmunds, 1424. R2/1/167
John, the elder, Sudbury, 1512. W1/9/39
Robert, Bury St. Edmunds, 1432. R2/1/199
Robert, skinner, Bury St. Edmunds, 1455. R2/2/50
Thomas, Old Newton, 1485. R2/11/336
PLOMMER, Edward, singleman, Dalham, 1638. A5/4/64
Robert, Dalham, 1578. R2/37/418; W1/36/154
see also Mylys als. Plomer
PLOMPEN, John, the elder, Nayland, 1548. R2/21/188; W1/10/163 & 165
PLOWMAN, Elisabeth, wid., Lakenheath, 1668. In. 3/13/80; A5/5/93, A4/6/41
Henry, husb., Barton Mills, 1652. In. 3/4/73; A5/4/142
Jane, als. Albery, Barton Mills, 1631. A5/4/12
PLOWRIGHT, John, wheelwright, Fordham, 1602. R2/45/99; W1/60/9
PLUMB(E), Edmund, carrier, Clare, 1671. R2/65/246; W1/123/124
Elizabeth, wid., Bury St. Edmunds, 1537. R2/7/46
Henry, Bury St. Edmunds, 1637. A5/4/54
James, tailor, Bury St. Edmunds, 1624. R2/53/140; W1/80/116
Lawrence, school master, Bury St. Edmunds, 1618. R2/51/191; W1/75/119
Margaret, wid., Thetford, 1526. R2/17/210; W1/23/21
Robert, Langham, 1578. R2/37/354; W1/36/221
see also Plome, Plum(e), Plumme, Clamtrey als. Plumbe
PLUMBER, John, yeo., Fornham All Saints, 1638. R2/57/340; W1/93/123
PLUM(E), Edmund, gent., Hawkedon, 1643. R2/59/15; W1/100/23
John, gent., Hawkedon, 1681. R2/68/224; W1/135/165

PLUM(E) continued
John, wool comber, Kentford, 1692. In. 3/24/44; A5/6/15, A4/34/35
Mary, singlewoman, Groton, 1627, (N). R2/54/19; W1/83/24
Robert, the elder, yeo., Barnardiston, 1640. R2/58/192; W1/96/116
Thomas, Stradishall, 1684. A5/6/77, A4/21/32
William, Barnham, 1682. R2/68/471; W1/136/147; In. 3/21/45; A5/6/64, A4/19/117
PLUMER, Edward, Bury St. Edmunds, 1674. A5/5/151, A4/11/76
Joan, Dalham, 1640. A5/4/78
John, Bury St. Edmunds, 1405. R2/1/106
John, yeo., Dalham, 1661. R2/62/245; W1/113/125; In. 3/6/159
Robert, cordwainer, Hunston, 1691. R2/71/522; W1/145/80
PLUMME, Edmund, the elder, gent., Hawkedon, 1682. R2/68/392; W1/136/93; In. 3/21/123
Robert, gent., Stansfield, 1679. R2/67/471; W1/133/192
PLUMMER, Anthony, bach., Ixworth, 1695. A5/6/180, A4/38/54
Edward, husb., Dalham, 1663. In. 3/8/194; A5/5/52
George, clerk, Little Thurlow, 1645, (N). R2/59/173; W1/102/2
John, yeo., Barnham, 1698. R2/73/327; W1/152/96
John, shepherd, Barningham, 1667. R2/64/228; W1/119/80; In. 3/12/90
Mary, wid., Barningham, 1677. A5/5/169, A4/14/31
Richard, gardener, Timworth, 1647. In. 3/2/153; A5/4/117
Robert, barber, Bury St. Edmunds, 1684. R2/69/210; W1/138/21
Thomas, yeo., Ashley, 1684. R2/69/365; W1/138/155
Thomas, Cowlinge, 1674. A5/5/145, A4/11/14
Thomas, yeo., Dalham, 1630. R2/55/66; W1/86/77
see also Plomer, Plumber, Plumer, Brown als. Plummer, Hardie als. Plummer
PLUMPTON, Edmund, Risby, 1690. A5/6/134, A4/32/34
George, Chevington, 1674. A5/5/149, A4/11/56
Henry, yeo., tailor, Fornham All Saints, 1699. R2/73/460; W1/153/96; In. 3/26/34
Thomas, Sudbury, 1483. W1/24/12
PLUMSTED, Edward, Old Newton, 1690. R2/71/426; W1/144/129
POCHER, Thomas, husb., West Stow, 1699. R2/74/123; W1/154/119
PODD, Agnes, wid., Stoke by Nayland, 1578. R2/37/329
John, Groton, 1573. R2/36/111; W1/32/10
Thomas, yeo., Elmsett, 1613. R2/48/259; W1/70/34
Thomas, singleman, Elmsett, 1636. R2/57/108; W1/92/127
William, glover, Stoke by Nayland, 1577. R2/37/295
PODDNYE, William, husb., Stoke by Nayland, 1597. W1/55/89
PODENEY, Robert, Bures, 1464. R2/10/323
POLARD, Charles, Little Thornham, 1661. R2/62/261; W1/113/152; In. 3/6/178
POLE, John, Stowmarket, 1494. R2/11/449
Margaret, wife of William, Finningham, 1551. R2/23/27; W1/11/50
Richard, Fordham, 1568. R2/33/41; W1/29/51
Thomas, Westhorpe, 1566. R2/32/285; W1/28/109
POLEY, Catherine, wid., Icklingham, 1560. R2/29/173
Edmund, Combs, 1552. R2/23/179; W1/12/12
Francis, esq., Boxted, 1567. A5/1/225
George, gent., Bury St. Edmunds, 1536. R2/7/34
John, esq., Boxted, 1580, (N). R2/38/204; W1/39/106
John, gent., usher of the privy chamber, Bury St. Edmunds, 1664. R2/63/216; W1/116/128
Katherine, wid. of John, knight, Bury St. Edmunds, 1670. R2/65/119; W1/122/143; In. 3/15/214
William, gent., Icklingham, 1557. R2/26/144; W1/20/107
POLEYN, John, cordwainer, Bury St. Edmunds, 1388. R2/1/55
POLINTON, James, labourer, Mildenhall, 1679. R2/67/370
POLLARD, John, Little Bradley, 1642. A5/4/93
John, husb., Mildenhall, 1584. R2/39/140; W1/42/185
John, priest, Preston, 1479. R2/12/3
Nicholas, husb., Little Wratting, 1677. In. 3/18/70; A5/5/167, A4/14/13
Peter, miller, Stoke by Clare, 1662. R2/62/404; W1/114/152; In. 3/7/194
Robert, sheepman, Freckenham, 1667. W8/22; In. 10/10

POLLARD continued
Thomas, yeo., Eye, 1666. R2/64/152; W1/118/118; In. 3/11/163
Thomas, Hinderclay, 1558. R2/27/281
William, yeo., Bacton, 1672. R2/65/294; W1/124/11; A5/5/140, A4/10/61
William, Little Thurlow, 1661. A5/5/18, A4/1/79
see also Polard
POLLE, Adam, Barnham, 1459. R2/9/257
William, Barnham, 1481. R2/11/223
POLLEN, John, the elder, weaver, Boxford, 1624. R2/53/10; W1/80/14
POLLENTON, Thomas, yeo., Mildenhall, 1695. R2/72/472; W1/149/28
William, thatcher, Mildenhall, 1602. R2/45/103; W1/60/14
POLLEY, Benjamin, grocer, Bures, 1693. R2/72/120
Mary, wid., Bures, 1687. A5/6/108, A4/108/8
Mary, spinster, Bures, 1692. R2/72/23; W1/146/22
Oliver, yeo., Long Melford, 1664. R2/63/213; W1/116/123; In. 3/9/174
William, husb., Bures, 1556. R2/25/147; W1/16/164
see also Pollie, Polly
POLLEYN, John, husb., Mildenhall, 1570. R2/35/27
POLLIE, Thomas, Little Cornard, 1584. A5/2/57
POLLIN, John, Mildenhall, 1571. R2/35/137; W1/36/79
POLLING, Nicholas, Flempton, 1558. R2/27/304
see also Poleyn, Pollen, Polleyn, Pollin, Pollyng
POLLINGTON, Edward, husb., Herringswell, 1627, (N). R2/54/13; W1/83/16
John, tailor, Mildenhall, 1629. R2/54/304; W1/85/20
John, thatcher, Mildenhall, 1636. R2/57/47; W1/92/57
John, tailor, Mildenhall, 1667. In. 3/12/54; A5/5/83, A4/5/31
Nicholas, Mildenhall, 1558. R2/27/31; W1/31/22
Susan, Mildenhall, 1669. In. 3/14/163; A5/5/108, A4/7/73
POLLINTON, John, wid., labourer, Mildenhall, 1680, (N). R2/67/749; W1/134/185; In. 3/20/36; A5/6/32, A4/17/18
see also Polinton, Pollenton, Pollyngton, Polyngton
POLLY, John, Long Melford, 1694. A5/6/168, A4/37/23
Thomas, Ballingdon, 1632. A5/4/20
POLLYNG, John, Chelsworth, 1567. A5/1/185
Nicholas, Bacton, 1531. R2/19/57
Thomas, Bacton, 1533. R2/19/186
POLLYNGTON, Robert, Wangford, 1575. R2/37/91
POLSTEDE, Agnes, Bury St. Edmunds, 1507. R2/4/193 (admon. only)
POLTER, Thomas, Exning, 1672. A5/5/131, A4/9/43
POLYCH, William, Oakley, 1454. R2/9/231
POLYNGTON, John, thatcher, Mildenhall, 1559. R2/28/293; W1/22/234
Richard, Mildenhall, 1549. R2/21/515; W1/8/54
POND, Ann, Haughley, 1588. A5/1/113a
Bartholomew, Bury St. Edmunds, 1637. A5/4/55
Edward, the elder, yeo., Gazeley, 1678. R2/67/3; W1/130/4; In. 3/19/3
Edward, Soham, 1644. A5/4/105
John, Chevington, 1558. R2/27/129
John, shepherd, Gazeley, 1598. R2/44/119; W1/56/118
John, yeo., Gazeley, 1679. R2/67/364; W1/133/121
John, Soham, 1639. R2/58/114; W1/94/189
Margaret, wid., Bury St. Edmunds, 1562. R2/8/375; W1/17/31
Mary, Soham, 1636. A5/4/42
Nicholas, Wickhambrook, 1540. R2/20/181; W1/4/147
Richard, Bury St. Edmunds, 1595. A5/1/210
Richard, Great Waldingfield, 1566. A5/1/178
Richard, husb., Rushbrook, 1608. R2/46/210; W1/65/99
Thomas, Wickhambrook, 1520. R2/15/18
William, husb., Soham, 1625. R2/53/397; W1/81/178
William, Wickhambrook, 1559. R2/28/405; W1/3/68
see also Poond
PONDER, Ambrose, Boxford, 1673. A5/5/137, A4/10/31
John, Ashfield, 1464. R2/10/367
John, Haughley, 1556. R2/25/143; W1/16/168
John, fuller, Sudbury, 1467. R2/10/403
John, Waldingfield, 1461. R2/9/300
Thomas, butcher, Haverhill, 1669. In. 3/14/18; A5/5/101, A4/7/3
William, Fordham, 1699. In. 3/26/28

PONGE, Agnes, Poslingford, 1446. R2/9/67
PONYARD, John, Stoke Ash, 1504. R2/12/31
POODE, John, Stoke by Nayland, 1484. R2/11/291
POOLE, Edith, wid., Rattlesden, 1609. A5/3/70
Edmund, tailor, Mildenhall, 1588. R2/41/69; W1/45/59
Elisabeth, singlewoman, Bury St. Edmunds, 1700. R2/74/72; W1/154/71
Francis, wheelwright, Shimpling, 1637. R2/57/124; W1/92/153
Grace, spinster, Bury St. Edmunds, 1700. R2/74/26; W1/154/25
John, Combs, 1556. R2/25/117; W1/16/128b
John, Fordham, 1485. R2/11/355
John, Fordham, 1533. W1/2/34
John, yeo., Wetherden, 1604. R2/45/361; W1/62/88
John, yeo., Wetherden, 1649. R2/60/203; W1/106/47
Margaret, singlewoman, Ashfield, 1629, (N). R2/54/312; W1/85/27
Margaret, Westhorpe, 1568, (N). R2/33/52; W1/29/68
Martin, Lavenham, 1635. A5/4/41
Philip, Rattlesden, 1686. A5/6/100, A4/26/80
Robert, wheelwright, Combs, 1555. R2/24/178; W1/15/15
Robert, Ixworth, 1573. A5/1/260
Robert, wheelwright, Rattlesden, 1599. R2/44/176; W1/57/8
Robert, Rattlesden, 1649. R2/60/221; W1/106/69
Robert, Wetherden, 1638. A5/4/57
Thomas, Buxhall, 1689. A5/6/125, A4/30/89
Thomas, yeo., Combs, 1604. R2/45/316
Thomas, Combs, 1632. R2/56/222; W1/89/143
Thomas, yeo., Combs, 1660. R2/62/91; W1/112/121; In. 3/5/142
Thomas, labourer, Exning, 1612. R2/48/160; W1/69/41
William, Finningham, 1547. R2/21/291
William, Fordham, 1460. R2/9/275
William, blacksmith, Harleston, 1650. R2/61/326; W1/107/24; In. 3/3/21
POOLEY, Alice, wid., Combs, 1578. R2/37/383; W1/36/192
Dorothy, spinster, Stowmarket, 1636. R2/57/81; W1/92/98
Edmund, the elder, yeo., Combs, 1622. R2/52/397; W1/78/32
James, husb., Groton, 1619. R2/51/299; W1/132/24
POOLY, Edmund, esq., Bury St. Edmunds, 1668. A4/6/26
Jane, spinster, Stowmarket, 1640. R2/58/130; W1/96/16
John, singleman, esq., Bury St. Edmunds, 1668. A5/5/92, A4/6/27
John, yeo., Combs, 1670, (N). R2/65/113; W1/122/136; In. 3/15/172
POOND, John, Bury St. Edmunds, 1406. R2/1/113
POOPE, Daniel, Walsham le Willows, 1677. R2/66/457; W1/129/35; In. 3/18/37
George, Wortham, 1579. A5/2/18 & 22
John, yeo., Stowupland, 1662. R2/62/371; W1/114/102; In. 3/7/131
John, the elder, Wortham, 1542. R2/22/43; W1/6/13
Thomas, gent., Mildenhall, 1579. R2/38/9; W1/39/70
Thomas, Redgrave, 1562. R2/31/112; W1/8/86
POORE, John, yeo., Rougham, 1556. R2/25/31; W1/16/33
POPE, Bartholomew, Mendlesham, 1645. R2/59/250; W1/102/71
Edmund, Redgrave, 1563. A5/1/151
Henry, Mellis, 1448. R2/9/79
Henry, esq., Mildenhall, 1537. R2/20/52; W1/4/42
Henry, Wortham, (1489). R2/13/10
Jane, wid., Badwell Ash, 1665. R2/63/345; W1/117/94; In. 3/10/99
John, chaplain, Bury St. Edmunds, 1515. R2/6/17
John, Eye, 1462. R2/10/376
John, Layham, 1573. A5/1/266
John, Walsham le Willows, 1558. R2/27/524
John, Wattisfield, 1450. R2/9/127
John, yeo., Westhorpe, 1594. R2/42/602; W1/53/5
Katherine, wife of Thomas, Fornham All Saints, 1668. R2/64/403; W1/120/126; In. 3/13/119
Margery, wife of Nicholas, Wyverstone, 1542. R2/22/52; W1/6/62
Martha, singlewoman, Thetford, 1629. R2/54/369; W1/85/67
Richard, Knettishall, 1457. R2/9/199
Robert, Bury St. Edmunds, 1361. R2/1/15
Robert, Westhorpe, 1553. R2/31/173; W1/13/115

POPE continued
Thomas, esq., Mildenhall, 1566. R2/32/360; W1/28/19
Thomas, Rattlesden, 1636. R2/57/11; W1/92/15
Thomas, Redgrave, 1474. R2/10/510
Thomas, Westhorpe, 1527. R2/17/241; W1/1/42
Unica, wid., Westhorpe, 1666. R2/64/136; W1/118/102; In. 3/11/153
Walter, Thrandeston, 1451. R2/9/137
William, Rickinghall, 1565. A5/1/168
William, yeo., Westhorpe, 1617. R2/50/292; W1/74/85
see also Poope
POPERYK, Margaret, Chippenham, 1483. R2/11/286
POPIE, Robert, the elder, Diss, 1559. R2/28/340; W1/19/67
POPLINGTON, Joan, wid., Stoke by Nayland, 1574. R2/37/68; W1/33/7
see also Wilkinson als. Poplington, Wilkinson als. Poplinton
POPYE, Elisabeth, spinster, Yaxley, 1589. A5/2/113b
see also Popie
PORDON, William, Clare, 1536. R2/14/100
PORRE, Edmund, Great Horningsheath, 1528. R2/15/216; R2/17/275
PORT(E), David, chaplain, Bury St. Edmunds, 1433. R2/1/204
Edmund, Honington, 1472. R2/10/462
John, Barningham, 1441. R2/9/22
John, Honington, 1475. R2/11/117
John, Weston, 1493. R2/13/8
Thomas, Barningham, (1482). R2/11/266
Thomas, Bury St. Edmunds, 1534. R2/7/16
William, Barningham, 1492. R2/13/5
PORTER, Ann, wid. of Edward, say maker, Lavenham, 1668. R2/64/314; W1/120/19; In. 3/13/19
Beatrice, Bury St. Edmunds, 1428. R2/1/181
Christopher, Chippenham, 1520. R2/15/68, R2/17/311; W1/23/12
Clare, wid., Barningham, 1553. R2/23/122; W1/11/126
Edward, say maker, Lavenham, 1667. R2/64/182; W1/119/20; In. 3/12/38
Gabriel, labourer, Lavenham, 1637. R2/57/226; W1/92/274
Gabriel, Stoke by Nayland, 1679. A5/6/25, A4/16/104
George, yeo., Stoke by Nayland, 1640. R2/58/148; W1/96/54
George, yeo., Stoke by Nayland, 1682. R2/68/473; W1/136/150; In. 3/21/29
George, comber, Sudbury, 1650. In. 3/3/100
Henry, Kedington, 1633. A5/4/26
John, Cavendish, 1684. A5/6/79, A4/21/57
John, Chelsworth, 1458. W2/9/238
John, Fordham, 1562. R2/31/5; W1/8/135
John, yeo., Fordham, 1683. R2/69/9; W1/137/9
John, sen., Groton, 1494. R2/13/17
John, Landwade, 1556. R2/25/133; W1/16/176
John, the elder, weaver, Lavenham, 1667. R2/64/254; W1/119/117; In. 3/12/159, In. 3/13/120
John, clothier, Lavenham, 1686. W1/140/64
John, yeo., Stoke by Nayland, 1604. W1/62/36a
John, Stoke by Nayland, 1649. A5/4/127
John, Thurston, 1571, (N). R2/35/259; W1/38/115; A5/1/223
Katherine, wid., Stoke by Clare, 1639, (N). R2/58/76; W1/94/131
Margaret, wid., Mildenhall, 1634, (N). R2/56/429; W1/90/214
Margaret, wid., Stoke, 1635. R2/56/480; W1/91/56
Marion, Chippenham, 1515. R2/12/115
Mary, wid., Cavendish, 1694. R2/72/418; W1/148/152
Mary, spinster, Chelsworth, 1669. R2/64/424; W1/121/7; In. 3/14/183
Richard, Bury St. Edmunds, 1394. R2/1/65
Richard, Bury St. Edmunds, 1607. A5/3/32
Richard, husb., Knettishall, 1691. R2/71/556; W1/145/108
Richard, Lakenheath, 1584. A5/2/63
Richard, husb., Stoke by Nayland, 1603. R2/45/221; W1/61/10
Robert, husb., Stoke by Nayland, 1523. R2/14/89
Robert, yeo., Stoke by Nayland, 1646. R2/59/303; W1/103/23
Robert, Stoke by Clare, 1650. A5/4/131
Simon, husb., Lakenheath, 1650. In. 3/3/33; A5/4/134
Stephen, Sudbury, 1587. A5/2/93
Thomas, freemason, Bury St. Edmunds, 1556. R2/8/295; W1/18/24

PORTER continued
Thomas, Fordham, 1557. R2/26/298; W1/20/219
Thomas, Horringer, 1531. R2/19/66 & 329
Thomas, Stoke by Clare, 1589. A5/2/126
Thomas, husb., Stoke by Nayland, 1583. R2/39/88; W1/42/23
Thomas, Sudbury, 1649. A5/4/131
Thomas, say maker, Sudbury, 1666. R2/64/104; W1/118/75; In. 3/11/109
Thomas, husb., Wicken, 1668. R2/64/306; W1/120/9; In. 3/13/7; A5/5/91, A4/6/12
William, Bury St. Edmunds, 1536. R2/7/39
William, sen., Fordham, 1506. R2/13/180
William, Fordham, 1553. R2/31/107; W1/13/74 & 75
William, yeo., Fordham, 1668. R2/64/399; W1/120/122; In. 3/13/156
William, husb., Lackford, 1640. R2/58/190; W1/96/111
William, Polstead, 1630. A5/4/1
PORTOR, Robert, husb., Stoke by Nayland, 1561. R2/30/58
PORTOUR, John, Bury St. Edmunds, 1420. R2/1/153
see also Clopton als. Porter, Palgrave, als. Porter
PORTWAY, Thomas, 1540. R2/21/384; W1/9/60, W1/38/73
William, Nayland, 1519. R2/15/3
PORYE, Elisabeth, wid., Ixworth Thorpe, 1589. A5/2/125
Thomas, singleman, Chippenham, 1559. R2/28/55; W1/22/58
POSFORD, Alice, wid., Bures, 1564. R2/32/124
Benedict, yeo., Semer, 1671. R2/65/276; W1/123/157
John, yeo., Great Thornham, 1661. R2/62/215; W1/113/80; In. 3/6/87
John, husb., Semer, 1550. R2/21/53
John, yeo., Semer, 1678. R2/67/188; W1/130/165; In. 3/19/211
Thomas, Bures, 1564. R2/32/124; W1/27/75; A5/1/161
William, Semer, 1641. A5/4/87
POSFORTH, Benedict, yeo., Semer, 1608. R2/46/211; W1/65/101
Hugh, husb., Semer, 1619. R2/51/432; W1/132/104
John, husb., Lindsey, 1615. R2/49/251; W1/72/36
POSTFORTH, Edmund, husb., Wetheringsett, 1618. R2/51/21; W1/75/11
POTAGER, Thomas, Walsham le Willows, 1496. R2/13/47
POTEER, William, Bures, 1455. R2/9/227
POTER, Alice, wid. of George, husb., Great Cornard, 1549. R2/21/503; W1/8/81
POTFEILD, John, Wissington, 1570. A5/1/221
POTFYLDE, John, Wissington, 1559. R2/28/89; W1/22/86
POTKIN, John, yeo., Bury St. Edmunds, 1555. R2/8/276; W1/18/5
POTKYN, Margaret, Bury St. Edmunds, 1556. R2/8/292; W1/18/19
Robert, parson, Tostock, 1575. W1/95/8
POTTALL, John, Clare, 1611. A5/3/110
John, butcher, Clare, 1678. R2/67/18; W1/130/17; In. 3/19/15
Katherine, wid., Clare, 1608. R2/46/200; W1/65/75
Thomas, als. Puttoe, Clare, 1642, (N). R2/58/381; W1/99/87
Thomas, butcher, Stoke by Clare, 1538. R2/20/78; W1/4/77 a & b (and inventory)
see also Puttoe als. Pottall
POTTAR, Joan, Bury St. Edmunds, 1545. R2/8/269
POTTER, Adam, Saxham, 1544. A5/1/20 & 21
Alice, spinster, Hundon, 1697. A5/7/1, A4/40/9
Diana, wid., Hundon, 1697. A5/7/1, A4/40/10
Dudley, gent., Mildenhall, 1681. R2/68/117; W1/135/89
Edward, yeo., Cheveley, 1647. In. 3/2/132; A5/4/118
Edward, yeo., Cheveley, 1678. R2/67/93; W1/130/77; In. 3/19/97
Edward, Fordham, 1685. A5/6/94, A4/24/101
Edward, Great Thurlow, 1563. R2/32/39; W1/26/98
Elisabeth, wid., Bures, 1694. A5/6/167, A4/37/11
Elisabeth, wid., Bury St. Edmunds, 1600. R2/45/82; W1/58/116
Francis, oatmeal maker, Bury St. Edmunds, 1699. R2/73/419; W1/153/61
George, yeo., Assington, 1645. R2/59/217; W1/102/42
George, Sudbury, 1650. A5/4/135
George, Thurlow, 1610. A5/3/108
Henry, Bury St. Edmunds, 1579. A5/2/16
Henry, Hinderclay, 1695. R2/72/524; W1/149/79

POTTER continued
Henry, Rede, 1530. R2/15/238, R2/17/309
Henry, husb., 1537. W1/51/5
Hugh, husb., Icklingham, 1663. In. 3/9/126; A5/5/46
James, Stoke by Nayland, 1643. A5/4/100
Jeffery, gent., Assington, 1640. R2/58/164; W1/96/77
Joan, wid., Great Saxham, 1556. R2/25/91; W1/16/115
John, weaver, Bures, 1553. R2/23/220; W1/12/41
John, yeo., Bures, 1684. R2/69/321; W1/138/117
John, currier, Bury St. Edmunds, 1419. R2/1/153
John, labourer, Fordham, 1684. R2/69/299; W1/138/95
John, yeo., Great Saxham, 1611, (N). R2/48/98; W1/68/115; A5/3/112
John, yeo., Great Thurlow, 1562. R2/31/72; W1/8/110
John, maltster, Hundon, 1682. In. 3/21/197; A5/6/59, A4/19/36
John, maltster, Isleham, 1685. W7/109; In. 9/68
John, husb., Little Saxham, 1548. R2/21/91; W1/9/76
John, yeo., Mildenhall, 1692. R2/72/180
John, Wicken, 1668. In. 3/13/29; A5/5/93, A4/6/36
Jonas, cordwainer, Soham, 1670. R2/65/132; W1/122/158; In. 3/15/203
Joseph, yeo., Great Saxham, 1683. R2/68/144; W1/137/118
Joseph, the elder, yeo., Hundon, 1696. R2/73/96; W1/150/110
Katherine, wid., Rede, 1558. R2/27/85; W1/36/57
Lucy, wid., Great Cornard, 1626. R2/53/463; W1/82/13
Marion, Clare, 1459. R2/9/242
Mary, als. King, Cowlinge, 1678. In. 3/19/223; A5/6/14, A4/15/120 & 121
Nicholas, yeo., Great Cornard, 1621. R2/52/328; W1/77/109 a & b
Patrick, husb., Assington, 1553. R2/23/234a; W1/11/125
Phybe, wid., Newton, 1541. W1/51/83
Richard, Assington, 1571. R2/35/149; W1/36/71
Richard, Hundon, 1668. A5/5/96, A4/6/70
Robert, baker, Bury St. Edmunds, 1401. R2/1/91
Robert, yeo., Bury St. Edmunds, 1537. R2/7/43
Robert, sen., Great Saxham, 1643. R2/59/9; W1/100/11
Robert, yeo., Great Saxham, 1663. R2/63/78; W1/115/125; In. 3/8/152; A5/5/50
Robert, husb., Hundon, 1668. R2/64/338; W1/120/48; In. 3/12/196
Roger, husb., Barrow, 1552. R2/31/55; W1/13/42
Roger, inn holder, Bury St. Edmunds, 1588. R2/41/9; W1/45/6
Roger, yeo., Rede, 1584. R2/39/165; W1/42/160
Stephen, Bury St. Edmunds, 1640. A5/4/84
Susan, wid., Great Saxham, 1681. R2/68/29; W1/135/25
Susan, wid., Icklingham, 1692. A5/6/150, A4/34/28
Thomas, singleman, Assington, 1661, (N). R2/62/217; W1/113/81; A5/5/16, A4/1/98
Thomas, Finningham, 1661. A5/5/22, A4/1/39
Thomas, Fordham, 1626, (N). R2/53/655; W1/82/178
Thomas, yeo., Great Cornard, 1617. R2/50/223; W1/74/14
Thomas, singleman, Great Cornard, 1647. R2/59/483; W1/104/118; In. 3/2/126
Thomas, carpenter, Haughley, 1613. R2/48/244; W1/70/2
Thomas, Mildenhall, 1558. R2/27/356
Thomas, gent., Mildenhall, 1673. R2/65/470
Thomas, yeo., Occold, 1684. R2/69/414; W1/138/193
Thomas, Rede, 1469. R2/10/433
Thomas, yeo., Rougham, 1625. R2/53/385; W1/81/162
Thomas, Wissington, 1479. R2/11/200
Thomas, Wissington, 1480. R2/11/220
William, Beyton, 1589. R2/41/264; W1/46/43
William, Bury St. Edmunds, 1609. A5/3/60
William, Great Saxham, 1541. R2/22/107; W1/10/36
William, yeo., Mildenhall, 1619. R2/51/373; W1/132/70
William, Mildenhall, 1672. A5/5/132, A4/9/57
William, gent., Mildenhall, 1679. R2/67/458; W1/133/183
William, hatter, Nayland, 1662. R2/62/427; W1/114/190; In. 3/7/229
see also Poteer, Potyer

POTTINGER, John, Fornham, 1590. A5/2/135
POTYER, John, sen., Bures, 1468. R2/10/407
Thomas, tailor, Sudbury, 1531. R2/19/53
POULE, John, singleman, Tuddenham, 1669. R2/64/446; W1/121/31
POULSON, Elisabeth, wid., Lavenham, 1696. R2/73/62; W1/150/104; In. 3/25/95
POULTER, Anne, wid., Cheveley, 1651. R2/61/436
Christopher, clerk, Great Wratting, 1698. R2/73/219; W1/152/1; A5/7/7
John, Exning, 1638. R2/57/246; W1/93/5
Mary, Exning, 1692. A5/6/149, A4/34/18
Ralph, miller, Burwell, 1672. R2/65/364; W1/124/100
Robert, yeo., Lidgate, 1686. R2/70/532; W1/140/136; In. 3/22/119
Thomas, yeo., Bury St. Edmunds, 1687. R2/70/573; W1/141/14
William, yeo., Cheveley, 1644. R2/59/84; W1/101/13
William, yeo., Cheveley, 1676. In. 3/17/61; A5/5/161, A4/13/31 & 32
see also Polter, Powlter
POULTON, Catherine, wid. of George, esq., Acton, 1678. In. 3/19/64; A5/6/4, A4/15/31
POULYN, Robert, Bury St. Edmunds, 1472. R2/2/166
POULYNGE, John, weaver, Chelsworth, 1542. R2/22/15; W1/6/5
POUNCY, Thomas, Wickhambrook, 1460. R2/10/373
POUND, John, Edwardstone, 1670. R2/65/4; W1/122/6; In. 3/15/44
POUNGE, Alexander, weaver, Long Melford, 1590. R2/41/438; W1/47/112
POUNSABYE, Robert, locksmith, Bury St. Edmunds, 1608. R2/46/167; W1/65/20
POWELL, Adam, grocer, Mildenhall, 1674. R2/66/11; W1/126/110
Barnaby, Barton Mills, 1602, (N). R2/45/201; W1/60/130
Francis, yeo., Mildenhall, 1660. W1/110/53
Francis, yeo., Mildenhall, 1661. R2/62/209; W1/113/72; In. 3/6/118
Nicholas, gardener, Denston, 1700. R2/74/100; W1/154/103
Richard, physician, Sudbury, 1559, (N). R2/28/233; W1/22/185
Roger, Drinkstone, 1610. A5/3/103
see also Powle
POWER, Alice, Langham, (1511). R2/13/202
Alice, singlewoman, Soham, 1688. In. 3/23/30; A5/6/117, A4/29/9
Elisabeth, Barway, 1677. R2/66/493; W1/129/91; In. 3/18/91
Henry, 1459. R2/9/246
John, Soham, 1672. R2/65/338; W1/124/68
Margaret, wife of Henry, Barton, 1472. R2/10/498
Nicholas, Rougham, 1478. R2/11/151
Thomas, sen., yeo., Barway, 1681. R2/68/15; W1/135/13; A5/6/44, A4/18/11
Thomas, Barway, 1695. A5/6/180, A4/38/49
POWERS, Mary, wid., Soham, 1680. R2/67/665; W1/134/127; In. 3/20/140
POWLE, Alice, als. Mason, wife of William, Exning, 1590. A5/2/144
Elisabeth, wid., Flempton, 1635. R2/56/462; W1/91/29
Elisabeth, wid. of William, Kentford, 1560. R2/29/77; W1/25/91
Harry, Kentford, 1559. R2/28/399; W1/3/121
John, yeo., Bury St. Edmunds, 1578. R2/37/374; W1/36/201
John, Whepstead, 1520. R2/15/118
Katherine, wid., Bury St. Edmunds, 1540. R2/8/249
Margery, wid., Bury St. Edmunds, 1579. R2/38/13; W1/39/63
Robert, Barnham, 1523. R2/17/28; W1/21/59
Thomas, Bury St. Edmunds, 1473. R2/2/172
Thomas, mercer, Bury St. Edmunds, 1570, (N). R2/35/40; W1/38/5; A5/1/234
William, Flempton, 1635. A5/4/37
William, yeo., Kentford, 1558. R2/27/593
William, Landwade, 1590. A5/2/144
William, Preston, (1484). R2/11/307

POWLING, William, clothworker, Bildeston, 1601. R2/44/346; W1/59/9
see also Poulyn, Powlyn
POWLTER, Christopher, blacksmith, Ashley, 1682. R2/68/260; W1/136/1
Elisabeth, wid., Cheveley, 1682. In. 3/21/81b; A5/6/57, A4/19/10
John, yeo., Kirtling, 1677. R2/66/452; W1/129/29; In. 3/18/31
Robert, als. Lewen, yeo., Cheveley, 1672. R2/65/302; W1/124/20
POWLTOR, Thomas, yeo., Cheveley, 1663. R2/63/22; W1/115/36; In. 3/8/29
POWLYE, Francis, esq., Boxted, 1570. A5/1/216
POWLYN, Emayn, wid., Bury St. Edmunds, 1479. R2/2/269
John, Timworth, 1457. R2/9/184
Katherine, 1457. R2/9/221
POWLYNG, Nicholas, husb., Mendlesham, 1610. R2/47/298; W1/67/189
Roger, tailor, Finningham, 1546. R2/21/650
William, weaver, Bildeston, 1556. R2/25/3
POWNDER, William, Bury St. Edmunds, 1503. R2/4/137
POWNGE, Thomas, Lavenham, 1519. R2/15/3; W1/26/108
POWRDE, Edmund, Botesdale, (1531). R2/19/80
POYE, Peter, Walsham le Willows, 1452. R2/9/111
POYK, Adam, Bury St. Edmunds, 1380. R2/1/44
POYKYN, John, Hitcham, 1612. R2/48/238; W1/69/137
William, Finningham, 1494. R2/13/14
POYNTE, George, Wortham, 1587. R2/40/253; W1/44/94
POYNTER, John, husb., Stanton, 1623. R2/52/680; W1/79/100
Susan, Stanton, 1630. A5/4/8
see also Scarlett als. Poynter
PRATEMAN, Peter, yeo., Bacton, 1559. R2/28/36; W1/22/38
PRATH, Richard, Ashley, 1444. R2/9/46
PRATT, Agatha, wid., Wood Ditton, 1590, (N). R2/41/430; W1/47/8
Agnes, als. Kinge, Lavenham, 1584. A5/2/56
Alice, wid., Kirtling, 1559. R2/28/324
Ann, singlewoman, Stowmarket, 1595. R2/43/66; W1/53/53
Christine, wife of Thomas, yeo., Wood Ditton, 1558. R2/27/407
Edward, inn holder, Newmarket, 1682. R2/68/279; W1/136/13; In. 3/21/214
Eleanor, wid., Redgrave, 1576. R2/37/169; W1/37/32; In. 3/1/84
Geoffrey, shepherd, Gazeley, 1695. R2/72/457; W1/149/12
Henry, yeo., Cheveley, 1591. R2/42/79; W1/48/66
Joan, wid., Liston, 1560. R2/29/132; W1/25/40
John, husb., Cheveley, 1637. R2/57/194; W1/92/231
John, labourer, Cowlinge, 1578, (N). R2/37/370; W1/36/205
John, Drinkstone, 1643. A5/4/98
John, minister, Kettlebaston, 1647. In. 3/2/149; A5/4/117
John, butcher, Lavenham, 1577. R2/37/251
John, carpenter, Little Bradley, 1665. R2/63/371; W1/117/121
John, Mildenhall, 1545. R2/19/558; W1/7/59
John, weaver, Redgrave, 1587. R2/40/298; W1/44/126
John, carpenter, Stradishall, 1665. In. 3/10/148
John, rector, Thorpe Morieux, 1673. R2/65/457; W1/125/90
John, the elder, Wheatacre Burgh, 1537. W1/51/19
John, Wood Ditton, 1551. R2/23/84; W1/11/51
John, Wood Ditton, 1579. A5/2/20
John, yeo., Wood Ditton, 1642. R2/58/340; W1/99/36
John, gent., Wood Ditton, 1661. R2/62/231; W1/113/102; In. 3/6/134
Katherine, wid., Cowlinge, (1535). R2/19/213; W1/3/161
Margaret, Gipping, 1594. A5/2/203
Margaret, wid., Mildenhall, 1555. R2/24/239; W1/15/68
Ralph, yeo., Cowlinge, 1628. R2/54/192; W1/84/68 a & b
Richard, bach., Burwell, 1681. A5/6/55, A4/18/137
Robert, Kirtling, 1581. A5/2/32
Robert, shoe maker, Nayland, 1663. R2/63/5; W1/115/9; In. 3/8/28

PRATT continued
Robert, yeo., Polstead, 1623. R2/52/555; W1/79/14
Robert, yeo., Polstead, 1692. R2/72/230; W1/147/119; In. 3/24/106
Robert, weaver, Stoke by Nayland, 1609. R2/47/23; W1/66/24
Robert, Stradishall, 1560, (N). R2/29/52; W1/25/125
Roger, Wood Ditton, 1506. R2/12/89
Samuel, carpenter, Chevington, 1679. R2/67/257; W1/133/50
Sarah, wid., Wood Ditton, 1686. R2/70/475; W1/140/87; In. 3/22/31
Susan, wid., Felsham, 1678. R2/67/102; W1/130/87; In. 3/19/115
Thomas, carpenter, Chevington, 1684. R2/69/399; W1/138/181
Thomas, Cowlinge, 1519. R2/15/9
Thomas, Dalham, 1697. A5/7/3, A4/40/57
Thomas, Long Melford, 1550, (N). R2/21/101; W1/9/103
Thomas, yeo., Polstead, 1585. R2/39/250; W1/42/323
Thomas, husb., Stradishall, 1599. R2/44/189; W1/57/16
Thomas, carpenter, Stradishall, 1651. R2/61/502; W1/108/92
Thomas, yeo., Wood Ditton, 1558. R2/27/406
Thomas, Wood Ditton, 1560. R2/29/136; W1/25/35
Walter, husb., Poslingford, (1551). R2/23/92; W1/11/52
Walter, the elder, yeo., Wood Ditton, 1620. R2/52/59; W1/76/48
Walter, the elder, gent., Wood Ditton, 1694. R2/72/315; W1/148/44
William, Kentford, 1638. A5/4/63
William, yeo., Kentford, 1685. R2/70/24; W1/139/23
William, Stradishall, 1642. A5/4/95
William, 1679. R2/67/209; W1/133/17
PRATTY, Thomas, Eye, 1583. R2/39/15; W1/42/82
PRATYMAN, Joan, wid., Bacton, 1546. R2/21/218; W1/10/77
John, yeo., Bacton, 1560. R2/29/75; W1/25/93
John, clerk, Wyverstone, 1545. R2/19/505; W1/7/74
William, sen., Bacton, 1564. R2/32/97; W1/27/46
PRECIOUS, Agnes, Bury St. Edmunds, 1380. R2/1/43
PRECYOUS, Walter, lime burner, Mildenhall, 1620. R2/52/91; W1/76/74
PREKE, Alice, wid. of John, Barrow, 1541. R2/21/350; W1/38/89
William, Barrow, 1527. R2/17/248; W1/1/33
PRENTES, William, Clare, 1474. R2/11/41
PRENTICE, Jane, wid., Mellis, 1674. A5/5/148, A4/11/50
John, hair weaver, Palgrave, 1682. R2/68/407; W1/136/102; In. 3/21/63
John, yeo., Wiston, 1630. R2/55/1; W1/86/2
Mary, wid., Poslingford, 1664. R2/63/229; W1/116/144; In. 3/9/223
Matthew, yeo., Clare, 1665. R2/63/296; W1/117/26; In. 3/10/32
Nicholas, the elder, yeo., Palgrave, 1651. R2/61/440
Robert, yeo., Palgrave, 1664. R2/63/165; W1/116/62; In. 3/9/72
Samuel, Kettlebaston, 1693. A5/6/159, A4/35/59
Thomas, Palgrave, 1643. A5/4/99
William, linen weaver, Palgrave, 1660. R2/62/63; W1/112/79; In. 3/8/52
William, Wyverstone, 1642. A5/4/99
PRENTIZE, John, the elder, yeo., Nayland, 1596. R2/43/212; W1/55/55
PRENTS, Cecily, wid., Sudbury, 1495. R2/13/25
PRENTYES, Katherine, Sudbury, 1445. R2/9/92
PRENTYS, Adam, Bury St. Edmunds, 1475. R2/2/205
George, Sudbury, 1484. R2/11/350
John, Nayland, 1479. R2/11/170
John, Palgrave, 1483. R2/11/296
John, Stoke Ash, 1572. W1/111/63
Margaret, wid., Bury St. Edmunds, 1475. R2/2/209
Nicholas, Stoke by Clare, 1480. R2/11/208
Robert, Palgrave, (1543). R2/19/377; W1/6/120
William, husb., Stoke Ash, (1552). R2/23/184
PRENTYZYS, John, Kersey, 1450. R2/9/122
see also Preyntese

PRESGRAVE, John, Stoke, (1456). W1/24/59
PRESSON, Richard, Newmarket, 1593. R2/42/426; W1/50/86
PRESTON, John, yeo., Bacton, 1619. R2/51/382; W1/132/75
John, miller, Eye, 1688. In. 3/23/65; A5/6/120, A4/29/54
Margaret, wid., Wickham Skeith, 1592. R2/42/256; W1/49/73
Nicholas, yeo., Finningham, 1559. R2/28/108; W1/22/107
Nicholas, Finningham, 1573. A5/1/258
Ralph, Stoke by Nayland, 1483. R2/11/316
Richard, Bury St. Edmunds, 1429. R2/1/189
Robert, Aspal, 1683. A5/6/66, A4/20/5
Robert, yeo., Finningham, 1675. R2/66/125; W1/127/3
Robert, worstead weaver, Finningham, 1676, (N). R2/66/329; W1/128/32; In. 3/17/47
Robert, blacksmith, Old Newton, 1679. R2/67/426; W1/133/160
Roger, Wicken, 1541. R2/20/184; W1/4/150
Thomas, Stradishall, 1485. R2/11/347
William, husb., Finningham, 1541. R2/21/363
William, Gislingham, 1592. A5/2/167
PRETT, Richard, 1582. W1/51/159
PRETTIE, Margaret, Eye, 1588. A5/2/105b
PRETTIMAN, Rachael, wid., Thelnetham, 1627. R2/54/2; W1/83/4
PRETTY, Barbara, wid., Edwardstone, 1688. R2/71/131; W1/142/119; In. 3/23/33
Edmund, Yaxley, 1660. In. 3/5/112; A5/5/5, A4/1/196
George, Edwardstone, 1673. R2/65/423; W1/125/51
Henry, woollen weaver, Thwaite, 1665. R2/63/382; W1/117/137; In. 3/10/173
John, woollen weaver, Eye, 1676. R2/66/414; W1/128/124; In. 3/17/175
Thomas, woollen weaver, Eye, 1630. R2/55/130; W1/86/146
see also Pratty, Prettie, Pyrty
PRETTYMAN, Elisabeth, wid., Newmarket, 1694. R2/72/410; W1/148/144
Henry, gent., Bacton, 1667. R2/64/185; W1/119/24
Jeremiah, Mildenhall, 1692. A5/6/150, A4/35/30
Thomas, Bury St. Edmunds, 1674. A5/5/151, A4/11/83
PRETYMAN, Clare, spinster, Bacton, 1700. R2/73/385; W1/153/37
George, gent., Bacton, 1688. R2/71/48; W1/142/45
John, the elder, yeo., Bacton, 1544. R2/19/433; W1/21/157
John, Bacton, (1587). R2/40/228
John, the elder, yeo., Bacton, 1593. R2/42/395; W1/50/120
Margaret, wid., Bacton, 1569. R2/33/97; W1/19/121
Richard, gent., Wyverstone, 1651. R2/61/446
Thomas, yeo., Bacton, (1543). R2/19/349; W1/6/136
William, the elder, yeo., Bacton, 1542. R2/22/36; W1/6/10
William, the elder, gent., Bacton, 1617. R2/50/296; W1/74/88
see also Prateman, Pratyman, Prettiman
PREWER, Thomas, husb., Haverhill, 1566. R2/32/342; W1/28/43
see also Pruer
PREYNTESE, John, Clare, 1454. R2/9/205
PRIAMUS, Lucian, weaver, Sudbury, 1620. R2/52/180; W1/76/162
PRICE, Margaret, wid., Bury St. Edmunds, 1673. R2/65/449; W1/125/77
Robert, yeo., Chelsworth, 1699. R2/73/415; W1/153/57; In. 3/26/19
PRICK(E), Alice, wid., Great Saxham, 1627. R2/54/8; W1/83/10
Ambrose, felt maker, Lavenham, 1631. R2/56/60; W1/87/86
Ann, wid., Chevington, 1680. R2/67/618; W1/134/84; In. 3/20/91
Anne, wid., Rattlesden, 1585. R2/39/357; W1/42/247
Beatrice, wid., Barrow, 1603. R2/45/227; W1/61/18
Charles, tailor, Barrow, 1599. R2/44/212; W1/57/35
Charles, the elder, Barrow, 1660. R2/62/134; W1/112/176; In. 3/6/15
Dorothy, wid., Barrow, 1630. R2/55/65; W1/86/75
Dorothy, singlewoman, Great Saxham, 1617, (N). R2/50/321; W1/74/109
Edward, Bury St. Edmunds, 1695. A5/6/177, A4/38/20
Edward, blacksmith, Wickhambrook, 1666. R2/64/112; W1/118/85; In. 3/11/131

PRICK(E) continued
Elisabeth, Saxham, 1622. R2/52/471; W1/78/85
Francis, cordwainer, Bury St. Edmunds, 1678. In. 3/19/128; A5/6/6, A4/15/47
George, smith, Barrow, 1611. R2/47/312; W1/68/7
George, blacksmith, Burwell, 1668. In. 3/13/41; A5/5/94, A4/6/49
George, yeo., Chevington, 1672. R2/65/353; W1/124/89
George, yeo., Chevington, 1690. R2/71/320; W1/144/23
George, labourer, Thurston, 1570. R2/35/32
James, Chevington, 1634. A5/4/34
John, Badingham, 1638. R2/57/350; W1/93/138
John, sen., Barrow, 1661. In. 3/6/267; A5/5/25, A4/1/9
John, carpenter, Bury St. Edmunds, 1624. R2/53/15; W1/80/23
John, carpenter, Bury St. Edmunds, 1678. R2/67/79; W1/130/61; In. 3/19/83
John, Chevington, 1630. A5/4/9
John, Gazeley, 1694, (N). R2/72/395; W1/148/126; A5/6/170, A4/37/48
John, yeo., Great Horningsheath, 1562. R2/31/52; W1/8/127
Jonathan, singleman, husb., Gazeley, 1668, (N). R2/64/316; W1/120/23; In. 3/13/57
Margaret, singlewoman, Chevington, 1635. R2/56/438; W1/91/1
Margaret, wife of Thomas, yeo., Chevington, 1679. R2/67/452; W1/133/178
Matthew, yeo., Mildenhall, 1692. R2/72/61; W1/146/59; In. 3/24/40; A5/6/150, A4/34/29
Nicholas, yeo., Gazeley, 1625. R2/53/343; W1/81/123
Richard, tailor, Barrow, 1625. R2/53/258; W1/81/48
Richard, yeo., West Stow, 1609, (N). R2/47/77; W1/66/90
Robert, carpenter, Dalham, 1583. R2/39/74; W1/42/33
Robert, husb., Needham, 1620. R2/52/78; W1/76/67
Robert, bach., Rougham, 1674. A5/5/151, A4/11/85
Sarah, als. Mason, Exning, 1666. A5/5/72, A4/4/6b
Simon, carpenter, Bury St. Edmunds, 1694. R2/72/277; W1/148/1
Simon, Chevington, 1670. In. 3/15/58; A5/5/113
Thomas, labourer, Fornham All Saints, 1611. R2/48/2; W1/68/17
Thomas, yeo., Gazeley, 1695. R2/72/581; W1/149/127
Thomas, labourer, Kettlebaston, 1609. R2/47/110; W1/66/126
Thomas, Tuddenham, 1637. A5/4/52
William, Cheveley, 1664. In. 3/9/204; A5/5/63, A4/2/101
see also Preke, Prik, Prycke, Pryke, Johnson als. Prick
PRICKET, Edmund, the elder, Bungay, (1574). W1/51/248
PRICKLES, William, Bury St. Edmunds, 1599. R2/44/233; W1/57/50
PRIEST, Henry, clerk, Great Livermere, 1680. In. 3/20/223; A5/6/42, A4/17/118
Thomas, Mildenhall, 1607. R2/46/135
PRIGG, Adam, tailor, Stradishall, 1631. R2/56/64; W1/87/93
Adam, Stradishall, 1689. A5/6/128, A4/30/37
Edmund, weaver, Stradishall, 1625. R2/53/242; W1/81/36
George, sen., Bury St. Edmunds, 1641. A5/4/92
George, glazier, Bury St. Edmunds, 1677. In. 3/18/101; A5/5/171, A4/14/47
George, tailor, Stansfield, 1634. R2/56/362; W1/90/135
John, Dalham, 1590. A5/2/131
Robert, clothworker, Sudbury, 1669. R2/64/465; W1/121/52
Roger, yeo., Lidgate, 1674. R2/66/99; W1/126/18
Simon, bach., weaver, Ballingdon, 1680. R2/67/763; W1/134/196; In. 3/20/22
Thomas, Dalham, 1589. A5/2/126
Thomas, the elder, tailor, Stradishall, 1645. R2/59/173; W1/102/1
Thomas, miller, Stradishall, 1668. R2/64/413; W1/120/135; In. 3/13/60
William, Stradishall, 1612. A5/3/118
see also Prygg
PRIK, William, Barrow, 1572. A5/1/250
PRIME, Anne, wid., Stoke by Clare, 1672. R2/65/337; W1/124/67
Margery, wid., Thrandeston, 1553. R2/31/18; W1/13/11
Samuel, Bildeston, 1697. A5/7/3, A4/40/50
William, gent., Stoke by Clare, 1685. In. 3/22/56; A5/6/88, A4/24/22
see also Pryme

PRINCE, John, Long Melford, 1612. R2/48/159; W1/69/40
see also Prynce
PRIOR, Edmund, Timworth, 1556. R2/25/134; W1/16/175
John, Cavenham, 1672. A5/5/131, A4/9/48
William, yeo., Bradfield St. George, 1632. R2/56/187; W1/89/96
William, Great Bradley, 1623. R2/52/697; W1/79/111
PRIOUR, William, Bury St. Edmunds, 1466. R2/2/94
see also Pryor
PRISTMAN, John, clerk, Nayland, 1537. R2/20/34; W1/4/26
PROCKTER, Solomon, the elder, clothier, Bildeston, 1676. R2/66/321; W1/128/26; In. 3/17/60
PROCTER, Bridget, wid., Bildeston, 1667. In. 3/12/109; A5/5/87, A4/81/67
Edward, yeo., Lakenheath, 1652. R2/61/539; W1/109/19; In. 3/4/10
PROCTOR, George, husb., Lakenheath, 1679. R2/67/285; W1/133/71
John, husb., Lakenheath, 1665. R2/63/350; W1/117/101; In. 3/10/127
William, Stradishall, 1670. In. 3/15/108; A5/5/115
PROFFET(T), John, Little Cornard, 1521. R2/14/137
Thomas, Bures, 1531. R2/19/76
PROFFIT, William, Bures, 1570. R2/34/15; W1/30/14; A5/1/220
PROM, John, Wetheringsett, 1454. R2/9/166
PROPHET(T), George, singleman, Great Cornard, 1559. R2/28/28; W1/22/32
John, Bures, 1531. R2/19/85
William, Great Cornard, 1549. R2/21/565; W1/8/59
see also Proffet(t)
PROVOST, William, gent., Great Thurlow, 1663. R2/63/100; W1/115/152
PROYE, Hugh, Bury St. Edmunds, 1406. R2/1/114
PRUDHOMME, John, smith, Bury St. Edmunds, 1394. R2/1/69
PRUER, Ann, wid., Withersfield, 1675. In. 3/16/10; A5/5/152, A4/12/3
Robert, joiner, Great Bradley, 1619. R2/51/319; W1/132/38
Thomas, the elder, yeo., Withersfield, 1690. R2/71/416; W1/144/119
PRUM, John, labourer, Bardwell, 1624. R2/53/70; W1/80/91 (and inventory)
PRUME, Elinor, wid., Mendlesham, 1556. R2/25/55; W1/16/63
PRYCKE, Edward, Lackford, 1533. R2/18/206, R2/19/139
John, carpenter, Barrow, 1551. R2/23/11; W1/11/53
John, yeo., Great Saxham, 1604. R2/45/352; W1/62/75
Richard, Bury St. Edmunds, 1427. R2/1/178
PRYGG, John, singleman, labourer, Sapiston, 1573, (N). R2/36/132; W1/32/21
Margaret, wid., Stradishall, 1616. R2/50/177; W1/73/169
Walter, Dalham, 1558. R2/27/390
PRYKE, Edward, Lackford, 1533. R2/19/135; W1/2/58
Elizabeth, wife of John, Great Horningsheath, 1540. R2/19/584, R2/20/115; W1/5/46
John, sen., Barrow, 1470. R2/10/482
John, husb., Barrow, 1584. R2/39/236; W1/42/95
Richard, Lavenham, 1504. R2/13/156
Simon, Shimpling, 1485. R2/11/329
William, Barrow, 1508. R2/13/175
William, carpenter, Barrow, 1567. R2/32/371; W1/3/8
see also Prick(e)
PRYME, Catherine, wid., Cambridge, 1664. R2/63/186; W1/116/90
Edmund, Thrandeston, 1567. A5/1/186
Elisabeth, wid., Thrandeston, 1589. A5/2/119
James, Thrandeston, 1452. R2/9/129
PRYNCE, Alice, wid., Haughley, 1481. R2/11/195
John, Bury St. Edmunds, 1416. R2/1/140
Laurence, Fornham All Saints, 1484. R2/11/371
Robert, Ixworth Thorpe, 1478. R2/11/176
Roger, Bury St. Edmunds, 1396. R2/1/77
Rose, wid., Troston, 1503. R2/13/141
Thomas, Fornham, 1473. R2/11/33
William, Fornham All Saints, 1503. R2/13/140

PRYNCHET, John, Chelsworth, 1441. R2/9/37
Thomas, Bury St. Edmunds, 1504. R2/4/154
PRYOR, Catherine, singlewoman, Haughley, 1666. A5/5/74, A4/4/25
Jane, Haughley, 1641. A5/4/89
Joan, Stoke by Nayland, 1562. R2/31/133; W1/26/14
John, Thurston, 1557. R2/26/222; W1/20/125
John, Thurston, 1580. A5/2/24
Margaret, wid., Haverhill, 1669. R2/64/452; W1/121/40
Robert, yeo., Haughley, 1697. R2/73/213; W1/151/99
Thomas, yeo., Haughley, 1669. R2/64/523; W1/121/112; In. 3/14/76
Thomas, Haverhill, 1670. In. 3/15/163; A5/5/117
Thomas, Haverhill, 1671. A5/5/122, A4/8/29
William, yeo., Fornham St. Genevieve, 1606. R2/46/15; W1/64/18
William, yeo., Haughley, 1645. R2/59/221; W1/102/46
William, husb., Pakenham, 1560. R2/29/124; W1/25/45
PRYOUR, Alice, wid., Bury St. Edmunds, 1470. R2/2/133
Richard, weaver, Bury St. Edmunds, 1466. R2/2/93
Robert, braider, embroiderer, Bury St. Edmunds, 1499. R2/4/76 (admon. only)
William, Great Cornard, (1457). R2/9/192
see also Prior
PRYTYLL, Robert, Stoke by Nayland, 1533. R2/19/180; W1/2/24
PUGH, Randolph, yeo., Exning, 1700. R2/74/60; W1/154/57
PULCOO, Harry, weaver, Lavenham, 1477. R2/11/102
Thomas, Semer, 1526. R2/17/212; W1/23/20a
see also Pulkoo
PULFORD, Ann, spinster, Combs, 1689. A5/6/128, A4/30/34
Christopher, Stowlangtoft, 1632. A5/4/22
Daniel, Creeting St. Peter, 1684. R2/69/343; W1/138/139; A5/6/77, A4/21/42
John, husb., Combs, 1616. R2/50/55; W1/73/66
John, singleman, Westhorpe, 1672, (N). R2/65/317; W1/124/40
Samuel, Rattlesden, 1691. A5/6/143, A4/33/54
Silas, Stowlangtoft, 1673. A5/6/141, A4/10/67
PULHAM, Christopher, Mellis, 1560. A5/1/101
George, gent., Mellis, 1554. R2/24/48; W1/14/38
John, cordwainer, Bury St. Edmunds, 1386. R2/1/52
Robert, freemason, Bury St. Edmunds, 1501. R2/4/117
Soames, Hundon, 1688. A5/6/121, A4/29/58
Thomas, Mellis, 1542. R2/22/65; W1/6/31
see also Harvy als. Pullam
PULKOO, John, Lavenham, 1447. R2/9/75
PULLEN, Katherine, wid., Assington, 1598, (N). R2/44/115; W1/56/122
PULLUM, Robert, Mellis, 1567. R2/32/374; W1/3/14
PULLYN, Adam, 1539. R2/20/95 & 200; W1/4/86
PUNCHARD, John, the elder, husb., Occold, 1584. R2/39/138; W1/42/188
PUNCHARTH, John, Yaxley, 1450. W1/24/95
PUNDER, Isabel, wid., Stanton, 1522. R2/15/47
John, Bury St. Edmunds, 1517. R2/6/42 (admon. only)
PUNDYR, John, cordwainer, Lavenham, 1504. R2/12/62
PUNG(E), Agnes, wid., Long Melford, 1525. R2/17/118; W1/21/115
James, yeo., Long Melford, 1682. In. 3/21/206; A5/6/57, A4/19/17
John, sen., carpenter, Stanstead, 1484. R2/11/372
Margaret, wid., Denston, 1611. R2/47/308; W1/68/4
Richard, Poslingford, 1441. R2/9/31a
William, Long Melford, 1521. W1/9/53
see also Ponge, Pounge, Pownge
PUNT, John, Palgrave, 1460. R2/9/275
Thomas, Occold, 1454. R2/9/231
PURCAS, Ann, Bury St. Edmunds, 1689. A5/6/130, A4/30/10
Henry, Sudbury, 1606. A5/3/11
John, sen., grocer, Bury St. Edmunds, 1698. R2/73/227; W1/152/9
Richard, Sudbury, 1673. A5/5/141, A4/10/76
Thomas, yeo., Thorpe Morieux, 1643. R2/59/51; W1/100/61
Thomas, the elder, yeo., Withersfield, 1670. R2/65/54; W1/122/65; In. 3/15/78

PURCHAS, Robert, Barking, 1361. R2/1/17
see also Purcus, Clarke als. Purchas, Gipps als. Purchas
PURCHE, John, Bildeston, 1559. R2/28/7; W1/22/7
PURCUS, Thomas, husb., Stoke by Nayland, 1671. R2/65/179; W1/123/49
PURDEY, James, Redgrave, 1560. R2/29/64; W1/25/107
Richard, yeo., Redgrave, 1684. R2/69/293; W1/138/88
PURDIE, Henry, yeo., Wortham, 1666. R2/64/79; W1/118/55; In. 3/11/67
Thomas, glazier, Bury St. Edmunds, 1592. R2/42/262; W1/49/80
William, sen., Bury St. Edmunds, 1558. R2/8/326; W1/18/62
PURDY, Anne, maid, Redgrave, 1547. R2/21/305; W1/10/134
Geoffrey, blacksmith, Boxford, 1575. W1/95/14
John, Redgrave, 1559. R2/28/140; W1/22/129
Margaret, Bury St. Edmunds, 1593. A5/2/182
Margaret, wid., Wortham, 1668. R2/64/338; W1/120/47; A5/5/92, A4/6/23
Richard, Polstead, 1611. A5/3/112
Thomas, mason, Bury St. Edmunds, 1561. R2/8/358; W1/17/47
Thomas, Redgrave, 1538. R2/20/84; W1/4/82 a & b (and inventory)
PURPLE, George, Mildenhall, 1568. A5/1/202
PURPYLL, Henry, Denham, 1444. R2/9/50
John, Ixworth Thorpe, 1476. R2/11/59
PURSE, Robert, husb., Ampton, 1536. R2/19/249
PURSER, John, Bury St. Edmunds, 1492. R2/4/6
John, Stoke by Nayland, 1452. R2/9/130
William, Stoke by Nayland, 1479. R2/12/2
PURSEY, John, Bury St. Edmunds, 1370. R2/1/21
PUSK, James, Kersey, 1447. R2/9/85
John, Kersey, 1463. R2/10/337
Roger, Bacton, 1480. R2/11/206
PUTTALL, see Puttoe als. Puttall
PUTTO(E), John, als. Puttall, the elder, yeo., Clare, 1597. R2/43/240; W1/55/22
Thomas, yeo., Long Melford, 1574. R2/37/40; W1/33/40
William, als. Pottall, yeo., Glemsford, 1640. R2/58/173; W1/96/91
see also Pottall als. Puttoe
PUTTOCK, Alice, Sudbury, 1578. A5/2/13
PUTTOK, Margaret, wife of Thomas, Ixworth, 1475. R2/11/54
Thomas, barker, Mildenhall, 1464. R2/10/353
William, Sudbury, 1573. A5/1/254
PYCHE, Thomas, Kirtling, 1480. R2/11/208
PYCHES, Richard, Kirtling, 1519. R2/14/135, R2/15/16; W1/26/109
Robert, Ashley cum Silverley, 1528. W1/19/11
PYCKRED, Thomas, Great Thornham, 1573. A5/1/254
PYCKRELL, Robert, husb., Thurston, 1566. R2/32/348; W1/28/34; A5/1/179
PYCOT, Margaret, Bury St. Edmunds, 1478. R2/2/251
PYDDE, John, Alpington, 1537. W1/51/17
PYDENALE, Adam, Ousden, 1468. R2/10/410
PYE, Alice, wid. of Thomas, Assington, 1470. R2/10/437
Edmund, Assington, 1457. R2/9/213
Edward, labourer, Sudbury, 1588. R2/41/79; W1/45/69
Edward, Tuddenham, 1638. A5/4/57
Frances, wid., Tuddenham, 1638. R2/57/268; W1/93/32
George, the elder, clothier, Lavenham, 1557. R2/26/312; W1/20/235
George, Lavenham, 1564. R2/32/106; W1/27/58
Henry, glover, Mildenhall, 1553. R2/31/176; W1/13/116
James, weaver, Sudbury, 1626. R2/53/621; W1/82/148
John, maltster, Bury St. Edmunds, 1557. R2/8/308; W1/17/36
John, Fornham All Saints, 1640, (N). R2/58/203; W1/96/134
John, Great Cornard, 1546. R2/21/182; W1/10/120
John, Icklingham, 1589. A5/2/117a
John, yeo., Wyverstone, 1560. R2/29/120; W1/25/48
Margaret, wid., Bury St. Edmunds, 1491. R2/4/1
Margaret, wife of John, Icklingham, 1589. A5/2/117a
Robert, Herringswell, 1558. R2/27/549

PYE continued
Thomas, Assington, 1443. R2/9/40
Thomas, parson, Flempton, 1560, (N). R2/29/3; W1/19/73
Thomas, smith, Hawstead, 1477. R2/11/129
Thomas, Icklingham, 1586. A5/2/82
Thomas, Tuddenham, 1631. A5/4/11
William, Dalham, 1536. R2/19/237
William, Herringswell, 1573. A5/1/259
William, 1626. R2/53/669; W1/82/193
PYERS, Anthony, linen weaver, Hopton, 1602. R2/45/166; W1/60/88
PYGAS, Robert, Brandon, 1496. R2/13/31
Robert, Brandon, (1519). R2/14/7
PYGHTLYN, Rose, wid., Horstead, 1575. W1/51/203
PYKE, John, Stanton, 1451. R2/9/135
Margaret, wid., Bury St. Edmunds, 1481. R2/2/318
William, butcher, Bury St. Edmunds, 1484. R2/2/199
PYKENHAM, Emma, wife of Roger, Bury St. Edmunds, 1370. R2/1/28
PYKERELL, John, Thurston, 1468. R2/10/406
Margaret, Ixworth, 1518. R2/12/104
Robert, Norton, 1453. R2/9/161
PYKHORN, William, Bury St. Edmunds, 1442. R2/1/258
PYKRELL, Thomas, Bury St. Edmunds, 1509. R2/4/208
PYLBAROW, John, singleman, Newton, 1581. R2/38/305; W1/40/48
William, husb., Buxhall, 1558. R2/27/304
PYLBOROW, Richard, Onehouse, 1596. R2/43/197; W1/54/77
William, husb., Buxhall, 1562. R2/31/20; W1/8/147
PYLCHE, Augustin, Lackford, 1528. R2/15/229
PYLCREKE, Edward, Great Thornham, 1566. A5/1/174
PYLE, Margaret, wid., Rickinghall Superior, 1679. R2/67/475; W1/133/196
Richard, clerk, Rickinghall Superior, 1674. R2/66/45; W1/126/75
PYLGEKE, Thomas, Long Melford, 1533. W1/2/35
PYM, Richard, baker, Boxford, 1668. R2/64/319; W1/120/26; In. 3/13/38
Richard, sen., Ixworth, 1643. A5/4/98
PYMAN, John, husb., Palgrave, 1690. R2/71/303; W1/144/3
John, Stowmarket, 1574. R2/37/33; W1/33/54
see also Piman
PYMPERNEL, Agnes, wid., Norton, 1609. A5/3/71
PYNCHBECK, Thomas, Kersey, 1593. A5/2/186
Thomas, Nayland, 1595. A5/2/204
PYNCHBEK, Jane, wid., Poslingford, 1536. R2/14/142
John, Poslingford, 1521. R2/15/169, R2/17/12; W1/21/75
PYNCHEBEK, John, currier, Bury St. Edmunds, 1523. R2/6/106
Richard, Bury St. Edmunds, 1436. R2/1/220
PYNCHUN, Walter, Bury St. Edmunds, 1361. R2/1/16
PYNDAR, Mary, wid., Kentford, 1633, (N). R2/56/302; W1/90/68
PYNGELLS, Thomas, Haverhill, 1545. A5/1/48
PYNHORN, Robert, Mildenhall, 1484. R2/11/307
PYNHYS, Thomas, Kirtling, 1521. R2/15/152, R2/17/331
PYNNER, Francis, the younger, Bury St. Edmunds, 1618. R2/51/58; W1/75/35
Francis, gent., Bury St. Edmunds, 1639. R2/58/61a; W1/94/113
PYPE, John, labourer, Soham, 1620. R2/52/94; W1/76/78
PYPER, Emota, wid., Thorpe Morieux, 1481. R2/11/203
Henry, Little Wratting, 1539. R2/19/322 & 602
John, Thorpe Morieux, 1462. R2/10/349
Nicholas, yeo., Hundon, 1640. R2/58/146; W1/96/48
Robert, als. Wayneflet, carpenter, Great Waldingfield, 1558. R2/27/279
Thomas, Thorpe Morieux, 1465. R2/10/382
PYRLYSTON, Walter, als. Wareyn, Acton, 1474. R2/11/142
PYRTON, John, Fordham, 1479. R2/11/217
PYRTY, Thomas, Thorndon, 1454. R2/9/169
PYRYE, Giles, Bury St. Edmunds, 1425. R2/1/168
Joan, wid., Bury St. Edmunds, 1426. R2/1/176
Thomas, Bury St. Edmunds, 1404. R2/1/105
PYRYN, William, leather worker, Bury St. Edmunds, 1540. R2/7/60
PYTCHER, Joan, wid., Edwardstone, 1605, (N). R2/45/458; W1/63/104; A5/3/4
PYTCHES, Ann, the younger, Kirtling, 1639. R2/58/108; W1/94/179

PYTCHES continued
Ellen, wid., Kirtling, 1574. A5/1/270
George, Hawstead, 1673. A5/5/135, A4/10/2
John, labourer, Ashley, 1593. R2/42/340; W1/50/4
John, the elder, yeo., Hundon, 1660. R2/62/124; W1/112/167; In. 3/8/43
John, Kirtling, 1573. R2/36/211; W1/32/138
Robert, Kirtling, 1559. R2/28/211; W1/22/193
Roger, ploughwright, Ashley, 1559. R2/28/174; W1/22/158
Samuel, scrivener, Wood Ditton, 1667. R2/64/272; W1/119/135; In. 3/12/135
Thomas, husb., Kirtling, 1521. R2/15/49, R2/17/152 & 331
PYTCHYS, Richard, Kirtling, 1521. R2/15/16, R2/14/135 (inventory only)
PYTMAN, Richard, shearman, Bury St. Edmunds, 1574. R2/37/72; W1/33/2
Richard, Mendlesham, 1496. R2/13/47
PYTT, John, sen., Wattisfield, 1458. R2/9/197
William, Wattisfield, 1471. R2/10/485
PYTTOCK, John, Snailwell, 1451. W1/24/103
PYZANE, Osmund, Eriswell, 1612. W1/95/113

Q

QUADWELL, Thomas, Bures, 1504. R2/12/39
see also Qwodwell
QUANTRELL, Thomas, Hopton, 1683. A5/6/70, A4/20/69
QUARLES, Elisabeth, wid. of Francis, clerk, Newton, 1674. R2/66/87; W1/126/31
Francis, gent., Haverhill, 1697. R2/73/217; W1/151/104
Mary, spinster, Newton, 1675. R2/66/242; W1/127/112; In. 3/16/157
Nathaniel, say maker, Sudbury, 1668. In. 3/13/78; A5/5/98, A4/6/88
QUARRE, Thomas, 1626, (N). R2/53/497; W1/82/39
QUARRY, Isabel, wid., Bacton, 1632. R2/56/199; W1/89/113
James, Finningham, 1632. A5/4/19
James, Woolpit, 1688. R2/71/56; W1/142/50; In. 3/23/23
Richard, Rickinghall Superior, 1689. A5/6/127, A4/30/40
Thomas, Drinkstone, 1530. R2/19/12
see also Qwarry
QUASER, Richard, Sudbury, 1480. R2/12/5
QUE, Max, Brandon, 1588. R2/41/122; W1/45/116; A5/2/105a
QUEYE, Robert, Bury St. Edmunds, 1361. R2/1/9
QUI, Stephen, Brandon, 1579. R2/38/86
QUIBLE, see Janings als. Quible, Janyn als. Qweybyll
QUINTIN, Anthony, Bildeston, 1677. In. 3/18/36; A5/5/168, A4/14/20
Elisabeth, wid., Layham, 1680. R2/67/701; W1/134/152; A5/6/40, A4/95/93
QUINTON, Dinah, wid., Eye, 1693. A5/6/158, A4/116/67
see also Quyntyn, Qwyntyn
QUYK, Andrew, rector, Honington, 1404. R2/1/101
John, Bury St. Edmunds, 1410. R2/1/127
see also Qwyk
QUYN, Marion, Thrandeston, 1457. R2/9/187
see also Qwyn
QUYNTYN, John, yeo., Stuston, 1576. R2/37/155; W1/37/23; In. 3/1/105
QWARRY, Geoffrey, Drinkstone, 1492. R2/13/117
Henry, Hitcham, 1461. R2/9/297
QWATLOK, Robert, Lawshall, 1477. R2/11/101
QWHELERE, John, Hundon, 1462. R2/10/330
QWHYGTH, John, Bures, 1482. R2/11/276
Walter, Clare, 1478. R2/11/154
QWODWELL, John, Polstead, 1480. R2/11/213
QWYK, William, Edwardstone, 1461. R2/9/307
QWYLT, Robert, Bures, 1472. R2/10/458
Thomas, Newmarket, 1471. R2/10/476
QWYN, Thomas, Eye, 1453. R2/9/168
QWYNTYN, Peter, Hitcham, 1463. R2/10/318
Stephen, Thwaite, 1466. W1/24/85
QWYTE, Cecily, Bury St. Edmunds, 1386. R2/1/51
QWYZTHAND, Sara, Icklingham, 1450. R2/9/124

R

RABET, Ralph, singleman, Aldeburgh, 1690. R2/71/370; W1/144/78
RABIE, Miles, clerk, Langham, 1577. W1/95/61
RABSHA, Grace, spinster, Newmarket, 1689. R2/71/205; W1/143/54
RABY, Denise, wid., Newmarket, 1675. In. 3/16/93
Jeremiah, husb., Mildenhall, 1676. In. 3/17/7; A5/5/159, A4/13/7
John, Newmarket, 1686. In. 3/22/96; A5/6/102, A4/26/64
John, yeo., Stowlangtoft, 1640. R2/58/208; W1/96/142
Mary, wid., Newmarket, 1695. R2/73/99; W1/150/113
Miles, brick maker, Stowlangtoft, 1663. R2/63/7; W1/115/12
Robert, goldsmith, Bury St. Edmunds, 1497. R2/4/61
William, the elder, baker, Mildenhall, 1689. R2/71/198; W1/143/48
William, yeo., Soham, 1698. R2/73/333; W1/152/102
see also Rabie
RACKE, William, yeo., Brandon, 1626. R2/53/650; W1/82/171
William, Brandon, 1661. In. 3/6/181; A5/5/20, A4/1/56
RACKET(T), John, lime burner, Bury St. Edmunds, 1695. In. 3/25/79; A5/6/181, A4/38/60
Thomas, clothier, Bury St. Edmunds, 1626, (N). R2/53/677; W1/82/197
RACKHAM, Thomas, yeo., Little Thornham, 1665. R2/63/312; W1/117/45; In. 3/10/69
RADCLYFF, Thomas, gent., Bury St. Edmunds, 1529. R2/6/157
see also Ratcliffe
RADFORD, Alexander, husb., Newton, 1610. R2/47/152; W1/67/33
Richard, pewterer, Newton, 1575. W1/95/19
RADIWELL, Henry, Occold, 1592. A5/2/163
RAFFE, Elizabeth, wid., Hitcham, 1631. R2/56/108; W1/87/166
John, husb., Naughton, 1557. R2/26/92; W1/20/53
John, Nedging, 1545. R2/19/550; W1/7/83
John, yeo., Wetherden, 1697. R2/73/153; W1/151/39
Nicholas, Hitcham, 1610. R2/47/229; W1/68/109
Rowse, yeo., Wetherden, 1673. R2/65/405; W1/125/22
Simon, Wattisfield, 1577. A5/2/2
William, Mendlesham, 1580. A5/2/23
William, yeo., Wetherden, 1683. R2/69/148; W1/137/121
RAGETT, John, Bury St. Edmunds, 1574. R2/37/21
RAGGETT, Christopher, yeo., Denham, 1615, (N). W1/95/106
RAGHETT, Timothy, Bury St. Edmunds, 1630. A5/4/5
RAINBERD, Laurence, singleman, Walsham le Willows, 1648. R2/60/119; W1/105/40
Nathaniel, yeo., Gislingham, 1691. R2/71/484; W1/145/41
Thomas, sen., freemason, Stowupland, 1633. R2/56/301; W1/90/66
RAINBIRD, John, sen., yeo., Walsham le Willows, 1676. R2/66/330; W1/128/34; In. 3/17/39
Mary, wid., Gislingham, 1673. R2/65/414; W1/125/37
Thomas, husb., Walsham le Willows, 1669, (N). R2/64/466; W1/121/53
RAINBURD, Richard, yeo., Walsham le Willows, 1685. R2/70/74; W1/139/67
see also Raynbard, Reynberd
RAINE, Christopher, clerk, Bures, 1589. A5/2/119
RAINEHAM, John, yeo., Brettenham, 1635. R2/56/444; W1/91/12
RAINER, Edward, weaver, Soham, 1611. R2/48/24; W1/68/47
Edward, shoe maker, Soham, 1618. R2/51/91; W1/75/57
RAISE, Robert, labourer, Exning, 1660. R2/62/56; W1/112/68; In. 3/5/63
RAKER, Hugh, Ixworth, 1595. A5/2/208
John, wid., Hepworth, 1680. A5/6/33, A4/17/24
Simon, Ixworth, 1647. R2/59/503; W1/104/143
RALFE, James, the elder, victualler, Mildenhall, 1687. R2/70/311; W1/141/55
RALPH, Edward, Walsham le Willows, 1639. A5/4/73
Samuel, Lavenham, 1698. A5/7/9
Thomas, yeo., Hitcham, 1693. R2/72/211; W1/147/104
William, singleman, Bacton, 1695. R2/72/549; W1/149/104
William, singleman, Bacton, 1697. R2/73/133; W1/151/22
see also Raffe, Raphe, Realph, Rolf(e)

RAMESDENE, Thomas, Bury St. Edmunds, 1361. R2/1/17
RAMPHOLY, Marion, Ixworth, 1484. R2/11/335
RAMPLE, William, husb., Rickinghall Superior, 1603. R2/45/284; W1/61/87
RAMPLEY, Alice, wid., Walsham le Willows, 1585. R2/39/349; W1/42/252
John, yeo., Tostock, 1667. R2/64/245; W1/119/108; In. 3/12/97
John, the elder, Walsham le Willows, 1585. R2/39/389; W1/42/218
Richard, the elder, yeo., Walsham le Willows, 1585. R2/39/363; W1/42/241
Thomas, the elder, Walsham le Willows, 1649. R2/60/220; W1/106/67
William, Walsham le Willows, 1557. R2/26/229; W1/20/117
RAMPLY, John, yeo., Walsham le Willows, 1613. R2/48/248a; W1/70/21
Katherine, wid. of John, Walsham le Willows, 1587. R2/40/123; W1/44/6
Rebecca, Walsham le Willows, 1680. A5/6/38, A4/17/77
Reginald, yeo., Walsham le Willows, 1590. R2/41/341; W1/47/34
Richard, husb., Great Fakenham, 1600. R2/45/89
William, husb., Rickinghall Superior, 1662. R2/62/349; W1/114/68; In. 3/7/95
RAMPOLY, John, Rickinghall Superior, 1448. R2/9/142
Richard, Walsham le Willows, 1513. R2/12/83
Thomas, Rickinghall, 1460. R2/9/281
RAMSBOTHOM, Abraham, draper, Woolpit, 1663. R2/63/38; W1/115/60; A5/5/45
RAMSEY, George, Felsham, 1482. R2/11/256
William, Bury St. Edmunds, 1562. A5/1/132
William, als. Cuttell, chaplain, Bury St. Edmunds, 1482. R2/2/333
William, yeo., thatcher, Combs, 1675. R2/66/280; W1/127/149; In. 3/16/187
RAMSIE, John, shearman, Newmarket, 1619. R2/51/455; W1/132/120
RAMMYSSEY, John, clerk, Bury St. Edmunds, 1473. R2/2/173
RANAMS, George, joiner, Mendlesham, 1662. In. 3/7/216
RAND, Adam, clothmaker, Bildeston, 1567. R2/32/378; W1/3/174
Dorothy, singlewoman, Rushbrook, 1613. R2/48/272; W1/70/47
Edmund, yeo., Aldham, 1608. R2/46/208; W1/65/94
Elisabeth, 1620. R2/52/116; W1/76/102
James, Isleham, 1560. W7/18
Joan, Little Waldingfield, 1452. R2/9/111
Joan, wid., Stoke, 1568. R2/33/58; W1/29/77
John, Semer, 1665. In. 3/10/171; A5/5/71, A4/3/83
Richard, jun., yeo., Aldham, 1637. R2/57/229; W1/92/279
Richard, yeo., Aldham, 1669. R2/64/556; W1/121/144; In. 3/14/157
Richard, blacksmith, Clare, 1599. R2/44/234; W1/57/51
Robert, Layham, 1697. A5/7/2, A4/40/32
Rose, wid., Sudbury, 1542. R2/22/91 & 116; W1/6/2 & 33
Thomas, Bury St. Edmunds, 1477. R2/2/242
Thomas, Clare, 1577. R2/37/282
William, Aldham, 1685. R2/70/51; W1/139/44
William, Soham, 1639. A5/4/76
William, Wixoe, 1638. A5/4/62
RANDALL, Anna, wid., Wickhambrook, 1615. R2/49/313; W1/72/92
Edmund, felt maker, Lavenham, 1674. R2/66/67; W1/126/49
Edward, Stowmarket, 1589. A5/2/122a
Elisabeth, wid., Great Finborough, 1680. R2/67/592; W1/134/68
Elisabeth, wid., Stanton, 1695. R2/72/461; W1/149/17
Gilbert, Little Thurlow (1550). R2/21/657
John, rector, Fornham St. Genevieve, 1680. R2/67/632; W1/134/98; In. 3/20/110
John, Fornham St. Martin, 1684. A5/6/76, A4/21/29
John, the elder, weaver, Great Waldingfield, 1549. R2/21/513; W1/8/55
John, Great Waldingfield, 1559. R2/28/25; W1/22/29
John, Great Waldingfield, 1594. A5/2/203
John, yeo., Pakenham, 1601. R2/44/397; W1/59/56

RANDALL continued
Joseph, Layham, 1664. In. 3/9/31; A5/5/55, A4/2/18
Nicholas, Thurston, 1582. W1/51/161
Oliver, husb., Great Finborough, 1665. In. 3/10/153; A5/5/70, A4/3/73
Parnell, wid., Wickhambrook, 1585. R2/39/283; W1/39/292
Richard, Bury St. Edmunds, 1645. A5/4/108
Robert, Brockford, 1694. R2/72/496; W1/149/50
Robert, Mendlesham, 1578. R2/37/377; W1/36/199
Thomas, tailor, Barrow, 1628, (N). R2/54/143; W1/84/13
Thomas, Bures, 1632. A5/4/19
Thomas, Wicken, 1648. A5/4/122
Thomas, the elder, yeo., Wickhambrook, 1559. R2/28/365; W1/3/3
William, Fordham, 1668. In. 3/13/187; A5/5/91, A4/6/13
RANDELL, Thomas, Isleham, 1672. In. 9/30
see also Randoll
RANDISDALE, John, Fordham, 1592. A5/2/170
RANDISDELL, Thomas, Fordham, 1527. R2/17/266; W1/1/11
RANDOLFE, John, Little Waldingfield, 1503. R2/12/63
RANDOLFF, Robert, Bury St. Edmunds, 1385. R2/1/46
Thomas, Stowmarket, 1527. R2/17/260; W1/1/19
Thomas, Sudbury, 1479. R2/11/162
RANDOLL, Charles, singleman, Mendlesham, 1596. R2/43/152; W1/54/29
Denise, wid., Fordham, 1673, (N). R2/65/412; W1/125/34
Edmund, Glemsford, 1609. A5/3/58
Elisabeth, wid., Stow, 1567. A5/1/182
James, Bury St. Edmunds, 1624, (N). R2/53/18; W1/80/27
John, carpenter, Stowmarket, 1558. R2/27/380
Rebecca, wife of William, yeo., Fordham, 1606. R2/46/22; W1/64/25
Robert, weaver, Great Waldingfield, 1559. R2/28/142; W1/22/131
William, weaver, Great Waldingfield, 1549. R2/21/142; W1/9/81
William, Wickhambrook, 1545. R2/19/511; W1/7/104
RANDS, John, singleman, Stowlangtoft, 1681. A5/6/46, A4/18/32
Rose, wid., Sudbury, 1533. W1/10/2
William, Thorpe, 1536. R2/19/254
RANDYSDALE, John, Fordham, 1531. R2/18/56, R2/19/52
RANGBELL, Joan, Burgate, 1561. A5/1/112
RANKYN, William, Downham, 1557. R2/26/258; W1/20/172
RANNEW, John, yeo., Burwell, 1615. R2/49/215; W1/72/8
Mary, Burwell, 1630. A5/4/1
William, Stetchworth, 1619. R2/51/364; W1/132/64
RANNOLDS, John, tailor, Denston, 1677. R2/66/451; W1/129/27; In. 3/18/55
RANNOWE, John, Burwell, 1603. R2/45/216; W1/61/2
Robert, Burwell, 1645. A5/4/109
Thomas, yeo., Burwell, 1602. R2/45/157; W1/60/78
Thomas, brazier, Burwell, 1647. R2/59/474; W1/104/108; In. 3/2/117
Thomas, wid., Burwell, 1687. A5/6/113, A4/27/76
RANOWE, Giles, Wickhambrook, 1676. R2/66/389; W1/128/99; In. 3/17/115; A5/5/164, A4/13/67
Joan, wid., Newmarket, 1603. R2/45/286; W1/61/89
Rose, wid., Kentford, 1508. R2/13/190
RANSALL, Katherine, wid., Euston, 1571. R2/35/307; W1/36/122
RANSDAILL, Alice, Fordham, 1552. R2/23/129; W1/11/106
RANSDALE, William, husb., Burwell, 1664. In. 3/9/20; A5/5/55, A4/2/10
RANSDALL, John, Wickhambrook, 1602, (N). R2/45/130; W1/60/47
RANSDAYLL, Robert, Brockley, 1643. R2/59/14; W1/100/21
RANSDELL, Ann, spinster, Wicken, 1693. R2/72/161
John, husb., Wicken, 1668. R2/64/308; W1/120/11; In. 3/13/11
see also Randisdale, Randysdale
RANSOLD, Thomas, Fornham, 1548. R2/21/393; W1/8/27
RANSOME, Thomas, Preston, 1641, (N). R2/58/261; W1/98/36
William, shepherd, Lakenheath, 1661. R2/62/279; W1/113/187; In. 3/6/245

RANSON, Adam, yeo., Preston, 1558. R2/27/312
Agnes, Kettlebaston, 1573. A5/1/257
Christopher, hoop maker, Gedding, 1687. R2/70/302; W1/141/45; In. 3/23/49; A5/6/116, A4/27/99 & 101
Christopher, husb., Kettlebaston, 1563. R2/31/144; W1/26/27
Dinah, wid., Preston, 1637. R2/57/129; W1/92/161
Edward, Hitcham, 1632. A5/4/20
Edward, yeo., Preston, 1679. R2/67/357; W1/133/115
George, singleman, Hitcham, 1599. R2/44/267; W1/57/73
John, hoop maker, Felsham, 1661. In. 3/6/276; A5/5/24, A4/1/23
John, yeo., Preston, 1629. R2/54/391; W1/85/85
John, Rattlesden, 1685. A5/6/86, A4/24/1
Lee, als. Blyse, 1644. A5/4/103
Margery, Kettlebaston, 1573. R2/36/105; W1/32/6
Rachael, Cockfield, 1634. A5/4/29
Richard, Hitcham, 1609. A5/3/80
Richard, yeo., Kettlebaston, 1568. R2/33/67; W1/29/87
Roger, felt maker, Mildenhall, 1680. R2/67/529; W1/134/13; In. 3/20/15
Samuel, husb., Onehouse, 1606. R2/46/26; W1/64/30
Thomas, yeo., Preston, 1699. R2/73/467; W1/153/103
William, Preston, 1594. A5/2/201
RAPHE, John, Nedging, 1544. A5/1/34
John, Nedging, 1545. A5/1/67
Nicholas, yeo., Bacton, 1629. R2/54/401; W1/85/93
RASBROOKE, Martin, Tostock, 1560. R2/29/61; W1/25/112
RASH, Mary, wid. of Robert, minister, Poslingford, 1685. R2/70/66; W1/139/57
Robert, clerk, Poslingford, 1681. R2/68/157; W1/135/119
RASSEBROOKE, Richard, Milden, 1554. R2/24/136
RASTALD, John, Coney Weston, 1480. R2/11/192
Robert, Bardwell, 1480. R2/11/272
RASTALL, John, Barningham, 1560. A5/1/104
John, Rishangles, 1584. R2/39/147; W1/42/178
Katherine, Fornham, 1594, (N). R2/42/526; W1/52/59; A5/2/203
see also Restall
RATCLIFFE, Thomas, Bury St. Edmunds, 1591. A5/2/150
RATCLYFF, Ann, wid., Stetchworth, 1472. R2/2/167
see also Radclyff, Ratlife
RATESDENE, Nicholas, Bury St. Edmunds, 1361. R2/1/8
RATLIE, John, labourer, Glemsford, 1608. R2/46/179; W1/65/40
RATLIFE, Rose, wid., Bury St. Edmunds, 1597, (N). R2/43/228; W1/55/13
RATLYFF, Thomas, yeo., Bury St. Edmunds, 1622. R2/52/427; W1/78/51
RAUKIN, Margery, wid., Downham, 1558. R2/27/454
RAUNDE, John, Little Wratting, 1444. R2/9/50
RAVELL, John, jun., Cavendish, 1679. A5/6/25, A4/94/107
John, clothier, Cavendish, 1693. R2/72/268; W1/147/156
RAVEN, John, wheelwright, Ashdon, 1628. R2/54/259; W1/84/117
John, Exning, 1516. R2/13/224
Thomas, Haverhill, 1545. R2/19/510; W1/7/30
RAVENS, Edward, Haverhill, 1586. A5/2/81
John, Edwardstone, 1607. A5/3/26
RAWE, Humphrey, tailor, Withersfield, 1604. R2/45/340; W1/62/58
Matthew, fustian weaver, Haverhill, 1683. R2/69/319; W1/138/115
see also Wraw
RAWLIN, John, woollen weaver, Bildeston, 1663. R2/63/118; W1/115/182
John, husb., Groton, 1639. R2/58/7; W1/94/11
Sarah, singlewoman, Brandon, 1683. A5/6/71, A4/20/87
Thomas, tailor, Brandon, 1669, (N). R2/64/476; W1/121/64; In. 3/14/75
Thomas, bach., Brandon, 1683. A5/6/72, A4/20/88
RAWLING, Thomas, Brandon, 1641. A5/4/92
Thomas, husb., Chippenham, 1558. R2/27/446
RAWLINS, John, Oakley, 1558. R2/27/191

RAWLYN, Isabella, Chippenham, 1464. R2/10/368
John, tailor, Bury St. Edmunds, 1522. R2/6/94
Robert, Chippenham, 1464. R2/10/345
William, Barnham, 1464. R2/10/328
RAWLYNG, William, Mildenhall, 1519. R2/14/12
see also Rewlying
RAY, Agnes, Wood Ditton, (1528). R2/9/286
Alice, wid., Hawkedon, 1650. R2/61/392; W1/107/95; In. 3/3/110
Ann, spinster, Glemsford, 1662. R2/62/357; W1/114/80; In. 3/7/111
Daniel, yeo., Stansfield, 1661. In. 3/6/122; A5/5/14, A4/1/118
Elisabeth, Denston, 1521. R2/14/112
Elisabeth, als. Garrard, Stanningfield, 1690. A5/6/135, A4/32/46
Elisabeth, wid., Stradishall, 1565. R2/32/259; W1/27/164
Elisabeth, wid., Whepstead, 1648, (N). R2/60/20; W1/105/30
Frances, Barrow, 1630. R2/55/98; W1/86/110
Francis, yeo., Denston, 1611. R2/48/49; W1/68/72
George, yeo., Cowlinge, 1680. R2/67/680; W1/134/136; In. 3/20/149
Gilbert, Chippenham, 1391. R2/1/59
Hester, wid., Stansfield, 1673. A5/5/142, A4/10/86
John, yeo., Cheveley, 1559. R2/28/213; W1/22/197
John, yeo., Clare, 1628. R2/54/243; W1/84/104
John, Denston, 1503. R2/12/54
John, Denston, 1636. R2/57/2; W1/92/1
John, Newmarket, 1460. R2/9/298
John, Old Newton, 1694. A5/6/171, A4/37/61
John, mercer, grocer, Sudbury, 1686. R2/70/542; W1/140/148; In. 3/22/43; A5/6/128, A4/30/35
John, Wickhambrook, 1452. R2/9/147
John, yeo., Wickhambrook, 1651. R2/61/426
John, the elder, yeo., Wickhambrook, 1666. R2/64/101; W1/118/72; In. 3/11/106
John, sen., Wickhambrook, 1681. R2/68/4; W1/135/4; In. 3/21/19; A5/6/61, A4/19/70
John, Wood Ditton, 1459. R2/9/269
John, yeo., Wood Ditton, 1481. R2/11/209
Joseph, wid., Wickhambrook, 1685. A5/6/87, A4/24/15
Margery, wid., Denston, 1484. R2/11/351
Nathaniel, mercer, Hawkedon, 1636. R2/57/80; W1/92/96
Philemon, yeo., Clare, 1679. R2/67/380; W1/133/132
Phillip, Sudbury, 1631. A5/4/9
Richard, singleman, Depden, 1676. In. 3/17/143; A5/5/163, A4/13/61
Richard, Depden, 1677. In. 3/18/85
Richard, singleman, Hundon, 1637. R2/57/199; W1/92/236
Richard, yeo., Nayland, 1682. In. 3/21/22; A5/6/65, A4/19/113
Richard, yeo., Stradishall, 1610. R2/47/292; W1/125/183
Richard, yeo., Stradishall, 1632. R2/56/122; W1/89/9
Richard, yeo., Whepstead, 1642. R2/58/359; W1/99/59
Robert, Denston, 1482. R2/11/275
Robert, clerk, Hawkedon, 1647. R2/59/388; W1/104/14; In. 3/2/21
Robert, Lakenheath, 1551. R2/23/90; W1/11/54
Robert, Newmarket, 1563. R2/32/24; W1/26/85
Robert, yeo., Wickhambrook, 1598. R2/44/60; W1/56/56
Robert, Wickhambrook, 1685. R2/70/59; W1/139/53
Simon, yeo., Hundon, 1626. R2/53/552; W1/82/76a & b
Simon, yeo., Hundon, 1682. In. 3/21/146; A5/6/61, A4/19/67
Thomas, Landwade, 1586. R2/40/31; W1/43/22
Thomas, yeo., Stradishall, 1552. R2/31/72; W1/13/52
William, clerk, Gislingham, 1557. R2/26/290; W1/20/210
William, Thelnetham, 1634. A5/4/34
see also Rey
RAYDON, John, yeo., Gipping, 1624. R2/53/75; W1/80/96
RAYLETT, Elisabeth, Haverhill, 1687. A5/6/115, A4/27/97
RAYMANT, Hugh, Clare, 1636. A5/4/43
Margaret, Chilton, 1637. A5/4/54
RAYMENT, Ann, wid., Wickhambrook, 1684. R2/69/238; W1/138/43
Edward, husb., Stoke by Clare, 1633, (N). R2/56/267; W1/90/31
Giles, husb., Great Thurlow, 1662. R2/62/410; W1/114/162; In. 3/7/195

RAYMENT continued
Hugh, 1617. R2/50/313; W1/74/100
John, labourer, Clare, 1581. R2/38/341; W1/40/80
John, tailor, Clare, 1630. R2/55/121; W1/86/136
John, tailor, Wickhambrook, 1648. R2/60/85; W1/105/103
John, Wickhambrook, 1681. A5/6/55, A4/18/142
John, Wickhambrook, 1685. R2/70/100; W1/139/90
John, Withersfield, 1647. In. 3/2/94; A5/4/117
Katherine, wid., Mildenhall, 1615. R2/49/236; W1/72/26
Peter, Landwade, 1640. A5/4/79
Richard, yeo., Barnardiston, 1602. R2/45/194; W1/60/122
Richard, Isleham, 1576, (N). W7/42
William, yeo., Clare, 1699. R2/73/405; W1/153/49
RAYMOND, George, Bury St. Edmunds, 1675. W1/312/4 (inventory only)
John, Burwell, 1691. A5/6/139, A4/33/13
Thomas, say maker, Clare, 1691. R2/71/459
William, Stowmarket, 1687. A5/6/115, A4/27/93
RAYMONT, Joan, wid., Burwell, 1692. R2/72/49; W1/146/44; In. 3/24/70
see also Reymond
RAYNAKER, John, Wattisham, 1559. R2/28/270
RAYNAM, Ralph, Sudbury, 1610. R2/47/247; W1/67/28
RAYNAR, Robert, lime burner, Sudbury, 1583. R2/39/74; W1/42/34
RAYNARD, John, fisherman, Soham, 1556. R2/25/135; W1/16/173
see also Raynerd
RAYNBARD, Edward, Thelnetham, 1597. R2/43/221; W1/55/6
RAYNBEARD, John, yeo., Hepworth, 1625. R2/53/357; W1/81/136
RAYNBERD, Elisabeth, spinster, 1644. A5/4/110
John, Badwell Ash, 1669. In. 3/14/61; A5/5/100, A4/6/113
John, Thelnetham, 1562. R2/31/45
John, Woolpit, 1683. A5/6/68, A4/20/28
Laurence, the elder, yeo., Walsham le Willows, 1631. R2/56/106; W1/87/163
Lawrence, yeo., Westhorpe, 1644. R2/59/125; W1/101/54
Richard, Bacton, 1623, (N). R2/52/589; W1/79/40
Thomas, yeo., Bacton, 1542. R2/22/50; W1/6/63
William, Walsham le Willows, 1597. R2/43/285; W1/55/61
RAYNEBARD, Thomas, the elder, butcher, Walsham le Willows, 1563. R2/31/159; W1/29/38
RAYNEBERD, John, yeo., Occold, 1638. R2/57/330; W1/93/113
Robert, yeo., Wyverstone, 1690. R2/71/398; W1/144/101
Thomas, Newton, 1566. A5/1/179
Thomas, husb., Stowupland, 1634. R2/56/395; W1/90/176
RAYNEBURD, Lawrence, gent., Westhorpe, 1669. R2/64/574; W1/121/163; In. 3/14/172
William, yeo., Walsham le Willows, 1675. R2/66/247; W1/127/116; In. 3/16/136
RAYNEHAM, Robert, Stoke by Nayland, 1540. R2/19/286
RAYNER, Andrew, Soham, 1458. R2/9/210
Andrew, Soham, 1566. R2/32/346; W1/28/37
Ann, singlewoman, Great Waldingfield, 1633. R2/56/254; W1/90/16
Ann, wid., Hartest, 1598. R2/44/152; W1/56/87
Clement, labourer, Stanton, 1619. R2/51/441; W1/132/110
Edward, cordwinder, Soham, 1660. R2/62/117; W1/112/157; In. 3/5/166
Eleanor, wid., Soham, 1595. R2/43/78; W1/53/72
Ellen, Soham, 1599. R2/44/259; W1/57/66
Erasmus, husb., Somerton, 1618. R2/51/215; W1/75/136
Francis, Soham, 1591. A5/2/145
Henry, yeo., Newmarket, 1640. R2/58/129; W1/96/15
Henry, labourer, Stanton, 1616. R2/50/50; W1/73/58
John, Bures, 1638. R2/57/361; W1/93/157
John, bach., Clare, 1682. In. 3/21/209; A5/6/59, A4/19/35
John, labourer, Hawkedon, 1606. W1/111/24
John, Sapiston, 1697. A5/7/2, A4/40/35
John, fisherman, Soham, 1589. R2/41/168; W1/46/117
Mary, wid., Soham, 1593. R2/42/344; W1/50/9
Nicholas, singleman, Eye, 1558. R2/27/363
Richard, fisherman, Soham, 1583. W1/42/62
Robert, Fordham, 1628. R2/54/196; W1/84/69
Robert, fisherman, Soham, 1558. R2/27/25
Robert, yeo., Wattisham, 1647. R2/59/431; W1/104/61; In. 3/2/73

RAYNER continued
Thomas, the elder, husb., Soham, 1620. R2/52/20; W1/76/19
William, tailor, Chippenham, 1636. R2/57/98; W1/92/116
William, Soham, 1642. R2/58/385; W1/99/97
William, Soham, 1642. R2/58/386; W1/99/95
William, Sudbury, 1593. A5/2/184
see also Rainer, Raynar, Raynor, Reyner, Ryner, Depenham als. Reyner
RAYNERD, William, labourer, Soham, 1563. R2/32/8; W1/26/65
RAYNES, William, Burwell, 1546. R2/19/495, R2/21/228 & 651. W1/10/102
RAYNHAM, John, yeo., Brettenham, 1694. R2/72/320; W1/148/49
John, the elder, yeo., Bury St. Edmunds, 1684. R2/69/236; W1/138/41
John, yeo., Bury St. Edmunds, 1698. R2/73/465; W1/153/102
John, yeo., Kettlebaston, 1683. R2/69/59; W1/137/45
see also Raineham, Ranams, Raynam, Rayneham, Raynum, Reinams, Reynham
RAYNOLD(S), Catherine, Hessett, 1631. A5/4/15
Henry, yeo., Hessett, 1623. R2/52/687; W1/79/106
Joan, wid., Woolpit, 1557. R2/26/298; W1/20/220
John, Bury St. Edmunds, 1557. R2/8/315; W1/18/45
John, Haverhill, 1563. R2/31/145; W1/26/26
John, Hopton, (1540), (N). R2/21/361
Nicholas, Bury St. Edmunds, 1580. A5/2/24
Susan, als. Worledge, Thelnetham, 1640. A5/4/86
Thomas, miller, Barnham, 1601. R2/44/345; W1/59/7
Thomas, Great Finborough, 1571. A5/1/234
Thomas, Haverhill, 1652. In. 3/4/25; A5/4/141
RAYNOR, John, fisherman, Soham, 1583. R2/39/45
John, yeo., Wattisham, 1557. R2/26/326; W1/20/255
Robert, shoe maker, Soham, 1602. R2/45/171; W1/60/93
William, translator, Mildenhall, 1676. R2/66/423; W1/128/133
RAYNOULDES, John, husb., Haughley, 1640. R2/58/148; W1/96/53
RAYNSON, James, Newmarket, 1521. R2/15/171
RAYNTHORPE, William, clerk, Kersey, 1560. R2/29/12; W1/25/169
RAYNUM, John, yeo., Bury St. Edmunds, 1644. R2/59/108; W1/101/35
RAYSIN, Mercy, wid., Hitcham, 1640, (N). R2/58/124; W1/96/6
William, Hitcham, 1639. A5/4/77
RAYSYN, William, husb., Hitcham, 1649, (N). R2/60/281; W1/106/153
REACH, Nicholas, weaver, Great Waldingfield, 1589. R2/41/248; W1/46/10
READ(E), Anne, wid., Stoke Ash, 1650, (N). R2/61/410; W1/107/114; In. 3/3/130
Bridget, wid., Bardwell, 1695. R2/72/578; W1/149/126
Daniel, singleman, Sudbury, 1638. A5/4/58
Eleanor, Gislingham, 1590. A5/2/130
Francis, Great Thornham, 1609. A5/3/77
George, Dalham, 1661. In. 3/6/44; A5/5/13, A4/1/125
Harry, Fordham, 1625, (N). R2/66/369; W1/81/146
Henry, Bury St. Edmunds, 1599. R2/44/301; W1/57/96
James, yeo., Brockford, 1698. R2/73/270; W1/152/47
James, Combs, 1564. W1/27/141
Jane, wid., Stowmarket, 1636, (N). R2/57/48; W1/92/58
John, the elder, husb., Bures, 1597. R2/43/322; W1/55/87
John, Bury St. Edmunds, 1635. A5/4/42
John, singleman, Bury St. Edmunds, 1649. R2/60/161; W1/106/5
John, husb., Combs, 1638. R2/57/398; W1/93/215
John, labourer, Eye, 1666. R2/64/90; W1/118/64; A5/5/76, A4/4/46
John, Fordham, 1661. A5/5/18, A4/1/77
John, Gedding, 1681. A5/6/56, A4/18/149
John, Great Finborough, 1679. A5/6/27, A4/16/124
John, Landwade, 1681. A5/6/49, A4/18/64
John, husb., Soham, 1631. R2/56/51; W1/87/70
John, wid., Stowupland, 1647. In. 3/2/146; A5/4/116
John, sen., Wetheringsett, 1693. R2/72/154
Katherine, Bures, 1590. A5/2/140
Mary, wid., Kedington, 1679. A5/6/23, A4/16/88
Paul, Stoke Ash, 1647. R2/59/404; W1/104/31; In. 3/2/138
Phillippa, wid., Wicken, 1684. R2/69/432; W1/138/210; A5/6/78, A4/21/48

READ(E) continued
Richard, bach., Gazeley, 1681. A5/6/52, A4/18/110
Robert, Lindsey, 1575. R2/37/85; W1/34/5
Robert, Withersfield, 1563. A5/1/146
Susan, wid., Great Finborough, 1670. R2/65/116; A5/5/118
Thomas, yeo., Cockfield, 1577. R2/37/284
Thomas, yeo., linen weaver, Gislingham, 1660. R2/62/45; W1/112/53; In. 3/5/52
Thomas, Great Thurlow, 1661. In. 3/6/147; A5/5/18, A4/1/78
Thomas, Hopton, 1679. A5/6/25, A4/16/109
Thomas, Kedington, 1593. R2/42/459; W1/50/122
Thomas, Onehouse, 1699. In. 3/27/70; A5/7/21 & 70, A4/41/8
Thomas, Redlingfield, 1639. A5/4/77
Thomas, Thorndon, 1580. A5/2/28
Thomas, Wetheringsett, 1611. A5/3/110
Thomas, Wicken, 1684. A5/6/75, A4/21/15
Walter, husb., Stoke Ash, 1632. R2/56/130; W1/89/18
William, Assington, 1649. A5/4/129
William, Gislingham, 1590. R2/41/347; W1/47/39
William, the elder, Hopton, 1590. R2/41/322; W1/47/11
William, Kedington, 1554. R2/24/8; W1/14/8
William, Kedington, 1557. R2/26/195; W1/20/135
William, Kedington, 1615. R2/49/345; W1/72/117
William, yeo., Kedington, 1662. In. 3/7/76; A5/5/30
William, Mildenhall, 1693. A5/6/163, A4/35/28b
William, Thornham, 1594. W1/51/115
see also Rede, Reed, Davy als. Reade, Sagon als. Rede
READER, Nicholas, Langham, 1609. A5/3/59
see also Reeder, Reder, Peers als. Reder
REAGEN, Beatrice, Bury St. Edmunds, 1606. A5/3/11
REALPH, Richard, husb., Great Wratting, 1604. R2/45/374; W1/62/103
REASON, Edmund, Layham, 1661. In. 3/7/84; A5/5/14, A4/1/110
John, tanner, Haverhill, 1519. R2/15/20
Richard, singleman, Layham, 1638. R2/57/436; W1/93/277
REAVE, Rose, wid., Thelnetham, 1680. R2/67/550; W1/134/34; In. 3/20/63; A5/6/32, A4/17/19
REAVELL, Bridget, wid., Chedburgh, 1694. R2/72/406; W1/148/138
George, yeo., Chedburgh, 1697. R2/73/113; W1/151/4
REAWSE, John, Stoke by Nayland, 1621. R2/52/316; W1/77/94
RECHARD, John, Bacton, (1471). R2/10/494
RECHE, Margery, wid., Boxford, 1457. R2/9/219
RECHEFORD, Margery, Worlington, 1458. R2/9/212
RECHESUN, John, Freckenham, 1672. In. 10/14
RECHYR, Martin, Buxhall, 1542. R2/22/65; W1/6/48
RECORD, Elisabeth, Newmarket, 1696. A5/6/186, A4/39/30
REDDE, Thomas, husb., Worlington, 1580. W1/39/159
REDDIE, Thomas, Mendlesham, 1672. R2/65/352; W1/124/88
REDDLESDALLE, John, husb., Lindsey, 1585. R2/40/38; W1/43/27
REDDOWCE, Ambrose, husb., Clare, 1622. R2/52/415; W1/78/43
REDE, Anne, wid., Shimpling, 1551. R2/23/42; W1/11/55 & 56
Geoffrey, collar maker, Bury St. Edmunds, 1519. R2/6/58
John, Cockfield, 1556. R2/25/82; W1/16/126
John, Kedington, 1562. R2/31/90; W1/8/99
John, fisherman, Soham, 1557. R2/26/256; W1/20/170b
John, Thornham, 1461. R2/9/295
Margaret, Cockfield, 1571. A5/1/237
Robert, husb., Thrandeston, 1573. R2/36/177; W1/52/84
Thomas, Bury St. Edmunds, 1557. R2/8/302; W1/18/30
Thomas, Hawstead, 1480. R2/11/197
William, painter, Bury St. Edmunds, 1453. R2/2/41
William, baker, Bury St. Edmunds, 1495. R2/4/41
William, glover, Bury St. Edmunds, 1500. R2/4/101
William, husb., Cockfield, 1548. R2/21/491; W1/10/164
William, Lawshall, 1519. R2/15/5; W1/26/107
see also Read(e)
REDELL, John, als. Lardener, Bury St. Edmunds, 1477. R2/2/236
REDELYSWORTH, William, Badwell Ash, 1462. R2/9/285
REDENHALE, John, Bury St. Edmunds, 1445. R2/2/15
REDER, John, Timworth, 1455. R2/9/177
Richard, Redgrave, 1462. R2/12/11
Simon, Bury St. Edmunds, 1446. R2/2/19

REDER continued
Thomas, Bury St. Edmunds, 1474. R2/2/187
Thomas, husb., Stowlangtoft, 1573. R2/36/187; W1/32/110
Walter, Bury St. Edmunds, 1426. R2/1/170
REDGEMAN, John, yeo., Bury St. Edmunds, 1475. R2/2/207
REDGEN, Bridget, wid., Fornham All Saints, 1638. R2/57/428; W1/93/265
Richard, husb., Fornham All Saints, 1640. R2/58/204; W1/96/136
Thomas, Timworth, 1639. A5/4/70
REDGIS, John, Bury St. Edmunds, 1437. R2/1/232
REDGRAVE, Clement, Great Livermere, 1439. R2/9/5
Edmund, Bury St. Edmunds, 1422. R2/1/162
John, chaplain, Bury St. Edmunds, 1432. R2/1/202
Richard, Great Livermere, 1474. R2/11/44
Timothy, Wiston, 1646. A5/4/114
REDGWELL, Alice, wid., Cavendish, 1625. R2/53/362; W1/81/141
William, yeo., Wickhambrook, 1641. R2/58/259; W1/98/32
REDGYS, Denise, wid., Bury St. Edmunds, 1449. R2/2/29
REDHOUSE, Thomas, yeo., Clare, 1626. R2/53/638; W1/82/162
see also Reddowce
REDINGTON, John, Exning, 1652. A5/4/142
Richard, Burwell, 1593. R2/42/417; W1/50/78
Richard, husb., Exning, 1662. In. 3/7/1; A5/5/28
REDLAND, Maria, Tuddenham, 1696. In. 3/25/102; A5/6/189, A4/36/64
Robert, Tuddenham, 1694. A5/6/170, A4/37/47
REDLEND, Ann, Mendlesham, 1571. W1/36/141
see also Ridlond
REDMAN, John, parson, Great Whelnetham, 1550. R2/21/54; W1/9/105
William, mercer, Exning, 1611. R2/48/23; W1/68/43
REDSTON, Ann, Boxted, 1567, (N). R2/32/401; W1/3/100
REDWYN, Anne, spinster, Bury St. Edmunds, 1684. A5/6/86, A4/21/131
REDYSDALE, Richard, Milden, 1538. R2/20/64; W1/4/57
REED, Jeffry, carpenter, Lavenham, 1587. R2/39/357; W1/42/246b; A5/2/88
John, Bures, 1554. A5/1/93
John, Clare, 1477. R2/11/78
John, chapman, Fordham, 1626. R2/53/654; W1/82/177
John, Stowmarket, 1606. A5/3/8
John, yeo., Stowmarket, 1630. R2/55/99; W1/86/111
John, als. Gooch, Wickhambrook, 1451. R2/9/105
Thomas, Market Weston, 1477. R2/11/49
see also Read(e)
REEDER, Henry, husb., Stradishall, 1619. R2/51/317; W1/132/37
Jonas, yeo., Hundon, 1692. R2/72/89; W1/146/83; In. 3/24/19
Robert, the elder, yeo., Brancaster, 1653. W1/110/37 & 39
Simon, mason, Bury St. Edmunds, 1444. R2/2/10
see also Reader
REEFE, William, 1508. W1/9/24
Thomas, Great Thurlow, 1606. A5/3/7
REEVE, Alice, Hopton, 1630. A5/4/4
Andrew, husb., Mildenhall, 1596. R2/43/199; W1/54/75
Ann, spinster, Finningham, 1680. A5/6/41, A4/17/111
Ann, wid., Isleham, 1628. R6/53
Bridget, Thelnetham, 1670. A5/5/118
Denise, wid., Bury St. Edmunds, 1503. R2/4/152
Edward, gent., Bury St. Edmunds, 1598. R2/44/90; W1/56/91
Edward, miller, Hundon, 1631. R2/56/25; W1/87/34
Elisabeth, wid., Finningham, 1672. A5/5/129, A4/9/25
Elisabeth, wid., Hundon, 1691, (N). R2/71/529; W1/145/85; A5/6/145, A4/33/78
Francis, singleman, Hepworth, 1631. R2/56/72; W1/87/109
George, esq., Lavenham, 1687. R2/70/314; W1/141/59
Isaac, cook, Botesdale, 1646. R2/59/319; W1/103/38
James, yeo., Hepworth, 1651. R2/61/449
Jane, Bury St. Edmunds, 1607. A5/3/23
John, yeo., Cheveley, 1682. R2/68/380; W1/136/83; In. 3/21/131
John, Clare, 1694. A5/6/173, A4/37/88
John, husb., Cowlinge, 1607. R2/46/114; W1/97/20
John, Great Livermere, 1631. A5/4/15
John, yeo., Great Wratting, 1638. R2/57/368; W1/93/169

REEVE continued
John, yeo., Hepworth, 1667. R2/64/278; W1/119/77; In. 3/12/143
John, Horningsheath, 1688. In. 3/23/25; A5/6/118, A4/29/24
John, miller, Hundon, 1688. R2/71/69; W1/142/61; In. 3/23/106
John, Knettishall, 1638. A5/4/67
John, shepherd, Mildenhall, 1634. R2/56/436; W1/90/221
John, Mildenhall, 1641. A5/4/92
John, yeo., Shelland, 1680. R2/67/604; W1/134/77
John, Thelnetham, 1679. A5/6/29, A4/16/149
John, singleman, Wetheringsett, 1669. R2/64/508; W1/121/99; In. 3/14/60
Jonathan, yeo., Hepworth, 1667. R2/64/224; W1/119/141; In. 3/12/144
Joseph, singleman, Thelnetham, 1648. A5/4/120
Judith, Mildenhall, 1607. A5/3/21
Margaret, wid., Thelnetham, 1671. A5/5/122, A4/8/23
Mary, wid., Bury St. Edmunds, 1603. R2/45/259; W1/61/63
Peter, labourer, Stradishall, 1599, (N). R2/44/253; W1/57/121a
Richard, labourer, Isleham, 1626. R6/46
Richard, miller, West Stow, 1620. R2/52/8; W1/76/6
Richard, miller, West Stow, 1666. R2/64/112; W1/118/86; In. 3/11/134
Robert, Isleham, 1624. R6/35
Robert, husb., Isleham, 1670. In. 9/27
Robert, Mildenhall, 1629. R2/54/311; W1/85/25
Roger, singleman, Ixworth Thorpe, 1650. In. 3/3/150; A5/4/137
Samuel, Soham, 1638, (N). R2/57/339; W1/93/121
Simon, husb., Barningham, 1627. R2/54/121; W1/83/118
Stephen, yeo., Eriswell, 1700. R2/74/20; W1/154/17; In. 3/27/81
Susan, wid., Wood Ditton, 1682. In. 3/21/47; A5/6/61, A4/19/65
Thomas, Thrandeston, 1648. A5/4/125
Thomas, sen., yeo., Wood Ditton, 1613. R2/48/323; W1/70/102
Timothy, Pakenham, 1636. A5/4/45
William, Haughley, 1687. A5/6/107, A4/26/2
William, husb., Rede, 1663. R2/63/69; W1/115/109; In. 3/8/135
William, Weston, 1651. A5/4/139
William, the elder, shepherd, Wood Ditton, 1638. R2/57/382; W1/93/190
Zachary, gent., Eye, 1631, (N). W1/111/67
see also Reave, Reefe, Reive, Reve, Bullock als. Reve, Cake als. Reve, Frances als. Reve, Francis als. Reeve, Francis als. Reve, Frannces als. Reve, Fraunces als. Reve, Wright als. Reve

REEVES, Elisabeth, the elder, wid., Stoke by Nayland, 1636. R2/57/75; W1/92/89

REFFHAM, John, Barwell, 1476. R2/11/120

REGEWYN, John, Sudbury, 1442. R2/9/49

REGIN, John, bricklayer, Bury St. Edmunds, 1600. R2/45/70; W1/58/99
see also Reagen, Redgen, Regyn, Rogen

REGNER, John, Bury St. Edmunds, 1447. R2/2/22

REGYN, Thomas, Fornham St. Martin, 1589, (N). R2/41/315; W1/47/2

REICROFTE, Edmund, weaver, Bildeston, 1603. R2/45/299; W1/61/107

REIGNOLD, Henry, Hopton, 1558. R2/27/370
John, yeo., Lawshall, 1626. R2/53/649; W1/82/169
William, tailor, Bury St. Edmunds, 1494. R2/4/32

REINAMS, George, Mendlesham, 1662. R2/62/415; W1/114/170

REINOLES, Alice, wid., Cowlinge, 1634. R2/56/391; W1/90/170

REIVE, Edmund, yeo., Lawshall, 1616. R2/50/87; W1/73/95
James, glover, Stanton, 1682. R2/68/324; W1/136/144; In. 3/21/193
William, als. Bullocke, tailor, Hartest, 1624. R2/53/34; W1/80/47

REKEDON, Margery, wife of John, Gazeley, 1453. R2/9/158

RELINGHAM, Robert, Soham, 1521. R2/15/126, R2/17/1

RELTON, Edward, shearman, Sudbury, 1682. R2/68/441; W1/136/125

REMINGTON, Bridget, wid., Wortham, 1663. In. 3/8/132; A5/5/49

RENAKERS, Robert, Wattisham, 1562. R2/31/6; W1/8/136

RENOLDS, Robert, husb., Westley, 1673. R2/65/437
RERY, John, mercer, Bury St. Edmunds, 1402. R2/1/94
RESAN, William, Fordham, 1480. W1/24/48
RESOLD, Roger, clothier, Bury St. Edmunds, 1598. R2/44/83; W1/56/79
RESSHEBROK, John, Combs, 1440. R2/9/8
RESSHEY, John, als. Barbour, sen., Bures, 1474. R2/11/144
RESTALL, Richard, miller, Fornham St. Genevieve, 1576. R2/37/135; W1/37/6; In. 3/1/115
RESUN, Robert, husb., Rattlesden, 1550. R2/21/171; W1/9/89
REVE, Alice, wid., Tuddenham, 1558. R2/27/367
Agnes, wife of Thomas, Sudbury, (1535). R2/18/108, R2/19/216; W1/3/53
Agnes, wid., Wicken, 1554. R2/24/19; W1/14/19
Andrew, Preston, 1603. R2/45/224; W1/61/14
Edmund, parson, Bury St. Edmunds, 1587. R2/40/189
Elisabeth, wid., Haughley, 1692. R2/72/91; W1/146/85; In. 3/24/13
Elisabeth, wid., Mildenhall, 1556. R2/25/153; W1/16/158
Elisabeth, wid., Thwaite, 1621. R2/52/279; W1/77/66
George, Hepworth, 1537. R2/20/53; W1/4/43
Henry, Wood Ditton, 1595. R2/43/98; W1/53/95
Isabel, Wickham, 1460. R2/9/256
James, Freckenham, 1556. W8/1
Joan, wid., Walsham le Willows, 1559. R2/28/306
John, yeo., Bramfield, 1575. W1/51/225
John, sen., Bury St. Edmunds, 1471. R2/2/138
John, Bury St. Edmunds, 1532. R2/7/7
John, Cavenham, 1511. R2/12/82
John, Clare, 1484. W1/24/78
John, Cowlinge, 1457. R2/9/185
John, sen., Downham, 1473. R2/11/8
John, Downham, 1488. R2/11/395
John, Fornham St. Martin, 1476. R2/11/48
John, the elder, Haverhill, 1489. R2/11/434
John, Hepworth, 1469. R2/10/430
John, the elder, yeo., Hepworth, 1597. R2/43/294; W1/55/67
John, Whepstead, 1446. R2/9/74
John, sen., Wickham, 1460. R2/9/252
John, Wood Ditton, 1549. R2/21/500; W1/28/150
Juliane, wife of William, Haverhill, 1525. R2/14/109
Lucy, Great Saxham, 1585. R2/39/366; W1/42/240
Margaret, wid., Bury St. Edmunds, 1549. R2/8/259
Mary, wid., Stanton, 1688. R2/71/51; W1/142/122; In. 3/23/45
Reginald, yeo., Hepworth, 1630. R2/55/21; W1/86/25
Richard, Kirtling, 1511. R2/12/81
Robert, Barningham, 1606. W1/111/25
Robert, gent., Bury St. Edmunds, 1615. R2/49/360; W1/72/130
Robert, Elveden, 1676. R2/66/392; W1/128/103; In. 3/17/127
Robert, als. Bocher, Great Waldingfield, 1554. A5/1/92
Robert, Hepworth, 1557. R2/26/149; W1/20/103
Robert, husb., Isleham, 1671. W7/78
Robert, Mildenhall, 1461. W1/24/51
Robert, Mildenhall, 1521. R2/15/175
Robert, husb., Troston, 1572, (N). R2/36/9; W1/31/133; A5/1/246
Robert, Tuddenham, 1554. R2/24/15; W1/14/15
Robert, Wicken, 1552. R2/23/187a; W1/12/15
Roger, gent., Bury St. Edmunds, 1607. R2/46/142
Thomas, labouring man, Brettenham, 1559. R2/28/257; W1/22/248
Thomas, sicklesmith, Haverhill, 1504. R2/13/158
Thomas, shoe maker, Haverhill, 1527. R2/17/267; W1/1/10
Thomas, yeo., Hopton, 1682. R2/68/489; W1/136/161; In. 3/21/16
Thomas, the elder, Soham, 1476. R2/11/119
Thomas, Thelnetham, 1505. R2/12/45
Walter, Hepworth, 1447. W1/24/184
William, the elder, Cheveley, 1550. R2/21/86; W1/9/113, 116 & 123
William, Cheveley, 1553. R2/31/139; W1/13/93
William, Cheveley, 1579. A5/2/21
William, yeo., Fordham, 1638. R2/57/245; W1/93/3

REVE continued
William, Freckenham, 1579. W8/12
William, als. Frances, Gazeley, 1582. A5/2/43
William, Great Livermere, 1497. R2/13/85
William, Haverhill, 1538. R2/20/60; W1/4/48
William, the elder, Hepworth, 1577. R2/37/290
William, Isleham, 1556. W7/3
William, priest, Mildenhall, 1546. R2/21/184; W1/10/81
William, als. Francis, Moulton, 1583. R2/39/101; W1/42/16
William, Wetherden, 1630. A5/4/2
William, Wicken, 1539. R2/19/304
William, Wicken, 1540. R2/20/165; W1/4/141
William, sen., Worlington, 1547. R2/21/308; W1/10/125
---, wife of George, Hepworth, 1559. W1/22/279
REVELL, Adam, Shimpling, 1481. R2/11/218
Alice, wid., Yaxley, 1698. A5/7/8
Ann, wid., Rede, 1681. R2/68/88; W1/135/66
Anne, wid., Bury St. Edmunds, 1586. R2/40/75; W1/43/59
Edmund, Great Waldingfield, 1608. A5/3/49
Henry, weaver, Mildenhall, 1615. R2/49/355; W1/72/125
Isaac, Rede, 1679. A5/6/16, A4/16/10
Joan, the younger, wid., Buxhall, 1521. R2/15/159
Joan, Buxhall, 1538. R2/20/65; W1/4/58
Joanna, wid., Wicken, 1679. A5/6/26, A4/16/122
John, Buxhall, 1521. R2/14/39
John, Bury St. Edmunds, 1416. R2/1/137
John, yeo., Cavendish, 1630. R2/55/110; W1/86/123
John, yeo., Chedburgh, 1690. R2/71/409; W1/144/113
John, husb., Great Cornard, 1571. R2/35/92; W1/36/99
John, yeo., Great Wratting, 1589. R2/41/304
John, Lawshall, 1484. R2/11/361
John, yeo., Rede, 1615. R2/49/346; W1/72/118
John, the elder, yeo., Rede, 1675. R2/66/163; W1/127/39; In. 3/16/45
John, fanwright, Yaxley, 1681. R2/68/187; W1/135/136
Margaret, wid., Bury St. Edmunds, 1664. R2/63/248; W1/116/170; In. 3/9/231
Mary, wid., Mellis, 1675. In. 3/16/23; A5/5/152, A4/11/90
Mirabel, wid., Chevington, 1631. R2/56/39; W1/87/55
Richard, glover, Bury St. Edmunds, 1583. R2/39/29; W1/42/38
Richard, Buxhall, 1530. R2/19/32
Richard, clothier, Cavendish, 1568. R2/33/7; W1/29/13
Richard, yeo., Hundon, 1593. R2/42/352; W1/50/20
Robert, labourer, Soham, 1588. R2/41/34; W1/45/27
Roger, Wicken, 1646. A5/4/111
Thomas, Cockfield, 1631. A5/4/12
Thomas, Soham, 1601, (N). R2/44/398; W1/59/53
Walter, Buxhall, 1521. R2/15/141, R2/17/331
Walter, Woolpit, 1521. R2/15/144
William, bachelor of civil law, Bury St. Edmunds, 1639. R2/58/72; W1/94/122
William, yeo., Chedburgh, 1528. R2/17/279
William, yeo., Wicken, 1678. R2/67/4; W1/130/5; In. 3/19/7
see also Ravell, Reavell, Ryvel
REVET(T), Dorothy, wid. of James, Fornham St. Martin, 1617. R2/50/271; W1/74/70
Elisabeth, wid., Braiseworth, 1700. A5/7/15, A4/41/97
Elisabeth, wid., Exning, 1570. R2/34/59
Elisabeth, wid., Pakenham, 1671. R2/65/186; W1/123/56
John, Hundon, 1693. A5/6/156, A4/35/84
John, yeo., Rishangles, 1562. R2/31/60; W1/8/117
John, gent., Rishangles, 1667. R2/64/235; W1/119/93; In. 3/12/85
Mary, singlewoman, Bildeston, 1637. R2/57/199; W1/92/237
Robert, husb., Bacton, 1567. R2/32/390
Robert, husb., Thorndon, 1558. R2/27/329
Samuel, yeo., Mendlesham, 1635. R2/56/548; W1/91/130
REVIT(T), John, Assington, 1670. In. 3/15/184; A5/5/118
John, singleman, Little Finborough, 1606. R2/46/19; W1/64/22
REWARD, Ralph, Bury St. Edmunds, 1443. R2/1/266
REWE, William, Thelnetham, 1457. R2/9/214
REWLE, Thomas, Kirtling, 1596. A5/2/220

REWLYNG, William, husb., Cavendish, 1559. R2/28/169; W1/22/153
REWSE, Alice, wid., Worlington, 1669, (N). R2/64/447; W1/121/33; In. 3/14/42
Bartholomew, Polstead, 1638. A5/4/60
Richard, ploughwright, Kirtling, 1609. R2/47/78; W1/66/91
Simon, yeo., Cheveley, 1601. R2/44/389; W1/59/48
Thomas, Icklingham, 1592. A5/2/166
Thomas, Kirtling, 1608. A5/3/53
Thomas, the elder, yeo., Kirtling, 1695. R2/72/460; W1/149/15
Thomas, the elder, husb., Polstead, 1581. R2/38/283; W1/40/29
REWYS, John, husb., Polstead, 1547. R2/21/300; W1/10/138
see also Reawse
REY, Agnes, wid., Denston, 1540. R2/19/274; W1/36/37
Richard, yeo., Eriswell, 1635. R2/56/476
Thomas, wood setter, Great Waldingfield, (1543). R2/19/407 & 436; W1/6/104; A5/1/34
REYDE, William, Shimpling, 1546. R2/21/649
REYFFHAM, William, sen., Fordham, 1454. R2/9/175
REYGHAM, Thomas, Waldingfield, 1451. R2/9/137
REYGHNOLD, Simon, Harleston, 1566. A5/1/171
REYGNOLD, John, sen., Boxford, 1504. R2/12/34
REYMOND, Frances, wid., Hartest, 1636, (N). R2/57/106; W1/92/124
REYNALD, Agnes, Bury St. Edmunds, 1569. W1/10/215
REYNBERD, Elisabeth, wid., Barton Mills, 1561. A5/1/111
John, husb., Occold, 1642. R2/58/396; W1/99/112
John, yeo., Westhorpe, 1683. R2/69/147; W1/137/120
Lawrence, singleman, Walsham le Willows, 1539. R2/20/42; W1/4/32
Margaret, wid., Walsham le Willows, (1504). R2/13/152
Robert, the elder, Bacton, 1562. R2/37/11; W1/8/140
Robert, Bacton, 1574. R2/37/26; W1/33/95
REYNBORD, William, parson, Hepworth, 1559. R2/28/114; W1/22/111
REYNEBERD, John, yeo., Walsham le Willows, 1597. R2/43/282; W1/55/59
Matilda, wid., Bacton, (1549). R2/21/56
REYNELERDE, Nicholas, husb., Finningham, 1605. R2/45/397; W1/63/26
REYNER, Edward, yeo., Elmsett, 1621. R2/52/252; W1/77/39
Harry, Bury St. Edmunds, 1504. R2/4/160
John, Preston, 1529. R2/18/26; W1/311/10
John, Thwaite, 1494. R2/13/71
Stephen, maltster, Bury St. Edmunds, 1648. R2/60/89; W1/105/110
William, the elder, Outwell, 1575. W1/51/221
REYNHAM, Joan, wid., Stoke by Nayland, 1548. R2/21/459; W1/38/109
REYNOLD(S), Alice, wid., Lavenham, 1627. R2/54/93; W1/83/92
Anne, wid., Woolpit, 1609. R2/47/1; W1/66/2
Anthony, cordwainer, Lavenham, 1627. R2/54/81; W1/83/82
Anthony, cordwinder, Little Waldingfield, 1648. R2/60/103; W1/105/123
Elisabeth, wid., Haverhill, 1672. R2/65/336; W1/124/65
Helen, Hepworth, 1545. A5/1/44
James, shepherd, Cavenham, 1696. In. 3/25/31; A5/6/187, A4/39/43
James, yeo., Woolpit, 1635. R2/56/446; W1/91/13
Joan, wid., Lawshall, 1638. R2/57/412; W1/93/234
John, linen draper, Bury St. Edmunds, 1430. R2/1/193
John, gent., Bury St. Edmunds, 1609. R2/47/27; W1/66/30
John, Stowmarket, 1610. A5/3/94
John, Stradishall, 1689. A5/6/126, A4/30/52
John, Wattisham, 1559. W1/22/218
John, Woolpit, 1471. R2/10/493
John, Woolpit, 1548. R2/21/436; W1/14/108
Margaret, wife of John, Woolpit, 1471. R2/10/493
Nicholas, Bury St. Edmunds, 1566. R2/8/403; W1/18/70
Richard, chaplain, Bocking, 1394. R2/1/64
Richard, inn holder, Haverhill, 1676. R2/66/424; W1/128/135; In. 3/17/178
Richard, Ingham, 1667. In. 3/12/162; A5/5/86, A4/5/56

REYNOLD(S) continued
Richard, Kedington, 1567. A5/1/188
Richard, Woolpit, 1498. R2/13/82
Richard, the elder, Woolpit, 1551. R2/23/78; W1/11/57
Richard, bladesmith, Woolpit, 1598. R2/44/17; W1/56/17
Robert, Barnham, 1617, (N). R2/50/357; W1/74/138
Robert, Wortham, 1689. A4/30/2
Thomas, inn holder, Haverhill, 1691. R2/71/482; W1/145/37
Thomas, Hopton, 1473. R2/11/38
Thomas, Stoke by Clare, 1576. In. 3/1/43
Thomas, husb., Stoke by Clare, 1623. W1/95/149
William, Woolpit, 1452. R2/9/121
William, tailor, Woolpit, 1600. R2/45/12; W1/58/18
see also Rannolds, Raynold(s), Raynouldes, Reignold, Reinoles, Renolds, Reyghnold, Reynald, Reynelerde
REYNOLDYSSON, Edward, Thurlow, 1450. R2/9/112
REYSHAY, Alice, Bures, 1482. R2/11/276
REYSON, Steven, Hawkedon, 1523. R2/14/87
William, Kedington, 1445. R2/10/417
William, 1465. R2/10/417
REYSYNG, Laurence, tailor, Bury St. Edmunds, 1556. R2/8/293; W1/18/21
RICARD, James, saddler, Bury St. Edmunds, 1576. R2/37/236
James, Bury St. Edmunds, 1685. W1/42/211
RICE, Nicholas, Wattisfield, 1668. A4/6/65
Thomas, yeo., Elmswell, 1686. R2/70/268; W1/140/36
William, yeo., Elmswell, 1662. R2/62/390; W1/114/133; In. 3/7/177
William, Walsham le Willows, 1686. A5/6/106, A4/26/9
see also Ryce, Ryece, Ryse, Rysse
RICH, John, yeo., Chevington, 1697. R2/73/146; W1/151/33
John, yeo., Flempton, 1669. In. 3/14/144; A5/5/109, A4/7/62
John, the elder, yeo., Hundon, 1662. R2/62/365; W1/114/94; In. 3/7/137
John, Soham, 1635. A5/4/41
Margaret, wid., Hundon, 1677. R2/66/534; W1/129/114
Robert, husb., Barnham, 1609. R2/47/79b; W1/66/94; A5/3/74
Roger, Bury St. Edmunds, 1415. R2/1/136
Stephen, yeo., Rougham, 1661, (N). R2/62/265; W1/113/159; In. 3/6/226
William, yeo., Stansfield, 1695. R2/72/564; W1/149/118
see also Reche, Ritche, Ryche
RICHAR, Agnes, wid., Great Finborough, 1628. R2/54/233; W1/84/95
RICHARD(S), Edward, Eye, 1667. A5/5/85 & 87, A4/5/63
Francis, Snailwell, 1693. A5/6/159, A4/35/54
Lewis, Chippenham, 1662. In. 3/7/49; A5/5/28
Margaret, wid. of William, Stansfield, 1558. R2/27/482
see also Rechard, Record, Ricard, Rickard, Rycard, Rychards
RICHARDSON, Alexander, husb., Hessett, 1559. R2/28/289
Edward, butcher, Clare, 1618. R2/51/64; W1/75/39
Frances, singlewoman, Kersey, 1695. R2/72/536; W1/149/91
George, Freckenham, 1660. W8/15; In. 10/2
George, yeo., Gislingham, 1637. R2/57/148; W1/92/184
George, Kersey, 1661. R2/62/268; W1/113/165; In. 3/6/241; A5/5/21, A4/1/38
George, Stowmarket, 1571. A5/1/241
George, wheelwright, Stowmarket, 1573. R2/36/140; W1/32/43
John, Freckenham, 1672, (N). W8/25
John, Soham, 1678. In. 3/19/202; A5/6/13, A4/15/108
John, Wicken, 1682. In. 3/21/174; A5/6/58, A4/19/26
Leonard, parson, Barton Mills, 1565. R2/32/228
Nicholas, the elder, yeo., Kersey, 1613. R2/48/318; W1/70/95
Nicholas, Kersey, 1637. A5/4/53
Robert, yeo., Soham, 1694. R2/72/400; W1/148/132
Roger, Rattlesden, 1584. A5/2/58
Rose, Kersey, 1562. A5/1/134
Solomon, clothier, Kersey, 1617. R2/50/232; W1/74/26
Stephen, yeo., Kersey, 1683. R2/69/157; W1/137/127
Thomas, carpenter, Gislingham, 1573. R2/36/175; W1/32/83
Thomas, Stowmarket, 1678. In. 3/19/139; A5/6/9, A4/15/75

RICHARDSON continued
William, yeo., Kersey, 1686. R2/70/505; W1/140/125; A5/6/104, A4/26/32, 33 & 34
William, Soham, 1679. A5/6/29, A4/16/157
see also Rechesun, Rekedon, Rychardson, Rycherdson, Barrett als. Richardson
RICHEMAN, Thomas, Stowmarket, 1543. R2/19/359; W1/6/137
RICHER, Agnes, Buxhall, 1556. R2/25/56; W1/16/66
Anthony, singleman, Hitcham, 1620. R2/52/142; W1/76/126
Henry, Buxhall, 1554. R2/24/55; W1/14/44
Henry, Rattlesden, 1613. R2/48/325; W1/70/107
John, yeo., Little Finborough, 1622. R2/52/385; W1/78/21
John, Stanton, 1540. R2/19/585; W1/5/49
Philip, Combs, 1696. A5/6/185, A4/39/15
Richard, Hitcham, 1589. A5/2/114b
Robert, yeo., Creeting St. Peter,1695. R2/72/477; W1/149/35
Thomas, weaver, Hepworth, 1684. R2/69/383; W1/138/167; A5/6/79, A4/21/54
see also Rechyr, Richar, Ricker, Ritcher, Rycher
RICHERS, Richard, Sudbury, 1544. R2/19/486
RICHMAN, Henry, Haughley, 1641, (N). R2/58/298; W1/98/84
Lawrence, cook, Woolpit, 1663. R2/63/57; W1/115/89; In. 3/8/110
Thomas, West Stow, 1592. A5/2/169
see also Richeman, Rycheman
RICHMOND, David, yeo., Exning, 1695. R2/72/499; W1/149/52
Robert, yeo., Stowmarket, 1638. R2/57/301; W1/93/74
Thomas, husb., Burwell, 1674. R2/66/9; W1/126/113
see also Ritchmond, Rychemonde
RICKARD, Robert, Mendlesham, 1673. A5/5/141, A4/10/72
see also Richard(s)
RICKER, Robert, Buxhall, 1673. A5/5/141, A4/10/68
RICKS, Anne, als. Folkes & Goodwyn, Burwell, 1574. R2/37/44; W1/33/35
John, Palgrave, 1665. In. 3/10/125; A5/5/69, A4/3/66
see also Rix
RIDDELSDALE, Lucy, als. Loker, wid., Bures, 1593, (N). R2/42/448; W1/50/108
RIDDISDALL, Henry, Winston, 1593. A5/2/189
RIDDLESDALE, Jasper, Kersey, 1680. In. 3/20/55; A5/6/34, A4/17/30
John, yeo., Polstead, 1663. R2/63/99; W1/115/151; In. 3/8/202
Richard, Assington, 1610. A5/3/107
Richard, Boxford, 1610. A5/3/86
see also Reddlesdalle, Redysdale, Ridelsdale, Ridsdale, Ryddyllesdale, Dynes als. Ryddlesdall
RIDELS, William, yeo., Stanton, 1625. R2/53/390; W1/81/168
RIDELSDALE, Jasper, Groton, 1641, (N). R2/58/269; W1/98/49
Joanna, Boxford, 1662. In. 3/7/247
John, Boxford, 1682. R2/68/294; W1/136/25; In. 3/21/196
RIDGEMAN, John, Bury St. Edmunds, 1484. R2/2/199
see also Redgeman
RIDGES, Agnes, wid., Bury St. Edmunds, 1495. R2/4/39
see also Redgis, Redgys, Ridgys
RIDGEWELL, William, vicar, Wood Ditton, 1618. R2/51/44; W1/75/24
see also Redgwell
RIDGYS, John, grocer, Bury St. Edmunds, 1464. R2/2/83
RIDLOND, William, Mendlesham, 1558. R2/28/245; W1/22/237
RIDNALL, Abraham, carpenter, Buxhall, 1660. In. 3/5/82
Ann, wid., Bradfield St. George, 1662. R2/62/390; W1/114/132; In. 3/7/162
Ann, Lavenham, 1633. A5/4/23
John, Gedding, 1567. A5/1/189
Richard, yeo., Lavenham, 1629. R2/54/366; W1/85/64
Robert, the elder, yeo., Mendlesham, 1631. R2/56/82; W1/87/123
Robert, Rattlesden, 1645. A5/4/108
see also Redenhale, Rodnall, Rydnale
RIDSDALE, Henry, yeo., Boxford, 1591. R2/42/127; W1/48/110
see also Riddlesdale

RIGG(S), Bevis, inn holder, Bury St. Edmunds, 1647. R2/59/377; W1/104/6; In. 3/2/7
John, grocer, Eye, 1623. R2/52/665; W1/79/87
Richard, Landwade, 1589. A5/2/124
see also Rygge
RIGHT, Gregory, husb., Kedington, 1636. R2/57/8; W1/92/11
RIGMAYDEN, Margaret, spinster, Bury St. Edmunds, 1690. R2/71/322; W1/144/25
RIKYNGHALE, Richard, Bury St. Edmunds, 1430. R2/1/193
see also Rykynghale
RILEY, Thomas, singleman, Little Waldingfield, 1639. R2/58/115; W1/94/192
RIMINGTON, John, yeo., Botesdale, 1680. R2/67/733; W1/134/174; In. 3/20/187
RINGBELL, Anne, wid. of William, Hepworth, 1617. R2/50/279; W1/74/78
Edward, labourer, Hepworth, 1638. R2/57/428; W1/93/264
John, linen weaver, Thelnetham, 1647. R2/59/463; W1/104/96; In. 3/2/82
William, carpenter, Hepworth, 1616. R2/50/49; W1/73/55
William, weaver, Thelnetham, 1663. R2/63/6; W1/115/10; In. 3/8/27
see also Ryngbell
RINGLAND, John, miller, Little Whelnetham, 1613. R2/48/286; W1/70/59
see also Rynglond, Pary als. Rynglonde
RIPER, John, singleman, Hinderclay, 1636. A5/4/43
RIPLEY, Ann, wid., Burwell, 1697. A5/7/3, A4/40/40
Edward, boatwright, Burwell, 1693. R2/72/206; W1/147/97
John, victualler, Bury St. Edmunds, 1700. R2/74/74; W1/154/75; A5/7/15
RIPPER, Robert, baker, Botesdale, 1679. R2/67/431; W1/133/163
RIPPINGALE, Edward, Clare, 1665, (N). R2/63/329; W1/117/74; In. 3/10/129
RIPPS, Thomas, Eye, 1563. A5/1/146
see also Ryppes
RIPPYN, Elisabeth, wid., Lavenham, 1586. R2/40/59; A5/2/78
RISBE, John, Lavenham, 1488. W1/24/185
RISBIE, Elisabeth, wid., Sudbury, 1576. R2/37/141; W1/37/92; In. 3/1/110
John, labourer, Mendlesham, 1601. R2/37/347; W1/59/10
RISBY, Edward, Buxhall, 1469. R2/10/435
Justinian, shearman, Sudbury, 1584. R2/39/192; W1/42/135
see also Rysby, Jermy als. Risby
RISING, John, the younger, wheelwright, Bradfield St. George, 1619. R2/51/255
Samuel, labourer, Fordham, 1693. R2/72/265; W1/147/152
see also Rysing, Rysyng, Clarke als. Ryssne
RITCHE, Margaret, wid., 1626. R2/53/578; W1/82/106
William, collar maker, Soham, 1582. R2/38/378; W1/41/61
RITCHER, John, Hitcham, 1631. A5/4/13
RITCHMOND, Edward, husb., Burwell, 1630. W1/95/67
RIVERS, Joseph, Assington, 1688. In. 3/23/10; A5/5/117, A4/29/5
Joseph, linen weaver, Great Ashfield, 1682. R2/68/486; W1/136/160; In. 3/21/8
RIVET(T), Edward, esq., Rattlesden, 1660. R2/62/135; W1/112/177
John, yeo., Wetheringsett, 1603. R2/45/292; W1/61/98
Mary, wid., Acton, 1666. In. 3/11/119; A5/5/78, A4/4/66
Philip, Glemsford, 1639. A5/4/77
Susan, wid., Occold, 1650. In. 3/3/149; A5/4/133
Thomas, yeo., Mendlesham, 1699. R2/73/389; W1/153/39; In. 3/26/49
Thomas, Rishangles, 1596. R2/43/174; W1/54/85
William, yeo., Braiseworth, 1699. In. 3/26/33; A5/7/11, A4/41/22
see also Ryvet(t)
RIX, Edmund, Palgrave, 1562. A5/1/138
Henry, yeo., Palgrave, 1645. R2/59/234; W1/102/58
John, yeo., Botesdale, 1679. R2/67/490
John, the elder, wheelwright, Palgrave, 1556. R2/25/54; W1/16/62

RIX continued
Miles, sen., labourer, Thelnetham, 1652. R2/61/590; W1/109/64; In. 3/4/88
Robert, yeo., Redgrave, 1668. In. 3/13/81; A5/5/98, A4/6/92
see also Ricks, Rycks, Rykkys, Ryxe
ROADS, Robert, Newmarket, 1630. A5/4/1
ROAFF, George, the elder, butcher, Lawshall, 1676. R2/66/321; W1/128/27; In. 3/17/24
ROASE, Ann, wid., Wetheringsett, 1609. A5/3/78
ROATH, Anthony, yeo., Combs, 1637. R2/57/241; W1/92/296
ROBARDS, Samuel, clothier, Bury St. Edmunds, 1691. R2/71/494; W1/145/54
ROBARTS, John, labourer, Brent Eleigh, 1578. R2/37/400; W1/36/175
John, Sudbury, 1571. R2/35/98; W1/36/111
William, tailor, Sudbury, 1601. R2/44/417; W1/59/93
ROBB, Christine, wid., Wetheringsett, 1563. W1/26/77
ROBBENS, Ann, wid., Stowmarket, 1598. R2/44/121; W1/56/116
ROBBISON, John, Isleham, 1678. In. 9/47
ROBENSON, John, yeo., Haughley, 1660. R2/62/45; W1/112/54; In. 3/5/113
ROBERD(S), Alan, Sudbury, 1441. R2/9/24
Alice, Sudbury, 1453. R2/9/145
Cicely, Sudbury, 1453. R2/9/159
Grace, wid., Eye, 1559. R2/28/328
John, Lawshall, 1474. R2/10/509
John, baker, Sudbury, 1494. R2/11/447
ROBERDSON, Elisabeth, wid., Chedburgh, 1592. R2/42/303; W1/49/124
Nicholas, Glemsford, 1473. R2/10/519
ROBERSON, Nicholas, yeo., Westhorpe, 1695. R2/72/488; W1/149/45
Thomas, yeo., Bradfield, 1661. R2/62/251; W1/113/133; In. 3/6/186
Thomas, Exning, 1646. A5/4/113
---, wid., Freckenham, 1663. In. 10/6
ROBERT(S), Alice, singlewoman, Downham, 1630, (N). R2/55/9; W1/86/11
Alice, Nayland, 1562. A5/1/130
Ann, wid., Great Waldingfield, 1679. R2/67/381; W1/133/133
Daniel, Great Waldingfield, 1678. In. 3/19/191; A5/6/12, A4/15/102
Edmund, Eye, 1558. R2/27/338
Edward, yeo., Glemsford, 1646. R2/59/287; W1/103/1
Florence, Hartest, 1533, (N). R2/19/144; W1/2/7
James, joiner, Mildenhall, 1686. R2/70/470; W1/140/81
Joan, wife of John, Sudbury, 1506. R2/13/183
John, yeo., Eye, 1596. R2/43/158; W1/54/39
John, oatmeal maker, Eye, 1673. R2/65/485; W1/125/124
John, Glemsford, 1519. R2/13/197
John, victualler, Soham, 1676. R2/66/347; W1/128/54; In. 3/17/62
Lawrence, yeo., Bury St. Edmunds, 1628. R2/54/197; W1/84/72
Matthew, wire drawer, Bury St. Edmunds, 1465. R2/2/85
Paul, Soham, 1685. A5/6/93, A4/24/90
Roger, yeo., Glemsford, 1639. R2/58/13; W1/94/23
Stephen, clothier, Glemsford, 1584. R2/39/144; W1/42/179
Thomas, Wissington, 1673. A5/5/141, A4/10/73b
William, Great Wratting, 1592. A5/2/164
see also Robards, Roberd(s), Robhard
ROBERTSON, Edward, husb., Oakley, (1546). R2/21/340; W1/10/96
Henry, husb., Stowmarket, 1680. In. 3/20/137; A5/6/37, A4/17/69
see also Roberdson
ROBHARD, Robert, Walsham le Willows, 1453. R2/9/159
ROBHOD, John, Walsham le Willows, 1459. R2/9/258
John, husb., Walsham le Willows, 1537. R2/20/16
ROBHOOD, Anne, wid., Walsham le Willows, (1548). R2/21/423; W1/8/12
Joan, wife of John, sen., Walsham le Willows, 1470. R2/10/434
John, Walsham le Willows, 1548. R2/21/442; W1/38/104

ROBINS, Ann, wid., Soham, 1682. R2/68/287; W1/136/19
Elisabeth, spinster, Wicken, 1680. R2/67/723; W1/134/165; In. 3/20/183
Katherine, wid., Soham, 1617. R2/50/408; W1/74/196
Oliver, Soham, 1608. A5/3/47
Oliver, Soham, 1670. R2/65/24; W1/122/26; In. 3/15/42
Thomas, wheeler, Soham, 1677. R2/66/512; W1/129/94; In. 3/18/117
see also Robbens, Robyn, Robynys
ROBINSON, Adam, Soham, 1593. A5/2/181
Ann, wid., Boxford, 1689. R2/71/155; W1/143/16
Benjamin, brick striker, Rede, 1686. In. 3/22/130; A5/6/104, A4/26/30
Cornelius, yeo., Drinkstone, 1620. R2/52/132; W1/76/116
David, inn holder, Bury St. Edmunds, 1696. R2/73/65; W1/150/92
Henry, gent., Sudbury, 1669. R2/64/522; W1/121/111; In. 3/14/153
Israel, shoe maker, Honington, 1651. R2/61/464
John, tallow chandler, Groton, 1608. R2/46/121; W1/97/38a
John, Haverhill, 1698. A5/7/9
John, yeo., Onehouse, 1664. In. 3/9/3; A5/5/54, A4/2/3
John, Wyverstone, 1580. R2/38/171; W1/39/127
Margaret, wid., Freckenham, 1663. W8/19
Margaret, wid., Gedding, 1666. In. 3/11/96; A5/5/75, A4/4/36
Martha, wid., Sudbury, 1675. R2/66/155; W1/127/29; In. 3/16/33
Martin, yeo., Creeting St. Peter, 1691. R2/71/463
Mary, wid., Rushbrook, 1695. A5/6/178, A4/38/32
Richard, clothworker, Boxford, 1674. R2/66/98; W1/126/19
Richard, Little Thurlow, 1616, (N). R2/50/50; W1/73/57
Richard, Rougham, 1570. R2/34/19; W1/30/18; A5/1/221
Robert, als. Sander, shepherd, Wangford, 1634. R2/56/405; W1/90/190
Susan, wid., Ixworth, 1685. A5/6/87, A4/24/8
Thomas, singleman, tanner, Bildeston, 1682. R2/68/330; W1/136/49; In. 3/21/207
Thomas, clothier, Bury St. Edmunds, 1622. R2/52/470
Thomas, the elder, carpenter, Combs, 1674. R2/66/93; W1/126/23; A5/5/146, A4/11/33
Thomas, Fordham, 1688. In. 3/23/108; A5/6/122, A4/29/77
Thomas, Needham Market, 1644. R2/59/89; W1/101/18
Thomas, gent., Sudbury, 1616. R2/50/99; W1/73/108
William, als. Cooper, Mildenhall, 1690. R2/71/371; W1/144/79
William, Rushbrook, 1684. A5/6/79, A4/21/63
William, Rushbrook, 1687. A5/6/107, A4/26/6
see also Robbison, Robynson, Cooper als. Robenson, Sanders als. Robinson
ROBSON, Edmund, gent., Stradishall, 1676. R2/66/333; W1/128/37; In. 3/17/37
John, yeo., Soham, 1631. R2/56/85; W1/87/128
Richard, als. Morrys, Sudbury, 1589. R2/41/194
Thomas, Elveden, 1642. A5/4/98
William, thatcher, Soham, 1614. R2/49/120; W1/71/87
see also Ropsone
ROBUCKE, William, Bures, 1584. A5/2/54
ROBWOD, Alice, 1602. R2/45/135; W1/60/55
ROBWOOD, John, yeo., Great Finborough, 1616. R2/50/41; W1/73/43
ROBYN, Richard, Rushbrook, 1471. R2/10/484
William, Exning, 1454. R2/9/200
ROBYNSON, Margaret, wid., Bury St. Edmunds, 1527. R2/6/135
Miles, Bury St. Edmunds, 1492. R2/4/14
Ralph, Bury St. Edmunds, 1506. R2/4/187
Ralph, Newmarket, 1533. R2/19/183; W1/2/28
Thomas, Groton, 1585. R2/39/262; W1/42/311
William, blacksmith, Ashley, 1616, (N). R2/50/197; W1/73/185
William, carpenter, Hopton, 1543. R2/19/389; W1/6/165
William, saddler, Newmarket, (1543). R2/19/406, R2/21/596; W1/6/104
ROBYNYS, Thomas, Bury St. Edmunds, 1458. R2/2/64
ROCHE, John, brazier, Bury St. Edmunds, 1427. R2/1/173
ROCHELL, Robert, husb., Dalham, 1606. R2/46/44; W1/64/60

ROCHER, Robert, Lindsey, 1578. R2/37/329; W1/36/246
ROCKELL, Agnes, wife of Richard, Little Waldingfield, 1558. R2/27/522
Richard, Little Waldingfield, 1558. R2/27/521
Thomas, Ousden, 1626. R2/53/611; W1/82/138
ROCKETT, Edmund, husb., Wortham, 1592. R2/42/309; W1/49/132
Henry, blacksmith, Palgrave, 1678. R2/67/81; W1/130/65; In. 3/19/89
Richard, Thelnetham, 1564. A5/1/156
Thomas, gent., Bury St. Edmunds, 1625. R2/53/220; W1/81/21
Thomasine, singlewoman, Wortham, 1674. A5/5/148, A4/11/48
William, gent., Bury St. Edmunds, 1665, (N). R2/63/343; W1/117/91; A5/5/67, A4/3/47
see also Rockytt, Rokytt
ROCKWELL, John, Ousden, 1693. A5/6/157, A4/116/77
Thomas, Ousden, 1694. R2/72/301; W1/148/29
ROCKYLL, Margaret, wid., Bury St. Edmunds, 1558. R2/8/321; W1/18/52
see also Rockell, Rokell
ROCKYTT, William, sen., Bury St. Edmunds, 1578. R2/37/404
RODE, Baldwin, Great Ashfield, 1459. W1/24/124
RODEKYSHAM, William, carpenter, Bury St. Edmunds, 1375. R2/1/35
RODELAND, John, sen., Kersey, (1459). R2/9/248
William, Great Waldingfield, 1451. R2/9/137
RODELOND, Joan, wife of John, Kersey, 1460. R2/9/245
RODGERS, John, Freckenham, 1646. W1/110/24
RODGIN, Joan, singlewoman, Fornham St. Martin, 1611. R2/48/121; W1/68/133
Miles, grocer, Mildenhall, 1667. R2/64/209; W1/119/59; In. 3/12/139
RODING, Henry, Little Saxham, 1526. R2/17/190; W1/23/43a
see also Rodyng, Roodyng
RODLAND, John, yeo., Groton, 1558. W1/28/1
RODNALL, Agnes, wid., Mendlesham, 1571. R2/35/363
RODWELL, James, grocer, Brandon, 1690. R2/71/371; W1/144/80
John, yeo., Westhorpe, 1682. R2/68/344; W1/136/59; In. 3/21/175
Mary, wid., Brockford, 1695. R2/72/520; W1/149/75
Robert, yeo., Wyverstone, 1686. R2/70/507; W1/140/113; In. 3/22/116
Samuel, Bacton, 1698. A5/7/8
Thomas, the elder, yeo., Westhorpe, 1669. R2/64/495; W1/121/90; In. 3/14/109
RODYNG, Adam, Horringer, 1474. R2/10/525
Alan, cordwainer, Bury St. Edmunds, 1435. R2/1/215
John, yeo., Horringer, 1550. R2/21/74; W1/9/118
Margery, wid. of John, Wetherden, 1470. R2/10/453
Robert, als. Baker, Stoke by Nayland, 1483. R2/11/313
RODYS, Nicholas, Combs, 1472. R2/10/463
ROFE, Ann, wid., Lawshall, 1638, (N). R2/57/419; W1/93/245
Thomas, yeo., Bury St. Edmunds, 1683. R2/69/71; W1/137/53
ROFFE, Eleanor, wid., Redgrave, 1603. R2/45/299; W1/61/108
John, Mildenhall, 1588. R2/41/112; W1/45/108
Robert, Sudbury, 1522. R2/14/48
William, waterman, Isleham, 1679. In. 9/51
ROGELL, John, weaver, Stanstead, 1566. R2/32/307; W1/28/85
ROGEN, Edene, wid., Fornham All Saints, 1609, (N). R2/47/1; W1/66/1; A5/3/57
John, the elder, Bardwell, 1557. R2/26/109; W1/20/63
John, bricklayer, Bardwell, 1573, (N). R2/36/178; W1/32/85
Thomas, Fornham, 1608. A5/3/41
see also Regin, Rodgin, Rogyn
ROGER(S), Abraham, Hartest, 1606. A5/3/7
Alice, wid., Wood Ditton, 1649. R2/60/163; W1/106/7
Andrew, als. Wever, Eye, 1451. R2/9/103
Arthur, yeo., Barrow, 1619. R2/51/455; W1/132/119
Arthur, Fornham All Saints, 1693. A5/6/155, A4/35/93
Bridget, wid., Bury St. Edmunds, 1623, (N). R2/52/635; W1/79/68
Christopher, Bury St. Edmunds, 1581. A5/2/34
Edmund, linen weaver, Thrandeston, 1662. R2/62/352; W1/114/71; In. 3/7/96

ROGER(S) continued
Edmund, linen weaver, Thrandeston, 1685. R2/70/6; W1/139/8
Francis, labourer, Stanton, 1627, (N). R2/54/128; W1/83/127
Francis, yeo., Stanton, 1693. R2/72/136
Geoffrey, Great Finborough, 1474. R2/10/510
George, yeo., Brockley, 1616. R2/50/187; W1/73/174
Gertrude, Fornham All Saints, 1695. A5/6/183, A4/38/84
Godfrey, Burwell, 1562. R2/31/73; W1/8/111
Godfrey, Burwell, 1637. A5/4/49 & 50
Harry, Ixworth, 1525. R2/12/136
Humfrey, yeo., Eye, 1615. R2/49/370; W1/72/144
James, yeo., Pakenham, 1633. R2/56/258; W1/90/24
James, labourer, Wood Ditton, 1638. R2/57/401; W1/93/220
Joan, wid., Bury St. Edmunds, 1473. R2/11/181
John, Burwell, (1528). R2/15/213; W1/19/32
John, scrivener, Bury St. Edmunds, 1465. R2/11/82
John, husb., Bury St. Edmunds, 1625. R2/53/270; W1/81/56
John, Combs, 1589. A5/2/117a
John, labourer, Higham, 1649. R2/60/225; W1/106/76
John, husb., Higham, 1696. R2/73/89; W1/150/105
John, Soham, 1452. R2/9/109
John, yeo., Stanton, 1673. R2/65/415; W1/125/38; A5/5/138, A4/88/36
John, singleman, Stanton, 1679. R2/67/237; W1/133/6
John, yeo., Stoke by Clare, 1680. R2/67/598; W1/134/73
John, Wickhambrook, 1532. R2/19/114; W1/3/11 & 140
John, Wickhambrook, 1590. R2/41/343; W1/47/36
Martin, Hartest, 1697. R2/73/140; W1/151/25
Matthew, yeo., Cowlinge, 1680. R2/67/596; W1/134/71; In. 3/20/78
Paul, Burwell, 1568. R2/33/16; W1/29/24
Reginald, brick maker, Barnardiston, 1648. R2/60/6; W1/105/10
Richard, Burwell, 1587. R2/40/246; W1/44/87
Robert, Ixworth, 1547. R2/21/298; W1/10/126
Robert, singleman, Ixworth, 1573. R2/36/135; W1/32/17
Robert, Ixworth, 1679. A5/6/21, A4/16/63
Robert, Stanton, 1560. R2/29/163; W1/25/12
Thomas, Burwell, 1521. R2/15/139
Thomas, Burwell, 1557. R2/25/165; W1/16/149
Thomas, yeo., Bury St. Edmunds, 1678. In. 3/19/23
Thomas, Cavenham, 1554. R2/24/112; W1/14/85
Thomas, cordwainer, Clare, 1669. In. 3/14/174; A5/5/109, A4/7/65
Thomas, labourer, Gazeley, 1557. R2/26/2; W1/20/8
Thomas, Gazeley, 1572. R2/36/32; W1/31/130
Thomas, yeo., Gazeley, 1625. R2/53/382; W1/81/159
Thomas, clerk, Horningsheath, 1616. R2/50/34; W1/73/33
Thomas, sen., tailor, Hundon, 1694. R2/72/287; W1/148/12
Thomas, Snailwell, 1462. R2/9/289
Thomas, the elder, Stoke by Clare, 1602. R2/45/149; W1/60/68
Thomas, brick maker, Stoke by Clare, 1622. R2/52/373; W1/78/13
Thomas, Worlington, 1578. R2/37/389; W1/36/183
William, the elder, yeo., Burwell, 1645. R2/59/241; W1/102/64
William, yeo., Burwell, 1666. R2/64/22; W1/118/22; In. 3/11/29
William, Dalham, 1566. R2/32/315; W1/28/79
William, husb., Hartest, 1573. R2/36/207; W1/32/103; A5/1/266
William, Little Saxham, 1539, (N). R2/19/296
William, husb., Pakenham, 1601. R2/44/378; W1/59/38
see also Rodgers, Rogger(s), Rorger, Kelde als. Rogers, Thomas als. Rogers

ROGERON, Emma, wid., Tuddenham, 1482. R2/11/281
Thomas, Hundon, 1480. R2/11/232

ROGGER(S), John, Fordham, 1576. R2/37/147; W1/37/16; In. 3/1/98
John, yeo., Great Thurlow, 1592. R2/42/238; W1/49/54
Thomas, Higham, 1677. R2/66/506; W1/129/87

ROGIER, Nicholas, cook, Bury St. Edmunds, 1467. R2/2/110

ROGLE, Thomas, Hartest, 1560. R2/29/63; W1/25/110
William, Long Melford, 1525. R2/12/131

ROGYLL, Thomas, Glemsford, 1464. R2/10/358
Thomas, Sudbury, 1547. R2/21/287; W1/38/65

ROGYN, John, Bardwell, 1573. A5/1/263
John, cordwainer, Bury St. Edmunds, 1464. R2/2/80
John, Rattlesden, 1458. R2/9/207

ROISSE, Robert, weaver, Exning, 1602. R2/45/100; W1/60/11
ROKEBY, William, Fordham, 1461. R2/9/295
ROKELL, Elisabeth, Hitcham, 1504. R2/12/28
John, Bury St. Edmunds, 1410. R2/1/121
John, Lavenham, 1454. R2/9/167
John, Long Melford, 1462. R2/10/324
Robert, Dalham, 1526. R2/17/145; W1/21/138
Thomas, Lavenham, 1447. R2/9/81
ROKELOND, William, Bury St. Edmunds, 1386. R2/1/49 & 50
ROKELY, Thomas, Chelsworth, 1546. R2/19/623, R2/21/190; W1/10/79
ROKEWOODE, Anne, singlewoman, Hartest, 1572. R2/19/67; W1/31/78
Roger, Euston, 1482. R2/11/263
ROKKER, Cristine, Bury St. Edmunds, 1469. R2/2/128
John, jun., webster, Bury St. Edmunds, 1434. R2/1/204
John, Bury St. Edmunds, 1434. R2/1/205
Margery, Bury St. Edmunds, 1438. R2/1/236
ROKWODE, Joan, wife of John, Stanningfield, 1391. R2/1/60
ROKYNGHAM, John, Burgate, 1519. R2/15/26
ROKYTT, William, 1578. W1/36/252
ROLEFF, Richard, yeo., Mildenhall, 1678. R2/67/123; W1/130/108
ROLEY, Alice, Burwell, 1540. R2/20/176
John, Burwell, 1540. R2/20/177
ROLF(E), Agnes, wid., Mildenhall, 1630. R2/55/22; W1/86/26
Alice, spinster, Burwell, 1664. In. 3/9/70; A5/5/57, A4/2/43
Andrew, sen., yeo., Lakenheath, 1682. R2/68/450; W1/136/133; In. 3/21/92
Edward, yeo., Lakenheath, 1689. R2/71/237; W1/143/76
Elisabeth, als. Bridge, Bury St. Edmunds, 1632. A5/4/17
George, Lawshall, 1634. A5/4/33
Hannah, spinster, Mildenhall, 1692. A5/6/152, A4/115/52
James, shearman, Sudbury, 1540. R2/20/256; W1/4/194
Joan, wid., Mildenhall, 1611. R2/47/309; W1/68/5
Joan, wid., Nedging, 1636. A5/4/45
John, Burwell, 1454. R2/9/231
John, Burwell, 1471. W1/24/132a
John, Burwell, 1477. R2/11/181
John, Burwell, 1597. R2/43/335; W1/55/101
John, the elder, water glover, Bury St. Edmunds, 1637. R2/57/202; W1/92/242
John, Heacham, 1594. W1/51/275
John, Mildenhall, 1521. R2/15/111
John, Mildenhall, 1546. R2/21/238; W1/10/73
John, the elder, yeo., Mildenhall, 1576. R2/37/181; W1/37/49; In. 3/1/55
John, yeo., Mildenhall, 1620. R2/52/2
John, husb., Mildenhall, 1620. R2/52/148; W1/76/132
John, husb., Mildenhall, 1635. R2/56/536; W1/91/118
John, Mildenhall, 1636. A5/4/44
John, als. Chapman, Mildenhall, 1638. A5/4/63
John, yeo., Mildenhall, 1686. R2/70/427; W1/140/48
Nicholas, Burwell, 1485. R2/11/322
Richard, Mildenhall, 1584. R2/39/206; W1/42/121
Richard, carpenter, Redgrave, 1582. R2/38/374; W1/41/65
Robert, Mildenhall, 1565. R2/32/250
Robert, the elder, yeo., Mildenhall, (1679). W1/312/26
Robert, Mildenhall, 1686. R2/70/263; W1/140/30
Robert, yeo., Mildenhall, 1686. R2/70/529; W1/140/130
Robert, Stowmarket, 1483. R2/11/315
Robert, Thorndon, 1485. R2/11/332
Roger, Fornham All Saints, 1665. R2/63/333; W1/117/79; In. 3/10/130
Roger, husb., Mildenhall, 1575. R2/37/83; W1/5/31, W1/34/1
Simon, husb., Mildenhall, 1628. R2/54/144; W1/84/15
Thomas, Burwell, 1457. R2/9/189
Thomas, Burwell, 1503. R2/13/171
Thomas, Burwell, 1552. R2/23/156; W1/11/107
Thomas, Exning, 1681. A5/6/52, A4/18/105
Thomas, yeo., Lawshall, 1593. R2/42/403; W1/50/65
Thomas, the elder, yeo., Mildenhall, 1553. R2/31/143; W1/13/96
Thomas, the elder, yeo., Mildenhall, 1591. R2/42/162; W1/48/83
Thomas, yeo., Mildenhall, 1609. R2/47/50; W1/66/57

ROLF(E) continued
  Thomasine, wid., Bury St. Edmunds, 1584, (N). R2/39/150; W1/42/172
  William, the younger, wid., Barton Mills, 1664. In. 3/9/119; A5/5/60, A4/2/67
  William, Burwell, 1461. W1/24/91
  William, waterman, Isleham, 1680. W7/94
  William, Snailwell, 1444. R2/9/45
  see also Ralfe, Rofe, Roleff, Rolph, Roulfe
ROLLECROS, Thomas, Stanton, 1453. R2/9/164
  Walter, Stanton, 1461. R2/9/284
ROLLES, Joan, wid., Clare, 1558. R2/27/378
ROLPH, Isaac, tailor, Mildenhall, 1666. R2/64/86; W1/118/61; In. 3/11/88
  Robert, yeo., Mendham, 1686. R2/70/550; W1/140/153
  William, Mildenhall, 1690. R2/71/356; W1/144/61
ROLYNGHAM, Robert, husb., Soham, 1521. R2/15/126, R2/17/1
ROMBALL, Margaret, Worlington, 1631. A5/4/14
  Robert, husb., Worlington, 1627. R2/54/50; W1/83/55
ROMBELOWE, Bartholomew, Kennett, 1572. A5/1/248
  Martin, Tuddenham, 1630. A5/4/4
  William, singleman, Barrow, 1573, (N). R2/36/154; W1/32/51
ROMBOWLE, John, cordwainer, Isleham, 1626. R6/43
ROMBYLOWE, John, Kentford, 1553. R2/31/112; W1/13/78
  John, Lackford, 1484. R2/11/307
  Margaret, wid., Dalham, 1617. R2/50/402; W1/74/186
  Margaret, singlewoman, Dalham, 1623. R2/52/577; W1/79/33
  Thomas, husb., Dalham, 1625. R2/53/400; W1/81/182
ROMPNALE, William, weaver, Bury St. Edmunds, 1479. R2/2/282
ROMYLOWE, William, Tuddenham, 1540. R2/20/203; W1/4/159
RONGNYNG, William, Little Bradley, 1452. R2/9/139
ROO, Clement, shearman, Bury St. Edmunds, 1423. R2/6/107 (admon. only)
  Edmund, Wangford, 1592, (N). R2/42/301; W1/49/120
  John, Brandon, 1527. R2/12/143
  Margaret, wid., Elmswell, 1592. R2/42/226; W1/49/45
  Robert, yeo., Elmswell, 1558. R2/27/313
  Robert, sen., yeo., Elmswell, 1588. R2/41/102; W1/45/97
  Robert, yeo., Elmswell, 1596. R2/43/140; W1/54/19
  Thomas, Elmswell, 1582. A5/2/42
  Thomas, carpenter, Weston, 1614. R2/49/72; W1/71/56
  William, Oakley, 1560. A5/1/108
ROODESE, John, glover, Ixworth, 1463. R2/10/316
  see also Bright als. Roodes
ROODYNG, Humphrey, Barrow, 1503. R2/13/131 & 133
ROOFE, Elisabeth, wid., Lawshall, 1690. A5/6/132, A4/32/7
ROOKE, Thomas, Palgrave, 1565. A5/1/164
ROOKES, Abraham, Bradley, 1697. A5/7/3, A4/41/44
  George, Whepstead, 1583. A5/2/49
  John, yeo., Reach, 1684. R2/69/201; W1/138/13
  Robert, Bardwell, 1694. A5/6/168, A4/37/26
ROOKEWOOD, Ann, wid., Bury St. Edmunds, 1685. A5/6/89
  Robert, esq., Stanningfield, 1602. R2/45/211; W1/60/145
ROOKWOOD, Edmund, Fornham St. Martin, 1661. R2/62/302; W1/113/221
  see also Rokewoode, Rokwode
ROOLE, Alice, Burwell, 1540. R2/21/372; W1/38/69
  Richard, Burwell, 1471. R2/10/477
ROOPE, Benjamin, grocer, Eye, 1697. R2/73/172; W1/151/55
  John, gent., Mellis, 1669. R2/64/434; W1/121/16; In. 3/14/23
ROOS(E), John, Nayland, 1461. R2/9/303
  John, Stoke by Nayland, 1479. R2/11/168
  John, Stowlangtoft, 1513. W1/9/45
  Robert, Saxham, 1544. A5/1/20
  Thomas, husb., Lawshall, 1574. R2/37/56; W1/33/21
ROOSHBROOK, John, Thurston, 1503. R2/13/132
ROOT(E), Agnes, Wicken, 1636. A5/4/42
  Ann, Wicken, 1668. R2/64/318; W1/120/25
  Avice, wid., Lakenheath, 1673. R2/65/445; W1/125/73
  Edward, shepherd, Eriswell, 1661. In. 3/6/51; A5/5/13, A4/1/126
  George, Wicken, 1607. R2/46/135; W1/97/66; A5/3/28
  Isabel, Wicken, 1564. A5/1/154
  John, shepherd, Eriswell, 1663. R2/63/85; W1/115/133; In. 3/8/158

ROOT(E) continued
John, Glemsford, 1454. R2/9/175
John, husb., Wicken, 1592. R2/42/235; W1/49/52
John, 1564. A5/1/162
Lawrence, Bradfield St. George, 1677. A5/5/169, A4/14/25
Martha, wid., Bradfield St. George, 1683. A5/6/71, A4/20/81
Michael, yeo., Long Melford, 1671. R2/65/173; W1/123/42
Nicholas, Nayland, 1585. R2/39/347; W1/42/253
Peter, singleman, Wicken, 1590. R2/41/427; W1/47/10
Peter, Wicken, 1668. R2/64/307; W1/120/10; In. 3/13/24
Peter, yeo., Wicken, 1674. R2/66/90; W1/126/30
Richard, Cavendish, 1503. R2/12/68
Richard, Glemsford, 1475. R2/11/114
Robert, Wicken, 1616. R2/50/108; W1/73/117
Thomas, Clare, 1602. R2/45/154; W1/60/75
Thomas, Glemsford, 1471. R2/10/476
Thomas, Wicken, 1625. R2/53/330; W1/81/113
William, Isleham, 1674. In. 9/37
William, carpenter, Lakenheath, 1620. R2/52/150; W1/76/135
William, husb., Wicken, 1598. R2/44/164; W1/56/44
see also Rote, Plesants als. Roote
ROPELEY, John, the younger, Walsham le Willows, 1557. R2/26/228; W1/20/113
ROPER, Alice, Lakenheath, 1567. A5/1/182
Catherine, wid., Lakenheath, 1689. R2/71/255; W1/143/93
Dorothy, spinster, Stanton, 1680. A5/6/42, A4/17/116
Elisabeth, wid., Langham, 1623. R2/52/664; W1/79/86
Ellen, wid., Lakenheath, 1687. R2/70/304; W1/141/47
George, Badwell Ash, 1664. In. 3/9/111; A5/5/59, A4/2/61
Henry, Langham, 1606. A5/3/11
James, sen., yeo., Bacton, 1670. R2/65/105; W1/122/127; In. 3/15/115
James, yeo., Bacton, 1697. R2/73/168; W1/151/52
James, Bury St. Edmunds, 1679. A5/6/24, A4/16/98
Jane, singlewoman, Westhorpe, 1644. R2/59/139; W1/101/63
John, Burwell, 1582. A5/2/39
John, als. Pegg, Bury St. Edmunds, 1500. R2/4/99
John, the elder, yeo., Lakenheath, 1660. R2/62/10; W1/112/9; In. 3/5/22
John, yeo., Lakenheath, 1664. R2/63/240; W1/116/160; In. 3/9/220
John, Nayland, 1459. R2/9/263
John, Wetherden, 1700. In. 3/27/52; A5/7/16, A4/41/121
Robert, Bury St. Edmunds, 1361. R2/1/8
Robert, Lakenheath, 1556. R2/25/111; W1/16/138
Robert, Lakenheath, 1696. A5/6/189, A4/39/71
Steven, Gazeley, 1537. R2/18/144
Thomas, labourer, Badwell Ash, 1593. R2/42/370; W1/50/38
Thomas, yeo., Barnham, 1665. R2/63/316; W1/117/52; In. 3/10/58
Thomas, Hopton, 1453. R2/9/164
Thomas, Lakenheath, 1562. R2/31/85; W1/8/170
Thomas, yeo., Lakenheath, 1680. R2/67/544; W1/134/28; In. 3/20/29
Thomas, tailor, Stanton, 1678. In. 3/19/136; A5/6/9, A4/15/77
Thomas, gent., Walsham le Willows, 1694. R2/72/140; A5/6/172, A4/37/74
Thomas, husb., Westhorpe, 1629, (N). R2/54/374; W1/85/72
William, Fordham, 1560. R2/29/103; W1/25/63
William, yeo., Lakenheath, 1677. R2/66/516; W1/129/98; In. 3/18/127
William, Lakenheath, 1684. A5/6/78, A4/21/49
see also Lotkyn als. Roper
ROPKYN, Nicholas, Thrandeston, 1473. R2/11/33
Roger, Thrandeston, 1452. R2/9/108
ROPSONE, Davie, labourer, Soham, 1559. R2/28/227; W1/22/179
RORGER, Robert, sen., butcher, Bury St. Edmunds, 1426. R2/1/171
William, Bury St. Edmunds, 1428. R2/1/182
ROSBROKE, Elizabeth, wid., Elmswell, 1536. R2/19/247
ROSBY, Henry, shepherd, Eriswell, 1601. R2/44/515; W1/59/140
Nicholas, carpenter, Mildenhall, 1592. R2/42/184; W1/49/5
ROSCHEBROKE, Ann, wid., Rattlesden, 1555. R2/24/194; W1/15/29
ROSE, Abraham, Culford, 1679. A5/6/23, A4/16/85
Alice, wid., Bacton, 1563. R2/32/1; W1/26/58
Arthur, yeo., Brockley, 1680. R2/67/698; W1/134/149; In. 3/20/167
Barnaby, bach., Cotton, 1678. A5/5/173, A4/14/65

ROSE continued
Edmund, Bacton, 1504. W1/7/5
Edmund, Elmswell, 1617. R2/50/343; W1/74/126
Edmund, Horningsheath, 1694. A5/6/172, A4/37/67
Edmund, yeo., Weston, 1671. R2/65/170; W1/123/36
Edward, weaver, Bury St. Edmunds, 1674. R2/66/43; W1/126/79
Edward, Cockfield, 1681. A5/6/45, A4/18/25
Ezechias, Great Ashfield, 1647. R2/59/412; W1/104/38; In. 3/2/54
Isaac, Nayland, 1588. A5/2/100
Joan, the elder, wid., Elmswell, 1652. R2/61/575; W1/107/48
John, Bardwell, 1586. A5/2/78
John, husb., Great Ashfield, 1639. R2/58/76; W1/94/130
John, Hopton, 1505. R2/12/44
John, husb., Lawshall, 1558. R2/27/388
John, tailor, Rattlesden, 1638, (N). R2/57/386; W1/15/197; A5/4/60
John, jun., Thurston, (1448). R2/9/119
John, Thurston, 1490. R2/13/3
Katherine, Bury St. Edmunds, 1411. R2/1/122
Margaret, wid., Fornham St. Genevieve, 1605, (N). R2/45/450; W1/63/97; A5/3/3
Martha, Cotton, 1631. A5/2/13
Richard, Wangford, 1483. R2/11/247
Robert, chandler, Bury St. Edmunds, 1471. R2/2/140
Robert, Cotton, (1542). R2/22/75; W1/6/43
Robert, tailor, Great Ashfield, 1618. R2/51/28; W1/75/15
Robert, yeo., Great Ashfield, 1684. R2/69/373; W1/138/161
Robert, miller, Hopton, 1634. R2/56/334; W1/90/101
Robert, yeo., Norton, 1676. R2/66/342; W1/128/50; In. 3/17/56
Robert, yeo., Rishangles, 1676. In. 3/17/159; A5/5/166, A4/13/91
Robert, Saxham, 1544. A5/1/21
Roger, Bury St. Edmunds, 1405. R2/1/104
Susan, wid., Wattisham, 1686. In. 3/22/36; A5/6/100, A4/26/82
Thomas, singleman, yeo., Bradfield St. Clare, 1677. R2/66/513; W1/129/95; In. 3/18/121
Thomas, yeo., Brockley, 1638. R2/57/325; W1/93/105
Thomas, Brockley, 1685. R2/70/50; W1/139/43
Thomas, potter, Bury St. Edmunds, 1390. R2/1/59
Thomas, Bury St. Edmunds, 1406. R2/1/108
Thomas, Bury St. Edmunds, 1678. R2/67/141; W1/130/126
Thomas, clothier, Chevington, 1688. R2/71/34; W1/142/33
Thomas, yeo., Elmswell, 1677. R2/66/482; W1/129/62; In. 3/18/74
Thomas, Polstead, 1585. A5/2/66
Thomas, Walsham le Willows, 1501. R2/13/124
Thomas, Whepstead, 1527. R2/17/251; W1/1/25
Valentine, Hepworth, 1573. R2/19/123; W1/32/23
William, Bacton, 1519. R2/12/107
William, brazier, Bury St. Edmunds, 1411. R2/1/122
William, Bury St. Edmunds, 1643. A5/4/100
William, yeo., Cotton, 1620. R2/52/175; W1/76/157
William, singleman, Cotton, 1678. A5/5/173, A4/14/64
William, the elder, yeo., Elmswell, 1670. R2/65/131; W1/122/157; In. 3/15/201
William, yeo., Fornham St. Martin, 1625. R2/53/374; W1/81/154
William, clerk, Timworth, 1692. R2/72/55; W1/146/57
William, yeo., Wattisham, 1686. R2/70/442; W1/140/57; A5/6/100, A4/26/81
Zachary, yeo., Great Ashfield, 1651. R2/61/501; W1/108/91

ROSELL, Joan, als. Sotyll, wife of James, Lavenham, 1503. R2/12/62

ROSER, Edmund, Haughley, 1562. R2/31/41
James, husb., Yaxley, 1552. R2/23/242; W1/12/52
Margaret, wid., Palgrave, 1574. R2/37/64
Robert, tanner, Wetherden, 1570. R2/34/35; W1/30/33

ROSHER, Joseph, weaver, Ballingdon, 1697. R2/73/173; W1/151/56
Joseph, say maker, Little Waldingfield, 1674. R2/66/92; W1/126/22
Richard, labourer, Semer, 1696. R2/73/66; W1/150/91

ROSHEY, Henry, yeo., Little Waldingfield, 1637. R2/57/163; W1/92/203
see also Rosshey

ROSIER, Edmund, tanner, Stowmarket, 1680. W1/134/178
George, singleman, Wetherden, 1636. A5/4/44
John, yeo., Nedging, 1619. R2/51/398; W1/132/85

ROSIER continued
Robert, labourer, Great Livermere, 1625. R2/53/304; W1/81/89
Robert, Stoke by Nayland, 1678. In. 3/19/101; A5/6/8, A4/15/64
Robert, yeo., Stowmarket, 1691. R2/71/533; W1/145/90; In. 3/24/8
Thomas, tailor, Elmsett, 1683. R2/69/416; W1/138/195
Thomas, Naughton, 1684. A5/6/75, A4/21/18
Thomas, yeo., Stoke by Nayland, 1662. In. 3/7/12; A5/5/27
Thomas, yeo., Wetherden, 1614. R2/49/39; W1/71/33
William, thatcher, Livermere, 1671. R2/65/210; W1/123/81
William, sen., Great Livermere, 1685. A5/6/89, A4/24/35
William, sen., carpenter, Stowmarket, 1639. R2/58/58; W1/94/108
William, pump maker, Stowmarket, 1667. R2/64/218; W1/119/70; In. 3/12/79
see also Rosyar, Rosyr
ROSLER, Valentine, labourer, Bury St. Edmunds, 1593. R2/42/435; W1/50/96
ROSS(E), Edward, Nayland, 1633. A5/4/24
John, Brent Eleigh, 1571. A5/1/234
John, Combs, 1578. A5/2/7
John, Stowlangtoft, 1555. R2/24/235; W1/15/64
Margery, wid., Cotton, 1546. R2/21/209; W1/10/110
Richard, Long Melford, 1590, (N). R2/41/325; W1/47/15
Robert, Nayland, 1553. R2/31/47; W1/13/36
Thomas, Bacton, 1572. R2/36/28; W1/31/138
Thomas, yeo., Polstead, 1585. R2/39/270; W1/42/304
Thomas, Stoke by Nayland, 1556. R2/25/171; W1/16/144; A5/1/97
William, Nayland, 1545. A5/1/35
William, clothier, Nayland, 1638. R2/57/429; W1/93/267
William, wool comber, Nayland, 1670. R2/65/82; W1/122/102; In. 3/15/132
ROSSHEY, Henry, the elder, yeo., Little Waldingfield, 1612. R2/48/149; W1/69/32
Richard, Glemsford, (1515). R2/14/8
ROSYAR, Thomas, knacker, Great Livermere, 1685. R2/70/116; W1/139/103
ROSYER, Nicholas, yeo., Wetherden, 1597. R2/43/356; W1/55/120
Walter, yeo., Wetherden, 1631. R2/56/75; W1/87/113
ROSYNGREY, Hugh, tailor, Bury St. Edmunds, 1469. R2/2/127
ROSYR, Richard, Wetherden, 1549. R2/21/164; W1/9/77
ROTE, Cristine, wife of John, Glemsford, 1443. R2/9/85
John, Glemsford, 1454. R2/9/205
John, mat maker, Soham, 1621. R2/52/269; W1/77/53
Matilda, Glemsford, 1453. R2/9/145
ROTHE, Katherine, wid., Bury St. Edmunds, 1470. R2/2/136
ROTHOWELL, William, carpenter, Bury St. Edmunds, 1600. R2/45/39; W1/58/56
ROTT(E), John, husb., Stoke by Nayland, 1575. W1/95/9
John, Wicken, 1553. R2/31/40; W1/13/29
Robert, Wicken, 1558. R2/27/504
ROUGE, William, cordwainer, Bury St. Edmunds, 1627. R2/54/10; W1/83/12
ROUGH, Christopher, Newmarket, 1613. R2/48/251; W1/70/9
ROUGHAM, Cecily, Bury St. Edmunds, 1438. R2/1/234
John, Bury St. Edmunds, 1501. R2/4/110
John, Bury St. Edmunds, 1516. R2/6/30
Margaret, Bury St. Edmunds, 1399. R2/1/88
William, rector, Sproughton, 1396. R2/1/76 & 77
see also Reffham, Reyffham, Rouham, Rugham
ROUGHT(E), John, baker, Bury St. Edmunds, 1573. R2/36/170; W1/32/72
William, the elder, Rickinghall, 1560. R2/29/122; W1/25/47
William, yeo., Rickinghall Superior, 1620. R2/52/83; W1/76/69
ROUGHTON, Stephen, Polstead, 1664. In. 3/9/148; A5/5/61, A4/2/81
ROUHAM, John, fisher, Bury St. Edmunds, 1361. R2/1/8
Richard, Bury St. Edmunds, 1410. R2/1/130
ROULES, Thomas, 1576. R2/37/219
ROULFE, Geoffrey, carpenter, Bury St. Edmunds, 1531. R2/7/10
ROULINSON, John, Bury St. Edmunds, 1677. In. 3/18/46; A5/5/168, A4/14/24
ROUNCTON, Robert, husb., Rattlesden, 1589. R2/41/299; W1/46/13

ROUNDIN, Thomas, linen weaver, Hopton, 1625. R2/53/370; W1/81/148
ROUNGTON, Matilda, Troston, 1459. R2/9/234
ROUS(E), Ann, spinster, Walsham le Willows, 1696. R2/73/49; W1/150/39
John, Brockley, 1441. R2/9/34
John, clerk, Downham, 1649. R2/60/223; W1/106/75
Lydia, spinster, Ixworth Thorpe, 1680. R2/67/702; W1/134/154; In. 3/20/174 a & b
Thomas, clerk, Ingham, 1672. A5/5/131, A4/9/42
William, Long Melford, 1461. R2/9/277
see also Rowes, Rowse
ROUSBROCK, John, shearman, Walsham le Willows, 1588. R2/41/103; W1/45/99
ROUT, Ann, Old Newton, 1686. R2/70/533; W1/140/135; In. 3/22/118
Eleazor, linen weaver, yeo., Wetheringsett, 1682. R2/68/418; W1/136/112; In. 3/21/94
Michael, the elder, Wicken, 1586. R2/40/108; W1/43/86
Thomas, husb., Barningham, 1640. R2/58/155; W1/96/61
see also Rought(e), Rowght, Rowte, Maskall als. Rowghte
ROW(E), Christopher, inn holder, Newmarket, 1670. In. 3/15/24; A5/5/112
Elisabeth, Coney Weston, 1607. A5/3/37
George, Bildeston, 1608. A5/3/53
George, bach., Newmarket, 1683. A5/6/73, A4/20/101
John, Bildeston, 1507. R2/13/70
John, Pakenham, 1460. R2/9/253
John, the elder, Rickinghall Inferior, 1676. R2/66/339; W1/128/45; In. 3/17/53
Jonas, butcher, Kersey, 1649. R2/60/272; W1/106/142
Katherine, wid., Newmarket, 1616. W1/95/79
Matthew, the elder, butcher, Kersey, 1672. R2/65/318; W1/124/42
Matthew, Kersey, 1678. R2/67/110; W1/130/95; In. 3/19/124
Michael, Bury St. Edmunds, 1606. A5/3/10
Peter, Wangford, 1559. R2/28/104; W1/22/103
Susan, Rickinghall, 1696. A5/6/188; A4/39/54
Thomas, Bury St. Edmunds, 1695. A5/6/182, A4/38/66
Thomas, Kedington, 1652. A5/4/141
Thomas, Stanton, 1666. In. 3/11/69; A4/4/17
see also Roo, Wroe, Wroo, Bullock als. Rowe
ROWELL, William, Bury St. Edmunds, 1519. R2/6/67 (admon. only)
ROWELLS, Robert, Haverhill, 1617. R2/50/242; W1/74/40
see also Rowles
ROWES, Elisabeth, wid., Newmarket, 1558. R2/27/386
ROWGE, Robert, husb., Bradfield St. Clare, 1617, (N). R2/50/408; W1/74/195
ROWGHT, Elizabeth, Bury St. Edmunds, 1536. R2/7/41
Richard, Mendlesham, 1559. R2/28/191; W1/22/172
Rose, wid., Bury St. Edmunds, 1596. R2/43/193; W1/54/80
Syvester, yeo., Rickinghall Superior, 1574. R2/37/48; W1/33/29
ROWHED, Thomas, the elder, Bury St. Edmunds, 1503. R2/4/129
William, Thorndon, 1457. R2/9/187
ROWHEY, William, Little Thurlow, 1462. R2/10/313
ROWLAND, Ann, wid. of Hugh, Haughley, 1639. R2/58/107; W1/94/176
George, Long Melford, 1634. A5/4/29
Hugh, yeo., Haughley, 1629. R2/54/329; W1/85/38
John, Bildeston, 1663. In. 3/8/210
John, tailor, Depden, 1610. R2/47/232; W1/67/112
John, Groton, 1558. R2/27/47
John, yeo., Haughley, 1620. R2/52/23; W1/76/21
John, Haughley, 1634. A5/4/30
Richard, the elder, yeo., Haughley, 1609. R2/47/7; W1/66/7
Richard, Haughley, 1634. A5/4/27
Richard, Haughley, 1679. A5/6/30, A4/94/164
Thomas, yeo., Cockfield, 1692. In. 3/24/66; A5/6/150, A4/34/32
ROWLAYE, Benedict, Burwell, 1549. R2/21/2; W1/10/171
ROWLES, George, yeo., Little Thurlow, 1652. R2/61/548; W1/109/30; In. 3/4/37
Robert, yeo., Haverhill, 1674. R2/66/81; W1/126/38
William, Haverhill, 1676. In. 3/17/126
ROWLEY, Thomas, husb., Wickhambrook, 1650. R2/61/330; W1/107/28; In. 3/3/36
William, Denston, 1661. In. 3/6/203; A5/5/21, A4/1/50
see also Roley, Rowlaye

ROWLINGSON, Bryant, 1617. R2/50/221; W1/74/11
John, Cavendish, 1559. R2/28/217; W1/22/199
John, weaver, Cavendish, 1578. R2/37/338
John, blacksmith, Glemsford, 1622. R2/52/359; W1/78/5
ROWLINSON, Henry, Haverhill, 1667. A5/5/81, A4/5/17
Lettice, Glemsford, 1639. A5/4/69
William, weaver, Haverhill, 1613. R2/48/280; W1/70/54
ROWLYNGSON, Andrew, blacksmith, Glemsford, 1603. R2/45/244; W1/61/43
see also Roulinson
ROWNEING, Phyllis, wid., Badlingham, 1638. R2/57/339; W1/93/122
Thomas, yeo., Wixoe, 1668. R2/64/353; W1/120/65; In. 3/13/102
William, Chippenham, 1641. A5/4/89
ROWNING, Alice, wid., Glemsford, 1620. R2/52/183; W1/76/165
Alice, wid., Hundon, 1619. R2/51/483; W1/132/141
Austin, the elder, yeo., Hundon, 1623. R2/52/570; W1/79/28
John, labourer, Chippenham, 1609. R2/47/79a; W1/66/92
John, yeo., Gazeley, 1680. R2/67/776; W1/134/207; In. 3/20/235; A5/6/43, A4/95/129
John, yeo., Hundon, 1609. R2/47/65; W1/66/75
John, yeo., Hundon, 1639. R2/58/100; W1/94/162
John, yeo., Hundon, 1661. R2/62/189; W1/113/47; In. 3/6/66
Margaret, wid., Hundon, 1690. R2/71/312; W1/144/11
Nathaniel, yeo., Hundon, 1683. R2/69/123; W1/137/99
Ralph, Ixworth, 1603. R2/45/285; W1/61/88
Samuel, bach., Barnardiston, 1677. In. 3/18/63; A5/5/170, A4/14/36
Thomas, yeo., Barnardiston, 1617. R2/50/281; W1/74/80
Thomas, yeo., Barnardiston, 1670. R2/65/15; W1/122/20; In. 3/15/23
Thomas, the elder, Hundon, 1588. R2/41/86; W1/45/82
Thomas, Hundon, 1593. A5/2/180
William, yeo., Chippenham, 1630. R2/55/72; W1/86/83
William, Hundon, 1607. A5/3/37
William, yeo., Hundon, 1650. R2/61/409; W1/107/116; In. 3/3/128
see also Rownyng, Brand als. Rowninge
ROWNTON, John, Lawshall, 1472. R2/10/498
ROWNYNG, Agnes, wid., Hundon, 1601. R2/44/366; W1/59/32
Henry, Hundon, 1567. R2/32/390; W1/3/29
John, Chippenham, 1554. R2/24/10; W1/14/11
John, the elder, yeo., Chippenham, 1592. R2/42/277; W1/49/94
John, Hundon, 1549. R2/21/525 & 553; W1/8/74
Thomas, yeo., Hundon, 1609. R2/47/83; W1/66/100
Thomas, singleman, Hundon, 1609. R2/47/88; W1/66/104
William, smith, Hundon, 1497. R2/13/43
ROWSE, Thomas, Lakenheath, 1642. A5/4/94
see also Rous(e)
ROWTE, Edmund, singleman, Wetheringsett, 1557. R2/26/74; W1/20/44
Joan, Wicken, 1559. R2/28/59; W1/22/63
John, Rattlesden, 1465. R2/10/379
Michael, Wicken, 1573. R2/36/210
Peter, Wicken, 1559. R2/28/390; W1/3/76
Richard, husb., Thorndon, 1566. R2/32/289; W1/28/105
Samuel, yeo., Mendlesham, 1649. R2/60/256; W1/106/119
Walter, Bury St. Edmunds, 1511. R2/5/4
see also Rout
ROWTH, John, Rickinghall Superior, 1505. R2/13/166
ROYDON, Jane, wid., Newmarket, 1650. In. 3/3/3
ROYSE, Henry, husb., Exning, 1634. R2/56/386; W1/90/165
Henry, husb., Exning, 1640. R2/58/162; W1/96/72
Henry, labourer, Exning, 1662. R2/62/314; W1/114/13; In. 3/7/14
William, Hessett, 1531. R2/12/109, R2/19/36
see also Roisse
ROYSSHBROOK, John, Buxhall, 1496. R2/13/31
John, Rattlesden, 1496. R2/13/38
John, Stowmarket, 1488. R2/11/423
Walter, Stowmarket, 1487. R2/11/426
ROYSTON, Oliver, Withersfield, 1671. A5/5/125, A4/86/57

RUDD(S), Henry, clerk, Bury St. Edmunds, 1506. R2/4/180
John, Aldeburgh, (1535). R2/19/214; W1/3/54
William, Fordham, 1521. R2/14/27
see also Ellis als. Rud
RUDDINGTON, Laurence, singleman, Fordham, 1607. R2/46/113
RUDDUCK, Richard, linen weaver, Hinderclay, 1679. R2/67/231; W1/133/1
RUDGELS, Thomas, tailor, Depden, 1610. R2/47/215; W1/67/93
RUDHAM, William, Great Barton, 1439. R2/9/5; W1/24/111
RUDLAND, Abraham, carpenter, Buxhall, 1660. R2/62/44; W1/112/52
Alice, wid., Edwardstone, 1602. R2/45/208; W1/60/140
Andrew, Ixworth, 1533. R2/19/151; W1/2/11
Augustine, Bradfield St. Clare, 1565. A5/1/164
Daniel, Milden, 1639. A5/4/71
Geoffrey, Wetheringsett, 1565. R2/32/217
James, Little Waldingfield, 1589. R2/41/140; W1/46/138
John, Groton, 1569. A5/1/211
John, Ixworth Thorpe, 1558. R2/27/555
John, labourer, Kersey, 1611. R2/48/15; W1/68/34
John, husb., Little Waldingfield, 1564. R2/32/92; W1/27/39
John, Pakenham, 1562. A5/1/132
Robert, Nowton, 1617. R2/50/278; W1/74/77
Thomas, weaver, Groton, 1617. R2/50/366; W1/74/149
Thomas, carpenter, Hitcham, 1628, (N). R2/54/239; W1/83/99
Thomas, Little Waldingfield, 1592. R2/42/287; W1/49/101
RUDLOND, Jacob, Little Waldingfield, 1478. R2/11/167
James, husb., Bures, 1612. R2/48/170; W1/69/49
James, Little Waldingfield, 1552. R2/31/128; W1/13/88
Joan, Ixworth Thorpe, 1503. R2/12/65
Joan, Little Waldingfield, 1554. R2/24/88; W1/14/67
Joan, wid., Wetheringsett, 1539. R2/19/295
John, yeo., Gipping, 1558. R2/27/382
Robert, Great Waldingfield, 1471. R2/10/484
Robert, Great Waldingfield, 1478. R2/11/180
William, singleman, Boxford, 1563. R2/31/124; W1/26/9
see also Rodeland, Rodland, Mathewe als. Rudland
RUFFELL, Lenten, yeo., Lavenham, 1619. R2/51/282; W1/132/18
William, Little Cornard, 1587. R2/40/282; W1/44/113
William, Milden, 1664. In. 3/9/71; A5/5/56, A4/2/20
William, Poslingford, 1617. R2/50/252; W1/74/50
RUFFLE, Ann, wid., Cockfield, 1691. R2/71/488; W1/145/48
George, yeo., Sudbury, 1633. R2/56/303; W1/90/69
Grace, wid., Sudbury, 1638. R2/57/266; W1/93/29
John, bricklayer, Little Cornard, 1616. R2/50/54; W1/73/64
John, husb., Little Cornard, 1616. R2/50/144; W1/73/147
Richard, yeo., Great Cornard, 1675. R2/66/172; W1/127/48; In. 3/16/50
Richard, husb., Sudbury, 1619. R2/51/273; W1/132/13
Samuel, yeo., Little Waldingfield, 1680. In. 3/20/212; A5/6/41, A4/17/110
William, yeo., Naughton, 1683. R2/69/107; W1/137/82
RUFFYN, John, Bury St. Edmunds, 1458. R2/2/59
RUGGELL(S), Mary, wid., Glemsford, 1605. R2/45/435; W1/63/48
Robert, husb., Denham, 1616. R2/50/91; W1/73/99
Robert, yeo., Lavenham, 1605. R2/45/405
RUGGLE(S), Thomas, Chelsworth, 1569. A5/1/212
Thomas, shoe maker, Stoke by Nayland, 1614. R2/49/169; W1/71/115
Thomas, Sudbury, 1638. A5/4/67
William, weaver, Glemsford, 1649. R2/60/162; W1/106/6
see also Rogell, Rogle
RUGHAM, William, cordwainer, Bury St. Edmunds, 1394. R2/1/65
RUGHE, Alice, spinster, Sudbury, 1595. A5/2/206
RUKKE, Joan, Wetheringsett, 1458. R2/9/208
RULE, Thomas, Great Wratting, 1634. A5/4/31
Thomas, labourer, Withersfield, 1672. R2/65/380; W1/124/123
Thomas, miller, Withersfield, 1688. R2/71/79; W1/142/71; In. 3/23/81
William, labourer, Withersfield, 1612. R2/48/216; W1/69/115
see also Rewle, Roole, Rulle
RULES, John, labouring man, Kedington, (1550). R2/21/168; W1/9/88
see also Roules

RULLE, Edward, yeo., Poslingford, 1682. R2/68/366; W1/136/74; In. 3/21/155
RUMBALL, William, husb., Wangford, 1634. R2/56/405; W1/90/191
RUMBELO(E), Alice, wid., Icklingham, 1676. In. 3/17/131; A5/5/164, A4/13/76 & 77
John, Gazeley, 1533. R2/19/202
Nathaniel, Freckenham, 1659. W8/16
Nathaniel, Freckenham, 1675. In. 10/19
RUMBELOW, Agnes, Lavenham, 1593. A5/2/185
Edmund, yeo., Dalham, 1630. R2/55/39; W1/86/45
Edward, Brandon, 1599. W1/57/99
John, Dalham, 1570. R2/34/24; W1/30/23; A5/1/222
John, Dalham, 1601. R2/44/377; W1/59/37
John, yeo., Dalham, 1641. R2/58/273; W1/98/55
John, the younger, yeo., Isleham, 1663. W7/66; In. 9/14
Margaret, wid., Isleham, 1617, (N). R6/16
Mary, singlewoman, Bury St. Edmunds, 1682. A5/6/61, A4/19/71
Mary, wid., Isleham, 1683. In. 9/55
Mary, wid., Isleham, 1685. W7/103
Mary, wid., Isleham, 1687. W7/115
Nicholas, Isleham, 1687. In. 9/74
Robert, singleman, Dalham, 1631. R2/56/28; W1/87/40
Robert, Isleham, 1619. R6/17
Robert, Isleham, 1675. In. 9/40
Susan, wid., Isleham, 1684. In. 9/63
Thomas, Great Thurlow, 1568. A5/1/201
William, husb., Isleham, 1661. W7/56; In. 9/4
see also Rombelowe, Romylowe, Rumbylowe
RUMBOLD, George, Mildenhall, 1567. R2/32/423; W1/19/99
James, Worlington, 1638. A5/4/60
see also Romball, Rumball
RUMBYLOWE, John, Gazeley, 1461. R2/9/274
RUNAKERS, Robert, the elder, yeo., Thrandeston, 1662. R2/62/332; W1/114/42
see also Raynaker, Renakers
RUNCKTON, Prudence, Felsham, 1635. A5/4/40
RUNCTON, John, Rattlesden, 1620. R2/52/127; W1/76/111
see also Rouncton, Roungton, Rungton
RUNEYE, William, Preston, 1458. R2/9/262
RUNGTON, John, chaplain, Bury St. Edmunds, 1473. R2/2/176
RUNKETLE, Robert, Mellis, 1582. R2/38/383; W1/41/54
RUSBROKE, William, Coney Weston, 1565, (N). R2/32/209; W1/27/132; A5/1/165
RUSBROOKE, William, yeo., Thurston, 1665. R2/63/274; W1/117/1; In. 3/10/6
RUSCHE, John, mercer, Rattlesden, 1553. R2/31/23; W1/13/15
RUSCHBROCKE, Thomas, Haughley, 1540. R2/19/619
RUS(E), Henry, husb., Kirtling, 1563. R2/32/26; W1/19/79
John, Woolpit, 1461. R2/10/314
Martin, Kirtling, 1607. A5/3/33
Thomas, gent., Hawstead, 1636. R2/57/107; W1/92/125
Thomas, clerk, Ingham, 1684. A5/6/76, A4/21/22
RUSFEILD, William, Assington, 1672. A5/5/130, A4/9/34
RUSH, Agnes, wid., Hitcham, 1580. R2/38/103; W1/39/173
Cicely, singlewoman, Great Thornham, 1592. R2/42/188; W1/49/7; In. 5/2/161
Edward, Buxhall, 1631. A5/4/16
Elisabeth, wid., Mellis, 1606. R2/46/3; W1/64/5
Francis, farmer, Aldham, 1691. R2/71/504; W1/145/65
Henry, Hitcham, 1580. A5/2/22
John, yeo., Hitcham, 1623. R2/52/538; W1/79/2
John, Mellis, 1637. A5/4/54
John, the elder, Rattlesden, (1553). R2/32/443; W1/17/62
John, the elder, Rattlesden, (1553). R2/21/664
Margery, singlewoman, Gislingham, 1689. R2/71/277; W1/143/113
Peter, Aldham, 1691. A5/6/141, A4/33/29
Robert, husb., Mellis, 1603, (N). R2/45/242; W1/61/40
Robert, Mendlesham, 1672. A5/5/130, A4/9/37
Robert, Stowmarket, 1697. A5/7/2, A4/40/33
Robert, Wyverstone, 1695. A5/6/178, A4/38/24
Thomas, Eye, 1628. R2/54/235; W1/84/97
Thomas, bach., Knettishall, 1682. A5/6/61, A4/19/58
see also Rusche, Russch

RUSHBROCKE, Elisabeth, wid., Coney Weston, 1566. R2/32/312; W1/28/80
RUSHBROKE, Bartholomew, Bury St. Edmunds, 1578. A5/2/12
  Benedict, Great Barton, (1546). R2/21/194; W1/10/58
  Robert, yeo., Haughley, 1598. R2/44/14; W1/56/21
  Simon, tailor, Bury St. Edmunds, 1591. R2/42/26; W1/48/17
RUSHBROOK(E), Alice, wid., Stowupland, 1679. R2/67/394; W1/133/143
  Ann, spinster, Stowmarket, 1679. A5/6/22, A4/16/71
  Christopher, Eriswell, 1663. R2/63/80; W1/115/129; In. 3/8/149
  Christopher, husb., Long Melford, 1632, (N). R2/56/226; W1/89/147
  Edward, Thelnetham, 1666. R2/64/76; W1/118/52; In. 3/11/70
  Elisabeth, wid., Sapiston, 1697. A5/7/4, A4/40/51
  Frances, weaver, Bury St. Edmunds, 1602. R2/45/150; W1/60/71
  George, tailor, Great Barton, 1637. R2/57/223; W1/92/270
  George, Thurston, 1633. A5/4/27
  Isolde, wid., Bury St. Edmunds, 1597. R2/43/228; W1/55/14
  John, yeo., Thurston, 1606. R2/46/46; W1/64/62
  John, yeo., Thurston, 1621. R2/52/311; W1/77/91
  John, clothier, Woolpit, 1603. R2/45/255; W1/61/56
  Prudence, wid., Great Fakenham, 1676. R2/66/314; W1/128/18
  Richard, Bury St. Edmunds, 1572. A5/1/247
  Richard, gent., Great Fakenham, 1692. R2/72/33; W1/146/32; In. 3/24/80
  Richard, gent., Woolpit, 1673. R2/65/486; W1/125/127
  Robert, gent., Honington, 1674. R2/66/33; W1/126/89
  Robert, Yaxley, 1668. A5/5/101, A4/6/117
  Thomas, gent., Eriswell, 1684. R2/69/309; W1/138/105
  William, the elder, gent., Bardwell, 1623. R2/52/672; W1/79/91
  William, the elder, yeo., Bardwell, 1652. R2/61/607; W1/109/87
  William, gent., Bardwell, 1692. R2/72/42; W1/146/38
  William, Great Barton, 1598. R2/44/146; W1/56/94
  William, the elder, carpenter, Stowupland, 1676. R2/66/374; W1/128/87; In. 3/17/102
  William, yeo., Thurston, 1630. R2/55/82; W1/86/90
  Zachary, yeo., Thurston, 1683. R2/69/168; W1/137/135
RUSHBRUCKE, Henry, Great Barton, 1605. R2/45/453; W1/63/99
RUSHEBROKE, Charity, wid., Bury St. Edmunds, 1591. R2/42/93; W1/48/139
  Stephen, Bildeston, (1551). R2/23/70; W1/11/58
RUSHEBROOKE, Ann, wid., Thurston, 1582, (N). R2/39/164; W1/42/162
RUSHEBRUKE, William, singleman, Thurston, 1578, (N). R2/37/400; W1/36/176
  see also Rasbrooke, Rassebrooke, Resshebrok, Rooshbrook, Rosbroke, Roschebroke, Rousbrock, Roysshbrook, Rusbroke, Ruschbrocke, Rysbroke, Ryshebrook, Hunt als. Rushbrooke & Gooch
RUSHEN, John, Bury St. Edmunds, 1689. A5/6/127, A4/30/45
RUSHFORD, Joan, als. Baron, wife of Richard, Hitcham, 1461. R2/9/297
  John, Sudbury, 1464. R2/10/365
RUSHINGE, John, the elder, barber, Bury St. Edmunds, 1676. R2/66/396; W1/128/107; In. 3/17/139
RUSSCH, John, Wetherden, 1452. R2/9/130
RUSSELL(S), Constance, wid., Icklingham, 1587. R2/40/256; W1/44/97
  Denise, wid., Bury St. Edmunds, 1512. R2/54/25
  Edward, Isleham, 1695. A12/13
  Elisabeth, Burwell, 1475. R2/11/115
  Henry, Dalham, 1633. A5/4/24
  John, Bury St. Edmunds, 1475. R2/2/196
  John, bach., Fordham, 1695. A5/6/176, A4/38/5
  John, sen., Great Waldingfield, 1470. R2/10/444
  John, yeo., Stowmarket, 1634. R2/56/423; W1/90/207
  John, wid., Wicken, 1680. In. 3/20/98; A5/6/36, A4/17/54
  John, yeo., Withersfield, 1644. R2/59/89; W1/101/20
  Mary, Old Newton, 1649. A5/4/128
  Richard, Woolpit, 1638. R2/57/436; W1/93/276
  Samuel, Wicken, 1683. A5/6/70, A4/20/58
  Sarah, spinster, Newmarket, 1690. A5/6/132, A4/32/8
  Susan, wid., Bury St. Edmunds, 1633. R2/56/286; W1/90/51
  Thomas, gent., Bury St. Edmunds, 1511. R2/5/7 (admon. only)
  Thomas, Hopton, 1650. In. 3/3/1; A5/4/133
  Thomas, Rickinghall Superior, 1661. In. 3/6/266; A5/5/24, A4/1/25
  William, Bury St. Edmunds, 1663. In. 3/8/82; A5/5/45
RUST, Agnes, Weston, 1584. R2/39/130; W1/42/201
  Ann, wid., Wattisfield, 1593. A5/2/191
  Ann, wid., Rickinghall Superior, 1663. R2/63/8; W1/115/14

RUST continued
Edith, wid., Clare, 1557. R2/26/276; W1/20/195
Edward, Bury St. Edmunds, 1698. A5/7/7
George, Ixworth, 1644. A5/4/106
Giles, Hepworth, 1573. R2/36/223; W1/32/96
Giles, Stanton, 1635. A5/4/35
Jeremiah, Hessett, 1672. A5/5/134, A4/9/74
Jeremy, gent., Hepworth, 1643. R2/59/33; W1/100/44
Jeremy, yeo., Rattlesden, 1624. R2/53/45; W1/80/66
Jeremy, the elder, Rattlesden, 1683. R2/69/91; W1/137/69; A5/6/69, A4/20/46
Jeremy, gent., Rattlesden, 1698. R2/73/229; W1/152/10
John, tanner, Clare, 1546. R2/21/224; W1/10/104
John, gent., Hepworth, 1627. R2/54/102; W1/83/102
John, Soham, 1610. A5/3/94
John, husb., Stanton, 1559. R2/28/156; W1/22/143
John, husb., Stanton, 1613. R2/48/302; W1/70/76
Jonathan, yeo., Rickinghall Superior, 1680. R2/67/636; W1/134/101; In. 3/20/109
Margaret, wid., Ampton, 1637. R2/57/171; W1/92/211
Margaret, wid., Stanton, 1554. A5/1/92
Philip, Harleston, 1595. A5/2/208
Richard, bach., Eriswell, 1678. In. 3/19/129; A5/6/8, A4/15/70
Robert, yeo., Market Weston, 1650. R2/61/406; W1/107/113; In. 3/3/127
Robert, labourer, Onehouse, 1564. R2/32/53; W1/51/268
Roger, Hepworth, 1503. R2/12/66
Roger, Wattisfield, 1571. R2/35/141; W1/36/76
Roger, yeo., Weston, 1616. R2/50/178; W1/73/170
Thomas, glover, Clare, 1589. R2/41/287; W1/46/24
Thomas, yeo., Rickinghall Superior, 1663. R2/63/8; W1/115/15; In. 3/8/9
Thomas, Stanton, 1508. W1/9/15
Thomasine, wid., Stoke by Nayland, 1635. R2/56/534; W1/91/116
Walter, gent., Rattlesden, 1661. R2/62/202; W1/113/66; In. 3/6/98
William, yeo., Botesdale, 1698. R2/73/232; W1/152/13
William, Hepworth, 1541. R2/21/356; W1/38/85
William, husb., Hepworth, 1575. R2/37/84; W1/34/3
William, yeo., Rickinghall Inferior, 1661. R2/62/293; W1/113/207

RUTLAND, Joan, wid., Boxford, 1648. R2/21/455; W1/38/108
Richard, Edwardstone, 1542. R2/22/68; W1/6/47

RUTLEDGE, Isabel, spinster, Ickworth, 1649. R2/60/265; W1/106/131
John, Thorndon, 1684. R2/69/300; W1/138/96

RUTLEY, Richard, gent., Mildenhall, 1640. R2/58/198; W1/96/126

RUTTER, Hannah, wid., Bury St. Edmunds, 1695. R2/72/509; W1/149/61

RUTTUR, John, Bury St. Edmunds, 1690. R2/71/401; W1/144/105

RYALL, John, yeo., Haughley, 1563. R2/31/161; W1/26/42

RYCARD, William, saddler, Bury St. Edmunds, 1575. R2/37/110; W1/34/69

RYCE, Agnes, wid., Bures, 1589. R2/41/271; W1/46/38
Daniel, Withersfield, 1668. A5/5/96
Thomas, yeo., Walsham le Willows, 1668. R2/64/305; W1/120/7; In. 3/13/82
Yan, Bures, (1521). R2/15/145
see also Rice

RYCHARDS, William, yeo., Stansfield, 1558. R2/27/324

RYCHARDSON, John, Billingford, 1574. W1/51/208a & b
William, Hundon, 1550. R2/21/39; W1/10/188

RYCHE, Alexander, baker, Bury St. Edmunds, 1427. R2/1/177
Thomas, Soham, (1550). R2/21/145

RYCHEMAN, Agnes, wid., Stanton, 1582. R2/38/409; W1/41/27
Ellen, Bury St. Edmunds, 1471. R2/2/148

RYCHEMONDE, William, Burwell, 1557. R2/26/54; W1/20/34

RYCHER, John, cordwainer, Bury St. Edmunds, 1444. R2/2/13
Margaret, wid., Hitcham, 1593. A5/2/181
Ralph, illuminator, Bury St. Edmunds, 1446. R2/2/20
Richard, Buxhall, 1565. A5/1/162
Walter, Cavendish, 1483. R2/11/400
William, draper, Bury St. Edmunds, 1461. R2/2/68

RYCHERDSON, Elisabeth, wid., Brandon, 1546. R2/21/195; W1/10/78

RYCHOLD, Isabel, Bury St. Edmunds, 1428. R2/1/181
Richard, Bury St. Edmunds, 1417. R2/1/144

RYCKS, Edmund, Palgrave, 1580. A5/2/29
Henry, wheelwright, Palgrave, 1556. R2/25/53; W1/16/61
Isabel, wid. of Henry, Palgrave, 1558. R2/27/119; W1/7/136

RYCROFT, Edmund, Bildeston, 1533. R2/18/213, R2/19/159; W1/2/90
John, husb., Barton Mills, 1589. R2/41/236; W1/46/56
Margery, wid., Bildeston, 1583. R2/39/63; W1/42/46
see also Reicrofte
RYDALE, Alice, wid., Bury St. Edmunds, 1465. R2/2/88
Edmund, Bury St. Edmunds, 1471. R2/2/155
Philip, lorrimer, Bury St. Edmunds, 1454. R2/2/44
see also Rydell
RYDDELEY, John, als. Gerrard, Wickhambrook, 1548. R2/21/439
RYDELL, John, Bury St. Edmunds, 1429. R2/1/192
RYDELS, William, Great Fakenham, 1571. R2/35/269; W1/38/114
see also Ridels
RYDER, James, Creeting All Saints, 1675. In. 3/16/35; A5/5/154, A4/12/16
RYDLESEWORTHE, Robert, Bury St. Edmunds, 1475. R2/2/214
see also Redelysworth
RYDNALE, Alice, wid., Hopton, 1525. R2/17/129, R2/15/214; W1/21/125
Thomas, Bury St. Edmunds, 1510. R2/4/213
RYDNALL, James, shearman, Haverhill, 1527. R2/17/239; W1/1/43
Robert, yeo., Buxhall, 1600. R2/45/11; W1/58/16
RYDDYLLESDALE, John, priest, Bury St. Edmunds, 1505. R2/4/173
RYDSDALLE, John, als. Locar, Bures, 1552. R2/23/195; W1/12/22
RYDYSDALE, Elisabeth, wid., Boxford, 1553. R2/31/77; W1/13/54
Jasper, husb., Boxford, 1552. R2/31/61; W1/13/46
RYE, Dorcas, wid., Bury St. Edmunds, 1700. R2/74/32
Robert, (1550). R2/14/128
RYECE, Robert, gent., Preston, 1638. R2/57/386; W1/93/199; A5/4/63
see also Rice
RYELAND, Ann, wid., Bury St. Edmunds, 1679, (N). R2/67/385; W1/133/137; A5/6/25, A4/16/106
RYGGE, John, Combs, 1464. R2/10/359
Thomas, Combs, 1528. R2/17/276
RYKKYS, Henry, Palgrave, 1518. R2/12/104
RYKYNGHALE, Agnes, wid., Bury St. Edmunds, 1459. R2/2/64
RYLAND, Alice, the elder, wid., Great Bradley, 1680. R2/67/679; W1/134/135; In. 3/20/148
Augustine, Barnardiston, 1606. A5/3/9
John, Great Bradley, (1675), (N). R2/66/209; W1/127/84; In. 3/16/109; A5/5/156, A4/12/43
RYLOND, Thomas, Great Thurlow, 1567. A5/1/191
see also Ryeland
RYMAN, Ann, spinster, Chippenham, 1640. R2/58/228; W1/96/176
RYMEL, Alice, wid., Glemsford, 1631. A5/4/11
RYMILL, Robert, shoe maker, Glemsford, 1630. R2/55/70; W1/86/81
RYNER, William, Sudbury, 1594. A5/2/201
RYNGAR, John, bricklayer, Stanton, 1618. R2/51/102; W1/75/63
RYNGBELL, Andrew, Hepworth, 1559. R2/28/205; W1/22/209
John, Coney Weston, 1557. R2/26/327; W1/20/245
Florence, wid. of John, Coney Weston, 1564. R2/32/65; W1/27/13
Robert, Coney Weston, 1484. R2/11/291
William, Hepworth, 1560. R2/29/37; W1/25/139
RYNGLAGE, John, Fornham, 1455. R2/9/229
RYNGLOND, John, Fornham St. Martin, 1498. R2/13/96
John, Fornham, 1566. R2/32/352; W1/28/28a
RYPPES, William, Eye, 1531. R2/19/58
RYSBROKE, Richard, Rattlesden, 1538. R2/20/146; W1/4/127
RYSBY, Agnes, wid., Lavenham, 1528. R2/15/195, 219 & 231; W1/19/51
John, Mendlesham, 1605. R2/44/347; A5/3/2
RYSE, John, Bures, 1554. R2/24/100; W1/14/78
Reginald, yeo., Wattisfield, 1614. R2/49/84; W1/71/65
William, shearman, Walsham le Willows, 1560. R2/29/73; W1/25/94
William, yeo., Walsham le Willows, 1613. R2/48/308; W1/70/81
RYSELY, William, yeo., Barnardiston, 1667. In. 3/12/119; A5/5/87, A4/5/64
RYSEWOLD, Richard, Mellis, 1493. R2/11/443
RYSHEBROOK, John, yeo., Buxhall, 1569. R2/33/134; W1/5/57
RYSHEY, Agnes, Bures, (1487). R2/13/11
John, barber, Bures, 1487. R2/11/444
RYSING, John, the elder, wheelwright, Bradfield Combust, 1595. R2/43/91; W1/53/90
John, wheelwright, Bradfield St. George, 1619. R2/51/461; W1/132/1a & b & 124
William, jun., Elmswell, 1545. A5/1/44

RYSSE, Thomas, Kedington, 1531. R2/19/69
RYSYNG, William, Mellis, 1455. R2/9/181
RYTCHEOLD, Thomas, Bury St. Edmunds, 1549. R2/8/256
RYVEL, Joan, Bury St. Edmunds, 1420. R2/1/152
RYVET(T), James, Rattlesden, 1589. R2/41/189; W1/46/96
John, yeo., Bacton, 1632. R2/56/184; W1/89/93
John, yeo., Eye, 1617. R2/50/249; W1/74/46
John, the elder, smith, Long Melford, 1531. R2/19/55
John, Stowmarket, 1608, (N). R2/46/160; W1/65/5
Mary, singlewoman, Yaxley, 1617, (N). R2/50/316; W1/74/103
William, Bacton, 1560. R2/29/34; W1/25/143
RYXE, William, yeo., Oakley, 1627. R2/54/27; W1/83/34

S

SABELOTT, John, Worlington, (1475). R2/11/141
SABYN, Thomas, husb., Isleham, 1620. R6/21
SACHE, Christine, wid. of Thomas, gent., Great Horningsheath, 1665. R2/63/329; W1/117/75; In. 3/10/110
Elisabeth, wid. of John, Little Whelnetham, 1647. R2/59/450; W1/104/83
SACKER, Thomas, maltster, Groton, 1686. R2/70/519
SADD, Charles, yeo., Cotton, 1648. R2/60/10; W1/105/13
James, yeo., Layham, 1648. R2/60/96; W1/105/115
John, Burgate, 1680. A5/6/40, A4/17/97
John, Bury St. Edmunds, 1370. R2/1/30
Matilda, Clare, 1455. R2/9/226
William, weaver, Bury St. Edmunds, 1498. R2/4/68
SADDELLER, Margaret, wid., Hawstead, 1650. R2/61/343; W1/107/38; In. 3/3/51
SADE, Richard, Shimpling, 1589. A5/2/117b
SADLER, Elisabeth, wid., Stradishall, 1638. A5/4/58
John, Cavenham, 1679. A5/6/16, A4/16/11
John, Stradishall, 1542. R2/22/16; W1/6/80
John, Stradishall, 1567. R2/32/410; W1/19/115b
John, yeo., Stradishall, 1626. R2/53/570; W1/82/96
John, Wickhambrook, 1650. In. 3/3/58; A5/4/133
Katherine, wid., Pakenham, 1590. R2/41/374; W1/47/68
Margaret, wid., Stradishall, 1670. R2/65/36; W1/122/41; In. 3/15/64
Richard, yeo., Great Bradley, 1690. R2/71/432; W1/144/137
Richard, yeo., Stradishall, 1664. R2/63/140; W1/116/30; In. 3/10/31
William, Hawstead, 1640, (N). R2/58/228; W1/96/175
see also Saddeller
SADLINGTON, Sarah, wid., Bury St. Edmunds, 1637. R2/57/120; W1/92/146
Sara, singlewoman, Bury St. Edmunds, 1639. R2/58/34; W1/94/62
Thomas, Fornham St. Martin, 1676. R2/66/358; W1/128/68; In. 3/17/86
SAER, John, Buxhall, 1551. R2/23/74; W1/11/59
John, husb., Withersfield, 1550. R2/21/41; W1/10/189
Mary, als. Hawkins, wid., Lavenham, 1665. In. 3/10/149; A5/5/68, A4/3/54
Susan, Groton, 1631, (N). R2/56/37; W1/87/50
SAGERDE, Robert, Stoke Ash, 1581. A5/2/33
SAGON, Henry, husb., Old Newton, 1564. R2/32/56
James, als. Rede, husb., Old Newton, 1565. R2/32/165; W1/27/103
ST. CLEERE, Amy, als. Smyth, Sudbury, 1612. A5/3/115
ST. CLERE, Amy, wife of John, Sudbury, 1609. A5/3/76
SAINTGENES, Bertram, als. Sengens, gent., Kirtling, 1666. R2/64/82; W1/118/57; In. 3/11/72
Mary, wid., Bury St. Edmunds, 1670. R2/65/117; W1/122/141
SAINTY, Robert, yeo., Bradfield Combust, 1678. In. 3/19/40
see also Sancte, Santie, Santy(e)
SAKE, Alexander, Great Cornard, 1479. R2/11/147
John, Great Cornard, 1550. R2/21/109; W1/9/139
John, Great Waldingfield, (1477). R2/11/149
SAKEIN, Robert, Isleham, 1650. A4/1/4
SAKEN, Richard, Isleham, 1628. R6/57
SAKENS, Richard, Wicken, 1675. R2/66/263; W1/127/132; In. 3/16/161
SAKER, Edmund, bach., Langham, 1680. A5/6/37, A4/17/65

SAKIN, Elisabeth, wid., Lidgate, 1662. R2/62/347; W1/114/65; In. 3/7/97
Leonard, Fordham, 1671. A5/5/124, A4/8/46
Robert, Isleham, 1674. W7/84; In. 9/36
Thomas, Great Thurlow, 1592. R2/42/310; W1/49/133
William, gent., Livermere, 1688. R2/71/124; W1/142/112
see also Sakein, Saykyn
SALADYN, Cicely, als. Clye, Chippenham, 1518. R2/15/6
SALE, John, shepherd, Great Fakenham, 1638. R2/57/265; W1/93/28
SALEMAN, Robert, Bury St. Edmunds, 1394. R2/1/67
SALISBURIE, John, the elder, husb., Great Barton, 1620. R2/52/61; W1/76/50
SALISBURY, Clement, Fornham St. Martin, 1682. In. 3/21/205; A5/6/58, A4/19/21
John, husb., Great Barton, 1557. R2/26/236; W1/20/110
John, yeo., Great Barton, 1691. R2/71/534; W1/145/91
John, Sapiston, 1683. A5/6/67, A4/20/20
John, Soham, 1555. A5/1/95
Thomas, yeo., Barton, 1661. In. 3/6/45; A5/5/13, A4/1/124
Thomas, the younger, Great Barton, 1652. A5/4/142
Thomas, Sapiston, 1607. A5/3/38
see also Sallysbury, Salsbury, Salusbury, Saulsburie, Honymull als. Salysbury
SALKELD, John, jun., Walsham le Willows, 1696. R2/73/83; W1/150/70
John, clerk, Walsham le Willows, 1699. R2/73/369; W1/153/27; In. 3/26/66
SALL, John, als. Cooke, Bildeston, 1471. R2/10/466
Simon, als. Cooke, Bildeston, 1520. R2/15/75
SALLET, Edward, Norton, 1669. In. 3/14/27; A5/5/103, A4/7/26
SALLEY, Thomas, Mendlesham, 1689. A5/6/127, A4/30/43
SALLMON, Richard, yeo., Wetherden, 1636. R2/57/20; W1/92/28
SALLYSBURY, John, yeo., Soham, 1559. R2/28/175; W1/22/160
SALMAN, Agnes, Bury St. Edmunds, 1412. R2/1/129
Henry, Sudbury, 1496. R2/13/78
Margaret, Bury St. Edmunds, 1443. R2/2/2
Margaret, wid., Bury St. Edmunds, 1500. R2/4/104
SALMON, Christine, Acton, 1630. A5/4/5
George, Bury St. Edmunds, 1697. A5/7/1, A4/40/13
Eli, fuller, Edwardstone, 1563. R2/31/171; W1/26/56
Elisabeth, wid., Stoke Ash, 1682. R2/68/346; W1/136/60; In. 3/21/162
John, husb., Bradfield St. George, 1559. R2/28/278; W1/22/210
John, yeo., Mendlesham, 1595. R2/43/68; W1/53/56
John, Mendlesham, 1634. A5/4/33
John, Nayland, 1662. In. 3/7/224; A5/5/39
John, Stoke Ash, 1675. In. 3/16/95; A5/5/155, A4/12/31
John, Stoke Ash, 1700. A5/7/17, A4/41/150
Mary, singlewoman, Mendlesham, 1688. R2/71/1; W1/142/1; In. 3/23/79
Mary, wid., Mildenhall, 1648. R2/60/3; W1/105/4
Peter, clothworker, Icklingham, 1611. R2/48/92; W1/68/110
Ralph, chaplain, Bury St. Edmunds, 1361. R2/1/25
Robert, yeo., Mendlesham, 1638. R2/57/329; W1/93/109
Thomas, cordwainer, Bury St. Edmunds, 1668. R2/64/348; W1/120/58; In. 3/13/40
Thomas, Euston, 1665. A5/5/68, A4/3/49 & 51
Thomas, Stowmarket, 1668. A5/5/92, A4/6/31
Walter, Bradfield St. George, 1609, (N). R2/47/10; W1/66/9
William, mariner, Burwell, 1552, (N). R2/23/167; W1/12/8
William, yeo., Rattlesden, 1619. R2/51/477; W1/132/138
see also Saleman, Sallmon, Sammon
SALOTT, Thomas, Brome, 1543. R2/19/347; W1/6/151
SALOWES, Jeffery, petty chapman, Sudbury, 1580. R2/38/234; W1/39/82
SALSBURY, Peter, husb., Soham, 1516. R2/12/123
Thomas, the elder, Barton, 1604. R2/45/318; W1/62/17
Thomas, the elder, cordwainer, Great Barton, 1669. R2/64/507; W1/121/98; In. 3/14/69
Thomas, yeo., Great Barton, 1690. R2/71/433; W1/144/138
SALTER, Agnes, Buxhall, 1566. A5/1/172
Alice, wid., Chelsworth, 1634. A5/4/29
Andrew, yeo., Buxhall, 1561. R2/30/92; W1/28/267

SALTER continued
Audrey, wife of John, cook, Bury St. Edmunds, 1581. R2/38/340; W1/40/79
Bernard, Bildeston, 1636. A5/4/44
Easter, singlewoman, Stowmarket, 1629. R2/54/378; W1/85/76
Edmund, Brome, 1614. R2/49/46; W1/71/39
Edmund, Buxhall, (1506). R2/13/180
Edmund, butcher, Buxhall, 1549. R2/21/140; W1/9/79
Elisabeth, wife of Edward, Stowmarket, 1633. A5/4/24
George, yeo., Buxhall, 1576. R2/37/146; W1/37/15
George, yeo., Great Finborough, 1623. R2/52/620; W1/79/65
George, singleman, Great Finborough, 1638. A5/4/65
Gregory, yeo., Buxhall, 1586. R2/40/114; W1/43/90
Henry, Buxhall, 1472. R2/10/501
James, Mildenhall, 1547. R2/21/290
James, husb., Mildenhall, 1587. R2/40/182; W1/44/53
Joan, wid., Badwell Ash, 1580. R2/38/161; W1/39/131
Joan, wid., Buxhall, 1625. R2/53/208; W1/80/12
John, husb., Badwell Ash, 1558. R2/27/63
John, Bury St. Edmunds, 1434. R2/1/208
John, barber, sen., Bury St. Edmunds, 1462. R2/2/71
John, Bury St. Edmunds, 1503. R2/4/141
John, sen., Buxhall, 1488. R2/11/427
John, Buxhall, 1508. W1/9/27a
John, Buxhall, 1533. R2/19/129; W1/2/100
John, the younger, Buxhall, 1533. R2/18/64; W1/2/97
John, butcher, Buxhall, 1560. R2/29/87; W1/25/78
John, the elder, yeo., Buxhall, 1576. R2/37/230; W1/37/90; In. 3/1/8
John, the elder, yeo., Buxhall, 1611. R2/48/27; W1/68/49
John, Cavenham, (1533). R2/19/144; W1/2/6
John, Great Finborough, 1639. A5/4/73
John, husb., Hitcham, 1650. R2/61/355; W1/107/51; In. 3/3/68
John, yeo., Honingham, (1594). W1/51/143
John, say maker, Sudbury, 1662. In. 3/7/210; A5/5/38
Margaret, wid., Bildeston, 1581. R2/38/257, R2/39/237; W1/40/8, W1/42/178
Margaret, wid., Buxhall, 1549. R2/21/143; W1/9/80
Margaret, wid., Hitcham, 1584. W1/42/202
Margery, wid., Great Finborough, 1560. A5/1/101
Mark, gent., Sudbury, 1691. R2/71/505; W1/145/66; A5/6/143, A4/33/57
Nicholas, Sudbury, 1634. A5/4/31
Peter, the elder, clothier, Lavenham, 1662. R2/62/401; W1/114/147; In. 3/7/209
Peter, Long Melford, 1685. A5/6/96, A4/24/122
Rachel, spinster, Sudbury, 1700. R2/74/81; W1/154/84
Richard, Buxhall, 1546. R2/21/185; W1/10/119
Robert, Combs, 1610. A5/3/87
Robert, miller, Lakenheath, 1680. R2/67/732; W1/134/173; In. 3/20/186
Susanna, wid., Chelsworth, 1694. R2/72/351; W1/148/77
Thomas, Bildeston, 1573. A5/1/255
Thomas, yeo., Buxhall, 1577. R2/37/299
Thomas, clothier, Chelsworth, 1613. R2/48/320; W1/70/97
Thomas, Chelsworth, 1687. A5/6/113, A4/27/66
Thomas, yeo., Rattlesden, 1648. R2/60/56; W1/105/74
William, sen., Buxhall, 1488. R2/11/427
William, Sudbury, 1532. R2/19/93
see also Saulter, Sawlter, Sowlter
SALUSBURY, Ambrose, clerk, rector, Whepstead, 1678. R2/67/86; W1/130/70
SALYSBERY, Ellen, wid., Soham, 1484. R2/11/305
Richard, Soham, 1455. R2/9/181
Thomas, Soham, 1474. R2/10/565
SALYSBURY, Geoffrey, Great Barton, 1519. R2/15/76; W1/26/121
Joan, wife of Richard, Soham, 1454. R2/9/170
Thomas, husb., Barton, 1620. R2/52/92; W1/76/75
SAME, Robert, chaplain, Bury St. Edmunds, 1519. R2/6/62
see also Seym
SAMFELDE, Elisabeth, wid., Little Wratting, 1555. A5/1/98

SAMFEILD, Alice, Little Wratting, 1596. R2/43/178; W1/54/58
Robert, husb., Stradishall, 1610. R2/47/216; W1/67/95
SAMFELD, Robert, the elder, Little Wratting, 1551. R2/23/24; W1/11/60
Thomas, Little Wratting, 1551. R2/23/26; W1/11/61
SAMFILDE, Robert, Little Wratting, 1593. A5/2/179
SAMISUM, William, Shimpling, 1487. R2/11/420
SAMMES, John, joiner, Hitcham, 1612. R2/48/142; W1/69/27
SAMMON, Edward, singleman, Lidgate, 1668. R2/64/365; W1/120/79
SAMMUNDE, John, Fordham, 1527. R2/17/268; W1/1/9
SAMON, Ralph, husb., Eriswell, 1572. R2/36/27; W1/31/141
SAMPFORTHE, Edmund, Rattlesden, 1564. R2/32/58; W1/27/5
SAMPSON, James, Bury St. Edmunds, 1468. R2/2/115
John, Burwell, 1553, (N). R2/23/253
John, Bury St. Edmunds, 1473. R2/2/177
John, mercer, Bury St. Edmunds, 1504. R2/4/149
John, Hinderclay, 1474. R2/10/582
John, the elder, esq., Kersey, 1647. R2/59/427; W1/104/57; In. 3/2/55
John, gent., Kersey, 1661. R2/62/218; W1/113/84; A5/5/17, A4/1/86
Nicholas, Bury St. Edmunds, 1586. A5/2/77
Nicholas, yeo., Stoke by Clare, 1547. R2/21/485
Richard, Stanningfield, 1494. R2/13/16
Robert, cordwainer, Bury St. Edmunds, 1516. R2/6/28
Susan, wid., Bury St. Edmunds, 1685. R2/70/180; W1/139/152
Thomas, als. Goore, Bardwell, 1474. R2/10/561
Thomas, Ixworth, 1519. R2/14/13, R2/15/24; W1/26/116
William, glover, Bury St. Edmunds, 1685. A5/6/96, A4/24/129
William, glover, Newmarket, 1632. R2/56/229; W1/89/152
William, Stoke by Clare, 1560. A5/1/101
see also Samisum, Sawmpson
SAMPYE, John, Bury St. Edmunds, 1551. R2/8/406; W1/21/186
SANCROFT, John, Tuddenham, 1682. In. 3/21/80; A5/6/64, A4/19/123
SANCTE, Robert, yeo., Bradfield St. George, 1678. R2/67/28; W1/130/27
SANCTY, Robert, yeo., Wickhambrook, 1631. R2/56/99; W1/87/151
SANDCROFT, Elisabeth, Market Weston, 1670. A5/5/116
Mary, Market Weston, 1670. A5/5/116
see also Sancroft
SANDER(S), Arthur, als. Robinson, Brandon, 1634. A5/4/28
Elisabeth, Brandon, 1631. A5/4/11
Elisabeth, wid., Soham, 1650. R2/61/385; W1/107/88; In. 3/3/96
Francis, Soham, 1647. In. 3/2/129; A5/4/118
John, carpenter, Shimpling, 1601. R2/44/463; W1/59/76
Martha, als. Skynner, Bury St. Edmunds, 1588. A5/2/111
Richard, glover, Wyverstone, 1565, (N). R2/32/244; W1/32/136
Robert, tallow chandler, Brandon, 1552. R2/23/128; W1/11/108
Thomas, Bury St. Edmunds, 1588. A5/2/111
Thomas, say maker, Bury St. Edmunds, 1613. R2/48/259; W1/70/33
Thomas, als. Hugh, Cotton, 1620. R2/52/138; W1/76/122
Thomas, joiner, Lavenham, 1622. R2/52/378; W1/78/16
William, husb., Bradwell, 1689. R2/71/286; W1/143/121
see also Robinson als. Sander
SANDERSON, Ann, wid., Great Bradley, 1693. R2/72/208; W1/147/100
John, Great Bradley, 1570. A5/1/219 & 220
Margaret, wid., Haverhill, 1580. R2/38/192; W1/39/114
Martin, the elder, yeo., Great Bradley, 1617. R2/50/248; W1/74/45
Martin, yeo., Great Bradley, 1682. R2/68/315; W1/136/40; In. 3/21/232
Philip, husb., Wood Ditton, 1668. R2/64/358; W1/120/70
Rebecca, singlewoman, Icklingham, 1623. R2/52/542; W1/79/5
Susan, spinster, Great Bradley, 1692. R2/72/49; W1/146/45
SANDES, Thomas, Kedington, 1573. A5/1/261
SANDOVER, William, Newmarket, 1691. A5/6/145, A4/33/82
SANDWICH, Elisabeth, spinster, Bury St. Edmunds, 1697. A5/6/191, A4/39/85
SANDWITH, Elisabeth, Bury St. Edmunds, 1646. A5/4/113
Thomas, woollen draper, Bury St. Edmunds, 1642. R2/58/366; W1/99/67
Thomas, Bury St. Edmunds, 1646. A5/4/113
Thomas, woollen draper, Bury St. Edmunds, 1650, (N). R2/61/383; W1/107/86
SANFEILD, Robert, yeo., Hawkedon, 1674. R2/66/95; W1/126/25
SANFORTH, Thomas, Cockfield, 1591. A5/2/154
SANGAR, James, yeo., Ixworth, 1700. R2/74/37; W1/154/37

SANNFORD, Thomas, Bury St. Edmunds, 1396. R2/1/83
SANTIE, John, yeo., Cheveley, 1675. R2/66/136; W1/127/16; In. 3/16/13
SANTON, Robert, Wangford, 1463. R2/10/320
William, Wangford, 1460. R2/9/252
SANTY(E), John, husb., Wickhambrook, 1637. R2/57/130; W1/92/162
Nicholas, gent., Cheveley, 1638. R2/57/355; W1/93/148
Sarah, wid., Cheveley, 1647. R2/59/493; W1/104/128; In. 3/2/122
Thomas, smith, Hargrave, 1574. R2/37/17; W1/33/74
SANTYLEY, Margaret, wife of Richard, Ashfield, 1504. W1/7/7
SAPIE, Augustine, Eye, 1573. A5/1/258 & 259
SARBE, William, Elmswell, 1611. R2/48/115; W1/68/127
SARE, Agnes, Barnardiston, 1592. A5/2/164
Alice, wid., Elmswell, 1466. R2/10/406
Ambrose, Newmarket, 1611. A5/3/109
Christopher, husb., Barnardiston, 1562. R2/31/15; W1/8/144
Cicely, wid., Cavendish, 1608. A5/3/49
David, clothier, Lavenham, 1695. R2/72/491; W1/149/49
Elisabeth, wid., Boxford, 1603. R2/45/241; W1/61/38
Elisabeth, wid., Newmarket, 1619. R2/51/450; W1/132/116
James, yeo., Herringswell, 1601. R2/44/431; W1/59/104b
John, yeo., Barnardiston, 1597. R2/43/339; W1/55/106
John, the elder, yeo., Barnardiston, 1611. R2/48/5; W1/68/23
John, Exning, 1583. A5/2/52
John, Herringswell, 1558. R2/27/558
John, als. Hawkyns, weaver, Lavenham, 1618. R2/51/14; W1/75/6
John, Withersfield, 1457. R2/9/221
Katherine, Little Thurlow, 1580. A5/2/23
Richard, Great Finborough, 1576. R2/37/144; W1/37/14; In. 3/1/106
Robert, Hundon, 1588. A5/2/112
Robert, Walsham le Willows, 1471. R2/10/470
Thomas, Barnardiston, 1553. R2/37/21; W1/13/14
Thomas, Kedington, 1608. A5/3/50
Thomas, Wood Ditton, 1698. W1/56/139
William, waterman, Burwell, 1671. R2/65/231; W1/123/107
SARESON, Thomas, Barningham, 1572. R2/36/22; W1/31/112
SARGANT, Emma, Great Finborough, 1582. R2/38/268; W1/41/74
Robert, tailor, Bury St. Edmunds, 1650. In. 3/3/92; A5/4/136
Robert, 1630, (N). R2/55/87; W1/86/95
Thomas, yeo., Hargrave, 1661. R2/62/251; W1/113/135; In. 3/6/191
SARGEANT, Faith, wid., Hargrave, 1644, (N). R2/59/81; W1/101/8
Mary, wid., Fordham, (1607). W1/111/33
Peter, yeo., Pakenham, 1624. R2/53/191; W1/80/164
Richard, the elder, husb., Fordham, 1607. R2/46/112; W1/97/13
Robert, yeo., Rougham, 1618. R2/51/240; W1/75/154
Thomas, Hargrave, 1641. R2/58/284; W1/98/70
Thomas, Snailwell, 1664. In. 3/9/74
William, Brettenham, 1558. R2/27/455
William, Norton, 1542. R2/22/83; W1/6/39
SARGENT, Abraham, sen., yeo., Hargrave, 1680. R2/67/770; W1/134/203
Andrew, the elder, clothworker, Mildenhall, 1612, (N). R2/48/131; W1/69/10
Gilbert, petty teacher, Bury St. Edmunds, 1578. R2/37/359; W1/36/216
John, Pakenham, 1662. In. 3/7/28; A5/5/27
Leonard, yeo., Coney Weston, 1599. R2/44/275; W1/57/78
Richard, blacksmith, Bury St. Edmunds, (1564). W1/17/13
Richard, Little Livermere, 1584. A5/2/59
Sara, wid. of Thomas, yeo., Bury St. Edmunds, 1670. R2/65/113; W1/122/135
Thomas, yeo., Bury St. Edmunds, 1670. R2/65/76; W1/122/94
Thomas, Stradishall, 1693. A5/6/163, A4/35/24
SARJEANT, John, Barrow, 1679. A5/6/28, A4/94/138
see also Sergant
SARLEY, Thomas, husb., Stanfield, 1574. W1/51/246
SARRE, Elisabeth, Great Wratting, 1632. A5/4/18
SARSON, Ann, wid., Wickhambrook, 1640. R2/58/135; W1/96/30
William, Bury St. Edmunds, 1633. A5/4/27
see also Sareson
SARTIE, Thomas, tailor, Ousden, 1641. R2/58/264; W1/98/38
SATCHFEILD, William, yeo., Wetherden, 1692. R2/72/80; W1/146/73
SATTEFAT, Andrew, yeo., Bardwell, 1681. R2/68/60; W1/135/47

SATTERFAT, Avice, wid., Coney Weston, 1615. R2/49/375; W1/72/143
Edward, Coney Weston, 1594. A5/2/199
SAULSBURIE, Joan, wid., Soham, 1589. R2/41/223; W1/46/64
SAULTER, Margaret, wid., Bildeston, 1585. W1/42/203
SAUNDER(S), John, draper, Brandon, 1554. R2/24/94; W1/14/72
John, Burgate, 1565. R2/32/353
Robert, Newton, 1688. A5/6/119, A4/29/29
Robert, Wangford, 1464. W1/24/123
Roger, Lidgate, 1697. A5/5/1, A4/40/11
Susan, wid., Bardwell, 1692. R2/72/3; W1/146/4
William, chandler, Bury St. Edmunds, 1557. R2/8/313; W1/18/42
William, blacksmith, Hengrave, 1648. R2/60/11; W1/105/15
see also Sawnder(s)
SAUNSON, Katherine, spinster, Bury St. Edmunds, 1469. R2/2/124
SAVAGE, Agnes, wid., Rickinghall Inferior, 1551. R2/23/47; W1/11/62
Walter, Barrow, 1612. A5/3/115
SAVEREY, William, mason, Bury St. Edmunds, 1432. R2/1/201 (probate only)
SAVERY, Alice, Chelsworth, 1580. A5/2/28
Ann, wid., Glemsford, 1557. R2/26/205; W1/20/150
Robert, Stansfield, 1497. R2/13/67
SAVILL, Henry, clothier, Stanstead, 1646. R2/59/316; W1/103/34
SAW, Elisabeth, Long Melford, 1649. R2/60/272
SAWARD, Joseph, plumber, Lavenham, 1686. R2/70/519; W1/140/121
see also Sayward
SAWEN, Margaret, Boxford, 1649. A5/4/126
Robert, Boxford, 1646. A5/4/113
see also Sawyn
SAWER, George, yeo., Wetheringsett, 1645. R2/59/174; W1/102/3
John, Thelnetham, 1503. R2/12/66
John, Wetherden, 1449. R2/9/95
Richard, Fordham, 1484. R2/11/301
Thomas, Great Whelnetham, 1668. A5/5/95, A4/6/56
Thomas, Thelnetham, 1458. R2/9/198
see also Sawyer
SAWGOR, John, Glemsford, 1480. R2/12/8
SAWKYNS, Edward, Hengrave, 1557. R2/26/269; W1/20/185
SAWLE, John, Nayland, 1480. R2/12/7
SAWLTER, John, cook, Bury St. Edmunds, 1576. R2/37/174; W1/37/38; In. 3/1/73
SAWMPSON, Thomas, Stansfield, 1452. R2/9/146 (probate only)
SAWNDER(S), Henry, clothier, Stanton, 1613. R2/48/294; W1/70/68
John, Bury St. Edmunds, 1610. A5/3/105
SAWNDRE, Edward, 1553. R2/31/193; W1/13/126
SAWNDYR, John, jun., Cheveley, (1464). R2/10/512
SAWNSUN, Laurence, Great Cornard, 1451. R2/9/134
SAWYER, George, als. Gylly, Bradfield St. George, 1476. R2/11/135
George, Brandon, 1591. A5/2/145
Gregory, Bildeston, 1534. R2/19/197
Jane, wid., Exning, 1589. A5/2/116
John, als. Gylly, Bradfield St. George, 1472. R2/10/529
John, Brockford, 1689. A5/6/128, A4/30/36
John, weaver, Ixworth, 1601. R2/44/434; W1/59/107
John, Lavenham, 1450. R2/9/104
Mary, wid. of John, blacksmith, Brockford, 1698. R2/73/238; W1/152/19; A5/7/9
Rose, Bury St. Edmunds, 1439. R2/1/239
Thomas, cordwainer, Bury St. Edmunds, 1437. R2/1/227
William, yeo., Great Horningsheath, 1633. R2/56/243; W1/90/5
William, husb., Whatfield, 1616. R2/50/112; W1/73/121
see also Sawer
SAWYN, Robert, Boxford, 1641. A5/4/93
SAXE, John, Eye, 1448. R2/9/94
SAXHAM, John, Bury St. Edmunds, 1355. R2/1/4
Roger, als. Taillour, Bury St. Edmunds, 1429. R2/9/187
Thomas, clerk, Bury St. Edmunds, 1364. R2/1/24
William, Bury St. Edmunds, 1386. R2/9/46
SAXIE, Augustine, Eye, 1573. R2/36/71; A5/1/260
Robert, yeo., Little Whelnetham, 1597. R2/43/366; W1/55/129
SAXSI, Clement, Eye, 1451. R2/9/133
SAXSY, John, Stanningfield, (1441). R2/9/44
see also Saxe

SAXTON, John, Burwell, 1458. W1/24/18
SAY(E), George, Soham, 1569. A5/1/210
James, Oakley, 1638. A5/4/67
Joan, wid., Newmarket, 1571. R2/35/179; W1/38/159
John, Newmarket, 1566. R2/32/339; W1/28/48
John, Newmarket, 1598. R2/44/83; W1/56/77
John, the elder, yeo., Redenhall, 1594. W1/51/132
Nicholas, Burwell, 1565. R2/32/168; W1/27/105
Roger, Bury St. Edmunds, 1393. R2/1/62
Thomas, Newmarket, 1606. R2/46/99; W1/64/119
William, chaplain, Bury St. Edmunds, 1400. R2/1/89
William, Wicken, 1474. R2/10/565
SAYARE, Joan, wid., Denston, 1539. R2/19/598
SAYDGE, John, Kirtling, 1569. A5/1/214
SAYER, Elizabeth, als. Mathew, Kersey, 1554. R2/24/130
Francis, 1625. W1/95/93
Jane, wid. of Richard, Bury St. Edmunds, 1643. R2/59/71; W1/100/82
John, yeo., Stanton, 1665. R2/63/281; W1/117/8; In. 3/10/44
John, cordwainer, Stowmarket, 1692. R2/72/44; W1/146/40; In. 3/24/87
Margaret, wid., Eye, 1695. A5/6/176; W4/38/6
Robert, yeo., Brome, 1683. R2/69/8; W1/137/8; In. 3/21/36
Thomas, singleman, Ixworth, 1668, (N). R2/64/380; W1/120/97
Thomas, Polstead, 1680. A5/6/35, A4/17/41
Thomas, Thorndon, 1640. A5/4/78
see also Saer, Sare, Sarre, Sayare, Seare, Seayr, Hawkins als. Saer, Hawkins als. Sare
SAYKYN, John, Bury St. Edmunds, 1396. R2/1/81
William, Thurston, 1478. R2/11/194
SAYWARD, William, plumber, Clare, 1678. R2/67/98; W1/130/82; In. 3/19/105
SCACE, Margaret, wid., Stanton, 1673. R2/65/436; W1/125/62
SCAEPIE, Thomas, slaughterman, Stowmarket, 1674. R2/66/3; W1/126/123
SCAFFE, John, the elder, yeo., Wortham, 1542. R2/22/84; W1/6/23
SCALDER, Margaret, wid., Sudbury, 1475. R2/11/90
see also Skalder
SCALPIE, Edward, Great Finborough, 1584. R2/39/141; W1/42/183
see also Skalpie
SCAPES, William, Combs, 1648. A5/4/122
SCAPY, Ann, Haughley, 1674. A5/5/147, A4/89/38
John, Combs, 1594. A5/2/203
Margaret, als. Lucas & Whiteing, wid., Stowmarket, 1683. A5/6/72, A4/20/93
see also Scaepie
SCARBOROUGH, John, Bures, 1639, (N). R2/58/24; W1/94/45
see also Skarburgh
SCARBOT, Thomas, webster, Bury St. Edmunds, 1415. R2/1/135
see also Skarbot
SCARFE, Augustin, husb., Stanton, 1630. R2/55/124; W1/86/139
George, wid., Thelnetham, 1662. In. 3/7/144; A5/5/33
Henry, husb., Bradfield Combust, 1642. R2/58/392; W1/99/106
Richard, Wattisfield, 1664. A4/2/113
Robert, Wattisfield, 1664. In. 3/9/225; A5/5/64
Roger, sen., Hinderclay, 1648. R2/60/123; W1/105/146
Susan, singlewoman, Thurston, 1692. R2/72/85; W1/146/79
Thomas, husb., Polstead, 1651. R2/61/484; W1/108/73
SCARLET(T), George, als. Poynter, Cavendish, 1610. A5/3/81
John, Nayland, 1571. A5/1/242
Mary, wid., Nayland, 1625. R2/53/421; W1/81/207
Mary, Nayland, 1640. A5/4/83
Philip, Bury St. Edmunds, 1642, (N). R2/58/345; W1/99/43
Thomas, shoe maker, Cavendish, 1606. R2/46/62; W1/64/86
see also Skarlett
SCARPE, Anthony, yeo., Bradfield Combust, 1691. R2/71/446
Cicely, wid., Brockley, 1665. In. 3/10/121; A5/5/68, A4/3/59
Elisabeth, singlewoman, Long Melford, 1568. R2/33/43; W1/29/53
Frances, wid., Felsham, 1636. R2/57/114; W1/92/138
George, yeo., Cockfield, 1693. R2/72/131
George, Hawstead, 1644. A5/4/106
George, Kettlebaston, 1665. In. 3/10/82; A5/5/67, A4/3/35
George, Layham, 1680. R2/67/535; W1/134/18; In. 3/20/19
Henry, yeo., Bradfield St. George, 1679. R2/67/363; W1/133/120

SCARPE continued
Joan, wid., Stanton, 1602. R2/45/174; W1/60/97
John, gent., Bradfield St. George, 1691. R2/71/477; W1/145/34
John, Rattlesden, 1646. R2/59/302; W1/103/21
John, Woolpit, 1567, (N). R2/32/418; W1/3/17
Martin, the elder, yeo., Great Whelnetham, 1666. R2/64/141; W1/118/110; In. 3/12/51
Mary, wid., Bradfield St. Clare, 1691. R2/71/448
Mary, wid., Great Whelnetham, 1692. R2/72/179
Rachael, wid., Rattlesden, 1674. R2/66/74; W1/126/47
Robert, yeo., Shimpling, 1669. R2/64/456; W1/121/44; In. 3/14/34
Thomas, singleman, Felsham, 1636. R2/57/71; W1/92/82
Thomas, tailor, Rattlesden, 1684. R2/69/358; W1/138/147
William, wid., Chelsworth, 1675. R2/66/231; W1/127/100; In. 3/16/128
William, Felsham, 1470. R2/10/482
William, Felsham, 1681. A5/6/55, A4/18/135
William, Gedding, 1559. R2/28/58; W1/22/62
see also Skarpe, Skerppe, Bentlie als. Scarpe
SCASE, Henry, Stanton, 1675. In. 3/16/100; A5/5/150, A4/11/69
Henry, husb., Wortham, 1613. R2/48/292; W1/70/65
Richard, husb., Wattisfield, 1667. R2/64/281; W1/119/145; In. 3/12/72
Robert, Stanton, 1665. R2/63/284; W1/117/13; In. 3/10/11
Robert, carpenter, Thrandeston, 1661. R2/62/228; W1/113/98; In. 3/6/145
William, yeo., Walsham le Willows, 1690. R2/71/307; W1/144/8
see also Scace, Skace
SCATERON, John, Elmswell, 1457. R2/9/203
see also Skateron
SCELIE, John, husb., Dalham, 1608. R2/46/209; W1/65/96
SCENDALL, Elisabeth, Saxham, (1677). W1/312/23
SCEPPYE, Thomas, timber man, Bury St. Edmunds, 1559. R2/8/348; W1/17/62 & 63 (and inventory)
SCHAFTYNG, Richard, Bury St. Edmunds, 1450. R2/2/33
SCHALDEFORD, Thomas, fuller, Bury St. Edmunds, 1415. R2/1/135
SCHALFORD, John, carpenter, Bury St. Edmunds, 1444. R2/2/13
Thomas, weaver, Bury St. Edmunds, 1443. R2/2/3
SCHANK, Agnes, (1449). W1/24/4
SCHAPMAN, John, cordwainer, Bury St. Edmunds, 1394. R2/1/71
John, Withersfield, 1471. R2/10/491
SCHARDELOWE, Joan, Bury St. Edmunds, 1382. R2/9/44
SCHARPE, Alice, Felsham, 1483. R2/11/317
John, Felsham, 1479. W1/24/55
John, yeo., Lavenham, 1548. W1/9/74
John, yeo., Wickhambrook, 1550. R2/21/64; W1/9/142
Richard, Hessett, 1537. R2/20/8
SCHAWCROSSE, Robert, Newmarket, 1532. R2/19/98; W1/3/119
SCHEDDE, William, Lavenham, 1469. R2/10/412
SCHELDRAKE, William, Waldingfield, 1441. R2/9/31a
SCHELFHANGYR, Christine, wife of William, Bury St. Edmunds, 1404. R2/1/101
SCHELTON, William, Stowmarket, 1462. R2/10/342
SCHELYNG, John, Lavenham, 1476. R2/11/63
SCHENE, Thomas, husb., Mildenhall, 1610. R2/47/281; W1/67/165
SCHEP, John, Woolpit, 1439. R2/9/2
SCHEPERDE, Thomas, Rickinghall Superior, 1503. R2/12/68
SCHEPEY, John, husb., Little Thornham, 1540. R2/19/615; W1/5/25
SCHERCROFT, Thomas, rector, Icklingham, 1474. R2/11/42
SCHERDE, Ralph, Cavendish, 1495. R2/13/50
SCHEREWYND, Robert, cordwainer, Bury St. Edmunds, 1446. R2/2/18
SCHERMAN, Geoffrey, Bury St. Edmunds, 1410. R2/1/121
SCHERPE, John, Stowmarket, 1552. R2/23/59; W1/11/109
SCHERWYN, Robert, Great Barton, 1524. R2/17/72; W1/21/19
SCHET, John, Boxford, 1521. R2/14/135
SCHIERCROFT, John, husb., Lackford, 1528. R2/15/207, R2/17/281; W1/19/22
SCHILLYNG, Margaret, wid., Lavenham, 1479. W1/24/35
SCHIRWODE, Joan, Bury St. Edmunds, 1442. R2/1/266
SCHOFILD, Ellen, wid., Stowlangtoft, 1621. R2/52/215; W1/77/13
SCHOLVER, Roger, 1579. R2/38/11; W1/39/67
SCHOMERE, John, Layham, 1445. R2/9/68
SCHORTH, John, yeo., Thorndon, 1529. R2/18/30
SCHORTHOSE, Thomas, Sudbury, 1459. R2/9/235
SCHOTTE, John, labouring man, Mildenhall, 1587. R2/40/209; W1/44/63

SCHOUTHAR, Geoffrey, Mellis, 1451. R2/9/107
SCHREVEYN, Henry, Bury St. Edmunds, 1402. R2/1/96
SCHUCFORD, Robert, Thelnetham, 1452. R2/9/110
SCHURLOKKE, John, Eriswell, 1477. R2/11/66
SCHYPLEY, Thomas, Sudbury, 1539. R2/20/9
SCHYRLOK, John, Cheveley, 1452. R2/9/153
SCHYWODE, William, Bury St. Edmunds, 1386. R2/1/48
SCOFEILD, Henry, labourer, Stowlangtoft, 1615, (N). R2/49/379; W1/72/146c
Thomas, Bury St. Edmunds, 1643. A5/4/98
William, cordwainer, Hargrave, 1691. A5/6/139, A4/33/12
see also Schofild, Skofeild
SCOLE, William, Sudbury, 1526. R2/17/199; W1/23/33
SCOOPES, William, collar maker, Combs, 1649. R2/60/237; W1/106/91
SCOOT(E), John, Hopton, 1459. R2/9/264
Robert, husb., Great Whelnetham, 1667. R2/64/201; W1/119/49; In. 3/12/63
William, yeo., Barnardiston, 1648. R2/60/5; W1/105/8
SCOTCHMER(E), Ann, wid., Rishangles, 1684. R2/69/189; W1/138/2
John, Thwaite, 1661. In. 3/6/73; A5/5/14, A4/1/111
Mary, Stowupland, 1669. A5/5/105, A4/7/42
William, yeo., Stowupland, 1672. R2/65/291; W1/124/8
SCOTCHMORE, John, husb., Layham, 1573. R2/36/193; W1/32/118
Thomas, wid., Stowmarket, 1679. A5/6/27, A4/16/127
see also Scothmer, Skottysmore
SCOTE, John, sawyer, Hundon, 1687. R2/70/379; W1/141/101
Robert, yeo., Fordham, 1684. R2/69/364; W1/138/153
SCOTEN, Peter, Stoke by Nayland, 1529. R2/15/199
SCOTHMER, William, tailor, Stowupland, 1645. R2/59/235; W1/102/59
SCOTT, Aggis, als. Gamblyn, Fordham, 1632. A5/4/18
Ambrose, Glemsford, 1668. In. 3/13/134; A5/5/96, A4/6/66
Amy, wid., Glemsford, 1620. R2/52/12; W1/76/12
Andrew, yeo., Glemsford, 1618. R2/51/244; W1/75/159
Ann, wid., Bury St. Edmunds, 1667. In. 3/12/59; A5/5/80, A4/81/4
Ann, als. Wright, Clare, 1642. A5/4/97
Anne, singlewoman, Bradfield St. George, 1639, (N). R2/58/21; W1/94/37
Austin, yeo., Chippenham, 1650. R2/61/356; W1/107/53
Avery, wid., Hundon, 1661. R2/62/195; W1/113/56; In. 3/6/74
Bartholomew, Haverhill, 1607. R2/46/114; W1/97/18
Clement, yeo., Great Thurlow, 1662. R2/62/429; W1/114/194; In. 3/7/258
Edmund, husb., Clare, 1571. R2/35/241
Edmund, yeo., Cowlinge, 1664. R2/63/161; W1/116/57; In. 3/9/63
Edmund, yeo., Wickhambrook, 1573. R2/36/150; W1/32/56
Edward, gent., Clare, 1640. R2/58/125; W1/96/8
Edward, Cowlinge, 1623, (N). R2/52/598; W1/79/48
Edward, the elder, Cowlinge, 1652. A5/4/142
Edward, yeo., Cowlinge, 1699. In. 3/26/25; A5/7/10, A4/41/1
Elisabeth, wid., Bradfield St. George, 1684. R2/69/415; W1/138/194
Elisabeth, wid., Horningsheath, 1606. A5/3/12
Elisabeth, wid., Long Melford, 1638. A5/4/60
George, tailor, Boxford, 1644, (N). R2/59/89; W1/101/19
George, Bradfield St. George, 1579. R2/38/80; W1/39/2
George, yeo., Gedding, 1629. R2/54/327; W1/85/36
George, yeo., Glemsford, 1602. R2/45/199; W1/60/128
George, yeo., Lavenham, 1696. R2/73/71; W1/150/85
George, yeo., Somerton, 1637. R2/57/136; W1/92/169
George, Somerton, 1666. In. 3/11/91; A5/5/75, A4/4/32
George, husb., Wiston, 1632, (N). R2/56/162; W1/89/68
Henry, yeo., Bradfield St. George, 1664. R2/63/167; W1/116/64; In. 3/9/87
Henry, Hartest, 1571. A5/1/239
Henry, Isleham, 1690. W7/117; In. 9/76
James, singleman, Chippenham, 1597. R2/43/263; W1/55/41
James, mason, Tostock, 1628. R2/54/170; W1/84/44
Jane, wid., Glemsford, 1736, (N). R2/57/139; W1/92/173
Jeremiah, Long Melford, 1638. A5/4/60
Joan, wid., Haverhill, 1628. R2/54/156; W1/84/28
John, singleman, Boxted, 1605. R2/45/471; W1/63/122
John, Bradley, 1673. A5/5/136, A4/10/9
John, yeo., Brettenham, 1681. R2/68/191; W1/135/140

SCOTT continued
John, Burgate, 1576. W1/37/19
John, yeo., Burgate, 1600. R2/45/16; W1/58/31
John, Great Finborough, 1574. R2/37/37; W1/33/44; A5/1/271
John, Great Whelnetham, 1669. In. 3/14/19; A5/5/103, A4/7/22
John, yeo., Lawshall, 1689. R2/71/146; W1/143/5
John, the elder, yeo., Troston, 1689. R2/71/246; W1/143/87
John, Tuddenham, 1633. A5/4/23
Margaret, Glemsford, 1609. A5/3/76
Margaret, wid., Great Bradley, 1675. In. 3/16/97; A5/5/156, A4/12/44
Margaret, wid., Soham, 1613. R2/48/334; W1/70/117
Matthew, gent., Hawstead, 1696. R2/73/91; W1/150/107
Nicholas, Stanton, 1681. A5/6/50, A4/18/76
Osmond, singleman, Brettenham, 1697. R2/73/157; W1/151/43
Richard, clothier, Glemsford, 1565. R2/32/171; W1/27/108
Richard, yeo., Glemsford, 1584. R2/39/155; W1/42/167
Richard, singleman, Hartest, 1685. A5/6/87, A4/24/10
Richard, Honington, 1684. A5/6/77, A4/21/36
Robert, husb., Boxted, 1635, (N). R2/56/473; W1/91/44; A5/4/36
Robert, Bradfield, 1559. R2/28/252; W1/22/244
Robert, tailor, Bury St. Edmunds, 1405. R2/1/105
Robert, inn holder, Bury St. Edmunds, 1648. R2/60/128; W1/105/152
Robert, inn holder, Bury St. Edmunds, 1662. R2/62/428; W1/114/193; In. 3/7/255
Robert, husb., Chippenham, 1596. R2/43/202; W1/54/72
Robert, yeo., Cockfield, 1625. R2/53/381; W1/81/158
Robert, yeo., Cockfield, 1660. R2/62/123; W1/112/166; In. 3/5/183
Robert, labourer, Fornham St. Martin, 1687. R2/70/337; W1/141/75
Robert, the elder, wheelwright, Hessett, 1638. R2/57/414; W1/93/236
Robert, husb., Little Bradley, 1673. R2/65/484; W1/125/123
Robert, husb., Little Waldingfield, 1638. R2/57/424; W1/93/258
Robert, Pakenham, 1650. In. 3/3/64; A5/4/134
Robert, the elder, butcher, Stanton, 1652. R2/61/567; W1/109/42
Robert, bricklayer, Wickhambrook, 1600. R2/45/58; W1/58/82
Roger, wheelwright, Rattlesden, 1677. R2/66/445; W1/129/19; In. 3/18/43
Samuel, inn holder, Ballingdon, 1684. R2/69/299; W1/138/94
Thomas, Cavendish, 1610. A5/3/107
Thomas, Glemsford, 1529. R2/18/9
Thomas, Haverhill, 1632. A5/4/20
Thomas, yeo., Hessett, 1596, (N). R2/43/163; W1/54/43; A5/3/221
Thomas, yeo., Pakenham, 1651. R2/61/485; W1/108/75
Thomasine, wid., Cowlinge, 1662, (N). R2/62/331; W1/114/39; In. 3/7/35; A5/5/27, A4/2/51
William, Beyton, 1667. In. 3/12/137; A5/5/89, A4/5/82
William, tailor, Chippenham, 1661. R2/62/173; W1/113/26; In. 3/6/28
William, husb., Clare, 1625. R2/53/356; W1/81/135
William, Great Thornham, 1643. A5/4/100
William, tailor, Soham, (1613). W1/111/54
William, Wattisham, 1674. A5/5/147, A4/11/25
William, Wickhambrook, 1554. R2/24/2; W1/14/3
see also Scote, Scutt, Skott, Barnes als. Scott, Brook als. Scott, Hill als. Scott
SCRAGG, Margaret, wid., Long Melford, 1692. R2/72/108; W1/146/99; In. 3/24/27
Richard, Long Melford, 1673. A5/5/136, A4/10/11
SCREFYNE, Thomas, Stradishall, 1546. R2/21/244; W1/10/95
SCREVENER, John, Wickhambrook, 1462. R2/9/290
SCREVIN, Alice, Stradishall, 1558. R2/27/470
SCREVYN(E), Alexander, Stradishall, 1560. A5/1/104
Alice, wid., Wickhambrook, 1548. W1/8/32
SCRIVEN, Richard, gent., Stradishall, 1636. R2/57/81; W1/92/99
see also Schreveyn, Screfyne, Screvin, Skryveyn
SCRIVENER, John, Bury St. Edmunds, 1610. A5/3/89
Robert, broad weaver, Nayland, 1638. R2/57/302; W1/93/75
Robert, say worker, Stoke by Nayland, 1641. R2/58/261; W1/98/35
Thomas, Bures, 1695. A5/6/179, A4/38/41
see also Screvener, Skrevener
SCROGGS, John, husb., Brandon, 1616. R2/50/131; W1/73/137
SCROOPE, Henry, husb., Mildenhall, 1631, (N). R2/56/102; W1/87/166
SCROOTON, John, mercer, Bildeston, 1539. R2/19/290

SCRUTTON, John, husb., Culford, 1650. R2/61/362; W1/107/58; In. 3/3/73
Richard, yeo., Stowupland, 1700. R2/74/91; W1/154/94; In. 3/27/55
SCUDAMORE, George, carpenter, Newmarket, 1678. In. 3/19/170; A5/6/11, A4/15/95
SCULTHORPE, George, Bury St. Edmunds, 1680. In. 3/20/146; A5/6/38, A4/17/72
George, yeo., Thurston, 1660. R2/62/147; W1/112/191; In. 3/5/209; A5/5/9, A4/1/163
Thomas, Thurston, 1677. In. 3/18/81; A5/5/166, A4/14/4
William, Kennett, 1677. R2/66/459; W1/129/38; In. 3/18/80
see also Skolthorpe
SCULTOCK, John, linen weaver, Bury St. Edmunds, 1604, (N). R2/45/307
John, the elder, yeo., Euston, 1649. R2/60/239; W1/106/97
Robert, the elder, Sapiston, 1686. R2/70/264; W1/140/31; In. 3/22/42
William, weaver, Bury St. Edmunds, 1551. R2/8/229
SCUTT, Ann, singlewoman, Thrandeston, 1678. R2/67/171; W1/130/151; In. 3/19/210
Gilbert, Bury St. Edmunds, 1444. R2/2/8
John, Bury St. Edmunds, 1604. R2/45/327; W1/62/38
Thomas, Soham, 1444. R2/9/45
SEABROOK(E), John, Cowlinge, 1699. In. 3/26/20; A5/7/11, A4/41/19
Thomas, gent., Barnardiston, 1661. R2/62/234; W1/113/106; In. 3/6/141
SEADON, Daniel, joiner, Ixworth, 1665. R2/63/349; W1/117/104
Martin, hosier, Bury St. Edmunds, 1669. R2/64/562; W1/121/151; In. 3/14/143
SEAGAR, John, miller, Cavendish, 1639, (N). R2/58/21; W1/94/35
SEAGER, John, bay maker, Stanstead, 1602. R2/45/114; W1/60/28
see also Segar, Seger, Segore, Segyr, Barker als. Segar
SEAGO(E), John, Barton, 1697. A5/7/1, A4/40/18
John, Pakenham, 1681, (N). R2/68/56; W1/135/44; A5/6/46, A4/18/31
see also Sego(e), Sigo, Sygo
SEAGRAVE, Robert, yeo., Brettenham, 1660. R2/62/118; W1/112/159; In. 3/5/162
see also Segrave
SEALE, Henry, yeo., Great Livermere, 1680. R2/67/694; W1/134/145; In. 3/20/165
see also Seele
SEALLER, Richard, Haughley, 1606. R2/46/27; W1/64/32
SEAMAN, Ann, wid., Bacton, 1684. A5/6/84, A4/21/114
Anthony, yeo., Bacton, 1680. R2/67/734; W1/134/175; In. 3/20/11
Christine, singlewoman, Wattisfield, 1634, (N). R2/56/429; W1/90/213
Cicely, Walsham le Willows, 1631. A5/4/12
Edmund, yeo., Rickinghall Inferior, 1639. R2/58/46; W1/94/84
Edmund, clerk, Wortham, 1645. A5/4/110
George, the elder, yeo., Bradfield Combust, 1595. R2/43/40; W1/53/32
George, yeo., Palgrave, 1649. R2/60/261; W1/106/123
Gilbert, singleman, Mendlesham, 1634. R2/56/324; W1/90/90
Jane, wid., Wattisfield, 1617. R2/50/209; W1/74/2
John, Hinderclay, 1669. R2/64/513; W1/121/106; In. 3/14/91
John, yeo., Mendlesham, 1606. R2/46/101; W1/64/122
John, jun., Rickinghall Inferior, 1664. A5/5/64, A4/2/112
John, grocer, Stanton, 1680. R2/67/572; W1/134/52; In. 3/20/54
John, grocer, Stanton, 1683. R2/69/61; W1/137/46
John, yeo., Thelnetham, 1645. R2/59/225; W1/102/51
John, yeo., Thelnetham, 1680. R2/67/656; W1/134/118; In. 3/20/125
John, the elder, yeo., Wattisfield, 1627. R2/54/23; W1/83/30
Margaret, Bacton, 1644. A5/4/102
Ralph, smith, Bury St. Edmunds, 1634. R2/56/424; W1/90/208
Ralph, Great Thurlow, 1687. A5/6/108, A4/108/12
Ralph, tailor, Stowmarket, 1690. R2/71/325; W1/144/27
Richard, Wiston, 1636. A5/4/46
Robert, citizen of London, fishmonger, Rickinghall Inferior, 1650. R2/61/381; W1/107/83
Roger, yeo., Botesdale, 1641. R2/58/281; W1/98/65
Samuel, woollen draper, Botesdale, 1693. R2/72/266; W1/147/154
Stephen, bach., Stanton, 1681. A5/6/44, A4/18/8
Thomas, singleman, Bacton, 1638. R2/57/323; W1/93/102
Thomas, yeo., Rickinghall Inferior, 1642. R2/58/317; W1/99/3
Thomas, sen., Stanton, 1690. A5/6/134, A4/32/28

SEAMAN continued
William, yeo., Bacton, 1638. R2/57/246; W1/93/6
William, husb., Coney Weston, 1590. R2/41/356; W1/47/53
William, yeo., Cotton, 1639. R2/58/31; W1/94/56
William, yeo., Rickinghall Inferior, 1644. R2/59/106; W1/101/33
William, yeo., West Creeting, 1645. R2/59/226; W1/102/52
SEAMON, Roger, the elder, yeo., Rickinghall Inferior, 1624. R2/53/50; W1/80/74
William, Cotton, 1647. A5/4/118
see also Seman, Semman, Seymon
SEARE, Thomas, the younger, clothier, Boxford, 1598. R2/44/57
Thomas, the younger, Boxford, 1598. R2/44/153; W1/56/48
SEARGENT, Thomas, Little Bradley, 1608. A5/3/45
William, husb., Norton, 1583. R2/39/112; W1/42/7
SEARLES, John, linen weaver, Hopton, 1679. R2/67/483; W1/133/202
Thomas, the elder, yeo., Occold, 1671. R2/65/226; W1/123/100
see also Serle
SEAWELL, Thomas, Great Thornham, 1661. R2/62/173; W1/113/27; In. 3/6/37
SEAYR, Robert, Mildenhall, 1630. A5/4/4
SEBOROWE, John, Little Cornard, 1540. R2/19/611
SECKER, John, Elveden, 1537. R2/20/1 & 15; W1/4/9
John, Elveden, 1537. R2/19/576; W1/3/7
Richard, shearman, Bury St. Edmunds, 1595, (N). R2/43/71; W1/53/59
Robert, yeo., Lakenheath, 1692. R2/72/68; W1/146/66; In. 3/24/84
Thomas, clothier, Great Waldingfield, 1639. R2/58/52; W1/94/97
see also Sekker
SEDDON, Mercy, wid., Walsham le Willows, 1636. R2/57/9; W1/92/13
see also Seadon
SEDEMAN, Robert, Wangford, 1551. R2/23/51
SEELE, Joan, Brettenham, 1569. W1/19/123
SEELEY, Susan, spinster, Dalham, 1696. A5/6/190, A4/39/78
SEELY, Clement, tailor, Dalham, 1671. R2/65/150; W1/123/10
James, carpenter, Gazeley, 1663. In. 3/8/144; A5/5/48
John, singleman, Denston, 1668. In. 3/13/121; A5/5/95, A4/6/61
John, Denston, 1670. A5/5/117
Richard, miller, Denston, 1648. R2/60/84; W1/105/102
Richard, Denston, 1670. In. 3/15/173
Robert, Dalham, 1633. A5/4/23
Timothy, yeo., Dalham, 1664. R2/63/219; W1/116/131; In. 3/9/184
see also Ceelie, Cely, Scelie, Seley, Selye
SEFFERY, George, Great Barton, 1604. W1/62/92
Josias, yeo., Stradishall, 1670. R2/65/98; W1/122/120; In. 3/15/147
Samuel, Groton, 1640. A5/4/86
see also Seffray
SEFFORTHE, Thomas, chaplain, Bury St. Edmunds, 1467. R2/2/109
SEFFRAY, Thomas, shop keeper, Hundon, 1692. In. 3/24/55; A5/6/151, A4/34/42
Thomas, husb., Hunston, 1582. R2/38/379; W1/41/60
SEFFREY, John, sen., Bardwell, 1493. R2/11/447
John, the elder, Bardwell, 1499. R2/13/102
John, Great Horningsheath, 1541. R2/22/99; W1/10/4
Robert, Bury St. Edmunds, 1529. R2/6/160
Rose, Great Horningsheath, 1540. W1/5/11
Thomas, Bardwell, 1521. R2/15/107
William, the elder, Bardwell, 1504. R2/13/111
SEGAR, Henry, yeo., Stowlangtoft, 1669. R2/64/488; W1/121/82
Richard, inn holder, Sudbury, 1623. R2/52/536; W1/79/1
SEGBROOK, John, Stowmarket, 1471. R2/10/479
SEGER, John, Tuddenham, 1468. R2/10/413
Robert, inn holder, Sudbury, 1588. R2/41/7; W1/45/5b
William, Lavenham, 1488. R2/11/431
SEGGAR, John, Wickhambrook, 1580. A5/2/22
SEGGES, Robert, Sudbury, 1583. A5/2/46
SEGO(E), John, yeo., Blakenham, 1604. R2/45/328; W1/62/39
John, labourer, Hawstead, 1600. R2/45/55; W1/58/76
John, Pakenham, 1620. R2/52/80; W1/76/68
John, husb., Rougham, 1620. R2/52/129; W1/76/114
Peter, Ixworth, 1578. A5/2/10
SEGORE, William, Stradishall, 1465. R2/10/393

SEGRAVE, Abednego, yeo., Great Waldingfield, 1670. R2/65/4; W1/122/5
Michael, yeo., Boxted, 1610. R2/47/192; W1/67/71
Rose, wid., Hartest, 1619. R2/51/464; W1/132/127
SEGYR, John, Cowlinge, (1458). R2/11/412
SEKKER, Christopher, priest, Bury St. Edmunds, 1503. R2/4/124
Thomas, weaver, Bury St. Edmunds, 1496. R2/4/47
SEKYLMER, Thomas, Bacton, 1523. R2/17/38; W1/21/49
SELBY, Martin, yeo., Great Wratting, 1624. R2/53/14; W1/80/22
SELERS, Agnes, Bury St. Edmunds, 1498. R2/4/70
SELEY, Henry, miller, Lidgate, 1605. R2/45/405; W1/63/49
SELIE, Edward, Soham, 1591. A5/2/153
SELL, Leonard, priest, Bury St. Edmunds, 1536. R2/7/38
SELLAR, John, say weaver, Bury St. Edmunds, 1677. R2/66/475; W1/129/56
see also Sealler, Selers
SELLET, ---, wid. of Henry, Horringer, 1670. In. 3/15/110
SELLOND, Joan, wid., 1583, (N). R2/39/72; W1/42/37 (and inventory)
see also Selond
SELLOWES, Ann, als. Smith, singlewoman, Great Finborough, 1639, (N).
R2/58/92; W1/94/156
John, yeo., Great Finborough, 1608. R2/46/169; W1/65/24
John, yeo., Great Finborough, 1641. R2/58/256; W1/98/28
Robert, yeo., Great Finborough, 1592. R2/42/199; W1/49/24
Thomas, als. Smythe, Buxhall, 1596. R2/43/213; W1/54/52
Winifred, singlewoman, Bury St. Edmunds, 1653, (N). W1/110/43
see also Selos, Selowes, Smith als. Sellowes
SELLYNG, Agnes, Bury St. Edmunds, 1458. R2/2/57
SELOND, Robert, Bury St. Edmunds, 1512. R2/5/16
SELOS, John, Great Finborough, 1493. R2/11/444
SELOTT, Isabel, wid., Bardwell, 1486. R2/11/320
Robert, Bury St. Edmunds, 1422. R2/1/159
John, tailor, Bardwell, 1485. R2/11/328; W1/24/52
John, the elder, Bardwell, 1545. R2/19/544
SELOWES, William, woollen weaver, Stowmarket, 1587. R2/40/243;
W1/44/83
SELOWSE, Thomas, als. Smith, yeo., Great Finborough, 1568. R2/33/4;
W1/29/10
SELYE, Thomas, Denham, 1548. R2/21/422
SEMAN, Anne, wid. of James, Eye, 1561. R2/30/4; W1/28/206
Anne, wid., Great Wratting, 1614. R2/49/71; W1/71/55
Augustine, Eye, 1557. R2/26/31; W1/20/16
Charles, Mendlesham, 1591. A5/2/152
Elisabeth, Bury St. Edmunds, 1470. R2/2/132
Henry, Barnardiston, 1571. R2/35/253
James, mercer, Eye, 1557. R2/26/117; W1/20/69
John, Acton, 1559. R2/28/12; W1/22/16
John, Bury St. Edmunds, 1462. R2/2/72
John, sen., Drinkstone, 1463. R2/10/311
John, yeo., Great Wratting, 1613. R2/48/334; W1/70/118
John, yeo., Mendlesham, 1626. R2/53/604; W1/82/130
John, Stoke by Nayland, 1559. R2/28/16; W1/22/21
Margaret, wid., Wetheringsett, 1559. R2/28/14; W1/22/18
Margery, Stanton, 1579. A5/2/17
Peter, Barnardiston, 1595. R2/43/76; W1/53/68
Ralph, baker, Stowmarket, 1665. R2/63/319; W1/117/58; In. 3/13/28
Robert, Coney Weston, 1557. R2/26/273; W1/20/191
Roger, Bury St. Edmunds, 1471. R2/2/147
Roger, Drinkstone, 1479. R2/11/236
Thomas, glover, Bury St. Edmunds, 1572. R2/36/10; W1/31/131
Thomas, ploughwright, Hinderclay, 1608. R2/46/170; W1/65/26
Thomas, yeo., Rickinghall Inferior, 1586. R2/40/43; W1/43/31
Thomas, Thelnetham, 1442. R2/9/39
Thomas, the elder, yeo., Walsham le Willows, 1619. R2/51/266;
W1/132/9
Thomas, Woolpit, (1507). R2/13/192
William, tailor, Bury St. Edmunds, (1557). R2/8/319; W1/18/50
William, Eye, 1477. R2/11/43
William, Little Cornard, 1447. R2/9/75
William, the elder, husb., Mendlesham, 1558. R2/27/95
SEMANCROFTH, John, Redgrave, 1464. R2/10/367
SEMAR, Alice, wid., Hawstead, 1552. R2/23/166; W1/12/7
Robert, labourer, Little Whelnetham, 1550. R2/21/55; W1/8/83
SEMARKE, Henry, freemason, Bury St. Edmunds, 1534. R2/7/21

SEMER, Nicholas, Sudbury, 1482. R2/11/259
SEMMAN, Robert, Thorndon, 1693. R2/72/172
SEMPER, John, Bury St. Edmunds, 1506. R2/4/178
SEMYCROFT, Robert, Bury St. Edmunds, 1519. R2/6/58
see also Semancrofth
SENDALL, Daniel, Stoke by Nayland, 1690. A5/6/136, A4/32/53
John, Stoke by Nayland, 1676. In. 3/17/27; A5/5/160, A4/13/13
Roger, yeo., Assington, 1578. R2/37/422; W1/36/151
SENDELL, Robert, clerk, Cheveley, 1623. R2/52/611; W1/79/58
SENEKERE, Henry, Bury St. Edmunds, 1364. R2/1/25
SENGELTON, Elisabeth, wid. of William, Walsham le Willows, 1559. R2/28/15; W1/22/19
SENGENS, see Saintgenes als. Sengens
SENGYLTON, Thomas, Stowmarket, 1437. W1/24/144
SENNOW, William, Bury St. Edmunds, 1482. R2/2/337
SENOWE, Christian, wid., Bury St. Edmunds, 1498. R2/4/63
SENTER, John, Sudbury, 1585. R2/39/244; W1/42/329
SENTWYN, Alice, Burwell, 1547. R2/21/292
SENYHALL, see Wylling als. Senyhall
SEPHAR, Alice, Barnham, 1457. R2/9/183
SERGANT, Robert, Stoke by Nayland, 1667. R2/64/211; W1/119/61; In. 3/12/70
SERGAUNT, Nicholas, Thurston, 1490. R2/11/454
Thomas, Norton, 1492. R2/13/4
William, yeo., Brandon, 1582. R2/38/412; W1/41/22
William, Lawshall, 1490. R2/13/10
---, Thurston, 1482. R2/13/13
SERGEANT, Andrew, the elder, clothworker, Mildenhall, 1662. R2/62/328; W1/114/35; In. 3/7/55
Anne, wid., Long Melford, 1617. R2/50/266; W1/74/66
Edmund, the elder, Coney Weston, 1618, (N). R2/51/229; W1/75/145
Elisabeth, wid., Hopton, 1684. A5/6/84, A4/21/105
John, the elder, husb., Pakenham, 1559. R2/28/136
John, yeo., Pakenham, 1610. R2/47/186; W1/67/63
John, husb., Stradishall, 1631. R2/56/24; W1/87/31
Philemon, wid., Bury St. Edmunds, 1678. A5/6/14, A4/15/118
Philippa, spinster, Mildenhall, 1691. A5/6/143, A4/33/53
Thomas, wid., Bury St. Edmunds, 1679. A5/6/20, A4/16/57
Thomas, yeo., Fordham, 1664. R2/63/149; W1/116/39
Thomas, yeo., Fordham, 1688. R2/71/54; W1/142/49; In. 3/23/9
Thomas, husb., Thorpe, 1550. R2/21/123; W1/9/93
SERGEAUNT, John, chandler, Bury St. Edmunds, 1496. R2/4/78
Nicholas, Bury St. Edmunds, 1503. R2/4/138
Roger, Thurston, 1503. R2/13/139
SERGENT, Henry, yeo., Hopton, 1667. In. 3/12/45; A5/5/83, A4/5/72
Robert, Burwell, 1566. R2/32/348; W1/28/33
Thomas, Little Bradley, 1608, (N). R2/46/180; W1/65/44
SERIANT, Giles, Lawshall, (1532). R2/19/88 & 182
Richard, husb., Great Thornham, 1608. R2/46/191; W1/65/56
SERIAUNT, Agnes, wid., Bury St. Edmunds, 1507. R2/4/192
Richard, labourer, Bury St. Edmunds, 1447. R2/2/21
William, Pakenham, 1503. R2/13/131
SERIAWNT, John, Thurston, 1546. R2/21/250; W1/10/48
Nicholas, Drinkstone, 1520. R2/15/73
William, Stoke by Nayland, 1441. R2/9/34
SERJEANT, Edmund, yeo., Coney Weston, 1662. R2/63/27; W1/115/43; In. 3/8/50
Edward, husb., Exning, 1692. R2/72/99; W1/146/91; In. 3/24/15
Phyllis, wid., Stradishall, 1631. R2/56/47; W1/87/65
see also Sargant, Seargent, Sergant, Sirgant
SERLE, John, Great Wratting, 1458. R2/9/262
John, Hundon, 1458. R2/9/198
John, Stanton, 1452. R2/9/139
SEROKE, Joan, wid., Eye, 1567, (N). R2/32/380; W1/3/13
SETON, Felicity, wid., Bury St. Edmunds, 1509. R2/4/203 (admon. only)
SEUELES, John, Great Finborough, (1550). R2/21/58; W1/8/82
SEUELLE, Gregory, Bury St. Edmunds, 1471. R2/2/143
SEWALE, Agnes, wid., Bury St. Edmunds, 1464. R2/2/79
James, saddler, Bury St. Edmunds, 1454. R2/2/46
James, saddler, Bury St. Edmunds, 1484. R2/2/199
John, barber, Bury St. Edmunds, 1444. R2/2/14
John, cordwainer, Stowmarket, 1455. R2/9/228

SEWALE continued
John, Stowmarket, 1481. R2/11/195
Katherine, wid., Bury St. Edmunds, 1476. R2/2/224
Robert, Great Barton, 1465. R2/10/391
Robert, Hinderclay, 1505. R2/12/43
Roger, Bury St. Edmunds, 1403. R2/1/97
Thomas, Bury St. Edmunds, 1386. R2/1/47
SEWALL, William, Hopton, 1544. R2/21/589
SEWELL, Alexander, yeo., Braiseworth, 1667. R2/64/197; W1/119/42; In. 3/12/36
Edward, husb., Hepworth, 1673. R2/65/464; W1/125/99
Elisabeth, wid., Ixworth Thorpe, 1612. R2/48/191; W1/69/78
Frances, husb., Thelnetham, 1640. R2/58/180; W1/96/99
Henry, Botesdale, 1608. A5/3/40
John, Redgrave, 1607. A5/2/36
John, yeo., Ixworth Thorpe, 1612. R2/48/127; W1/69/5
Luke, husb., Thelnetham, 1638. R2/57/369; W1/93/170
Mary, wid., Chevington, 1663. R2/63/10; W1/115/19; In. 3/8/19
Peter, Sudbury, 1637. A5/4/50
Peter, singleman, Thelnetham, (1633). W1/111/82
Ralph, Chevington, 1648. A5/4/121
Robert, husb., Fornham St. Martin, 1596. R2/43/157; W1/54/37
Robert, Rickinghall Superior, 1590. A5/2/137
Thomas, woollen draper, Bury St. Edmunds, 1644. R2/59/103; W1/101/29
Thomas, Bury St. Edmunds, 1650. A5/4/135
Thomas, Bury St. Edmunds, 1693. A5/6/160, A4/116/51
Thomas, the elder, labourer, Icklingham, 1614. R2/49/2; W1/71/3
Thomas, grocer, Soham, 1700. R2/74/46; W1/154/45; In. 3/27/63
Thomas, Stowmarket, 1533. W1/2/51
William, thatcher, Harleston, 1603. R2/45/290; W1/61/95
William, grocer, Soham, 1695. R2/72/503; W1/149/56
---, Rougham, 1572. W1/31/91
see also Seawell, Seueles, Sueell
SEXDEN, Robert, Lavenham, 1545. R2/19/497; W1/7/95
SEXTEN, Agnes, wid., Lavenham, 1558. R2/27/125
Edmund, Haughley, 1583. A5/2/48
John, Lavenham, 1557. R2/26/329; W1/20/249
Susan, Combs, 1634. A5/4/33
Thomas, parson, Fornham St. Genevieve, 1556. R2/25/87; W1/16/122
William, Sudbury, (1505). R2/13/174
SEXTON, Richard, Lidgate, 1679. R2/67/216; W1/133/23
Robert, Lavenham, 1533. R2/19/154 & 170; W1/2/12 & 39
SEYDEY, James, husb., Great Waldingfield, 1575. W1/95/13
SEYM, William, chaplain, Bury St. Edmunds, 1370. R2/1/31
SEYMON, John, Stradishall, (1546). R2/21/480, R2/23/194; W1/38/98
SEYMOR, John, jun., Pakenham, 1477. R2/11/194
SEYMOUR, John, Stanningfield, 1484. R2/11/288
SEYMOWR, John, sen., Stanningfield, 1449. R2/9/95
see also Semar, Semer
SHACKELTON, Thomas, vicar, Kenton, 1594. W1/51/257
SHACKLES, John, als. Jons, upholsterer, Bury St. Edmunds, 1629. R2/54/328; W1/85/37
SHADE, Richard, Edwardstone, 1572. A5/1/244
Thomas, Stoke by Nayland, 1572. A5/1/249
Willose, 1678. In. 11/2
SHAFTEN, John, butcher, Mildenhall, 1663. R2/63/29; W1/115/47; In. 3/8/49
SHAFTYNG, Amy, wid., Bury St. Edmunds, 1518. R2/6/54
John, butcher, Bury St. Edmunds, 1512. R2/5/20
Richard, mercer, Bury St. Edmunds, 1522. R2/6/95
see also Schaftyng
SHALDEFORD, John, mercer, Bury St. Edmunds, 1403. R2/1/98
John, weaver, Bury St. Edmunds, 1459. R2/2/67
John, Bury St. Edmunds, 1460. R2/2/28
Roger, webster, Bury St. Edmunds, (1426). R2/1/206
SHALES, Mary, wid., Eye, 1639. R2/58/7; W1/94/9
William, yeo., New Buckenham, 1594. W1/51/148
SHALFORD, Agnes, wife of Thomas, Bury St. Edmunds, 1429. R2/1/190
see also Schaldeford, Shaldeford
SHAMFIELD, Josias, yeo., Alpheton, 1692. R2/72/24; W1/146/24; In. 3/24/57

SHANKES, Thomas, Soham, 1689. A5/6/124, A4/30/69
see also Schank
SHANSFEILD, William, yeo., Alpheton, 1661. R2/62/147; W1/112/190; In. 3/5/204
William, labourer, Long Melford, 1617. R2/50/376; W1/74/158
SHARDELOWE, Ella, wife of Robert, Bury St. Edmunds, 1457. R2/2/57
see also Schardelowe
SHARECROFT, Samuel, Nayland, 1699. A5/7/12, A4/41/29
SHAREMAN, Jane, wid., Haughley, 1688. R2/71/99; W1/142/89
SHARLYE, Margaret, wid., Sudbury, 1585. R2/39/252; W1/42/322
SHARMAN, Christopher, Wangford, 1617. R2/50/352; W1/74/133
SHARP(E), Andrew, Isleham, 1685, (N). W7/112
Andrew, Freckenham, 1687. In. 10/32
Barbara, wid., Bury St. Edmunds, 1571. R2/35/295; W1/36/143
Benjamin, bach., Isleham, 1699. In. 9/102; A12/17
Catherine, singlewoman, Hawstead, 1651. R2/60/433
Dorothy, wid., 1634. R2/56/338; W1/90/105
Everard, Euston, 1567. A5/1/193
Francis, Bury St. Edmunds, 1611. A5/3/111
Grace, wid., Bury St. Edmunds, 1644, (N). R2/59/171; W1/101/100
Henry, mason, Bury St. Edmunds, 1607. R2/46/118; W1/97/30
Henry, mercer, Ixworth, 1616. R2/50/119; W1/73/126
Henry, husb., Lakenheath, 1623. R2/52/614; W1/79/59
Henry, yeo., Lawshall, 1645. R2/59/223; W1/102/49
Henry, husb., Wickhambrook, 1681. R2/68/222; W1/135/163
James, yeo., Freckenham, 1693. W8/34; In. 10/34
James, gingbread baker, Mildenhall, 1637. R2/57/134; W1/92/165
Jane, wid., Isleham, 1687. W7/114
Jasper, Bury St. Edmunds, 1644. A5/4/103
Jasper, woollen draper, Bury St. Edmunds, 1663. R2/63/112; W1/115/169; In. 3/8/183
Jasper, joiner, Bury St. Edmunds, 1697. In. 3/25/78; A5/6/19, A4/39/88
Joan, wid., Isleham, 1692. In. 9/86
John, parson, Bacton, 1558. R2/27/565; W1/31/30
John, baker, Bury St. Edmunds, 1664. R2/63/261; W1/116/188; In. 3/9/209
John, Bury St. Edmunds, 1679. A5/6/28, A4/16/135
John, the elder, clothier, Bury St. Edmunds, 1686. R2/70/425; W1/140/47
John, Great Wratting, 1595. A5/2/209
John, Haverhill, 1544. R2/21/606
John, miller, Haverhill, 1662. R2/62/431; W1/114/198; In. 3/7/253
John, miller, Haverhill, 1682. In. 3/21/187; A5/6/59, A4/19/38
John, yeo., Honington, 1639. R2/58/81; W1/94/140
John, yeo., Norton, 1593. R2/42/400; W1/50/64
John, gent., Norton, 1688. R2/71/10; W1/142/8
John, yeo., Old Newton, 1629. R2/54/331; W1/85/39
John, curate, Wickham Skeith, 1637. R2/57/207; W1/92/249
John, blacksmith, Worlington, 1608. R2/46/162; W1/65/11
Judith, wid., Bury St. Edmunds, 1680. R2/67/607; W1/134/79; In. 3/20/84
Martine, wid., Bury St. Edmunds, 1691. R2/71/553; W1/145/106
Maud, wid., Isleham, 1625. R6/36
Philip, Isleham, 1673. W7/80; In. 9/32
Phoebe, singlewoman, Bury St. Edmunds, 1644. R2/59/169; W1/101/98
Ralph, Norton, 1566. R2/32/291; W1/28/102
Richard, yeo., Brent Eleigh, 1544. R2/19/437
Richard, yeo., Hessett, 1635. R2/56/496; W1/91/72
Richard, grocer, Ixworth, 1697. R2/73/175; W1/151/59
Robert, mercer, Bury St. Edmunds, 1557. R2/8/309; W1/18/37
Robert, shearman, Bury St. Edmunds, 1624. R2/53/120; W1/80/120
Robert, gent., Bury St. Edmunds, 1693. R2/72/183; W1/147/73
Robert, cordwainer, Woolpit, 1606. R2/46/45; W1/64/61
Roger, maltster, Bury St. Edmunds, 1631. R2/56/7; W1/87/10
Roger, singleman, Bury St. Edmunds, 1636. R2/57/73; W1/92/86
Roger, Hessett, 1566. R2/32/327; W1/28/61
Simon, yeo., Bury St. Edmunds, 1641. R2/58/306; W1/98/102
Susan, Isleham, 1682. In. 9/84; A12/11
Thomas, husb., Haughley, 1557. R2/26/172; W1/20/94
Thomas, grocer, Isleham, 1672. In. 9/29; A12/9
Thomas, clothier, Stanstead, 1649. R2/60/249; W1/106/109

SHARP(E) continued
Thomas, als. Smart, shoe maker, Wetherden, 1593. R2/42/337; W1/50/1
Thomas, carpenter, Wickhambrook, 1556. R2/25/172; W1/19/64
Thomas, the elder, husb., Wickhambrook, 1638. R2/57/408; W1/93/228
William, Badwell Ash, 1580. A5/2/22
William, Haughley, 1553. R2/31/48; W1/13/37
William, the elder, Isleham, 1665. W7/69; In. 9/16
William, gent. Isleham, 1678. W7/91; In. 9/49
William, the younger, gent., Isleham, 1697. W7/132; In. 9/100
William, Stanstead, 1645. A5/4/111
William, als. Smart, potter, Stowmarket, 1590. R2/41/420; W1/47/28
see also Scharpe, Scherpe, Meadow als. Sharpe
SHARPELYS, Gilbert, tailor, Bury St. Edmunds, 1471. R2/2/148
SHARPINGTON, John, Cavendish, 1594. R2/42/584; W1/52/11
SHARPLIN, Thomas, Bildeston, 1606. A5/3/9
SHARPULL, Robert, shearman, Bury St. Edmunds, 1515. R2/6/16
SHARWOOD, John, miller, Great Finborough, 1662. In. 3/7/4; A5/5/26
SHASTYNE, John, Bury St. Edmunds, 1559. W1/17/75
SHAVE, Alice, wid., Sudbury, 1666. R2/64/50; W1/118/44; In. 3/11/38
Ann, wid., Exning, 1699. R2/73/412; W1/153/53; In. 3/26/58
Elisabeth, Harleston, 1699. A5/7/11, A4/41/15
George, yeo., Great Waldingfield, 1649, (N). R2/60/273; W1/106/144
Isaac, yeo., Edwardstone, 1689. R2/71/235; W1/143/73
Jane, singlewoman, Alpheton, 1609. R2/47/54; W1/66/62; A5/3/66
John, husb., Glemsford, 1587. R2/40/120; W1/44/2
John, Stansfield, 1573. A5/1/255
Richard, yeo., Little Cornard, 1617. R2/50/373; W1/74/154
Robert, Exning, 1681. A5/6/44, A4/18/12
Robert, carpenter, Preston, 1613. R2/48/244; W1/70/15
Thomas, cordwainer, Newmarket, 1675. R2/66/227; W1/127/97; In. 3/16/181
Thomas, Shelland, 1638. A5/5/67
Thomas, Shelland, 1687. A5/6/111, A4/27/45
William, yeo., Alpheton, 1607. R2/46/117; W1/97/29
William, Harleston, 1690. A5/6/136, A4/32/50
William, carpenter, Long Melford, 1604. R2/45/344; W1/62/63
William, carpenter, Long Melford, 1648. R2/60/46; W1/105/60
William, fishmonger, Sudbury, 1627. R2/54/95; W1/83/94
Winifred, wid., Great Waldingfield, 1649. A5/4/132
SHAW, Alice, wid., Bury St. Edmunds, 1594. R2/42/580; W1/52/15
Charles, Chevington, 1643. R2/59/69; W1/100/79
Edward, clerk, Great Saxham, 1678. R2/67/75; W1/130/59; In. 3/19/78
Edward, Oakley, 1634. A5/4/33
Elisabeth, Long Melford, 1649. R2/60/272; W1/106/143
George, shoe maker, Stanstead, 1630. R2/55/177; W1/86/194
Giles, labourer, Acton, 1596, (N). R2/43/185; W1/54/91
Giles, Long Melford, 1560. R2/29/58; W1/25/116
Joan, wid., Oakley, 1615. R2/49/311; W1/72/90
John, goldsmith, Bury St. Edmunds, 1563. R2/8/379; W1/17/27
John, Bury St. Edmunds, 1675. A5/5/159, A4/12/80
John, Bury St. Edmunds, 1679. A5/6/19, A4/16/48
John, husb., Cavendish, 1662. R2/62/381; W1/114/117; In. 3/7/151
Margery, singlewoman, Bury St. Edmunds, 1645, (N). R2/59/275; W1/102/90
Richard, Burwell, 1697. A5/6/191, A4/39/92
Richard, Oakley, 1608. A5/3/42
Robert, Long Melford, 1539. R2/19/321
Simon, Bury St. Edmunds, 1636. A5/4/45
Thomas, Soham, (1639). W1/110/52
Thomas, yeo., Thorndon, 1684, (N). R2/69/337; W1/138/132; A5/6/75, A4/21/16
SHAWBERY, Anne, wid., Fornham St. Martin, 1647. R2/59/423; W1/104/53
George, baker, Hopton, 1664. R2/63/139; W1/116/27; In. 3/9/7
John, the elder, gent., Bury St. Edmunds, 1637. R2/57/235; W1/92/289
Thomas, locksmith, Bury St. Edmunds, 1470. R2/2/132
Thomas, gent., Bury St. Edmunds, 1644, (N). R2/59/80; W1/101/7
SHAWBURY, Anne, Hopton, 1671. A5/5/121, A4/8/14
SHAXTON, Thomas, Bale, 1537. W1/51/37

SHEAD, Charles, labourer, Barningham, 1700. R2/74/122; W1/154/118
John, blacksmith, Barningham, 1692. R2/72/64; W1/145/63; In. 3/24/37
Richard, husb., Barningham, 1660. R2/62/60; W1/112/75
Thomas, blacksmith, Barningham, 1650. R2/61/307; W1/107/2; In. 3/3/2
Thomas, blacksmith, Coney Weston, 1682. In. 3/21/46; A5/6/62, A4/19/84
see also Shedd
SHEAPEARD, Margaret, wid., Long Melford, 1647. R2/59/429; W1/104/59; In. 3/2/63
SHEARMAN, Alice, wid., Soham, 1583, (N). R2/39/73; W1/42/36
Christopher, maltster, Newmarket, 1663. R2/63/14; W1/115/24; In. 3/8/22
Christopher, Thorndon, 1575. R2/37/94; W1/34/36
Walter, husb., Thorndon, 1571. R2/35/287; W1/36/118
SHEARWEN, George, yeo., Mendlesham, 1650. R2/61/344; W1/107/40; In. 3/3/60
SHEATHER, Ann, Lavenham, 1637. R2/57/230; W1/92/280
Robert, Stoke by Nayland, 1570. A5/1/223
Walter, mercer, Lavenham, 1641. R2/58/297; W1/98/83
see also Schedde, Shethar
SHEDD, William, Bures, 1635. A5/4/38
SHEDE, Thomas, blacksmith, Barningham, 1627. R2/54/46; W1/83/51
SHEEN, George, gent., Freckenham, 1695. W8/37
Thomas, yeo., Chippenham, 1631. R2/56/103; W1/87/158; A5/4/21
William, currier, Bury St. Edmunds, 1570. R2/35/35
SHEEP, Anne, wid., Burwell, 1631. R2/56/50; W1/87/68
Edward, singleman, Woolpit, 1562. R2/31/22; W1/8/149
Thomas, husb., Rickinghall Inferior, 1570. R2/34/44; W1/30/40
see also Schep, Shepe, Shepp
SHEEPWRYTH, Agnes, wife of Nicholas, Burwell, 1476. R2/11/63
SHEET, Daniel, Ousden, 1650. R2/61/359; W1/107/56; In. 3/3/70
William, yeo., Acton, 1590. R2/41/369; W1/47/65; A5/2/114a
see also Schet, Shete
SHEFFEILD, George, Sudbury, 1671. R2/65/273; W1/123/153
SHEIFFEILD, Edmund, Ballingdon, 1630. A5/4/7
SHELDON, Edward, gunlock maker, Sudbury, 1650. In. 3/3/42; A5/4/134
SHELDRAKE, Ann, wid. of John, yeo., Kedington, 1603. R2/45/256; W1/61/59
Edward, Clare, 1612. A5/3/117
Francis, Kedington, 1635. A5/4/40
Giles, yeo., Clare, 1617. R2/50/218; W1/74/10
Giles, Great Waldingfield, 1588. A5/2/111
Henry, glover, Kedington, 1572. R2/36/66; W1/31/73
Hugh, als. Cuttyng, smith, Clare, 1515. R2/15/12
Joan, wid., Great Waldingfield, 1593. R2/42/438; W1/50/119
Joan, wid., Stoke by Nayland, 1579. R2/38/60; W1/39/19
John, husb., Assington, 1618. R2/51/9; W1/75/2
John, Clare, 1551. R2/23/53; W1/11/64
John, Clare, 1561. R2/30/115
John, yeo., Kedington, 1573. R2/36/115; W1/32/14
John, Little Waldingfield, 1458. R2/9/238
John, Stoke by Nayland, 1472. R2/10/464
John, labourer, Wetheringsett, 1590. R2/41/336; W1/47/27
John, sen., Wissington, 1664. In. 3/9/33; A5/5/55, A4/2/11
Martha, Waldingfield, 1460. R2/9/277
Richard, Clare, 1575. R2/37/102; W1/34/43
Simon, Clare, 1489. R2/11/411
Stephen, Stoke by Nayland, 1479. R2/12/3
Thomas, Clare, 1635. R2/56/444; W1/91/11
William, labourer, Great Wratting, 1661. R2/62/231; W1/113/101; In. 3/7/251; A5/5/40
---, Clare, 1564. W1/28/282
SHELDRICKE, John, Sudbury, 1649. R2/60/301; W1/106/179
see also Scheldrake, Shildracke
SHELFORTH, John, Bury St. Edmunds, (1500). R2/13/108
SHELL, William, Pakenham, 1582. A5/2/39
SHELLAYE, Richard, Exning, 1569. R2/33/88; W1/28/203
SHELLEY, John, yeo., Exning, 1620. R2/52/179; W1/76/161
John, wool comber, Mildenhall, 1679. R2/67/222; W1/133/31
Nicholas, Chilton, 1612. R2/48/158; W1/69/39
Robert, Exning, 1579. R2/38/30; W1/39/46

SHELLIE, Ralph, Soham, 1583. A5/2/51
SHELLYE, Nicholas, tailor, Isleham, 1621. R6/24
Nicholas, tailor, Isleham, 1669. W7/75
SHELTON, Martha, wid. of Maurice, esq., Barningham, 1688. R2/71/112; W1/142/100
Robert, Nayland, 1592. R2/42/192; W1/49/15
see also Schelton
SHELTRUM, Christopher, Bury St. Edmunds, 1618. R2/51/190; W1/75/118
SHELVERDEN, William, Cowlinge, 1634. A5/4/32
SHELVERTON, Roger, Hargrave, 1642. A5/4/96
Timothy, Hargrave, 1663. In. 3/8/215; A5/5/53
SHELYNG, Richard, Bury St. Edmunds, 1512. R2/5/21
SHENE, Edward, Worlington, 1674. A5/5/145, A4/8/17
John, Mildenhall, 1558. R2/27/143
John, Mildenhall, 1607. A5/3/32
John, jun., yeo., Stowupland, 1693. R2/72/127; A5/6/164, A4/35/16
Nicholas, clothier, Stoke Ash, 1628. R2/54/156; W1/84/27
Reginald, Wangford, 1559. R2/28/102; W1/22/100
Robert, Chippenham, 1609. A5/3/76
Robert, clothier, Eye, 1568. R2/33/76; W1/29/99
William, Chippenham, 1637. A5/4/55
SHEPARD, Richard, Long Melford, 1644. A5/4/106
Thomas, singleman, Mildenhall, 1641. R2/58/307; W1/98/104
Thomas, Redgrave, 1460. R2/9/273
Thomas, husb., Rickinghall Superior, 1571. R2/35/47
William, Mendlesham, 1538. R2/18/149
SHEPE, Thomas, the elder, Long Melford, (1519). R2/15/90
Thomas, singleman, Wattisham, 1566. R2/32/356; W1/28/22
SHEPEARD, Millicent, spinster, Rickinghall Inferior, 1621. R2/52/345; W1/77/124
SHEPERD, Agnes, Hessett, 1557. R2/26/280; W1/20/200
John, Hessett, 1553. R2/31/45; W1/13/34
Nicholas, surgeon, Bildeston, 1574. R2/37/43; W1/33/34
SHEPERED, John, als. Askewe, Great Wratting, 1552. R2/23/249; W1/12/57
SHEPEY, John, sen., carpenter, Bury St. Edmunds, 1528. R2/6/146
see also Schepey
SHEPHARD, Henry, yeo., Wetheringsett, 1596. R2/43/149; W1/54/27
John, Lavenham, 1700. A5/7/14, A4/41/77
Richard, Redgrave, 1645. R2/59/236; W1/102/60
SHEPHEARD, Andrew, yeo., Hepworth, 1651. R2/61/504; W1/108/93
Benjamin, Gislingham, 1688. A5/6/120, A4/29/47
Henry, Ballingdon, 1691. A5/6/139, A4/33/2
John, Acton, 1632. A5/4/20
John, Bury St. Edmunds, 1641. A5/4/91
John, bach., Long Melford, 1690. A5/6/137, A4/32/75
John, Stowmarket, 1633. A5/4/24
John, Sudbury, 1638. A5/4/65
Robert, husb., Stowmarket, 1615. W1/127/157
Thomas, butcher, Cavendish, 1678. R2/17/8; W1/130/10; In. 3/19/16
Thomas, the elder, linen weaver, Rickinghall Superior, 1663. In. 3/8/16; A5/5/42
William, Long Melford, 1611. A5/3/114
William, wid., Long Melford, 1650. In. 3/3/91; A5/4/136
William, gent., Thorndon, 1660. In. 3/5/51b; A5/5/5, A4/1/204
William, husb., Wetheringsett, 1630. R2/55/20; W1/86/22
SHEPHERD, Jasper, draper, Bury St. Edmunds, 1663. R2/63/55; W1/115/87; In. 3/8/108
John, Ballingdon, 1673. A5/5/139, A4/10/46
Margaret, wid., Sudbury, 1472. R2/10/524
Margaret, 1564. R2/32/55; W1/27/2
Nicholas, Mildenhall, 1575. R2/37/93; W1/34/18
Robert, clerk, Hepworth, 1675. R2/66/257; W1/127/126; In. 3/16/166
Robert, singleman, Redgrave, 1598. R2/44/24; W1/56/19
Thomas, linen weaver, Rickinghall Superior, 1693. R2/72/247; W1/147/137
see also Scheperde, Sheapeard, Shepard, Shepeard, Shephard, Sheppard
SHEPP, Robert, rector, Rickinghall Superior, 1474. R2/11/14
William, Hartest, 1651. A5/4/138
SHEPPARD, Agnes, Redgrave, 1539. R2/20/100 & 210; W1/4/89
Edmund, Redgrave, 1523. R2/17/317
Edmund, wheelwright, Redgrave, 1631. R2/56/11; W1/87/14

SHEPPARD continued
Elisabeth, wid., Mendlesham, 1612. R2/48/187; W1/69/71
Elisabeth, wid., Mendlesham, 1630. R2/55/164; W1/86/181
Frances, wid., Acton, 1638. R2/57/366; W1/93/166
Francis, gent., Cotton, 1662. A5/5/33
Henry, brickmaker, Sudbury, 1662. R2/62/374; W1/114/109; In. 3/7/126
John, Alpheton, 1606. A5/3/8
John, Bury St. Edmunds, 1447. R2/2/23
Katherine, wid., Aspal, 1558. R2/27/416
Richard, Aspal, 1550. R2/21/26; W1/10/194
Richard, husb., Wetheringsett, 1578. R2/37/368; W1/36/207
Robert, Redgrave, 1560. R2/29/161; W1/25/13
Rose, wid., Long Melford, 1541. R2/22/96; W1/10/21
Thomas, Long Melford, 1472. R2/10/554
Thomas, yeo., Long Melford, 1541. R2/21/576; W1/36/48
Thomas, Mendlesham, 1633. R2/56/276; W1/90/43
Thomas, husb., Rickinghall Superior, 1610. R2/47/226; W1/67/106
William, the elder, blacksmith, Ixworth, 1609. R2/47/67; W1/66/77
William, yeo., Mendlesham, 1636. R2/57/108; W1/92/128
SHEPPERD, Henry, 1562. W1/95/48
John, Redgrave, 1529. R2/18/39; W1/311/12
John, the elder, Waldingfield, 1484. R2/11/350
Robert, husb., Mendlesham, 1570. R2/34/31; W1/30/29
SHEPPORD, John, Rickinghall, 1534. R2/19/202
SHERCROFT, Francis, singleman, husb., Wissington, 1677. In. 3/18/49; A5/5/69, A4/14/30
John, Little Waldingfield, 1663. In. 3/8/231; A5/5/54
John, blacksmith, Nayland, 1672. R2/65/332; W1/124/59
Matthew, weaver, Bildeston, 1584. R2/39/124; W1/42/99 & 213
William, blacksmith, Bures, 1648. R2/60/5; W1/105/7
see also Schercroft, Schiercroft, Sharecroft, Sherecroft
SHERD, Bridget, singlewoman, Great Livermere, 1630, (N). R2/55/32; W1/86/37
John, Elmsett, 1588. A5/2/99
Simon, tailor, Ixworth, 1613. R2/48/243a; W1/70/14
see also Scherde
SHERE, John, yeo., Wickhambrook, 1640. R2/58/144; W1/96/44
Thomas, yeo., Old Newton, 1637. R2/57/200; W1/92/238
SHERECROFT, Francis, Bures, 1638. A5/4/63
John, weaver, Bures, 1597. R2/43/375; W1/55/138
John, Bures, 1626, (N). R2/53/558; W1/82/82
Thomas, Nayland, 1647. A5/4/115
SHEREMAN, Thomas, husb., Brandon, 1639. R2/58/24; W1/94/44
SHERESON, William, Sudbury, 1562, (N). R2/31/28; W1/8/184
SHEREWEN, Alice, wid., Nayland, 1577. R2/37/316
SHERIFF, John, Assington, 1612. A5/3/118
SHERLYNG, Ralph, Stowmarket, 1472. R2/10/501
SHERMAN, Amy, singlewoman, Gislingham, 1618. R2/51/76; W1/75/44
Dorothy, wid., Eye, (1647). W1/110/14
Elisabeth, wid. of John, doctor of divinity, Sudbury, 1663, (N). R2/63/62; In. 3/8/128; A5/5/49
James, Yaxley, 1577. R2/37/287
Jane, Haughley, 1688. In. 3/23/102
Jane, wid., Stowmarket, 1668. In. 3/14/48; A5/5/98, A4/6/87
Joan, Bury St. Edmunds, 1435. R2/1/215
John, singleman, Barningham, 1668. A5/5/91, A4/6/8
John, miller, Stowmarket, 1665. In. 3/10/118; A5/5/68, A4/3/60
John, Stowmarket, 1669. A5/5/101, A4/7/2
John, Thorndon, 1595. A5/2/209
John, husb., Thorndon, 1602. R2/45/105; W1/60/16
John, shepherd, Wangford, 1624. R2/53/94; W1/80/107
John, miller, Woolpit, 1662. R2/62/382; W1/114/121
John, Yaxley, 1465. R2/10/384
Richard, Wattisham, 1470. R2/10/447
Robert, Troston, 1557. R2/26/14; W1/20/26
Roger, Rickinghall Superior, 1681. A5/6/45, A4/18/22
Thomas, husb., Barnham, 1607. R2/46/120; W1/97/34
Thomas, clothworker, Bildeston, 1592. R2/42/287; W1/49/100
Thomas, clothier, Stoke by Nayland, 1650, (N). R2/61/417; W1/107/124; In. 3/3/138
William, wid., Stowmarket, 1683. A5/6/70, A4/20/73
William, Sudbury, 1684. A5/6/81, A4/21/73
see also Scherman, Shareman, Sharman, Shearman, Shereman

SHERROCK, Edward, yeo., Freckenham, 1574. W8/10
SHERWOOD, Henry, Wiston, 1580. A5/2/30
Jane, wid., Little Waldingfield, 1668, (N). R2/64/351; W1/120/62; In. 3/13/143; A5/5/97, A4/6/81
Richard, chandler, Little Waldingfield, 1665. R2/63/349; W1/117/99; In. 3/10/90
Sarah, spinster, Great Finborough, 1688. R2/71/12; W1/142/11
see also Schirwode, Schywode, Sharwood, Shirwode
SHERWYN, John, Bury St. Edmunds, 1454. R2/2/45
William, Timworth, 1533. R2/19/152; W1/2/99
see also Scherewynd, Scherwyn, Shearwen, Sherewen
SHERYNGHAM, William, yeo., Wood Norton, 1574. W1/51/206 a - d
SHERYNGTON, William, Wetheringsett, 1474. R2/10/583
SHETE, Agnes, Stoke by Nayland, 1523. R2/14/73
SHETHAR, Robert, rector, Rishangles, 1648. R2/60/133; W1/105/159
SHILBURNE, Roger, carpenter, Snailwell, 1618. R2/51/171; W1/75/104
see also Shylborne
SHILDRACKE, William, als. Cutting, Stoke by Nayland, 1564. R2/32/131
SHILLING, Dorothy, wid., Dalham, 1619, (N). R2/51/436; W1/132/107
John, Lidgate, 1692. A5/6/152, A4/34/49
Katherine, wid., Bury St. Edmunds, 1699. R2/73/448; W1/153/88
Martin, gent., Dalham, 1629. R2/54/340; W1/85/48
Thomas, als. Baker, Fornham St. Martin, 1564. A5/1/161
see also Schelyng, Schillyng, Shelyng, Sherlyng, Shyllyng
SHINGLES, Robert, carpenter, Ixworth, 1616. R2/50/51; W1/73/59
SHINGLEWOOD, Thomas, Bury St. Edmunds, 1692. A5/6/146, A4/33/86
SHINN, Clement, husb., Soham, 1641. R2/58/269; W1/98/48
Elisabeth, wid., Soham, 1693. R2/72/126
Francis, Soham, 1681. A5/6/51, A4/18/89
Grace, wid., Soham, 1662. R2/62/391; W1/114/135; In. 3/7/178
John, Mildenhall, 1687. A5/6/111, A4/27/48
John, labourer, Mildenhall, 1692. In. 3/24/59; A5/6/151, A4/34/44
Owen, Hopton, 1694. A5/6/172, A4/37/69
Robert, sen., inn holder, Lakenheath, 1688. R2/71/32; W1/142/130; In. 3/23/69
William, Brockley, 1695. A5/6/182, A4/38/72
see also Schene, Sheen, Shene, Shyn
SHIPABOTOM, James, beer brewer, Brandon, 1587. R2/40/188; W1/44/47
SHIPDAM, Godwin, chaplain, Bury St. Edmunds, 1471. R2/2/146
SHIPP, Ann, spinster, Mendlesham, 1671. R2/65/275; W1/123/156
Ann, Rickinghall Superior, 1640. A5/4/84
Edward, yeo., Hessett, 1682. R2/68/288; W1/136/20; In. 3/21/219; A5/6/57, A4/19/13
Henry, tailor, Burwell, 1619. R2/51/447; W1/132/114
Hugh, Kirtling, 1608, (N). R2/46/163; W1/65/14
John, grocer, Bacton, 1624. R2/53/40; W1/80/57
John, Cheveley, 1683. R2/69/107; W1/137/83
John, Kirtling, 1648. A5/4/124
John, yeo., Old Newton, 1648. R2/60/22; W1/105/33
John, singleman, Old Newton, 1665. In. 3/10/167; A5/5/71, A4/3/80
John, yeo., Stoke Ash, 1680. R2/67/622; W1/134/88; In. 3/20/101
Peter, husb., Barnham, 1665, (N). R2/63/308; W1/117/38; In. 3/10/12; A5/5/64, A4/3/3
Timothy, smith, Cheveley, 1670. R2/65/114; W1/122/137; In. 3/15/169
Timothy, the elder, blacksmith, Kirtling, 1664. R2/63/180; W1/116/80
see also Shypp
SHIPWRIGHT, see Sheepwryth, Askyll als. Shypwryght
SHIRWODE, John, barker, Bury St. Edmunds, 1437. R2/1/233
SHOKEFORD, Margery, wid., Thelnetham, 1559. R2/28/118; W1/22/112
SHOKEFORTH, John, Thelnetham, 1559. R2/28/285; W1/22/260
William, Weston, 1488. R2/11/401
SHOLVARD, Richard, Wetheringsett, 1567. A5/1/186
SHOLVER, Elisabeth, Great Livermere, 1583. A5/2/53
William, yeo., Mellis, 1648. R2/60/71; W1/105/88
SHOMERE, Katherine, Layham, 1457. R2/9/215
see also Schomere
SHOOSMITH, James, Rushbrook, 1660. A5/5/1, A4/1/252
Thomas, tailor, Rushbrook, 1694. R2/72/387; W1/148/115

SHORDE, John, fuller, Cavendish, 1559. R2/28/318
Ralph, weaver, Hundon, 1596. R2/43/203; W1/54/71
Thomas, cloth maker, Cavendish, 1552. R2/23/100; W1/11/110
SHORT, Alice, als. Couldham, Bury St. Edmunds, 1682. A5/6/63, A4/19/86
Bridget, wid., Bury St. Edmunds, 1649. R2/60/164; W1/106/10
Catherine, Exning, 1560. R2/29/147; W1/25/26
Daniel, Mildenhall, 1630. A5/4/2
George, Exning, 1554. A5/1/95
Joan, wid., Bury St. Edmunds, 1533. R2/7/12
John, baker, Bury St. Edmunds, 1551. R2/8/240
John, gent., Great Saxham, 1630. A5/4/3 & 112
John, Risby, 1650. A5/4/137
John, Thorndon, 1584. A5/2/58
Margaret, wife of Richard, doctor of medicine, Risby, 1638. R2/57/399; W1/93/217
Maud, wid., Thorndon, 1560. R2/29/64; W1/25/108
Peregrine, Bury St. Edmunds, 1679. R2/67/456; W1/133/181
Richard, the elder, Bury St. Edmunds, 1668. A5/5/92, A4/6/30
Thomas, yeo., Bury St. Edmunds, 1603. R2/45/289; W1/61/94
see also Schorth, Schotte
SHORTEN, Elisabeth, wid., Stowmarket, 1683. R2/69/142; W1/137/116
SHORTER, Charles, Bury St. Edmunds, 1689. A5/6/129, A4/30/18
SHORTLIN, John, Stowmarket, 1679. A5/6/27, A4/16/128
SHRAGGER, see Fyssher als. Shraggere
SHRIVE, John, Boxford, 1676. A5/5/162, A4/13/35 & 36
John, wid., Boxford, 1683. A5/6/68, A4/20/39
Robert, Newton, 1676. A5/5/162, A4/13/38
Thomas, yeo., Newton, 1676. In. 3/17/151; A5/5/165, A4/13/85a
SHUCKFORD, James, Eye, 1662. In. 3/8/222; A5/5/32
John, husb., Badwell Ash, 1607. R2/46/151; W1/97/97
SHUCKFORTH, Hannah, spinster, Long Melford, 1680. R2/67/604; W1/134/76
John, Eye, 1675. A5/5/158, A4/12/74 & 75
Thomas, Thelnetham, 1524. R2/17/78; W1/21/13
William, Thelnetham, 1558. R2/27/61
SHUKEFORTT, John, Thelnetham, 1541. R2/22/93 & 111; W1/10/32
SHUKFORD, John, Langham, (1511). R2/13/188a
John, Thelnetham, 1471. R2/10/491
John, Thelnetham, 1472. R2/10/572
Robert, Langham, 1464. R2/10/371
see also Schucford, Shokeford
SHULVARD, Ralph, yeo., Langham, 1665. R2/63/313; W1/117/46; In. 3/10/54
SHULVER, Daniel, card maker, Great Ashfield, 1622. R2/52/421; W1/78/48
John, Wattisfield, 1649. A5/4/131
Roger, bach., Stowlangtoft, 1682. In. 3/21/79; A5/6/64, A4/19/121
see also Scholver, Sholvard
SHURLOKE, John, Lakenheath, 1455. W1/24/182
see also Schurlokke, Schyrlok
SHYLBERWYTH, Robert, Bury St. Edmunds, 1361. R2/1/13
SHYLBORNE, James, als. Parker, Fordham, 1485. R2/11/363
SHYLLE, Thomas, Ixworth, 1485. R2/11/339
SHYLLYNG, Thomas, Flempton, 1477. R2/11/105
SHYN, Henry, Soham, 1674. A5/5/150, A4/11/66
SHYPP, Thomas, husb., Woolpit, 1556. R2/25/151; W1/16/160
SHYTTE, John, yeo., Kersey, 1558. R2/27/528
Thomas, Assington, (1518). R2/15/27
SIBBLIE, Henry, yeo., Cheveley, 1605. R2/45/432; W1/63/75
SIBBLY, Thomas, inn holder, Newmarket, 1625. R2/53/228; W1/81/25
SIBBS, Alice, wid., Tostock, 1650. In. 3/3/148; A5/4/135
John, gent., Thurston, 1673. R2/65/432; W1/125/56; A5/5/140, A4/10/60
Paul, yeo., Thurston, 1610. R2/47/287; W1/67/176
Robert, thatcher, Tostock, 1637. R2/57/225; W1/92/272
Thomas, yeo., Rattlesden, 1669. R2/64/421; W1/121/3; In. 3/14/35
Thomas, yeo., Tostock, 1690. R2/71/335; W1/144/38
SIBIS, Thomas, labourer, Pakenham, 1559. R2/28/136; W1/22/125
see also Sybbes
SIBLE, Edward, Newmarket, 1662. R2/62/307; W1/114/1; In. 3/7/15
Elisabeth, Newmarket, 1685. R2/70/67; W1/139/58
Henry, husb., Mildenhall, 1620. R2/52/105; W1/76/92

SIBLEY, Joan, wid., Cheveley, 1620. R2/52/140; W1/76/124
Joan, wid., Great Bradley, 1666. R2/64/85; W1/118/60; In. 3/11/78
Margaret, wid., Newmarket, 1610. R2/47/166; W1/67/44
Roger, inn holder, Newmarket, 1661. In. 3/6/227; A5/5/23, A4/1/33
Roger, inn holder, Newmarket, 1698. R2/73/268; W1/152/43
William, yeo., Cheveley, 1573. R2/36/135; W1/32/16
William, husb., Cheveley, 1612. R2/48/235; W1/69/133
SIBLIE, John, husb., Cheveley, 1586. R2/40/54; W1/43/41
see also Sibblie, Sibly, Sybely, Syblie
SIBLING, Edward, yeo., Glemsford, 1647. R2/59/375
SIBLY, Mary, Cheveley, 1594. A5/2/195
SIDAY, Edmund, gent., Occold, 1680. In. 3/20/159; A5/6/38, A4/17/80
SIDEY, Elisabeth, wid., Sudbury, 1693. R2/72/121
John, Bures, 1664. In. 3/9/117; A5/5/60
John, the elder, Great Waldingfield, 1535. R2/19/212, R2/20/119; W1/4/99, W1/3/58
Margaret, wid., Bures, 1606. R2/46/89; W1/64/106
see also Seydey, Syday, Sydey, Benskin als. Syday, Briscoe als. Siday
SIER, John, yeo., Great Finborough, 1690. R2/71/339; W1/144/44
Peter, Great Finborough, 1662. In. 3/8/17; A5/5/33
SIFFOKS, Agnes, Bury St. Edmunds, 1354. R2/1/3
SIGGAR, Ann, Boxford, 1674. A5/5/144, A4/89/4
Robert, Great Waldingfield, 1571. A5/1/234
SIGO, Robert, Mildenhall, 1498. R2/13/80
William, yeo., Pakenham, 1569, (N). R2/33/88; W1/19/118
SILL, William, bach., Burwell, 1626, (N). R2/53/533; W1/82/62
SILLAT, Robert, carpenter, Rickinghall Superior, 1587. R2/40/292; W1/44/123
SILLETT, Edward, yeo., Great Horningsheath, 1603. R2/45/237; W1/61/31
Edward, yeo., Great Horningsheath, 1632. R2/56/227; W1/89/151
Henry, yeo., Horningsheath, 1670. R2/65/74; W1/122/90
James, Fornham All Saints, 1610. R2/47/134; W1/67/14
John, yeo., Bardwell, 1652. R2/61/559; W1/109/37; In. 3/4/44
John, gent., Bardwell, 1678. R2/67/49; W1/130/49
Joshua, singleman, Horningsheath, 1678. R2/67/30; W1/130/30; In. 3/19/41
Miles, yeo., Bardwell, 1677. R2/66/530; W1/129/111
Richard, yeo., Great Horningsheath, 1642. R2/58/367; W1/99/69
Stephen, yeo., Bardwell, 1664. R2/63/172; W1/116/70; In. 3/9/134
SILLIOTT, Thomas, tailor, Botesdale, 1647. R2/59/443; W1/104/73; In. 3/2/76
SILLITT, Richard, yeo., Bardwell, 1609. R2/47/28; W1/66/31
see also Sellett, Selott, Sillott, Syllett, Sylote
SILLMAN, Richard, als. Sowman, husb., Acton, 1627. R2/54/49; W1/83/54
SILLOTT, John, yeo., Bardwell, 1619. R2/51/315; W1/132/34
Richard, yeo., Horningsheath, 1687. R2/70/392; W1/141/115
Thomas, yeo., Coney Weston, 1685. R2/70/208; W1/139/176
Thomas, Stanton, 1523. R2/17/36; W1/21/50
William, yeo., Bardwell, 1650. R2/61/352; W1/107/49
SILOTT, Thomas, husb., Bardwell, 1552. R2/23/158
SILVESTER, Elisabeth, wid., Haughley, 1669. R2/64/560; W1/121/148
James, Haughley, 1673, (N). R2/65/475; W1/125/111; A5/6/143, A4/10/93
James, thatcher, Whepstead, 1597. R2/43/329; W1/55/95
Robert, Haughley, 1664. In. 3/9/53; A5/5/56, A4/2/24
Thomas, yeo., Depden, 1678. R2/67/24; W1/130/23; In. 3/19/29
William, husb., Pakenham, 1590. R2/41/383
SILVEY, Edward, Clare, 1637. A5/4/53
SIMKINS, John, Mildenhall, 1578. A5/2/10
SIMMS, Charles, als. Thatcher, husb., Great Thornham, 1608. R2/46/191; W1/65/57
Edward, clerk, Stoke by Clare, 1667. R2/64/338; W1/120/46; In. 3/12/194; A5/5/90, A4/6/3
Nicholas, als. Thatcher, labourer, Great Thornham, 1619. R2/51/265; W1/132/7
SIMON, Henry, tailor, Cavenham, 1608. R2/46/206; W1/65/92
SIMOND(S), Bridget, wid., Bury St. Edmunds, 1665, (N). R2/63/381; W1/117/134; A5/5/71
John, Barton, 1464. R2/10/353
John, Redgrave, 1461. R2/9/280

SIMOND(S) continued
John, Snailwell, 1668. R2/64/383; W1/120/102
Jonathan, Rickinghall Inferior, 1666. In. 3/11/71; A5/5/73, A4/4/9
Lydia, wid., Chippenham, 1679. A5/6/17, A4/16/20
Robert, Ampton, 1569. A5/1/212
Robert, clothier, Ipswich, 1574. W1/51/241
Thomas, husb., Boxford, 1637. R2/57/144; W1/92/180
Thomas, the elder, yeo., Great Barton, 1623. R2/52/705; W1/79/119
Thomas, the elder, Rougham, 1572. R2/36/49; W1/31/91
SIMONT(S), Gilbert, labourer, Withersfield, 1647. R2/59/465; W1/104/101; In. 3/2/101
Roger, als. Drue, weaver, Long Melford, 1597. R2/43/285; W1/55/60
see also Symmonds
SIMPER, Ann, als. Baker, wid., Hepworth, 1666. A5/5/74, A4/4/20
Matthew, yeo., Culford, 1683. R2/69/126; W1/137/102
Silas, yeo., Hepworth, 1671. R2/65/153; W1/123/14
see also Symper
SIMPKIN, Roger, Cheveley, 1681. A5/6/52, A4/18/99
see also Edgar als. Sympkyn
SIMPSON, Alice, Bury St. Edmunds, 1684. A5/6/83, A4/21/102
Ann, spinster, Great Bradley, 1661. In. 3/6/268; A5/5/24, A4/1/15
Edward, Brent Eleigh, 1652. A5/4/142
George, singleman, Wetheringsett, 1667. A5/5/86, A4/5/50
Isaac, yeo., Bures, 1678. R2/67/99; W1/130/83; In. 3/19/107
John, yeo., Chelsworth, 1663. R2/63/117; W1/115/179; In. 3/8/233
John, yeo., Poslingford, 1700. R2/74/44; W1/153/43; In. 3/27/32
John, Walsham le Willows, 1672. A5/5/132, A4/9/59
Joseph, say maker, Great Waldingfield, 1684. R2/69/324; W1/138/120
Mary, wid., Newmarket, 1692. R2/72/106; W1/146/96
Matthew, yeo., Poslingford, 1688. R2/71/63; W1/142/55; In. 3/23/4
Mordecai, Great Cornard, 1649. A5/4/131
Mordecai, singleman, Sudbury, 1670, (N). R2/65/31; W1/122/35
Ralph, gent., Bures, 1682. R2/68/297; W1/136/28; In. 3/21/208
Robert, yeo., Chelsworth, 1603. R2/45/245; W1/61/44
Samuel, Naughton, 1675. A5/5/157, A4/12/50
Thomas, butcher, Palgrave, 1686. A5/6/103, A4/26/47
William, shoe maker, Hawkedon, 1627. R2/54/59; W1/83/63
William, butcher, Lawshall, 1668. R2/64/374; W1/120/92; In. 3/13/87
William, Mildenhall, 1664. In. 3/9/90; A5/5/59, A4/2/54
William, Newmarket, 1678. A5/6/7, A4/15/56
SIMSON, Edward, inn holder, Bury St. Edmunds, 1690. R2/71/327; W1/144/30
John, husb., Great Waldingfield, 1590. R2/41/345; W1/47/37
John, Somerton, 1691. R2/71/493; W1/145/52
Thomas, Great Barton, 1695. In. 3/25/69; A5/6/184, A4/38/92
see also Sympson
SINDERLAND, George, clothier, Nayland, 1634. R2/56/349; W1/90/118
SINGLETON, Elisabeth, Ixworth Thorpe, 1639. A5/4/77
Mary, wid., Botesdale, 1687. R2/71/305; W1/141/48
see also Sengelton, Sengylton
SIRE, Reginald, yeo., Great Ashfield, 1614. R2/49/125; W1/71/90
SIRGANT, John, yeo., Bardwell, 1681. R2/68/100; W1/135/75
SISCAM, Alexander, Long Melford, 1648. A5/4/123
SISER, John, Cheveley, 1678. R2/67/6; W1/130/8; In. 3/19/10
John, Kedington, 1637. A5/4/52
SIZAR, Lambert, Soham, 1697. A5/7/4, A4/40/70
Simon, shepherd, Cheveley, 1629. R2/54/341; W1/85/49
SIZER, John, Exning, 1651. R2/61/424
John, yeo., Wicken, 1685. R2/70/170; W1/139/141
Margaret, Cheveley, 1647. In. 3/2/127; A5/4/118
Roger, yeo., Dalham, 1686. R2/70/481; W1/140/95
Walter, husb., Snailwell, 1664. R2/63/149; W1/116/40; In. 3/9/77
SKALDER, Adam, Bury St. Edmunds, 1406. R2/1/110
SKALES, Reynold, labourer, Great Fakenham, 1562. R2/31/59; W1/8/171
SKALPIE, Nicholas, Combs, 1561, (N). R2/30/103
SKARBOT, Andrew, Bury St. Edmunds, 1474. R2/2/189
John, Bury St. Edmunds, 1479. R2/2/287
SKARBURGH, Alexander, parson, Rockland, 1531. W1/51/2

SKARLETT, Robert, yeo., Assington, 1622. R2/52/460; W1/78/75
Robert, Ixworth, 1573. R2/36/130; W1/32/32
SKARPE, Anthony, yeo., Felsham, 1607. R2/46/139
Cicely, wid. of William, Felsham, 1481. R2/11/196
John, husb., Felsham, 1532. R2/19/107; W1/3/112 & 134
John, Fornham All Saints, 1464. R2/2/81
Martin, Woolpit, 1589, (N). R2/41/168; W1/46/116
Michael, Rattlesden, 1602. R2/45/186; W1/60/112
Richard, Norton, (1530). R2/19/31
Robert, Norton, (1494). R2/11/448
Robert, tailor, Tostock, 1571. R2/33/87, R2/35/173; W1/28/200
Samuel, Preston, 1661. In. 3/6/27; A5/5/12, A4/1/130
William, Rattlesden, 1506. R2/13/170
William, Tostock, 1593. R2/42/372; W1/50/39
SKACE, John, carpenter, Thrandeston, 1675. R2/66/169; W1/127/46; In. 3/16/52
SKATERON, Edmund, yeo., Elmswell, 1567. R2/32/384; W1/3/185
Thomas, yeo., Elmswell, 1568. R2/33/43; W1/29/54
SKEALIS, Robert, singleman, Brandon, 1576. R2/37/213; W1/37/73; In. 3/1/23
SKEATH, Robert, yeo., Sudbury, 1616. R2/50/62; W1/73/73
SKEET, Alice, wife of Robert, Great Livermere, 1465. R2/10/384
John, barker, Bury St. Edmunds, 1462. R2/2/75
Margaret, Bury St. Edmunds, 1394. R2/1/73
Thomas, Kersey, 1608. A5/3/47
William, merchant, Bury St. Edmunds, 1392. R2/1/61
see also Skete, Skette, Skeytt
SKEGGES, Lawrence, tanner, Mildenhall, (1553). R2/31/96; W1/13/67
SKEITONE, Henry, dornick weaver, Bury St. Edmunds, 1603. R2/45/242; W1/61/39
SKELES, Thomas, singleman, Brandon, 1585. R2/39/266; W1/42/307
SKELTON, John, draper, Bury St. Edmunds, 1528. R2/6/145
John, Hengrave, (1473). R2/11/27
John, Little Thornham, 1562. A5/1/133
Robert, Hengrave, 1525. R2/17/83; W1/21/8
William, shearman, Bury St. Edmunds, 1607. R2/46/117; W1/97/27
see also Skilton, Skylton
SKELY, William, Brandon, 1612. A5/3/115
SKENER, George, Wickhambrook, 1555. R2/24/190; W1/15/24
SKEPER, John, carpenter, Felsham, 1568. R2/33/57
SKEPPER, Ann, wid., Felsham, 1635. A5/4/36
Constance, wid., Thurston, 1637. R2/57/225; W1/92/271
Edmond, blacksmith, Felsham, 1620, (N). R2/52/104; W1/76/90
Edmund, husb., Thurston, 1589, (N). R2/41/195; W1/46/92
George, yeo., Thurston, 1631. R2/56/47; W1/87/66
George, yeo., Thurston, 1660. R2/62/125; W1/112/168
Henry, vicar, Lakenheath, 1578. R2/37/406; W1/36/166
John, labourer, Bardwell, 1616. R2/50/74; W1/73/83, W1/74/3
John, yeo., Drinkstone, 1617. R2/50/210
John, Gedding, 1563. A5/1/144
John, Woolpit, 1462. R2/10/317
Margaret, wife of John, Thornham, 1559. R2/28/190; W1/22/170
Ralph, reeder, Bury St. Edmunds, 1479. R2/2/282
Robert, labourer, Drinkstone, 1557. R2/26/68; W1/20/42
Thomas, Barnham, 1473. R2/11/39
Thomas, Cowlinge, 1589. A5/1/205
Thomas, carpenter, Stradishall, (1625). W1/111/65
Thomas, Stradishall, 1632. R2/56/196; W1/89/109
Thomas, Thurston, 1698. A5/7/8
William, Buxhall, 1569. R2/33/116; W1/28/179
SKERPPE, Joan, Felsham, 1538. R2/20/138; W1/4/119a & b (and inventory)
SKETE, John, Kersey, (1505). R2/13/161
Richard, Ilketshall St. Margaret, 1422. W1/9/1a
Thomas, Downham, (1515). R2/13/221
SKETH, Katherine, wid. of Thomas, Stanton, 1469. W1/10/454
Margaret, Stanton, 1472. R2/10/549
see also Skeyth
SKETTE, William, husb., Kersey, 1559. R2/28/143; W1/22/132
SKETTON, James, clothier, Bury St. Edmunds, 1615. R2/49/348; W1/72/120
see also Skeitone

SKEVEN, Alice, wid., Wickhambrook, 1548. R2/21/411
SKEVINGTON, Nicholas, the elder, yeo., Brandon, 1611. R2/48/69; W1/68/86
Nicholas, Brandon, 1630, (N). R2/55/135; W1/86/151
SKEYTH, Thomas, Stanton, 1462. R2/12/12
SKEYTT, John, Bildeston, 1504. R2/12/28; W1/7/10
Robert, Great Finborough, 1522. R2/14/70, R2/17/19; W1/21/68
SKILTON, Anne, wid., Bury St. Edmunds, 1628. R2/54/182; W1/84/60
SKINNER, Ann, wid., Bury St. Edmunds, 1664. In. 3/9/42; A5/5/57, A4/2/32
Christine, wife of George, Icklingham, 1632. R2/56/197; W1/89/111
Edward, weaver, Sudbury, 1687. R2/70/349; W1/141/84
Elisabeth, wid., Icklingham, 1679. A5/6/19, A4/16/45
Elisabeth, Icklingham, 1687. A5/6/116, A4/27/104
George, Icklingham, 1640. R2/58/222; W1/96/160
Isaac, butcher, Gedding, 1687. R2/70/295; W1/141/39
James, husb., Icklingham, 1667. R2/64/214; W1/119/66; In. 3/12/64
John, husb., Icklingham, 1640. R2/58/191; W1/96/115
John, yeo., Icklingham, 1663. R2/63/97; W1/115/148; In. 3/8/197
John, Icklingham All Saints, 1683. A5/6/67, A4/20/15
Rachel, wid., Sudbury, 1698. R2/73/268; W1/152/44
Thomas, husb., Icklingham, 1678. R2/67/187; W1/130/163; In. 3/19/224
Thomas, Icklingham, 1681. A5/6/55, A4/18/143b
Timothy, grocer, Long Melford, 1698. R2/73/293; W1/152/64
William, the elder, yeo., Icklingham, 1648. R2/60/42; W1/105/53
William, yeo., Icklingham, 1676. R2/66/353; W1/128/61; In. 3/17/77
William, yeo., Icklingham, 1679. R2/67/258; W1/133/51; A5/6/19, A4/16/43
William, fuller, Stoke by Clare, 1533. R2/19/170; W1/2/19
William, yeo., Withersfield, 1686. R2/70/236; W1/140/6
see also Skener, Skynner, Sander als. Skynner
SKIPWITH, Mercy, wid., Lakenheath, (1675), (N). R2/66/244; W1/127/114; A5/5/157, A4/12/57
SKOFEILD, Mary, wid., Bury St. Edmunds, (1642). W1/110/16
William, clothier, Stoke by Nayland, 1596. R2/43/209; W1/54/60
SKOLER, John, priest, Thurston, 1556. R2/25/50; W1/16/57
SKOLTHORPE, Simon, shoe maker, Drinkstone, 1558. R2/27/359
SKOPES, William, Coney Weston, 1553. R2/23/253
SKOPPES, Edmund, husb., Creeting All Saints, 1559. R2/28/163
SKORELL, William, Hitcham, 1484. R2/11/311
SKOTT, Adam, Bradfield St. George, 1474. R2/11/44
Agnes, wid., Mildenhall, 1575. R2/37/87; W1/34/4
Andrew, ploughwright, Depden, 1580. R2/38/194
Christopher, tailor, Fordham, 1603. R2/45/230; W1/61/23
Edmund, Elveden, 1561. A5/1/116
George, cooper, Bury St. Edmunds, 1519. R2/6/59
George, yeo., Hessett, 1610. R2/47/156; W1/67/38
Harry, Felsham, 1551. R2/23/58; W1/11/65
Henry, yeo., Rattlesden, 1624. R2/53/117; W1/80/118
Henry, thatcher, Shimpling, 1605. R2/45/425; W1/63/70
Isabel, Felsham, 1571. R2/35/247; W1/38/120
John, inn holder, Bury St. Edmunds, 1587. R2/40/173; W1/44/45
John, Felsham, 1475. R2/11/142
John, Felsham, 1597. R2/43/291; W1/55/65
John, Fordham, 1576. R2/37/151; In. 3/1/102
John, yeo., Glemsford, 1524. R2/17/325
John, labourer, Hawkedon, 1631. R2/56/39; W1/87/54
John, Old Newton, 1478. R2/11/175
Lettice, wid., Clare, 1563. R2/32/8; W1/26/66
Nicholas, Bradfield St. Clare, 1563. R2/31/164; W1/26/45
Nicholas, spicer, Bury St. Edmunds, 1468. R2/2/120
Richard, the elder, Boxted, 1560. R2/29/26; W1/25/153
Robert, singleman, Bures, 1550. R2/21/168; W1/9/125
Robert, cooper, Bury St. Edmunds, 1552. R2/8/54; W1/21/187
Robert, Clare, 1581. A5/2/38
Robert, Fordham, 1587. R2/40/178; W1/44/52
Susan, singlewoman, Stanton, 1589, (N). R2/41/184; W1/46/102

SKOTT continued
Thomas, Bury St. Edmunds, 1471. R2/2/142
Thomas, Bury St. Edmunds, 1479. R2/2/288
Thomas, wid., Felsham, 1521. R2/15/122
Thomas, yeo., Felsham, 1618. R2/51/120; W1/75/75
Thomas, Lavenham, 1546. A5/1/67
Thomas, Mildenhall, 1545. R2/19/522; W1/7/106
Thomas, Stowlangtoft, 1476. R2/11/77
William, bricklayer, Bury St. Edmunds, 1554. R2/8/271; W1/18/1
William, Elveden, 1569. A5/1/214
William, Glemsford, 1498. R2/13/79
William, Glemsford, 1559. R2/28/23; W1/22/27
SKOTTYSMORE, John, Walsham le Willows, 1559. R2/28/185; W1/22/288
SKOYLE, Alexander, Lavenham, 1476. R2/11/64
John, Brockley, 1451. R2/9/105
SKREVENER, John, fuller, Bildeston, 1475. R2/11/436
William, Bury St. Edmunds, 1439. R2/1/241
SKREVEYNER, Thomas, Stradishall, 1493. R2/13/6
SKREVYNER, Edward, the elder, Wickhambrook, 1533. W1/2/29
SKROOKE, John, Eye, 1596. A5/2/220
SKRYVEYN, Robert, Bury St. Edmunds, 1380. R2/1/39
SKURRE, John, priest, Long Melford, 1545. R2/19/529; W1/7/41
SKYLTON, Henry, Withersfield, 1557. R2/26/163; W1/20/99
SKYNALL, Richard, Snailwell, 1462. R2/10/309
SKYNNER, Andrew, singleman, Icklingham, 1623. R2/52/663; W1/79/84
Dorothy, singlewoman, Tuddenham, 1663, (N). R2/63/37; W1/115/58; In. 3/8/10; A5/5/40 & 42
George, husb., Icklingham St. James, 1622. R2/52/400; W1/78/34
Harry, Layham, 1480. R2/11/272
Henry, gent., Bacton, 1650. R2/61/330; W1/107/27; In. 3/3/39
James, Bury St. Edmunds, 1632. A5/4/20
James, Little Cornard, 1640. A5/4/80
John, clothmaker, Boxford, 1530. R2/19/30
John, tailor, Bury St. Edmunds, 1479. R2/2/278
John, baker, Bury St. Edmunds, 1500. R2/4/95
John, Icklingham, 1594. A5/2/201
John, Stoke by Nayland, 1460. R2/9/275
John, Stoke by Nayland, (1487). R2/11/396
John, gent., Sudbury, 1645. R2/59/273; W1/102/88
Margaret, wid., Bury St. Edmunds, 1524. R2/6/120
Margery, Botesdale, 1561. A5/1/114
Margery, wid., Icklingham St. James, 1626. R2/53/447; W1/82/4
Nicholas, chandler, Bury St. Edmunds, 1454. R2/2/45
Richard, Bury St. Edmunds, 1477. R2/2/233
Richard, Bury St. Edmunds, 1487. R2/2/199
Richard, sen., Bury St. Edmunds, 1512. R2/5/20
Richard, husb., Bury St. Edmunds, 1520. R2/6/79
Richard, gent., alderman, Sudbury, 1640. R2/58/190; W1/96/112
Robert, currier, Bury St. Edmunds, 1499. R2/4/85
Robert, metalman, Redgrave, 1618. R2/51/47; W1/75/25
Thomas, Clare, 1516. R2/12/117
Thomas, yeo., Lackford, 1573. R2/36/221
Thomas, Rougham, 1472. R2/10/535
Walter, Rickinghall Inferior, 1455. R2/9/233
William, fuller, Bury St. Edmunds, 1429. R2/1/188
William, Kedington, 1439. R2/9/5
William, Layham, 1490. W1/24/66
SKYPPYNG, Robert, Haverhill, 1454. R2/9/205
SKYRBECKE, John, weaver, Great Waldingfield, 1556. R2/25/55; W1/16/64
SLACK, Joseph, Herringswell, 1699. In. 3/26/42; A5/7/12, A4/41/35
SLADE, Edmund, Assington, 1532. R2/19/101; W1/3/65
Edward, Stoke, 1460. R2/9/271
SLAKE, Jeremy, the elder, yeo., Soham, 1691. R2/71/497; W1/145/58
SLANY, William, Snailwell, 1595. A5/2/210
SLATER, John, clothier, Lavenham, 1686. R2/70/453
SLAUGHTER, John, Bury St. Edmunds, 1435. R2/1/213
SLAW, Matilda, Redgrave, 1457. R2/9/189
SLEIGHTON, John, gent., Chippenham, 1700. R2/74/36; W1/154/35
see also Slighton
SLEYE, John, rector, Whatfield, 1565. A5/1/167
SLIGH, Richard, Bacton, 1610. A5/3/88

SLIGHTON, James, gent., Chippenham, 1661. In. 3/6/59; A5/5/11, A4/1/149
SLINGER, Richard, glazier, Lavenham, 1667. R2/64/262; W1/119/124; In. 3/12/169
SLIPPER, Thomas, labourer, Groton, 1615. R2/49/337; W1/72/109
SLONE, Rachel, wid., Little Thurlow, 1678. In. 3/19/158; A5/6/10, A4/15/86
SLOWGRAVE, John, Clare, 1592. R2/42/304; W1/49/125
William, sen., Sudbury, 1663. R2/63/10; W1/115/17; A5/5/44
SLYE, Elisabeth, wid., Bacton, 1611. R2/48/20; W1/68/40
Thomas, Great Wratting, 1586. R2/40/45; W1/43/33
see also Sligh
SMALBEROWE, Walter, Wortham, (1494). R2/13/18
SMAL(E), Ann, wid., Kersey, 1608, (N). R2/46/178; W1/65/38
Joan, wid., Exning, 1614, (N). R2/49/111; W1/71/82
John, yeo., Bury St. Edmunds, 1450. R2/2/33
Richard, tailor, Exning, 1604. R2/45/374; W1/62/104
SMALL, Francis, Exning, 1601. R2/44/359; W1/59/25
see also Bole als. Small, Smorne als. Small, Smyrne als. Smale
SMALLBONE, John, Sudbury, 1512. W1/9/42
SMALLHODE, Margaret, Hinderclay, (1536). R2/19/232
SMALLWOOD, Lydia, singlewoman, Elmswell, 1681. A5/6/47, A4/18/40
SMALWODE, Bennet, Hepworth, 1529. R2/18/35
Isabel, Bradfield St. George, 1472. R2/10/498
SMALWOOD, Bennet, Bradfield St. George, 1484. R2/11/346
see also Barbor als. Smalwode
SMART, Ezekial, singleman, clerk, Rede, 1650. In. 3/3/12; A5/4/133
Robert, Stoke by Nayland, 1569. A5/1/208
Roger, labourer, Ixworth, 1613. R2/48/312; W1/70/85
Thomas, Lackford, 1679. A5/6/20, A4/87/52
William, Lackford, 1670, (N). R2/65/48; W1/122/55; In. 3/15/73
see also Sharpe als. Smart
SMEARE, Stephen, gent., Gislingham, 1663. R2/63/96; W1/115/147; In. 3/8/171
John, the elder, yeo., Gislingham, 1669. R2/64/568; W1/121/158; In. 3/14/155
see also Smere
SMEATH, Henry, husb., Nayland, 1596. R2/43/129; W1/54/7
SMEE, Edward, carpenter, Great Waldingfield, 1640. R2/58/163; W1/96/73
Richard, Sudbury, 1683. A5/6/66, A4/20/13
Susan, wid., Hawstead, 1650. R2/61/331; W1/107/29; In. 3/3/34
see also Smy
SMEETH, John, Great Wratting, 1568. A5/1/203
William, Hawstead, 1638. A5/4/62
William, Long Melford, 1569. A5/1/211
SMERE, Katherine, wid., Bury St. Edmunds, (1527). R2/6/142
SMETH(E), Agnes, wid., Glemsford, 1555. R2/24/186; W1/15/21
Elisabeth, wid., Ashfield, 1604. R2/45/342; W1/62/62
Geoffrey, Bures, 1472. R2/10/577
John, Kedington, 1477. R2/12/19
John, Kedington, 1573. A5/1/261
Marion, Barrow, 1561. R2/30/67
Peter, butcher, Nayland, 1585. R2/39/345; W1/42/255
Robert, Great Cornard, 1484. R2/11/374
Robert, yeo., Pakenham, 1582. R2/38/385; W1/41/52
Robert, Withersfield, 1526. R2/17/210; W1/23/22
Thomas, Newton, 1477. R2/12/19
William, Cowlinge, 1452. R2/9/121
William, Isleham, 1556. W7/4
SMETON, see Cowper als. Smeton
SMEY, Richard, barber, Sudbury, 1673. R2/65/398; W1/125/13
SMITH, Abraham, webster, Wickhambrook, 1681. R2/68/174; W1/135/128; A5/6/51, A4/18/98
Alice, Polstead, 1639. A5/4/71
Ambrose, blacksmith, Boxted, 1686. R2/70/424; W1/140/46; In. 3/22/75
Andrew, Somerton, 1678. In. 3/19/85; A5/6/6, A4/15/42
Ann, Cockfield, 1637. A5/4/53
Ann, spinster, Mellis, 1643. R2/59/45; W1/100/53
Ann, wid., Semer, 1638. R2/57/258; W1/93/21
Ann, wid., Soham, 1681. R2/68/193; W1/135/141

SMITH continued
Ann, wid. of Lionel, Stradishall, 1581. R2/38/328; W1/40/70
Ann, wid., Whatfield, 1639, (N). R2/58/55; W1/94/101
Anne, wid., Risby, 1627, (N). R2/54/69; W1/83/72
Anne, wid., Walsham le Willows, 1610. R2/47/249; W1/67/132
Catherine, wid., Stowlangtoft, 1638. A5/4/65
Christopher, yeo., Great Wratting, 1583. R2/39/7; W1/42/87
Daniel, Newton, 1684. R2/69/297; W1/138/92
David, Icklingham, 1698. A5/7/8
Dorothy, wife of Thomas, the elder, Lawshall, 1677. R2/66/503; W1/129/84
Edmund, gent., Cheveley, 1700. R2/74/117; W1/154/114a; A5/7/14, A4/41/92
Edmund, als. Barker, husb., Kedington, 1588. R2/41/94; W1/45/90
Edmund, yeo., Rushbrook, 1632. R2/56/120; W1/89/7
Edward, the elder, Ousden, 1615. R2/49/264; W1/72/48
Edward, Shimpling, 1647. In. 3/2/161; A5/4/113
Edward, Woolpit, 1669. In. 3/14/55; A5/5/106, A4/7/51
Ellen, als. Arnold, wife of Thomas, Assington, 1619. W1/95/63
Gilbert, husb., Lakenheath, 1589. R2/41/283; W1/46/26
Grace, wid., Wickhambrook, 1669. R2/64/473; W1/121/61
Hannah, als. Gardner, wid., Gipping, 1679. A5/6/16, A4/16/7
Henry, Buxhall, 1699. A5/7/11, A4/41/25
Henry, Stoke by Clare, 1683. A5/6/71, A4/20/86
Henry, Tuddenham, 1639. A5/4/76
Hugh, Bildeston, 1679. A5/6/17, A4/16/26
James, husb., Ixworth, 1639. R2/58/8; W1/94/15
Jeffery, Clare, 1575. In. 3/1/76
Joan, Cockfield, 1561. R2/30/120
John, Assington, 1672. A4/9/27
John, Ballingdon, 1668. In. 3/13/144; A5/5/96, A4/6/71
John, the elder, yeo., Barrow, 1612. R2/48/134; W1/69/14
John, Bradfield Combust, 1593. R2/42/438; W1/50/100
John, husb., Bradfield St. George, 1604. R2/45/333; W1/62/47
John, bricklayer, Burwell, 1663. R2/63/48; W1/115/76; In. 3/8/94
John, parson, Cockfield, 1676. R2/66/344; W1/128/51; In. 3/17/57
John, gardener, Dalham, 1687. R2/70/300 & 579; W1/141/43
John, apothecary, Eye, 1698. R2/73/251; W1/152/29
John, Great Bradley, 1686. A5/6/102, A4/26/61
John, husb., Great Thurlow, 1648. R2/60/17; W1/105/25
John, baker, Groton, 1652. R2/61/602; W1/109/80; In. 3/4/84
John, Haughley, 1691. A5/6/142, A4/33/44
John, yeo., Higham, 1664. R2/63/193; W1/116/99; In. 3/9/154
John, yeo., Hopton, 1663. In. 3/8/33; A5/5/44
John, sen., yeo., Hopton, 1663. R2/63/98; W1/115/149; In. 3/8/212
John, Icklingham St. James, 1668. In. 3/13/136; A5/5/92, A4/6/24
John, clerk, Kedington, 1618. R2/51/64; W1/75/38
John, yeo., Lawshall, 1629. R2/54/399; W1/85/91
John, als. Barker, Little Bradley, 1523. R2/17/316
John, husb., Mellis, 1554. R2/24/125; W1/14/99
John, Naughton, 1622, (N). R2/52/522; W1/78/120
John, Redgrave, 1534. R2/19/192
John, blacksmith, Shimpling, 1688. R2/71/123; W1/142/111; In. 3/23/110
John, Stansfield, (1542). R2/19/338; W1/9/62
John, Stoke by Nayland, 1638. A5/4/63
John, sen., husb., Stoke by Nayland, 1693. R2/72/194; W1/147/84
John, yeo., Thrandeston, 1646. R2/59/333; W1/103/49
John, yeo., Thrandeston, 1652. R2/61/520; W1/109/5
John, Weston, 1684. A5/6/82, A4/21/86
John, Wetherden, 1694. A5/6/168, A4/37/22
John, yeo., Wickhambrook, 1581. R2/38/336; W1/40/77
Joseph, wheelwright, Acton, 1618. R2/51/115; W1/75/71
Joseph, Great Cornard, 1684. A5/6/82, A4/21/92
Joseph, Mellis, 1679. A5/6/24, A4/16/93
Joseph, yeo., Soham, 1632. R2/56/220; W1/89/139
Katherine, Hengrave, 1610. A5/3/106
Leonard, Wood Ditton, 1610. A5/3/92
Margaret, wid., Bury St. Edmunds, 1621, (N). R2/52/264; W1/77/48

SMITH continued
Margaret, wid., Ousden, 1627. R2/54/120; W1/83/117
Margaret, wid., Sible Hedingham, 1539. R2/19/297
Margaret, wid., Wickhambrook, 1682. R2/68/396; W1/136/96 (and inventory); A5/6/62, A4/19/81
Margery, wid., spinster, Icklingham, 1660. R2/62/84; W1/112/109; In. 3/5/123
Mary, wid., Elmsett, 1632. R2/56/174
Mary, Fordham, 1700. A5/7/15, A4/41/115
Mary, wid., Mellis, 1602. R2/45/97; W1/60/6
Matilda, wid., Redgrave, 1575, (N). R2/37/94; W1/28/35
Matthew, Bury St. Edmunds, 1681. A5/6/54, A4/18/132
Mildred, wid., Troston, 1642. R2/58/395; W1/99/111
Nicholas, worstead weaver, Stowupland, 1638. R2/57/323; W1/93/101
Philip, Elmsett, 1679. R2/67/415; W1/133/152
Philip, husb., Kedington, 1634. R2/56/416; W1/90/189
Philip, Whatfield, 1631, (N). R2/56/72; W1/87/107
Philippa, wid., Great Livermere, 1661. In. 3/6/281; A5/5/23, A4/1/27
Ralph, yeo., Stowmarket, 1666. In. 3/11/140; A5/5/80, A4/4/75
Richard, Cavendish, 1640. A5/4/84
Richard, Depden, 1664. R2/63/231; W1/116/147; In. 3/9/197; A5/5/63, A4/2/98
Richard, als. Sellowes, yeo., Great Finborough, 1624. R2/53/57; W1/80/82
Richard, weaver, Haverhill, 1648. R2/60/79; W1/105/95
Richard, Nayland, 1527. R2/17/242; W1/1/41
Richard, husb., Ormesby St. Margaret, 1575. W1/51/224
Richard, Stoke Ash, 1631, (N). R2/56/72; W1/87/108
Richard, yeo., Stoke by Clare, 1689. R2/71/217; W1/143/61
Richard, gent., Wickhambrook, 1683. R2/69/156; W1/137/126
Richard, husb., Wickhambrook, 1685. R2/70/163; W1/139/136
Richard, yeo., Wortham, 1662. R2/62/413; W1/114/167; In. 3/7/218
Robert, Aldham, 1639. A5/4/74
Robert, shepherd, Bacton, 1628. R2/54/268; W1/84/123
Robert, Bacton, 1662. In. 3/7/119; A5/5/33
Robert, thatcher, Botesdale, 1636. R2/57/111; W1/92/133
Robert, Combs, 1610. A5/3/82
Robert, timberman, Great Wratting, 1639. R2/58/76; W1/94/129
Robert, thatcher, Haverhill, 1624, (N). R2/53/43; W1/80/61
Robert, yeo., Kedington, 1685. R2/70/122; W1/139/110
Robert, Lakenheath, 1612. R2/48/186; W1/69/69
Robert, yeo., Lawshall, 1660. A5/5/7, A4/1/183
Robert, grocer, Long Melford, 1686. R2/70/456; W1/140/69; In. 3/22/143
Robert, wid., Norton, 1679. A5/6/21, A4/16/65
Robert, labourer, Semer, 1615. R2/49/250; W1/72/34
Robert, Shimpling, 1593. R2/42/339; W1/50/3
Robert, Stowupland, 1681. A5/6/50, A4/18/78
Robert, yeo., Wickhambrook, 1558. R2/27/485
Roger, yeo., Cockfield, 1624. R2/53/37; W1/80/54
Roger, husb., Long Melford, 1676. R2/66/339; W1/128/46; In. 3/17/52
Ruth, wid., Alpheton, 1694. R2/72/358; W1/148/84
Samuel, Bury St. Edmunds, 1666. In. 3/11/112; A5/5/76, A4/4/48
Samuel, yeo., Capel, 1661. R2/62/164; W1/113/13; In. 3/6/5
Samuel, yeo., Clare, 1682. R2/68/291; W1/136/23
Samuel, Groton, 1688. In. 3/23/34; A5/6/118, A4/29/22
Samuel, yeo., Kedington, 1681. R2/68/99; W1/135/73
Samuel, wid., Old Newton, 1698. A5/7/7
Sophia, Polstead, 1531. R2/56/104; W1/87/159
Stephen, Mellis, 1611. R2/48/70; W1/68/87
Steven, labourer, Great Livermere, 1608. W1/111/56
Susan, wid., Bury St. Edmunds, 1672. R2/65/328; W1/117/54
Thomas, the elder, blacksmith, Bacton, 1671. R2/65/146; W1/123/3
Thomas, blacksmith, Bacton, 1690. R2/71/354; W1/144/59
Thomas, collar maker, Barnham, 1643. R2/59/50; W1/100/59
Thomas, carpenter, Chevington, 1671. R2/65/161; W1/123/27
Thomas, the elder, yeo., Chevington, 1680. R2/67/548; W1/134/31
Thomas, yeo., Great Ashfield, 1604. R2/45/304; W1/62/1

SMITH continued
Thomas, carpenter, Hartest, 1685. R2/70/128; W1/139/114; A5/6/93, A4/105/87
Thomas, yeo., Hundon, 1668. R2/64/330; W1/120/36; In. 3/13/67
Thomas, carpenter, Kersey, 1638, (N). R2/57/419; W1/93/247
Thomas, the elder, yeo., Lawshall, 1677. R2/66/522; W1/129/103; In. 3/18/134
Thomas, grocer, Lawshall, 1689. R2/71/231; W1/143/69
Thomas, Layham, 1570. A5/1/219
Thomas, butcher, Long Melford, 1625. R2/53/301; W1/81/87
Thomas, Long Melford, 1638. A5/4/63
Thomas, Long Melford, 1685. A4/24/107a, b & 138
Thomas, yeo., Mildenhall, 1620. R2/52/11; W1/76/11
Thomas, cordwainer, Mildenhall, 1683. R2/69/170; W1/137/136
Thomas, Onehouse, 1694. A5/6/175, A4/37/108
Thomas, miller, Semer, 1684. R2/69/291; W1/138/86
Thomas, sen., blacksmith, Stanstead, 1674. R2/66/15; W1/126/107
Thomas, gent., Stradishall, 1680. R2/67/737; W1/134/177; In. 3/20/189
Thomas, gent., Thrandeston, 1666. R2/64/51 - 64; W1/118/45; In. 3/11/51
Thomas, Wickhambrook, 1636. A5/4/43
Thomas, Wixoe, 1670. In. 3/15/87; A5/5/111
Thomas, the elder, butcher, Woolpit, 1625. R2/53/432; W1/81/213
Timothy, Fornham, 1681. A5/6/46, A4/18/30
William, tailor, Barnham, 1601. R2/44/364; W1/59/31
William, yeo., Barningham, 1669. R2/64/511; W1/121/102; In. 3/14/122
William, husb., Burwell, 1632. R2/56/136; W1/89/26
William, felt maker, Bury St. Edmunds, 1670. In. 3/15/217; A5/5/113
William, Exning, 1534. R2/19/193
William, the elder, Eye, 1681. A5/6/46, A4/18/36
William, als. Sellowes, yeo., Great Finborough, 1624. R2/53/3; W1/80/5
William, clerk, Hepworth, 1686. R2/70/423; W1/140/45
William, carpenter, Icklingham, 1647. R2/59/488; W1/104/123; In. 3/2/134
William, inn holder, Icklingham, 1694. R2/72/415; W1/148/148
William, wid., Kirtling, 1690. A5/6/137, A4/32/61
William, Long Melford, 1520. R2/15/124
William, Long Melford, 1608. A5/3/39
William, the younger, butcher, Long Melford, 1667. R2/64/238; W1/119/98; In. 3/12/102
William, maltster, Newton, 1696. In. 3/25/71; A5/6/190, A4/39/80
William, husb., Ousden, 1660. R2/62/85; W1/112/111; In. 3/5/126
William, husb., Soham, 1670. R2/65/78; W1/122/96; In. 3/15/106
William, Soham, 1680. In. 3/20/219; A5/6/42, A4/17/115
William, husb., Soham, 1694. R2/72/432; W1/148/164
William, blacksmith, Stanstead, 1630. R2/55/2; W1/86/3
William, husb., Stoke by Nayland, 1665. In. 3/10/134
William, Thelnetham, 1681. A5/6/51, A4/18/97
William, the younger, wheelwright, Walsham le Willows, 1603. R2/45/252; W1/61/53
William, Wickhambrook, 1643. R2/59/20; W1/100/31
see also Smeath, Smeeth, Smeth(e), Smyth(e), Agnis als. Smith, Annis als. Smith, Balden als. Smith, Hovell als. Smith, Sellowes als. Smith, Selowse als. Smith
SMITTEN, Edward, carpenter, Exning, 1599. R2/44/232; W1/57/49
SMORNE, Robert, als. Small, Stowupland, 1641. R2/58/292; W1/98/80; In. 3/2/46
SMY, Edward, Combs, 1684. A5/6/82, A4/21/85
John, carpenter, Great Waldingfield, 1607. R2/46/118
see also Smee, Smey
SMYETH, George, singleman, Wickhambrook, 1574. R2/37/5
John, sen., Sudbury, 1483. R2/11/306
Thomas, Felsham, 1564, (N). R2/32/97
SMYRNE, William, als. Smale, Stowmarket, 1610. A5/3/99
SMYTH(E), Agnes, wid., Bures, 1556. R2/25/44; W1/16/49
Agnes, Bury St. Edmunds, 1473. R2/2/181
Agnes, wid., Bury St. Edmunds, 1551. R2/8/241
Agnes, wid., Kedington, 1533. R2/19/131; W1/2/94

SMYTH(E) continued
Agnes, wid., Mildenhall, 1570. R2/35/26
Agnes, wid., Palgrave, 1531. R2/19/75
Alice, wife of Robert, Bury St. Edmunds, 1435. R2/1/213
Alice, wid., Bury St. Edmunds, 1554. R2/8/99; W1/21/170
Alice, wid., Groton, 1513. R2/12/87
Alice, als. Tyler, Groton, 1558. R2/27/257
Alice, Hartest, 1609. W1/95/108
Alice, wid., Kedington, 1537. R2/20/61; W1/4/51
Alice, als. Jefferie, wid., Lavenham, 1569. R2/33/138; W1/5/66
Alice, wife of John, Lawshall, 1477. R2/11/440
Alice, als. Elmes, Little Livermere, 1589. A5/2/126
Andrew, Bures, 1662. In. 3/7/212; A5/5/39
Andrew, blacksmith, Somerton, 1615. R2/49/229; W1/72/19
Ann, als. Springe, Chelsworth, 1630. A5/4/3
Ann, Great Bradley, 1588. A5/2/99
Ann, als. Barbar, Great Cornard, 1563. R2/31/142; W1/26/23
Ann, Preston, 1583. A5/2/49
Ann, Shimpling, 1631. W1/111/88
Ann, Wissington, 1562. A5/1/131
Anne, als. Ganyll, wife of Richard, Boxford, 1504. R2/12/62
Anthony, mercer, Bury St. Edmunds, 1644. R2/59/137; W1/101/62
Arthur, Badwell Ash, 1558. R2/27/445
Avice, wid., Bury St. Edmunds, 1559. W1/17/65
Barnaby, Hengrave, 1573. R2/36/174; W1/32/79
Bartholomew, ploughwright, Stradishall, 1640. R2/58/162
Beatrice, wid., Bury St. Edmunds, 1579. R2/38/17
Bridget, singlewoman, Wortham, 1660. R2/62/81; W1/112/106; In. 3/5/122
Catherine, wid., Eye, 1555. R2/24/208; W1/15/41
Catherine, wid., Eye, 1568. R2/33/6; W1/29/12
Charles, yeo., Barnardiston, 1677. R2/66/479; W1/129/59; In. 3/18/75
Christian, wid., Whatfield, 1559. R2/28/389; W1/3/77
Cicely, Burwell, 1441. R2/9/13
Cicely, Bury St. Edmunds, 1494. R2/4/30
Dionysius, Eriswell, 1441. R2/9/31a
Dorothy, Snailwell, 1558. R2/27/25
Edmond, Lavenham, 1531. R2/12/109, R2/19/77
Edmund, Hitcham, 1546. A5/1/67
Edmund, Pakenham, 1545. W1/9/67
Edmund, yeo., Shelland, 1662. R2/62/326; W1/114/32; In. 3/7/52
Edmund, als. Baker, Thurlow, 1525. R2/14/111
Edmund, yeo., Thurston, 1600. R2/44/341; W1/59/3
Edward, als. Ernold, Assington, 1476. R2/11/56
Edward, yeo., Cockfield, 1651. R2/61/483; W1/108/72
Edward, Gazeley, 1663. R2/63/25; W1/115/41; In. 3/8/53
Edward, gent., Great Waldingfield, 1684. R2/69/230; W1/138/36
Edward, Lakenheath, 1568. R2/33/69; W1/29/90
Edward, yeo., Shelland, 1610. R2/47/301; W1/67/192
Edward, husb., Stoke by Nayland, 1574. R2/37/56; W1/33/23
Eleanor, Nayland, 1469. R2/10/449
Elisabeth, wid., Bury St. Edmunds, 1647. R2/59/438; W1/104/68
Elisabeth, wid., Great Finborough, 1564. R2/32/60; W1/27/8
Elisabeth, spinster, Groton, 1593. A5/2/180
Elisabeth, Stoke by Clare, 1668. A5/5/93, A4/6/43
Ellen, wid., Preston, 1621, (N). R2/52/309; W1/77/88a & b
Emma, wid., Bures, 1616. R2/50/8; W1/73/11
Fabian, Polstead, 1588. R2/41/11; W1/45/9
Francis, Soham, 1591. A5/2/146
Francis, Woolpit, 1608. A5/3/57
Geoffrey, als. Tostoke, Barningham, 1489. R2/11/389
Geoffrey, Long Melford, 1482. R2/11/259
George, linen weaver, Badwell Ash, 1673, (N). R2/65/407; W1/125/25; A5/5/137, A4/10/26
George, dornick weaver, Bildeston, 1622. R2/52/439; W1/78/61
George, husb., Great Cornard, 1599. R2/44/244; W1/57/57
George, Stoke by Nayland, 1542. R2/22/68; W1/6/46
George, husb., Stoke by Nayland, 1558. R2/27/368
George, yeo., Wickhambrook, 1576. R2/37/171; W1/37/34; In. 3/1/79
Harry, Gedding, (1497). R2/13/69

SMYTH(E) continued
Harry, Rattlesden, 1459. R2/9/268
Henry, Bury St. Edmunds, 1476. R2/2/218
Henry, Bury St. Edmunds, 1590. A5/2/140
Henry, Bury St. Edmunds, 1632. A5/4/21
Henry, the elder, husb., Great Finborough, 1540. R2/19/264 & 620; W1/3/136
Henry, husb., Great Finborough, 1548. R2/21/490
Henry, Great Finborough, 1550. R2/21/27; W1/10/180
Henry, als. Tostock, yeo., Hopton, 1606. R2/46/80; W1/64/99
Henry, labourer, Kirtling, 1608, (N). R2/46/194
Henry, yeo., Shimpling, 1632. R2/56/141; W1/89/36
Henry, West Stow, 1453. R2/9/147
Hugh, husb., Layham, 1545. R2/19/507; W1/7/89
Hugh, yeo., Redgrave, 1603. R2/45/286; W1/61/90
Humfrey, Haverhill, 1593. A5/2/179
Humphrey, husb., Barnham, 1545. R2/19/514; W1/7/33
Isabel, Bury St. Edmunds, 1473. R2/2/171
Isabel, Great Finborough, 1462. R2/10/352
James, Barton Mills, 1674. A5/5/146, A4/11/36
James, Eriswell, 1446. R2/9/74
James, inn holder, Newmarket, 1693. R2/72/155
Jane, wid., Bury St. Edmunds, 1624. R2/53/179; W1/80/154a
Jane, wid., Gislingham, 1611. R2/48/58; W1/68/81
Jeffery, tanner, Bury St. Edmunds, 1579. R2/38/47; W1/39/29
Jeremy, baker, Bures, 1676, (N). R2/66/363; W1/128/73; In. 3/17/87; A5/5/162, A4/13/52
Joan, als. Cook, wid., Bury St. Edmunds, 1514. R2/6/10
Joan, singlewoman, Cotton, 1568. A5/1/200
Joan, wid. of John, Eye, 1495. R2/13/75
Joan, wid., Eye, 1540. R2/19/608, R2/20/278
Joan, Great Wratting, 1544. A5/1/46
Joan, wid., Lavenham, 1540. R2/20/112; W1/4/96
Joan, singlewoman, Long Melford, 1588. R2/41/106; W1/45/101 & 102
Joan, wid. of Robert, Nayland, 1480. R2/11/213
Joan, wid., Stowmarket, 1485. R2/11/339
John, yeo., Assington, 1668. R2/64/310; W1/120/15; In. 3/13/27
John, Assington, 1672. A5/5/130
John, Bacton, 1525. R2/17/93; W1/21/89
John, rector, Bacton, 1565. A5/1/167
John, Badmondisfield, 1451. R2/9/103
John, Barnardiston, 1460. R2/9/245
John, Barnardiston, 1472. R2/10/526
John, Barrow, 1557. R2/26/25; W1/20/19
John, Beyton, 1439. R2/9/9
John, Botesdale, (1445). W1/24/53
John, sen., Botesdale, 1462. R2/10/415; W1/24/168
John, Botesdale, 1468. R2/10/408 & 415
John, Bradfield St. George, 1652. In. 3/4/19; A5/4/141
John, Bradley, 1594. A5/2/194
John, Brandon, 1459. W1/24/125
John, Brandon, 1641. A5/4/91
John, husb., Bures, 1614. R2/49/35; W1/71/30
John, Bury St. Edmunds, 1444. R2/2/8
John, weaver, Bury St. Edmunds, 1452. R2/2/39
John, cordwainer, Bury St. Edmunds, 1462. R2/2/74
John, esq., Bury St. Edmunds, 1481. R2/2/304
John, mercer, Bury St. Edmunds, 1509. R2/4/205
John, mason, Bury St. Edmunds, 1513. R2/5/30
John, yeo., Bury St. Edmunds, 1539. R2/7/57
John, scrivener, Bury St. Edmunds, 1560. R2/8/355; W1/17/50
John, Bury St. Edmunds, 1587. A5/2/93
John, singleman, Buxhall, 1540. R2/20/171; W1/4/145
John, Chelsworth, 1542. R2/22/80; W1/6/20
John, Chelsworth, 1578. A5/2/12
John, yeo., Chelsworth, 1621. R2/52/260; W1/77/46
John, Clare, 1462. R2/12/11
John, husb., Cockfield, 1569. R2/33/126; W1/28/193
John, Coney Weston, 1673. A5/6/138, A4/10/42
John, Dalham, 1557. R2/26/156; W1/20/90
John, als. Cordar, Denston, 1580. R2/38/157; W1/39/133
John, gent., Eriswell, 1670. R2/65/110; W1/122/132; In. 3/15/164

SMYTH(E) continued
John, Exning, 1458. R2/9/267
John, Exning, 1482. R2/11/261
John, Exning, (1512). R2/13/212
John, Exning, 1557. R2/26/64; W1/20/38
John, Eye, 1558. R2/27/334
John, Fornham St. Martin, 1661. R2/62/197; W1/113/60
John, Glemsford, 1479. R2/11/189
John, husb., Great Cornard, 1560. R2/29/23; W1/25/158
John, yeo., Great Horningsheath, 1557. R2/26/210; W1/20/155
John, Great Livermere, 1645. A5/4/110
John, husb., Great Livermere, 1662. R2/62/352; W1/114/72; In. 3/7/80
John, weaver, Great Waldingfield, 1583, (N). R2/39/106; W1/42/12
John, Great Waldingfield, 1593. R2/42/376; W1/50/41
John, Haughley, 1565. A5/1/167
John, gent., Haughley, 1691. R2/71/484; W1/145/42; A5/6/142
John, Hundon, 1455. R2/9/176
John, the elder, Hundon, 1521. R2/15/124
John, Hundon, 1592. A5/2/174
John, gent., Hundon, 1603. R2/45/234; W1/61/28
John, Kersey, 1457. R2/9/189
John, Kirtling, 1461. R2/9/299
John, yeo., Lidgate, 1630. R2/55/91; W1/86/101
John, Lindsey, 1443. R2/9/57
John, sen., Little Cornard, 1635. A5/4/39
John, Long Melford, 1503. R2/12/57
John, smith, Long Melford, 1505. R2/12/46
John, Long Melford, 1591. A5/2/157
John, wid., Mellis, 1529. W1/311/3
John, yeo., Mellis, 1661. R2/62/164; W1/113/14; In. 3/6/10
John, gent., Mellis, 1679. R2/67/491; W1/133/209
John, shoe maker, Mildenhall, 1474. R2/11/23
John, the elder, Mildenhall, 1556. R2/25/18; W1/16/18
John, Nayland, 1539. R2/20/39
John, Nayland, 1590. A5/2/130
John, Polstead, 1451. R2/9/137
John, the elder, Polstead, 1575. W1/95/16
John, carpenter, Preston, 1582. R2/38/412; W1/41/23
John, miller, Rattlesden, 1588. R2/41/54; W1/45/47
John, Redlingfield, 1631, (N). R2/56/26; W1/87/36
John, clerk, Rickinghall Inferior, 1615. R2/49/302; W1/72/82
John, Ringshall, 1575. W1/51/195
John, Semer, 1590. A5/2/136
John, Shimpling, (1528). R2/17/275
John, Soham, 1470. R2/10/432
John, als. Hyll, Soham, 1475. R2/11/137
John, Stansfield, 1465. R2/10/388
John, Stansfield, 1597. R2/43/300 & 321; W1/55/69
John, Stanton, 1471. R2/10/492
John, Stoke by Clare, 1562. R2/31/86
John, Stoke by Nayland, 1455. R2/9/224
John, labourer, Stoke by Nayland, 1581. R2/38/253; W1/40/4
John, Stowmarket, 1529. W1/311/7
John, husb., Stradishall, 1632. R2/56/191; W1/89/101
John, Sudbury, 1440. R2/9/27
John, miller, Thurston, 1566. R2/32/276; W1/28/117
John, Whepstead, 1482. R2/11/281
John, Wickhambrook, 1451. R2/9/137
John, Wickhambrook, 1485. R2/11/366
John, the elder, yeo., Wickhambrook, 1550. R2/21/79; W1/9/116b
John, Wixoe, 1612. A5/3/116
John, Wixoe, 1630. A5/4/5
John, Woolpit, 1689. A5/6/128, A4/30/38
John, butcher, Woolpit, 1690. R2/71/333; W1/144/37; A5/6/135, A4/32/42
Katherine, Boxted, 1573. A5/1/254
Katherine, wid. of John, sen., Polstead, 1577. R2/37/319
Lawrence, mercer, Bury St. Edmunds, 1481. R2/2/325
Margaret, als. Arnolde, Assington, 1531. R2/19/86
Margaret, als. Arnoulde, Assington, 1617. R2/50/237; W1/74/33
Margaret, wid., Boxford, 1444. R2/9/62

SMYTH(E) continued
Margaret, wid., Bury St. Edmunds, 1473. R2/2/179
Margaret, wid., Great Ashfield, 1564. R2/32/119
Margaret, Newton, 1560. A5/1/102
Margaret, wid., Woolpit, 1615. R2/49/316; W1/72/95
Margery, wid., Nayland, 1637. R2/57/136; W1/92/168
Marian, als. Hauke, wid. of John, Bradfield Combust, 1562. R2/31/9
Marion, als. Barbour, Stowmarket, 1440. R2/9/28
Martha, wid., Finborough, 1685. A5/6/95, A4/24/119
Martin, Exning, 1567. R2/32/372; W1/3/22
Martina, Rattlesden, 1583. A5/2/46
Mary, wid., Bacton, 1680. In. 3/20/51; A5/6/30, A4/16/158
Mary, wid., Buxhall, 1626. W1/95/91
Mary, wid., Kettlebaston, 1650. R2/61/390; W1/107/94; In. 3/3/113
Mary, Long Melford, 1632. A5/4/19
Mary, wid., Long Melford, 1652. R2/61/527; W1/109/13; In. 3/4/8
Mary, wid., Rattlesden, 1638. R2/57/280; W1/93/49
Mary, wid. of Bartholomew, Stradishall, 1630. R2/55/28; W1/86/33
Matthew, Rickinghall Superior, 1586. A5/2/80
Michael, say weaver, Sudbury, 1642. R2/58/403; W1/99/121
Nicholas, als. Arnould, Bures, 1585. R2/39/253; W1/42/321
Nicholas, husb., Hitcham, 1574. R2/37/7; W1/33/89
Nicholas, Hundon, 1649. A5/4/126
Nicholas, Stowmarket, 1473. R2/11/9
Nicholas, Walsham le Willows, 1461. R2/9/280
Rachel, sen., wid., Long Melford, 1670. R2/65/15; W1/122/21; In. 3/15/47
Ralph, Bildeston, 1472. R2/10/553
Ralph, Newton, 1522. R2/14/69
Reginald, labourer, Sudbury, 1602. R2/45/139; W1/60/58
Richard, Great Bradley, 1540. R2/19/610; W1/5/17
Richard, Great Livermere, 1458. R2/9/203
Richard, als. Nycholl, Icklingham, 1525. R2/17/82; W1/21/6
Richard, Ixworth, 1672. A5/5/132, A4/5/52
Richard, Lavenham, 1673. A5/5/144, A4/10/103
Richard, labourer, Long Melford, 1558. R2/27/567; W1/31/28
Richard, Long Melford, 1607. A5/3/19
Richard, yeo., Mellis, 1558. R2/27/465
Richard, Newton, 1561. R2/30/55
Richard, Shimpling, 1441. R2/9/31a
Richard, husb., Soham, 1609. R2/47/52; W1/66/58
Richard, Tuddenham, 1439. R2/9/2
Richard, Westley, 1471. R2/10/467
Richard, Wissington, 1559. R2/28/380; W1/3/129
Robert, yeo., Bacton, 1567. R2/32/421; W1/19/107
Robert, Badwell, 1560. R2/29/6; W1/25/177
Robert, cordwainer, Bildeston, 1580. R2/38/231; W1/39/85
Robert, Brettenham, 1562. A5/1/132
Robert, Brettenham, 1563. A5/1/141
Robert, Brome, 1560. R2/29/36; W1/25/140
Robert, Bury St. Edmunds, 1354. R2/1/3
Robert, carpenter, Bury St. Edmunds, 1551. R2/8/242
Robert, Bury St. Edmunds, 1587. A5/1/91
Robert, Cockfield, 1554. R2/24/79; W1/14/61
Robert, the elder, husb., Cockfield, 1580. R2/38/225
Robert, Felsham, 1523. R2/14/90
Robert, Great Ashfield, 1578. A5/2/6
Robert, carpenter, Great Waldingfield, 1589. R2/41/273; W1/46/34
Robert, labourer, Ixworth, 1617. R2/50/361; W1/74/145
Robert, yeo., Kettlebaston, 1613. R2/48/312; W1/70/86
Robert, husb., Lakenheath, 1614. R2/49/114; W1/71/84
Robert, Little Cornard, 1671. A5/5/127, A4/8/74
Robert, Mellis, 1651. A5/4/140
Robert, Nayland, 1448. W1/24/189
Robert, Palgrave, 1474. R2/11/3
Robert, Preston, 1583. R2/39/40; W1/42/59
Robert, Semer, 1571. A5/1/237
Robert, the elder, husb., Shimpling, 1575. W1/95/17
Robert, husb., Stoke Ash, 1496. W1/24/131
Robert, Sudbury, 1649, (N). R2/60/215; W1/106/62
Robert, Wyverstone, 1440. R2/9/11

SMYTH(E) continued
Roger, Barnardiston, 1451. R2/9/137
Roger, Troston, 1642, (N). R2/58/404; W1/99/123
Rose, Bury St. Edmunds, 1603, (N). R2/45/217; W1/61/5
Rose, wid., Clare, 1557. R2/26/254; W1/20/169
Rose, wid., Long Melford, 1674. A5/5/146, A4/11/34
Samuel, gent., Mellis, 1622. R2/52/429; W1/78/52
Sara, Ingham, 1631. A5/4/16
Seman, Great Finborough, 1464. R2/10/357
Simon, als. Arnold, Boxford, 1610. R2/47/243; W1/67/125
Simon, als. Steynore, Gislingham, 1578. R2/37/344
Simon, Stanton, 1538. R2/20/126; W1/4/104
Simon, Worlington, 1459. R2/9/248
Stephen, Stradishall, 1486. R2/11/321
Steven, als. Tostok, Barningham, 1521. R2/15/105, R2/17/327
Thomas, Assington, 1526. R2/17/184; W1/23/49
Thomas, butcher, Badwell Ash, 1544. R2/19/472; A5/1/39
Thomas, Bildeston, 1558. R2/27/557
Thomas, gent., Bury St. Edmunds, 1671. R2/65/210; W1/123/82
Thomas, singleman, Cockfield, 1561, (N). R2/30/31; W1/28/221
Thomas, Cockfield, 1641. A5/4/91
Thomas, Denston, 1671. A5/5/123, A4/9/32
Thomas, Gipping, 1554. A5/1/93
Thomas, Gislingham, 1496. R2/13/34
Thomas, yeo., Great Ashfield, 1648. R2/60/33; W1/105/44
Thomas, Great Finborough, 1577. R2/37/306
Thomas, the elder, Great Finborough, 1583. R2/39/69; W1/42/42
Thomas, yeo., Great Finborough, 1611. R2/48/82; W1/68/100
Thomas, Great Waldingfield, 1580. A5/2/23
Thomas, rope weaver, Hessett, 1455. R2/9/177 & 223
Thomas, Honington, (1487). R2/11/428
Thomas, Hopton, 1552. R2/23/237; W1/12/50
Thomas, carpenter, Kersey, 1666. R2/64/20; W1/118/20; In. 3/11/28
Thomas, Lawshall, 1640. A5/4/86
Thomas, husb., Lawshall, 1683. R2/69/163; W1/137/130
Thomas, Long Melford, 1482. R2/11/259
Thomas, Long Melford, 1671. A5/5/124, A4/8/40
Thomas, Nayland, 1553. R2/31/189; W1/13/124
Thomas, Pakenham, 1504. R2/13/156
Thomas, Palling, 1535. W1/51/26
Thomas, husb., Poslingford, (1551). R2/23/57
Thomas, Poslingford, 1661. A5/5/12, A4/1/134
Thomas, husb., Preston, 1619. R2/51/428; W1/132/102
Thomas, Soham, 1520. R2/15/32
Thomas, husb., Soham, 1545. R2/19/534; W1/7/109
Thomas, Soham, 1633. A5/4/26
Thomas, Stansfield, 1464. R2/10/345
Thomas, Sudbury, 1580. A5/2/23
Thomas, gent., Sudbury, 1632. R2/56/146; W1/89/43
Thomas, the elder, yeo., Thelnetham, 1614. R2/49/6; W1/71/6
Thomas, Westley, 1442. R2/9/18
Thomas, the elder, Wickhambrook, 1601, (N). R2/44/427; W1/59/102
Thomas, Wissington, 1670. In. 3/15/189; A5/5/119
Thomas, yeo., Woolpit, 1691. R2/71/500; W1/145/61
Thomas, yeo., Wyverstone, 1557. R2/26/193; W1/20/136
Thomasine, Dalham, 1641. A5/4/90
Walter, Stanton, 1528. R2/15/215
William, the elder, Assington, 1510. R2/12/79
William, Assington, 1545. A5/1/38
William, Bacton, 1554. A5/1/88
William, yeo., Badwell Ash, 1545. R2/19/501; W1/7/101
William, husb., Badwell Ash, 1628. R2/54/145; W1/84/16
William, Brandon, 1643. A5/4/98
William, Bures, 1473. R2/10/527
William, yeo., Burwell, 1693. R2/72/202; W1/147/94
William, wright, Bury St. Edmunds, 1458. R2/2/59
William, merchant, Bury St. Edmunds, 1679. R2/67/296; W1/133/80
William, yeo., Cavendish, 1629. R2/54/295; W1/85/13
William, Cavendish, 1644. R2/59/108; W1/101/34
William, als. Tyrle, Dalham, 1603. R2/45/249; W1/61/50
William, Denham, 1641. R2/58/260; W1/98/34

SMYTH(E) continued
William, esq., Elmsett, 1662. R2/62/389; W1/114/130; In. 3/8/60
William, Exning, 1563. A5/1/153
William, cloth maker, Glemsford, 1545. R2/19/561; W1/7/60
William, yeo., Great Ashfield, 1540. R2/20/182
William, Haughley, 1563. A5/1/140
William, Hockwold, 1666. In. 3/11/48
William, tanner, Kirtling, 1642. R2/58/357; W1/99/56
William, Langham, 1563. R2/31/142; W1/26/22
William, yeo., Lawshall, 1684. R2/69/337; W1/138/131
William, Little Cornard, 1574. R2/37/11; W1/33/82
William, the elder, butcher, Long Melford, 1668. R2/64/332; W1/120/38; In. 3/13/43
William, Norton, 1590. A5/2/130
William, Palgrave, (1546). R2/21/644
William, yeo., Palgrave, 1624. R2/53/160; W1/80/142
William, Redgrave, 1545. R2/19/568; W1/7/68
William, yeo., Redlingfield, 1578. R2/37/354; W1/36/220
William, yeo., Rickinghall Inferior, 1558. R2/27/69
William, yeo., Sudbury, 1578, (N). R2/37/343; W1/36/231
William, sen., Thorpe, 1454. R2/9/174
William, Walsham le Willows, 1579. A5/2/14
William, yeo., Wetherden, 1643. R2/59/68; W1/100/78
William, yeo., Wickhambrook, 1589. R2/41/177; W1/46/108
William, Wreningham, (1533). W1/51/61
see also Smith, Smyeth, Symeth, Anows als. Smyth, Aums als. Smythe, Barker als. Smyth, Curteys als. Smyth, Denny als. Smyth, Gardiner als. Smyth, Hovell als. Smyth, Howell als. Smyth, Ketle als. Smyth, Lawrence als. Smyth, Nevell als. Smythe, Orbell als. Smyth, St. Cleere als. Smyth, Sellowse als. Smythe, Stowers als. Smyth, Watlok als. Smyth
SNARE, George, barber, Mildenhall, 1662. In. 3/7/109
John, barber, Mildenhall, 1662. R2/62/358; W1/114/83
John, barber, Mildenhall, 1684. R2/69/430; W1/138/209; A5/6/192
SNAWE, John, Nayland, 1451. W1/24/141
John, Nayland, 1455. R2/9/181
SNELL, Alice, Cockfield, 1611. A5/3/110
Anne, Cockfield, 1673. R2/36/123; W1/32/26
Henry, Denston, 1667. In. 3/12/29; A5/5/82
James, husb., Cockfield, 1661. In. 3/6/8; A5/5/12, A4/1/142
John, the elder, husb., Cockfield, 1569. R2/33/115; W1/28/178
John, yeo., Cockfield, 1610. R2/47/247; W1/67/130
William, yeo., Cockfield, 1685. R2/70/152; W1/139/131
SNELLING, Abraham, yeo., Great Waldingfield, 1680. R2/67/777; W1/134/208; In. 3/20/234
Edward, brick maker, Woolpit, 1605. R2/45/468; W1/63/117
Elisabeth, wid., Whatfield, 1563. R2/32/30; W1/26/89
Henry, yeo., Great Waldingfield, 1650. R2/61/380; W1/107/82; In. 3/3/98
Isaac, clothier, Sudbury, 1683. R2/69/179; W1/137/139
James, tailor, Bildeston, 1695. R2/72/294; W1/148/20
John, yeo., Bildeston, 1661. R2/62/242; W1/113/121; In. 3/6/155
Richard, husb., Acton, 1637. R2/57/161; W1/92/201
Robert, sen., yeo., Drinkstone, 1685. R2/70/159; W1/139/135
Robert, Drinkstone, 1700. In. 3/27/24; A5/7/17, A4/14/142
Robert, Great Waldingfield, 1637. A5/4/48
Robert, Whatfield, 1584. R2/39/184; W1/42/141
Rose, wid., Elmsett, 1598. R2/44/136; W1/56/99
Rose, wid., Sudbury, 1663. R2/63/16; W1/115/29; In. 3/9/35
Simon, clothier, Edwardstone, 1588. R2/41/10; W1/45/7
Thomas, Drinkstone, 1541. R2/21/387
Walter, Elmsett, 1532. R2/19/94
SNELLYNG, Alexander, Elmsett, 1474. R2/11/109
SNESSE, Richard, cooper, Wortham, 1566. R2/32/323; W1/28/64
SNODE, Richard, Great Saxham, (1503). R2/13/135
Richard, Westley, 1446. R2/9/77 & 146
Robert, Westley, 1452. R2/9/131
SNOKESHULL, John, esq., (1432). R2/1/204
SNOW, John, skinner, Bury St. Edmunds, 1434. R2/1/203
Robert, yeo., Barnham, 1648, (N). R2/60/27; W1/105/38
William, shepherd, Elveden, 1665. R2/63/322; W1/117/63
see also Fuller als. Snow, Fullor als. Snowe

SNOWDEN, Edward, Bury St. Edmunds, 1631. R2/56/7; W1/87/9
Edward, Cockfield, 1590. A5/2/131
Henry, Botesdale, 1679. A5/6/28, A4/16/141
SNOWDON, Prudence, wid., Stansfield, 1609. W1/111/59
SOAME, Elisabeth, wid., Little Thurlow, 1668. R2/64/400; W1/120/123
John, gent., Little Bradley, 1672. R2/65/367; W1/124/106
Richard, gent., Little Bradley, 1647. R2/59/373; W1/104/1; In. 3/2/12
Thomas, gent., Kedington, 1690. A5/6/134, A4/32/37
William, knight, Haughley, 1685. R2/70/151; W1/139/128
William, sen., gent., Hundon, 1632. R2/56/218; W1/89/138
SOAR, James, Ingham, 1685. A5/6/94, A4/24/102
SOHAM, William, spicer, Bury St. Edmunds, 1396. R2/1/79
SOKERMAN, Andrew, Mildenhall, 1544. R2/19/448
SOLAWE, John, Botesdale, 1442. R2/9/48
Walter, Botesdale, 1445. R2/9/87
SOLES, Robert, Long Melford, 1630. A5/4/7
SOMER, Elisabeth, singlewoman, Beyton, 1625, (N). R2/53/313; W1/81/97
John, smith, Bacton, 1601. R2/44/472; W1/59/81
John, Rougham, 1630, (N). R2/55/35; W1/86/38b
Robert, smith, Bacton, 1542. R2/22/22; W1/6/75
William, tailor, Bury St. Edmunds, 1473. R2/2/185
SOMERS, Thomas, Clare, 1700. A5/7/15, A4/41/107
SOMERSET, Henry, Sudbury, 1665. R2/63/291; W1/117/21; In. 3/10/24
Mary, wid., Acton, 1690. R2/71/431; W1/144/135
Thomas, gent., Acton, 1678. R2/67/95; W1/130/79; In. 3/19/111
SOMERSON, Francis, Great Waldingfield, 1626. R2/53/504; W1/82/45
John, Waldingfield, 1579. R2/38/25; W1/39/55
SOMERTON, Gilbert, governor of the hospital, Long Melford, 1632. R2/56/212; W1/89/130
John, gent., Bury St. Edmunds, 1428. R2/1/180
Robert, Chevington, 1445. R2/9/64
SOMMERS, Mary, als. Jackson, wife of Thomas, Timworth, 1665. In. 3/10/23; A5/5/66, A4/3/20
SONDAY, John, Newton, 1532. R2/19/110; W1/3/135
SONNER, Matthew, blacksmith, Bacton, 1591. R2/42/135; W1/48/105
SOPER, Adam, Bury St. Edmunds, 1370. R2/1/33
Robert, Barton Mills, 1439. R2/9/7; W1/24/115
Thomas, Pakenham, (1531). R2/19/81
SOPP, John, weaver, Brandon, 1554. R2/24/3; W1/14/4
SORR, Elisabeth, wid., Timworth, 1685. R2/70/91; W1/139/82
Thomas, yeo., Timworth, 1685. R2/70/1; W1/139/1
SORRELL, James, gent., Cavenham, 1670. R2/65/3; W1/122/3; In. 3/15/12
John, Chelsworth, 1452. R2/9/111
Thomas, gent., Lavenham, 1688. R2/71/78; W1/142/70
Thomas, yeo., Old Newton, 1559. R2/28/282; W1/22/257
William, gent., Gazeley, 1619. R2/51/339; W1/132/48
SORRILL, William, Cavenham, 1642. A5/4/97
SOTHERTON, Henry, Newmarket, 1689. R2/71/263; W1/143/100
SOTYLL, Hugh, draper, Lavenham, 1557. R2/26/93; W1/20/54
see also Rosell als. Sotyll
SOUGATE, Humphrey, yeo., Cockfield, 1623. R2/52/716; W1/79/128
Robert, yeo., Earl Stonham, 1691. R2/71/538; W1/145/95
William, Buxhall, 1648, (N). R2/60/147; W1/105/176
SOULE, William, Soham, 1583. R2/39/73; W1/42/35
see also Sowle
SOUTER, Edward, yeo., Cavenham, 1620. R2/52/6; W1/76/4
John, clothier, Little Waldingfield, 1638. R2/57/299; W1/93/72
Mary, wid., Little Waldingfield, 1641. R2/58/248; W1/98/18
Philip, Rattlesden, 1643, (N). R2/59/30; W1/100/41
see also Sowter
SOUTH, Dorothy, wid., Brandon, 1664. In. 3/9/158
Francis, Bury St. Edmunds, 1587. A5/2/85
John, singleman, Burwell, 1686. R2/70/452; W1/140/62; In. 3/22/45
Robert, wid., Felsham, 1681. A5/6/54, A4/18/131
Thomas, Haughley, 1536. R2/19/243
William, Burwell, 1632. A5/4/18
William, husb., Gedding, 1559. R2/28/200; W1/22/167
William, the younger, husb., Soham, 1677. R2/66/474; W1/129/55; In. 3/18/68
see also Sowth, Bysowth als. Sowth

SOUTHFOLK, William, Bury St. Edmunds, 1416. R2/1/137
see also Siffoks, Sutfolke
SOUTHGATE, Richard, yeo., Tostock, 1700. R2/74/40; W1/154/41; In. 3/27/30
see also Sowgate
SOUTHOUS, William, clerk, Brandon, 1660. R2/62/74; W1/112/94; In. 3/5/108; A4/2/84
SOUTHOWSE, Dorothy, wid., Brandon, 1674. A5/5/150, A4/11/71
Margaret, Brandon, 1664. A5/5/61
William, Brandon, 1674. A5/5/150, A4/11/72
SOWDEN, John, Rickinghall, 1699. In. 3/26/62; A5/7/13, A4/41/55
SOWDON, Anthony, Rickinghall Superior, 1666. R2/64/137; W1/118/103; In. 3/11/145
SOWGATE, Elisabeth, singlewoman, Great Finborough, 1617. R2/50/239; W1/74/36
Emily, spinster, Buxhall, 1611. R2/48/42; W1/68/63
George, yeo., Rattlesden, 1643. R2/59/41; W1/100/50
Humphrey, husb., Felsham, 1600. R2/45/5; W1/58/8
John, grocer, Felsham, 1660. R2/62/60; W1/112/76
John, Stowmarket, 1521. R2/15/160
John, Stowupland, 1681. A5/6/50, A4/18/83
John, yeo., Stowupland, 1688. R2/71/93; W1/142/84; In. 3/23/104
Joseph, Combs, 1685. A5/6/96, A4/24/123
Joseph, Combs, 1688. In. 3/23/20; A5/6/118, A4/29/20
Robert, Creeting St. Peter, 1693. A5/6/156, A4/35/82
Robert, yeo., Great Barton, 1669. R2/64/527; W1/121/117; In. 3/14/129
Robert, singleman, Hessett, 1620. R2/52/179; W1/76/160
Robert, yeo., Norton, 1688. R2/71/130; W1/142/118
Thomas, Thurston, 1691. A5/6/145, A4/33/80
William, yeo., Combs, 1660. R2/62/40; W1/112/47
William, yeo., Combs, 1678. R2/67/2; W1/130/3; In. 3/19/31
William, yeo., Felsham, 1625. R2/53/294; W1/81/83
William, yeo., Rattlesden, 1613. R2/48/293; W1/70/66
William, singleman, Stowupland, 1647. R2/59/403; W1/104/29; In. 3/2/147
see also Sougate, Southgate, Suggate
SOWLE, Frances, wid., Nayland, 1615. R2/49/341; W1/72/113
Marian, wid., Bury St. Edmunds, 1552. R2/8/79; W1/21/212
SOWLTER, Prudence, wid., Rattlesden, 1638. R2/57/263; W1/93/24
SOWMAN, John, husb., Acton, 1593. R2/42/380; W1/50/45
see also Sillman als. Sowman
SOWTER, Edward, husb., Rattlesden, 1660. R2/62/86; W1/112/113; In. 3/5/125
George, yeo., Ixworth, 1569. R2/33/119; W1/28/185
Henry, Combs, 1640. R2/58/133; W1/96/24
John, yeo., Fornham St. Genevieve, 1593. R2/42/416; W1/50/76
John, yeo., Rattlesden, 1627. R2/54/94; W1/83/93
John, sen., Thurston, 1477. R2/11/123
John, Thurston, 1491. R2/11/459
John, husb., Thurston, 1577. R2/37/287
Margaret, wid., Rattlesden, 1673. R2/65/421; W1/125/46
Robert, Thurston, 1517. R2/13/224
Rose, wid., Horringer, 1631. R2/56/104; W1/87/160
Samuel, Bury St. Edmunds, 1687. R2/70/280; W1/141/23
Thomas, Thurston, 1591. A5/2/151
---, wid., Thurston, (1526). W1/19/10
see also Souter, Ward als. Sowter
SOWTH, Elisabeth, Burwell, 1637. A5/4/48
Robert, waterman, Burwell, 1617. R2/50/400; W1/74/185
Robert, Cowlinge, 1570. R2/35/36
William, waterman, Burwell, 1604. R2/45/331; W1/62/45
William, husb., Felsham, 1520. R2/15/69
SPALDEING, Bridget, wid., Great Horningsheath, 1639. R2/58/84; W1/94/143
SPALDEN, John, Naughton, 1631. A5/4/10
SPALDIN, Edward, basket maker, Exning, 1663. R2/63/57; W1/115/90; In. 3/8/120
Henry, husb., Wicken, 1650. R2/61/367; W1/107/62; In. 3/3/88
William, linen weaver, Wortham, 1663. R2/63/58; W1/115/91; In. 3/8/131

SPALDING, Ann, Tuddenham, 1633. A5/4/26
Audrey, Bury St. Edmunds, 1700. A5/7/17, A4/41/149
Augustine, husb., Timworth, 1626. R2/53/628; W1/82/152
Cicely, singlewoman, Wortham, 1663, (N). R2/63/4; W1/115/7; In. 3/8/15; A5/5/42
Clement, Bury St. Edmunds, 1592. A5/2/160
Edward, Exning, 1630. R2/55/162; W1/86/179
Elisabeth, Hawstead, 1604. R2/45/308; W1/62/7
Francis, Tuddenham, 1630. R2/55/125; W1/86/141
Gilbert, yeo., Hartest, 1634. R2/56/362; W1/90/136
Gilbert, yeo., Hawstead, 1632. R2/56/192; W1/89/104
Henry, husb., Ickworth, 1572. R2/36/81; W1/31/52
John, Ampton, 1689. A5/6/130, A4/30/8
John, Bury St. Edmunds, 1578. R2/37/401; W1/36/173
John, Exning, 1630. A5/4/4
John, yeo., Fornham St. Martin, 1608. R2/46/189; W1/65/53
John, Great Livermere, 1591. A5/2/158
John, yeo., Risby, 1650. R2/61/322; W1/107/17; In. 3/3/27
Robert, yeo., Bury St. Edmunds, 1591. R2/42/173; W1/48/74
Robert, Bury St. Edmunds, 1636. A5/4/45
Robert, Bury St. Edmunds, 1668. In. 3/13/103; A5/5/95, A4/6/59
Robert, yeo., Wortham, 1572. R2/36/37; W1/31/47
Roger, the elder, maltster, Bury St. Edmunds, 1688. R2/71/25; W1/142/23
Samuel, yeo., Bury St. Edmunds, 1637. R2/57/214; W1/92/255
Thomas, husb., Timworth, 1573. R2/36/143; W1/32/53
Thomas, Walsham le Willows, 1552. R2/23/239
William, husb., Exning, 1650, (N). R2/61/326; W1/107/22; In. 3/3/23
William, the elder, husb., Fornham All Saints, 1588, (N). R2/41/90; W1/45/86
William, Fornham All Saints, 1612. A5/3/118
William, yeo., Fornham All Saints, 1674. R2/66/109; W1/126/12; A5/5/146, A4/11/19
William, the elder, labourer, Gazeley, 1685. R2/70/76; W1/139/68; A5/6/88, A4/24/21
William, yeo., Great Barton, 1626. R2/53/586; W1/82/116
William, yeo., Timworth, 1599. R2/44/304; W1/57/97
SPALDYNG, Annice, wid., Fornham All Saints, 1482. R2/11/199
Gilbert, husb., Fornham All Saints, 1546. R2/21/203; W1/10/68
John, Bury St. Edmunds, 1416. R2/1/138
John, Bury St. Edmunds, 1506. R2/4/173
John, bladesmith, Bury St. Edmunds, 1515. R2/6/19
John, Fornham All Saints, 1521. R2/15/129, R2/17/328
John, Fornham All Saints, 1523. R2/14/78
John, husb., Timworth, 1535. R2/19/211; W1/3/160
John, Wortham, 1460. R2/9/244
John, Wortham, 1518. R2/12/105
Robert, Barton, 1525. R2/17/123; W1/21/120
Thomas, maltster, Bury St. Edmunds, 1571. R2/35/247; W1/38/121
Walter, Fornham All Saints, 1473. R2/11/16
see also Spaulding
SPALL, John, Mildenhall, 1695. A5/6/180, A4/38/50
SPAREMAN, William, Wicken, 1631. R2/56/92; W1/87/139
SPAREPOYNT, John, weaver, Long Melford, 1571. R2/35/177; W1/38/161
Thomas, weaver, Sudbury, 1590. R2/41/340; W1/47/33
SPARHALKE, John, yeo., Mildenhall, 1700. R2/74/9; W1/154/10
Thomas, husb., Mildenhall, 1569. R2/33/120; W1/28/185
SPARHAM, John, Long Stratton, 1532. W1/51/16
SPARHAUKE, John, yeo., Mildenhall, 1600. R2/45/7; W1/58/11
Lettice, wid., Hengrave, (1679). W1/312/22
Philip, wid., Mildenhall, 1602. R2/45/209
Thomas, brewer, Hengrave, 1679. R2/67/268; W1/133/57; A5/6/19 & 24, A4/16/49 & 90
SPARHAWKE, Francis, Bury St. Edmunds, 1679. A5/6/24, A4/16/95
John, Culford, 1662. In. 3/7/213; A5/5/39
John, Mildenhall, 1559. R2/28/157; W1/22/144
John, jun., Mildenhall, 1681. A5/6/54, A4/18/129
Richard, Thorndon, 1689. A5/6/128, A4/30/29
Robert, bach., Culford, 1695. A5/6/179, A4/38/46
Robert, yeo., Mildenhall, 1696. R2/73/26; W1/150/5
Thomas, husb., Mildenhall, 1610. R2/47/251; W1/67/133
Thomas, Pulham St. Mary, (1536). W1/51/9
see also Sparhalke

SPARK(E), Adam, Little Saxham, 1477. R2/11/152
Andrew, Hartest, 1565. R2/32/178
Andrew, husb., Haughley, 1556. R2/25/69; W1/16/86
Andrew, Hawstead, 1503. R2/13/127
Ann, Bury St. Edmunds, 1594. A5/2/204
Ann, singlewoman, Hawstead, 1592. R2/42/242; W1/49/56
Ann, wid., Hawstead, 1652. R2/61/570; W1/109/44; In. 3/4/76
Anne, wife of John, Rougham, 1632. R2/56/156; W1/89/61
Anthony, Hawstead, 1675. In. 3/16/134; A5/5/157, A4/12/56
Bridget, als. Harvey, Depden, 1669. R2/64/563; W1/41/152; A5/5/109, A4/7/60
Cicely, wid., Great Bradley, 1620. R2/52/147; W1/76/130
Edmund, Hartest, 1596. A5/2/221
Edmund, yeo., Hawkedon, 1641. R2/58/303; W1/98/92
Edward, blacksmith, Hawstead, 1689. R2/71/215; W1/143/59
Francis, yeo., Great Whelnetham, 1637. R2/57/167; W1/92/207
Francis, Hawstead, 1651. A5/4/138
George, Bures, 1639. A5/4/74
Henry, Badwell Ash, 1590. A5/2/129
Henry, yeo., Hawstead, 1634. R2/56/399; W1/90/182
Henry, yeo., Somerton, 1647. R2/59/461; W1/104/94; In. 3/2/44
James, Flempton, 1585. A5/2/65 & 84
James, yeo., Hartest, 1663. R2/63/64; W1/115/103; In. 3/8/126
Janis, singlewoman, Lawshall, 1567. R2/32/408; W1/19/82
John, Ballingdon, 1697. A5/7/3, A4/40/45
John, miller, Bury St. Edmunds, 1520. R2/6/81
John, the elder, freemason, Bury St. Edmunds, 1531. R2/7/5
John, the younger, weaver, Bury St. Edmunds, 1534. R2/7/21
John, the elder, weaver, Bury St. Edmunds, 1537. R2/7/45
John, Combs, 1488. R2/11/397
John, Fornham St. Martin, 1685. R2/70/179; W1/139/151
John, gent., Great Ashfield, 1681. R2/68/95; W1/135/70
John, Hartest, 1585. R2/39/300; W1/42/280
John, Hartest, 1681. A5/6/48, A4/18/55
John, Hawstead, 1540. R2/19/269; W1/36/33
John, Hawstead, 1639, (N). R2/58/93; W1/94/158
John, blacksmith, Hawstead, 1669. R2/64/459; W1/121/48; In. 3/14/150
John, Hitcham, 1639. A5/4/78
John, yeo., Honington, 1696. R2/73/59; W1/150/102; In. 3/25/80
John, yeo., Rougham, 1640. R2/58/143; W1/96/42
John, the younger, gent., Rougham, 1696. R2/73/47; W1/150/42
John, gent., Rougham, 1699. R2/74/328
John, gent., Rougham, 1699. R2/73/456; W1/153/94
John, yarn man, Somerton, 1692. R2/72/19; W1/146/16
John, Thorpe Morieux, (1643). W1/110/13
John, yeo., Walsham le Willows, 1565. R2/32/189; W1/27/24
John, Wetheringsett, 1458. R2/9/188
John, blacksmith, Whepstead, 1692. R2/72/232; W1/147/122; In. 3/24/60
Katherine, wid., Barrow, 1480. W1/24/34
Katherine, Bury St. Edmunds, 1610. A5/3/88
Margaret, wid., Hawstead, 1565. R2/32/265; W1/27/162
Margaret, wid., Little Saxham, 1586. R2/40/96; W1/43/73; A5/2/85
Margery, wid. of Andrew, Hartest, 1577. R2/37/289
Marian, wid., Hawstead, 1609. R2/47/77; W1/66/89
Martha, spinster, Bury St. Edmunds, 1673. R2/65/477; W1/125/116
Mary, wid., Wetherden, 1688. In. 3/23/105; A5/6/124, A4/29/92
Nicholas, Stoke by Clare, 1630. A5/4/4
Ralph, yeo., Great Whelnetham, 1693. R2/72/131
Ralph, Hawstead, 1561. R2/30/11; W1/28/207
Ralph, bach., Hawstead, 1693. A5/6/155, A4/35/87
Ralph, Saxham, 1544. R2/19/477; W1/5/74
Rebecca, singlewoman, Hawstead, 1669. R2/64/478; W1/121/69; In. 3/14/77
Richard, Clare, 1610. R2/47/289; W1/67/178
Robert, Bury St. Edmunds, 1477. R2/2/240
Robert, baker, Bury St. Edmunds, 1600. R2/45/32; W1/58/48
Robert, skinner, Bury St. Edmunds, 1624. R2/53/146; W1/80/134
Robert, Bury St. Edmunds, 1643, (N). R2/59/19; W1/100/28
Robert, say weaver, Bury St. Edmunds, 1690. R2/71/318; W1/144/19

SPARK(E) continued
Robert, clock maker, Cockfield, 1648. R2/60/19; W1/105/29
Robert, the elder, yeo., Depden, 1669. In. 3/14/49; A5/5/102, A4/7/14
Robert, Haughley, 1522. R2/14/49
Robert, husb., Hawstead, 1578. R2/37/398; W1/36/177
Robert, yeo., Lawshall, 1618. R2/51/91; W1/75/56
Robert, yeo., Lawshall, 1648. R2/60/92; W1/105/113
Robert, Long Melford, 1663. R2/63/34; W1/115/53
Rose, servant, spinster, Fornham St. Martin, 1650, (N). R2/61/416; W1/107/121
Rose, wid., Hawstead, 1554. R2/24/61; W1/14/47
Thomas, Badwell Ash, 1613. R2/48/261; W1/70/35
Thomas, yeo., Lawshall, 1627. R2/54/87; W1/83/88
Thomas, Mildenhall, 1638. R2/57/377; W1/93/181
Thomas, miller, Pakenham, 1681. R2/68/119; W1/135/91
Thomas, yeo., Stowupland, 1683. R2/69/35; W1/137/29
Thomas, yeo., Wyverstone, 1640. R2/58/127; W1/96/11
William, Bury St. Edmunds, 1438. R2/1/236
William, yeo., Cavendish, 1680. R2/67/662; W1/134/124; In. 3/20/136
William, wid., Cockfield, 1681. A5/6/47, A4/18/52
William, Drinkstone, 1608. A5/3/51
William, Great Whelnetham, 1648. A5/4/120
William, blacksmith, Hawstead, 1582. R2/38/398; W1/41/41
William, Lavenham, 1662. R2/62/313; W1/114/11; In. 3/7/17
William, Lodden, (1531). W1/51/43
William, wid., Long Melford, 1684. A5/6/76, A4/21/25
William, Shimpling, 1641. A5/4/91
William, yeo., Walsham le Willows, 1576. R2/37/187; W1/37/54; In. 3/1/51
---, Hartest, 1565. W1/27/113
---, Little Saxham, 1476. R2/11/48
see also Sperk, Gault als. Sparke, Stebbin als. Sparke
SPARLING, James, Stoke by Nayland, 1681. A5/6/51, A4/18/92
Matthew, labourer, Assington, 1642. R2/58/376; W1/99/80
Sarah, Westhorpe, 1625. R2/53/241; W1/81/35
SPARMAN, John, Clare, 1679. A5/6/29, A4/16/154
Phillip, Groton, 1455. R2/9/228
SPAROW, Agnes, wid., Rede, 1570. R2/34/11; W1/30/11a
Alice, wid., Stansfield, 1559. R2/28/283; W1/22/258
Anthony, the elder, Depden, 1570. R2/34/61; W1/38/127
John, sen., Chedburgh, (1506). R2/13/192
John, Denston, 1520. R2/15/22
John, Hartest, 1503. R2/13/128
John, yeo., Stansfield, 1559. R2/28/1
John, yeo., Stansfield, 1562. R2/31/38; W1/8/162
Richard, Ousden, 1591. R2/42/69; W1/48/58
Richard, Rede, 1559. R2/28/219; W1/22/201
Robert, Long Melford, 1470. R2/10/576
Sara, Sudbury, 1485. R2/11/334
Thomas, husb., Great Saxham, 1632. R2/56/138; W1/89/29
Thomas, Long Melford, 1559. R2/28/410; W1/3/108
Thomas, yeo., Stansfield, 1559. R2/28/20; W1/22/24
William, Chedburgh, 1503. R2/13/129
SPARPOINT, Henry, Sudbury, 1589, (N). R2/41/148; W1/46/132
SPARROW, Agnes, wid. of Martin, Wixoe, 1617. R2/50/252; W1/74/51
Alice, wid. of Nicholas, Wickhambrook, 1599. R2/44/211; W1/57/32
Anne, wid. of George, Chevington, 1570, (N). R2/35/1; W1/38/133
Anthony, yeo., Chevington, 1631. R2/56/107; W1/87/165
Anthony, yeo., Chevington, 1687. R2/70/375; W1/141/97
Anthony, yeo., Depden, 1617. R2/50/327; W1/74/115
Dorothy, spinster, wid. of Samuel, gent., Rede, 1690. R2/71/319; W1/144/20
Elisabeth, wid. of Anthony, yeo., Rede, 1671. R2/65/258; W1/123/139
Elisabeth, wid., Woolpit, 1662. R2/62/351; W1/114/70; A5/5/22 & 31, A4/1/47a & b
Elizabeth, wid., Chedburgh, 1584. R2/39/209; W1/42/117
Erasmus, yeo., Chedburgh, 1608. R2/46/202; W1/65/78
Francis, yeo., Onehouse, 1686. R2/70/525; W1/140/127
George, baker, Bury St. Edmunds, 1634. R2/56/361; W1/90/134

SPARROW continued

George, husb., Cavenham, 1676. R2/66/356; W1/128/63; In. 3/17/72
George, yeo., Chevington, 1609. R2/47/71; W1/66/83
George, yeo., Chevington, 1650. R2/61/414; W1/107/120; In. 3/3/137
George, yeo., Langham, 1630. R2/55/131; W1/86/147
Henry, the elder, yeo., Cheveley, 1662. R2/62/364; W1/114/93; In. 3/7/140
Henry, yeo., Shimpling, 1696. R2/73/74; W1/150/80
Isabel, wid. of Robert, Depden, 1565. R2/32/219; W1/27/180
Joan, wid., Elmsett, 1599. R2/44/337; W1/59/2
John, the elder, carpenter, Ballingdon, 1695. R2/72/518; W1/149/72
John, Bury St. Edmunds, 1444. R2/2/7, R2/9/53
John, labourer, Cheveley, 1640. R2/58/202; W1/96/132
John, yeo., Chevington, 1675. In. 3/16/89; A5/5/154, A4/12/15
John, the elder, yeo., Chevington, 1686. R2/70/460; W1/140/73; In. 3/22/33
John, yeo., Denham, 1674. R2/66/76; W1/126/45
John, yeo., Depden, 1553. R2/23/94; W1/11/127
John, Depden, 1679. R2/67/320; W1/133/94
John, tanner, Hawkedon, 1612. R2/48/209; W1/69/101
John, sen., Ousden, 1680. R2/67/707; W1/134/156; In. 3/20/173
John, yeo., Rede, 1598. R2/44/87; W1/56/86
John, baker, Stowmarket, 1692. R2/72/52; W1/146/48
John, yeo., Whepstead, 1688. R2/71/105; W1/142/96; In. 3/23/100
John, Wixoe, (1585). R2/39/304; W1/42/273
John, bach., Wortham, 1679. A5/6/30, A4/16/160
John, yeo., Wortham, 1680. In. 3/20/49
Katherine, wid., Chedburgh, 1614. R2/49/14; W1/71/10
Katherine, spinster, Lidgate, 1690, (N). R2/71/357; W1/144/62; A5/6/134, A4/32/27
Margaret, wid., Rede, 1688. R2/71/91; W1/142/83
Matthew, yeo., Little Thurlow, 1593. R2/42/356; W1/50/23
Michael, Depden, 1592. R2/42/317; W1/49/139
Miles, Long Melford, 1642. A5/4/96
Nicholas, yeo., Wickhambrook, 1598. R2/44/8; W1/56/9
Nicholas, Wickhambrook, 1645. A5/4/108
Oliver, the elder, yeo., Chedburgh, 1582. R2/38/352
Oliver, yeo., Ousden, 1699. R2/73/348; W1/153/8
Phillip, yeo., Stansfield, 1570. R2/35/57
Rebecca, spinster, Whepstead, 1690. R2/71/331; W1/144/35
Richard, clothier, Boxford, 1591. R2/42/126; W1/48/111
Richard, the elder, Cowlinge, 1678. In. 3/19/4; A5/6/1, A4/15/3
Richard, husb., Elmsett, 1551. R2/23/2; W1/11/66
Richard, tanner, Onehouse, 1588. R2/41/119; W1/45/113
Richard, yeo., Ousden, 1616. R2/50/126; W1/73/134
Richard, Stansfield, 1521. R2/14/39, R2/17/12; W1/21/76
Richard, Thorpe Morieux, 1558. R2/27/253
Robert, Bures, 1640. A5/4/78
Robert, Depden, (1552). R2/23/150 & 205; W1/12/32
Robert, husb., Lavenham, 1616. R2/50/27; W1/73/27
Robert, Long Melford, 1470. R2/10/448
Robert, Stansfield, 1563. R2/32/23; W1/26/84
Robert, gent., Wickhambrook, 1684. R2/69/396; W1/138/179
Robert, singleman, Wickhambrook, 1690. A5/5/135, A4/32/40
Samuel, yeo., Depden, 1650. R2/61/333; W1/107/32; In. 3/3/15
Samuel, gent., Depden, 1683. R2/69/92; W1/137/70
Samuel, gent., Rede, 1682. R2/68/359; W1/136/71; In. 3/21/158
Sarah, Bury St. Edmunds, 1378. R2/1/42
Simon, yeo., Milden 1665. R2/63/289; W1/117/19; In. 3/10/16
Simon, Sudbury, 1474. R2/11/145
Stephen, yeo., Brockley, 1603. R2/45/255; W1/61/57
Thomas, tailor, Barrow, 1608. R2/46/175; W1/65/33
Thomas, yeo., Hargrave, 1629. R2/54/338; W1/85/47
Thomas, Hawkedon, 1644. A5/4/106
Thomas, singleman, Long Melford, 1661. R2/62/213; W1/113/77; In. 3/6/101
Thomas, saddler, Mildenhall, 1565, (N). R2/32/253; W1/27/167
Thomas, yeo., Rede, 1651. R2/61/471
Thomas, husb., Wood Ditton, 1617, (N). R2/50/404; W1/74/189

SPARROW continued
Titus, yeo., Rede, 1632. R2/56/161; W1/89/67
Walter, Boxford, 1447. R2/9/82
William, clerk, Bildeston, 1685. R2/70/11; W1/139/12
William, Bury St. Edmunds, 1589. A5/2/114b & 117b
William, yeo., Chevington, 1585. R2/39/379; W1/42/229
William, bach., Lawshall, 1679. A5/6/26, A4/16/113
William, Naughton, 1681. A5/6/55, A4/18/141
William, Rede, 1640. R2/58/210; W1/96/144
William, yeo., Woolpit, 1661. R2/62/206; W1/113/68; In. 3/6/84
see also Sparow
SPAULDING, Ann, singlewoman, Risby, 1606. R2/46/44; W1/64/59
William, Fornham St. Martin, 1565. R2/32/177; W1/27/112
SPEARE, Benjamin, Timworth, 1678. In. 3/19/143; A5/6/11, A4/15/92
see also Spere
SPEAREMAN, John, Burwell, 1613. W1/95/126
SPEARMAN, Roland, Burwell, 1625. R2/53/255; W1/81/45
Thomas, Burwell, 1642. A5/4/94
see also Spareman, Sparman, Sperman, Day als. Spearman
SPEARPOYNT, Joshua, say maker, weaver, Sudbury, 1682. R2/68/296; W1/136/27; In. 3/21/212
see also Sparepoynt, Sparpoint, Sperpoint
SPEDE, John, Bury St. Edmunds, 1473. R2/2/184
Richard, Nayland, 1542. R2/22/70; W1/6/44
SPEDIER, Lancelot, weaver, Sudbury, 1615. R2/49/260; W1/72/43
SPEED, Anthony, Nayland, 1592. R2/42/281; W1/49/97
Daniel, gent., Lavenham, 1688. In. 3/23/28; A5/6/126, A4/30/56
Estofidelis, wid., Great Saxham, 1697. R2/73/119; W1/151/9
William, Little Saxham, 1443. R2/9/46
see also Spede
SPEILMAN, Edward, Exning, 1661. R2/62/253; W1/113/137; In. 3/6/185
SPELLMAN, Robert, Soham, 1569. R2/33/132
Thomas, Soham, 1561. R2/30/69; W1/28/241
Thomas, Soham, 1570. R2/34/48; W1/30/43
SPENCAR, Joan, Nayland, 1573. R2/36/194; W1/32/127
SPENCELY, Martin, gent., Bury St. Edmunds, 1698. R2/73/312; W1/152/78
Thomas, the younger, Bury St. Edmunds, 1635. R2/56/524; W1/91/131
SPENCER, Elisabeth, wid., Groton, 1648. R2/60/135; W1/105/162
Elisabeth, wid., Layham, 1684. A5/6/78, A4/21/51
Francis, clerk, Flempton, 1631, (N). R2/56/110
Hannah, Hartest, 1682. A5/6/61, A4/19/63
Henry, Soham, 1665. A5/5/64, A4/3/1
Henry, pail maker, Wortham, 1678. R2/67/181; W1/130/159; In. 3/19/222
Isabel, wid., Bardwell, (1498). R2/13/93
James, wid., Hengrave, 1679. A5/6/20, A4/16/60
John, gent., yeo., Bacton, 1675. R2/66/136; W1/127/15; In. 3/16/17
John, yeo., Fornham St. Martin, 1660. A5/5/8, A4/1/179
John, Ousden, 1449. W1/24/152
Richard, yeo., Edwardstone, 1610. R2/47/234; W1/67/114
Robert, singleman, Boxford, 1647. In. 3/2/43; A5/4/116
Robert, Rickinghall, 1669. In. 3/14/151; A5/5/103, A4/7/27
Robert, Stanstead, 1699. A5/59/13
Thomas, Bardwell, 1471. R2/10/505
Thomas, Bury St. Edmunds, 1462. R2/2/72
Thomas, the elder, Dalham, 1633. R2/56/302; W1/90/67
Thomas, singleman, Haughley, 1598. R2/44/39; W1/56/30
Thomas, collar maker, Hopton, 1566. R2/32/343; W1/28/42
Thomas, cordwainer, Sudbury, 1647. R2/59/396; W1/104/22; In. 3/2/32
Thomas, Thelnetham, (1560). W1/36/8
Thomasine, Long Melford, 1584. A5/2/55
Walter, Ousden, 1441. R2/9/30
William, chaplain, Bury St. Edmunds, 1448. R2/2/27
William, Fordham, (1498). R2/13/110
see also Spencar, Spensar
SPENDELOVE, John, Nayland, 1474. R2/11/109
SPENDLEA, Christopher, Burwell, 1558. R2/27/469
SPENDLOVE, Harry, Acle, 1540. W1/51/86 & 87a & b
John, Old Newton, 1674. A5/5/146, A4/11/31
see also Spendelove, Spenlove

SPENEYE, Agnes, Bury St. Edmunds, 1411. R2/1/123
SPENLOVE, Anna, wid., Occold, 1679. R2/67/240; W1/133/10
SPENSAR, John, butcher, Nayland, 1562. R2/31/76; W1/8/191
SPENSER, Alice, Fordham, 1506. R2/13/181
Elisabeth, wid., Bury St. Edmunds, 1506. R2/4/174
Elisabeth, wid., Nayland, 1566. R2/32/314; W1/28/78
Gilbert, tailor, Bury St. Edmunds, 1469. R2/2/129
Henry, Ickworth, 1631. A5/4/15
John, gent., Boxford, 1643. R2/59/48; W1/100/58
John, Dalham, 1459. R2/9/240
John, husb., Hartest, 1603. R2/45/213; W1/61/8
Richard, Haughley, (1508). R2/13/176a
Thomas, weaver, Bury St. Edmunds, 1462. R2/2/76
Thomas, Haverhill, 1577. A5/2/1
Thomas, Little Cornard, 1580. A5/2/30
Thomas, Norton, 1557. R2/26/315; W1/20/237
William, Fordham, 1498. R2/13/109
William, Little Cornard, 1584. A5/2/62
SPERE, John, Bury St. Edmunds, 1584. A5/2/63
Thomas, pewterer, Bury St. Edmunds, 1531. R2/7/1
Thomas, Bury St. Edmunds, 1579. A5/2/17
SPERK, Robert, smith, Little Saxham, 1503. R2/13/138
SPERLING, John, carpenter, Bury St. Edmunds, 1557. R2/8/312; W1/18/40
Robert, husb., Stoke by Nayland, 1526. R2/17/212; W1/23/19
SPERLYNG, John, Stoke by Nayland, 1458. R2/9/262
John, Stoke by Nayland, 1473. R2/10/519
John, Stoke by Nayland, 1520. R2/15/27
Katherine, Combs, 1464. R2/10/368
see also Sparling
SPERMAN, John, Edwardstone, 1480. R2/12/5
SPERPOINT, Thomas, Long Melford, 1565. R2/32/170; W1/27/106
SPETYLMAN, Joan, wid., Buxhall, 1484. R2/11/330
Robert, Burgate, 1483. R2/11/359
William, Glemsford, 1440. R2/9/29
William, Norton, 1460. R2/9/271
SPICER, Aby, wid., Isleham, 1683. In. 9/60
Alice, spinster, Lakenheath, 1650. In. 3/3/34; A5/4/134
Edward, yeo., Ashley, 1694. R2/72/361; W1/148/87
Elisabeth, wid. of Thomas, Isleham, 1683. W7/100
John, the elder, gent., Wattisfield, 1686. R2/70/237; W1/140/7; In. 3/22/74
John, Wattisfield, 1692. A5/6/146, A4/33/94
Robert, Cheveley, 1700. A5/7/14, A4/41/135
Thomas, labourer, Isleham, 1685. W7/106; In. 9/58
Thomas, yeo., Newton, (1552). R2/21/622
William, Bury St. Edmunds, 1402. R2/1/94
see also Spissowr, Spycer, Spyser
SPILLMAN, Richard, husb., Soham, 1650. R2/61/375; W1/107/74; In. 3/3/94
Robert, Soham, 1679. A5/6/29, A4/16/148
Thomas, husb., Soham, 1677. R2/66/473; W1/129/54; In. 3/18/69
SPILMAN, Edward, Bury St. Edmunds, 1686. A5/6/105, A4/26/24
Edward, the elder, yeo., Soham, 1638. R2/57/404; W1/93/224
John, Soham, 1591. R2/42/97; W1/48/134
John, husb., Soham, 1624. R2/53/86; W1/80/101
Richard, tailor, Lavenham, 1699. R2/73/375; W1/153/30
Thomas, labourer, Exning, 1662. R2/62/411; W1/114/164; In. 3/7/225
Thomas, yeo., Soham, 1663. R2/63/36; W1/115/55; In. 3/8/61
William, Brandon, 1577. A5/2/3
see also Speilman, Spyleman
SPINCKE, Richard, carpenter, Ixworth, 1634. R2/56/419; W1/90/203
SPINK(E), Alice, Little Livermere, 1599. W1/57/101
Edmund, Beyton, 1691. A5/6/140, A4/33/24
Henry, Buxhall, 1589. A5/2/119
Humfrey, Bury St. Edmunds, 1660. R2/62/109; W1/112/144; In. 3/5/168
John, Badwell Ash, 1645. A5/4/108
Richard, husb., Walsham le Willows, 1561. R2/30/96; W1/28/277
Robert, yeo., Great Saxham, 1630. R2/55/96; W1/86/107
Thomas, wheelwright, Barningham, 1618. R2/51/243; W1/75/158

SPINK(E) continued
Thomas, linen weaver, Thelnetham, 1695. R2/72/559; W1/149/114
William, singleman, Eriswell, 1671. R2/65/272; W1/123/152
William, yeo., Thorpe, 1630. R2/55/95; W1/86/106; A5/4/121
see also Spyncke
SPISSOWR, Ellen, wid., Lakenheath, 1587. R2/40/129; W1/44/11
SPITE, Christopher, Whepstead, 1645. A5/4/109
SPITLEHOUSE, Margaret, wid., Bury St. Edmunds, 1605. R2/45/459; W1/63/107
SPITLEHOWSE, Thomas, yeo., Bury St. Edmunds, 1600. R2/45/48; W1/58/69
SPONER, Ann, wid., Bury St. Edmunds, 1660. R2/62/116; W1/112/154; In. 3/5/160
Edward, Honington, 1504. R2/12/41
Edward, Sudbury, 1480. R2/12/9
Geoffrey, Long Melford, 1584. A5/2/61
Isabel, Sapiston, 1465. R2/10/396
Joan, wid., Kirtling, 1583. R2/39/85; W1/42/26
John, singleman, Bardwell, 1533. R2/19/169; W1/2/18
John, Honington, 1495. R2/13/75
John, Honington, 1556. R2/25/134; W1/16/174
John, Stuston, 1555. R2/24/157; W1/15/5
Peter, Sapiston, 1455. R2/9/181
Robert, Bardwell, 1495. R2/13/73
William, Bardwell, 1545, (N). R2/19/501; W1/7/24
William, the elder, husb., Newton, 1555. R2/24/174; W1/15/13
---, 1452. R2/9/132
SPOONER, Edward, Wood Ditton, 1631. R2/56/49; W1/87/67
Elisabeth, als. King, Bury St. Edmunds, 1662. In. 3/7/25; A5/5/27
Elisabeth, wid., Wood Ditton, 1687. R2/70/313; W1/141/57
William, Wood Ditton, 1680. In. 3/20/69; A5/6/34, A4/95/39
see also Jeferye als. Spooner
SPORE, John, Bury St. Edmunds, 1370. R2/1/28
SPORLE, John, Burgate, 1474. R2/10/551
John, pattern maker, Bury St. Edmunds, 1494. R2/4/31
Robert, the elder, Hempnall, 1536. W1/51/23
Robert, yeo., Shottesham, 1594. W1/51/123
Walter, Bury St. Edmunds, 1421. R2/1/157
William, Bury St. Edmunds, 1507. R2/4/194
SPORYER, see Chapman als. Sporyer, Penteney als. Sporyer
SPRAGGE, Thomas, husb., Tostock, 1585, (N). R2/39/279; W1/42/297; A5/2/66
SPRAGY, Laurence, Haughley, (1469). R2/10/477
SPRAYE, Thomas, Combs, 1592. A5/2/161
SPRING, Elisabeth, wid. of William, Pakenham, 1677. R2/67/462; W1/133/186
Jeremy, gent., Lavenham, 1605, (N). R2/45/444; W1/63/88
Joanna, wid., Creeting All Saints, 1671. R2/65/174; W1/123/44
John, gent., Chelsworth, 1667. A5/5/86, A4/5/60
Katherine, wife of John, gent., Troston, 1575, (N). R2/37/101; W1/34/40
Mary, wid., Isleham, 1670. W7/77
Robert, gent., Hessett, 1690. R2/71/358; W1/144/64
Sarah, wid. of William, Pakenham, 1690. R2/71/372; W1/144/81
Thomas, Creeting All Saints, 1675. In. 3/16/2; A5/5/152, A4/12/2
Thomas, yeo., Isleham, 1661. In. 9/1; A5/5/11, A4/1/139
Thomas, gent., Wattisham, 1608. R2/46/207; W1/65/93
William, Thurston, 1700. In. 3/27/18; A5/7/17, A4/41/158
see also Spryng, Smyth als. Springe
SPRINGAT, John, yeo., Little Cornard, 1606. R2/46/69; W1/64/74
SPRINGETT, James, yeo., Boxford, 1637. R2/57/233; W1/92/286
SPRITE, Mary, Tuddenham, 1591. A5/2/155
SPROT(T), John, Sudbury, 1452. R2/9/156
John, tiler, Sudbury, 1494. R2/13/19
SPROUT, Richard, Clare, 1464. R2/10/356
SPRUNTE, John, yeo., Thetford, 1544. R2/19/463
Mariot, wid. of Richard, Clare, 1472. R2/10/529
Thomas, Lavenham, 1533. R2/18/215, R2/19/178
SPRYE, John, Lavenham, 1480. R2/12/8
SPRYNG, Robert, als. Wededeyn, Brockford, 1473. R2/10/591
Thomas, Lavenham, 1441. R2/9/19
William, Soham, 1457. R2/9/186

SPRYNGOLF, John, mariner, Cromer, (1531). W1/51/54
SPURDANCE, Elisabeth, spinster, Thrandeston, 1670. R2/65/10; W1/122/14; In. 3/15/30
SPURGEN, Ann, wid., Felsham, 1687. R2/70/381; W1/141/103
Henry, yeo., Gedding, 1663. R2/63/42; W1/115/65; In. 3/8/68
John, yeo., Hopton, 1587. R2/40/217; W1/44/67
Richard, Hopton, 1581. R2/38/276; W1/40/24
Thomas, singleman, Bury St. Edmunds, 1638. R2/57/315; W1/93/91
SPURGEON, Daniel, Sudbury, 1681. A5/6/45, A4/18/19
Edmund, yeo., Harleston, 1598. R2/44/53; W1/56/42
Henry, Hopton, 1551. R2/23/98; W1/11/67
SPURGIN, Stephen, yeo., Hopton, 1571. R2/35/52
SPURGYN, Robert, vicar, Foulden, 1582. W1/51/152
SPURLING, Robert, the elder, yeo., Beyton, 1670. R2/65/44; W1/122/51; In. 3/15/68
Sarah, 1684. R2/71/562; W1/145/113
Stephen, wheelwright, Ixworth, 1663. R2/63/53; W1/115/84; In. 3/9/183
Thomas, wheelwright, Ixworth, 1699. In. 3/26/64; A5/7/13, A4/41/66
SPYCER, Isabel, wid., Bury St. Edmunds, 1481. R2/2/317
John, Nowton, 1557. R2/26/41; W1/20/10
John, Walsham le Willows, 1465. R2/10/361
Robert, husb., Bury St. Edmunds, 1570. R2/35/41; W1/38/144
Robert, Fornham St. Martin, 1480. R2/11/191
William, Bury St. Edmunds, 1580. R2/38/128; W1/39/154
SPYLEMAN, John, Thrandeston, 1542. R2/22/31; W1/6/30
SPYLLMAN, Adam, husb., Soham, 1592. R2/42/307; W1/49/130
Agnes, wid., Soham, 1574. R2/37/64; W1/33/13
SPYLMAN, Henry, Soham, 1503. R2/12/52
John, husb., Stoke, 1601. R2/44/416; W1/59/92
John, Woodbridge, (1525). W1/5/33
Nicholas, singleman, Soham, 1592. R2/42/324; W1/49/146
SPYNCKE, John, husb., Preston, 1553. R2/23/110; W1/11/128
William, wheelwright, Ixworth, 1597. R2/43/348; W1/55/112
SPYNK(E), Henry, lime burner, Sudbury, 1551. R2/23/1; W1/11/68
Margaret, wid., Stoke by Nayland, 1495. R2/13/26
Thomas, the elder, yeo., Thorpe Morieux, 1620. R2/52/136; W1/76/120
Thomas, yeo., Thorpe Morieux, 1645. R2/59/244; W1/102/67
William, husb., Pakenham, 1558. R2/27/235
SPYSALL, Richard, Haverhill, 1539. R2/20/222
SPYSER, John, Bildeston, 1457. R2/9/185
Thomas, Lakenheath, 1579. R2/38/27; W1/39/52
SQUIRE, Edmund, Wixoe, 1592. A5/6/166
SQUIRRELL, Edmund, Stowmarket, 1573. R2/36/191; W1/32/115
SQUORRELL, Henry, yeo., Hitcham, 1664. R2/63/215; W1/116/126; In. 3/9/175
STABLE, William, Wicken, 1630. A5/4/8
STABLER, Robert, chaplain, Bury St. Edmunds, 1394. R2/1/66
STACE, Matilda, Sudbury, 1467. R2/10/403
STACY, John, clerk, Bury St. Edmunds, 1573. R2/36/173; W1/32/78
John, Thurston, 1449. R2/9/95
Robert, Barway, 1474. R2/10/582
Thomas, sen., grocer, Bury St. Edmunds, 1559. R2/8/344; W1/17/69
Thomas, Bury St. Edmunds, 1584, (N). R2/39/141; W1/42/184
see also Stasy
STAFFORD, Frances, wid., Pakenham, 1677. R2/66/432; W1/129/114; In. 3/18/2
Francis, als. Storey, husb., Mildenhall, 1673. R2/65/433; W1/125/57
Jeremy, yeo., Gislingham, 1616. R2/50/31; W1/73/31
Margery, wid., Gislingham, 1583. R2/39/3; W1/42/91
Richard, yeo., Buxhall, 1682. R2/68/464; W1/136/142; In. 3/21/72
Richard, yeo., Gislingham, 1555. R2/24/210; W1/15/43
Robert, clerk, Pakenham, 1661. In. 3/6/143
Thomas, (1396). R2/1/82
William, yeo., Gislingham, 1632. R2/22/165; W1/89/73
STAFFOURTHE, John, husb., Gislingham, 1571. R2/35/111 & 383; W1/36/92
see also Stoffer
STAGELL, John, Rattlesden, 1521. R2/14/40

STAKWODE, John, Long Melford, 1522. R2/15/40
STALEY, Richard, Thorndon, 1472. R2/10/581
STALHAM, John, sen., Mildenhall, 1461. R2/10/341
see also Stalonn
STALLWORTHY, John, Rickinghall Inferior, 1591. R2/42/42; W1/48/34
STALONN, John, Mildenhall, 1452. R2/9/148
STALPY, Edward, husb., Combs, 1560. R2/29/138; W1/25/32
STALVERS, John, Newmarket, 1594. A5/2/204
STAMAGE, Elinor, Haverhill, 1541. R2/22/91, 106 & 115; W1/10/33 & 34
Thomas, Haverhill, 1540, (N). R2/19/279; W1/36/40
STAMMER(S), Elisabeth, wid., Great Bradley, 1697. R2/73/205; W1/151/91
Joseph, Brettenham, 1663. In. 3/8/143; A5/5/49
Judith, wid., Denham, 1667. R2/64/202; W1/119/51
Robert, the elder, carpenter, Bury St. Edmunds, 1695. R2/72/481; W1/149/38
Robert, Bury St. Edmunds, 1698. A5/7/7
STANARD, Agnes, wid., Bury St. Edmunds, 1505. R2/4/172
Charity, Haughley, 1608. A5/3/26
STANBORNE, John, Clare, 1527. R2/17/246; W1/1/35
STANBOWE, John, Great Livermere, 1458. R2/9/238; W1/24/15
STANDE, Robert, Bures, 1565. R2/32/216
STANDLY, see Longtot als. Standly
STANERDE, Robert, Haughley, 1594. A5/2/201
STANFEILD, Robert, als. Bud, Exning, 1608. A5/3/40
STANFELD, John, Eye, 1504. R2/12/35
STANLEY, Joan, Bury St. Edmunds, 1528. R2/6/145 (admon. only)
STANLY, Thomas, Stoke by Nayland, 1668, (N). R2/64/404; W1/120/127; In. 3/13/86; A5/5/98, A4/6/84
STANNARD, Alice, Great Ashfield, 1638. A5/4/59
Anthony, yeo., Eye, 1689. R2/71/181; W1/143/38
Jeremiah, clerk, Lackford, 1687. A5/6/109, A4/27/26
John, butcher, maltster, Bury St. Edmunds, 1680. R2/67/559; W1/134/42; In. 3/20/44
John, woollen draper, Bury St. Edmunds, 1682. In. 3/21/151
John, blacksmith, Mildenhall, 1681. R2/68/74; W1/135/58
Nicholas, Bury St. Edmunds, 1505. R2/4/166
Peter, Haughley, 1598. R2/44/99; W1/56/137
Richard, husb., Eye, (1549). R2/21/562; W1/8/36
Robert, servant, Bury St. Edmunds, 1538. R2/7/50
Thomas, chapman, Eye, 1698. R2/73/323; W1/152/90
Thomas, Haughley, 1530. R2/19/20
William, singleman, Bury St. Edmunds, 1647. R2/59/421; W1/104/50
William, husb., Haughley, 1600. R2/45/31; W1/58/47
see also Stanard, Stanerde
STANNESBY, Roger, Bildeston, 1594. A5/2/199
STANSBY, Elisabeth, wid., Glemsford, 1609. R2/47/53; W1/66/60
Frances, wid., Stansfield, 1698. A5/7/6
Joan, wid. of Robert, Glemsford, 1585. R2/39/385; W1/42/221 a & b
John, Bildeston, 1559. R2/28/9; W1/22/11
John, Brent Eleigh, 1670. In. 3/15/52; A5/5/111
Robert, Glemsford, 1560. R2/29/22; W1/25/157
Sara, Brent Eleigh, 1671. A5/5/127, A4/8/67
see also Stanysbye
STANSTED, Robert, husb., Polstead, 1528. R2/15/190; W1/19/38
STANTLY, Thomas, Lavenham, 1594. A5/2/201
STANTON, Abraham, husb., Marham, 1585. W1/51/181
Adam, chaplain, Bury St. Edmunds, 1370. R2/1/34 (and inventory)
Adam, furbisher, Bury St. Edmunds, (1393). R2/1/70
Ann, wid., Bury St. Edmunds, 1665. A5/5/65, A4/3/18
Ann, Hawstead, 1588. A5/2/113a
Ann, Rougham, 1641. A5/4/93
Ann, wid., Rickinghall Superior, 1678. R2/67/132; W1/130/118
Benjamin, bach., Rickinghall Superior, 1683. A5/6/69, A4/20/53
Edmund, husb., Rougham, 1498. R2/4/63
Edward, Wattisham, 1607. A5/3/20
Elisabeth, Bures, 1668. A5/5/101, A4/6/121
Elisabeth, singlewoman, Rickinghall Superior, 1681. R2/68/115; W1/135/87; In. 3/21/42
George, clerk, Icklingham, 1665. R2/63/281; W1/117/9; In. 3/10/30

STANTON continued
Henry, mercer, Bury St. Edmunds, 1629, (N). R2/54/276; W1/85/1
James, Brome, 1458. R2/9/188
Joan, Bury St. Edmunds, 1405. R2/1/105
Joan, wid., Bury St. Edmunds, 1503. R2/4/127
John, Bury St. Edmunds, 1497. R2/4/54
John, Clare, 1452. R2/9/139
John, tailor, Fordham, 1648. R2/60/63; W1/105/80
John, grocer, Rickinghall Superior, 1682. R2/68/403; W1/136/100; In. 3/21/40
John, Rougham, 1459. R2/9/236
Leonard, clerk, Landwade, 1608. R2/46/214; W1/65/106
Lucy, wid., Stoke by Nayland, 1555. W1/95/38 & 39
Margaret, wid., Great Livermere, 1679. R2/67/499; W1/133/215
Martha, spinster, Bury St. Edmunds, 1668. R2/64/331; W1/120/37
Ralph, chaplain, Bury St. Edmunds, 1364. R2/1/25
Richard, Burwell, 1575. R2/37/92; W1/34/16
Robert, Bury St. Edmunds, 1499. R2/4/86
Robert, tanner, Bury St. Edmunds, 1550. R2/8/21
Robert, tailor, Great Livermere, 1678. R2/67/152; W1/130/136; In. 3/19/186
Robert, porter at college of St. John Baptist, Stoke, 1520. R2/15/68, R2/17/311; W1/23/11
Robert, the elder, husb., Stoke by Nayland, 1523. R2/14/87
Roger, Rougham, 1503. R2/13/149
Susan, als. Laurence, Burwell, 1611. A5/3/112
Thomas, mercer, Great Horningsheath, 1635. R2/56/497; W1/91/73
Venus, wid., Wattisham, 1617. R2/50/309; W1/74/97
William, Haverhill, 1543. R2/19/363; W1/6/150
William, Hawstead, 1579. R2/38/66; W1/39/16
see also Harkewood als. Stanton, Leather als. Stanton, Parkins als. Stanton
STANYSBYE, Richard, gent., Bildeston, 1552. R2/23/124; W1/11/111
STAPLE, Thomas, husb., Soham, 1604. R2/45/335; W1/62/49
STAPLEDON, Elisabeth, wid., Flempton, 1589. R2/41/310
STAPLES, Edward, the younger, yeo., Soham, 1673. R2/65/479; W1/125/118 & 130
Edward, the elder, Soham, 1693. R2/72/138; A5/6/161, A4/35/43
Ellis, yeo., Soham, 1641. R2/58/277; W1/98/62
Ellis, Soham, 1676, (N). R2/66/370; W1/128/81; In. 3/17/94; A5/5/163, A4/13/58
Grace, Soham, 1681. A5/6/46, A4/18/38
Thomas, yeo., Soham, 1678. R2/67/168; W1/130/148; In. 3/19/201
Thomas, Soham, 1696. In. 3/25/17; A5/6/187, A4/39/36
William, Glemsford, 1584. R2/39/203; W1/42/124
STAPLETON, Elisabeth, wid., Timworth, 1599. R2/44/334; W1/57/109
John, yeo., Flempton, 1618. R2/51/217; W1/75/137
Miles, yeo., Flempton, 1596. R2/43/165; W1/54/46
Miles, husb., Timworth, 1575. R2/37/74; W1/34/25
William, soldier, Stowmarket, 1652. In. 3/4/38; A5/4/141
STAPYLTON, Brian, gent., Bury St. Edmunds, 1516. R2/6/28 (admon. only)
see also Stapledon, Baxter als. Stapleton
STARKEY, John, Little Wratting, 1684. A5/6/84, A4/21/112
STARLING, Barnaby, Burwell, 1648. A5/4/121
Henry, Occold, 1647. A5/4/119
John, inn holder, Bury St. Edmunds, 1664. R2/63/161; W1/116/58
John, husb., Mildenhall, 1638. R2/57/243; W1/93/1
Robert, Mildenhall, 1675. R2/66/186; W1/127/112; In. 3/16/75
Robert, Nayland, 1632. A5/4/20
STARLYNG, Anthony, Occold, 1648. A5/4/125 & 131
Robert, weaver, Nayland, 1600. R2/45/2; W1/58/3
STARR, John, Great Bradley, 1694. A5/6/171, A4/37/55
William, Haverhill, 1693. R2/72/173
START, John, the elder, husb., Soham, 1620. R2/52/167; W1/76/150
Richard, tailor, Soham, 1598. R2/44/35; W1/56/37b
Thomas, Acton, 1638. A5/4/64
STARTHANT, John, Boxford, 1440. R2/9/28
STARTUPPE, Henry, Stoke by Nayland, 1559. R2/28/74; W1/22/76
STASY, Joan, wid., Bury St. Edmunds, 1590. R2/41/353; W1/47/47
STAVER(S), Ann, Newmarket, 1584. A5/2/62
Richard, clothier, Bury St. Edmunds, 1617. R2/50/238; W1/74/35
Thomas, Newmarket, 1585. A5/2/69

STAWFORD, John, Newmarket, 1560. R2/29/117; W1/25/50
STEAD, Ann, Long Melford, 1689. A5/6/126, A4/30/51
Mary, Long Melford, 1694. A5/6/166, A4/37/4
Richard, yeo., Barton Mills, 1697. R2/73/201; W1/151/84
William, clerk, Rishangles, 1621. R2/52/331; W1/77/111
STEADMAN, John, Weston, 1609. A5/3/77
Richard, Naughton, 1597. R2/43/293; W1/55/66
Thomas, als. Cutberde, yeo., Risby, 1592. R2/42/248; W1/49/65
William, yeo., Beyton, 1678. R2/67/61; W1/130/47; In. 3/19/53
STEARE, Thomas, Bures, 1606. A5/3/10
STEARNE, Edmund, clerk, Bury St. Edmunds, 1607. R2/46/135; W1/97/64
James, singleman, Bury St. Edmunds, 1670. R2/65/49; W1/122/58; In. 3/15/75
Nathaniel, Bury St. Edmunds, 1700. A5/7/16, A4/41/124
Rebecca, wid., Whepstead, 1678. R2/67/134; W1/130/119; In. 3/19/167
Thomas, Soham, 1637. A5/4/56
William, the elder, yeo., Hartest, 1678. R2/67/179; W1/130/157; In. 3/19/221
see also Sterne
STEAVENS, John, blacksmith, Cavendish, 1636. R2/57/40; W1/92/49
STEBEN, Daniel, yeo., Little Cornard, 1686. R2/70/211; W1/139/178; In. 3/22/17
STEBBEN, John, labourer, Hepworth, 1692. R2/72/90; W1/146/84; In. 3/24/25
John, sen., clothier, Stanstead, 1627. R2/54/47; W1/83/52
STEBBIN, Andrew, Long Melford, 1681. A5/6/51, A4/18/91
Francis, Walsham le Willows, 1689. A5/6/126, A4/30/54
Hester, als. Sparke, Badwell Ash, 1678. In. 3/19/162; A5/6/11, A4/15/89
Richard, yeo., Cockfield, 1638. R2/57/264; W1/93/26
Thomas, Bardwell, 1683. A5/6/73, A4/20/104
STEBBING, Abraham, Stanstead, 1694. A5/6/169, A4/37/43
Charles, woollen weaver, Bury St. Edmunds, 1678. R2/67/150; W1/130/134; In. 3/19/185
Edmund, Bury St. Edmunds, 1681. A5/6/54, A4/18/126
Henry, mercer, Long Melford, 1670. R2/65/57; W1/122/68; In. 3/15/102
James, yeo., Palgrave, 1664. R2/63/191; W1/116/94; In. 3/9/132
James, clothier, Stanstead, 1603, (N). R2/45/241; W1/61/36
John, yeo., Fordham, 1640. R2/58/181; W1/96/100
John, Hepworth, 1640. A5/4/80
John, yeo., Little Wratting, 1687. R2/70/563; W1/141/2
Margaret, wid., Bury St. Edmunds, 1680. R2/67/702; W1/134/153; In. 3/20/172
Robert, yeo., Bures, 1641. R2/58/244; W1/98/14
Sarah, wid., Stanstead, 1696. R2/73/78; W1/150/75
Thomas, Old Newton, 1565. R2/32/261; W1/27/160
William, Bardwell, 1691. A5/6/140, A4/33/23
William, 1691. R2/71/456
STEBBYN, Elisabeth, wid., Glemsford, 1565. R2/32/196; W1/27/183
James, Great Thornham, 1596. A5/2/217
STEBBYNG, Robert, Glemsford, 1561. R2/30/103; W1/28/253
William, Bury St. Edmunds, 1442. R2/1/262
STEBING, Agnes, wid., Cockfield, 1638. R2/57/322; W1/93/100
George, Barnardiston, 1597. R2/43/263; W1/55/42
STECKLES, Robert, Bury St. Edmunds, 1650. A5/4/136
STED(E), Emily, Brockley, 1522. R2/14/67
Nicholas, yeo., Shimpling, 1565. R2/32/229; W1/27/149
Richard, parish priest, Kentford, 1538. R2/18/190
Thomas, Kersey, 1590. A5/2/133
Thomas, Warham, 1504. W1/9/8
STEDGALL, John, yeo., Stanton, 1613. R2/48/316; W1/70/92
STEDMAN, Bridget, wid., Beyton, 1682. A5/6/62, A4/19/72
Cuthbert, husb., Nowton, 1540. R2/20/202
Edmund, Onehouse, 1648. A5/4/119
Ellen, wid., Nowton, 1591. R2/42/61; W1/48/49a
Elisabeth, wid., Onehouse, 1681. R2/68/106; W1/135/80
John, Great Barton, 1589. A5/2/122a
Richard, Gazeley, 1667. In. 3/12/110; A5/5/85, A4/5/42
Richard, yeo., Timworth, 1649. R2/60/166; W1/106/13

STEDMAN continued
Robert, Higham, 1641. A5/5/90
Sarah, spinster, Thurston, 1676. R2/66/424; W1/128/137
William, the elder, baker, Bury St. Edmunds, 1700. R2/74/13; W1/154/13
William, yeo., Fordham, 1694. R2/72/361; W1/148/88
William, yeo., Tostock, 1630. R2/55/78; W1/86/88
see also Steadman, Steedmaune, Browning als. Steadman
STEED, John, Ixworth, 1630. A5/4/8
John, glazier, Long Melford, 1695. R2/72/473; W1/149/29; In. 3/25/5
John, yeo., Shimpling, 1619. R2/51/326; W1/132/42
Nicholas, glazier, Stanstead, 1625. R2/53/346; W1/81/126
Thomas, Long Melford, 1692. In. 3/24/22; A5/6/148, A4/34/8
see also Stead, Sted(e), Steyd
STEEDMANNE, Richard, yeo., Naughton, 1588. R2/41/115; W1/45/110
STEEL(E), Barbara, wid., Mildenhall, 1677. R2/66/469; W1/129/50; In. 3/18/65
George, yeo., Long Melford, 1684. R2/69/362; W1/138/152
Henry, the elder, bricklayer, Bury St. Edmunds, 1631. R2/56/36; W1/87/48
Henry, husb., Herringswell, 1631. R2/56/13; W1/87/17
Joan, wid., Hundon, 1651. A5/4/139
John, Sudbury, 1546. R2/21/182; W1/10/121
Robert, labourer, Ashley, 1589. R2/41/200
Thomas, husb., Mildenhall, 1670. R2/65/39; W1/122/43; In. 3/15/63
Thomas, yeo., Mildenhall, 1673. R2/65/422; W1/125/48
see also Stele
STEFF(E), James, smith, Stowmarket, 1521. R2/15/158
John, als. Carter, Bury St. Edmunds, 1515. R2/6/19 (admon. only)
Richard, wid., Barningham, 1683. A5/6/73, A4/20/105
Robert, Fornham St. Martin, 1439. R2/9/4
Simon, Icklingham, 1473. R2/11/38
Simon, smith, Woolpit, 1535. R2/18/138
William, Icklingham, 1483. R2/11/309
STEGALL, Hannah, wid., Stanton, 1694. R2/72/423; W1/148/157; In. 3/26/23
STEGELL, Ann, wid., Troston, 1570. R2/34/9; W1/30/8
Edmund, Redgrave, 1554. R2/24/122; W1/14/94
John, tanner, Elmswell, 1688. R2/71/101; W1/142/91; In. 3/23/94
STEGGALL, Ann, wid., Old Newton, 1686. A5/6/100, A4/26/85
Daniel, Old Newton, 1686. A5/6/100, A4/26/86
John, husb., Elmswell, 1631, (N). R2/56/52; W1/87/72
John, Polstead, 1640. A5/4/80 & 82
Lawrence, Bury St. Edmunds, 1685. A5/6/87, A4/24/11
Philip, Lavenham, 1660. In. 3/5/181; A5/5/9, A4/1/164
Thomas, husb., Elmsett, 1597, (N). R2/43/336; W1/55/102
Thomas, Ingham, 1640. A5/4/82
Thomas, shepherd, Little Livermere, 1687. R2/70/567; W1/141/6
William, singleman, Aldham, 1639. A5/4/72
STEGGELL, Ann, widow, Elmswell, 1679. R2/67/433; W1/133/165; A5/6/27, A4/16/126
Anne, wid., Elmswell, 1678. A5/5/173, A4/14/58
Dennis, Pakenham, 1613. R2/48/324; W1/70/103
Laurence, husb., Ixworth Thorpe, 1666. R2/64/3; W1/118/4; In. 3/11/10
Simon, carpenter, Bury St. Edmunds, 1566. R2/8/401; W1/36/61
William, yeo., Elmswell, 1630. R2/55/52; W1/86/62
STEGGILL, Thomas, yeo., Stanton, 1687. R2/70/409; W1/141/133
STEGILL, Robert, the elder, tanner, Elmswell, 1660. R2/62/9; W1/112/8; In. 3/5/3
STEGGLES, Robert, Bury St. Edmunds, 1694. A5/6/173, A4/37/86
STEGGOLD, Henry, yeo., Stowupland, 1664. R2/63/258; W1/116/184
John, yeo., Stanton, 1660. R2/62/61; W1/112/77; In. 3/5/43
STEGGOLL, Nicholas, husb., Coney Weston, 1662. R2/62/371; W1/114/103; In. 3/7/122
STEGLE, Edmund, Elmswell, 1601. R2/44/509; W1/59/132
Simon, husb., Norton, 1635, (N). R2/56/543; W1/91/125
STEGOLD, John, husb., Wetheringsett, 1577. R2/37/317
Richard, labouring man, Combs, 1571. R2/35/149; W1/36/72
STEKELL, Simon, husb., Great Ashfield, 1558. R2/27/550
Thomas, Elmswell, 1588. R2/41/63; W1/45/52
see also Steckles, Stedgall, Stegall, Steykele, Stigall

STELE, Thomas, Bury St. Edmunds, 1513. R2/5/25
STEPHAN, Thomas, husb., Lindsey, 1558. R2/27/119; W1/7/138
STEPHEN(S), Alice, wid., Whatfield, 1558. R2/27/29
Arthur, Mendlesham, 1631. A5/4/15
Elizabeth, wid., Bradfield St. George, 1585, (N). R2/39/383; W1/42/224
Joan, wid., Preston, 1619. R2/51/301; W1/132/26
John, Clare, 1633. A5/4/24
John, als. Cater, Denston, 1583. R2/39/84; W1/42/28
John, Worlingworth, 1424. R2/1/170
Samuel, Bildeston, 1631. A5/4/14
Thomas, yeo., Preston, 1618. R2/51/111; W1/75/69
see also Steven(s), Howe als. Stephens, Howys als. Stephen, Jerrarde als. Stephan
STEPHYNSON, Thomas, draper, Sudbury, 1553. R2/31/180; W1/13/119
see also Stevenson
STEPPEN, Joan, Burwell, 1585. R2/39/377; W1/42/231
STEPPYNGTON, Richard, Exning, 1487. R2/11/421
STEPVENS, Walter, Bury St. Edmunds, 1475. R2/2/210
STERE, William, Sprowston, 1585. W1/51/180
STERLING, George, gent., Nacton, 1660. R2/62/55; W1/112/67
Robert, mercer, woollen draper, Eye, 1678. R2/67/191; W1/130/167; In. 3/19/230
see also Sterlyng
STERLOND, Richard, Icklingham, 1482. R2/11/277
William, Icklingham, 1461. R2/9/300
STERLYNG, John, Eriswell, 1580, (N). R2/38/227; W1/39/89
John, Thelnetham, 1562. R2/31/38; W1/8/169
Simon, Stoke by Nayland, 1485. R2/11/354
Thomas, husb., Eriswell, 1581. R2/38/263; W1/40/11
STERNE, Adam, weaver, Bury St. Edmunds, 1498. R2/4/73
Agnes, wid., Denston, 1564. R2/32/107; W1/27/59
Amy, wid., Elmswell, 1598. R2/44/2; W1/56/3
Charles, yeo., Aldham, 1662. In. 3/7/130; A5/5/33
Charles, yeo., Cockfield, 1628. R2/54/185; W1/84/62
Charles, yeo., Stowmarket, 1668. R2/64/379; W1/120/96
Edmund, Barnham, 1599. R2/44/271; W1/57/75
George, gent., Newmarket, 1699. A5/7/10, A4/41/5
Henry, yeo., Norton, 1626. R2/53/494; W1/82/36
John, yeo., Brandon, 1679. R2/67/346; W1/133/108
John, Chelsworth, 1634. A5/4/34
John, yeo., Felsham, 1685. A5/6/92, A4/24/73
John, yeo., Whepstead, 1613. R2/48/284; W1/70/58
Margaret, wid., Woolpit, 1648. R2/60/131; W1/105/156
Martin, maltster, Bury St. Edmunds, 1663. In. 3/8/136; A5/5/48
Mary, wid., Cockfield, 1634. R2/56/364; W1/90/138
Mary, wid., Monks Eleigh, 1646. R2/59/297; W1/103/14
Nathaniel, Bradfield Combust, 1673. A5/5/135, A4/10/3
Nathaniel, clerk, Stuston, 1675. R2/66/199; W1/127/76; In. 3/16/57
Richard, draper, Bury St. Edmunds, 1472. R2/2/165
Richard, husb., Denston, 1564. R2/32/95; W1/27/44
Richard, Great Barton, 1497. R2/13/57
Richard, Nowton, 1596. A5/2/220
Richard, gent., Pakenham, 1561. R2/30/22; W1/28/215
Roger, Bury St. Edmunds, 1467. R2/2/95
Thomas, Bradfield St. Clare, 1646. A5/4/112
Thomas, Great Barton, 1482. R2/11/252
Thomas, Haverhill, 1487. R2/11/425
William, yeo., Bury St. Edmunds, (1551). R2/8/244
William, Denston, 1558. R2/27/401
William, Nowton, 1544. R2/19/467
see also Stearne
STERR(E), John, thatcher, Bury St. Edmunds, 1512. R2/4/212, R2/5/11
Richard, thatcher, Bury St. Edmunds, 1492. R2/4/21
STETILL, John, Alpheton, 1522. R2/14/71
STETTELL, John, Stradishall, 1586. A5/2/75
STEVANSON, John, Fordham, 1532. R2/19/93
STEVEN(S), Agnes, als. Jarrold, wid., Stoke by Clare, 1567. R2/32/424; W1/19/83
Dorothy, wid., Clare, 1610. A5/3/104
Edmund, wool comber, Bildeston, 1697. R2/73/148; W1/151/34

STEVEN(S) continued
Edmund, Lavenham, 1580. A5/2/26
Francis, blacksmith, Clare, 1595. R2/43/84; W1/53/80
Francis, Clare, 1639. A5/4/70
George, blacksmith, Cavendish, 1582. R2/38/420; W1/41/13
George, singleman, Cavendish, 1583. R2/39/22; W1/42/78
Henry, Newmarket, 1660. In. 3/5/73; A5/5/3, A4/1/223
Joan, wid., Bury St. Edmunds, 1460. R2/2/65
Joan, wid., Bury St. Edmunds, 1469. R2/2/122
Joan, wid. of Richard, Cockfield, 1558. R2/27/316
John, Bury St. Edmunds, 1587. A5/2/92
John, Drinkstone, 1610. A5/3/94
John, Great Horningsheath, 1567. R2/32/406; W1/19/85 & 113a
John, Ixworth, 1458. R2/9/196
John, husb., Lindsey, 1584. R2/39/224; W1/42/103
Leonard, collar maker, Withersfield, 1614. R2/49/1; W1/71/1
Margaret, Bury St. Edmunds, 1588. A5/2/103
Nicholas, Whatfield, 1587, (N). R2/40/286; W1/44/117
Peter, labourer, Lindsey, 1610. R2/47/185; W1/67/62; A5/3/84
Richard, husb., Stanningfield, 1557. R2/26/225; W1/20/121
Robert, Ardleigh, 1667. In. 3/12/81
Robert, Rougham, 1636. A5/4/44
Roger, labourer, Denston, (1620). W1/95/83
Thomas, Bildeston, 1611. A5/3/112
Thomas, tailor, Long Melford, 1617. R2/50/395; W1/74/178
see also Steavens, Stephen(s), Stepvens, Stevenys, Stevyn, Howe als. Steven, Howse als. Steven, Jerald als. Stevyn
STEVENSON, Alice, wid., Bury St. Edmunds, 1528. R2/6/146 (admon. only)
Ann, wid., Mildenhall, 1664, (N). R2/63/162; W1/116/59; In. 3/9/65
Ann, wid., West Stow, 1684. R2/69/303; W1/138/99
Philip, victualler, Worlington, 1677. R2/66/477; W1/129/58
Richard, Newton, 1481. R2/11/198
Stephen, yeo., Mildenhall, 1663, (N). R2/63/17; W1/115/31; A5/5/43
Thomas, yeo., Stanton, 1680. R2/67/754; W1/134/189; In. 3/20/209
Thomas, bricklayer, West Stow, 1680. In. 3/20/199; A5/6/31, A4/17/6
William, Freckenham, 1693. In. 10/37
William, singleman, Mildenhall, 1686. W11/4
see also Stephynson, Stevanson, Stevinson, Stevynesson
STEVENYS, Nicholas, Bury St. Edmunds, 1512. R2/5/11
STEVINSON, William, Bury St. Edmunds, 1503. R2/4/132
STEVYN, William, Elmsett, 1564. R2/32/67; W1/27/16
William, Stoke by Clare, 1571. R2/35/225; W1/38/155
STEVYNESSON, John, Woolpit, 1451. R2/9/105
STEWARD, Agnes, wid., Cockfield, 1572. R2/36/36; W1/31/104
Agnes, singlewoman, Whepstead, 1636. R2/57/91; W1/92/107
Alice, wid., Lindsey, 1679. R2/67/378; W1/133/130
Ann, spinster, Whepstead, 1660. R2/62/20; W1/112/20; In. 3/5/27
Anne, spinster, Great Saxham, 1617. R2/50/259; W1/74/59
Anthony, Lawshall, 1646. A5/4/112
Charles, grocer, Bury St. Edmunds, 1679. R2/67/269; W1/133/58; A5/7/16, A4/41/146
Charles, singleman, Sudbury, 1683. R2/69/74; W1/137/55
Francis, Little Barton, 1635. R2/56/505; W1/91/84
Giles, the elder, bellows maker, Bury St. Edmunds, 1662. R2/62/388; W1/114/128
Giles, the elder, bellows maker, Bury St. Edmunds, 1690. R2/71/329; W1/144/32
Giles, yeo., Whepstead, 1629. R2/54/361; W1/85/60
Giles, yeo., Whepstead, 1685. R2/70/188; W1/139/157
Helen, als. Day, Ely, 1667. A5/5/88, A4/5/72
Henry, Mildenhall, 1664. In. 3/9/80; A5/5/55, A4/2/47
Henry, say maker, Sudbury, 1683. R2/69/72; W1/137/54
Henry, Wicken, 1673. A5/5/136, A4/10/20
Humphrey, Brandon, 1622. R2/52/523; W1/78/121
James, glazier, Bury St. Edmunds, 1693. R2/72/246; W1/147/135
John, beer brewer, Bury St. Edmunds, 1501. R2/4/113
John, carpenter, Bury St. Edmunds, 1630. R2/55/41; W1/86/48
John, the elder, husb., Lawshall, 1599. R2/44/257; W1/57/64
John, yeo., Lawshall, 1676. R2/66/381; W1/128/94; In. 3/17/117

STEWARD continued
John, husb., Newton, 1475. R2/11/140
John, husb., Whepstead, 1599. R2/44/230; W1/57/48
John, yeo., Whepstead, 1603. R2/45/247; W1/61/46
John, singleman, Whepstead, 1647. In. 3/2/72; A5/4/116
Margaret, wid., Bury St. Edmunds, 1678. In. 3/19/149; A5/6/9, A4/15/79
Margaret, wid., Whepstead, 1697. R2/73/197; W1/151/79
Margery, wid., Sudbury, (1519). R2/14/8
Mary, als. Bulbrooke, wid., Horningsheath, 1682. In. 3/21/211; A5/6/58, A4/19/23
Robert, Cockfield, 1611. A5/3/114
Robert, Hessett, 1610, (N). R2/47/189; W1/67/65; A5/3/82
Robert, Horringer, 1680. R2/67/634; W1/134/99; In. 3/20/113
Robert, yeo., Market Weston, 1671. R2/65/252; W1/123/131
Robert, Whepstead, 1528. R2/15/228
Roger, yeo., husb., Tuddenham, 1660. R2/62/95; W13112/128; In. 3/5/159
Roger, yeo., Whepstead, 1604. R2/45/329; W1/62/43
Roger, Whepstead, 1633. A5/4/23
Rose, wid., Cockfield, 1649. R2/60/207; W1/106/53
Susan, wid., Bury St. Edmunds, 1691. R2/71/545; W1/145/100
Thomas, esq., Barton Mills, 1647. R2/59/490; W1/104/126
Thomas, yeo., Brockley, 1630. R2/55/54; W1/86/64
Thomas, sen., Brockley, 1686. R2/70/551; W1/140/154; In. 3/22/149
Thomas, Rushbrook, 1609. A5/3/58
Thomas, husb., Whepstead, 1616. R2/50/114; W1/73/122
Thomas, gent., Whepstead, 1679. R2/67/313; W1/133/92
Thomas, the elder, husb., Wickhambrook, 1652, (N). R2/61/576; W1/109/49; In. 3/4/52
Thomasine, wid., Whepstead, 1616, (N). W1/73/39
William, singleman, Hawkedon, 1629. R2/54/291; W1/85/9
see also Stiward, Stuard, Styward
STEWSON, John, cook, Poslingford, 1573. R2/36/102
STEYD, Edmund, Sudbury, 1557. R2/26/218; W1/20/123
STEYKE, Thomas, fuller, Bury St. Edmunds, 1406. R2/1/109
STEYKELE, John, Woolpit, 1485. R2/11/336
STEYLL, Edward, Herringswell, 1546. R2/21/270; W1/10/56
STEYNORE, see Smyth als. Steynore
STIGALL, Richard, Stanton, 1605. R2/45/398; W1/63/29
STIGELL, Richard, Coney Weston, 1597. R2/43/369; W1/55/131
STIGLE, George, yeo., Great Horningsheath, 1619. R2/51/474; W1/132/134
STIGOOD, Edward, yeo., Stradishall, 1667. R2/64/172; W1/119/5; In. 3/12/5
James, sen., gelder, Stradishall, 1625. R2/53/264; W1/81/53
James, the elder, yeo., Stradishall, 1651. R2/60/484; W1/108/74
see also Stygood
STILEMAN, John, yeo., Great Whelnetham, 1694. R2/72/352; W1/148/78
see also Styleman
STILE(S), Edward, Haverhill, 1688. A5/6/122, A4/29/72
Thomas, Bury St. Edmunds, 1455. R2/2/48
see also Style, Stylys
STINNETT, John, clerk, Bacton, 1695. R2/72/558; W1/149/113
see also Stynett
STINTON, Samuel, Burwell, 1650. R2/61/402; W1/107/107; In. 3/3/123
Thomas, Burwell, (1575). R2/37/124
STIRRIE, Alexander, Stoke by Clare, 1591. R2/42/27; W1/48/16
STIWARD, John, Nayland, 1449. R2/9/123
STOAKES, Edward, Great Wratting, 1642. A5/4/93
Frances, wid., Great Wratting, 1648. R2/60/44; W1/105/57
Geoffrey, Sudbury, 1606. A5/3/9
STOBEN, Robert, Stoke by Clare, 1541. R2/20/232; W1/4/170a & b (and inventory)
STOBHAWE, William, Bury St. Edmunds, 1473. R2/2/170
STOCK, John, Burwell, 1553. R2/23/135; W1/11/129
Thomas, tanner, Stradishall, 1664. In. 3/9/163; A5/5/62, A4/2/97
see also Stockes, Stok(k)
STOCKDAILE, Ann, wid., Rattlesden, 1650. R2/61/332; W1/107/30; In. 3/3/20
STOCKDALE, Geoffrey, haberdasher, Debenham, 1594. W1/51/140

STOCKDELL, Edmund, grocer, Rattlesden, 1651. R2/61/453
STOCKEN, Hugh, Mildenhall, 1593. A5/2/182
John, Fornham All Saints, 1590. R2/41/398; W1/47/82
John, Fornham All Saints, 1592. R2/42/268; W1/49/87
John, weaver, Glemsford, 1632. R2/56/188; W1/89/98
John, maltster, Mildenhall, 1589. R2/41/144; W1/46/134
Mary, wid., Glemsford, 1649. R2/60/193; W1/106/35
Robert, husb., Mildenhall, 1586. R2/40/52; W1/43/40
STOCKES, John, yeo., Wetherden, 1558. R2/27/83; W1/36/52
see also Stokes
STOCKING, Elisabeth, wid., Fornham, 1610. R2/47/281; W1/67/166
George, weaver, Glemsford, 1610. R2/47/211; W1/67/88
James, yeo., Fornham All Saints, 1646. R2/59/358; W1/103/72
Robert, yeo., Fornham All Saints, 1588. R2/41/36; W1/45/31
William, Kirtling, 1579. A5/2/15
William, Kirtling, 1581. A5/2/32
see also Stocken, Stockynge, Stokine, Stokynge, Storken
STOCKWOOD, Faith, wid., Long Melford, 1688. R2/71/13; W1/142/12; In. 3/23/32
Margaret, spinster, Long Melford, 1685. R2/70/41; W1/139/34
STOCKYNGE, Joan, wid., Fornham All Saints, 1556. R2/25/5; W1/16/2
STOCTUM, Roger, Wicken, 1540. R2/20/193
STOFFER, Robert, Gislingham, 1572. R2/36/51; W1/31/90
STOFFORDE, William, husb., Gislingham, 1575, (N). R2/37/76; W1/34/23
STOK(K), Joan, wid., Bury St. Edmunds, 1537. R2/7/42
Richard, Bury St. Edmunds, 1511. R2/5/5
STOKDON, Alice, wid., Bury St. Edmunds, 1514. R2/6/8
John, shoe maker, Bury St. Edmunds, 1512. R2/5/1
STOKE, Joan, wid., Lavenham, 1478. R2/11/161
Joan, wid., Lavenham, 1557. R2/26/284; W1/20/205
see also Aldred als. Stoke
STOKEAS, Roger, yeo., Wetherden, 1579. R2/38/45; W1/39/37
STOKES, Robert, yeo., Wetherden, 1605. R2/45/436; W1/63/80
Simon, Bury St. Edmunds, 1364. R2/1/23
see also Stoakes, Stockes, Stokys, Stookes
STOKINE, Robert, herdman, Risby, 1598. R2/44/37; W1/56/31
STOKINGE, Anne, wid., Cockfield, 1578. R2/37/416; W1/36/156; In. 3/1/64
STOKKYNG(E), John, Hopton, 1530. R2/19/4
Richard, Hopton, 1495. R2/13/20
Thomas, the elder, Fornham All Saints, 1526. R2/17/138; W1/21/134
STOKTON, John, Wicken, 1546. R2/21/641
see also Stoctum, Stokdon
STOKYNGE, John, Hopton, 1551. R2/23/73; W1/11/69
STOKYS, John, als. Halibred, doctor of divinity, Clare, 1538. R2/20/137; W1/4/117
STON, Margery, wid., Chevington, 1605. A5/3/1
STONARD, Agnes, Bures, (1534). R2/19/199
John, weaver, Bury St. Edmunds, 1471. R2/2/151 & 199
Richard, Bury St. Edmunds, 1442. R2/1/258
Robert, carver, Bury St. Edmunds, 1510. R2/5/2
see also Stonnard
STONE, see Olyver als. Stone, Olyver als. Stonne
STONEHAM, Robert, Lawshall, (1526). R2/17/167 & 233; W1/1/51, W1/23/66
STONHAM, Agnes, wid., Tuddenham, 1552. R2/23/141; W1/11/112
Elias, yeo., Preston, 1632. R2/56/224; W1/89/145
Elias, jun., husb., yeo., Preston, 1660. R2/62/75; W1/112/96; In. 3/5/87
Elias, yeo., Preston, 1660. In. 3/5/101; A5/5/5, A4/1/206
Peter, Cockfield, 1601, (N). R2/44/488; W1/59/115
Peter, Thorndon, 1472. R2/10/570
Robert, yeo., Hawstead, 1614. R2/49/27; W1/71/22
William, Bury St. Edmunds, 1437. R2/1/229
William, cordwainer, Bury St. Edmunds, 1440. R2/1/249
William, husb., Hawstead, 1567. R2/32/401
William, husb., Hawstead, 1568. R2/33/71; W1/29/92
see also Stonom
STONNARD, Sybil, wid., Yaxley, 1594. R2/42/525; W1/52/60
STONNAWAY, Lambert, Lavenham, 1608. A5/3/52
STONOM, Peter, husb., Whepstead, 1595. R2/43/106; W1/53/106

STOOKES, John, Wetherden, 1606. R2/46/25; W1/64/29
STORER, William, priest, Lavenham, 1543. R2/19/364; W1/6/154
STORIE, Joan, wid., Mendlesham, 1558. R2/27/463
 John, husb., Mendlesham, 1558. R2/27/466
STORKE, John, Burgate, 1608. A5/3/42
 Simon, Walsham le Willows, 1597. R2/43/260; W1/55/39
STORKEN, Bridget, wid., Mildenhall, 1599. R2/44/200; W1/57/26
STORY, Henry, Wattisfield, 1470. R2/10/436
 see also Storie, Stafford als. Storey
STOUDDE, William, Brettenham, 1554. A5/1/88
STOWARS, Richard, yeo., Nayland, 1646. R2/59/361; W1/103/75
STOW(E), Bartholomew, Bury St. Edmunds, 1465. R2/2/83
 Jacob, carpenter, Polstead, 1692. R2/72/10; W1/146/9; In. 3/24/50
 John, weaver, als. Benet, Stoke by Nayland, 1571. R2/35/343; W1/35/135
 Martha, Polstead, 1684. A5/6/82, A4/21/90
STOWER(S), Arcolas, yeo., Newton, 1660. R2/62/138; W1/112/178; In. 3/6/206
 Archelaus, Newton, 1676. A4/13/56
 Edward, blacksmith, Bures, 1606. R2/46/72; W1/64/77
 George, wheelwright, Stoke by Nayland, 1633, (N). R2/56/258; W1/90/22
 John, Nayland, 1661. R2/62/174; W1/113/29; In. 3/6/41; A5/5/11, A4/1/140
 Susan, als. Smyth, Nayland, 1661. A5/5/11, A4/1/141
STOWR(E), Agnes, wid., Little Cornard, 1559. R2/28/89; W1/22/87
 Christian, wid., Sudbury, 1482. R2/11/268
 Henry, Bures, 1518. R2/12/102
 Thomas, Little Cornard, 1554. A5/1/92
STRACHY, Edward, Sudbury, 1539. R2/20/61; W1/4/49
STRAND, Bartholomew, husb., Stoke by Clare, 1621. W1/77/5
 Joan, wid., Stoke by Nayland, 1599, (N). R2/44/228; W1/57/46
 John, Stoke by Clare, 1554. W1/14/114
 Mark, yeo., Stoke by Clare, 1671. R2/65/176; W1/123/46
 Robert, Stoke by Nayland, 1697. A5/7/1, A4/40/6
STRANGAM, John, Redgrave, 1618. R2/51/93; W1/75/58
STRANGEMAN, Joan, wid., Bildeston, 1504. W1/7/4
STRANGMAN, John, gent., Redgrave, 1676. R2/66/349; W1/128/56; In. 3/17/69
STRATFORD, John, rector, (1396). R2/1/82
STRATTON, Henry, Downham, 1640. A5/4/80
STRAWE, John, Glemsford, 1489. R2/11/434
 William, Glemsford, 1543. R2/19/382; W1/6/107
 see also Laurence als. Strawe, Lawrence als. Strawe, Lorence als. Strawe
STRAYLES, Thomas, fuller, Bury St. Edmunds, 1495. R2/4/40
STREATON, Paul, blacksmith, Kersey, 1626. R2/53/454; W1/82/9
STREET(E), George, yeo., Felsham, 1682. R2/68/338; W1/136/55; In. 3/21/184
 Nicholas, yeo., Brettenham, 1663. R2/63/26; W1/115/42; In. 3/8/55
 Richard, clothier, yeo., Rattlesden, 1665. R2/63/368; W1/117/119; In. 3/10/140
 see also Strete, Stryt
STREETMAN, Thomas, als. Bennet, Mendlesham, 1611. A5/3/113
STRETE, John, Sudbury, 1527. R2/17/236; W1/1/47
STRETT, Daniel, Little Cornard, 1662, (N). R2/62/342; W1/114/55; A5/5/29
STRETTON, Phillippa, wife of Francis, saltpetre maker, Sudbury, 1615. R2/49/371; W1/72/140
STRIBLING, Joseph, Stowmarket, 1694. A5/6/173, A4/37/90
STRICKLAND, Roger, maltster, Sudbury, 1580. R2/38/99; W1/39/178
STRONG, James, Mildenhall, 1641. R2/58/273; W1/98/56
 Simon, Mildenhall, 1631. A5/4/13
 Simon, Troston, 1696. In. 3/25/42; A5/6/188, A4/39/55
 William, Mildenhall, 1630. R2/55/144; W1/86/161
STROUD, Bartholomew, Stoke by Clare, 1592. R2/42/246; W1/49/63
 John, Stoke by Clare, 1521. R2/14/25, R2/17/333
 Nicholas, als. Tayloure, Stoke by Clare, 1472. R2/10/518
 Richard, Stoke by Clare, 1522. R2/14/51
 Thomas, Stoke by Clare, 1586. R2/40/59; W1/43/46
STRUTE, Richard, Occold, 1578. A5/2/7
STRUTH, Thomas, Hartest, 1449. R2/9/101

STRUTON, Catherine, wid., Little Thurlow, 1665. R2/63/347; W1/117/97; In. 3/10/95
STRUTT, Alice, wid., Bildeston, 1469. R2/10/402
Benjamin, Lavenham, 1643. A5/4/100
Christopher, yeo., Buxhall, 1628. R2/54/133; W1/84/4
Edward, Bures, 1669. In. 3/14/102; A5/5/108, A4/7/53
Elisabeth, spinster, Bardwell, 1660. R2/62/15; W1/112/14
Elisabeth, wid., Glemsford, 1526. R2/17/208; W1/23/25
Erasmus, Glemsford, 1558. R2/27/115; W1/7/144
John, yeo., Clare, 1605. R2/45/422; W1/63/67
John, yeo., Glemsford, 1591. R2/42/24; W1/48/15b
John, the elder, Poslingford, 1537. R2/19/52, R2/20/18; W1/3/167
Mary, wid., Lavenham, 1643. R2/59/47; W1/100/56
Otwell, yeo., Rattlesden, 1592, (N). R2/42/268; W1/49/86
Richard, Redlingfield, 1565. R2/32/240; W1/27/138
Robert, Acton, 1454. R2/9/169
Robert, collar maker, Eye, 1674. R2/66/2; W1/126/124
Silvester, yeo., Poslingford, 1638. R2/57/299; W1/93/73
Sarah, wid., Bury St. Edmunds, 1694. R2/72/401; W1/148/133
Thomas, gent., Bury St. Edmunds, 1682. R2/68/469; W1/136/146
Thomas, knacker, Eye, 1686. R2/70/480; W1/140/94; In. 3/22/39
Thomas, yeo., Mellis, 1607. R2/46/141; W1/97/78
Thomas, Mellis, 1643. A5/4/99
Thomas, yeo., Poslingford, 1564. R2/32/61; W1/27/9a & b
Thomas, gent., Rede, 1700. R2/74/9; W1/154/11
STRUTTER, John, Bacton, 1648. A5/4/124
Thomas, Bacton, 1594. A5/2/202
STRUTTON, George, Chevington, 1697. A5/6/191; A4/39/89
John, mason, Little Thurlow, 1636. R2/57/39; W1/92/48
see also Struton
STRYNGER, Peter, husb., Elveden, 1560. R2/29/155; W1/25/19
STRYT, Richard, carpenter, Sudbury, 1564. R2/32/53; W1/27/1
STUARD, Alice, Whepstead, 1544. R2/36/447
John, tailor, Bury St. Edmunds, 1580. R2/38/238; W1/39/77
John, yeo., Whepstead, 1551. R2/23/106; W1/11/70
Robert, yeo., Nowton, 1664. R2/63/191; W1/116/95; In. 3/9/138
Thomas, Whepstead, 1554. R2/24/114; W1/14/87
STUART, John, yeo., Lawshall, 1641. R2/58/272; W1/98/54
William, gent., Whepstead, 1680. R2/67/584; W1/134/61
see also Steward
STUBBARD, Agnes, Bury St. Edmunds, 1422. R2/1/158
Stephen, Bury St. Edmunds, 1396. R2/1/80
Thomas, Rattlesden, 1483. R2/11/282
see also Grigg als. Stubberd
STUBBEN, Robert, yeo., Fordham, 1620. R2/52/151; W1/76/136
William, Snailwell, 1620. R2/52/102; W1/76/87
STUBBIN, Edmund, clerk, Naughton, 1638. R2/57/438; W1/93/137
Susanna, wid., Drinkstone, 1690. R2/71/383; W1/144/90
William, Stansfield, 1602. R2/45/131; W1/60/49
William, Stanton, 1700. A5/7/17; A4/41/171
STUBBING, Edmund, clothier, Bury St. Edmunds, 1685. R2/70/166; W1/139/138
John, yeo., Depden, 1640. R2/58/202; W1/96/133
John, grocer, Groton, 1669. R2/64/561; W1/121/149; In. 3/14/123
John, Haverhill, 1558. R2/27/572
John, husb., Hundon, 1669. In. 3/14/50; A5/5/103, A4/7/20
John, yeo., Little Wratting, 1661. R2/62/181; W1/113/37; In. 3/6/43; A5/5/13, A4/1/128
Lewis, husb., Stoke by Clare, 1609. R2/47/50; W1/66/56
Mary, wid., Stoke, 1662. R2/62/411; W1/114/163; In. 3/7/236; A5/5/38
Robert, Fornham, 1639. A5/4/71
Robert, Wicken, 1632. R2/56/203; W1/89/118
William, yeo., Stoke by Clare, 1675. R2/66/265; W1/127/134; In. 3/16/159
see also Stubbyn
STUBBLEFEILD, Thomas, Burwell, 1695. A5/6/176, A4/38/1
STUBBS, Osborn, labourer, Sapiston, 1631. R2/56/46; W1/87/64
William, husb., Sapiston, 1648. R2/60/142; W1/105/170
STUBBYN, Giles, yeo., Soham, 1598. R2/44/56; W1/56/49
STUBINN, John, miller, Fordham, 1608. R2/46/213

STUDD, Edmund, blacksmith, Buxhall, 1608. R2/46/193; W1/65/60
John, Buxhall, 1632. A5/4/17
Robert, blacksmith, Haughley, 1647. R2/59/398; W1/104/20; In. 3/2/31
Robert, Old Newton, 1673. A5/5/136, A4/10/22
Robert, tailor, Thorpe Morieux, 1691. R2/71/486; W1/145/45
Stephen, yeo., Semer, 1696. R2/73/73; W1/150/81
Thomas, Semer, 1684. A5/6/83, A4/21/101
STUDGEON, John, the elder, yeo., Thelnetham, 1689. R2/71/204; W1/143/53
STUDLIE, Edmund, fishmonger, Sudbury, 1621. R2/52/275; W1/77/61
STURDY, John, Kedington, 1461. R2/10/341
STURGEN, Edmund, Bures, 1684. A5/6/81, A4/21/80
John, Hawstead, 1686. In. 3/22/26; A5/5/99, A4/30/96
STURGEON, Anne, wid., Lawshall, 1607. R2/46/143
Joan, wid., Brockley, 1582. R2/38/397; W1/41/42a
John, Rougham, 1687. A5/6/108, A4/27/14
John, yeo., Whepstead, 1589. R2/41/217; W1/46/67
Margaret, wid., Whspstead, 1581. R2/38/315; W1/40/58
Matthew, Great Cornard, 1679. A5/6/17, A4/16/25
Philip, Whepstead, 1643, (N). R2/59/18; W1/100/27
Robert, miller, Rattlesden, 1652. R2/61/569; W1/109/43; In. 3/4/27
Roger, gent., Herringswell, 1684. R2/69/257; W1/138/58; A5/6/84
Roger, husb., Lawshall, 1605. R2/69/447; W1/63/92
Roger, Whepstead, 1551. R2/23/37; W1/11/71
Roger, Whepstead, 1691. A5/6/141, A4/33/40
Susan, wid., Whepstead, 1684. R2/69/253; W1/138/56; A4/21/106
William, Stansfield, 1667. In. 3/12/165; A5/5/88, A4/5/76
William, Whepstead, 1488. W1/24/172
STURGION, John, husb., Bardwell, 1668. R2/64/395; W1/120/117; In. 3/13/104
Roger, yeo., Pakenham, 1651. R2/61/454
STURGON, Ellen, wid., Hitcham, 1699. R2/73/417; W1/153/58
John, the elder, yeo., Whepstead, 1562. R2/31/33; W1/8/158
STURMYN, Agnes, als. Fuller, wid., Lavenham, 1538. R2/20/86
Christine, Lavenham, 1457. R2/9/203
Christine, Lavenham, 1458. R2/9/211
Robert, Lavenham, 1484. R2/11/335
STURT(T), Jeffery, labouring man, Soham, 1585. R2/39/257; W1/42/317
Stephen, wid., Newmarket, 1698. A5/7/6
STUSTON, Thomas, Oakley, 1451. R2/9/135
William, Oakley, 1458. R2/9/194
STUTEFELDE, Elisabeth, wid., Wetherden, 1549. R2/21/558; Wi/8/39
STUTEVILLE, John, esq., Norton, 1671. R2/65/177; W1/123/47
Judith, wid. of Thomas, esq., Dalham, 1696. R2/73/55; W1/150/100
Thomas, esq., Dalham, 1649. R2/60/247; W1/106/107; In. 3/3/45
STUTFILDE, Robert, Wetherden, (1542). R2/19/336 & 367
STUTFYLLD, Margery, Burwell, 1552, (N). R2/23/166; W1/12/6
STUTTER, John, husb., Ixworth Thorpe, 1664. R2/63/222; W1/116/134; In. 3/9/171
John, labourer, Troston, 1596, (N). R2/43/156; W1/54/35
John, Troston, 1642. A5/4/97
Mary, wid., Ixworth Thorpe, 1673, (N). R2/65/419; W1/125/42
STYGOOD, John, cooper, Stradishall, 1674. R2/66/64; W1/126/53
Thomas, yeo., Stradishall, 1639. R2/58/69; W1/94/118
STYLE, Thomas, Bury St. Edmundsl, 1443. R2/2/3
William, fuller, Bury St. Edmunds, 1436. R2/1/226
see also Stile
STYLEMAN, John, the younger, Bradfield St. George, 1686, (N). R2/70/477; W1/140/90
STYLYS, Robert, merchant, Bury St. Edmunds, 1479. R2/2/288
STYNGE, John, coverlet weaver, Bury St. Edmunds, 1507. R2/4/193
Thomas, coverlet weaver, Bury St. Edmunds, 1531. R2/7/3; W1/9/55
STYNNETT, Mary, wife of John, clerk, Bacton, 1681. R2/68/249; W1/135/189
STYWARD, John, the elder, Cockfield, 1558. R2/27/237
SUBBERN, Edmund, Rickinghall Inferior, 1476. R2/11/135
SUCCERMAN, Simon, yeo., Mildenhall, 1605. R2/45/400; W1/63/38
SUCK, Clara, wid., Great Thurlow, 1687. A5/6/112, A4/27/60
SUCKERMAN, Andrew, yeo., Mildenhall, 1603. R2/45/264; W1/61/72
Christopher, Isleham, 1557. W7/9
Elisabeth, wid., Great Livermere, 1698. A5/7/9
Francis, Mildenhall, 1645. R2/59/264; W1/102/79

SUCKERMAN continued
James, Mildenhall, 1638. R2/57/385; W1/93/195
John, the elder, Brandon, 1559. R2/28/295; W1/22/233
John, Brandon, 1570. R2/32/438; W1/19/124
John, yeo., Great Livermere, 1697. R2/73/117; W1/151/8; A5/7/15, A4/41/98
Robert, the elder, yeo., Mildenhall, 1649. R2/60/214; W1/106/61
Robert, maltster, Mildenhall, 1694. R2/72/419; W1/148/154
Robert, the elder, yeo., Mildenhall, 1699. R2/73/343; W1/153/2
Simon, yeo., Mildenhall, 1624. R2/53/176; W1/80/151
Simon, sen., yeo., Mildenhall, 1674. R2/66/18; W1/126/103
Simon, singleman, Mildenhall, 1678. R2/67/155; W1/130/139; In. 3/19/192
see also Sokerman, Succerman
SUCKLING, John, Great Fakenham, 1660. R2/62/105; W1/112/137
John, Ingham, 1580, (N). R2/38/117; W1/39/161
SUDBURY, Christopher, Bury St. Edmunds, 1640. A5/4/82
Isaac, Sudbury, 1638. R2/57/290; W1/93/61
Simon, Sudbury, 1694. In. 3/25/56; A5/6/175, A4/37/104
William, Kettleborough, 1459. R2/9/266
SUDD, Agnes, wid., Glemsford, 1522. R2/15/38
SUEELL, Margaret, wid., Hopton, 1549. R2/21/543; W1/8/71
SUGG(E), Anabelle, wife of Seman, Edwardstone, 1444. R2/9/45
Thomas, Boxford, 1557. R2/26/218; W1/20/126
SUGGATE, William, yeo., Combs, 1660. In. 3/5/68
see also Sowgate
SULMAN, John, the elder, yeo., Boxford, 1673. R2/65/456; W1/125/89
SULYARD, Edward, esq., Haughley, 1691. R2/71/511; W1/145/70
SUMERS, Mary, wid., Fornham St. Martin, 1687. R2/70/365; W1/141/93
SUMMER(S), Dorothy, wid., Brettenham, 1683. R2/69/98; W1/137/75
Edmund, inn holder, Bury St. Edmunds, 1661. R2/62/281; W1/113/189; In. 3/6/244
John, blacksmith, Ickworth, 1673. R2/65/455; W1/125/87
John, West Stow, 1679. A5/6/21, A4/16/62
Richard, Culford, 1680. R2/67/749; W1/134/184; In. 3/20/193
Thomas, Timworth, 1681. R2/68/61; W1/135/48
SUMPTER, Reginald, carpenter, Bury St. Edmunds, 1412. R2/1/129
SUNNER, Thomas, labourer, Stowmarket, 1573. R2/36/190; W1/32/114
SURMAN, John, blacksmith, Norwich, 1582. W1/51/151
SURMYN, John, Hartest, 1561. R2/30/74; W1/28/242
SURREY, Henry, Groton, 1634. A5/4/31
SURRYE, Henry, the elder, Groton, 1625. R2/53/280; W1/81/69
SUSAN, Alice, Cockfield, 1439. R2/1/1
SUSSUMS, William, silk weaver, Hessett, 1689. R2/71/205; W1/143/55
SUTFEILDE, Edward, als. Wallys, ploughwright, Elmswell, 1566. R2/32/354; W1/28/24
SUTFOLKE, Geoffrey, Icklingham, 1527. R2/17/248; W1/1/31
SUTHILL, Arnold, husb., Barnardiston, 1632. R2/56/202; W1/89/116
SUTTELL, Ellen, wid., Fordham, 1609. R2/47/73; W1/66/85
John, Gazeley, 1581. A5/2/34
SUTTILL, Anne, wid., Lavenham, 1560. R2/29/81
SUTTLE, Arnold, husb., Cowlinge, 1661. In. 3/6/70; A5/5/14, A4/1/114
Nicholas, Fordham, 1592. A5/2/170
SUTTON, Anthony, maltster, Barningham, 1691. R2/71/475; W1/145/33
Clementia, Bradfield, 1455. R2/9/180
Daniel, clerk, Chilton, 1681. A5/6/53, A4/18/115
Douglas, Rushbrook, 1688. R2/74/269
Edward, Wetheringsett, 1635. A5/4/41
Elisabeth, wid., Eriswell, 1695. R2/72/474; W1/149/30
James, weaver, Occold, 1649. R2/60/231; W1/106/84
Joan, wid., Mildenhall, 1636. R2/57/3
John, Bury St. Edmunds, 1361. R2/1/18
John, Bury St. Edmunds, 1394. R2/1/69
John, Bury St. Edmunds, 1479. R2/2/291
John, Cavendish, 1585. A5/2/65
John, labourer, Long Melford, 1616. R2/50/8; W1/73/10
John, yeo., Stanton, 1649. R2/60/242; W1/106/101
John, Stanton, 1674. A5/6/151, A4/11/77
Lawrence, 1581. R2/38/268; W1/40/17
Margaret, Tuddenham, 1457. R2/9/213
Martin, Bradfield St. George, 1679. R2/67/464; W1/133/187
Mary, spinster, Acton, 1670. In. 3/15/25; A5/5/112

SUTTON continued
Mary, wid., Eriswell, 1664. In. 3/9/199; A5/5/62, A4/2/94
Richard, Oxborough, 1451. R2/9/107
Robert, Bury St. Edmunds, 1386. R2/1/53
Robert, the younger, Wetheringsett, 1637, (N). R2/57/200; W1/92/239
Samuel, sen., clerk, Eriswell, 1649. A5/4/128
Samuel, gent., Eriswell, 1688. R2/71/127; W1/142/115
Stephen, Great Barton, 1675. In. 3/16/168; A5/5/159, A4/12/81
Thomas, Bury St. Edmunds, 1361. R2/1/26
Thomas, Lakenheath, 1649. A5/4/129
Thomas, yeo., Timworth, 1684. R2/69/326; W1/138/121
Thomasine, wid., Brandon, 1690. A5/6/134, A4/32/36
William, Brandon, 1648. A5/4/121
William, the elder, Bury St. Edmunds, 1570. R2/65/68; W1/122/82
William, Mildenhall, 1474. R2/10/523
SWAFTON, John, mason, Bury St. Edmunds, 1479. R2/2/272
SWAINE, Agnes, Bures, 1577. A5/2/1
Ann, wid., Coney Weston, 1677. R2/66/467; W1/129/48
Jacobine, wid., Fornham St. Genevieve, 1662. R2/62/424; W1/114/184; In. 3/7/232
see also Swane, Swayne, Sweyn
SWALLOW, Thomas, yeo., Elmswell, 1630. R2/55/146; W1/86/163
SWANE, Richard, Stowmarket, (1499). W1/24/148
SWAN(N), Alice, Creeting St. Peter, 1458. R2/9/211
John, Acle, (1534). W1/51/6 (quitclaim only)
Margery, Haughley, 1482. R2/11/264
Robert, wheelwright, Badwell Ash, 1668. R2/64/388; W1/120/109; In. 3/13/166
Robert, husb., Glemsford, 1618. R2/51/196; W1/75/124
Thomas, Thorndon, 1444. R2/9/45
William, blacksmith, Mildenhall, 1640. R2/58/223; W1/96/162
SWANTON, Anthony, Kentford, 1610, (N). R2/47/285; W1/67/170
Catherine, wid., Bury St. Edmunds, 1610. W1/95/130
Edmund, tailor, Lavenham, 1588. R2/41/74; W1/45/63
Edmund, tailor, Lavenham, 1620. R2/52/177; W1/76/159
Edmund, Lavenham, 1630. A5/4/1
Elisabeth, Whepstead, 1577. A5/2/2
Henry, Botesdale, 1469. R2/10/425
Isabel, Botesdale, 1471. R2/10/487
Joan, wid. of William, Depden, 1471. R2/10/538
John, yeo., Bury St. Edmunds, 1551. R2/8/223
John, Bury St. Edmunds, 1610. A5/3/101
John, carpenter, Lavenham, 1616. R2/50/194; W1/73/182
John, Lavenham, 1633. A5/4/27
John, singleman, Lavenham, 1636. R2/57/37; W1/92/45
John, carpenter, Lavenham, 1673. R2/65/459; W1/125/92
John, Rede, 1471. R2/10/538
John, shepherd, Rushbrook, 1605. R2/45/409; W1/63/54
Stephen, priest, Bury St. Edmunds, 1479. R2/2/279
Thomas, Bradfield St. George, 1577. R2/37/281
Thomas, Bury St. Edmunds, 1394. R2/1/63
Thomas, smith, Bury St. Edmunds, 1407. R2/1/114
Thomas, Bury St. Edmunds, 1509. R2/4/206
William, Depden, 1469. R2/10/421
William, Denston, 1452. R2/9/153
see also Swauntone
SWARE, Richard, yeo., Combs, 1645. R2/59/210; W1/102/36
SWARTHE, Thomas, priest, Sudbury, 1539. R2/19/303
SWATONE, Richard, husb., Fordham, 1559. R2/28/398; W1/3/130
SWAUNTONE, Agnes, wife of Thomas, Bury St. Edmunds, 1417. R2/1/142
SWAYLES, see Lenenede als. Swayles
SWAYNE, Alice, Creeting St. Peter, 1458. R2/9/211
Joan, wid., Ashfield, 1559. R2/28/123; W1/22/115
Joan, wid., Ashfield, 1564. R2/32/75
Michael, shearman, Elmswell, 1567. R2/32/431; W1/19/93
Robert, husb., Ashfield, 1564. R2/32/88; W1/27/36 a & b
Robert, slaughterman, Stowmarket, 1639. R2/58/86; W1/94/146
Samuel, Stoke by Nayland, 1593. A5/2/189
Thomas, labourer, Stoke by Nayland, 1570. R2/34/15; W1/30/15
William, servant, Great Cornard, 1566. R2/32/368; W1/28/9
William, Lavenham, 1554. R2/24/25; W1/14/24
William, basket maker, Long Melford, 1641, (N). R2/58/277; W1/98/61
see also Swaine

SWAYTES, Jane, wid., Mildenhall, 1626, (N). R2/53/559; W1/82/84
 Leonard, husb., Mildenhall, 1580. R2/38/200; W1/39/108
SWAYTS, William, husb., Lakenheath, 1662. W11/1
 William, Lakenheath, 1674. A5/5/151, A4/89/84
SWEARE, Mary, wid., Combs, 1660. R2/62/89; W1/112/117
 see also Sware
SWEATE, Thomas, Elveden, 1550. R2/21/167
SWEETEMAN, William, yeo., Lindsey, 1620. R2/52/62; W1/76/51
SWEETMAN, Joan, als. Bennytt, wid., Mendlesham, 1618. R2/51/72; W1/75/42
 Susan, spinster, Lindsey, 1629. R2/54/342; W1/85/50
 Thomas, als. Bennett, Bacton, 1637. A5/4/51
 see also Swetman
SWEIFTE, Margaret, wid., Hopton, 1585, (N). R2/39/240; W1/42/334
SWETALL, John, Thurlton, 1537. W1/51/15
SWETMAN, Alice, wife of William, Buxhall, 1525. W1/5/37b
 Bennet, Beyton, 1529. R2/18/23
 William, Buxhall, 1525. W1/5/37b
SWEYN, James, Glemsford, 1464. R2/10/358
 John, Creeting, 1452. R2/9/139
 John, Lavenham, 1441. R2/9/30
 John, sen., Lavenham, 1471. R2/10/478
 John, Rattlesden, 1452. R2/9/121
 Thomas, Creeting St. Peter, 1471. R2/10/462
 Thomas, Mildenhall, 1462. R2/10/374
SWIFT, Susan, singlewoman, Onehouse, 1637, (N). R2/57/156; W1/92/194
 see also Sweifte, Swyfte
SWORTON, William, Sudbury, 1587. R2/40/280; W1/44/111
 William, Sudbury, 1612. A5/3/116
SWYFTE, Jeffery, woollen weaver, Stowmarket, 1611. R2/48/85; W1/68/101
 John, Walsham le Willows, 1465. R2/10/388
 Thomas, Long Melford, 1459. R2/9/246
 William, chaplain, Bury St. Edmunds, 1465. R2/2/87
 William, Stowmarket, 1570. R2/34/5; W1/30/4
SYAR, Hugh, husb., Great Ashfield, 1575. R2/37/111; W1/34/52
SYBBES, Robert, yeo., Coney Weston, 1581. R2/38/296; W1/40/39; In. 5/2/36
 Robert, Coney Weston, 1594. A5/2/200
SYBBYS, Alice, Coney Weston, 1461. R2/9/307
 John, Coney Weston, 1494. R2/13/17
SYBELY, William, Cheveley, 1496. R2/13/54
SYBLEY, Edward, husb., Cheveley, 1549. R2/21/132; W1/9/85
SYBETONE, John, Bury St. Edmunds, 1375. R2/1/35
YBLIE, Henry, the elder, husb., Cheveley, 1581. R2/38/291; W1/40/35
 Martin, singleman, Hundon, 1597, (N). R2/43/304 & 376; W1/55/73
YBLY, John, Cheveley, 1457. R2/9/218
 Thomas, husb., Exning, 1591. R2/42/30; W1/48/21
YBOTSON, William, clerk, Hawstead, 1565. R2/32/152; W1/27/95
YDAY, Alice, Long Melford, 1639. A5/4/71 & 75
 Catherine, wid., Somerton, 1648. A5/4/123
 John, Bures, 1674. A5/6/149, A4/11/59
 John, Great Waldingfield, 1462. R2/10/377
 John, Great Waldingfield, 1487. R2/11/417
 John, husb., Great Waldingfield, 1556. R2/25/40; W1/16/45
 Robert, husb., Great Waldingfield, 1572. R2/36/49; W1/31/93
 Sarah, wid., Barrow, 1700. R2/74/74; W1/154/74
 Walter, Sudbury, 1549. R2/21/552; W1/8/66
YDDALL, James, cordwainer, Woolpit, 1585. R2/39/372; W1/42/236
YDEY, John, weaver, Great Waldingfield, 1450. R2/9/116
 John, the elder, yeo., Great Waldingfield, 1625. R2/53/410; W1/81/191
 Mary, wid., Stowmarket, 1660. R2/62/102; W1/112/134
 William, Bures, 1665. In. 3/10/156; A4/3/74
YDOLSMERE, John, Bury St. Edmunds, 1382. R2/1/44
YER, Agnes, Soham, 1539. R2/20/71 & 200
 Bridget, wid., Langham, 1680. R2/67/517; W1/134/6; In. 3/20/13
 Edward, tailor, Great Finborough, 1683. R2/69/145; W1/137/119
 Elizabeth, wid., 1564. R2/32/68; W1/27/17
 Frances, wid., Great Ashfield, 1639. R2/58/22; W1/94/40
 Henry, husb., Great Ashfield, 1556. R2/25/81; W1/16/75

SYER continued
Henry, Great Ashfield, 1616. R2/50/64; W1/73/75
Joan, wid., Great Ashfield, 1603. R2/45/269; W1/61/74
Joan, Langham, 1644. A5/4/102
John, yeo., Ashfield, 1618. R2/51/109; W1/75/68
John, yeo., Badwell Ash, 1675. R2/66/273; W1/127/141; In. 3/16/173
John, chirurgeon, Bury St. Edmunds, 1685. R2/70/57; W1/139/50
John, yeo., Great Livermere, 1696. In. 3/25/70; A4/38/95
John, blacksmith, Hitcham, 1699. R2/73/354; W1/153/13; In. 3/26/65; A5/7/11, A4/41/26
John, bach., Langham, 1678. In. 3/19/26; A5/6/2, A4/15/14
John, yeo., Onehouse, 1616. R2/50/133; W1/73/139
John, yeo., Pakenham, 1556. R2/25/96; W1/16/108
John, Tostock, 1677. In. 3/18/30; A5/5/168, A4/14/16
Katherine, wid., Onehouse, 1620. R2/52/29; W1/76/26
Mary, spinster, Woolpit, 1697. A5/7/5, A4/40/76
Mirabel, wid., Stowmarket, 1632. R2/56/217; W1/89/136
Nathaniel, Onehouse, 1639. A5/4/71
Ralph, cordwainer, Woolpit, 1679. R2/67/244; W1/133/13
Richard, Combs, 1649. A5/4/127
Richard, shoe maker, Great Finborough, 1678. R2/67/79; W1/130/62; In. 3/19/84
Richard, butcher, Kersey, 1546. R2/21/272; W1/10/55
Robert, gent., Badwell Ash, 1660. R2/62/18; W1/112/18; In. 3/5/15
Robert, Stowmarket, 1697. A5/7/2, A4/40/27
Robert, Walsham le Willows, 1687. A5/6/109, A4/27/23
Robert, blacksmith, Walsham le Willows, 1694. R2/72/368; W1/148/97
Susan, spinster, Ixworth, 1647. In. 3/2/16; A5/4/115
Susan, wid., Ixworth, 1676. R2/66/331; W1/128/35
Thomas, yeo., Buxhall, 1627. R2/54/38; W1/83/46
Thomas, yeo., Haughley, 1666. In. 3/11/83; A5/5/75, A4/4/35
Thomas, Ixworth, 1688. In. 3/23/53; A5/6/120, A4/29/43
Thomas, the elder, yeo., Langham, 1638. R2/57/381; W1/93/188
Thomas, the elder, gent., Langham, 1667. R2/64/170; W1/119/3; In. 3/12/50
William, butcher, Ashfield, 1632. R2/56/152; W1/89/54
William, husb., Buxhall, 1595. R2/43/59; W1/53/40
William, blacksmith, Hitcham, 1690. R2/71/407; W1/144/111
William, grocer, Ixworth, 1669. R2/64/471; W1/121/58; In. 3/14/52
William, yeo., Shelland, 1623. R2/52/721; W1/79/134a & b
see also Sier, Sire, Syar, Syor, Aleyn als. Syer
SYGER, Joan, wid., Polstead, 1568. R2/33/46; W1/29/59
William, Burwell, 1477. R2/11/80
SYGO, Agnes, wife of Robert, Mildenhall, 1484. R2/11/302
John, priest, Bury St. Edmunds, 1516. R2/6/20
John, Worlington, 1470. R2/10/446
Robert, Mildenhall, 1440. R2/9/11
Robert, husb., Pakenham, 1560. R2/29/100; W1/25/66
William, draper, Bury St. Edmunds, 1482. R2/2/330
SYLCOCKE, Thomas, husb., Mildenhall, 1553. R2/31/164; W1/13/106
SYLLETT, Francis, beer brewer, Bury St. Edmunds, 1621. R2/52/231; W1/77/23
James, cordwainer, Horningsheath, 1605. R2/45/379; W1/63/1
Richard, sen., 1633. W1/111/85
SYLLIOT, Robert, carpenter, Rickinghall Superior, (1609). W1/95/80
SYLLOTT, Judith, wid., Coney Weston, 1687. A5/6/112, A4/27/52
SYLOM, John, tailor, Bury St. Edmunds, 1669. R2/2/127
SYLOTE, Alice, wid., Bardwell, 1540. R2/20/283; W1/4/212
SYLVER, John, labourer, Rougham, 1623, (N). R2/52/718; W1/79/131
SYMETH, Richard, Bury St. Edmunds, 1361. R2/1/8
SYMMETT, John, Wicken, 1539. R2/19/306
SYMMONDS, Ann, singlewoman, Stowmarket, 1685. R2/70/204; W1/139/171
SYMOND(S), Agnes, Newmarket, 1582. A5/2/42
Agnes, wid., Thurston, 1556. R2/25/146; W1/16/165
Alice, wid., Gislingham, 1678. R2/67/118; W1/130/101; In. 3/19/134
Alice, singlewoman, Gislingham, 1688. R2/71/115; W1/142/104; In. 3/23/112
Ann, Eriswell, (1626). W1/95/143
Ann, wid., Great Thornham, 1611. A5/3/111
Anne, wid., Bacton, 1582. R2/38/400; W1/41/25

SYMOND(S) continued

Bridget, Bury St. Edmunds, 1667. A5/5/86, A4/5/59
Christopher, shoe maker, Stowmarket, 1585. R2/39/342; W1/42/258
Constance, Eriswell, 1581. A5/2/37
George, yeo., Langham, 1648. R2/60/138; W1/105/165
Helen, wid., Gislingham, 1679. R2/67/290; W1/133/76
Henry, inn holder, fishmonger, Bury St. Edmunds, 1661. R2/62/176; W1/113/31; In. 3/6/35
Henry, the younger, fishmonger, Bury St. Edmunds, 1669. R2/64/561; W1/121/150; In. 3/14/147
Henry, yeo., Cavenham, 1567. R2/32/375; W1/3/18
Henry, cordwainer, Eye, 1670. R2/65/81; W1/122/100; In. 3/15/126
Henry, sen., Glemsford, 1677. In. 3/18/2; A5/5/167, A4/14/10
Henry, labourer, Newton, 1584. R2/39/137; W1/42/191
Joan, wid., Cotton, 1608. R2/46/199
John, Bacton, 1572. R2/36/52; W1/31/82
John, yeo., Bacton, 1594. R2/42/578; W1/52/16
John, Bury St. Edmunds, 1646. A5/4/113
John, yeo., Cavenham, 1588. R2/41/92
John, yeo., Cavenham, 1678. R2/67/177; W1/130/156; In. 3/19/217
John, yeo., Cotton, 1675. R2/66/175; W1/127/50; In. 3/16/61
John, Gazeley, 1482. R2/11/309
John, Great Barton, 1489. R2/11/461
John, Lavenham, 1586. A5/2/78
John, Rickinghall Inferior, 1640. A5/4/80
Katherine, wid., Ashfield, 1561. R2/32/443; W1/19/77
Katherine, wid., Eriswell, 1564. R2/32/128
Margaret, wid., Cavenham, 1603. R2/45/215; W1/61/1
Mark, Cavenham, 1591. A5/2/159
Richard, Mildenhall, 1538. R2/20/135; W1/4/115
Richard, the elder, Stowmarket, 1599. R2/44/311; W1/57/117
Robert, Bacton, 1551. R2/23/85; W1/11/72
Robert, apothecary, Botesdale, 1692. R2/72/40; W1/146/37
Robert, Bury St. Edmunds, 1479. R2/2/276
Robert, tanner, Langham, 1632. R2/56/206; W1/89/124
Robert, yeo., Lavenham, 1578. R2/37/342; W1/36/232
Robert, Mildenhall, 1514. R2/12/126
Robert, yeo., Market Weston, 1670. R2/65/1; W1/122/1; In. 3/15/17; A5/5/111
Roger, the elder, yeo., Bacton, 1610. R2/47/130; W1/67/12
Roger, Thorndon, 1634. A5/4/31
Roger, husb., Thurston, 1531. R2/19/66
Roger, clerk, Wetheringsett, 1544. R2/19/493
Susan, wid., Bury St. Edmunds, 1677. A5/5/169, A4/14/29
Susan, wid., Market Weston, 1671, (N). R2/65/230; W1/123/105; A5/5/125, A4/8/55
Susan, wife of John, Timworth, 1666. In. 3/11/73; A5/5/75, A4/4/31
Susan, Weston, 1671. A5/5/125
Thomas, Bacton, 1573. R2/36/186; W1/32/109
Thomas, Bacton, 1623. R2/17/39; W1/21/49
Thomas, Bury St. Edmunds, 1642. A5/4/97
Thomas, husb., Cheveley, 1526. R2/17/168; W1/23/64
Thomas, tailor, Glemsford, 1611. R2/48/19; W1/68/38; A5/3/111
Thomas, Great Barton, 1521. R2/14/16, R2/17/334; W1/14/115
Thomas, yeo., Great Barton, 1610. R2/47/261; W1/67/144
Thomas, mason, Groton, 1566. R2/32/305; W1/28/88
Thomas, Hinderclay, 1631. R2/56/38; W1/87/53
Thomas, husb., Icklingham, 1558. R2/27/177
Thomas, sen., Mildenhall, 1477. R2/11/87
Thomas, husb., Rickinghall Inferior, 1662. In. 3/7/90; A5/5/30
Thomas, Rougham, 1460. R2/9/302
Thomas, Thelnetham, 1461. R2/9/276
Thomas, yeo., Weston, 1613. R2/48/287; W1/70/61
Thomas, 1462. R2/9/291
Vinca, wid., Bacton, 1618. R2/51/36; W1/75/19
William, Bury St. Edmunds, 1473. R2/2/175
William, blacksmith, Bury St. Edmunds, 1591. R2/42/171; W1/48/75
William, ironmonger, Bury St. Edmunds, 1626. R2/53/678; W1/82/201
William, Gazeley, 1503. R2/13/130
William, sen., yeo., Market Weston, 1676. R2/66/365; W1/128/77; In. 3/17/103

SYMOND(S) continued
  William, Mildenhall, 1461.   R2/9/293
  William, the elder, yeo., Withersfield, 1681.   R2/68/146; W1/135/110
SYMON(S), Agnes, wid., Withersfield, 1614.   R2/49/12; W1/71/8
  Constance, singlewoman, Eriswell, 1582.   R2/38/369; W1/41/72
  Henry, Polstead, 1601.   R2/44/351; W1/59/14
  Joan, Wicken, (1518).   R2/15/72
  John, yeo., Chippenham, 1668.   In. 3/13/181
  Mary, wid., Bury St. Edmunds, 1620.   R2/52/125; W1/76/109
  Robert, Cavendish, 1589.   R2/41/298; W1/46/15
  Thomas, Stowmarket, 1579.   A5/2/15
SYMONT, Andrew, Eriswell, 1506.   R2/13/179
  Henry, Lavenham, 1543.   R2/19/353; W1/6/147
  James, labourer, Cavenham, 1610.   R2/47/191; W1/67/70
  Lawrence, Wicken, 1518.   R2/14/6
  Ralph, Wicken, 1540.   R2/21/370; W1/38/79
  see also Simond(s)
SYMPER, John, the elder, yeo., Hunston, 1680.   R2/67/557; W1/134/40; In. 3/20/43
SYMPSON, Edward, tailor, Felsham, 1638, (N).   R2/57/399; W1/93/216
  Emily, wid., Bures, 1618.   R2/51/88; W1/75/54
  John, shoe maker, Bures, 1614.   R2/49/36; W1/71/31
  Margery, wid., Little Saxham, 1625, (N).   R2/53/319; W1/81/103
  Robert, Bury St. Edmunds, 1611.   A5/3/109
  Thomas, Little Saxham, 1624.   R2/53/28; W1/80/37
  Walter, Cockfield, 1593.   A5/2/187
SYMSON, Thomas, vicar, Islington, 1538.   W1/51/21 & 96
  William, Long Melford, 1480.   R2/12/6
SYNGE, Edward, husb., Isleham, (1659).   W1/312/41
SYNTON, William, Sudbury, 1463.   R2/10/315
SYOR, Thomas, blacksmith, Pakenham, 1566.   R2/32/362; W1/28/17
SYRE, John, Ashfield, 1487.   R2/13/2
  Margaret, Great Ashfield, 1469.   R2/10/430
  Nicholas, tiler, Bury St. Edmunds, 1479.   R2/2/276
  Robert, Ashfield, 1473.   R2/10/519
  William, Glemsford, 1443.   R2/9/47
  William, the elder, Great Ashfield, 1544.   R2/19/425
SYRYTH, John, Nayland, 1452.   R2/9/156
SYSSANCE, Agnes, Fordham, 1580.   A5/2/27
SYWARDE, John, fuller, Icklingham, 1562.   R2/31/13; W1/8/141
  Richard, barber, Bury St. Edmunds, 1479.   R2/2/281
  Richard, weaver, Bury St. Edmunds, 1479.   R2/2/285

T

TABARD, Richard, Mildenhall, 1559.   R2/28/179; W1/22/161
  Richard, als. Burgies, yeo., Mildenhall, 1611.   R2/48/11; W1/68/29
TABBARD, Walter, West Stow, 1461.   R2/24/113
  see also Taberd
TABBEL, Simon, yeo., Mildenhall, 1699.   R2/73/363; W1/153/23
TABER, Thomas, inn holder, Stoke by Clare, 1625.   R2/53/236; W1/81/32
  William, yeo., Stoke by Clare, 1645.   R2/59/204; W1/102/30
TABERD, William, als. Burges, husb., Mildenhall, 1599.   R2/44/181; W1/57/11
TABERHAM, Elizabeth, wife of John, Great Waldingfield, 1469. R2/10/402
  Joan, wid., Wicken, 1648.   R2/60/145; W1/105/184
  John, husb., Wicken, 1671.   R2/65/239; W1/123/119
  Margaret, wid., Wicken, 1596.   R2/43/137; W1/54/13
TABOR, Ann, wid., Boxford, 1636.   R2/57/72; W1/92/84
  Thomas, shoe maker, Boxford, 1628.   R2/54/266; W1/84/122
  see also Taber
TABRAHAM, John, the elder, yeo., Wicken, 1643.   R2/59/61; W1/100/69
TABRAM, John, blacksmith, Soham, 1631.   R2/56/51; W1/87/69
  Robert, husb., Wicken, 1639.   R2/58/73; W1/94/124
  Thomas, husb., Wicken, 1589.   R2/41/245; W1/46/18
  see also Taberham
TABUT, Luke, husb., Fordham, 1622.   R2/52/447; W1/78/66
TAILER, Robert, Norton, 1638.   A5/4/61
  Thomas, singleman, Great Fakenham, 1665.   In. 3/10/27; A5/5/64, A4/3/10

TAILER continued
Thomas, labourer, Mildenhall, 1584. R2/39/172; W1/42/155
William, Ixworth, 1573. R2/36/130; W1/32/30
TAILLOUR, William, Sudbury, 1443. R2/9/36
TALANTE, George, wheelwright, Wetherden, 1624. R2/53/175; W1/80/150
TALBANE, Robert, Boxted, 1562. R2/31/26; W1/8/155
TALBONE, Catherine, wid., Assington, 1625. R2/53/293; W1/81/82
William, blacksmith, Assington, 1624. R2/53/89; W1/80/103
see also Tawbonne
TALBOT(T), Ann, wid., Bacton, 1559. R2/28/56; W1/22/59
Ann, wife of Paul, yeo., Mildenhall, 1664. R2/63/189; W1/116/93; In. 3/9/131
David, Saxham, 1596. A5/2/220
Edward, Cavenham, 1698. A5/7/9
Isabel, wid., Fordham, 1626. R2/53/471; W1/82/18
Joan, Wyverstone, 1522. R2/14/127, R2/15/47
John, Bury St. Edmunds, 1692. A5/6/146, A4/33/90
John, Cavenham, 1593. R2/42/433; W1/50/94
John, Cavenham, 1683. A5/6/71, A4/20/80
John, Cavenham, 1687. R2/70/562
John, yeo., Cavenham, 1696. R2/73/100; W1/150/115; In. 3/25/96
John, Fordham, 1563. A5/1/151
John, husb., Fordham, 1606. W1/111/26
John, Glemsford, 1635. A5/4/40
John, Icklingham, 1555. R2/24/177
John, husb., Mildenhall, 1579. R2/38/22; W1/39/36
John, yeo., Timworth, 1554. R2/24/27
John, yeo., Wicken, 1632. R2/56/230; W1/89/153
Katherine, Cavenham, (1546). R2/21/642
Lewis, gent., Brandon, 1555. R2/24/159; W1/15/6
Mary, Bury St. Edmunds, 1692. A5/6/151, A4/34/41
Nicholas, Bury St. Edmunds, 1501. R2/4/114
Paul, yeo., Icklingham, 1670. R2/65/93; W1/122/113; In. 3/15/141
Richard, yeo., Worlington, 1681. R2/68/94; W1/135/69
Richard, 1484. R2/11/346
Robert, Bacton, 1566. A5/1/180
Robert, tanner, Bury St. Edmunds, 1565. R2/8/393; W1/17/9a & b (and inventory)
Robert, Chevington, 1612. A5/3/118
Thomas, the elder, yeo., Bury St. Edmunds, 1552. R2/8/68; W1/21/202
Thomas, Cavenham, 1544. R2/19/431; W1/21/154
Thomas, Cavenham, 1593. R2/42/361; W1/50/29
Thomas, yeo., Finningham, 1610. R2/47/222; W1/67/100
Thomas, the elder, Fordham, 1520. R2/15/70
Thomas, yeo., Wyverstone, 1568. R2/33/83; W1/29/2
---, Botesdale, 1611. A5/3/113
TALBUT(T), Edmund, husb., Fordham, 1616. R2/50/92; W1/73/100
Elisabeth, wid., Isleham, 1685. W7/107; In. 9/62
Helen, wife of Paul, yeo., Mildenhall, 1660. R2/62/71; W1/112/91; A5/5/3, A4/1/220
Thomas, shepherd, Barton Mills, 1632. R2/56/227; W1/89/150
see also Tabut, Tawbot
TALLANT, Martha, Little Waldingfield, 1631. A5/4/11
Richard, yeo., Edwardstone, 1606. R2/46/55; W1/64/71
Stephen, Waldingfield, 1630. A5/4/3
William, Edwardstone, 1607. A5/3/19
TALLENTE, Benedict, Milden, 1587. A5/2/94
see also Talante
TALLWORDIE, Edmund, tailor, Cockfield, 1559. R2/28/323; W1/22/278
TALMACHE, Thomas, Great Finborough, 1551. R2/23/40; W1/11/73
TALMAGE, John, Great Finborough, 1478. R2/11/238
Katherine, Bury St. Edmunds, 1449. R2/2/30a
Michael, Great Finborough, 1568. R2/33/30; W1/29/45
see also Tollemache
TALWARDIE, Ambrose, singleman, Chippenham, 1652. R2/61/592; W1/109/67; In. 3/4/72
TALWIN, Arthur, husb., Mendlesham, 1675. R2/66/261; W1/127/129; In. 3/16/164
Sarah, wid., Mendlesham, 1697. R2/73/198; W1/151/80
Thomas, yeo., Mendlesham, 1666. R2/64/49; W1/118/43; In. 3/11/45
Thomas, Wyverstone, 1695. R2/72/510; W1/149/62; In. 3/25/39

TALWORTH, Abigail, Great Wratting, 1667. R2/64/268; W1/119/130; In. 3/12/131
George, Great Wratting, 1640. R2/58/216; W1/96/153
Henry, Great Wratting, 1631. A5/4/12
Henry, Little Wratting, 1685. A5/6/88, A4/24/23
John, 1454. R2/9/175
Jonas, yeo., Great Wratting, 1682. R2/68/409; W1/136/103; In. 3/21/113
Peter, husb., Great Wratting, 1568. R2/33/23; W1/29/35
see also Taylworth

TALWORTHY, Thomas, yeo., Brockley, 1624. R2/53/107; W1/80/114
William, Brockley, 1551. R2/23/72; W1/11/74
William, thatcher, Brockley, 1602. R2/45/213; W1/60/142
see also Tolworthy

TALYOUR, John, jun., Thorndon, 1453. R2/9/168
William, Eriswell, 1452. R2/9/156

TALYOWE, John, Bradfield, 1451. R2/9/104

TANEY, John, Troston, 1678. In. 3/19/125; A5/6/8, A4/15/68

TANFELD, Agnes, wid., Exning, 1560. R2/29/66; W1/25/105
Robert, Exning, 1557. R2/26/301; W1/20/241

TANFILDE, George, shepherd, Exning, 1593. R2/42/427; W1/50/87

TANGY, Agnes, Lavenham, 1476. R2/11/119

TANNER, Andrew, Occold, 1632. R2/56/131; W1/89/19
Anne, wid., Little Cornard, 1589. R2/41/234; W1/46/58
Dorcas, Great Cornard, 1671. A5/5/125, A4/8/51
Elisabeth, wid., Kennett, 1685. R2/70/22; W1/139/21
Emily, wid. of Henry, Great Cornard, 1593. R2/42/356; W1/50/24
Francis, Combs, 1651. A5/4/138
Francis, say maker, Sudbury, 1646, (N). R2/59/292; W1/103/7
Geoffrey, yeo., Bures, 1631. R2/56/14; W1/87/18
Geoffrey, yeo., Bures, 1683. R2/69/23; W1/137/18
Geoffrey, yeo., Great Cornard, 1639. R2/58/115; W1/94/191
Henry, Bures, 1651. A5/4/139
Henry, yeo., Great Cornard, 1593. R2/42/357; W1/50/25
Henry, sen., yeo., Great Cornard, 1623. R2/52/701; W1/79/116
Henry, yeo., Great Cornard, 1647. R2/59/481; W1/104/116
Jeffery, Little Cornard, 1583. A5/2/48
John, Bures, 1638. A5/4/63
John, yeo., Bures, 1666. R2/64/98; W1/118/69; In. 3/11/74; A5/5/74, A4/4/21
John, yeo., Bures, 1668. R2/64/308; W1/120/12; In. 3/13/145
Susannah, wid., Great Cornard, 1641. R2/58/312; W1/98/116
William, yeo., Bures, 1603. R2/45/251; W1/61/52
see also Waltham als. Tanner

TAPLEE, Margaret, wid., Newmarket, 1610. R2/47/287; W1/67/175

TAPYR, Nicholas, Hopton, 1532. R2/19/89

TARRY, Richard, yeo., Chevington, 1667. R2/64/212; W1/119/63; In. 3/12/78

TARVER, Christopher, Finningham, 1540. R2/21/376; W1/38/54
John, weaver, Lavenham, 1696, (N). R2/73/38; W1/150/54; In. 3/25/91
Margery, wid., Finningham, 1552. R2/23/131; W1/11/113
Susan, wid., Stowmarket, 1692. R2/72/9; W1/146/8; A5/6/148, A4/34/14

TASSELL, Edmund, gent., Bardwell, (1532). R2/19/102; W1/3/107
Simon, Bury St. Edmunds, R2/4/144
William, husb., Stowupland, 1599. R2/44/236; W1/57/53

TASTARD, John, Stowmarket, 1505. W1/9/11
Robert, Combs, 1561. A5/1/116
Robert, the elder, Combs, 1620. R2/52/47
Thomas, Combs, (1531). R2/18/124
Thomas, the elder, yeo., Combs, 1638. R2/57/320; W1/93/98
Thomas, gent., Combs, 1641. R2/58/307; W1/98/105
Thomas, the younger, Combs, 1643. A5/4/99

TATERSALL, Roger, Haverhill, 1595. A5/2/212

TATHAM, John, husb., Ixworth, 1608. R2/46/209; W1/65/95

TATTERSALL, Ann, wid., Great Wratting, 1671, (N). R2/65/251; W1/123/128; A5/5/127, A4/8/70
Benedict, glazier, Newmarket, 1644. R2/59/147; W1/101/71
Robert, the elder, plumber, Haverhill, 1650. R2/61/313; W1/107/12; In. 3/3/19

TATTERSELL, Thomas, carpenter, Great Wratting, 1686. R2/70/501; W1/140/106; In. 3/22/83
TATTERSHALL, John, plumber, Newmarket, 1610. R2/47/266; W1/67/148
TATTERSOLDE, William, Newmarket, 1592. A5/2/170
TATTERSOLE, Margaret, wid., Haverhill, 1669. R2/64/475; W1/121/63
see also Tatersall
TATUM, Thomas, singleman, Lavenham, 1693. R2/72/246; W1/147/136
William, Lavenham, 1697. A5/7/4, A4/40/62
TAVERHAM, Alice, Bury St. Edmunds, 1467. R2/2/108
TAVERNE, Robert, baker, Stoke by Clare, 1660. R2/62/145; W1/112/187
TAVERNER, Alan, Bury St. Edmunds, (1372). R2/1/37
TAWBONNE, William, blacksmith, Sudbury, 1600. R2/45/67; W1/58/95
TAWBOT, John, Cavenham, 1546. R2/21/265; W1/10/88
John, husb., Fordham, 1556. R2/25/145; W1/16/166
Thomas, Fordham, 1537. R2/20/6; W1/4/4
TAWNEY, Susan, wid., Rougham, 1633. R2/56/252; W1/90/14
Thomas, shepherd, Rougham, 1632. R2/56/211; W1/89/128
Thomas, Rougham, 1634. A5/4/34
TAYLER, Agnes, wid., Tuddenham, 1591. R2/42/92; W1/48/140
Ann, Brockley, 1700. A5/7/15, A4/41/102
Anne, wid., Combs, 1560. R2/29/139; W1/25/33
Christopher, wid., Occold, 1601, (N). R2/44/355; W1/59/19
Edmund, Ashley, 1678. R2/67/115; W1/130/99
Edmund, husb., Snailwell, 1590. R2/41/370; W1/47/71
Elisabeth, Fordham, 1580. A5/2/23
Elisabeth, Stowmarket, 1573. R2/36/129; W1/32/31
Frances, wid., Bradfield, 1622. R2/52/480; W1/78/92
George, gent., Lidgate, 1621. R2/52/281; W1/77/69
Giles, husb., Haverhill, 1558. R2/27/547
Helena, Exning, 1581. A5/2/34
Henry, Bildeston, 1589. A5/2/114b
James, Kirtling, 1628. R2/54/177; W1/84/53
James, Kirtling, 1666. In. 3/11/147; A5/5/79, A4/4/84
James, yeo., Mildenhall, 1676. R2/66/319; W1/128/25; In. 3/17/25; A5/5/159, A4/12/82 & 83a
Joan, wid., Hundon, (1575), (N). R2/37/82; W1/34/32
John, Ashley, 1677. In. 3/18/19; A5/5/167, A4/14/6
John, Bury St. Edmunds, 1590. A5/2/144
John, shearman, Clare, 1652. In. 3/4/58; A5/4/142
John, Exning, 1556. R2/25/124; W1/16/187
John, Exning, 1573. R2/36/147; W1/32/50
John, Gazeley, 1566. A5/1/179
John, Haverhill, 1582. A5/2/40
John, yeo., Haverhill, 1628. R2/54/215; W1/84/78
John, yeo., Hundon, 1666. R2/64/149; W1/118/116
Margaret, wid., Hundon, 1601. R2/44/359; W1/59/24
Margaret, wid., Nayland, 1671. R2/65/145; W1/123/1
Martin, oatmeal maker, Nayland, 1650. R2/61/347; W1/107/42; In. 3/3/66
Ralph, husb., Wicken, 1601. R2/44/350; W1/59/13
Richard, yeo., Hundon, 1574. R2/37/69
Richard, Hundon, 1585. A5/2/73
Richard, singleman, Whepstead, 1675. R2/66/236; W1/127/108; In. 3/15/145
Robert, Bacton, 1638. A5/4/66
Robert, Rougham, 1588. A5/2/108
Robert, husb., Soham, 1571. R2/35/121; W1/36/87
Roger, Hitcham, 1610. A5/3/84
Stephen, Chippenham, 1573. R2/36/153; W1/32/59
Stephen, Stanton, 1606. R2/46/42; W1/64/56
Thomas, als. Clarke, Bildeston, 1553. R2/31/135; W1/13/91
Thomas, Clare, 1562. R2/31/66; W1/8/113
Thomas, shepherd, Downham, 1598, (N). R2/44/20; W1/56/20
Thomas, husb., Mildenhall, 1599. R2/44/199; W1/57/23
Thomas, yeo., Thelnetham, 1635. R2/56/544; W1/91/127
Thomas, wheelwright, Woolpit, 1649. R2/60/253; W1/106/114
William, carpenter, Barnardiston, 1592. R2/42/190; W1/49/13
William, Bury St. Edmunds, 1580. A5/2/25
William, shepherd, Fordham, 1683. R2/69/109; W1/137/85
William, Hundon, 1567. R2/32/425; W1/19/95

TAYLER continued
William, the elder, yeo., Hundon, 1663. R2/63/29; W1/115/48; In. 3/8/48
William, husb., Soham, 1613. R2/48/328; W1/70/111
William, yeo., Stoke by Nayland, 1603. R2/45/220; W1/61/9
William, Woolpit, 1556. R2/25/37; W1/14/40
TAYLLAYR, William, Layham, 1562. R2/31/14; W1/8/142
TAYLOR, Agnes, wid., Eriswell, 1532. R2/19/101; W1/3/111 & 137
Alice, Bradfield St. George, 1472. R2/10/533
Alice, wid., Bury St. Edmunds, 1567. W1/10/199
Alice, wid., Bury St. Edmunds, 1606. R2/46/34; W1/64/46
Alice, Haverhill, 1577. A5/2/4
Ann, Bradfield St. Clare, 1667. A5/5/86, A4/5/87
Ann, wid., Bradfield St. Clare, 1667. A5/5/90, A4/5/54
Edmund, the elder, shearman, Bury St. Edmunds, 1558. R2/8/322; W1/18/55
Edmund, Bury St. Edmunds, 1573. R2/36/188; W1/32/111
Edmund, Groton, 1579. A5/2/19
Edward, grocer, Bury St. Edmunds, 1669, (N). R2/64/456; W1/121/43; In. 3/14/37; A5/5/104, A4/7/38
Edward, yeo., Stanton, 1603. R2/45/229; W1/61/22
Elisabeth, wid., Polstead, 1598, (N). R2/44/40; W1/56/35
Elisabeth, wid., Wetheringsett, 1609. R2/47/48; W1/66/55
Francis, yeo., Horningsheath, 1661. R2/62/193; W1/113/52; In. 3/6/61
Francis, Withersfield, 1640. A5/4/85
George, gent., Lidgate, 1634. R2/45/318; W1/90/85
Giles, yeo., Barnardiston, 1692. R2/72/87; W1/146/81; In. 3/24/12
Henry, Bildeston, 1565. R2/32/184; W1/27/120
Henry, yeo., Mildenhall, 1629. R2/54/287; W1/85/6
Hugh, blacksmith, Nayland, 1665. R2/63/386; W1/117/141; In. 3/10/175
Hugh, Oakley, 1540. R2/20/168; W1/4/143
James, Gazeley, 1591. A5/2/153
Joan, wid., Stoke by Nayland, 1600. R2/45/69; W1/58/97
Joan, wife of John, Stoke Ferry, 1536. R2/19/242
Joan, Thorndon, 1573. A5/1/265
John, Buxhall, 1462. R2/9/278
John, Buxhall, 1554. R2/24/34
John, Bury St. Edmunds, 1523. R2/6/106
John, husb., Chippenham, 1646. R2/59/341; W1/103/54
John, webster, Clare, 1686. R2/70/248; W1/140/18; In. 3/22/40
John, gent., Cockfield, 1667. R2/64/213; W1/119/65; In. 3/12/47
John, shepherd, Fordham, 1636. R2/57/4; W1/92/4
John, Honington, 1584. A5/2/63
John, husb., Ixworth, 1572. R2/36/18; W1/31/117
John, singleman, Lackford, 1617. R2/50/383; W1/74/168
John, als. Wyllyamsone, Mildenhall, 1460. R2/9/255
John, blacksmith, Nayland, 1669. R2/64/538; W1/121/129; In. 3/14/64
John, husb., Newton, 1511. R2/12/111
John, Stoke by Nayland, 1564. A5/1/153
John, Thelnetham, 1633. A5/4/24
John, Thorndon, 1463. R2/10/347
Katherine, wid., Stoke by Nayland, 1566. R2/32/282; W1/28/112
Leame, Hessett, 1641. A5/4/89
Luke, Bury St. Edmunds, 1698. A5/7/8
Margaret, wid., Clare, 1563. R2/31/160; W1/26/41
Margaret, wid., Lidgate, 1602. R2/45/95; W1/60/3
Margaret, wid., Rattlesden, 1630. A5/4/8
Martin, oatmeal maker, Nayland, 1611. R2/48/73; W1/68/90
Mary, wid., Bildeston, 1694. R2/72/407; W1/148/140
Mildred, wid., Fordham, 1667. R2/64/177; W1/119/9; In. 3/12/18
Nicholas, yeo., Ixworth, 1597. R2/43/271; W1/55/48
Philip, Soham, 1692. In. 3/24/108; A5/6/152, A4/34/50
Ralph, Cowlinge, 1521. R2/15/171
Richard, Bury St. Edmunds, 1587. R2/40/153; W1/44/36
Richard, glazier, Clare, 1638. R2/57/355; W1/93/149
Robert, Fakenham, 1667. In. 3/13/23; A5/5/89, A4/5/77
Robert, Gazeley, (1543). R2/19/411; W1/6/122

TAYLOR continued
Robert, the elder, yeo., Gazeley, 1587. R2/40/266; W1/44/104
Robert, als. Woodale, tailor, Hopton, 1549. R2/21/559; W1/8/38
Robert, knacker, Norton, 1695. R2/72/515; W1/149/68
Robert, husb., Soham, 1642, (N). R2/58/391; W1/99/104
Robert, Stowmarket, 1525. R2/17/114; W1/21/111
Simon, Hundon, 1559. R2/28/260; W1/22/108
Susan, wid., Nayland, 1664. R2/63/148; W1/116/37
Susan, wid., Wood Ditton, 1685. A5/6/87, A4/24/12
Thomas, mason, Burwell, 1632. R2/56/137; W1/89/28
Thomas, tailor, Chippenham, 1609. R2/47/30; W1/66/34
Thomas, husb., Chippenham, 1610. R2/47/117; W1/67/2
Thomas, Fordham, 1483. R2/11/372
Thomas, mason, Fordham, 1663. R2/63/44; W1/115/70; In. 3/8/90
Thomas, singleman, Gislingham, 1663. R2/63/109; W1/115/165; In. 3/8/187
Thomas, husb., Higham, 1687. R2/70/338; W1/141/77
Thomas, wheelwright, Hundon, 1597. R2/43/337; W1/55/104
Thomas, Hundon, 1693. A5/6/165, A4/35/8
Thomas, yeo., Isleham, 1690. W7/118; In. 9/75
Thomas, Lavenham, 1462. R2/10/376
Thomas, bay maker, Lavenham, 1625, (N). R2/53/278; W1/81/66
Thomas, tailor, Mildenhall, 1591. R2/42/143; W1/48/101
Thomas, Withersfield, 1684. A5/6/80, A4/4/71
Thomas, singleman, Woolpit, 1660. R2/62/57; W1/112/71
William, Bildeston, 1511. R2/12/94
William, Exning, 1603. R2/45/224; W1/61/13
William, Gazeley, 1558. R2/27/314
William, weaver, Glemsford, 1614, (N). R2/49/99; W1/71/74
William, the elder, yeo., Hundon, 1549. R2/21/524; W1/8/50
William, yeo., Norton, 1566. R2/32/292; W1/28/101
William, Poslingford, 1634. A5/4/31
William, yeo., Redlingfield, 1662. R2/62/333; W1/114/43; In. 3/7/44
William, the elder, husb., Soham, 1610. R2/47/154; W1/67/35
William, Soham, 1672. A5/5/133, A4/87/66
William, Stoke by Nayland, 1589. A5/2/120
William, Wicken, 165-. W1/111/9
TAYLOUR, Cecilia, 1445. W1/9/67
Edward, husb., Tuddenham, 1577. R2/37/293
Henry, Wetheringsett, 1461. R2/9/296
Joan, wid., Polstead, 1562. R2/31/96; W1/8/95
John, yeo., Bildeston, 1553. R2/31/116; W1/13/82
John, husb., Hundon, 1594. R2/42/551; W1/52/42
Richard, Bildeston, 1574. R2/37/55
Richard, Hundon, 1500. R2/13/113
Richard, parson, Little Wratting, 1557. R2/26/147; W1/20/104
Robert, Lavenham, 1446. R2/9/91
Robert, Wissington, 1531. R2/36/58
Simon, Hundon, 1491. R2/13/104
Thomas, singleman, Fordham, 1664. R2/63/182; W1/116/85; In. 3/9/113
Thomas, Hitcham, 1458. R2/9/188
William, priest, Bury St. Edmunds, 1511. R2/5/9
William, Preston, 1455. R2/9/233
---, 1574. W1/33/25
see also Tailer, Talyour, Taylyer, Teyler, Aleyn als. Tayleyour, Saxham als. Taillour, Stroud als. Tayloure
TAYLWORTH, Margaret, wid., Great Wratting, 1636. R2/57/110; W1/92/131
TAYLYER, John, Wicken, 1594. R2/42/566; W1/52/30
TAYLYOR, Henry, Wood Ditton, 1552. R2/23/201; W1/12/27
TAYLYWRE, Richard, Wissington, 1482. R2/11/271
TEBALD, John, yeo., Chippenham, 1605. R2/45/384; W1/63/13
Thomas, Barnham, 1538. R2/20/75; W1/4/72a & b (and inventory)
TEBAWDE, John, Fordham, 1464. R2/10/365
TEBB, John, als. Kyrtelynge, Stoke by Clare, 1450. R2/9/112
William, Bury St. Edmunds, 1368. R2/1/28
TEBBALD, Henry, shepherd, Cheveley, 1639. R2/58/90; W1/94/152
TEBBALL, Ann, spinster, Great Bradley, 1676. R2/66/423; W1/128/134; In. 3/17/165

TEBBETT, John, Soham, 1693. R2/72/232; W1/147/121
Joseph, singleman, Chippenham, 1675. R2/66/153; W1/127/25; In. 3/16/26
Robert, yeo., Chippenham, 1668. R2/64/347; W1/120/56; In. 3/13/158; A5/5/94, A4/6/53
Robert, singleman, yeo., Chippenham, 1682. R2/68/379; W1/136/82; In. 3/21/141
Susan, wid., Chippenham, 1662. In. 3/7/142; A5/5/34
TEBBITT, Avis, spinster, Soham, 1683. A5/6/66, A4/20/14
John, the elder, Hessett, 1681. A5/6/53, A4/18/114
William, yeo., Soham, 1698. R2/73/330; W1/152/100
see also Tebboot, Tebet, Thebott
TEBBOLD, Leonard, yeo., Mendlesham, 1642. R2/58/399; W1/99/115
Thomas, yeo., Barnardiston, 1543. R2/19/385; W1/6/92
Thomas, the elder, yeo., Barnardiston, 1586. R2/40/25; W1/43/18
William, tailor, Glemsford, 1635. R2/56/513; W1/91/96
TEBBOOT, Robert, husb., Soham, 1609. R2/47/36; W1/66/41
TEBBOT, John, labourer, Soham, 1626. R2/53/470; W1/82/17
Richard, husb., Soham, 1616. R2/50/190; W1/73/179 (and inventory)
TEBBOULD, John, Cheveley, 1605, (N). R2/45/383; W1/63/12
William, Glemsford, 1568. R2/33/49; W1/29/62
TEBET, John, labourer, Soham, 1670. R2/65/24; W1/122/25; In. 3/15/54
TEBINGTON, William, labourer, Exning, 1556. R2/25/20; W1/16/20
TEBOLD, Agnes, wid., Barnardiston, 1546. R2/21/639; W1/21/184a
Edmund, Barnardiston, 1520. W1/23/1
Edmund, Brandon, 1520. R2/15/88, R2/17/315; W1/23/1
Edward, Barnardiston, 1612. A5/3/116
Henry, Tuddenham, 1594. W1/95/25
John, the elder, Burwell, 1543. R2/22/40; W1/6/105
Roger, Barnham, 1540. R2/19/612; W1/5/21
Thomas, Cavenham, 1550. R2/21/106; W1/9/99
Thomas, tailor, Great Bradley, 1592, (N). R2/42/259; W1/49/77
Thomas, Tuddenham, 1591. A5/2/153
William, weaver, Bildeston, 1564. R2/32/76; W1/27/28
William, Diss, (1519). W1/51/40
William, Wickhambrook, 1648. A5/4/123
---, Cheveley, 1610. A5/3/88
TEBOLL, John, yeo., Great Bradley, 1619. W1/95/153
TEBOULL, Thomas, husb., Great Bradley, 1620, (N). W1/95/102
TEBOWLD, John, yeo., Great Bradley, 1590. R2/41/328; W1/47/20
TEDER, William, husb., Hundon, 1670. In. 3/15/88; A5/5/115
TEGGE, William, Bury St. Edmunds, 1579. A5/2/19
TEGO, Thomas, weaver, Mildenhall, 1625. R2/53/299; W1/81/85
TELLER, John, husb., Soham, 1553. R2/31/120; W1/13/85
TEMBES, Richard, yeo., Dalham, 1619. R2/51/268; W1/132/10
TEMPLE, John, clerk, Bury St. Edmunds, 1674. R2/66/118; W1/126/1; A5/5/144, A4/11/1
Ursula, wid., Edwardstone, 1589, (N). R2/41/166; W1/46/119
TEMPLEMAN, John, labourer, Palgrave, 1589, (N). R2/41/154; W1/46/128
TENANT, Henry, clothier, Edwardstone, 1664. In. 3/9/22; A5/5/55, A4/2/7
see also Tenent
TENDALL, William, Long Melford, 1613. R2/48/323; W1/70/101
TENENT, Henry, Hopton, 1580. R2/38/141; W1/39/147
TENWYNTER, Margaret, wid., Lavenham, 1476. R2/11/99
TERINGTON, Constance, wid., Eriswell, 1545. R2/19/495
Robert, Eriswell, 1544. R2/19/427; W1/21/147
see also Terryton, Teryngton, Tyryngton, Balkey als. Teryngton
TEROLD, Alice, Walsham le Willows, 1524. R2/17/63; W1/21/30
James, Wortham, 1689. R2/71/260; W1/143/98
TERRELL, Robert, painter, Soham, 1567. R2/32/422
TERRETT, Herod, yeo., Soham, 1670. In. 3/15/121; A5/5/115
TERRY, Robert, Burgate, 1540. R2/19/618
TERRYTON, Richard, Rattlesden, 1533. W1/2/38
TERWIKE, Robert, Stowmarket, 1521. R2/14/117
see also Tyrwite
TERYNGTON, Isabel, wid., Bury St. Edmunds, 1468. R2/2/117
Margery, wid., Bury St. Edmunds, 1471. R2/2/150
Nicholas, butcher, Bury St. Edmunds, 1471. R2/2/137
Robert, Mendlesham, 1473. R2/11/40

TESTARD, Roger, Chelsworth, 1464. W1/24/143
TESTWODE, see Odeham als. Testwode
TETLEY, Thomas, Brandon, 1700. A5/7/18, A4/41/164
TETRELL, Jane, als. Janckes, Acton, 1571. R2/35/335; W1/36/129
TETSALL, Agnes, wid., Burwell, 1573. R2/36/216; W1/32/180
John, the elder, husb., Burwell, 1614. R2/49/195; W1/71/128
John, Burwell, 1557. R2/25/167; W1/16/147
John, yeo., Chippenham, 1698. R2/73/320; W1/152/86
Thomas, Burwell, 1578. R2/37/407; W1/36/163
Thomas, husb., Burwell, 1591. R2/42/103; W1/48/127
Thomas, singleman, Cowlinge, 1612. R2/48/219; W1/69/119
TEVERSAM, Robert, husb., Cowlinge, 1624. R2/53/20; W1/80/30
TEVERSON, Nicholas, Horringer, 1583. A5/2/53
TEVERY, Henry, als. Cooke, Stoke by Nayland, 1527. R2/17/230; W1/1/54
TEVIS, William, baker, Botesdale, 1663. R2/63/45; W1/115/72; In. 3/8/172
TEYE, Anne, the elder, Stanton, 1623, (N). R2/63/680
TEYLER, John, yeo., Norton, 1569. R2/33/123; W1/28/188
TEYLUR, John, wid., Hundon, 1535. R2/18/128
TEYPE, William, Soham, 1474. R2/11/2
THAINE, John, linen weaver, Thelnetham, 1697. R2/73/94; W1/150/108
THAKE, Ann, wid., Hundon, 1650. A5/4/138
Richard, labourer, Bury St. Edmunds, 1585. R2/39/288; W1/42/289
THATCHER, see Thaxter, Simms als. Thatcher, Woodcroft als. Thatcher
THAWBERY, Thomas, locksmith, Bury St. Edmunds, 1470. R2/2/132
THAWLINGE, John, Redgrave, 1593. A5/2/186
THAXTER, Richard, blacksmith, Stowlangtoft, 1605. R2/45/404; W1/63/47
THAYTH, Thomas, Thrandeston, 1510. W1/9/29
THEBOLL, Mary, wid., Finningham, 1650. R2/61/396; W1/107/102; In. 3/3/122
THEBOTT, John, husb., Soham, 1588. R2/41/23; W1/45/17
THEKESTON, William, Bury St. Edmunds, 1649. A5/4/126
THELNETHAM, Adam, Bury St. Edmunds, 1380. R2/1/39
THEOBALD, Anthony, gent., Durham, 1635. R2/56/464; W1/91/33
Anthony, barber, Eye, 1684. R2/69/345; W1/138/140
Anthony, the elder, Ringshall, 1621. R2/52/226; W1/77/19
Elisabeth, spinster, Eye, 1667. A5/5/82, A4/5/20
Henry, joiner, Stowmarket, 1681. R2/68/32; W1/135/27
John, singleman, yeo., Great Ashfield, 1685. R2/70/192; W1/139/163; A5/6/111
John, bach., Great Ashfield, 1687. A5/6/111, A4/27/44
Thomas, yeo., Great Ashfield, 1679. R2/67/404; W1/133/147
Thomas, singleman, Harleston, 1678. R2/67/129; W1/130/114
William, bach., Ashfield, 1694. A5/6/168, A4/37/33
see also Tebald, Tebbald, Tebbold, Tebbould, Tebold, Theboll, Tobald, Torbold, Cokkow als. Thebolde
THERLYNG, William, Little Thurlow, 1462. R2/9/289
THETFORD, Arthur, butcher, Stradishall, 1670. In. 3/15/167; A5/5/116
Francis, Glemsford, 1647, (N). R2/59/416; W1/104/43; In. 3/2/50
Francis, yeo., Stoke, 1685. R2/70/220; W1/139/183
John, husb., Cavendish, 1577. R2/37/248
John, yeo., Cavendish, 1605. R2/45/466; W1/63/115
William, barker, Bury St. Edmunds, 1406. R2/1/108
THETFORTH, John, labourer, Cavendish, 1623, (N). R2/52/643; W1/79/71
William, Cavendish, 1531. R2/19/71
THEYN, William, tailor, Bury St. Edmunds, 1528. R2/6/149
THINGE, Joan, spinster, Haughley, 1581. R2/38/323; W1/40/66
Joan, wid., Old Newton, 1626. R2/53/593; W1/82/122
John, Haughley, 1572. A5/1/252
John, the elder, husb., Haughley, 1602. R2/45/157; W1/60/79
Marion, wid., Haughley, 1554. A5/1/90
Thomas, tailor, Old Newton, 1629. R2/54/312; W1/85/28
see also Thyng
THIRKETLE, John, carpenter, Norwich, (1594). W1/51/98
see also Thyrketyll
THIRLOE, Margaret, Mendlesham, 1642, (N). R2/58/342; W1/99/39
THIRSTONE, John, yeo., Cavenham, 1667. R2/64/193; W1/119/39; In. 3/12/8

THOMAS, Ann, wid., Denham, 1661. R2/62/259; W1/113/148; In. 3/6/209
Father, Bury St. Edmunds, 1572, (N). R2/36/49; W1/31/94
John, als. Rogers, Wickhambrook, 1636. R2/57/67; W1/92/78
Roger, yeo., Wickhambrook, 1609. R2/47/68; W1/66/78
William, servant, Ingham, 1555. R2/24/193; W1/15/27
THOMBE, Agnes, Long Melford, 1477. W1/24/19
THOMLINGSON, Thomas, rector, Milden, 1566. A5/1/174
THOMPSON, Adam, Aldham, 1631. A5/4/14
Alice, Burwell, 1587. A5/2/90
Anthony, butcher, Boxford, 1564. R2/32/70; W1/27/20
Edmund, Soham, 1582. A5/2/41
Edmund, clothier, Stanstead, 1661, (N). R2/62/296; W1/113/212; In. 3/6/274; A5/5/25, A4/1/7
Edward, clog maker, Bury St. Edmunds, 1635. R2/56/489; W1/91/65
Edward, inn holder, Bury St. Edmunds, 1693. R2/72/170
George, Great Waldingfield, 1635. A5/4/35
Henry, Downham, 1641. A5/4/92
James, Layham, 1683. A5/6/71, A4/20/79
Joan, wid., Boxford, 1589. A5/2/123
John, husb., Cavendish, 1606. R2/46/51; W1/64/65
John, Groton, 1666. A5/5/77, A4/80/63
John, clerk, Icklingham St. James, 1556. R2/25/21; W1/16/22
John, Kersey, 1563. A5/1/144
John, Newmarket, 1577. In. 3/1/29; A5/2/1
John, Onehouse, 1678. R2/67/138; W1/130/132; In. 5/6/12; A4/15/99
John, husb., Soham, 1544. R2/19/490
John, yeo., Soham, 1593. R2/42/392; W1/50/60
Oliver, miller, Burwell, 1647. R2/59/435; W1/104/66; In. 3/2/67
Richard, Hundon, 1683. R2/69/34; W1/137/27
Robert, yeo., Stanton, 1663, (N). R2/63/42; W1/115/64; In. 3/8/67
Thomas, Soham, 1524. R2/17/326
William, Lavenham, 1577. A5/2/5
William, husb., Soham, 1547. R2/21/313; W1/10/128
William, Soham, 1576. In. 3/1/82
William, Soham, 1660. In. 3/5/35; A5/5/2, A4/1/229
William, Whatfield, 1638. A5/4/64
THOMSON, Alexander, Brandon, 1457. R2/9/183
John, yeo., Cavendish, 1680. R2/67/661; W1/134/123; In. 3/20/135
Mary, wid., Cavendish, 1681. R2/68/215; W1/135/158
Robert, clerk, Soham, 1583. R2/39/93; W1/42/20a, b & c
Sarah, wid., Sudbury, 1663, (N). R2/63/110; W1/115/167; In. 3/9/79; A5/5/53
Thomas, husb., Barrow, 1638. R2/57/273; W1/93/39
Thomas, Burwell, 1612. A5/3/119
Thomas, Soham, 1611. A5/3/114
Thomas, singleman, Soham, 1613. R2/48/336; W1/70/120
William, gent., Cotton, 1685. R2/70/7; W1/139/9
William, tanner, Rattlesden, 1560. R2/29/95; W1/25/73
see also Tompson
THOMYSTON, John, chandler, Bury St. Edmunds, 1370. R2/1/31
THORGUR, Robert, Great Waldingfield, 1568. W1/95/51 & 52
THORINGTON, Martha, wid., Sudbury, 1695. A5/6/180, A4/38/48
THORMOD(E), John, the elder, husb., Combs, 1545. R2/19/516; W1/7/99
Robert, Thorpe Morieux, 1481. R2/11/274; W1/24/31
THORN(E), Edward, Ixworth Thorpe, 1570. R2/34/52; W1/30/47
Edward, gent., Mildenhall, 1633. R2/56/269; W1/90/34
Simon, fletcher, Bury St. Edmunds, 1458. R2/2/60
William, fletcher, Bury St. Edmunds, 1499. R2/4/77
William, Bury St. Edmunds, 1609. R2/47/82; W1/66/98
William, Pakenham, 1497. R2/13/36
THORNDON, Robert, wid., Fordham, 1691. A5/6/140, A4/33/17
THORNETON, John, Icklingham, 1593. A5/2/188
John, Lawshall, 1591. R2/42/15; W1/48/11
THORNTON, Daniel, Newmarket, 1668. In. 3/13/176; A5/5/96, A4/6/64
James, Clare, 1581. A5/2/37

THORNTON continued
Jane, Mildenhall, 1690. A5/6/132, A4/32/17
John, husb., Clare, 1620. R2/52/155; W1/76/140
John, Sudbury, 1694. A5/6/171, A4/37/63
Samuel, Snailwell, 1672. A5/5/130, A4/9/26
Thomas, Soham, 1520. R2/15/34
William, husb., Clare, 1626. R2/53/451; W1/82/7
THOROLD, Edmund, gent., Wortham, 1684. R2/69/216; W1/138/26
THOROUGOOD, Joan, wid., Elmswell, 1676. R2/66/412; W1/128/123; In. 3/17/160
THOROWGOOD, William, glover, Haughley, 1677. R2/66/517; W1/129/100
THORPE, Amy, spinster, Stowupland, 1668. R2/64/303; W1/120/3
Andrew, point maker, Sudbury, 1637. R2/57/201; W1/92/240
Daniel, Combs, 1640. A5/4/79
Daniel, farmer, Combs, 1685. R2/70/168; W1/139/139
Daniel, Combs, 1700. A5/7/16, A4/41/113
Elisabeth, wid., Wickhambrook, 1592. R2/42/243; W1/49/58
John, yeo., Assington, 1643. R2/59/31; W1/100/42
John, yeo., Bury St. Edmunds, 1558. W1/95/43
John, comber, Sudbury, 1671. R2/65/202; W1/123/72
John, yeo., Takeley, 1558. R2/27/45
Thomas, Soham, 1691. A5/6/140, A4/33/19
William, Combs, 1546. R2/21/236; W1/10/75
William, Combs, 1585. A5/2/70
William, yeo., Combs, 1607. R2/46/149
see also Bolle als. Thorp
THORROLD, Nicholas, yeo., Stoke by Nayland, 1663. R2/63/4; W1/115/8
see also Thorold, Turrold
THRECHER, John, Clare, 1442. R2/9/49
THREGALL, Thomas, Nayland, 1564. A5/1/160
THRESSER, John, Long Melford, 1522. R2/15/37
THRESSHER, Clemency, wid., Long Melford, 1526. R2/17/172; W1/23/60
Roger, Bradfield St. George, 1484. R2/11/361
see also Threcher
THROSTYLL, Thomas, Bury St. Edmunds, 1460. R2/2/66
THROVER, Thomas, sen., yeo., Newmarket, 1522. R2/14/67
THROWAR, Elisabeth, Bury St. Edmunds, 1605. R2/45/379; W1/63/2
THROWARD, Robert, weaver, Ousden, 1651, (N). R2/61/421
THROWER, Alice, wid. of Simon, Bury St. Edmunds, 1464. R2/2/80
Dorothy, Eye, 1630. A5/4/2
John, yeo., Eye, 1611. R2/48/108; W1/68/125
Joseph, maltster, Haughley, 1680. R2/67/572; W1/134/51; In. 3/20/53
Richard, gent., Eye, 1648. R2/60/51; W1/105/68
Richard, sen., Eye, 1649. A5/4/127
Robert, the elder, Eye, 1531. R2/19/84, R2/20/106; W1/4/93
Thomas, cook, Bury St. Edmunds, 1669. R2/64/451; W1/121/39; In. 3/14/10
Thomas, husb., Elmswell, 1598. R2/44/55; W1/56/52
William, Bildeston, 1559. R2/28/287; W1/22/261
William, singleman, Westhorpe, 1679. R2/67/282; W1/133/70
THRUSTON, John, mercer, Bury St. Edmunds, 1464. R2/2/80
John, mercer, Bury St. Edmunds, 1503. R2/4/125
Margaret, wid., Bury St. Edmunds, 1472. R2/2/164
William, yeo., Bury St. Edmunds, 1474. R2/2/194
THRYSTON, Alice, wid., Cheveley, 1520. R2/15/30
THURBERN, Richard, gent., Cotton, 1478. R2/11/172
Roger, Cotton, 1579. R2/38/42; W1/39/28
THURBORNE, Thomazine, wid., Bury St. Edmunds, 1648. A5/4/123
THURGO, Robert, Great Waldingfield, 1575. R2/37/96; W1/34/39
THURGOOD, Lawrence, yeo., Great Waldingfield, 1621. R2/52/293; W1/77/74
Robert, miller, Buxhall, 1700. R2/74/6; W1/154/5
THURGOR, James, Acton, 1474. R2/10/524
John, Waldingfield, 1458. R2/9/209
Robert, Acton, 1462. R2/10/312
Roger, Kettlebaston, 1506. R2/13/176b
THURGURE, William, Great Waldingfield, 1464. R2/10/357
THURKLYS, John, Kings Lynn, (1530). R2/19/44

THURLOE, Thomas, Thorndon, 1639, (N). R2/58/106; W1/94/173
Thomas, singleman, Wortham, 1698. A5/7/9
THURLOO, James, Wortham, 1571. R2/35/243; W1/38/149
THURLOWE, Geoffrey, Mendlesham, 1593. A5/2/180
Thomas, Great Thornham, 1636. A5/4/45
see also Thirloe, Thyrlowe
THURMEWALD, John, Combs, 1564. A5/1/155
THURMOD, John, Bildeston, 1460. R2/9/304
John, Great Finborough, 1473. R2/11/13
John, Thorpe Morieux, 1453. R2/9/160
Richard, Thorpe Morieux, 1455. R2/9/225
THURMOOD, Edith, wid., Stowmarket, 1580. R2/38/164; W1/39/130
Robert, yeo., Stowupland, 1682. R2/68/414; W1/136/108; In. 3/21/119; A5/6/63, A4/19/90
see also Thormod(e)
THURSTON, Ann, singlewoman, Cavenham, 1682. A5/6/56, A4/19/4 & 8
Ann, singlewoman, Eye, 1696. R2/73/10; W1/150/20; In. 3/25/41
Anne, wid., Mildenhall, 1644. R2/59/152; W1/101/77
Edmund, husb., Brandon, 1628, (N). R2/54/154; W1/84/25
Elisabeth, wid., Freckenham, 1616. R6/9
Ellen, wid., Bury St. Edmunds, 1512. R2/5/19
Grace, ----. W1/95/100
John, the elder, Bury St. Edmunds, 1498. R2/4/73
John, singleman, Cavenham, 1698. A5/7/8
John, Hoxne, 1640. A5/4/80
John, carpenter, Lidgate, 1615. R2/49/344; W1/72/116
John, Little Waldingfield, 1683. A5/6/70, A4/20/63
John, Mildenhall, 1681. A5/6/50, A4/18/74
John, Sapiston, 1697. In. 3/25/89; A5/6/192
John, Sudbury, 1537. R2/18/146
Katherine, wid., Woolpit (1548). R2/21/395
Marion, singlewoman, Mildenhall, 1595. R2/43/78; W1/53/71
Ralph, Layham, 1527. R2/17/219; W1/1/67
Robert, Mildenhall, 1673. A5/5/139, A4/10/56, A4/19/22a & b
Robert, Little Waldingfield, (1494). R2/13/23
Samuel, Mildenhall, 1608. A5/3/56
Thomas, shepherd, Freckenham, 1662. W8/18; In. 10/4
Thomas, yeo., Mildenhall, 1626. R2/53/636; W1/82/161
Thomas, yeo., Mildenhall, 1644. R2/59/111; W1/101/37
Thomas, husb., Mildenhall, 1662. R2/62/320; W1/114/20; In. 3/7/51
Thomas, labourer, Ousden, 1603. R2/45/293; W1/61/100
Thomas, West Stow, 1679. A5/6/15, A4/16/3
see also Thirstone
THURTON, Peter, Brandon, 1641. R2/58/305; W1/97/99
THWAITE, John, Thrandeston, 1573. A5/1/258
THWAYTE, Thomas, Thrandeston, 1544. R2/19/491
THWEYT, Matthew, Wetheringsett, 1453. R2/9/180
THWEYTS, Thomas, Bildeston, 1474. R2/10/584
THYKNESSE, John, inn holder, Bury St. Edmunds, 1499. R2/4/90
John, Newmarket, 1460. R2/9/277
THYNG, Elisabeth, wid., Wetherden, 1552. R2/23/236; W1/12/48
John, Wetherden, 1552. R2/23/235; W1/12/47
Stephen, als. Martin, yeo., Great Thurlow, 1625. R2/53/324; W1/81/108
William, Elmswell, 1559. R2/28/68; W1/22/71
William, the elder, Haughley, 1528. R2/15/220
THYRKETYLL, Richard, vicar, Eye, 1565. R2/32/204; W1/27/129
THYRKYLL, Rowland, shearman, Bury St. Edmunds, 1500. R2/4/97
THYRLOWE, John, Wortham, 1536. R2/18/142
THYSTELDEN, Alice, als. Kent, Stowmarket, 1470. R2/10/444
TIBNAM, Susan, spinster, Hargrave, 1663. In. 3/8/211; A5/5/53
TICKOE, John, yeo., petty chapman, Mellis, 1670. R2/65/115; W1/122/139; In. 3/15/181; A5/5/118
TIDD, Thomas, Mildenhall, 1570. A5/1/232
see also Tydde
TIFFIN, John, yeo., Newton, 1685. R2/70/69; W1/139/61
Peter, Felsham, 1690. A5/6/137, A4/32/70
Richard, weaver, Groton, 1613. R2/48/318; W1/70/96
Robert, yeo., Hundon, 1630. R2/55/88; W1/86/97
see also Tyffen

TIFFORD, Thomas, clerk, Pakenham, 1672. A5/5/135
TILBROOK, John, parish clerk, Brandon, 1634. R2/56/332; W1/90/95
Peter, Kirtling, 1445. R2/9/69
see also Tylbroke
TILER, Ann, Cavendish, 1636. A5/4/45
Henry, goldsmith, Bury St. Edmunds, 1664. In. 3/9/179; A5/5/62, A4/2/90
Richard, Brent Eleigh, 1638. R2/57/384; W1/93/194
Thomasine, wid., Depden, 1622. R2/52/401; W1/78/36
see also Tyler
TILL, Edward, Little Cornard, 1631. A5/4/15
Helen, Little Cornard, 1609. A5/3/57
John, Little Cornard, 1521. R2/14/114
John, dyer, Sudbury, 1460. R2/9/305
Richard, yeo., Little Cornard, 1618. R2/51/51; W1/75/29
see also Tyll(e)
TILLET(T), Agnes, wid., Bury St. Edmunds, 1678. R2/67/180; W1/130/158; A5/6/14, A4/15/122
Agnes, wid., Rushbrook, 1597. R2/43/334; W1/55/100
Anthony, Troston, 1665. A5/5/68, A4/3/50
Catherine, singlewoman, Rickinghall Inferior, 1633. R2/56/299; W1/90/63
Edmund, yeo., Rougham, 1589. R2/41/195; W1/46/90
George, weaver, Rougham, 1616. R2/50/96; W1/73/105
Grace, wid., Bardwell, 1696. R2/73/3; W1/150/31; In. 3/25/50
Henry, labourer, Hawstead, 1678. R2/67/153; W1/130/137; In. 3/19/188
John, yeo., Beyton, 1672. R2/65/324; W1/124/49
John, the elder, yeo., Bradfield St. George, 1673. R2/65/453; W1/125/85
John, Drinkstone, 1700. R2/74/99; W1/154/102
Robert, Bradfield St. Clare, 1661. In. 3/6/275; A5/5/25, A4/1/17
Thomas, the elder, yeo., Fornham St. Martin, 1621. R2/52/320; W1/77/99
Thomas, yeo., Wetherden, 1607. R2/46/124; W1/97/45
William, shoe maker, Bardwell, 1665. In. 3/10/166; A5/5/70, A4/3/8
TILLITT, Dorothy, wid., Brandon, 1634. R2/56/335; W1/90/100
TILLOT(T), Abigail, spinster, Pakenham, 1697. R2/73/120; W1/151/10
Agnes, wid., Bury St. Edmunds, 1636. R2/57/101; W1/92/119
Alice, wid., Bury St. Edmunds, 1635. R2/56/490; W1/91/66
Alice, wid., Walsham le Willows, 1639, (N). R2/58/29; W1/94/53
Ann, wid., Beyton, 1621. R2/52/252; W1/77/38
Ann, wid., Bradfield St. George, 1691. R2/71/470
Ann, wid., Bury St. Edmunds, 1679. R2/67/448; W1/133/176; In. 3/20/9
Anne, wid., Rougham, 1625. R2/53/275; W1/81/62
Anne, wid., Stowlangtoft, 1596. R2/43/154; W1/54/31
Edmond, yeo., Rougham, 1599. W1/57/104
Edmund, gent., Rougham, 1625. R2/53/253; W1/81/43
Edmund, Rougham, 1632. A5/4/19
Elena, Bury St. Edmunds, 1370. R2/1/24
Elisabeth, Rougham, 1596. A5/2/221
Faith, wid., Beyton, 1650. R2/61/313; W1/107/8
Henry, yeo., Rougham, 1609. R2/47/113; W1/66/129
Henry, Walsham le Willows, 1619, (N). R2/51/255; W1/132/2
John, Bury St. Edmunds, 1465. R2/2/90
John, singleman, Fornham St. Genevieve, 1592. R2/42/260; W1/49/78
John, yeo., Pakenham, 1644. R2/59/145; W1/101/69
John, Rougham, 1639. A5/4/71
John, yeo., Rushbrook, 1666. R2/64/108; W1/118/79; In. 3/11/154
John, gent., Woolpit, 1671. R2/65/180; W1/123/51
Leonard, gent., Rougham, 1663. R2/63/30; W1/115/49; In. 3/8/241
Margaret, wid. of George, yeo., Rougham, 1642. R2/58/321; W1/99/10
Martha, wid., Rougham, 1648. R2/60/94; W1/105/114
Mary, spinster, Beyton, 1646. A5/4/115
Mary, spinster, Wetherden, 1673. R2/65/399; W1/125/14
Priscilla, spinster, Beyton, 1646. A5/4/115
Reginald, gent., Bury St. Edmunds, 1660. R2/62/111; W1/112/149; In. 3/5/174

TILLOT(T) continued
Reginald, Rougham, 1557. R2/26/267; W1/20/183
Reginald, gent., Troston, 1619, (N). R2/51/357; W1/132/59 a & b
Robert, yeo., Brandon, 1681. R2/68/167; W1/135/125
Roger, carpenter, Rougham, 1649. R2/60/230; W1/106/83
Thomas, yeo., Beyton, 1616. R2/50/152; W1/73/152
Thomas, Botesdale, 1643. A5/4/101
Thomas, Botesdale, 1672. A5/5/130, A4/9/30
Thomas, Bury St. Edmunds, 1438. R2/1/235
Thomas, sen., tanner, Bury St. Edmunds, 1661. R2/62/260; W1/113/149
Thomas, collar maker, Bury St. Edmunds, 1676. In. 3/17/107; A5/5/163, A4/13/62
Thomas, Bury St. Edmunds, 1692. In. 3/24/72; A5/6/153, A4/34/59
Thomas, the elder, husb., Rougham, 1638. R2/57/344; W1/93/129
Thomas, the elder, yeo., Rougham, 1648. R2/60/144; W1/105/172
William, singleman, gent., Bury St. Edmunds, 1666. In. 3/11/79; A5/5/75, A4/4/30
William, maltster, Groton, 1671. R2/65/218; W1/123/92
William, Old Newton, 1694. A5/6/172, A4/37/75
William, singleman, Rushbrook, 1693. R2/72/235; W1/147/125
William, yeo., Thurston, 1674. R2/66/28; W1/126/96
see also Tyllett

TILNEY, Nicholas, yeo., Bury St. Edmunds, 1552. R2/8/73; W1/21/206
see also Tylney

TILSON, John, Mildenhall, 1649. A5/4/129
see also Tylson

TINCKLER, Edward, cordwainer, Mildenhall, 1692. R2/72/53; W1/146/49
George, singleman, Stowmarket, 1664. A5/5/61, A4/2/80

TINKER, see Havell als. Tynkar

TINKLER, Richard, Mildenhall, 1692. In. 3/24/61

TINN, Thomas, Freckenham, 1668. In. 10/12; A5/5/91, A4/6/15
see also Tynne

TIPLOCK, Joan, wid., Boxford, 1645. A5/4/111

TIPPLE, Robert, linen weaver, Botesdale, 1680. R2/67/525; W1/134/10; In. 3/20/14
Robert, yeo., Burgate, 1653. W1/110/41
Simon, linen weaver, Botesdale, 1694. R2/72/397; W1/148/128

TIPSHEW, Robert, Bury St. Edmunds, 1632. A5/4/21

TIPTOD, John, sen., butcher, Rickinghall, 1646. R2/59/354; W1/103/68

TIPTOT(T), Christopher, Clare, 1630. A5/4/2
Henry, tailor, Bury St. Edmunds, 1593. R2/42/404; W1/50/66
John, the elder, Rickinghall, 1536. R2/19/235
John, sen., yeo., Rickinghall Superior, 1642. R2/58/375; W1/99/79
John, husb., Rickinghall Superior, 1673. R2/65/450; W1/125/78
see also Typtode

TIRELL, James, clerk, Newton, 1567. R2/32/414; W1/3/116
Robert, gent., Gipping, 1681. R2/68/168; W1/135/126
Robert, gent., Gipping, 1681. R2/70/581
Thomas, esq., Gipping, 1678. R2/67/135; W1/130/120; In. 3/19/168
Tierce, wid. of James, esq., Gipping, 1661. R2/62/285; W1/113/196; In. 3/6/258

TIRRELL, Francis, gent., Stowmarket, 1665. In. 3/10/132; A5/5/68, A4/3/62
William, gent., Mildenhall, 1583. R2/39/66; W1/42/43

TIRROLD, Edward, husb., Thrandeston, (1625). W1/111/47
see also Tyrell

TITTELE, Phillippa, wid. of John, Bury St. Edmunds, 1493. R2/4/20 (admon. only)

TITTERELL, Mary, Great Bradley, 1625. R2/53/260; W1/81/50

TITTRILL, John, husb., Great Bradley, 1616. R2/50/49; W1/73/56

TOBOLD, Thomas, yeo., Barnardiston, 1609. R2/47/62; W1/66/70

TOCKE, Richard, parson, Great Livermere, 1558. R2/27/471b

TODD, Alice, wid., Bramfield, 1575. W1/51/218
Ann, wid., Bury St. Edmunds, 1695. R2/72/483; W1/149/40
Harry, parson, Buxhall, 1556. R2/25/99; W1/16/103
James, husb., Culford, 1559. R2/28/48; W1/22/51
John, Bury St. Edmunds, 1687. A5/6/115, A4/27/89

TODD continued
Robert, Bury St. Edmunds, 1691. A5/6/144, A4/33/66
Thomas, yeo., Cavendish, 1700. R2/74/148
Thomas, Eye, 1673. A5/5/136, A4/10/17
William, tailor, Alpheton, 1671. R2/65/199; W1/123/68
TOFFAY, Alice, Bardwell, 1478. R2/11/158
John, Great Livermere, 1483. R2/11/304
Thomas, Bardwell, 1464. R2/10/357
TOFT, William, Bury St. Edmunds, 1471. R2/2/154
TOFTES, Reginald, Elveden, (1464). R2/10/364
see also Toftys
TOFTWOOD, John, singleman, Mellis, 1605. R2/45/461; W1/63/109; A5/3/4
Robert, Eye, 1636. A5/4/44
Thomas, gent., Eye, 1639. R2/58/55; W1/94/104
Thomas, Mellis, 1605. A5/3/3
TOFTYS, John, West Stow, 1469. R2/10/402
Thomas, als. Wysbeche, tailor, Bury St. Edmunds, 1466. R2/2/93
TOKELY, Henry, Bury St. Edmunds, 1634. A5/4/29
TOLER, Joseph, yeo., Stoke by Nayland, 1649. R2/60/200; W1/106/43
TOLEYN, Ellen, wid. of Hugh, Brandon, 1506. R2/13/178
TOLLARD, Arnold, tailor, Bury St. Edmunds, 1471. R2/2/145
TOLLARE, Agnes, wid., Downham, 1557. R2/26/6; W1/20/4
TOLLEMACHE, Robert, Bury St. Edmunds, 1673. R2/65/460
see also Talmache
TOLLER, Alice, singlewoman, Isleham, 1662. A5/5/34, A12/1
Edmund, Nayland, 1662. In. 3/7/79; A5/5/29
James, Downham, 1580. A5/2/29
John, Brandon, 1556. R2/25/100; W1/16/102
John, Bury St. Edmunds, 1398. R2/1/85
John, husb., Chippenham, 1606. R2/46/86; W1/64/102
John, husb., Chippenham, 1616. R2/50/102; W1/73/110
John, Lakenheath, 1569. R2/33/117; W1/28/180
John, Worlington, 1544. R2/19/481
Margaret, wid., Downham, 1504. R2/13/147
Oliver, yeo., Whepstead, 1672, (N). R2/65/301; W1/124/19
Reginald, Horringer, 1542, (N). R2/22/30; W1/6/68
Robert, Wangford, 1464. R2/10/345
Thomas, Worlington, 1558. R2/27/496
William, shepherd, Brandon, 1550. R2/21/20; W1/10/185
William, Downham, 1503. R2/13/143
see also Toler, Tollare, Tollor, Towler
TOLLERTON, Christopher, Cavendish, 1556. R2/25/36; W1/16/39
TOLLOR, Robert, Fordham, 1553. R2/31/21; W1/13/13
Thomas, Lackford, 1553. R2/31/16; W1/13/10
TOLLWORTHY, John, Fordham, 1687. A4/27/68
TOLWARDIE, Ambrose, weaver, Chippenham, 1640. R2/58/165; W1/96/78
TOLWARDY, John, shepherd, Exning, 1632. R2/56/149; W1/89/48
Richard, Exning, 1579. R2/38/32; W1/39/44
William, Wixoe, 1636. A5/4/45
TOLWORDEY, John, Wicken, 1673. A5/5/136, A4/10/18
TOLWORDIE, Thomas, husb., Badingham, 1673. R2/65/413; W1/125/35
TOLWORTHY, Ann, wid., Chippenham, 1696. R2/73/50; W1/150/37
Isaac, tailor, Chippenham, 1691. R2/71/451
Thomas, Wicken, 1638. A5/4/57
William, yeo., Chippenham, 1696. R2/73/30; W1/150/63
see also Tallwordie, Talwardie, Talworthy, Tollworthy, Towlardie, Towlerdey
TOLY, Edmund, Bury St. Edmunds, 1399. R2/1/87
John, Bury St. Edmunds, 1467. R2/2/108
John, fishmonger, Bury St. Edmunds, 1468. R2/2/111
Margaret, Barnham, 1455. R2/9/233
Margaret, wid., Bury St. Edmunds, 1476. R2/2/200 & 224
Richard, barker, Bury St. Edmunds, 1469. R2/2/128
Robert, Bury St. Edmunds, 1432. R2/1/200
Simon, butcher, Bury St. Edmunds, 1429. R2/1/188
William, Barnham, 1454. R2/9/200
William, grain picker, Bury St. Edmunds, 1441. R2/1/257
TOMBLIN, John, Brandon, 1667. R2/64/192; W1/119/35
TOMELYNSON, John, shearman, Bury St. Edmunds, 1519. R2/6/67

TOMLIN, Elisabeth, wid., Sudbury, 1693. R2/72/119
Thomas, say weaver, Sudbury, 1696. R2/73/72; W1/150/83
TOMLINSON, Elisabeth, wid., Haverhill, 1606. R2/46/96; W1/64/115
John, yeo., Barnham, 1667. In. 3/12/33
TOMLYNSON, Robert, Stoke by Clare, 1578. R2/37/335; W1/36/240
see also Thomlingson, Tomelynson, Babington als. Tomlinson
TOMMES, Margaret, wid., Sudbury, 1584. R2/39/133; W1/42/197
Thomas, shoe maker, Sudbury, 1582. R2/38/359; W1/41/85
TOMMYS, Edmund, Pakenham, 1533. R2/19/178; W1/2/23
TOMPSON, Edmund, yeo., Soham, 1579. R2/38/37; W1/39/41
Edward, yeo., Cavendish, 1637. R2/57/183; W1/92/219
Edward, Cavendish, 1640, (N). R2/58/133; W1/96/25
Edward, gent., Sudbury, 1660. R2/62/100; W1/112/133; In. 3/6/204
Isabel, wid., Soham, 1582. R2/38/381; W1/41/55
James, yeo., Layham, 1672. R2/65/297; W1/124/12
Joan, wid., Belchamp Otten, 1639. R2/58/43; W1/94/77
John, Bury St. Edmunds, 1495. R2/4/38
John, the elder, tailor, Hindolveston, 1585. W1/51/182
John, yeo., Norton, 1635. R2/56/469; W1/91/36
Richard, Burwell, 1650. In. 3/3/131; A5/4/137
Richard, 1627. R2/54/128; W1/83/128a & b
Robert, Langham, 1594. A5/2/194
Thomas, yeo., Elmswell, 1660. R2/62/146; W1/112/188; In. 3/5/220
Thomas, husb., Soham, 1558. R2/27/439
Thomas, husb., Soham, 1590. R2/41/415; W1/47/92
William, yeo., Beccles, 1582. W1/51/170
William, yeo., Boxford, 1619. R2/51/463; W1/132/126
TOMSON, Alice, Haverhill, 1461. R2/9/296
Daniel, weaver, Great Cornard, 1644. R2/59/90; W1/101/21
James, Boxford, 1647. In. 3/2/109; A5/4/118
John, the elder, bricklayer, Glemsford, 1690. R2/71/346; W1/144/50
John, miller, Isleham, 1627. R6/47
John, Soham, 1501. R2/13/118
John, husb., Soham, 1567. R2/32/386; W1/3/26
John, singleman, Wicken, 1582. R2/38/268; W1/41/73
Margery, wid., Lavenham, 1560. R2/29/14; W1/25/167
Miles, smith, Sudbury, 1540. R2/20/253; W1/4/191
Robert, Sudbury, 1543. R2/19/363; W1/6/159
Thomas, Bury St. Edmunds, 1534. R2/7/20
William, husb., Eriswell, 1613. R2/48/325; W1/70/104
TONE, John, barber, Bury St. Edmunds, 1354. R2/1/1
Solris, Little Whelnetham, 1458. R2/9/206
TONGE, John, Mildenhall, 1596. A5/2/217
TONGETT, Thomas, the elder, Lavenham, 1568. R2/33/1; W1/29/6
TONGUET, Thomas, butcher, Lavenham, 1650. In. 3/3/54
TONNEYE, Julian, weaver, Bury St. Edmunds, 1583, (N). R2/39/149; W1/42/173
TONNYE, Stephen, Kedington, 1595. A5/2/211
Thomas, Bury St. Edmunds, 1597. R2/43/325; W1/55/91
TOOLEY, Joseph, Combs, 1692. A5/6/146, A4/31/85
Philip, Groton, 1661. A5/5/18, A4/1/82
TOOT, Alice, wid., Bury St. Edmunds, 1463. R2/2/78
William, tailor, Bury St. Edmunds, 1454. R2/2/43
TOPLE, Margaret, wid., Timworth, 1613. R2/48/256; W1/70/30
William, Hundon, 1563. R2/32/9; W1/26/67
TOPLEY, John, husb., Hundon, 1626. R2/53/682; W1/82/64
TOPPER, Matthew, inn holder, Groton, 1668, (N). R2/64/304; W1/120/5; In. 3/13/2
TOPPESSFYLD, William, Gislingham, 1480. R2/11/216; W1/24/110
TOPYSFELD, Ralph, gent., Bury St. Edmunds, 1479. R2/2/285
TORALD, Joan, Thornham, 1457. R2/9/220
John, Great Thornham, (1484). R2/11/330
TORBOLD, Philip, yeo., Wetheringsett, 1663. In. 3/8/182; A5/5/52
TORBOLT, John, timberman, Wetheringsett, 1589. R2/41/205; W1/46/79
TORELL, Margaret, wid., Soham, 1584. R2/39/150; W1/42/174
TORINGTON, John, labourer, Lakenheath, 1609. R2/47/52; W1/66/59
TORKINGTON, Robert, gent., Brettenham, 1693. R2/72/274; W1/147/159
TORNER, Edmund, priest, Brockley, 1540. R2/19/589; W1/5/7
Thomas, the elder, yeo., Lindsey, 1567. R2/32/434; W1/19/110

TORNOR, Agnes, wid., Drinkstone, 1556. R2/25/57; W1/16/73
Hugh, Stoke by Clare, 1535. R2/18/131
John, Depden, 1462. R2/10/322
Thomas, Bildeston, 1528. R2/15/191
TORNOUR, Simon, Bury St. Edmunds, 1406. R2/1/109
TOROLD, Alice, wid., Great Thornham, 1544. R2/19/424; W1/21/150a
John, Great Thornham, 1532. R2/19/99; W1/3/156
Robert, Great Thornham, 1433. W1/24/164
Robert, yeo., Thrandeston, 1555. R2/24/154; W1/15/3
Roger, Bury St. Edmunds, 1519. R2/6/63
TORRELL, John, painter, Soham, 1598. R2/44/134; W1/56/102
TORRILLE, James, labourer, Soham, 1616. R2/50/122; W1/73/128
see also Torell
TOSTOCK, Henry, singleman, Hopton, 1662. In. 3/7/148; A5/5/35
John, the elder, yeo., Hopton, 1664. R2/63/133; W1/116/21; In. 3/9/44
Margaret, wid., Thelnetham, 1675. R2/66/183; W1/127/56; In. 3/16/70
TOSTOK, Robert, husb., Hopton, 1571. R2/35/54; W1/36/65
Stephen, Hopton, 1568. R2/33/33; W1/29/47
see also Smyth als. Tostock, Smyth als. Tostoke
TOTAY, Robert, Bury St. Edmunds, 1468. R2/2/112
TOTNALL, John, thatcher, Soham, 1576, (N). R2/37/162; W1/37/27; In. 3/1/92
TOTNAM, William, Sudbury, 1579. A5/2/21
TOTTEY, John, Sudbury, 1682. In. 3/21/122; A5/6/63, A4/19/92
TOTTY, Henry, sen., yeo., Lawshall, 1662. R2/62/415; W1/114/171; In. 3/7/221
John, husb., Sudbury, 1593. R2/42/418; W1/50/80
TOULLER, Thomas, Bury St. Edmunds, 1568. A5/1/200
TOUNNES, Henry, Little Livermere, 1561. A5/1/121
TOWERS, Humphrey, Sudbury, 1610. R2/47/304; W1/67/195
TOWLARDIE, Thomas, carpenter, Exning, 1620. R2/52/171; W1/76/154
TOWLE, John, Kedington, 1559. R2/28/182; W1/22/163
TOWLER, Agnes, wid., Mildenhall, 1618. R2/51/95; W1/75/59
Ann, wid., Ixworth, 1665. R2/63/308; W1/117/37; In. 3/10/53
Christopher, Pakenham, 1665. R2/63/376; W1/117/127
George, husb., Ampton, 1625. R2/53/288; W1/81/78
James, yeo., Ixworth, 1693. R2/71/115
Joan, wid., Kirtling, 1572. R2/36/17; W1/31/116
John, Kirtling, 1567. A5/1/186
John, yeo., Pakenham, 1669. In. 3/14/162; A5/5/107, A4/7/66
John, Stanton, 1696. A5/6/185, A4/39/12
Margaret, Bury St. Edmunds, 1631. A5/4/14
Robert, Ampton, 1697. A5/7/2, A4/40/25
Robert, yeo., Whepstead, 1684. R2/69/204; W1/138/16
William, Downham, 1543. R2/19/374; W1/6/109
William, yeo., Lakenheath, 1584. R2/39/202; W1/42/125
William, yeo., Pakenham, 1625. R2/53/430; W1/81/212
William, the elder, yeo., Pakenham, 1690. R2/71/420; W1/144/125
see also Toller, Touller, Towllor
TOWLERDEY, William, Stoke by Clare, 1681. A5/6/44, A4/18/15
TOWLERDY, John, Wicken, 1693. A5/6/159, A4/35/60
TOWLEWORDE, John, Chippenham, 1661. R2/62/281; W1/113/190; In. 3/6/239
TOWLLOR, Richard, shepherd, Downham, 1566. R2/32/354; W1/28/25
TOWLSON, John, Stowmarket, 1638. R2/57/375; W1/93/178
TOWNE, Isabel, Fakenham, 1579. A5/2/20
Robert, Finningham, 1673. A5/5/138, A4/10/34
TOWNES, James, Polstead, 1674. A5/5/149, A4/11/60
John, Assington, 1671. A5/5/123, A4/8/36
TOWNSEN, Samuel, yeo., Stanton, 1674. R2/66/4; W1/126/120
TOWNESENDE, Matilda, wid., Walsham le Willows, 1539. R2/19/300
TOWNESHENDE, William, clerk, Rougham, 1545. R2/19/540; W1/7/46
TOWNSEND, John, Great Livermere, 1572. A5/1/256
Stephen, Bardwell, 1608. A5/3/39
Thomas, yeo., Great Livermere, 1621. R2/52/304; W1/77/84
William, yeo., Great Livermere, 1572. R2/36/75; W1/31/51
William, Great Thornham, 1662. In. 3/7/93; A5/5/31
TOWNSON, Edward, rector, Herringswell, 1578. A5/2/7
TOWVYLL, Robert, Wetheringsett, 1522. R2/15/42
TOXTON, John, Sudbury, 1601. R2/44/513; W1/59/138

TRACE, William, yeo., Smallburgh, 1582, (N). W1/51/153 & 154
TRAICE, Elisabeth, wid., Lakenheath, 1697. A5/7/5, A4/40/67
TRAISE, Thomas, Ampton, 1690. A5/6/138, A4/32/80
Thomas, Lakenheath, 1690. A5/6/132, A4/32/15
see also Trayce, Trayse
TRANNUM, William, Kersey, 1684. A5/6/81, A4/21/74
TRANYELL, Agnes, wid., Bury St. Edmunds, 1494. R2/4/32
TRAPET(T), Adam, chaplain, Bury St. Edmunds, 1378. R2/1/42
Edmund, Hinderclay, 1561. R2/30/94
John, the elder, Hepworth, 1505. R2/13/159
John, Wattisfield, 1558. R2/27/503
Margaret, wife of John, Hepworth, 1465. R2/10/392
Ralph, Hepworth, 1463. R2/10/327
Ralph, Hepworth, 1485. R2/11/347
Thomas, Hepworth, 1460. R2/9/254
Thomas, Wattisfield, 1552. R2/23/120; W1/11/114
Walter, Hinderclay, 1501. R2/13/120
William, Hepworth, 1474. R2/11/20
William, Wattisfield, 1524. R2/17/39; W1/21/48
TRAPPETT, Lettice, Hepworth, 1495. R2/13/7
Lucy, wid., Hinderclay, 1555. A5/1/97
TRAPPIT, Anne, wid., Eye, 1616. R2/50/188; W1/73/176
TRAVELL, Thomas, husb., Lakenheath, 1668. In. 3/13/70; A5/5/99, A4/6/96
TRAVIS, George, tailor, Bury St. Edmunds, 1684. R2/69/347; W1/138/142
James, Fornham All Saints, 1695. A5/6/182, A4/38/74 & 85
James, Fornham All Saints, 1695. A5/6/183
TRAY, Josias, husb., Troston, 1633, (N). R2/56/259; W1/90/25
Moses, husb., Chelsworth, 1662. R2/62/359; W1/114/85
Thomas, parchment maker, Bury St. Edmunds, 1632. R2/56/182; W1/89/91
William, Chelsworth, 1637. A5/4/48
TRAYCE, Robert, labourer, Brandon, 1664. R2/63/171; W1/116/67; In. 3/9/88
TRAYLE, Robert, Bury St. Edmunds, 1558. R2/8/328; W1/18/63
TRAYSE, John, Hengrave, 1673. A5/5/135, A4/88/8
John, Lakenheath, 1645. A5/4/108
Thomas, yeo., Lakenheath, 1652. R2/61/534; W1/109/18; In. 3/4/90
TREBECK, Edith, wid., Kennett, 1680. R2/68/448; W1/136/132; In. 3/21/89
TREDGET, Edward, Withersfield, 1663, (N). R2/63/43; W1/115/66; In. 3/8/76; A5/5/46
TREE, Walter, Brandon, 1520. R2/15/96
TREKAR, John, Stanton, 1525. R2/17/90; W1/21/2
TREKER, Isabel, Stowmarket, (1531). R2/18/125
John, husb., Combs, 1535. R2/14/143, R2/18/105, R2/19/216; W1/3/6
TREMBLE, Peter, tanner, Bury St. Edmunds, 1622, (N). R2/52/436; W1/78/57
TREVE, Nicholas, barker, Bury St. Edmunds, 1457. R2/2/55
William, Bury St. Edmunds, 1479. R2/2/291
TREW, Mary, als. Mudd, Great Barton, 1663. A5/5/52
TREWPENY, John, Mildenhall, 1472. R2/10/560
Richard, labourer, Mildenhall, (1537). R2/19/576, R2/20/193; W1/3/43
TREWYNARD, Thomas, priest, Bury St. Edmunds, 1492. R2/4/13
TREYLYS, William, Palgrave, 1462. R2/10/374
TRICKAR, Edmund, yeo., Stanton, 1595. R2/43/1; W1/53/1
TRICKER, Alice, wid., Combs, 1605. R2/45/402; W1/63/44
Edmund, the elder, Combs, 1607. R2/46/155
Edward, husb., Stanton, 1596. R2/43/156; W1/54/34
Kathleen, wid., Stanton, 1605. R2/45/450; W1/63/98
Richard, yeo., Stanton, 1616. R2/50/192; W1/73/151
see also Trekar, Triker
TRIGG, William, Burwell, 1698. A5/7/6
TRIKER, Richard, husb., Kettlebaston, 1602. R2/45/190; W1/60/116
TRIPPE, Roger, Lavenham, 1555. A5/1/97
William, yeo., Cockfield, 1617. R2/50/214; W1/74/7
see also Tryppe, Gronger als. Tripp
TROGYTT, John, Hundon, 1531. R2/19/73

TROISE, Robert, labourer, Lakenheath, 1593, (N). R2/42/428; W1/50/88
William, husb., Lakenheath, 1663. In. 3/8/88; A5/5/47
TROLLE, John, fletcher, Newmarket, 1540. R2/20/242; W1/4/181
TROOLL, Stephen, Wickhambrook, 1458. R2/9/212
TROTT, John, husb., Stoke by Clare, 1544. R2/19/461
TROUGHTON, Phillipa, wid., Nayland, 1640. R2/58/144; W1/96/43
see also Trowton
TROUNDEL, Thomas, husb., Mildenhall, 1676. R2/66/338; W1/128/44; In. 3/17/42
TROVY, Henry, Stradishall, 1466. W1/24/153
William, Stradishall, 1518. R2/14/2
TROWELL, Francis, clothier, Soham, 1700. In. 3/27/3; A5/7/18, A4/41/165
Thomas, blacksmith, Isleham, 1619. R6/19
Thomas, the elder, gent., Soham, 1695. R2/72/553; W1/149/108
TROWLE, John, yeo., Cowlinge, 1620. R2/52/18; W1/76/17
Richard, linen draper, Newmarket, 1594. R2/42/523
TROWLL, Edward, Whepstead, (1525). W1/5/40
TROWSE, Robert, Lakenheath, 1540. R2/19/611; W1/5/19
Thomas, Lakenheath, 1539. R2/19/307
TROWTON, Thomas, Sudbury, 1598. R2/44/159; W1/56/45
TROYES, Helen, wid., Lakenheath, 1661. In. 3/6/103; A5/5/16, A4/1/102
TROYSE, Robert, Lakenheath, 1567. R2/32/398; W1/3/172
Robert, yeo., Lakenheath, 1614. R2/49/44; W1/71/38
William, yeo., Lakenheath, 1640. R2/58/161; W1/96/68
see also Troise, Trowse
TRULL, John, Norwich, 1580. W1/51/188
TRUMPOOR, Thomas, als. Euston, Sudbury, (1503). R2/13/144
TRUNDLE, Joel, butcher, Bures, 1649. R2/60/270; W1/106/139
Samuel, Fornham All Saints, 1634. A5/4/28
TRUPENE, Thomas, labourer, Mildenhall, 1525. W1/21/124
see also Trewpeny
TRUSE, Isaac, Bury St. Edmunds, 1689. A5/6/130, A4/30/11
TRUSSE, David, yeo., Lavenham, 1675. R2/66/269; W1/127/137; In. 3/16/152
David, Lavenham, 1695. A5/6/183, A4/38/80
John, Cockfield, 1673. A5/5/144, A4/10/104
William, carpenter, Hundon, 1626. R2/53/569; W1/82/95
TRUST, Thomas, Bury St. Edmunds, 1446. R2/2/18
TRUSTON, Simon, cordwainer, Bury St. Edmunds, 1419. R2/1/147
TRYEARE, Elisabeth, Stanton, 1557. R2/26/13; W1/20/27
TRYGGER, Thomas, Tuddenham, 1545. A5/1/54
TRYKELOFFE, Joan, wid. of John, Stoke by Clare, (1518). R2/15/86
TRYPER, Katherine, Walsham le Willows, 1521. R2/15/134, R2/17/329
TRYPPE, Will, Wickham Skeith, 1480. R2/11/220
TUBBY, Richard, barker, Bury St. Edmunds, 1458. R2/2/60
William, Wortham, 1454. R2/9/231
TUCKE, John, Downham, 1666. In. 3/11/75; A4/4/18
Laurence, singleman, Pakenham, 1584. R2/39/201; W1/42/126
Lawrence, Great Livermere, 1559. R2/28/226; W1/22/191
TUDOR, James, upholsterer, Little Thurlow, 1640. R2/58/225; W1/96/169
TUFFEILD, Edmund, tailor, Barton, 1630. R2/55/68; W1/86/79
Jane, wid., Kennett, 1626, (N). R2/53/651; W1/82/173
Susan, Thurston, 1643. A5/4/100
Thomas, carpenter, Icklingham, 1621. R2/48/86; W1/68/104
William, Great Barton, 1666. A5/5/80
TUFFELD, Agnes, wid., Great Livermere, 1564. R2/32/93; W1/27/40
Alice, Whepstead, 1444. R2/9/50
Francis, yeo., Wangford, 1625. R2/53/270; W1/81/55
John, tailor, Great Barton, 1621. R2/52/342; W1/77/120
John, sen., Whepstead, 1462. R2/10/362
TUFFILD, Edward, Ixworth, 1645. R2/59/257; W1/102/85
William, shepherd, Barton, 1637. R2/57/142; W1/92/177
TUFFILL, James, yeo., Hawstead, 1645. R2/59/225; W1/102/50
TUFFYLL, John, tailor, Great Livermere, 1561. R2/30/57; W1/28/234

TUMMETT, Margaret, Drinkstone, 1634. A5/4/30
TUNBRIDGE, Simon, bach., Denston, 1692. A5/6/153, A4/115/61
TUNGETT, George, butcher, Lavenham, 1647. R2/59/498; W1/104/138
Thomas, Lavenham, 1650. A5/4/135
see also Tongett
TUNMAN, James, Westhorpe, 1472. R2/10/463
TUNMER, John, yeo., Cotton, 1682. R2/68/402; W1/136/99; In. 3/21/144
TUNMORE, Edward, glazier, Badwell Ash, 1697. R2/73/205; W1/151/90
John, Badwell Ash, 1696. A5/6/188, A4/39/44
TUNNELL, John, Lakenheath, 1646. A5/4/112
TURBOLL, Walter, Whatfield, 1558. R2/27/43
TURLEY, Thomas, Isleham, 1557. W7/8
TURNAY, Richard, chaplain, 1396. R2/1/75
TURNER, Abigail, wid., Nayland, 1692. R2/72/60; W1/146/58; In. 3/24/46
Adam, Bury St. Edmunds, 1411. R2/1/123
Agnes, wid., Kedington, (1558). W1/95/40
Agnes, wid., Wickhambrook, 1559. R2/28/255; W1/22/247
Alice, spinster, Kirtling, 1632. R2/56/117; W1/89/2
Alice, wid., Nayland, 1591. R2/42/152; W1/48/92
Alice, spinster, Wood Ditton, 1669, (N). R2/64/526; W1/121/116; In. 3/14/107; A5/5/108, A4/7/49
Andrew, doctor of physic, Bury St. Edmunds, 1623. R2/52/624; W1/79/67
Andrew, gent., Stoke by Clare, 1647. R2/59/385; W1/104/13; In. 3/2/22
Ann, wid., Chippenham, 1684. R2/69/386; W1/138/169
Ann, wid., Mildenhall, 1688. R2/71/82; W1/142/74; In. 3/23/59; A5/6/120, A4/29/99
Anne, wid., Rickinghall Inferior, 1624. R2/53/76; W1/80/97
Anthony, thatcher, Lidgate, 1697. R2/73/111; W1/151/1
Charles, yeo., Norton, 1645. R2/59/252; W1/102/72
Christopher, Nayland, 1638. R2/57/259; W1/93/22
Daniel, cordwainer, Burwell, 1677. R2/66/446; W1/129/21; In. 3/18/23
David, Bradfield St. Clare, 1664. R2/63/150; W1/116/41; In. 3/9/82
Edward, butcher, Kirtling, 1664, (N). R2/63/182; W1/116/84; In. 3/9/101; A5/5/59, A4/2/57
Elisabeth, wid., Clare, 1682. In. 3/21/30; A5/6/59, A4/19/34
Elisabeth, Hawstead, 1689. A5/6/125, A4/30/58
Elisabeth, wid., Sudbury, 1674. R2/66/60; W1/126/57
Emmie, wid., Acton, 1663. R2/63/63; W1/115/102; In. 3/8/127
Francis, Westhorpe, 1667. R2/64/186; W1/119/25; In. 3/12/22
George, clothier, Bures, 1592. R2/42/325; W1/49/147
George, yeo., Bures, 1639. R2/58/54; W1/94/99
George, yeo., Clare, 1651. R2/61/496; W1/108/87
George, the younger, Clare, 1651. A5/4/140
George, husb., Clare, 1680. R2/67/571; W1/134/50; In. 3/20/52
George, yeo., Cockfield, 1626. R2/53/575; W1/82/101
George, yeo., Drinkstone, 1627. R2/54/110; W1/83/109
George, husb., Lakenheath, 1626. R2/53/656; W1/82/182
George, yeo., Stowmarket, 1663. R2/63/1; W1/115/1; In. 3/8/7
George, yeo., Stowmarket, 1700. In. 3/27/26; A5/7/16, A4/41/147
George, yeo., Thorpe Morieux, 1647. R2/59/402; W1/104/27; In. 3/2/42
Gregory, Stoke by Clare, 1638. A5/4/62
Hannah, singlewoman, Stowmarket, 1691. R2/71/499; W1/145/60
Henry, Great Fakenham, 1680. A5/6/42, A4/17/119
Henry, labourer, Lidgate, 1640. R2/58/223; W1/96/163
Henry, Little Thurlow, 1595. A5/2/217
Henry, Little Wratting, 1571. R2/35/359; W1/36/132
Henry, Wickhambrook, 1691. A5/6/143, A4/33/59
Hosea, tailor, Clare, 1671. R2/65/196; W1/123/65
James, wid., Mildenhall, 1690. R2/71/427; W1/144/131
James, Sudbury, 1650. A5/4/134
James, Thwaite, 1601. R2/44/387; W1/59/46
Jane, wid., Wetherden, 1636. R2/57/61; W1/92/69

TURNER continued
Joan, wife of James, Woolpit, 1528. R2/15/223; W1/19/46
John, Bacton, 1635. A5/4/34
John, Bury St. Edmunds, 1688. A5/6/123, A4/29/80
John, Cowlinge, 1695. A5/6/176, A4/38/2
John, Dalham, 1672, (N). R2/65/367; W1/124/105
John, Depden, 1522. R2/14/55
John, singleman, Felsham, 1661. In. 3/6/116; A5/5/18, A4/1/75
John, yeo., Great Horningsheath, 1543. R2/19/384; W1/6/162
John, labourer, Hartest, 1645. R2/59/257; W1/102/74
John, Icklingham, 1611. A5/3/114
John, labourer, Kirtling, 1625. R2/53/436; W1/81/219
John, Kirtling, 1649. A5/4/128
John, Mildenhall, 1682. In. 3/21/25; A5/6/64, A4/19/120
John, Mildenhall, 1683. A5/6/67, A4/20/21
John, jun., shearman, Nayland, 1618. R2/51/83; W1/75/51
John, weaver, Nayland, 1620. R2/52/71; W1/76/61
John, Oakley, 1555. R2/24/150; W1/15/84
John, Stoke by Clare, 1592. R2/42/300; W1/49/118
John, Sudbury, 1476. R2/11/50
John, husb., Wood Ditton, 1628. R2/54/218; W1/84/82
Jonathan, Botesdale, 1674. R2/66/55; W1/126/64
Jonathan, baker, Walsham le Willows, 1681. R2/68/136; W1/135/104
Martha, Brockford, 1684. A5/6/75, A4/21/13
Martin, Depden, 1652. R2/61/513; W1/109/2; In. 3/4/82
Martin, gent., Great Bradley, 1682. R2/68/459; W1/136/139; In. 3/21/39
Mary, spinster, Bury St. Edmunds, 1674. A5/5/151, A4/11/80
Mary, singlewoman, Haughley, 1662, (N). R2/62/323; In. 3/7/85; A5/5/29
Mary, Stanton, 1604. R2/45/317
Mary, spinster, Wetherden, 1671. A5/5/122, A4/8/24
Osbert, Lakenheath, 1651. A5/4/139
Philip, the elder, Ixworth, 1553. R2/31/151
Philip, Ixworth, 1562. A5/1/135
Richard, Bardwell, 1606. R2/46/28; W1/64/35
Richard, yeo., Barton Mills, 1649. R2/60/220; W1/106/68
Richard, Bures, 1577. A5/2/6
Richard, husb., Chippenham, 1668. In. 3/13/106; A5/5/99, A4/6/99
Richard, Fornham All Saints, 1648. R2/60/2; W1/105/3
Richard, Lackford, 1588. A5/2/113a
Richard, yeo., Walsham le Willows, 1662. R2/62/337; W1/114/47
Richard, labourer, Wood Ditton, 1619, (N). W1/111/64
Robert, Bury St. Edmunds, 1675. In. 3/16/193; A5/5/157, A4/12/49
Robert, husb., Fordham, 1625. R2/53/683; W1/81/187
Robert, Fordham, 1691. A5/6/140, A4/33/18
Robert, Kedington, 1639. A5/4/69
Robert, yeo., Lidgate, 1663. R2/63/24; W1/115/39; In. 3/8/47
Robert, yeo., Newmarket, 1662. R2/62/375; W1/114/110; In. 3/7/145
Robert, Soham, 1592, (N). R2/42/309; W1/49/131
Robert, Stoke Ash, 1661, (N). R2/62/174; W1/113/28; In. 3/6/39; A5/5/12, A4/1/133
Robert, yeo., Stoke by Nayland, 1571. R2/35/283; W1/36/114
Robert, Stowmarket, 1586. A5/2/81
Robert, yeo., Wickhambrook, 1613. R2/48/251a; W1/70/24
Robert, the elder, yeo., Wickhambrook, 1690. R2/71/360; W1/144/65
Robert, Worlington, 1691. R2/71/482; W1/145/38
Roger, Brent Eleigh, 1653. W1/110/40
Roger, husb., Clare, 1675. R2/66/204; W1/127/80; In. 3/16/91
Sarah, spinster, Bury St. Edmunds, 1679. R2/67/437; W1/133/167
Thomas, Barrow, 1609. A5/3/69
Thomas, Great Saxham, 1642. A5/4/97
Thomas, yeo., Horningsheath, 1672. R2/65/311; W1/124/35
Thomas, husb., Mildenhall, 1602. R2/45/217; W1/61/4
Thomas, husb., Mildenhall, 1625, (N). R2/53/369; W1/81/147
Thomas, Newmarket, 1563. R2/32/25; W1/26/86
Thomas, Redgrave, 1600. R2/45/13; W1/58/20

TURNER continued
Thomas, wheelwright, Stowlangtoft, 1679. R2/67/236; W1/133/5
Thomas, yeo., Stowupland, 1680. R2/67/686; W1/134/142; In. 3/20/162
Thomas, turner, Wickhambrook, 1610. R2/47/299; W1/67/190
Thomas, Wickhambrook, 1673. A5/5/137, A4/10/32
Valentine, tanner, Woolpit, 1576. In. 3/1/2
William, the elder, Bures, 1533. R2/19/148; W1/2/73
William, sen., clothier, Bures, 1608. R2/46/182; W1/65/48
William, yeo., Bures, 1665. R2/63/341; W1/117/90; In. 3/10/104
William, singleman, Bury St. Edmunds, 1637. A5/4/52
William, gent., Bury St. Edmunds, 1678. R2/67/197; W1/130/169b
William, miller, Freckenham, 1675. W8/26; In. 10/18
William, Glemsford, 1630. A5/4/5
William, haberdasher, Lindsey, 1586. R2/40/15; W1/43/12
William, Long Melford, 1691. A5/6/145, A4/33/72
William, yeo., Wetherden, 1670. R2/65/50; W1/122/60; In. 3/15/79
William, Wickhambrook, 1587. A5/2/92
---, wid., Long Melford, 1588. A5/2/112

TURNOR, Agnes, Kedington, 1560. A5/1/102
Anne, wid., Little Wratting, 1586. R2/40/107; W1/43/83
Charles, gent., Norton, 1692. R2/71/4; W1/146/5
Elizabeth, Burwell, 1636, (N). R2/57/7; W1/92/8
Helen, Chevington, 1558. R2/27/318
Henry, als. Dyer, Long Melford, 1461. R2/9/279
James, Woolpit, 1528. R2/15/206
Joanna, wid., Bury St. Edmunds, 1681. R2/68/245; W1/135/186
John, clothier, Bures, 1580. R2/38/206; W1/39/103
John, Chedburgh, 1631. A5/4/11
John, Depden, 1476. W1/24/109
John, sen., Kirtling, 1465. R2/10/395
John, smith, Lavenham, 1476. R2/11/99
John, Norton, 1460. R2/9/281
John, Woolpit, 1540. R2/19/284; W1/36/38
Mary, wid., Haverhill, 1630. R2/55/91; W1/86/100
Matthew, Stuston, 1562. A5/1/121
Richard, Kedington, 1558. R2/27/310
Richard, gent., Pakenham, 1587. R2/40/126; W1/44/9; A5/2/96
Robert, Kirtling, 1557. R2/26/5; W1/20/5
Robert, Kirtling, 1578. R2/37/403; W1/36/170
Robert, Stuston, 1559. R2/28/284; W1/22/259
Susan, wid., Lindsey, 1597. R2/43/350; W1/55/114
Thomas, Hopton, 1564. A5/1/156
Thomas, Horringer, 1563. A5/1/149
Thomas, Kirtling, 1506. W1/36/7
Thomas, Lindsey, 1540. R2/21/381; W1/38/59
Thomas, Newmarket, (1547). R2/21/488
Thomas, husb., Polstead, 1580. R2/38/101; W1/39/177
Thomas, yeo., Stanton, 1592. R2/42/201; W1/49/26
Thomas, Wickhambrook, 1571. A5/1/234
Thomas, husb., Wiston, 1585. R2/39/258; W1/42/316
William, Westhorpe, 1624. R2/53/206; W1/81/10

TURNOUR, Alice, wid., Sudbury, (1456). R2/10/544
Beatrix, Woolpit, 1454. R2/9/167
Isabel, wife of Simon, Bury St. Edmunds, 1412. R2/1/126
James, Drinkstone, 1448. R2/9/97
John, fishmonger, Bury St. Edmunds, 1480. R2/2/293
John, Chippenham, 1472. R2/10/566
John, the elder, Depden, 1496. R2/13/37
John, Drinkstone, 1497. R2/13/59
John, gent., Great Thurlow, 1471. R2/10/506
John, Kirtling, 1480. R2/11/202
John, Whepstead, 1457. R2/9/183
John, Woolpit, 1439. R2/9/10
John, 1445. R2/9/67 (probate only)
Robert, Eye, 1470. R2/10/436
Simon, Combs, 1472. R2/10/502
Thomas, Sudbury, 1447. R2/9/80
Walter, fuller, Bury St. Edmunds, 1468. R2/2/117

TURNOUR continued
William, Bury St. Edmunds, 1469. R2/2/126
William, Bury St. Edmunds, 1474. R2/2/195
William, Depden, 1500. R2/13/113
William, Walsham le Willows, 1471. R2/10/470
see also Torner, Church als. Turner, Cossett als. Turnor, Cossett als. Turnour, Cossit als. Turnur, Cossey als. Turner, Newman als. Turner, Nowce als. Tourner
TURPEN, Elisabeth, wid., Wickham Skeith, 1540. W1/4/169
TURPIN, John, baker, Clare, 1688. R2/71/45; W1/142/43; In. 3/23/72
John, bach., Hundon, 1694. A5/6/173, A4/37/82
Mary, Wickham Skeith, 1697. R2/73/186; W1/151/70
Richard, Fornham, 1641. A5/4/90
TURPYN, Edward, Wickham Skeith, 1626. R2/53/498; W1/82/40
John, Bury St. Edmunds, 1521. R2/6/85 (admon. only)
Thomas, yeo., Bardwell, 1664. R2/63/156; W1/116/50; In. 3/9/59
Thomas, Mendlesham, 1586. R2/40/73; W1/43/58
see also Tyrpen
TURRELL, Nicholas, Stoke by Nayland, 1663. In. 3/8/39
TURRINGTON, John, husb., Lakenheath, 1682. R2/68/494; W1/136/164; In. 3/21/26
see also Torington
TURROLD, Edward, yeo., Eye, 1563. R2/32/46; W1/26/104
Katherine, wid., Great Thornham, 1565. R2/32/247
Margaret, wid., Palgrave, 1571. R2/35/101 & 383; W1/36/97
William, Rishangles, 1635. A5/4/38
TURROWLD, William, yeo., Thrandeston, 1618. R2/51/62; W1/75/37
see also Terold, Thorrold, Torald, Torold, Turrell
TURTELL, William, joiner, Stradishall, 1567. R2/32/415; W1/3/178
TURTLE, Elisabeth, wid., Bury St. Edmunds, 1681. R2/68/1; W1/135/1; A4/19/59
Henry, butcher, Bury St. Edmunds, 1684. R2/69/247; W1/138/52
Mary, wid., Bury St. Edmunds, 1698. R2/73/294; W1/152/65
Thomas, labourer, Bury St. Edmunds, 1633, (N). R2/56/242; W1/90/2
Thomas, cordwainer, Bury St. Edmunds, 1669. R2/64/482; W1/121/74; In. 3/15/175
William, husb., Bury St. Edmunds, 1676. R2/66/319; W1/128/24; In. 3/17/21
William, parson, Little Wratting, 1567. R2/32/418; W1/19/86; A5/1/189
William, Naughton, 1609. A5/3/74
TURTYLL, John, bach., Chippenham, 1563. R2/31/155; W1/26/35
TUTHILL, Edward, Tuddenham, 1664. In. 3/9/43; A5/5/57, A4/2/35
TUTTYS, Thomas, Bury St. Edmunds, 1506. R2/4/183 (admon. only)
TWAITS, William, oatmeal maker, Eye, 1650. R2/61/329; W1/107/26; In. 3/3/26
TWEED, Robert, yeo., Stanstead, 1685. R2/70/88; W1/139/79
Thomas, yeo., Cockfield, 1696. R2/73/30; W1/150/64
TWELLS, Godfrey, the elder, gent., Haverhill, 1650. R2/61/409 & 411; W1/107/117; In. 3/3/133
Godfrey, Haverhill, 1695. A5/6/177, A4/38/18
TWID(E), John, Stoke by Clare, 1590. A5/2/142
Ralph, yeo., Hartest, 1637. R2/57/219; W1/92/263
Robert, yeo., Stanstead, 1619. R2/51/361; W1/132/62
TWINN, Joan, wid., Glemsford, 1627. R2/54/48; W1/83/53
Margaret, wid., Glemsford, 1684. R2/69/201; W1/138/12
Thomas, clothier, Glemsford, 1616. R2/50/168; W1/73/162
see also Twyne
TWISSE, Samuel, glover, Wetheringsett, 1674. R2/66/98; W1/126/20
TWITCHETT, John, Whepstead, 1670. In. 3/15/5; A5/5/111
TWYBLE, John, als. Jarvyn, Brettenham, 1555, (N). R2/24/182
TWYD, William, husb., Glemsford, 1571. R2/35/103; W1/36/96
TWYNE, Jeremy, clothier, Haughley, 1618. R2/51/106; W1/75/66
Robert, clothier, Glemsford, 1631. R2/56/41; W1/87/59
Thomas, Glemsford, 1661. In. 3/6/150; A5/5/17, A4/1/90
TWYSE, Francis, husb., Lakenheath, 1626. R2/53/629; W1/82/153
Robert, Lakenheath, 1569. A5/1/214

TYBBIE, see Hubberd als. Tybbie
TYDDE, Henry, Mildenhall, 1473. R2/11/32
Martha, wid., Bury St. Edmunds, 1509. R2/4/202
Matilda, Bury St. Edmunds, 1509. R2/2/339
Richard, Mildenhall, 1488. W1/24/157
Thomas, Mildenhall, 1463. R2/12/12
TYDEMAN, Ann, wife of Nathaniel, Cotton, 1676. In. 3/17/71; A5/5/162, A4/13/50 & 51
TYDY, Richard, Bury St. Edmunds, 1444. R2/2/13
TYE, Andrew, smith, Bury St. Edmunds, 1538. R2/7/52
George, Stanton, 1614. R2/49/110; W1/71/81
John, Bury St. Edmunds, 1458. R2/2/60
John, Haverhill, 1525. R2/17/95
John, Mildenhall, 1454. R2/9/152
John, Poslingford, 1454. R2/9/200
John, singleman, Stanton, 1662. R2/62/329; W1/114/37; In. 3/7/41
Margaret, Sudbury, 1464. R2/10/359
Robert, Lavenham, 1459. R2/9/248
Robert, Mildenhall, 1452. R2/9/128
Robert, yeo., Stanton, 1672. R2/65/376; W1/124/119
Thomas, labourer, Barnham, 1609. R2/47/63; W1/66/71; A5/3/69
Thomas, Bury St. Edmunds, 1508. R2/4/200
TYELL, William, Stoke by Clare, 1450. R2/9/112
TYFFEN, Robert, Hundon, 1674. A5/5/149, A4/11/61
TYFFYN, Peter, yeo., Hundon, 1609. R2/47/29; W1/66/33
TYLAR, Ambrose, yeo., Stowupland, 1626. R2/53/485; W1/82/30
TYLBROKE, Edward, Kirtling, 1579. W1/38/122; A5/2/16
Joan, Cowlinge, 1567. A5/1/181
John, Kirtling, 1471. R2/10/472
Thomas, Cowlinge, 1566. R2/32/291; W1/28/104
TYLBROOK(E), John, thatcher, Snailwell, 1623. R2/52/568; W1/79/26
Thomas, Kirtling, 1472. R2/10/507
TYLER, Adam, Drinkstone, 1587. A5/2/88
Agnes, wid., Sudbury, 1576. R2/37/195; W1/37/61
Alice, Wetheringsett, 1457. R2/9/187
Anthony, Denham, 1669. A5/5/106, A4/7/47
Edward, Depden, 1586. A5/2/83
Elisabeth, Depden, 1588. A5/2/112
Elisabeth, wid., Isleham, 1649. W7/48
Francis, gent., Chippenham, 1651. R2/61/476; W1/108/67
Grace, wid., Isleham, 1626. R6/46
Joan, wid., Bury St. Edmunds, 1503. R2/4/153
John, Bildeston, 1612. A5/3/116
John, Burwell, 1556. R2/25/66; W1/16/90
John, sen., cordwainer, Burwell, 1694. R2/72/310; W1/148/38
John, yeo., Bury St. Edmunds, 1501. R2/4/113
John, Cavendish, 1503. R2/13/148
John, Hitcham, 1592. A5/2/178
John, Soham, 1683. A5/6/70; A4/20/59
John, Stowlangtoft, 1530. R2/19/10
John, the elder, weaver, Sudbury, 1683. R2/69/166; W1/137/132
John, tailor, Thorndon, 1683. R2/69/117; W1/137/93
John, Westley, 1462. R2/10/348
Margaret, wid., Stowupland, 1629. R2/54/420; W1/85/106
Richard, als. Alefownder, husb., Sudbury, 1587. R2/40/254; W1/44/95
Robert, Isleham, 1662. In. 9/3
Robert, the elder, husb., Isleham, 1662. W7/62
Robert, als. Alffunder, Long Melford, 1574. R2/37/41; W1/33/38
Robert, husb., Long Melford, 1635. R2/56/439; W1/91/3
Robert, husb., Woolpit, 1542. R2/22/64; W1/6/16
Roger, gent., Soham, 1635. R2/56/528; W1/91/111
Simon, Bury St. Edmunds, 1428. R2/1/184
Simon, Bury St. Edmunds, 1432. R2/1/201
Steven, yeo., Bacton, 1626. R2/53/479; W1/82/23
Thomas, yeo., Ixworth, 1681. R2/68/127; W1/135/97
Thomas, Rickinghall Superior, 1671. A5/5/125, A4/8/50
Thomas, yeo., Walsham le Willows, 1637. R2/57/233; W1/92/285
Thomas, Westley, 1461. R2/9/283

TYLER continued
Thomasine, wid., Bury St. Edmunds, 1641. R2/58/254; W1/98/25
Valentine, Sudbury, 1580. A5/2/27
Walter, rector, Bradfield St. George, 1469. R2/2/126
William, Creeting St. Peter, 1442. R2/9/38
see also Tiler, Tylar, Tyller, Tylor, Alefounder als. Tyler, Freman als. Tyler, Smyth als. Tyler
TYLKYS, John, Glemsford, 1462. R2/10/312
TYLL(E), Agnes, Preston, 1464. R2/10/353
Emily, wid. of Richard, Little Cornard, 1538. R2/4/133
Helen, wid., Little Cornard, 1605. R2/45/383; W1/63/10
Henry, Bures, 1561. A5/1/106
John, Boxford, 1442. R2/9/39
John, sen., Boxford, 1475. R2/11/119
John, dyer, Boxford, 1477. R2/11/124
John, husb., Little Cornard, 1554. R2/24/52; W1/14/40
John, Rattlesden, 1453. R2/9/159
John, Sudbury, 1472. R2/10/532
Margaret, wid., Buxhall, 1553. R2/37/156; W1/13/103
Peter, husb., Bures, 1556. R2/25/29; W1/16/29
Richard, husb., Hartest, 1598, (N). R2/44/142; W1/56/96
Richard, Little Cornard, 1538. R2/20/121; W1/4/100
Robert, Cornard, 1593. A5/2/181
Robert, yeo., Little Cornard, 1563. R2/32/31; W1/26/91
William, Brettenham, 1444. W1/24/160
William, singleman, Bures, (1556). R2/25/29; W1/16/31
TYLLER, William, Drinkstone, 1521. R2/15/122
TYLLETT, Augustus, Bury St. Edmunds, 1584. A5/2/56
Thomas, Bradfield St. Clare, 1591. A5/2/148
TYLLOT(T), Agnes, wid., Rougham, 1559. R2/28/309; W1/22/280
Ann, spinster, Rougham, 1679, (N). R2/67/307; W1/133/89; A5/6/21, A4/16/68
Audrey, wid., Beyton, 1628. R2/54/131; W1/84/2
Edmund, Wetherden, 1685. A5/6/96, A4/24/126
Elisabeth, Bury St. Edmunds, 1494. R2/4/29
Harry, the elder, yeo., Rougham, 1557. R2/26/226; W1/20/114
Henry, the younger, husb., Rougham, 1609. R2/47/69; W1/66/80
John, husb., Beyton, 1619. R2/51/401; W1/132/86
John, Bury St. Edmunds, 1448. R2/2/24
John, Great Barton, 1472. R2/11/146
John, jun., Great Barton, 1532. R2/19/103; W1/3/125 & 157
John, Rickinghall Inferior, 1564. R2/32/77; W1/27/30
John, Pakenham, 1687. A5/6/109, A4/27/19
John, Rougham, 1538. R2/20/117; W1/4/97
John, maltster, Rougham, 1556. R2/25/113; W1/16/134
John, yeo., Rougham, 1574. R2/37/27; W1/33/63
John, the elder, Rougham, 1578. R2/37/387; W1/36/186
John, the elder, yeo., Rougham, (1609). W1/95/133
John, Rushbrook, 1596. A5/2/219
Margaret, wid., Finningham, 1589. R2/41/147; W1/46/133
Margery, Great Barton, 1442. R2/9/58
Margery, wid., Rougham, (1513). R2/13/197 & 216; W1/9/46
Robert, mason, Bury St. Edmunds, 1452. R2/2/38
Robert, mercer, Rattlesden, 1609. R2/47/37; W1/66/44
Roger, Rougham, 1459. R2/9/247
Samuel, yeo., Rattlesden, 1618. R2/51/140; W1/75/87
Samuel, Rattlesden, 1631. A5/4/12
Thomas, shearman, Bury St. Edmunds, 1573. R2/36/196; W1/32/126; A5/1/267
Thomas, the elder, gent., Bury St. Edmunds, 1643. R2/59/9; W1/100/12
Thomas, Bury St. Edmunds, 1672. A5/5/132, A4/9/55
William, the elder, yeo., Barton, 1626. R2/53/630; W1/82/154
William, wheelwright, Beyton, 1651. R2/61/465
TYLLY, John, Tostock, 1487. R2/11/425
TYLMAN, John, Great Thurlow, 1563, (N). R2/32/77; In. 3/1/78; A5/1/152
TYLNEY, Cicely, wid., Bury St. Edmunds, 1553. R2/8/84; W1/21/213
John, scrivener, Bury St. Edmunds, 1553. R2/8/50; W1/21/190
Nicholas, Bury St. Edmunds, 1491. R2/4/2

TYLOR, Agnes, wid., Pakenham, 1574, (N). R2/37/39; W1/33/46
Richard, yeo., Preston, 1602. R2/45/170; W1/60/92
Robert, butcher, Isleham, 1692. W7/120 & 121; In. 9/83
Thomas, husb., Drinkstone, 1559. R2/28/367; W1/3/1
TYLSON, William, Mildenhall, 1595. A5/2/215
TYM(E), Henry, yeo., Bardwell, 1621. R2/52/247; W1/77/33
Richard, maltster, Burwell, 1592. R2/42/220; W1/49/39
TYMBYRMAN, John, sen., Mildenhall, 1472. R2/10/531
John, Mildenhall, 1481. R2/11/214
TYMBEWELL, William, Stowmarket, 1462. R2/9/290
TYMINGE, William, shearman, Hopton, 1618. R2/51/230; W1/75/146
TYMTON, John, Great Finborough, 1461. R2/9/273
TYMWORETH, Roger, husb., Icklingham, 1565. R2/32/222
TYMWORTH, John, husb., Icklingham, 1594. R2/42/560; W1/52/34; A5/2/200
John, Timworth, 1451. R2/9/104
William, husb., Icklingham, 1570. R2/34/21; W1/30/19
TYNDALL, John, Long Melford, 1669. In. 3/14/192; A5/5/102, A4/7/12
William, priest, Elveden, (1548). R2/21/451; W1/38/36
William, Long Melford, 1585. A5/2/73
see also Tendall
TYNNE, Richard, Burwell, 1568. R2/33/16; W1/29/25
TYNTON, Agnes, wid., Rougham, (1486). R2/11/444
John, Finborough, 1476. R2/11/46
John, the elder, Rickinghall Inferior, 1563. R2/32/18; W1/26/78
Robert, Rickinghall Inferior, 1525. R2/17/92; W1/21/88
TYNWYNTER, Nicholas, als. Clarke, carver, Finningham, 1566, (N). R2/32/276; W1/28/116
Robert, Buxhall, 1539. R2/19/315
see also Tenwynter
TYPPYNG, John, chaplain, Bury St. Edmunds, 1492. R2/4/11 & 12
TYPSHETH, Robert, Redgrave, 1552. R2/23/207; W1/12/34
William, Bardwell, 1592. R2/42/311; W1/49/135
TYPTODE, John, Rickinghall Superior, 1610. R2/47/227; W1/67/107
TYPTOT(T), Alice, singlewoman, Bury St. Edmunds, 1597, (N). R2/43/224; W1/55/8
Edmund, yeo., Rickinghall Superior, 1601. R2/44/396; W1/59/55
Elisabeth, Rickinghall Superior, 1628. R2/54/257; W1/84/114
John, yeo., Botesdale, 1574. R2/37/52; W1/33/28
John, tailor, Bury St. Edmunds, 1530. R2/6/162
John, the elder, yeo., Rickinghall Superior, 1573. R2/36/166; W1/32/71
John, the younger, yeo., Rickinghall Superior, 1579. R2/38/35; W1/39/34
John, the elder, yeo., Rickinghall Superior, 1608. R2/46/178; W1/65/39
John, yeo., Rickinghall Superior, 1633. R2/56/287; W1/90/52
TYRELL, Charles, gent., Gipping, 1608. R2/46/171; W1/65/29
Edmund, esq., Gipping, 1689. R2/71/201; W1/143/52
Francis, gent., Gipping, 1669. R2/64/512; W1/121/104; In. 3/14/203
Philip, gent., Old Newton, 1614. R2/49/11; W1/71/7
Robert, collar maker, Bury St. Edmunds, (1625). W1/111/69
see also Terrell, Tirell, Tyrrell, Smyth als. Tyrle
TYRER, John, Little Thurlow, 1660. In. 3/5/193; A5/5/10
TYRPEN, Edward, Mendlesham, 1604. R2/45/357
TYRRELL, Katherine, wid., Mildenhall, 1558. R2/27/165; W1/7/134
Mary, wid. of Thomas, esq., Gipping, 1621. R2/52/287; W1/77/72
TYRRILL, James, husb., Soham, 1635. R2/56/495; W1/91/71
TYRTON, Thomas, Haughley, 1533. R2/19/145; W1/2/43
TYRWITE, Agnes, Stowmarket, 1559. R2/28/386; W1/3/82
see also Terwike
TYRYNGTON, John, butcher, Bury St. Edmunds, 1450. R2/2/34
TYSO, John, Drinkstone, 1464. R2/10/370
Margery, Drinkstone, 1458. R2/9/188
Thomas, Drinkstone, 1458. R2/9/212
TYTTER, Robert, Langham, 1592. A5/2/177

U

UDALL, Thomas, als. Godsoule, Great Fakenham, 1560. R2/29/99; W1/25/69
UFFORD, Robert, Hundon, 1457. R2/9/218
ULFE, Edmund, Yaxley, 1582. R2/38/377; W1/41/62
Thomas, Bury St. Edmunds, 1525. R2/6/121
ULLET(T), Ann, Bury St. Edmunds, 1641. A5/4/91
John, Bury St. Edmunds, 1681. A5/6/49, A4/18/68
Thomas, Bury St. Edmunds, 1651. A5/4/139
William, the elder, Bury St. Edmunds, 1591. W1/95/62
William, yeo., Bury St. Edmunds, 1633, (N). W1/95/161
ULLIT, George, Walsham le Willows, 1690. R2/71/348; W1/144/52; A5/6/133, A4/32/26
ULLYT, Robert, victualler, Ixworth, 1616. R2/50/139; W1/73/143
ULSSEBY, William, 1406. R2/1/113
ULSTOFFE, John, yeo., Gipping, 1645. R2/59/194; W1/102/23
UMFERY, Agnes, wid., Stowlangtoft, 1563. R2/32/33; W1/26/69
UMFREY, David, miller, Bury St. Edmunds, 1499. R2/4/80
George, husb., Hitcham, 1548. R2/21/413; W1/8/29
Isabel, Sapiston, 1460. R2/9/248; W1/24/40
John, Little Saxham, 1477. R2/11/437
John, Stowmarket, (1508). R2/13/200
Stephen, Drinkstone, 1474. R2/11/29
William, Stowmarket, 1531. R2/18/126
UMFRY, John, husb., Risby, 1573. R2/36/138; W1/32/38
UMPHREY, John, yeo., Haughley, 1580. R2/38/202
Thomas, Glemsford, 1648. A5/4/125
UNDERLEY, Thomas, draper, Bury St. Edmunds, 1559. R2/8/348; W1/17/60
Thomas, Bury St. Edmunds, 1587. A5/2/90
UNDERWODE, Thomas, yeo., Bures, 1625. R2/53/413; W1/81/195
UNDERWOOD, Abraham, rector, Chevington, 1692. R2/72/7; W1/146/7
Agnes, wid., Cornard, 1533. R2/19/136; W1/2/98
Alice, wid., Lawshall, 1592. R2/42/225; W1/49/44
Augustine, clerk, Chevington, 1630. R2/55/112; W1/86/126
Elisabeth, wid., Chevington, 1694. R2/72/381; W1/148/110
Francis, tailor, Barningham, 1660. R2/62/90; W1/112/118; In. 3/5/139
Joan, Little Cornard, 1566. A5/1/176
John, yeo., Brettenham, 1633. R2/56/283; W1/90/47
John, yeo., Brettenham, 1683. R2/69/101; W1/137/77
John, joiner, Bures, 1614. W1/111/62
John, baker, Bury St. Edmunds, 1675. R2/66/223; W1/127/94; In. 3/16/120
John, gent., Bury St. Edmunds, 1692. R2/72/46; W1/146/42; In. 3/24/75
John, the elder, yeo., Hartest, 1669. R2/64/501; W1/121/95; In. 3/14/70
John, husb., Little Cornard, 1542. R2/56/19; W1/6/77
John, Little Cornard, 1566. A5/1/175
Katherine, wid., Chevington, 1648. R2/60/124; W1/105/147
Luke, husb., Whepstead, 1649, (N). R2/60/266; W1/106/133
Mary, wid., Chevington, 1693. R2/72/115
Mary, singlewoman, Gislingham, (1613). W1/111/41
Mary, wid., Sudbury, 1692. R2/72/28; W1/146/26
Richard, yeo., Little Cornard, 1625. R2/53/367; W1/81/145
Richard, say maker, Sudbury, 1639. R2/58/116; W1/94/195
Richard, husb., Thorpe Morieux, 1593. R2/42/342; W1/50/6
Robert, Burgate, 1561. A5/1/122
Robert, yeo., Great Waldingfield, 1615. R2/49/351; W1/72/123
Thomas, Bures, 1531. R2/19/86
Thomas, gent., Chevington, 1666. R2/64/30; W1/118/28; In. 3/3/22
Thomas, husb., Great Cornard, 1625. R2/53/395; W1/81/175
Thomas, the elder, yeo., Hartest, 1631. R2/56/92; W1/87/140
Thomas, the elder, yeo., Hartest, 1651. R2/61/495; W1/108/85
Thomas, the younger, singleman, Hartest, 1660. In. 3/5/189; A5/5/9, A4/1/162
Thomas, Little Cornard, 1571. A5/1/234

UNDERWOOD continued
William, the elder, Brockley, 1582. R2/38/416; W1/41/17 & 18
William, Burgate, 1474. R2/10/552
William, Kirtling, 1551. R2/23/19; W1/11/76
William, Somerton, 1551. R2/23/13; W1/11/75
UNDICK, William, Mildenhall, 1617. W1/74/20
UNDYRWOD, John, the younger, husb., Burgate, (1521). R2/14/19
UNDYRWOODE, Edmund, Assington, 1482. R2/11/265
UNGELLS, Nicholas, yeo., Barrow, 1624. R2/53/166; W1/80/146
UNGER, Joan, wid., Woolpit, 1624. R2/53/43; W1/80/62
John, clothworker, Woolpit, 1610. R2/47/228; W1/67/108
John, yeo., Woolpit, 1637. R2/57/206; W1/92/246
Thomas, yeo., Woolpit, 1558. R2/27/77; W1/36/58
UNGLES, William, Barrow, 1646. A5/4/112
UNWIN, Ann, wid., Lidgate, 1688. In. 3/23/13
Frances, wid., Glemsford, 1700. R2/74/25; W1/154/23; In. 3/27/19
UPCHER, John, wid., Lavenham, 1681. A5/6/56, A4/18/122 & 150
UPSHER, Mary, wid., Nayland, 1639. R2/58/54; W1/94/100
UPSON, James, Little Cornard, 1640. A5/4/86
Stephen, husb., Haughley, 1640. R2/58/146; W1/96/50
UPTON, Robert, parson, Eriswell, 1564. R2/32/118; W1/27/70
USHER, John, clothier, Bury St. Edmunds, 1688. R2/71/61; W1/142/54; In. 3/23/29
John, Wattisham, 1603. R2/45/243; W1/61/41
Thomas, minister, Hargrave, 1672. R2/65/358; W1/124/94
William, yeo., Edwardstone, 1678. R2/67/119; W1/130/102; In. 3/19/137
USHERWOOD, Alice, wid., Acton, 1609. R2/47/116; W1/67/1
George, Acton, 1599. R2/44/184; W1/57/14
UTTRIDGE, William, Timworth, 1663, (N). R2/63/28; W1/115/45; In. 3/8/46; A5/5/45

V

VAISEY, Edmund, Exning, 1663. In. 3/8/237; A5/5/54
see also Vasey, Vazey, Vesey
VALE, Alice, wid., Bury St. Edmunds, 1494. R2/4/29
Alice, singlewoman, Ousden, 1627, (N). R2/54/101; W1/83/101
Anne, wid., Groton, 1626. R2/53/537; W1/82/66
Edward, als. Hobys, smith, Bury St. Edmunds, 1476. R2/2/229
Henry, husb., Great Bradley, 1678. R2/67/63; W1/130/49
John, Lavenham, 1565. A5/1/164
John, Long Melford, 1441. R2/9/13
Margaret, wid., Groton, 1698. R2/73/234; W1/152/15
Rose, wid., Boxford, 1663. R2/63/23; In. 3/8/26
Samuel, servant, Elmswell, 1649. R2/60/180; W1/106/25
Sebastian, Little Livermere, 1634. A5/4/29
William, the elder, cooper, Groton, 1631. R2/56/4; W1/87/6
William, Kentford, 1610. R2/47/214; W1/67/92
VALEAUNT, Simon, Rickinghall Superior, 1529. R2/18/44
VALL, Anne, singlewoman, Norton, 1618. R2/51/201
Edward, baker, Groton, 1690. R2/71/397; W1/144/100
VALLIANT, Thomas, husb., Stanton, 1687. R2/70/387; W1/141/111
see also Valeaunt, Waleant
VANCY, William, Wood Ditton, 1550. R2/21/156; W1/9/133
VANSEY, William, yeo., Wood Ditton, 1616. R2/50/42; W1/73/45
VARBY, Nicholas, Hawstead, 1589. A5/2/114a
Robert, Bury St. Edmunds, 1666. A5/5/77, A4/2/103, A4/4/58
Robert, husb., Thurston, 1581. R2/38/335; W1/40/75
Thomas, yeo., Thurston, 1644. R2/59/162; W1/101/90
William, Thurston, 1558. R2/27/20
VARVY, John, Hessett, 1663. A5/5/50
Thomas, Bury St. Edmunds, 1664. In. 3/10/164; A5/5/63
VASEY, Margaret, Landwade, 1683. A5/6/69, A4/20/50
Thomas, Landwade, 1683. A5/6/66, A4/20/7
VASSE, Thomas, yeo., Benhall, 1536. R2/19/250
VAUNCY, John, Wood Ditton, 1490. R2/11/377
see also Vancy
VAZEY, Thomas, Landwade, 1693. R2/72/262; W1/147/149a
VEALE, Edward, Wickhambrook, 1619. R2/51/279; W1/132/15
Hester, als. Archer, wid., Bury St. Edmunds, 1680.

VEALE continued
In. 3/20/118; A5/6/36, A4/17/61
John, Bury St. Edmunds, 1676. In. 3/17/144; A5/5/166, A4/13/90
Robert, bach., Dalham, 1679. A5/6/26, A4/16/120
Thomas, Haverhill, 1663. In. 3/8/238; A5/5/51, A4/2/17
VEER, Margaret, wid., Eye, 1540. R2/20/276; W1/4/208
Roger, Eye, (1539). R2/20/204; W1/4/160
VELERS, John, the elder, Bury St. Edmunds, 1522. R2/6/98
VENALL, Thomas, Mildenhall, 1555. R2/24/144; W1/15/97
VENOLDE, Margaret, wid., Mildenhall, 1555. R2/24/241; W1/15/71
VENOR, George, Cornard, 1458. R2/9/207
John, husb., Little Cornard, 1546. R2/21/212; W1/10/67
VENOUR, John, Bures, 1487. R2/13/2
VERDON, John, clothmaker, Lavenham, 1554. R2/24/75; W1/14/56
Thomas, gent., Eye, 1679. A5/6/23, A4/16/87
VERE, William, Bury St. Edmunds, 1361. R2/1/12
see also Veer
VERLEY, George, Acton, 1530. R2/19/41
VERNON, Elisabeth, wid., Fordham, 1625. R2/53/381; W1/81/157
VERTU, Robert, shepherd, Downham, 1569. R2/33/134; W1/28/204
VESEY, Alice, 1579. A5/2/20
Thomas, gent., Aldham, 1681. R2/68/103; W1/135/78
William, Wattisfield, 1662. A5/5/32
VESY, Thomas, gent., Burgh, 1616. R2/50/171; W1/73/164
VEYZZEY, William, Brent Eleigh, 1625. R2/53/288; W1/81/77
see also Vaisey
VIALL, Francis, potter, Woolpit, 1620. R2/52/65; W1/76/52
see also Vyall, Vyell
VICE, John, Exning, 1588. A5/2/107
Sarah, als. Brodishe, Eye, 1584. A5/2/59
see also Vise
VILETT, Adam, Botesdale, 1562. A5/1/128
see also Vylet, Vyolette
VINCE, Anthony, yeo., Kersey, 1641. R2/58/268; W1/98/46
Daniel, cordwainer, Kersey, 1697, (N). R2/73/145; W1/151/31; A5/6/190
Elisabeth, wid., Kersey, 1699. R2/73/468; W1/153/104; In. 3/26/14
VINCENT, Augustin, woollen weaver, Walsham le Willows, 1599. R2/44/172; W1/57/4
Austin, labourer, Walsham le Willows, 1619. R2/51/339; W1/132/49
Elisabeth, Stowmarket, 1697. A5/7/3, A4/40/71
James, Bury St. Edmunds, 1692. In. 3/24/65; A5/6/152, A4/34/45
John, tailor, Assington, 1694. R2/72/337; W1/148/72
John, sen., Ixworth, 1637. A5/4/55
John, singleman, Stanton, 1579. R2/38/37; W1/39/35
John, husb., Walsham le Willows, 1598. R2/44/12; W1/56/11
John, yeo., Walsham le Willows, 1599. R2/44/324; W1/57/123
John, yeo., Walsham le Willows, 1669. R2/64/544; W1/121/134; In. 3/14/113
John, yeo., West Stow, 1694. R2/72/307; W1/148/35
Julia, wid., Walsham le Willows, 1617. R2/50/324; W1/74/111
Margaret, wid., Stowmarket, 1634. R2/56/360; W1/90/133
Nicholas, Redgrave, 1651. A5/4/138
Robert, copper smith, Bury St. Edmunds, 1690. R2/71/341; W1/144/45
Stephen, Great Livermere, 1690. A5/6/131, A4/32/5
Stephen, Walsham le Willows, 1665. R2/63/333; W1/117/80; In. 3/10/114
Stephen, grocer, Walsham le Willows, 1672. R2/65/351; W1/124/85
Thomas, Mendlesham, 1692. R2/72/48; W1/146/43; In. 3/24/101
Thomas, yeo., Stowmarket, 1641. R2/58/246; W1/98/17
Thomas, Walsham le Willows, 1564. R2/32/51
Thomas, Walsham le Willows, 1631. A5/4/11
William, tanner, Botesdale, 1690. R2/71/402; W1/144/106
William, Little Fakenham, 1582. R2/38/357; W1/95/21
VINSENT, Elisabeth, wid., Hitcham, 1662. R2/62/411; W1/114/165
John, the elder, Walsham le Willows, 1574. R2/37/25; W1/33/66
Stephen, Walsham le Willows, 1593. R2/42/348; W1/50/16 & 17
William, shepherd, Tuddenham, 1617. R2/50/404; W1/74/190
see also Vyncent

VISE, Joan, Burwell, 1598. R2/44/98; W1/56/135
Thomas, the elder, yeo., Burwell, 1630. R2/55/18; W1/86/20
VIVIAN, John, the elder, Bury St. Edmunds, 1698. R2/73/265; W1/152/40
VOICE, Hannah, wid., Great Cornard, 1693. A5/6/160, A4/35/1
Richard, husb., Soham, 1585. R2/39/293; W1/42/284
Roger, Soham, 1649. R2/60/299; W1/106/176
VOYCE, Richard, Soham, 1535. R2/18/133
Roger, husb., Soham, 1647. R2/59/474; W1/104/107; In. 3/2/120
William, yeo., West Stow, 1636. R2/57/95; W1/92/111
VOYSE, Agnes, wid., Soham, 1546. R2/21/258
John, Soham, 1474. R2/11/2
John, Soham, 1582. A5/2/44
William, Soham, 1541. R2/20/233; W1/4/172
VYALL, Margaret, als. Walman, Fornham All Saints, 1572. A5/1/248
Roger, Fornham All Saints, 1572. A5/1/249
Roger, Fornham All Saints, 1589. A5/2/118
Thomas, yeo., Wickhambrook, 1581. R2/38/300; W1/40/42
VYCARY, John, husb., Soham, 1548. R2/21/484; W1/38/94
VYELL, Thomas, the elder, Ixworth, 1472. R2/10/555
Thomas, Ixworth, (1479). R2/10/587
VYLET, Adam, labourer, Redgrave, 1565. R2/32/249; W1/27/169
VYNCENT, Edward, Great Fakenham, 1595. A5/2/207
John, husb., Walsham le Willows, 1497. R2/13/69
Katherine, wid., Walsham le Willows, 1561. R2/30/105; W1/28/255
Nicholas, the elder, yeo., Bildeston, 1553. R2/31/169; W1/13/114
Stephen, yeo., Walsham le Willows, 1550. R2/21/32; W1/10/181
Thomas, Walsham le Willows, 1537. R2/18/159
Thomas, blacksmith, Bacton, 1631. R2/56/46; W1/87/63
Walter, Wangford, 1593. A5/2/189
William, smith, Bury St. Edmunds, 1402. R2/1/94
William, Coney Weston, 1565. R2/32/223; W1/27/157
William, the elder, Walsham le Willows, 1529. R2/18/20; W1/311/5
William, the elder, husb., Walsham le Willows, 1557. R2/26/259; W1/20/174
William, tailor, Walsham le Willows, 1570. R2/35/38; W1/38/140
VYNSENT, Andrew, yeo., Bildeston, 1581. R2/38/274; W1/40/23
VYNT, John, cordwainer, Bury St. Edmunds, 1434. R2/1/212
VYOLETTE, Anthony, yeo., Nettlestead, 1562. R2/31/48; W1/8/129
see also Vilett
VYPOUND, Stephen, Lidgate, 1464. R2/10/365

W

WABOW, Robert, cordwainer, Bury St. Edmunds, 1445. R2/2/15
WABY, William, shepherd, Barnham, 1680. R2/67/773; W1/134/204; In. 3/20/231
WACE, Charles, yeo., Thelnetham, 1648. R2/60/136; W1/105/163
James, yeo., Chevington, 1635. R2/56/546; W1/91/129
John, yeo., Occold, 1684. R2/69/263; W1/138/63
Leonard, yeo., Ixworth Thorpe, 1632. R2/56/125; W1/89/13
Martha, Thrandeston, 1637. A5/4/53
Richard, husb., Wortham, 1636. R2/57/44; W1/92/54
Robert, yeo., Shelland, 1680. R2/67/640; W1/134/105
Roger, Ixworth Thorpe, 1563. A5/1/146
Thomas, husb., Eye, 1640. R2/58/159; W1/96/65
Thomas, husb., Wortham, 1622. R2/52/491; W1/78/100
William, husb., Great Livermere, 1688. R2/71/40; W1/142/39
William, Wortham, 1559. R2/28/313; W1/22/286
see also Waese, Wase, Wasse
WACHE, Edmund, husb., Shelland, 1557. R2/26/215; W1/20/131
WACRING, Richard, Stoke by Clare, 1558. R2/27/213
WACY, John, Bury St. Edmunds, 1551. R2/8/228
Margaret, wid., Bury St. Edmunds, 1552. R2/8/75; W1/21/208
see also Wasye
WADDELOWE, Elisabeth, wid. of Richard, clerk, Wilby, 1681. R2/68/71; W1/135/56

WADDINGTON, Henry, gent., Long Melford, 1685. R2/70/108; W1/139/95
John, yeo., Long Melford, 1695. R2/72/528; W1/149/82
WADE, Agnes, wid., Bildeston, 1533. R2/19/104
Agnes, wid., Bury St. Edmunds, 1479. R2/2/279
Alice, Old Newton, 1650. W1/110/57
Alice, Woolpit, 1469. R2/10/425
Ann, singlewoman, Old Newton, 1666. In. 3/11/89; A5/5/74, A4/4/24
Ann, singlewoman, Redgrave, 1667. A5/5/85, A4/5/46
Ann, wid., Thrandeston, 1680. R2/67/649; W1/134/114; In. 3/20/130
Bartholomew, Badwell Ash, 1698. A5/7/7
Caleb, yeo., Buxhall, 1660. In. 3/5/153; A5/5/7, A4/1/184
Clement, Bury St. Edmunds, 1386. R2/1/48
Edward, yeo., Great Bradley, 1662. R2/62/433; W1/114/200; In. 3/7/252
Henry, yeo., Naughton, 1641. R2/58/245; W1/98/15
Henry, husb., Stoke by Clare, 1612. R2/48/190; W1/69/75
James, Woolpit, 1452. R2/9/121
Joan, Wiston, 1563. R2/31/132; W1/26/13
John, Bildeston, 1535. R2/19/587; W1/5/52
John, yeo., Brandon, 1664. R2/63/158; W1/116/53; In. 3/9/19; A5/5/56, A4/2/21
John, sen., Bury St. Edmunds, 1392. R2/1/61
John, tailor, Bury St. Edmunds, 1431. R2/1/197
John, Bury St. Edmunds, 1435. R2/1/217
John, spurrier, Bury St. Edmunds, 1455. R2/2/47
John, chaplain, Bury St. Edmunds, 1458. R2/2/59
John, Clare, 1660. A5/5/9, A4/1/161
John, Creeting, 1455. R2/9/177
John, husb., Great Ashfield, 1688. R2/71/83; W1/142/76; In. 3/23/82
John, Kersey, 1531. R2/32/445
John, yeo., Newton, 1652. R2/61/557; W1/109/35; In. 3/4/46
John, yeo., Old Newton, 1676. In. 3/17/124; A5/5/164, A4/13/71
John, yeo., Woolpit, 1558. R2/27/81
John, yeo., Woolpit, 1589. R2/41/150 & 174; W1/46/109 & 129
John, yeo., Woolpit, 1599. R2/44/263; W1/57/71
Margaret, Gislingham, 1633. A5/4/25
Mary, spinster, Great Bradley, 1666. R2/64/15; W1/118/16; In. 3/11/27
Mary, singlewoman, Redgrave, 1627. R2/54/80; W1/83/81
Michael, Wattisham, 1595. R2/43/87; W1/53/84
Richard, the elder, husb., Woolpit, 1595. R2/43/28; W1/53/25
Richard, inn holder, Woolpit, 1626. R2/53/585; W1/82/115
Robert, Bildeston, 1521. R2/14/32, R2/17/5; W1/21/82
Robert, Bildeston, 1563. W1/26/82
Robert, Bury St. Edmunds, 1455. R2/2/50
Robert, Rattlesden, 1642. A5/4/96
Robert, Wissington, 1561. A5/1/116
Robert, the elder, Woolpit, 1557. R2/26/296; W1/20/217
Robert, the elder, Woolpit, 1600. R2/45/13; W1/58/22
Sarah, Lindsey, 1666. R2/64/106; W1/118/77; In. 3/11/161
Simon, yeo., Old Newton, 1639. R2/58/49; W1/94/90
Simon, the elder, tanner, Sudbury, 1622. R2/52/406; W1/78/39
Thomas, Bildeston, 1570. R2/34/45; W1/30/41
Thomas, Hitcham, 1578. R2/37/363; W1/36/211
Thomas, husb., Kedington, 1649. R2/60/187; W1/106/30
Thomas, Naughton, 1606. A5/3/10
Thomas, yeo., Wixoe, 1660, (N). R2/62/149; W1/112/195; In. 3/5/201; A5/5/10, A4/1/158
William, linen weaver, Old Newton, 1626, (N). R2/53/664; W1/82/189
William, husb., Stansfield, 1699. R2/73/464; W1/153/101; In. 3/26/9
WADSELL, John, Stradishall, 1464. R2/10/368
WADYLOVE, Margaret, wid., Wetheringsett, 1597. R2/43/273; W1/55/49
WAESE, John, shepherd, Ixworth, 1616. R2/50/191; W1/73/180

WAFORD, Robert, Flempton, 1591. R2/42/66; W1/48/55
Thomas, blacksmith, Long Melford, 1626. R2/53/598; W1/82/126 a & b
WAGE, Ann, wid., Stowmarket, 1629. R2/54/424; W1/85/107
Edmund, Haughley, 1477. R2/11/43
John, yeo., Stowmarket, 1561. R2/30/13; W1/26/209
John, inn holder, Stowmarket, 1624. R2/53/11; W1/80/17
John, Wetherden, 1487. R2/11/415
Prudence, singlewoman, Great Finborough, 1583, (N). R2/39/7; W1/42/89; A5/2/45
Thomas, Haughley, 1562. R2/31/22; W1/8/183
William, Stowmarket, 1671. A5/5/121, A4/8/12
see also Wayge
WAGGARD, Davy, Sapiston, 1457. R2/9/213
John, Great Fakenham, 1458. R2/11/182
WAGGE, John, Haverhill, 1457. R2/9/220
WAGON, John, Timworth, 1458. R2/9/216
WAINFLETT, John, Groton, 1586. A5/2/77
see also Waneflet, Waynfleet, Piper als. Wainflett, Pyper als. Wayneflet
WAINFORD, Bridget, Fornham St. Martin, 1666. A4/4/41
John, husb., Soham, 1625. R2/53/684; W1/81/188
see also Waynford
WAITES, Francis, Wicken, 1625. R2/53/387; W1/81/164
see also Wayte, Whaightes, Whayte
WAKE, Annice, wid., Soham, 1553. R2/31/110; W1/13/77
Christian, wid., Soham, 1675. R2/66/154; W1/127/26; In. 3/16/41
Edmund, husb., Soham, 1542. R2/19/335
Edmund, Soham, 1575. R2/37/126
Edmund, Soham, 1578. A5/2/5
Edmund, Soham, 1649. A5/4/129
Edward, yeo., Soham, 1661. R2/62/210; W1/113/73; In. 3/6/95
Edward, Soham, 1663, (N). R2/63/67; W1/115/107; In. 3/8/242; A5/5/49
John, Bury St. Edmunds, 1528. R2/6/150 (admon. only)
John, husb., Soham, 1556. R2/25/138 & 140; W1/16/171
John, Soham, 1587. A5/2/96
Richard, husb., Soham, 1556. R2/25/61; W1/16/68
Susan, wid., Great Wratting, 1700. R2/74/117; W1/154/113
Thomas, yeo., Soham, 1628. R2/54/240; W1/86/101
Thomas, yeo., Soham, 1677. R2/66/502; W1/129/83; In. 3/18/102
Thomas, the elder, labourer, Soham, 1678. R2/67/170; W1/130/150; In. 3/19/207
Walter, chandler, Bury St. Edmunds, 1436. R2/1/224
William, Soham, 1541. R2/22/89 & 96; W1/10/14
WAKEFELD, John, labourer, Haverhill, 1557. R2/26/155; W1/20/91
Thomas, shepherd, Herringswell, 1591. R2/42/114; W1/48/119
WAKEFEILD, Thomas, yeo., Lidgate, 1662. R2/62/388; W1/114/129
WAKEFIELD, George, the elder, carpenter, Dalham, 1679. R2/67/335; W1/133/103
WAKEFYLDE, Elizabeth, Haverhill, 1566. R2/32/291; W1/28/103
WAKELIN, Thomas, inn holder, Haverhill, 1680. R2/67/657; W1/134/119; A5/6/37, A4/17/68
WAKELYNE, Alice, wid., Great Thurlow, 1617. R2/50/231; W1/74/25
see also Waklen
WAKERINGE, Ralph, Hundon, 1589. A5/2/128
see also Wacring, Wakeryng
WAKERLEY, Sybil, Burwell, 1542. R2/22/77; W1/6/42
WAKERLY, John, smith, Burwell, 1541. R2/21/578; W1/28/156
WAKERYNG, Thomas, Hundon, 1490. R2/11/408
Thomas, Stoke by Clare, 1520. R2/15/100
WAKLEN, Edmund, carpenter, Hundon, 1640. R2/58/169; W1/96/84
WALBY, John, the elder, shepherd, Icklingham, 1660. R2/62/46; W1/112/55; In. 3/5/59
Richard, shepherd, Barnham, 1662. R2/62/307; W1/114/2; In. 3/7/20; A5/5/26
Richard, Barnham, 1677. In. 3/18/5; A5/5/166, A4/14/2

WALCARD, William, sen., Risby, 1475. R2/11/145
WALDEGRAVE, Agnes, wid., Eye, (1675). R2/66/311; W1/128/13; In. 3/17/128
Elisabeth, wid., Bures, 1652, (N). R2/61/574; W1/109/46
WALDEN, Benjamin, gent., Brandon, 1663. R2/63/111; W1/115/168
John, Brandon, 1482. R2/11/250
John, clerk, Mildenhall, 1558. R2/27/105
John, yeo., Stowupland, 1609. R2/47/64; W1/66/74
Robert, mercer, Brandon, 1543. R2/19/417; W1/6/95
see also Waldyn
WALDENFIELD, Richard, yeo., Freckenham, 1628. R6/56
WALDINGFIELD, Christopher, Bury St. Edmunds, 1608. R2/46/157; W1/65/1
see also Wallyngfylld, Anmer als. Waldingfild
WALDYN, Richard, Chippenham, 1573. R2/36/136; W1/32/35
WALE, John, sen., Great Thornham, 1448. R2/9/162
John, Little Thornham, 1454. R2/9/205
WALEANT, William, Rickinghall Superior, 1539. R2/19/317
WALENGER, John, carpenter, Bardwell, 1478. R2/11/173
Nicholas, Nayland, 1443. R2/9/36
WALER, John, Bardwell, 1527. R2/17/271; W1/1/6
WALES, Ann, wid. of William, Redgrave, 1664. R2/63/223; W1/116/136; In. 3/9/185
John, labourer, Hartest, 1604. R2/45/351
Margaret, wid., Haughley, 1537. R2/18/146
William, Burwell, 1527. R2/17/260; W1/1/18
WALESDENE, John, Bury St. Edmunds, 1370. R2/1/25
WALEYS, Alice, Soham, 1457. R2/9/219
John, Hundon, 1452. R2/9/145
Walter, Thorndon, 1452. R2/9/128
WALFORD, Henry, Ixworth, 1638. A5/4/66
Henry, yeo., Wattisfield, 1679. R2/67/278; W1/133/67
Robert, gent., Hunston, 1644. R2/59/154; W1/101/81
Thomas, cordwainer, Sudbury, 1684. R2/69/225; W1/138/30
WALGORE, John, glover, Ixworth, 1550. R2/21/154; W1/9/154
WALHEDE, Thomas, parson, Bildeston, (1531). R2/19/81
WALKEFAR, Richard, Hitcham, 1451. R2/9/107
WALKER, Edmund, husb., Boxted, 1692. R2/72/21; W1/146/19; In. 3/24/36
Edward, husb., Lakenheath, 1610. R2/47/245; W1/67/127
Edward, Little Waldingfield, 1581. A5/2/31
Edward, singleman, Milden, 1615. R2/49/298; W1/72/77
Henry, gent., Bury St. Edmunds, 1644. R2/59/112; W1/101/38
James, Lakenheath, 1687. A5/6/112, A4/27/57
Jesse, labourer, Worlington, 1611. R2/48/13; W1/68/32
John, parson, Bradfield St. Clare, 1556. R2/25/103; W1/16/98
John, husb., Lackford, 1696. In. 3/25/29; A5/6/188, A4/39/47
John, Mildenhall, 1684. A5/6/80, A4/21/69
Lucretia, wid., Bury St. Edmunds, 1618. R2/51/245; W1/75/160
Margaret, wid., Great Cornard, 1601. R2/44/506; W1/59/129
Margaret, wid., Lakenheath, 1676. R2/66/334; W1/128/38; In. 3/17/33
Martha, spinster, Bury St. Edmunds, 1665. R2/63/366; W1/117/118
Mary, wid., Bury St. Edmunds, 1690. R2/71/140 & 438; W1/144/146
Mary, wid., Mildenhall, 1697. R2/73/218; W1/151/105
Mary, singlewoman, Somerton, 1610. R2/47/305; W1/67/197
Osbert, wid., Lakenheath, 1688. In. 3/23/91; A5/6/123, A4/29/81
Richard, Bury St. Edmunds, 1610. R2/47/206; W1/67/87
Richard, yeo., Stowmarket, 1613. R2/48/286; W1/70/60
Robert, yeo., Combs, 1608. R2/46/160; W1/65/4
Robert, husb., Great Cornard, 1602. R2/45/210; W1/60/147
Robert, grocer, Mendlesham, 1698. R2/73/334; W1/152/103
Thomas, labourer, Cavenham, 1608. R2/46/205; W1/65/89
Thomas, Culford, 1579. R2/38/68; W1/39/13
Thomas, vicar, Stowmarket, 1545. R2/19/552; W1/7/88
Thomasine, wid., Bury St. Edmunds, 1671. R2/65/240; W1/123/120
William, fletcher, Bury St. Edmunds, 1539. R2/7/54
William, yeo., Lakenheath, 1606. R2/46/76; W1/64/95

WALKER continued
William, husb., Lakenheath, 1665. R2/63/348; W1/117/100; In. 3/10/133
William, yeo., Mendlesham, 1666. R2/64/47; W1/118/41; In. 3/11/42
William, the elder, yeo., Stowmarket, 1576. R2/37/233; W1/37/91; In. 3/1/7
William, yeo., Stowmarket, 1621. R2/52/234; W1/77/26
William, yeo., Thorndon, 1691. R2/71/467
WALL, Anne, singlewoman, Norton, 1618. R2/51/201; W1/75/128
John, Boxford, 1450. R2/9/131
John, Bury St. Edmunds, 1465. R2/2/87
John, Bury St. Edmunds, 1476. R2/2/222
John, miller, Bury St. Edmunds, 1504. R2/4/151
John, miller, Bury St. Edmunds, (1540). R2/8/12
John, 1567. A5/1/186
see also Whale
WALLAR, John, husb., Lavenham, 1557. R2/26/163; W1/20/100
WALLER, Andrew, yeo., Elmswell, 1683. R2/69/80; W1/137/61
Ann, wid., Hopton, 1695. R2/72/459; W1/149/14
David, tailor, Bardwell, 1624. R2/53/153
David, Bardwell, 1667. In. 3/12/58; A5/5/85, A4/5/41
Edmund, yeo., Stanton, 1695. R2/72/536; W1/149/92
James, master of arts, Rattlesden, 1697. R2/73/121; W1/151/11
John, labourer, Bardwell, 1648. R2/60/140; W1/105/168
John, linen weaver, Bardwell, 1684. R2/69/262; W1/138/62
John, shoe maker, Bury St. Edmunds, 1579. R2/38/29; W1/39/49
John, Bury St. Edmunds, 1638. A5/4/67
John, Bury St. Edmunds, 1645. A5/4/109
John, miller, Ixworth, 1556. R2/25/49; W1/16/56
John, shepherd, Ixworth, 1591. R2/42/100; W1/48/131
John, Little Bradley, 1686. In. 3/22/11; A5/6/98, A4/26/106
John, Rickinghall Superior, 1635. A5/4/35
John, the elder, husb., Stanton, 1615. R2/49/307; W1/75/87
John, the elder, yeo., Stanton, 1678. R2/67/154; W1/130/138; In. 3/19/189
John, Stanton, 1693. A5/6/159, A4/35/58
Mark, Wickhambrook, 1687. A5/6/114, A4/27/86
Phoebe, spinster, Rattlesden, 1699. A5/7/13, A4/41/64
Ralph, yeo., Drinkstone, 1614. R2/49/179; W1/71/121
Ralph, yeo., Drinkstone, 1630. R2/55/6; W1/86/9
Richard, linen weaver, Hessett, 1672. R2/65/288; W1/124/4
Richard, Walsham le Willows, 1559. R2/28/304
Robert, the elder, Rattlesden, (1553). R2/21/664, R2/31/102
Stephen, cordwainer, Bardwell, 1685. R2/70/58; W1/139/52
Susan, wid. of John, Bury St. Edmunds, 1663. R2/63/73; W1/115/116
Susan, Walsham le Willows, 1558. R2/27/306
Thomas, Fornham St. Martin, 1471. R2/10/471
Thomas, husb., Stoke by Nayland, 1533. R2/19/177; W1/2/21
Thomas, gent., Stoke by Nayland, 1649. R2/60/296; W1/106/172
William, Walsham le Willows, 1562. R2/31/18; W1/8/179
see also Waler, Wallor, Walour
WALLES, Thomas, husb., Mildenhall, 1615. R2/49/235; W1/72/25
WALLEYS, Thomas, Burwell, 1472. R2/10/515
WALLGRAVE, Mary, gentlewoman, Thrandeston, 1620. R2/52/98; W1/76/84
WALLINGTON, Simon, rector, Westhorpe, 1570. A5/1/224
WALLIS, Ann, wid., Hartest, 1698. A5/7/6
Avis, wid., Great Fakenham, 1638. R2/57/433; W1/93/272
Christopher, joiner, Hartest, 1682. R2/68/462; W1/136/141; In. 3/21/32
Dorothy, wife of John, gent., Burwell, 1663. R2/63/61; W1/115/98; In. 3/8/146
John, Burwell, 1667. In. 3/12/89; A5/5/85, A4/5/45
Margery, wid., Mildenhall, 1624. R2/53/46; W1/80/68
Mary, als. Warman, wife of Thomas, Cavendish, 1650. A5/4/133
William, yeo., Bury St. Edmunds, 1604. R2/45/309; W1/62/8
see also Wales, Waleys, Walles, Walys, Waules, Sutfeilde als. Wallys
WALLOR, Nicholas, Walsham le Willows, 1557. R2/26/17; W1/20/23
WALLOURE, Thomas, Wattisfield, 1474. R2/10/562

WALLYNGFYLLD, Gregory, Freckenham, 1568. W8/9
WALMAN, Cicely, wid., Eye, 1589. R2/41/155; W1/46/127
Henry, mason, Eye, 1584. R2/39/147; W1/42/177
Henry, Soham, 1679. A5/6/29, A4/16/147
John, husb., Fornham All Saints, 1570. R2/34/63; W1/38/129; A5/1/255
Robert, Ousden, 1693. A5/6/155, A4/35/88
see also Vyall als. Walman
WALOUR, Nicholas, Weston, 1458. R2/9/194
WALPOLE, Edward, Ixworth, 1475. R2/11/140
WALPOOL, Amy, Bury St. Edmunds, 1443. R2/2/1
Emma, Bury St. Edmunds, 1434. R2/1/209
John, carpenter, Bury St. Edmunds, 1435. R2/1/213
William, Bury St. Edmunds, 1406. R2/1/107
WALSH, John, East Harling, 1531. R2/19/60
WALSHAM, John, Bury St. Edmunds, 1469. R2/2/127
John, Pakenham, 1469. R2/10/400
Simon, pelter, Bury St. Edmunds, 1390. R2/1/57
WALSOM(E), Christopher, Newmarket, 1580, (N). R2/38/178; W1/39/123
John, Woolpit, 1444. R2/9/54
WALSYNGHAM, Agnes, wid., Thrandeston, 1553. R2/31/163
Thomas, the elder, Thrandeston, 1552. R2/23/230; W1/12/45
WALTAR, Richard, Hopton, 1527. R2/17/235; W1/1/48
WALTER(S), Hugh, Mildenhall, 1661. A5/5/22
Isaac, Assington, 1612. A5/3/118
Isabel, Coney Weston, 1482. R2/11/257
John, Elmswell, 1478. R2/11/162
John, Hepworth, 1563. A5/1/150
John, sen., Hopton, 1443. R2/9/55
John, sen., Hopton, 1446. R2/9/66
John, husb., Knettishall, 1585. R2/39/287; W1/42/290
John, carpenter, Rattlesden, 1550. R2/21/128; W1/9/91
John, Wicken, 1590. R2/41/407; W1/47/87
Margaret, als. Hert, wife of Edmund, Bury St. Edmunds, 1479. R2/2/267
Margaret, wid., Hepworth, (1542). R2/19/336
Marion, wid., Elmsett, 1559. R2/28/87; W1/22/85
Nicholas, the elder, Stowmarket, 1611. R2/48/10; W1/68/28; A5/3/110
Richard, Coney Weston, 1469. R2/10/399
Richard, Great Fakenham, 1504. R2/13/148
Richard, beer brewer, Stoke by Nayland, 1570. R2/34/16; W1/30/16; A5/1/221
Richard, Sudbury, 1592. A5/2/166
Thomas, Isleham, 1560. W7/20
Walter, Coney Weston,1472. R2/10/500
William, husb., Rattlesden, 1661. R2/62/223; W1/113/90; In. 3/6/119
William, Weston, 1554. R2/24/83; W1/14/64
WALTHAM, John, als. Mason, Mildenhall, 1559. R2/28/22; W1/22/26
John, als. Mason, Stoke by Clare, 1477. R2/11/103
Nicholas, als. Tanner, yeo., Kedington, 1648. R2/60/111; W1/105/131
Simon, als. Mason, Mildenhall, 1565. A5/1/167
Susan, wid., Bildeston, 1667, (N). R2/64/178; W1/119/10; In. 3/12/25; A5/5/82, A4/5/12
WALTON, Giles, Cotton, 1581. A5/2/35
Giles, yeo., Wyverstone, 1662, (N). R2/62/372; W1/114/105; In. 3/7/120; A5/5/33
James, yeo., Wyverstone, 1640. R2/58/142; W1/96/41
John, als. Jenking, labouring man, Mildenhall, 1588. R2/41/134; W1/46/143
John, Stoke by Nayland, 1565. R2/32/169
Leonard, Tuddenham, 1555. A5/1/96
Margery, wid., Thwaite, 1591. R2/42/9; W1/48/7
WALYS, John, labourer, Brandon, 1557. R2/26/302; W1/20/224
John, Wangford, 1560. R2/29/167; W1/25/7
WANEFLET, Peter, als. Piper, Lavenham, 1607. A5/3/19
WANT(E), John, Soham, 1545. R2/19/532; W1/7/112
Richard, Soham, 1590. R2/41/454; W1/47/96

WANTLOND, Robert, fuller, Bury St. Edmunds, 1443. R2/2/5
WANTON, Andrew, Stanton, 1507. R2/13/189
Edmond, Bury St. Edmunds, 1518. R2/6/53
Robert, Stanton, 1459. R2/9/266
Roger, Stanton, (1533). W1/2/32
Thomas, Kersey, 1585. A5/2/77
WAPPOLODE, William, Bury St. Edmunds, 1394. R2/1/68
WARAN, Robert, Somerton, 1560. R2/29/84; W1/25/82
WARBURTON, Dennis, Langham, 1511. R2/13/204
WARD, Abigail, wid., Little Waldingfield, 1681. A5/6/50, A4/18/75
Adam, Wicken, 1605. R2/45/418; W1/63/64
Alice, Fornham, 1439. R2/9/2
Alice, Stoke by Nayland, 1607. A5/3/19
Alice, wid., Tuddenham, 1567. R2/32/437; W1/19/91
Ambrose, husb., Rattlesden, 1671. R2/65/258; W1/123/138
Amy, wid., Hepworth, 1573. R2/36/132; W1/52/22
Ann, wid., Coney Weston, 1661. In. 3/6/235; A5/5/23, A4/1/37
Barnaby, Groton, 1608. A5/3/54
Christian, wid., Great Waldingfield, 1624. R2/53/69; W1/80/90
Christian, wid., Mellis, 1664. R2/63/232; W1/116/149; In. 3/9/202; A5/5/63, A4/2/102
Christine, wid., Bury St. Edmunds, 1559. R2/8/338; W1/17/82
Christopher, Elmswell, 1547. R2/21/335; W1/10/158
Clarissa, Barrow, 1467. W1/24/75
Edmund, tailor, Bury St. Edmunds, 1558. R2/8/333; W1/17/88
Edmund, Hitcham, 1496. R2/13/40
Edmund, Lackford, 1666. In. 3/11/104
Edmund, yeo., Layham, 1588. R2/41/74; W1/45/64
Edmund, miller, Wissington, 1652. R2/61/523; W1/109/8; In. 3/4/91
Edward, als. Dryver, husb., Assington, 1565. R2/32/171; W1/27/107
Edward, yeo., Lackford, 1666. R2/64/135; W1/118/101
Elisabeth, wid., Bury St. Edmunds, 1629. R2/54/383; W1/85/80
Elisabeth, wid., Coney Weston, 1638. R2/57/388; W1/93/200
Francis, husb., Icklingham, 1652. R2/61/599; W1/109/76; In. 3/4/83
George, yeo., Bildeston, 1666. R2/64/121; W1/118/93; In. 3/11/127
George, yeo., Bradfield St. George, 1623. R2/52/622; W1/79/66
George, yeo., Brettenham, 1664. R2/63/126; W1/116/10; In. 3/9/24; A4/3/34
George, miller, Creeting All Saints, 1632. R2/56/119
Henry, yeo., Hawstead, 1631. R2/56/79; W1/87/119
Hugh, Hepworth, 1569. A5/1/213
James, yeo., Coney Weston, 1664. R2/63/174; W1/116/72; In. 3/9/123
James, yeo., Great Waldingfield, 1650. R2/61/316; W1/107/10; In. 3/3/18
James, Hartest, 1488. R2/11/452
James, als. Innold, Sudbury, 1552. R2/31/94; W1/13/66
James, barber, Sudbury, 1598. R2/44/81; W1/56/72
Joan, wid., Glemsford, 1520. R2/15/78
John, Assington, 1555. R2/24/196; W1/15/30
John, Bradfield St. George, 1562. R2/31/88; W1/8/100
John, Cheveley, 1528. R2/15/179; W1/19/48
John, yeo., Coney Weston, 1640. R2/58/210; W1/96/145
John, Creeting All Saints, 1536. R2/14/100, R2/19/69
John, yeo., Glemsford, 1528. R2/15/221
John, Great Waldingfield, 1612. R2/48/135; W1/69/15
John, Icklingham, 1534. R2/19/196
John, shearman, Icklingham, 1551. R2/23/90; W1/11/79
John, husb., Icklingham, 1572. R2/36/90; W1/31/41
John, yeo., Icklingham, 1647. R2/59/404; W1/104/30; In. 3/2/36
John, Kersey, 1531. W1/19/54
John, Langham, 1593. A5/2/183
John, beer brewer, Lavenham, 1553. R2/31/203

WARD continued
John, als. Ford, the elder, yeo., Nowton, 1601. R2/44/503; W1/59/127
John, Soham, 1644. A5/4/106
John, husb., Soham, 1649. R2/60/163; W1/106/8
John, Stansfield, 1496. R2/13/44
John, carpenter, Stoke by Nayland, 1581. R2/38/255; W1/40/7
John, als. Innolde, Sudbury, 1551. R2/23/14; W1/11/78
John, Wicken, 1625. R2/53/340; W1/81/121
John, yeo., Wickham Skeith, 1559. R2/28/40; W1/22/42
John, Wood Ditton, 1448. R2/9/94
Joseph, yeo., Mellis, 1660. R2/62/68; In. 3/5/102
Juliana, Stoke by Nayland, 1565. A5/1/167
Lancelot, carpenter, Stoke by Nayland, 1592. R2/42/258; W1/49/76
Margaret, wid., Elmsett, 1568. R2/33/51; W1/29/66
Margaret, Haverhill, 1469. R2/10/413
Margaret, Rickinghall Inferior, 1559. R2/28/74; W1/22/77
Margaret, wid., Sudbury, 1606. R2/46/61; W1/64/85
Margery, wid., Assington, 1644. R2/59/150; W1/101/75
Philip, the elder, yeo., Little Whelnetham, 1670. R2/65/92; W1/122/112; In. 3/15/134
Phillip, the elder, yeo., Bradfield Combust, 1632. R2/56/125; W1/89/12
Richard, yeo., Bradfield St. George, 1667. R2/64/292; W1/119/155; In. 3/12/182a
Richard, Bury St. Edmunds, 1662. A5/5/38
Richard, clerk, Buxhall, 1580. R2/38/109; W1/39/168
Richard, Icklingham, 1483. R2/11/247
Richard, Lawshall, 1669. A4/7/63
Richard, husb., Mildenhall, 1634. R2/56/345; W1/90/115
Richard, the elder, yeo., Pakenham, 1674. R2/66/52; W1/126/67
Richard, brewer, Stoke, 1598. R2/44/86; W1/56/134
Robert, husb., Assington, 1596. R2/43/208; W1/54/63
Robert, Brandon, 1497. R2/13/64
Robert, Euston, 1565. A5/1/163
Robert, carpenter, Fornham St. Martin, 1651. R2/61/459
Robert, Glemsford, 1472. R2/11/126
Robert, Kersey, 1588. R2/41/46; W1/45/40
Robert, Walsham le Willows, 1459. R2/9/210
Roger, als. Sowter, husb., Bradfield, 1556. R2/25/174
Roger, also. Driver, yeo., Creeting All Saints, (1640). W1/110/1
Samuel, gent., Lidgate, 1695. R2/72/461; W1/149/18
Stephen, felt maker, Stowmarket, 1648. R2/60/12; W1/105/17
Susan, wid., Norton, 1680. In. 3/20/156; A5/6/38, A4/17/76
Thomas, husb., Assington, 1626. R2/53/551
Thomas, Bradfield St. George, 1602, (N). R2/45/96; W1/60/4
Thomas, yeo., Coney Weston, 1610. R2/47/176; W1/67/53
Thomas, Elmsett, 1476. R2/11/67
Thomas, cordwainer, Fornham St. Genevieve, 1624. R2/53/66; W1/80/87
Thomas, inn holder, Groton, 1688. R2/71/90; W1/142/82; In. 3/23/103
Thomas, cordwainer, Hitcham, 1663. R2/63/62; W1/115/101
Thomas, Kersey, 1587. A5/2/86
Thomas, yeo., Mellis, 1700. R2/74/249
Thomas, shoe maker, Mildenhall, 1616. R2/50/3; W1/73/5
Thomas, Nayland, 1638. A5/4/61
Thomas, husb., Nayland, 1667. In. 3/12/112; A5/5/87, A4/5/69
Thomas, Sudbury, 1489. R2/11/376
Thomas, Tostock, 1523. R2/17/27; W1/21/60
Thomas, Wattisham, 1647. In. 3/2/91; A5/4/117
Ursula, wid., Thelnetham, 1616. R2/50/30; W1/73/29
Walter, Elmsett, 1485. R2/11/343
William, yeo., Bradfield St. George, 1644. R2/59/123; W1/101/50
William, chaplain, Bury St. Edmunds, 1417. R2/1/146
William, Bury St. Edmunds, 1421. R2/1/156
William, husb., Chelsworth, 1564. R2/32/67; W1/27/15

WARD continued
William, yeo., Coney Weston, 1670. In. 3/15/8; A5/5/107, A4/7/61
William, yeo., Hundon, (1620). W1/111/4
William, labourer, Lakenheath, 1607. R2/46/110; W1/97/10
William, husb., Layham, 1551. R2/23/66; W1/11/77
William, carpenter, Long Melford, 1568. R2/33/20; W1/29/30
William, Preston, 1641. A5/4/92
William, husb., Rickinghall Inferior, 1573. R2/36/169; W1/32/73
William, Stoke by Nayland, 1574. A5/1/270
William, singleman, Stoke by Nayland, 1697. A5/7/2, A4/120/39
William, wid., Woolpit, 1682. In. 3/21/125; A5/6/60, A4/19/54
see also Craton als. Warde, Manning als. Warde, Wade als. Ward

WARDALL, Agnes, Great Wratting, 1578. A5/2/12
Thomas, tanner, Great Wratting, 1562. R2/31/115; W1/8/168
Thomas, Hawstead, 1592. R2/42/230; W1/49/49
William, Soham, 1590. A5/2/128

WARDELL, William, tanner, Eye, 1682. In. 3/21/189; A5/6/59, A4/19/39

WARDEN, William, Mendlesham, 1566. A5/1/180

WARDLEY, Joan, wid. of Thomas, Timworth, 1560. R2/29/115; W1/25/53
Thomas, Timworth, 1560. R2/29/115; W1/25/54

WARDLY, Thomas, Ixworth, 1633. A5/4/25

WARDSWORTH, Isaac, yeo., Yaxley, 1660. R2/62/94; W1/112/127

WARDWELL, William, Thorpe Morieux, 1630. A5/4/2

WARE, Christopher, Boxford, 1687. A5/6/114, A4/27/83
James, linen weaver, Thelnetham, 1672. R2/65/320; W1/124/45
John, Milden, 1524. R2/17/51; W1/21/36
Joseph, inn holder, Boxford, 1695. R2/72/468; W1/149/23
Richard, Lawshall, 1669. In. 3/14/178; A5/5/109
Robert, Boxford, 1685. A5/6/89 & 90, A4/24/42 & 139
Samuel, joiner, Sudbury, 1685. R2/70/121; W1/139/108
Thomas, the elder, hair weaver, Newmarket, 1693. R2/72/234; W1/147/123

WAREING, Richard, gent., Groton, 1696. R2/73/84; W1/150/68; In. 3/27/41

WAREN, Abigail, wid., Nayland, 1647. R2/59/462; W1/104/95; In. 3/2/71
Adam, labourer, Alpheton, 1573. R2/36/174; W1/32/80
Barbara, wid., Eye, 1563. R2/32/38; W1/26/97
Edward, Nayland, 1576, (N). R2/37/176; W1/37/42; In. 3/1/65
Elisabeth, wid., Wissington, 1605. R2/45/395; W1/63/27
Joan, wid., Sudbury, 1526. R2/17/140; W1/21/136
John, Bury St. Edmunds, 1505. R2/4/167
John, lime burner, Bury St. Edmunds, 1567. W1/10/200
John, Great Bradley, 1538. R2/19/604, R2/20/96; W1/3/41
John, Kirtling, 1559. R2/28/51; W1/22/55
John, husb., Stoke by Nayland, 1576. R2/37/142; W1/37/12; In. 3/1/109
Katherine, Kirtling, 1560. R2/29/10
Robert, husb., Barrow, 1530. R2/19/26
Robert, Kirtling, 1542. R2/22/53; W1/6/60
Samuel, Nayland, 1637, (N). R2/57/226; W1/92/273
Thomas, husb., Wissington, 1559. R2/28/57; W1/22/61
Thomas, yeo., Wiston, 1603. R2/45/288; W1/61/93
William, Bures, 1554. A5/1/92

WAREYN, Agnes, wid., Bury St. Edmunds, 1498. R2/4/63
Amfritha, Sudbury, 1463. R2/10/315
Bennet, coverlet weaver, Bury St. Edmunds, 1495. R2/4/34
Henry, Combs, 1452. R2/9/156
John, Bildeston, 1446. R2/9/91
John, Brettenham, 1454. R2/9/175
John, Burgate, 1498. R2/13/96
John, fisher, Bury St. Edmunds, 1446. R2/2/17
John, als. Baker, Clare, 1482. R2/11/262 & 265
John, Groton, 1477. R2/11/99
John, Kersey, 1485. R2/11/348
John, jun., Long Melford, 1453. R2/9/163
John, sen., Mildenhall, 1461. R2/9/300
John, Mildenhall, 1472. R2/10/518

WAREYN continued
John, barker, Nayland, 1441. R2/9/20
John, fuller, Stoke by Nayland, 1441. R2/9/60
John, Stowmarket, 1468. R2/10/407
Margaret, spinster, Eye, 1672. R2/65/319; W1/124/44
Margaret, Long Melford, 1458. R2/9/188
Richard, smith, Bury St. Edmunds, 1482. R2/2/331
Richard, Long Melford, 1460. R2/9/271
Robert, Ashfield, 1460. R2/9/254
Robert, Kirtling, 1461. R2/9/299
Rose, Kersey, 1447. R2/9/84
Simon, coverlet weaver, Bury St. Edmunds, 1513. R2/5/28
Thomas, Bury St. Edmunds, 1459. R2/2/66
Thomas, the elder, Bury St. Edmunds, 1523. R2/6/105
Thomas, Haughley, 1471. R2/10/487
William, Cotton, 1478. R2/11/154
William, Stuston, 1506. R2/12/49
William, chandler, Sudbury, 1497. R2/13/55
WARFORD, John, yeo., Norwich, 1594. W1/51/97
WARING, Robert, butcher, Burwell, 1675. R2/66/162; W1/127/37; In. 3/16/40
Walter, Brettenham, 1531. R2/19/73
see also Wareing, Warren
WARLEY, Clemency, wid., Thurston, 1559. R2/28/398; W1/3/150
WARLYCHE, Richard, Wickhambrook, 1536. R2/18/106, R2/19/243
WARMAN, George, Cavendish, 1650. A5/4/133
John, husb., Cavendish, 1606. R2/46/9; W1/64/11
Thomas, Cavendish, 1563. R2/31/170; W1/26/54
see also Wallis als. Warman
WARNAR, John, yeo., Barrow, 1557. R2/26/299; W1/20/221
Marion, Denston, 1521. R2/14/112
WARNE, Elisabeth, wid., Eye, 1693. R2/72/115
John, yeo., Gislingham, 1608. R2/46/181; W1/65/46
John, singleman, Thrandeston, 1681. R2/68/233; W1/135/174
Richard, Eye, 1693. A5/6/164, A4/35/18
Robert, Stoke Ash, 1681. A5/6/50, A4/18/80
Thomas, gent., Bury St. Edmunds, 1668. R2/64/412; W1/120/134; In. 3/14/41
Thomas, gent., Great Ashfield, 1697. R2/73/162; W1/151/48
Thomas, yeo., Thrandeston, 1628. R2/54/226; W1/84/90
Timothy, singleman, Thelnetham, 1699. R2/73/382; W1/153/35; In. 3/27/78
William, yeo., Thrandeston, 1625. R2/53/397; W1/81/177
WARNER, Abraham, carpenter, Nayland, 1682. In. 3/21/116; A5/6/61, A4/19/61
Alice, wid., Bardwell, 1540. R2/20/150 & 152; W1/4/189
Alice, Elmswell, 1455. R2/9/177
Bartholomew, Soham, 1632. A5/4/21
Clement, Thelnetham, 1671. A5/5/122, A4/8/26
Dorothy, wid., Bardwell, 1625. R2/53/360; W1/81/139
Edmund, singleman, Sudbury, 1693. A5/6/158, A4/116/63
Edward, yeo., Great Finborough, 1665. R2/63/361; W1/117/111; A5/5/70, A4/3/72
Edward, tailor, Lawshall, 1678. R2/67/103; W1/130/88; In. 3/19/121
Edward, esq., Mildenhall, 1618. R2/51/89; W1/75/55
Elisabeth, singlewoman, Bardwell, 1627. W1/95/66
George, labourer, Lavenham, 1686, (N). R2/70/419; W1/140/42; In. 3/22/86
Gregory, yeo., Great Finborough, 1663. R2/63/40; W1/115/63; In. 3/8/69
Gregory, Great Finborough, 1688. In. 3/23/63; A5/6/120, A4/29/55
Joan, wid., Clare, 1543. R2/19/415; W1/6/160
Joan, singlewoman, Nayland, 1585. R2/39/248; W1/42/325
John, Bardwell, 1593. R2/42/419; W1/50/79; A5/2/212
John, Barrow, 1452. R2/9/109
John, Clare, 1539. R2/19/307
John, Fornham All Saints, 1650. A5/4/137
John, Great Livermere, 1472. R2/10/503
John, Hargrave, (1538). R2/19/439 & 601; W1/5/55
John, Nayland, 1477. R2/11/57

WARNER continued
John, Whelnetham, 1638. A5/4/61
Katherine, wid., Docking, 1594. W1/51/271
Katherine, Great Livermere, 1474. R2/10/568
Margaret, Barrow, 1439. R2/9/10
Richard, yeo., Bardwell, (1613). W1/111/38
Richard, yeo., Burgate, 1694. A5/6/172, A4/37/71
Robert, tailor, Bardwell, 1673. R2/65/467; W1/125/102
Robert, Barrow, 1524. R2/17/321; W1/21/179
Robert, brander, Bury St. Edmunds, 1429. R2/1/188
Robert, sen., Walsham le Willows, 1695. A5/6/177, A4/38/15
Rose, als. Chambers, wife of William, husb., Botesdale, 1676. R2/66/386; W1/128/97; In. 3/17/135
Simon, Stowmarket, 1691. A5/6/144, A4/33/61
Thomas, Bardwell, 1471. R2/10/481
Thomas, Bardwell, 1573. R2/36/113; W1/32/12
Thomas, the elder, Bardwell, 1614. R2/49/70; W1/71/54
Thomas, Bardwell, 1667. A5/5/88
Thomas, Bardwell, 1667. In. 3/13/66; A5/5/99, A4/6/100
Thomas, tailor, Bury St. Edmunds, 1516. R2/6/29
Thomas, Denston, 1497. R2/13/57
Thomas, singleman, Little Saxham, 1558. R2/27/203
Thomas, Soham, 1665, (N). R2/63/323; W1/117/65; In. 3/10/86, A5/5/67
Thomas, Soham, 1670. In. 3/15/183; A5/5/118
Thomas, cordwainer, Walsham le Willows, 1690. R2/71/355; W1/144/60
William, tailor, Bardwell, 1625. R2/53/383; W1/81/160
William, husb., Barrow, 1605. R2/45/465; W1/63/114
William, Bradfield, 1462. R2/10/325
William, yeo., Coney Weston, 1556. R2/25/33; W1/16/35
William, Soham, 1465. R2/10/380
William, Soham, 1533. R2/19/176; W1/2/20
William, weaver, Sudbury, 1692. W1/146/33
William, yeo., Westhorpe, 1566. R2/32/359; W1/28/20
see also Warnar, Worner
WARNES, Richard, baker, Sudbury, 1641. R2/58/303; W1/98/93
WARRAN, Robert, husb., Stanton, 1557. R2/26/12; W1/20/28
WARRE, John, Stoke by Clare, 1482. R2/11/315
Robert, als. Foxerde, Bures, 1527. R2/17/252; W1/1/24
WARREN, Adam, husb., Stradishall, 1610. R2/47/226; W1/67/96
Alice, wid., Bury St. Edmunds, 1567. W1/10/202
Ann, wid., Downham, 1694. R2/72/332; W1/148/66
Denise, wid., Newmarket, 1675. R2/66/203; W1/127/79
Edward, Bury St. Edmunds, 1648. A5/4/119
Edward, Clare, 1631. A5/4/15
Edward, yeo., Lidgate, 1587. R2/40/170; W1/44/42
Edward, Thorpe Morieux, 1639. A5/4/69
Edward, Worlington, 1628. R2/54/171; W1/84/45
Elisabeth, wid., Bury St. Edmunds, 1675. R2/66/254; W1/127/125; In. 3/16/158
Elisabeth, als. Whitehead, Great Bradley, 1640. A5/4/85
Erasmus, yeo., Fordham, 1649. R2/60/169; W1/106/16
George, clerk, Barton Mills, 1662. R2/62/328; W1/114/36; In. 3/7/2
George, the elder, yeo., Kirtling, 1631. R2/56/78; W1/87/118
Giles, shepherd, Bury St. Edmunds, 1648. R2/60/37; W1/105/46
Henry, Bury St. Edmunds, 1637. A5/4/54
James, clothier, Bury St. Edmunds, 1696. R2/73/53; W1/150/96
James, yeo., Wissington, 1594. R2/42/514; W1/52/70; A5/2/199
Joan, Thwaite, 1581. A5/2/35
John, Bury St. Edmunds, 1699. A5/7/13, A4/41/54
John, Edwardstone, 1664. A5/5/64, A4/2/108
John, Glemsford, 1638. A5/4/63
John, yeo., Great Bradley, 1596. R2/43/135; W1/54/11
John, yeo., Great Bradley, 1641. R2/58/298; W1/98/85
John, Kirtling, 1598. R2/44/27; W1/56/23
John, barber, Long Melford, 1680. In. 3/20/39; A5/6/33, A4/17/23
John, cordwinder, Pakenham, 1669. R2/64/541; W1/121/131; In. 3/14/100

WARREN continued
John, husb., Pakenham, 1685. R2/70/71; W1/139/63
John, Thelnetham, 1697. A5/7/5, A4/40/77
Katherine, Bures, 1592. A5/2/178
Katherine, wid. of John, yeo., Great Bradley, 1611. R2/47/315; W1/68/12
Lydia, wid., Pakenham, 1685. R2/70/3; W1/139/4
Margery, wid., Worlington, 1615. R2/49/290; W1/72/71
Martin, cordwainer, Bury St. Edmunds, 1690. R2/71/331; W1/144/34
Martin, gent., Fordham, 1683. A5/6/72, A4/20/96
Martin, yeo., Snailwell, 1600. R2/45/51; W1/58/73
Martin, gent., Snailwell, 1688. R2/71/96; W1/142/87; In. 3/23/97
Mary, wid., Glemsford, 1621, (N). R2/52/327; W1/77/107
Mary, wid., Semer, 1671. R2/65/169; W1/123/35
Matthias, tanner, Bury St. Edmunds, 1686. R2/70/259; W1/140/27
Nathaniel, butcher, Nayland, 1682. R2/68/385; W1/136/88; In. 3/21/118
Nicholas, Shimpling, 1596. A5/2/219
Peter, Thorndon, 1595. A5/2/212
Phillippa, wid., Lavenham, 1591. R2/42/162; W1/48/84
Robert, Bury St. Edmunds, 1693. A5/6/162, A4/35/32
Robert, Hinderclay, 1542. R2/22/85; W1/6/38
Robert, labourer, Icklingham, 1588. R2/41/20; W1/45/15
Robert, yeo., Isleham, 1679. W7/93; In. 9/50
Robert, singleman, Kirtling, 1552. R2/31/69; W1/13/50
Robert, the elder, butcher, Lavenham, 1584. R2/39/199; W1/42/127
Robert, Stoke by Nayland, 1641. A5/4/87
Robert, cooper, Stuston, 1553. R2/31/187; W1/13/123
Robert, Whatfield, 1553. R2/31/80; W1/13/55
Robert, Wissington, 1544. R2/19/488
Simon, Nayland, 1599. R2/44/192; W1/57/19
Simon, yeo., Nayland, 1690. R2/71/307
Simon, husb., Wissington, 1607. R2/46/129
Stephen, Snailwell, 1635. A5/4/39
Stephen, yeo., Snailwell, 1641. R2/58/310; W1/98/109
Thomas, Bacton, 1566. R2/32/286; W1/28/108
Thomas, Great Bradley, 1628. R2/54/162; W1/84/35
Thomas, Hinderclay, 1582. A5/2/41
Thomas, yeo., Kirtling, 1609. R2/47/13; W1/66/12
Thomas, shearman, Nayland, 1566. R2/32/313; W1/28/76
Thomas, yeo., Stoke by Nayland, 1559. R2/28/84; W1/22/81
Thomas, yeo., Thurston, 1624. R2/53/132; W1/80/127
Walter, Isleham, 1691. In. 9/81
William, Burwell, 1599. R2/44/282; W1/57/83
William, Hawstead, 1680. In. 3/20/150; A5/6/37, A4/17/63
William, husb., Nayland, 1600. R2/45/79; W1/58/113
William, shepherd, Rushbrook, 1671. R2/65/168; W1/123/34
William, Stoke by Nayland, 1689. A5/6/125, A4/30/67
William, weaver, Sudbury, 1692. R2/72/35
William, Thwaite, 1579. A5/2/14
William, Woolpit, 1523. R2/17/22; W1/21/64
see also Waran, Waren, Waring, Warran, Warrin, Waryn, Worren, Pyrlyston als. Wareyn
WARRICK, Roger, say maker, Sudbury, 1616. R2/50/181; W1/73/171
WARRIN, Charles, yeo., Thurston, 1664. R2/63/265; W1/116/194; In. 3/9/243
WARRINER, Thomas, Ampton, 1626. R2/53/612; W1/82/140
WARRINGTON, see Harrison als. Warrington
WARRY, Thomas, Boxford, 1480. R2/11/219
WARTON, John, Milden, 1452. R2/9/111
WARWELL, Alice, wid., Lavenham, 1630. R2/55/181; W1/86/198
James, rector, Boxford, 1663. R2/63/87; W1/115/136
Richard, gent., Bury St. Edmunds, 1687. R2/70/323; W1/141/67
William, Polstead, 1460. R2/9/304
see also Worwell

WARYN, Edward, carpenter, Bury St. Edmunds, 1469. R2/2/124
Jasper, gent., Great Thurlow, 1611. R2/48/124; W1/68/135
John, the younger, Haughley, 1519. R2/12/125
John, sen., fuller, Long Melford, 1451. R2/9/106
Katherine, Bures, 1570. R2/35/20; W1/38/6
Richard, Bury St. Edmunds, 1460. R2/2/65
Thomas, sen., Bacton, 1560. R2/29/16; W1/25/164
Thomas, Preston, 1524. W1/5/47
WASBOURNE, Marion, wid., Wattisfield, 1524. R2/17/324b
WASCHERE, William, Boxford, 1516. R2/12/98
WASCHEPOKE, Eleanor, wife of William, Haverhill, 1452. R2/9/108
William, Haverhill, 1452. R2/9/108
WASE, Joan, wid., Ixworth Thorpe, 1589. R2/41/129; W1/46/1
John, Thurston, 1559. W1/95/45
Margery, wid., Edwardstone, 1599. R2/44/296; W1/57/93
Mary, Great Livermere, 1642. A5/4/98
Mary, als. Greene, Ixworth Thorpe, 1644. A5/4/105
Peter, husb., Redgrave, 1597. R2/43/362; W1/55/125
Stephen, Sudbury, 1591. A5/2/152
Thomas, Brandon, 1533. R2/19/161; W1/2/15
Thomas, husb., Edwardstone, (1640). W1/110/5
William, Great Livermere, 1638. A5/4/58
William, husb., Wortham, 1648. R2/60/149; W1/105/179
WASHBURN, Robert, Hinderclay, 1533. R2/19/140; W1/2/81
see also Wasbourne, Waysborn
WASHMAN, Katherine, Lavenham, 1441. R2/9/30
WASHSCHER, Robert, Boxford, 1470. R2/10/450
see also Waschere
WASHYNGTON, George, Burgh Castle, (1535). R2/19/214; W1/3/56
George, clerk, Wheatacre, 1535. W1/51/29
WASPE, Elizabeth, wid., Buxhall, 1698. A5/7/8
John, wid., Naughton, 1679. A5/6/18, A4/16/42
Richard, Great Cornard, (1496). R2/13/38
Robert, Aldham, 1632. A5/4/20
Robert, weaver, Groton, 1609. R2/47/115; W1/66/131
Thomas, Polstead, 1680. A5/6/39, A4/17/89
WASSE, Ellen, wid., Eye, 1541. R2/22/108; W1/10/9
Mary, wid., Groton, 1697. R2/73/172; W1/151/54
Robert, husb., Great Waldingfield, 1615. R2/49/271; W1/72/57
Robert, Groton, 1683. A5/6/66, A4/20/10
Thomas, carpenter, Edwardstone, 1586. R2/40/44; W1/43/32
WASSEN, John, Burwell, 1592. R2/42/219; W1/49/38
WASTELL, John, Bury St. Edmunds, 1515. R2/6/15
WASTELING, William, yeo., Bures, 1576. R2/37/176; W1/37/41; In. 3/1/67
WASYE, Richard, Bury St. Edmunds, 1550. R2/8/7
WATCHAM, John, yeo., Bacton, 1632. R2/56/124; W1/89/66b
Thomas, yeo., Wickham Skeith, 1683. R2/69/95; W1/137/73
WATCHEKOCKE, Robert, Redgrave, 1552. R2/23/190; W1/12/19
WATERBURY, John, yeo., Felsham, 1661. R2/62/230; W1/113/100; In. 3/6/139
Mary, wid., Preston, 1684. R2/69/273; W1/138/70
Robert, yeo., Assington, 1700. R2/74/94; W1/154/96
WATERHOUSE, Ann, wid., West Creeting, 1694. R2/72/336; W1/148/71
John, Bury St. Edmunds, 1644. A5/4/102
Tabitha, wid., Bury St. Edmunds, 1610. W1/111/37
WATERLEY, William, Hundon, 1488. R2/11/410
WATERS, Henry, Wicken, 1604. R2/45/347; W1/62/67
John, Bildeston, 1583. A5/2/50
John, pattern maker, Bury St. Edmunds, 1523. R2/6/107
John, Little Cornard, 1660. In. 3/6/207; A5/5/8, A4/1/146
John, Wicken, 1546. R2/21/225
Lydia, wid., Bury St. Edmunds, 1693. R2/72/197; W1/147/89
Robert, Mendlesham, 1560. R2/29/107; W1/25/60
Robert, Thwaite, 1583. A5/2/49
Susan, Mendlesham, 1606. A5/3/17
Thomas, turner, Haughley, 1660. R2/62/103; W1/112/135
Thomas, Haverhill, 1608. R2/46/205; W1/65/90
Thomas, Mendlesham, 1579. A5/2/18 & 22

WATERS continued
William, Bury St. Edmunds, 1470. R2/2/137
William, carpenter, Bury St. Edmunds, 1689. R2/71/239; W1/143/79
William, yeo., Eriswell, 1635. R2/56/443; W1/91/10a & b
see also Watyr
WATERTON, Alice, Bury St. Edmunds, 1595. A5/2/208
WATERWARD, Adam, Bury St. Edmunds, 1412. R2/1/127
Joan, Bury St. Edmunds, 1422. R2/1/161
WATHAM, John, Gazeley, 1478. R2/11/160
WATKINSON, Ambrose, clothier, Glemsford, 1680. In. 3/20/202; A5/6/41, A4/17/104
WATLIN, Henry, Eye, 1679. A5/6/15, A4/16/2
WATLING, Philip, Redlingfield, 1681. A5/6/49
see also Wattling
WATLOK, John, als. Smyth, Rede, 1458. R2/9/196
see also Whatlock
WATSON, Alice, wid., Soham, 1687. A5/6/110, A4/27/30
Edward, labourer, Exning, 1590. R2/41/437; W1/47/113
Henry, Exning, 1544. R2/19/445
Henry, Fordham, 1648. R2/60/22; W1/105/32
James, Isleham, 1677. In. 9/44; A12/10
James, husb., Oakley, 1622. R2/52/503; W1/78/106
John, whitener, Bury St. Edmunds, 1534. R2/7/18
John, wheelwright, Cockfield, 1558. R2/27/141; W1/7/131
John, Mildenhall, 1673. A5/5/140, A4/10/65
John, miller, Soham, 1625, (N). R2/53/386; W1/81/163
John, glover, Sudbury, 1565. R2/32/180
John, clerk, Woolpit, 1647. R2/59/374; W1/104/3; In. 3/2/8
Margaret, Haughley, 1567. R2/32/412
Margery, wid., Nayland, 1636. R2/57/5; W1/92/6
Mary, spinster, Soham, 1687. A4/27/31
Parnell, als. Browne, wife of Thomas, tanner, Mildenhall, 1573 (N). R2/36/214; W1/32/145; A5/1/266
Robert, Mildenhall, 1627. R2/54/88; W1/83/89
Samuel, weaver, Sudbury, 1666. In. 3/11/32; A5/5/73, A4/4/7
Thomas, Bury St. Edmunds, 1693. A5/6/160, A4/35/47
Thomas, Exning, 1553. R2/31/168; W1/13/112
Thomas, Haughley, 1565. R2/32/183; W1/27/118
Thomas, tanner, Kirtling, 1681. R2/68/186; W1/135/135
Thomas, yeo., Oakley, 1625. R2/53/332; W1/81/116
Thomas, yeo., Wilton, 1594. W1/51/124
see also Wattson
WATTERMAN, Henry, pail maker, Nayland, 1638. R2/57/285; W1/93/58
WATTIS, Roger, Wicken, 1539. R2/19/287, R2/20/207
WATTISFILDE, Agnes, Bacton, 1579. A5/2/19
WATTLING, John, yeo., Redlingfield, 1668. R2/64/400; W1/120/124; In. 3/13/83
John, yeo., Redlingfield, 1681. R2/68/122; W1/135/93
WATTON, George, priest, Bury St. Edmunds, 1504. R2/4/161
John, the elder, Bury St. Edmunds, 1501. R2/4/110
John, weaver, Bury St. Edmunds, 1505. R2/4/164
John, Cockfield, 1497. R2/13/80
Marian, wid., Bury St. Edmunds, 1556. R2/8/289 & 376
Robert, parson, Lawshall, 1585. R2/39/303; W1/42/278
Thomas, mercer, Bury St. Edmunds, 1459. R2/2/63
William, saddler, Bury St. Edmunds, 1422. R2/1/159
WATTS, Charles, yeo., Hopton, 1687. R2/70/385; W1/141/108
Charles, Wetheringsett, 1694. A5/6/166, A4/37/3
Dorothy, wid., Brandon, 1613, (N). R2/48/325; W1/70/105
Edward, Sudbury, 1590. A5/2/132
Eustace, blacksmith, Groton, 1698. R2/73/319; W1/152/85
Henry, husb., Wyverstone, 1624. R2/53/17; W1/80/26
James, Bury St. Edmunds, 1635. A5/4/40
Joan, wid., West Stow, 1600. R2/45/19; W1/58/26
John, Wicken, 1546. W1/10/105
Thomas, Barnham, 1591. A5/2/154
Thomas, Brandon, 1690. A5/6/132, A4/32/11

WATTS continued
Thomas, singleman, Downham, (1698), (N). R2/73/269; W1/152/46; A5/7/8
Thomas, Finningham, 1631. A5/4/16
Thomas, Hopton, 1675. In. 3/16/58; A5/5/153, A4/12/14
Thomas, Hopton, 1683. A5/6/70, A4/20/67
Thomas, Worlington, 1648. A5/4/121
William, husb., Lakenheath, 1665. R2/63/332; W1/117/77; In. 3/10/135
see also Wattis, Wattys
WATTSON, Diana, singlewoman, Elmswell, 1615, (N). R2/49/325; W1/72/103
Henry, clerk, Rickinghall Superior, 1560. R2/29/116; W1/25/51
William, Haverhill, 1560, (N). R2/29/21; W1/25/160
Winifred, wid., Soham, 1635. R2/56/470; W1/91/40
WATTYS, Robert, Tostock, 1490. R2/11/377
Simon, Downham, 1462. R2/12/22
WATYR, John, Burgate, 1504. R2/12/31
John, Eye, 1469. R2/10/451
Margaret, sen., Mendlesham, (1488). R2/11/388
William, Layham, 1503. R2/12/69
WATYRNAS, John, Norton, 1460. R2/9/281
WAULES, Henry, herdsman, Icklingham, 1568. R2/33/56; W1/29/73
WAUNCY, Edmund, Bury St. Edmunds, 1375. R2/1/36
WAYGE, John, servant, Mendlesham, 1573. R2/36/183; W1/32/97
WAYLONDE, Richard, cooper, Bures, 1608. R2/46/182; W1/65/49
WAYNE, Jane, wid., 1564. W1/27/26
WAYNER, William, Haverhill, (1483). R2/11/296
WAYNFLEET, John, als. Pyper, Boxford, 1551. R2/23/77; W1/11/80
Margaret, als. Pyper, Boxford, 1559. R2/28/402; W1/3/152
William, als. Pyper, 1626, (N). R2/53/556
WAYNFORD, Peter, sen., yeo., Soham, 1695. R2/72/474; W1/149/31
WAYSBORN, John, Hinderclay, 1474. R2/10/585
WAYTE, Alice, Bury St. Edmunds, 1431. R2/1/196
Robert, cordwainer, Bury St. Edmunds, 1370. R2/1/21
see also Marham als. Wayte
WEALDE, John, the elder, Long Melford, 1553. R2/23/97; W1/11/129
WEALY, Daniel, Mendlesham, 1673. A5/5/141, A4/10/77
Matthias, yeo., Mendlesham, 1662. R2/62/425; W1/114/186; In. 3/7/238
WEASENAM, John, labourer, Soham, 1591. R2/42/39; W1/48/30
WEAVER, Anne, wid., Little Thurlow, 1637. R2/57/221; W1/92/266
Jeffery, say weaver, Polstead, 1675. R2/66/156; W1/127/30; In. 3/16/21
John, Little Thurlow, 1611. A5/3/109
John, sen., Little Thurlow, 1638. A5/4/65
John, yeo., Little Thurlow, 1661. In. 3/6/289; A5/5/24, A4/1/14
Lambert, yeo., Little Thurlow, 1639. R2/58/36; W1/94/65
see also Wevour, Roger als. Wever
WEBB, Abigail, wid., Hundon, 1676. R2/66/411; W1/128/122; In. 3/17/156
Adam, husb., Cowlinge, 1559. R2/28/150; W1/22/137
Adam, yeo., Cowlinge, 1638. R2/57/403; W1/93/228
Adam, Lidgate, 1535. R2/19/222; W1/3/163
Agnes, als. Clarke, Barton Mills, 1573. R2/36/163; W1/32/69
Alice, Palgrave, 1465. R2/10/387
Alice, wid., Preston, 1576. R2/37/216; W1/37/77; In. 3/1/17
Ambrose, yeo., Cowlinge, 1684. R2/69/223; W1/138/29
Ann, singlewoman, Bury St. Edmunds, 1675. R2/66/130; W1/127/8; In. 3/16/38a
Ann, wid., Exning, 1680. R2/67/531; W1/134/14; In. 3/20/16
Ann, singlewoman, Wickhambrook, 1692. In. 3/24/11; A5/6/147, A4/34/5

WEBB continued

Catherine, Cowlinge, 1699. A5/7/13, A4/41/50
Christopher, yeo., Mildenhall, 1684. R2/69/251; W1/138/54
Diana, wid., Withersfield, 1660. In. 3/5/165; A5/5/8, A4/1/176
Dorothy, wid., Wickhambrook, 1676. R2/66/380; W1/128/93; In. 3/17/121
Edith, wid., Stoke, 1545. R2/19/515; W1/7/36
Edmund, Brandon, 1638. R2/57/278; W1/93/46
Edmund, Risby, 1522. R2/14/45
Edward, Kedington, 1631. A5/4/10
Edward, als. Clarke, yeo., Stradishall, 1607. R2/46/108
Elisabeth, wid., Haverhill, 1675. W1/127/155
Elisabeth, spinster, Stradishall, 1645. R2/59/268; W1/102/83
Elisabeth, wid., Wickhambrook, 1666. In. 3/11/36; A5/5/73, A4/4/13
Faith, Kersey, 1603. R2/45/256; W1/61/58
Francis, yeo., Cowlinge, 1614. R2/49/165; W1/71/112
Francis, Great Bradley, 1660. In. 3/5/198; A5/5/10, A4/1/154
Gardiner, jun., gent., Elmswell, 1669. R2/64/505; W1/121/97; A4/5/14
George, husb., Rede, 1623. R2/52/718; W1/79/130
Henry, Wickhambrook, 1679. A5/6/16, A4/16/9
Henry, yeo., Withersfield, 1647. R2/59/465; W1/104/100; In. 3/2/100
Henry, Thorpe Morieux, 1630. A5/4/3
Isaac, yeo., Burwell, 1693. R2/72/189; W1/147/79
Isabel, wid., Wickhambrook, 1556. R2/25/78; W1/16/78
James, chaplain, Bury St. Edmunds, 1428. R2/1/185
Jeffery, the elder, yeo., Wickhambrook, 1668. In. 3/13/69; A5/5/98, A4/6/90
John, Chevington, 1587. A5/2/88
John, Cowlinge, 1699. R2/73/410; W1/153/51; In. 3/26/41
John, Elmswell, 1471. R2/10/505
John, Gazeley, 1637. R2/57/203; W1/92/244
John, the elder, shearman, Glemsford, 1602. R2/45/170; W1/60/91
John, husb., Glemsford, 1647, (N). R2/59/494; W1/104/129
John, the elder, yeo., Great Bradley, 1649. R2/60/229; W1/106/81
John, Kennett, 1687. A5/6/111, A4/27/42
John, the elder, Lidgate, 1559. R2/28/408
John, Mildenhall, 1496. R2/13/76
John, sen., Palgrave, 1459. R2/9/271
John, yeo., Risby, 1587. R2/40/210; W1/44/64
John, Soham, 1545. R2/19/563; W1/7/118, W1/9/69
John, yeo., Wickhambrook, 1637. R2/57/196; W1/92/234
John, Wickhambrook, 1648. A5/4/119
John, smith, Withersfield, (1535). R2/18/140
John, yeo., Worlington, 1558. R2/27/372
Katherine, singlewoman, Bury St. Edmunds, 1675. R2/66/131; W1/127/9; In. 3/16/38b
Katherine, wid., Eye, 1562. R2/31/69; W1/8/101
Katherine, Worlington, (1542). R2/19/337
Laurence, Mildenhall, 1633, (N). W1/95/160a & b (and admon.)
Margaret, wid., Elveden, 1571. R2/35/281
Margaret, wid. of Adam, Lidgate, (1544). R2/19/431; W1/21/155
Margaret, wid., Wickhambrook, 1629. R2/54/413; W1/85/101
Nicholas, Norton, 1463. W1/24/142
Richard, Kentford, 1591. R2/42/161; W1/48/85; A5/2/159
Richard, Mildenhall, 1563, (N). R2/32/7; W1/26/63
Richard, the elder, yeo., Stansfield, 1670. R2/65/81; W1/122/99; In. 3/15/138
Richard, yeo., Wickhambrook, 1687. R2/70/571; W1/141/12
Richard, yeo., Wickhambrook, 1695. R2/72/502; W1/149/54
Robert, yeo., Barnardiston, 1663. R2/63/18; W1/115/33
Robert, tailor, Freckenham, 1628. R6/53
Robert, tailor, Glemsford, 1690. R2/71/316; W1/144/17
Robert, Risby, 1556. R2/25/7; W1/16/4
Robert, Thurlow, 1447. R2/9/86
Robert, baker, Wickhambrook, 1610. R2/47/256; W1/67/136
Robert, edge tool smith, Withersfield, 1618. R2/51/164; W1/75/100
Robert, clerk, Woolpit, (1464). R2/10/512
Robert, Worlington, 1541. R2/22/112; W1/10/16

WEBB continued
Robert, labourer, Worlington, 1563. R2/31/138; W1/26/19
Robert, clerk, Worlington, 1652. R2/61/522; W1/109/7; In. 3/4/6
Roger, Barnardiston, 1697. A5/7/1, A4/40/7
Roger, yeo., Kirtling, 1684. R2/69/219; W1/138/27
Susan, wife of John, Bradley, 1636. A5/4/45
Thomas, gent., Cowlinge, 1664. R2/63/183; W1/116/86; In. 3/10/5; A5/5/61, A4/2/78
Thomas, fustian maker, Haverhill, 1664. R2/63/181; W1/116/82; In. 3/9/161
Thomas, husb., Hawkedon, 1661. In. 3/6/161; A5/5/19, A4/1/67
Thomas, the elder, yeo., Hundon, 1663. R2/63/60; W1/115/96; In. 3/8/106
Thomas, yeo., Hundon, 1695. R2/72/516; W1/149/70
Thomas, Lidgate, 1458. R2/9/207
Thomas, husb., Mildenhall, 1559. R2/28/101; W1/22/101
Thomas, als. Clarke, cordwainer, Mildenhall, 1627. R2/54/20; W1/83/26
Thomas, fishmonger, Norwich, 1574. W1/51/240
Thomas, yeo., Wickhambrook, 1622. R2/52/398; W1/78/33
Thomas, yeo., Wickhambrook, 1648. R2/60/78; W1/105/94
Thomas, yeo., Worlington, 1580. R2/38/117; W1/39/160; A5/2/24
William, Ashley, 1686. In. 3/22/133; A5/6/106, A4/26/19
William, yeo., Barrow, 1584. R2/39/221; W1/42/105
William, the elder, yeo., Cowlinge, 1649. R2/60/244; W1/106/104
William, the elder, yeo., Cowlinge, 1696. R2/73/4; W1/150/130
William, Exning, 1679. A5/6/28, A4/16/137
William, Lidgate, 1527. R2/17/245; W1/1/37
William, tailor, Little Thurlow, 1678. R2/67/93; W1/130/76
William, Long Melford, 1450. R2/9/114
William, yeo., Mildenhall, 1603. R2/45/300; W1/61/109
William, Preston, 1568. R2/33/49; W1/29/63
William, yeo., Wickhambrook, 1583. R2/39/39; W1/42/66
see also Clarke als. Webbe, Clerke als. Webbe, Woodman als. Webbe
WEBBER, Robert, Elveden, 1557. R2/26/107; W1/20/61
William, Woolpit, 1682. In. 3/21/164; A5/6/49, A4/18/72
WEBESTER, Agnes, wid., Earl Soham, 1582. W1/51/168
WEBSTAR, Helen, wife of Robert, Chippenham, 1595. A5/2/213
Robert, vicar, Chippenham, 1595. A5/2/213
WEBSTER, Alexander, Bury St. Edmunds, 1398. R2/1/85
John, reeder, Brumstead. W1/51/117
John, parson, Langham, 1556. R2/25/49; W1/16/55
John, yeo., Mildenhall, 1643. R2/59/22; W1/100/32
Richard, Ixworth, 1451. R2/9/133
Robert, Fornham St. Martin, 1429. W1/24/43
WEBYSTERE, Peter, chaloner, Bury St. Edmunds, 1361. R2/1/9
WEDEDYN, see Spryng als. Wededyn
WEDEN, Hugh, husb., Long Melford, 1617. R2/50/295; W1/74/87
WEDERNS, John, Mildenhall, 1528. W1/19/18
WEDERTON, Richard, Hitcham, 1461. R2/10/363
WEDING, John, blacksmith, Boxford, 1661. R2/62/194; W1/113/54; In. 3/6/83
WEDYR, John, Clare, 1467. W1/24/134
John, Elmswell, 1461. R2/9/307
Robert, Norton, 1445. R2/9/69
WEDYRDENE, Mariola, Bildeston, 1449. R2/9/143
WEEDEN, Abraham, Little Cornard, 1697. A5/7/1, A4/40/5
Henry, Dalham, 1638. A5/4/58
Robert, 1651. R2/61/430
WEEDIN, William, wheelwright, yeo., Dalham, 1667. R2/64/242; W1/119/103; In. 3/12/111
WEEDING, Augustine, wheelwright, Dalham, 1663. R2/63/101; W1/115/153; In. 3/8/186
John, Depden, 1631. A5/4/16

WEEDING continued
John, Newton, 1668. A5/5/92, A4/6/32 & 33
Timothy, Chedburgh, 1636. A5/4/47
WEEDON, John, Newmarket, 1685. A5/6/94, A4/24/94
John, singleman, Soham, 1679. R2/67/472; W1/133/193
Thomas, Soham, 1672. A5/5/129, A4/9/23
WEEKES, William, Ashfield, 1585. R2/39/123; W1/42/214
see also Weikes, Wekes
WEETEN, William, husb., Barningham, 1602. R2/45/105; W1/60/15
WEETING, Alice, wid., Redgrave, 1635. R2/56/523; W1/91/107
Anne, Hepworth, 1606, (N). R2/46/27; W1/64/33
Elisabeth, wid., Redgrave, 1633. R2/56/296; W1/90/60
John, carpenter, Redgrave, 1625. R2/53/423; W1/81/208
Jonathan, yeo., Hinderclay, 1661. R2/62/299; W1/113/217; In. 3/6/263
Richard, Fakenham, 1607. A5/3/26
Robert, linen weaver, Redgrave, 1631. R2/56/22; W1/87/28
Robert, linen weaver, Redgrave, 1661. R2/62/283; W1/113/192; In. 3/6/253
WEFYN, Robert, Hawstead, 1528. R2/15/210; W1/19/24
Roger, Whepstead, 1524. R2/17/73; W1/21/18
WEGYN, William, Bures, 1477. R2/11/148
WEILOT, John, Little Saxham, 1586. R2/40/76; W1/43/60
WEKES, James, inn holder, Bury St. Edmunds, 1677. In. 3/18/56; A5/5/169, A4/14/28
WEKYS, Catherine, Great Livermere, 1522. R2/14/69
Robert, husb., Troston, 1500. R2/13/103
WELBANCKE, Leonard, Bures, 1579. A5/2/19
WELBELYE, John, Barnham, 1556. R2/25/45; W1/16/51
WELBERY, Robert, yeo., Bury St. Edmunds, 1556. R2/8/295; W1/18/25
WELBIE, John, Acton, 1553. R2/31/204
WELCH, Alice, wid., Little Wratting, (1601). R2/45/213; W1/60/143
Henry, Mildenhall, 1673. A5/5/141, A4/10/73a
Roger, Little Wratting, 1585. R2/39/234; W1/42/330
WELCHAM, John, Bury St. Edmunds, 1357. R2/1/6b
WELCHEMAN, see Gybbyn als. Welcheman
WELD, Ada, wid. of John, Woolpit, 1453. R2/9/161
Alice, Sudbury, 1571. A5/1/239
Eleanor, wid., Bildeston, 1686. R2/70/461; W1/140/74
John, clerk, Bildeston, 1665. R2/63/300; W1/117/30; In. 3/10/79, In. 3/11/100
John, Woolpit, 1442. R2/9/49
Margery, singlewoman, Long Melford, 1561. R2/30/75; W1/28/247
Sarah, Sudbury, 1637. A5/4/48
William, clothier, Boxford, 1592. R2/42/312; W1/49/136
WELETT, Margery, wid., Gislingham, 1545. R2/19/543; W1/7/70
WELHAM, Alice, wid. of Thomas, Bury St. Edmunds, 1499. R2/4/56
Ann, wid., Horningsheath, 1693. R2/72/181; W1/147/71
Daniel, Old Newton, 1685. A5/6/92, A4/24/67
Francis, Icklingham, 1698. A5/7/6
James, Layham, 1686. In. 3/22/105; A5/6/103, A4/26/51
John, baker, Bury St. Edmunds, 1401. R2/1/89
John, the elder, Horningsheath, 1559. R2/28/333; W1/22/264
John, jun., Icklingham, 1685. A5/6/90, A4/24/45
John, Icklingham, 1692. In. 3/24/76; A5/6/152, A4/34/48
Margaret, wid., Bury St. Edmunds, 1455. R2/2/47
Margaret, wid., Bury St. Edmunds, 1699. A5/7/12; A4/41/34
Nicholas, Combs, 1631. A5/4/13
Richard, butcher, Bury St. Edmunds, 1651. R2/61/472; W1/108/60
Richard, Hitcham, 1488. R2/11/431
Robert, Aldham, 1580. A5/2/28
Robert, Bildeston, (1508). R2/13/191
Robert, butcher, Bury St. Edmunds, 1696. R2/73/23; W1/150/9
Robert, husb., Combs, 1669. R2/64/480; W1/121/73; In. 3/14/117

WELHAM continued
Robert, husb., Great Horningsheath, 1601. R2/44/432; W1/59/106
Robert, the elder, husb., Hitcham, 1550. R2/21/68; W1/9/119
Thomas, weaver, Icklingham, 1694. R2/72/390
Thomas, Lackford, 1685. A5/6/94, A4/24/97
William, Bury St. Edmunds, 1524. R2/6/118
William, labourer, Bury St. Edmunds, 1581, (N). R2/38/308; W1/40/51
William, Great Horningsheath, 1462. R2/10/309
William, yeo., Great Horningsheath, 1535. R2/19/215; W1/3/180
see also Wellam
WELKISDALE, John, carver, Sudbury, 1548. R2/21/501; W1/28/151
WELL, Thomas, Walsham le Willows, 1452. R2/9/121
WELLAM, Ann, Kentford, 1530. R2/19/13
Henry, Hitcham, 1625. R2/53/432; W1/81/214
John, Hitcham, 1453. R2/9/160
John, husb., Hitcham, 1591. R2/42/55; W1/48/44
John, carpenter, Little Finborough, 1557. R2/26/249; W1/20/163
Michael, shepherd, West Stow, 1600. R2/45/17; W1/58/23
Richard, husb., Hitcham, 1557. R2/26/102; W1/20/58
Richard, singleman, Hitcham, 1606. R2/46/97; W1/64/116
Robert, Bury St. Edmunds, 1632. A5/4/21
Robert, Combs, 1599. R2/44/221; W1/57/41
Robert, Combs, 1610. R2/47/133; W1/67/13
Robert, Hitcham, 1591. R2/42/124; W1/48/113
Robert, Old Newton, 1640. A5/4/86
Thomas, Hitcham, 1557. R2/26/165; W1/20/97
Thomas, Hitcham, 1571. R2/35/177; W1/38/160
Thomas, Horningsheath, 1630. A5/4/8
Thomas, Kettlebaston, 1612. A5/3/115
WELLHAM, Isaac, jun., gent., Thorndon, 1677. R2/66/453; W1/129/30; In. 3/18/32
John, Horringer, 1564, (N). R2/32/115
John, husb., Kettlebaston, 1652. R2/61/579; W1/109/53; In. 3/4/64
Thomas, Bury St. Edmunds, 1570. A5/1/218
Thomas, the elder, webster, Great Horningsheath, 1678. R2/67/184; W1/130/162
William, Hitcham, 1527. R2/17/235
WELLIS, Agnes, wid., Walsham le Willows, 1521. R2/15/109, R2/17/4; W1/21/84
Matilda, Bardwell, 1452. R2/9/100
WELLS, Ann, wid., Dalham, 1700. R2/74/61; W1/154/59
Ann, wid., Rattlesden, 1693. R2/72/121
Catherine, wid., Isleham, 1631. R6/62
Christian, wid., Stanningfield, 1585. R2/39/277; W1/42/299
Edmund, husb., Stowupland, 1609. R2/47/18; W1/66/20
Edward, yeo., Dalham, 1685. R2/70/183; W1/139/154
Eleanor, wid., Lavenham, 1686. In. 3/22/57
Ellen, wid., Wicken, 1667. R2/64/262; W1/119/125; In. 3/12/114
Frances, wid., Bury St. Edmunds, 1688. A5/6/119, A4/29/100
George, yeo., Stowupland, 1602. R2/45/106; W1/60/18
George, yeo., Stowupland, 1664. In. 3/9/91; A5/5/58, A4/2/53
George, yeo., Stowupland, 1671. R2/65/206; W1/123/76
George, lime burner, Sudbury, 1665. R2/63/294; W1/117/24; In. 3/10/36
Gilbert, clothier, Lavenham, 1680. In. 3/20/33; A5/6/32, A4/17/16
Giles, clerk, Stowmarket, 1558. R2/27/296
James, yeo., Ingham, 1681. R2/68/125; W1/135/96
James, husb., Lawshall, 1594. R2/42/553; W1/52/40; A5/2/199
James, Rougham, 1612, (N). R2/48/211; W1/69/105
James, miller, Rattlesden, 1684. R2/69/330; W1/138/124

WELLS continued
James, sawyer, Sudbury, 1611. R2/48/7; W1/68/24
Joan, Stowmarket, 1582. R2/38/403; W1/41/33
John, clerk, Bildeston, 1666. A5/5/78, A4/4/68
John, Bury St. Edmunds, 1452. R2/2/39
John, yeo., Fornham St. Genevieve, 1638. R2/57/423; W1/93/255
John, hosier, Lavenham, 1686. R2/70/474; W1/140/86; In. 3/22/79
John, husb., Occold, 1559. R2/28/66; W1/22/68
John, husb., Redgrave, 1615. R2/49/321; W1/72/99
John, Stowmarket, 1543. R2/19/393; W1/6/128
John, Stowmarket, 1554. A5/1/89
John, the elder, Stowmarket, 1570. R2/34/4; W1/30/3; A5/1/218
John, husb., Stowmarket, 1593. R2/42/442
John, Sudbury, 1635. A5/4/36
Margaret, als. Gan, wid., Long Melford, 1598. R2/44/36; W1/56/28
Peter, husb., Edwardstone, 1603. R2/45/226; W1/61/16
Ralph, cooper, Badwell Ash, 1682. R2/68/270; W1/136/7; In. 3/21/210
Robert, Isleham, 1649. A4/1/1
Robert, Newton, 1450. R2/9/104
Robert, Redgrave, 1644. R2/59/119; W1/101/47
Robert, gent., Rougham, 1661. R2/62/161; W1/113/10; In. 3/6/36
Robert, Stowmarket, 1554. A5/1/89
Roger, Brockley, 1564. R2/32/122; W1/27/73
Roger, carpenter, Sudbury, 1666. R2/64/24; W1/118/24; In. 3/11/5
Simon, doctor of divinity, parson, Brockley, 1635, (N). R2/56/536; W1/91/117; A5/4/37
Susan, wid., Ingham, 1682. R2/68/495; W1/136/165; In. 3/21/28
Thomas, Brent Eleigh, 1680. A5/6/40, A4/17/96
Thomas, Chelsworth, 1557. R2/26/89; W1/20/51
Thomas, Fornham, 1612. A5/3/117
Thomas, sen., Isleham, 1694. In. 9/90
Thomas, Newton, 1665. In. 3/10/112; A5/5/67, A4/3/37
Thomas, Risby, 1672. A5/5/132, A4/9/51
Thomas, Risby, 1682. In. 3/21/61
Thomas, inn holder, Sudbury, 1634. R2/56/434; W1/90/219; A5/4/31
William, husb., Isleham, (1693). W7/123; In. 9/89
William, husb., Stanningfield, 1583. R2/39/9; W1/42/85; A5/2/65
William, yeo., Stowmarket, 1630. R2/55/127; W1/86/144
see also Well, Wellis, Wellys, Whiting als. Welles
WELLYE, John, Clare, 1467. W1/24/105
WELLYNG, Robert, esq., Lavenham, 1460. W1/24/20
WELLYS, John, the elder, Brockley, 1526. R2/17/188
John, tailor, Bury St. Edmunds, 1537. R2/7/42
John, the elder, Stowmarket, 1559. R2/28/290; W1/22/253
Katherine, Old Newton, 1512. R2/13/205
Margery, wife of Robert, Hartest, 1457. R2/9/216
Robert, Bury St. Edmunds, 1492. R2/4/12
Robert, Coney Weston, 1445. R2/9/67
Robert, Hartest, 1453. R2/9/145
Simon, Woolpit, 1453. R2/9/149
Thomas, Combs, 1519. R2/14/9
Thomas, Stoke by Nayland, 1462. R2/9/289
William, Bardwell, 1463. R2/10/311
William, Bury St. Edmunds, 1521. R2/6/85
WELTON, John, Cheveley, 1449. R2/9/141
John, sen., husb., Wortham, 1546. R2/21/260; W1/10/61
Nicholas, Wortham, 1559. R2/28/194; W1/22/173
Richard, husb., Wortham, 1560. R2/29/166; W1/25/8
William, husb., Burgate, 1616. R2/50/38; W1/73/38
WELWRYTHE, Bartholomew, Bury St. Edmunds, 1356. R2/1/5
WELYE, William, Mendlesham, 1559. R2/28/317; W1/22/292

WELYNGHAM, Clemency, wife of John, Glemsford, 1476. R2/11/72
Edmund, draper, Bury St. Edmunds, 1404. R2/1/102
Joan, Bury St. Edmunds, 1401. R2/1/92
John, chaplain, Bury St. Edmunds, 1420. R2/1/150
Margaret, wid., Westley, 1400. R2/1/89
WEMESE, Katherine, Ixworth, 1544. R2/19/476
WENCHARD, John, Haughley, 1633. A5/4/27
WENDEN, Christine, Bures, 1504. R2/12/34
Emma, Bures, 1444. R2/9/52
Joan, wid., Bures, 1483. R2/11/313
John, Bures, 1631. A5/4/12
WENDYE, John, sen., Clare, 1551. R2/23/11; W1/11/81
WENEFFE, John, Brettenham, 1526. R2/17/185; W1/23/48
Margaret, wid., Preston, 1559. R2/28/278; W1/22/211
WENIFFE, Robert, Lindsey, 1610. A5/3/99
see also Wenyffe, Winniffe
WENLOCK, Robert, Hepworth, 1629. R2/54/415; W1/85/103
WENNARD, Hugh, parson, Mellis, 1558. R2/27/474
WENNELL, Joan, wid., Palgrave, 1560. R2/29/99; W1/25/68
WENTE, John, Nayland, 1477. R2/11/82
Thomas, Bury St. Edmunds, 1361. R2/1/9
WENTWORTH, Thomas, gent., Bury St. Edmunds, 1517. R2/6/40
WENYFFE, George, gent., Brettenham, 1619. R2/51/479; W1/132/139
John, yeo., Troston, 1542. R2/22/2; W1/6/175
Robert, yeo., Troston, 1580. R2/38/176; W1/39/138
WEPPED, John, Bury St. Edmunds, 1370. R2/1/30
WEPSTED, John, Brettenham, 1469. R2/10/401
WERKETON, Peter, Bury St. Edmunds, 1439. R2/1/239
WERMOTHE, Richard, smith, Bury St. Edmunds, 1501. R2/4/111 (admon. only)
WESLEY, Joan, wid., Barnardiston, 1606. R2/46/74; W1/64/92
WESLY, Robert, Barnardiston, 1694. R2/72/418; W1/148/151; A5/6/173, A4/37/84
see also Westley
WESNUM, Stephen, husb., Soham, 1623. R2/52/675; W1/79/93
WEST, Ann, Ixworth, 1595. A5/2/206
Ann, singlewoman, Wyverstone, 1643. A5/4/100
Charles, singleman, Bardwell, 1599. R2/44/219; W1/57/40
Edene, wid., Oakley, 1671. A5/5/121, A4/8/11a
Edmund, clerk, 1594. W1/51/260
Edward, Bury St. Edmunds, 1694. A5/6/166, A4/35/4
Elisabeth, wid., Fornham All Saints, 1673. R2/65/393; W1/125/5
Eustace, husb., Brandon, 1573. R2/36/219; W1/32/154; A5/1/266
Henry, weaver, Badwell Ash, 1576. R2/37/151; W1/37/20; In. 3/1/99
Henry, yeo., Rickinghall Superior, 1665. R2/63/370; W1/117/120; In. 3/10/165
Henry, yeo., Wyverstone, 1625. R2/53/259; W1/81/49
Henry, yeo., Wyverstone, 1640. R2/58/128; W1/96/12
James, scrivener, Bury St. Edmunds, 1509. R2/4/209
John, the elder, Bardwell, 1557. R2/26/20; W1/20/22
John, Bardwell, 1585. R2/39/285; W1/42/291
John, draper, Bildeston, 1531. R2/18/70
John, Wyverstone, 1643. A5/4/100
Margaret, Barton Mills, 1390. R2/1/54
Nathaniel, Rickinghall, 1649. A5/4/130 & 131
Nicholas, Knettishall, 1668. In. 3/12/195; A5/5/96, A4/6/67
Richard, Ixworth, 1541. R2/22/103; W1/10/23
Richard, Long Melford, 1592. A5/2/177
Robert, husb., Wetheringsett, 1544. R2/19/479
Thomas, Bury St. Edmunds, 1646. A5/4/112
Thomas, Lakenheath, 1583. A5/2/51
William, Pakenham, 1543. R2/19/355; W1/6/148
William, Rickinghall Inferior, 1641. A5/4/90
William, husb., Wetheringsett, 1559. R2/28/64; W1/22/67
see also Baly als. West
WESTBROM, William, Wetherden, 1469. R2/10/410
WESTERBY, Ann, Bury St. Edmunds, 1685. A5/6/97, A4/24/134
Richard, cordwainer, Bury St. Edmunds, 1693. R2/72/185; W1/147/74
WESTEWOODE, Thomas, Bury St. Edmunds, 1471. R2/2/167
WESTFEILD, William, Soham, 1630. A5/4/5

WESTGATE, Andrew, Loddon, 1537. W1/51/51
Henry, yeo., Skeyton, 1574. W1/51/236
Isaac, butcher, Newmarket, 1651. R2/61/491; W1/108/82
Joseph, Burwell, 1650. A5/4/136
WESTHROPP, John, yeo., Hundon, 1635. R2/56/449; W1/91/14
John, yeo., Hundon, 1662. R2/62/323; W1/114/25; In. 3/7/63
John, yeo., Hundon, 1698. R2/73/314; W1/152/80
Joseph, yeo., Kedington, 1669. R2/64/467; W1/121/55; In. 3/14/32
Mary, wid., Kedington, 1678. R2/67/25; W1/130/25; In. 3/19/34
Thomas, gent., Hundon, 1675. R2/66/238; W1/127/109; In. 3/16/147
WESTHRUPPE, Robert, Stansfield, 1566. R2/32/318; W1/28/72
see also Westrop(e), Casgorne als. Westhorpe
WESTLEY, Henry, husb., Withersfield, 1558. R2/27/508
Nathaniel, Kentford, 1642. R2/58/351; W1/99/50
Nicholas, Withersfield, 1606. R2/46/83; W1/64/100
Robert, the elder, husb., Barnardiston, 1630. R2/55/176; W1/86/193
William, Barnardiston, 1588. A5/2/99
WESTLY, Catherine, wid., Kentford, 1648. A5/4/124
John, Great Wratting, 1668. In. 3/13/131; A5/5/100, A4/6/112
Mary, singlewoman, Soham, 1649. A5/4/130
Robert, husb., Clare, 1668. In. 3/13/147; A5/5/94, A4/6/52
William, yeo., Wickhambrook, 1699. R2/73/344; W1/153/3
see also Wesley
WESTON, Henry, Mildenhall, 1637, (N). R2/57/238; W1/92/292
John, draper, Bildeston, 1531. R2/19/62
John, Bury St. Edmunds, 1417. R2/1/140
John, Bury St. Edmunds, 1437. R2/1/227
Margery, wid., Nayland, 1620. R2/52/42; W1/76/38
William, Hempnall, (1530). W1/51/88
WESTROP(E), George, Exning, 1644. A5/4/105
John, yeo., Exning, 1647. R2/59/468; W1/104/105; In. 3/2/130
John, singleman, yeo., Exning, 1660. R2/62/59; W1/112/73; In. 3/5/64
John, Hundon, 1687. A5/6/113, A4/27/71
John, Stansfield, 1527. R2/17/258
Margery, wid., Stansfield, 1582. R2/38/426; W1/41/4
WESTROPP, Ambrose, Eye, 1639. A5/4/78
Frances, spinster, Exning, 1663, (N). R2/63/59; W1/115/93
Francis, Denston, 1646, (N). R2/59/370; W1/103/84
John, Poslingford, 1649. A5/4/126
Mary, spinster, Mildenhall, 1667. R2/64/174; W1/119/7; In. 3/12/6
Phillippa, wid., Exning, 1679. R2/67/422; W1/133/159
Simon, the elder, yeo., Exning, 1692. R2/72/82; W1/146/76; In. 3/24/4
Susan, wid., Denston, 1663. R2/63/60; W1/115/95; In. 3/8/107
Thomas, yeo., Stansfield, 1598. R2/44/70; W1/56/62
WETE, Adam, Wortham, 1501. R2/13/119
WETHEER, John, husb., Walsham le Willows, 1553. R2/31/134; W1/13/90
WETHERARD, John, sen., Stowmarket, 1453. R2/9/149
see also Wetherhard
WETHERBIE, James, husb., Haughley, 1558. R2/27/456
WETHERBY, James, wheelwright, Haughley, 1633. R2/56/251; W1/90/13
Jane, Chelsworth, 1523. R2/14/72
John, Haughley, 1647. In. 3/2/13; A5/4/112
Nicholas, Bacton, 1583. A5/2/49
Thomas, singleman, Stanton, 1664. R2/63/209; W1/116/118
see also Wethyrby, Witherbie
WETHERELL, John, wool comber, Stowmarket, (1695). R2/72/562; W1/149/116; A5/6/178, A4/38/31
WETHERHARD, John, Stowmarket, 1457. R2/9/191
Margaret, Stowmarket, 1458. R2/9/193 & 532
WETHERHED, Thomas, husb., Walsham le Willows, 1572. R2/36/43; W1/31/98
WETHER(S), Andrew, Honington, 1533. R2/19/149; W1/2/65
Edmund, Stanton, 1509. R2/12/78; W1/19/1
Edmund, Stanton, 1560. R2/29/166; W1/25/9
John, goldsmith, Bury St. Edmunds, 1568. W1/10/208
John, Honington, 1471. R2/10/479
John, yeo., Honington, 1623. R2/52/549; W1/79/9
John, Stanton, 1630. R2/55/84; W1/86/92
Matilda, wid., Stanton, 1545. R2/19/561; W1/7/61 & 62
Robert, Elmswell, 1457. R2/9/222

WETHER(S) continued
Robert, Walsham le Willows, 1477. R2/11/46
Rose, wid., Bury St. Edmunds, 1571. R2/35/265
Simon, Stanton, 1503. R2/12/57 & 62
William, Stanton, 1465. R2/10/388
WETHERYS, Andrew, singleman, Mildenhall, 1587. R2/40/183; W1/44/56
Nicholas, Mildenhall, 1559. R2/28/246; W1/22/238
WETHYR, Andrew, Stanton, 1475. R2/11/115
Edward, Elmswell, 1453. R2/9/147
John, sen., Elmswell, 1454. R2/9/152
John, Honington, 1497. R2/13/67
see also Wedyr, Wetheer, Weyther
WETHYRBY, Hugh, husb., Haughley, 1550. R2/21/162; W1/9/109
Maud, wid., Haughley, (1504). W1/7/21
WETTING, Margaret, Kersey, 1566. R2/32/280
WETTYNG, Peter, chaplain, Bury St. Edmunds, 1366. R2/1/19
WEVOUR, Richard, Great Cornard, 1452. R2/9/121
WEYLYE, William, Great Bradley, 1581, (N). R2/38/279; W1/40/25
WEYNEYLD, Simon, Chelsworth, 1464. R2/10/356
WEYTAN, Thomas, the elder, Wattisfield, 1543. R2/19/390
WEYTHER, Robert, mercer, Stanton, 1556. R2/25/94; W1/16/113
WHAIGHTES, John, labourer, Haughley, 1583. R2/39/2; W1/42/92
WHAITE, Mary, wid., Fakenham, 1687. A5/6/112, A4/27/61
WHAITES, William, yeo., Ixworth, 1698, (N). R2/74/268; A5/7/6
WHALE, Mary, Edwardstone, 1664. In. 3/9/78; A5/5/55, A4/2/12
Nicholas, yeo., Edwardstone, 1587. R2/40/175; W1/44/49
William, Boxford, 1645. A5/4/111
William, cordwainer, Edwardstone, 1697. R2/73/132; W1/151/20
Zachary, Edwardstone, 1664. A5/5/55, A4/2/13
WHALL, Margaret, als. Fuller, wid., Eye, 1680. A5/6/35, A4/17/45
WHAPLES, Hosea, yeo., Kirtling, 1622. R2/52/384; W1/78/20
Thomas, Kirtling, 1679. R2/67/385; W1/133/136
WHARTON, Ann, wid., Bury St. Edmunds, 1677. R2/66/514; W1/129/96; In. 3/18/123
John, Stuston, 1697. A5/7/5, A4/40/72
Richard, labourer, Bardwell, 1646. R2/59/369; W1/103/83
see also Warton, Worton
WHATLOCK, Robert, knacker, Rattlesden, 1622. R2/52/417; W1/78/45
Thomas, knacker, Rattlesden, 1608. R2/46/217; W1/65/120
WHATLOK, George, clothmaker, Clare, 1539. R2/20/37
John, sen., Bury St. Edmunds, 1450. R2/2/31
Margaret, wid., Lavenham, 1575. R2/37/116; W1/34/57
see also Qwatlok, Watlok
WHAYTE, Roger, the elder, husb., Ashfield, 1614. R2/49/181; W1/71/123
WHAYTES, Francis, yeo., Culford, 1621. R2/52/332; W1/77/112
WHEALAR, Margaret, Cavendish, 1553. R2/31/118
WHEATBREADE, John, clerk, Downham, 1563. A5/1/141
see also Whytbred
WHEATLEY, John, Bury St. Edmunds, 1551. R2/8/230
see also Whetele, Whytley
WHEELER, Edward, singleman, Barnardiston, 1625, (N). R2/53/280; W1/81/72
Edward, singleman, Hundon, 1665. R2/63/381; W1/117/135
Francis, miller, Exning, 1679. R2/67/222; W1/133/32
John, yeo., Hundon, 1620. R2/52/138; W1/76/121
Roger, blacksmith, Stowmarket, 1668. R2/64/394; W1/120/116; In. 3/13/161
Samuel, Sudbury, 1681. A5/6/44, A4/18/16
Thomas, yeo., Clare, 1662. In. 3/7/256; A5/5/40
Thomas, miller, Fordham, 1596. R2/43/192; W1/54/81
William, singleman, Clare, 1698. R2/73/270; W1/152/48
William, Polstead, 1638. A5/4/57
WHELER, Alice, spinster, Hundon, 1580, (N). R2/38/101; W1/39/176
WHELER, Edmund, husb., Polstead, 1585. R2/39/336; W1/42/260
Edward, yeo., Great Saxham, 1597. R2/43/338; W1/55/105
Henry, wheelwright, Alpheton, 1586. R2/40/5; W1/43/4
John, linen draper, Nayland, 1591. R2/42/34; W1/48/24
John, husb., Polstead, 1555. R2/24/139; W1/15/94
John, Stoke by Nayland, 1596. R2/43/207; W1/54/64
Robert, the elder, husb., Polstead, 1539. R2/19/313

WHELER continued
Robert, husb., Polstead, 1571. R2/35/71; W1/36/70
Roger, yeo., Polstead, 1598. R2/44/75; W1/56/75
Thomas, yeo., Barnardiston, 1619. R2/51/366; W1/132/65
Thomas, ploughwright, Hundon, 1558. R2/27/41; W1/36/55
Thomas, the elder, yeo., Hundon, 1599. R2/44/245; W1/57/58
Thomas, butcher, Stowmarket, 1696. R2/73/28; W1/150/2
William, Bury St. Edmunds, 1436. R2/1/223
William, husb., Hundon, 1558. R2/27/422
William, Hundon, (1610). W1/111/76
William, the elder, yeo., Hundon, 1617. R2/50/406; W1/74/191
William, husb., Polstead, 1579. R2/38/72; W1/39/11; A5/2/19
WHELLER, Edward, yeo., Hundon, 1640. R2/58/207; W1/96/140
Elisabeth, wid., Polstead, 1605. R2/45/424; W1/63/68
see also Qwhelere, Whealar
WHELWRYTH, William, Bury St. Edmunds, 1416. R2/1/137
see also Welwrythe
WHEPSTED, Hugo, Brettenham, 1476. R2/11/439
John, Brettenham, 1468. R2/10/407
see also Wepsted
WHETELE, Walter, singleman, Bury St. Edmunds, 1515. R2/6/18 (admon. only)
WHETLYE, Nicholas, gent., Rushbrook, 1569. R2/33/91; W1/5/58
WHETSTON, John, labourer, Burwell, 1675. In. 3/16/111; A5/5/156, A4/12/40
Katherine, wid., Burwell, 1693. R2/72/207; W1/147/98
WHIFFEN, Thomas, Horningsheath, 1685. A5/6/89, A4/24/30
WHIFFIN, Robert, Bury St. Edmunds, 1684. A5/6/86, A4/21/130
WHIFFYN, Edmund, ploughwright, Great Thurlow, 1565. R2/32/186; W1/27/174
WHIGHT, Alice, wid., Bures, 1634. R2/56/429; W1/90/216
Edward, weaver, Creeting St. Peter, 1599. R2/44/261; W1/57/68
George, Nowton, 1610. A5/3/85
George, Thelnetham, 1564. R2/32/65
Henry, yeo., Hopton, 1627. R2/54/85; W1/83/86
John, the elder, husb., Assington, 1590. R2/41/332; W1/47/24
John, labourer, Haughley, 1602, (N). R2/45/140; W1/60/59
Robert, husb., Hopton, 1600. R2/45/19; W1/58/27
Robert, the elder, linen weaver, Hopton, 1639. R2/58/2; W1/94/2
Robert, Soham, 1610, (N). R2/47/291; W1/67/181
Thomas, shearman, Bury St. Edmunds, 1583. R2/39/51; W1/42/56
Walter, husb., Botesdale, 1642. R2/58/350; W1/99/48
William, Lakenheath, 1560. A5/1/104
William, yeo., Rushbrook, 1622. R2/52/412; W1/78/42
WHIGHTING, Elias, miller, Wickhambrook, 1680. R2/67/685; W1/134/141; In. 3/20/161
William, yeo., Mendlesham, 1634. R2/56/371; W1/90/146
WHIGTEHED, Joan, wife of Robert, Bury St. Edmunds, 1443. R2/2/2
WHIGTHED, Robert, chandler, Bury St. Edmunds, 1442. R2/1/263
WHILES, Robert, Layham, 1556. R2/25/26; W1/16/26
WHIN, George, wool comber, Stoke by Nayland, 1696. In. 3/25/103; A5/6/185, A4/39/18
Mary, wid., Soham, 1639. R2/58/48; W1/94/87
WHINNEY, Robert, Troston, 1695. A5/6/177, A4/38/16
WHISKEN, Martha, wid., Hundon, 1673. R2/65/404; W1/125/21
Robert, Wickhambrook, 1673. A5/5/137, A4/10/30
WHISKIN, Thomas, tailor, Hundon, 1682. In. 3/21/227; A5/6/57, A4/19/14
WHISKING, Aaron, yeo., Hundon, 1670. R2/65/133; W1/122/160; In. 3/15/197
see also Wyskyn
WHISLAY, John, Little Waldingfield, 1672. R2/65/352; W1/124/87
Mary, wid., Long Melford, 1690. R2/71/357; W1/144/63
WHISTELEY, Robert, clothier, Lavenham, 1594. R2/42/558; W1/52/36
see also Whistlay
WHISTENE, Robert, blacksmith, Newton, 1624. R2/53/34; W1/80/48
WHISTLAY, Thomas, Little Waldingfield, 1672. A5/5/133, A4/9/67
WHISTLECROFT, Rachael, wid., Old Newton, 1673. R2/65/451; W1/125/82; A5/5/141, A4/10/70
WHISTLER, Henry, labouring man, Lakenheath, 1598. R2/44/92; W1/56/81
Richard, sen., Lakenheath, 1642. A5/4/94

WHITACKER, Thomas, labourer, Timworth, 1612. R2/48/208; W1/69/102
WHITACRE, Catherine, Bradfield St. George, 1633. A5/4/24
Samuel, Bradfield St. George, 1634. A5/4/31
WHITAKER, Ann, spinster, Braiseworth, 1680. R2/67/510; W1/134/1; In. 3/20/1
Martin, Timworth, 1615. R2/49/301; W1/72/81
William, sen., yeo., Dalham, 1688. R2/71/67; W1/142/59; In. 3/23/77
see also Whittacre, Whyteacre
WHITBEY, John, Brandon, 1577. A5/2/1
WHITBY, Susan, wid., Brandon, 1678. In. 3/19/25; A5/6/2, A4/15/13
see also Whytby, Whyttby, Witbey
WHITCROFT, George, Eye, 1635. A5/4/37
WHITE, Alice, wid., Clare, 1606. R2/46/70; W1/64/76
Anthony, carpenter, Bildeston, 1680. R2/67/546; W1/134/29; In. 3/20/31
Edward, clothier, Bury St. Edmunds, 1626. R2/53/538; W1/82/67
Edward, Soham, 1697. A5/7/5, A4/40/79
Elisabeth, wid., Herringswell, 1662. R2/62/331; W1/114/41; In. 3/7/43
Frances, wid., Thorpe Morieux, 1700. R2/74/414
George, husb., Polstead, 1602. R2/45/206; W1/60/137
Henry, rector, Rougham, 1661. R2/62/254; W1/113/140
John, Assington, 1631. A5/4/10
John, yeo., Assington, 1678. R2/67/99; W1/130/84; In. 3/19/110
John, inn holder, Bildeston, 1621. R2/52/218; W1/77/16
John, gent., Botesdale, 1652. R2/61/580; W1/109/54; In. 3/4/62
John, yeo., Brandon, 1646. R2/59/335; W1/103/51
John, yeo., Bures, 1638. R2/57/371; W1/93/174
John, gent., Bury St. Edmunds, (1672). W1/312/9
John, bach., Cotton, 1694, (N). R2/72/330; W1/148/64; A5/6/167, A4/37/16
John, husb., Newton, 1634. R2/56/421; W1/90/206
John, yeo., Thorpe Morieux, 1614. R2/49/29; W1/71/23
John, Thorpe Morieux, 1637. A5/4/49
John, yeo., Thorpe Morieux, 1673, (N). R2/65/429; W1/125/64; A5/5/139, A4/10/52
Jude, clothier, Bury St. Edmunds, 1661. R2/62/168; W1/113/19; In. 3/6/33
Margery, wid., Thelnetham, 1559. R2/28/123; W1/22/116
Mary, als. Cropley, wid., Soham, 1675. A5/5/152, A4/12/4
Nicholas, the elder, carpenter, Sudbury, 1625. R2/53/365; W1/81/144
Peter, Bures, 1554. A5/1/88
Robert, butcher, Bury St. Edmunds, 1690. R2/71/418; W1/144/122; A5/6/137, A4/32/74
Robert, Cotton, 1602. R2/45/101; W1/60/12
Robert, Great Cornard, 1649. A5/4/131
Robert, Little Cornard, 1631. A5/4/10
Samuel, Soham, 1665. R2/63/275; W1/117/2; In. 3/10/41
Sarah, singlewoman, Rattlesden, 1673, (N). R2/65/423; W1/125/49; A5/5/139, A4/10/50
Susan, spinster, Botesdale, 1644. R2/59/125; W1/101/53
Thomas, tailor, Brandon, 1669. R2/64/499; W1/121/93; In. 3/14/67
Thomas, Freckenham, 1674. In. 10/17
Thomas, clothier, Glemsford, 1592. R2/42/306; W1/48/127
Thomas, singleman, Hopton, 1690. R2/71/410; W1/144/114
Thomas, husb., Soham, 1676. In. 3/18/18
Thomas, husb., Soham, 1677. In. 3/18/141; A5/5/174, A4/14/71
Thomas, sen., husb., Soham, 1680. R2/67/532; W1/134/15; In. 3/20/17
Thomas, Soham, 1691. A5/6/140, A4/33/15
William, rector, Barnham, 1638. A5/4/68
William, yeo., Mendlesham, 1678. R2/67/36; W1/130/35
William, Stowmarket, 1584. R2/39/218; W1/42/108
see also Qwhygth, Qwyte, Whight, Whitte, Whyght, Whygth, Whyte, Whytt, Wight, Wite, Baker als. White, Bally als. White
WHITED, Thomas, yeo., Kedington, 1631. R2/56/65
WHITEFELD, Rowland, fuller, Bury St. Edmunds, 1513. R2/5/26
WHITEHAND, John, thatcher, Wattisfield, 1611. R2/48/75; W1/68/93, 94a & 95a
John, linen weaver, Wattisfield, 1646. R2/59/306; W1/103/26
see also Qwyzthand, Whithand, Whyghthand, Whytehand, Whythand, Wytehand

WHITEHEAD, Edmund, Stanton, 1625, (N). R2/53/419; W1/81/204
John, say maker, Lavenham, 1679. R2/67/306; W1/133/88
Robert, Barningham, 1662. In. 3/7/136; A5/5/33
Sara, Haverhill, 1641. A5/4/88
WHITEHED, William, clothier, Lavenham, 1664. R2/63/159; W1/116/55; In. 3/9/60; A5/5/57, A4/2/34
see also Whigtehed, Whited, Whithead, Whyghthede, Whythede, Warren als. Whitehead
WHITEING, John, grocer, Lavenham, 1686. In. 3/22/78; A5/6/101, A4/26/72
Thomas, Mendlesham, 1640. A5/4/81
Thomas, Troston, 1643, (N). R2/59/10; W1/100/15
WHITEMONTH, Thomas, Bury St. Edmunds, 1561. W1/95/47b
WHITER, George, husb., Cavendish, 1553. R2/31/52; W1/13/40
George, yeo., Risby, 1633. R2/56/249; W1/90/10
Margaret, wid., Risby, 1648. A5/4/122
Thomas, Cavendish, 1680. A5/6/38, A4/17/81
see also Whyter
WHITEROD, Richard, yeo., Hargrave, 1681. R2/68/218; W1/135/160
WHITEWOOD, Samuel, yeo., Wortham, 1687. A5/6/113, A4/27/74
Thomas, Wortham, 1683. A5/6/66, A4/20/6
see also Witwoode
WHITHAND, Thomas, carpenter, Wattisfield, 1586. R2/40/23; W1/43/17
William, linen weaver, Great Ashfield, 1692. R2/72/107; W1/146/97; In. 3/24/26
WHITHEAD, Robert, Mildenhall, 1696. R2/73/43; W1/150/47; In. 3/25/36
Thomas, grocer, Great Livermere, 1676. R2/66/363; W1/128/74; In. 3/17/91; A5/5/163, A4/13/53, 54 & 55
Thomas, the younger, glover, Kedington, 1626. R2/53/593; W1/82/123
WHITINE, Richard, 1614, (N). R2/49/198; W1/71/131
WHITING, Ann, wid., Mendlesham, 1639. R2/58/106; W1/94/174
Christian, wid., Mellis, 1566. A5/1/181
Edmund, yeo., Mendlesham, 1647. R2/59/402; W1/104/28; In. 3/2/40
Henry, Tuddenham, 1632. A5/4/19
John, Haverhill, 1639. A5/4/71
John, miller, Haverhill, 1651. R2/61/505; A5/4/138
John, husb., Icklingham, 1614. R2/49/151; W1/71/100
John, Occold, 1579. A5/2/14
Margaret, Kedington, 1578. R2/37/334; W1/36/241
Nathaniel, miller, Stoke by Clare, 1662, (N). R2/62/426; W1/114/189; In. 3/7/235; A5/5/39
Richard, Boxford, 1583. A5/2/51
Richard, Fundenhall, 1582. W1/51/160
Rose, als. Welles, Brockley, 1578. A5/2/6
Thomas, clothier, Boxford, 1593. R2/42/440; W1/50/102
Thomas, Mendlesham, 1590. A5/2/139
William, clothier, Groton, 1567. R2/32/436; W1/19/112
William, sen., carpenter, Mendlesham, 1584, (N). R2/39/154; W1/42/169a
William, the elder, Mendlesham, 1625. R2/53/234; W1/81/30
---, Elveden, 1630. A5/4/3
see also Whighting, Whiteing, Whitting, Whygtyng, Whyteing, Whyting, Scapy als. Lucas & Whiteing
WHITINGHAM, John, Eye, 1564. R2/32/56; W1/51/265
WHITLE, Richard, husb., Felsham, 1625. R2/53/436; W1/81/220
WHITOP, John, Bury St. Edmunds, 1429. R2/1/190
WHITTACRE, Richard, Ixworth, 1638. A5/4/58
William, Lidgate, 1630. A5/4/4
WHITTE, Christina, wid., Assington, 1592. A5/2/166
Thomas, yeo., Barton Mills, 1650. R2/61/326; W1/107/23; In. 3/3/22
WHITTELL, Edward, yeo., Acton, 1667. R2/64/140; W1/118/108; In. 3/12/28
William, yeo., Wattisham, 1682. R2/68/446; W1/136/130; In. 3/21/104
WHITTER, Justin, minister, Chilton, 1649. R2/60/174; W1/106/21
WHITTING, Peter, yeo., Newton, 1593. R2/42/425; W1/50/123 & 124
WHITTINGHAM, Ann, spinster, Great Cornard, 1665. In. 3/10/38
see also Whitingham, Wittingham, Whyttyngham

WHITTLE, George, yeo., Acton, 1685. R2/70/119; W1/139/106
Joan, wid., Long Melford, 1698. R2/73/266; W1/152/42
John, yeo., Lavenham, 1635. R2/56/480; W1/91/55
Judith, wid., Acton, 1683. R2/69/24; W1/137/19; In. 3/21/17
Thomas, yeo., Wattisham, 1649. R2/60/181; W1/106/27
see also Whitle, Whittell
WHITTRED, Anthony, pipe maker, Brandon, 1689. R2/71/165; W1/143/26
WHITWELL, Anne, wid., Worlington, 1596. R2/43/172; W1/54/50
see also Whytewell, Whytwell, Wyttewyll
WHODE, Ann, Long Melford, 1577. A5/2/4
WHOO, John, Redgrave, 1535. R2/19/221; W1/3/48
WHYGHT, James, Wissington, 1595. R2/43/98; W1/53/96
John, Newmarket, 1553. R2/31/154; W1/13/101
Robert, Thelnetham, 1557. R2/27/15; W1/20/24
WHYGHTHAND, Thomas, the elder, Wattisfield, 1543. R2/19/406; W1/6/99
WHYGHTHEDE, Robert, Great Wratting, 1545. R2/19/496; W1/7/71 & 100
WHYGTH, John, Fordham, 1504. R2/13/149
WHYGTYNG, William, cook, Bury St. Edmunds, 1449. R2/2/30a
WHYMERCKE, Robert, Chevington, 1557. R2/26/11; W1/20/3
WHYPHAM, Gilbert, Barnardiston, 1536. R2/18/133
James, yeo., Barnardiston, 1535. R2/18/130
WHYTBRED, Agnes, Eye, 1445. R2/9/65
WHYTBY, John, Kentford, 1573. A5/1/254
WHYTE, Elisabeth, wid., Cavendish, 1663, (N). R2/63/43; W1/115/67; In. 3/8/75
Henry, labourer, Buxhall, 1540. R2/19/619; W1/5/2
John, Bures, 1481. W1/24/94
John, yeo., Bury St. Edmunds, 1516. R2/6/27 (admon. only)
John, Hartest, 1558. R2/27/516
John, Hundon, 1516. R2/13/224
John, Kentford, 1457. R2/9/184
John, labourer, Soham, 1582. R2/38/365; W1/41/77
John, Tuddenham, 1530. R2/19/16
John, West Creeting, 1564. R2/32/112; W1/27/65
Richard, Stoke by Clare, 1476. R2/11/62
Thomas, Bury St. Edmunds, 1380. R2/1/41
Thomas, Haughley, 1462. R2/10/313
William, butler, Bury St. Edmunds, 1430. R2/1/192
William, rough mason, Mildenhall, 1563. R2/31/136; W1/26/18
William, Stowmarket, 1545. R2/21/621; W1/28/140
William, inn keeper, Sudbury, 1549. R2/21/556; W1/8/63
William, Wetheringsett, 1472. R2/10/501
WHYTEACRE, Alexander, Woodbridge, 1538. R2/20/138; W1/4/121, W1/9/58
WHYTEHAND, Robert, Culford, 1568. A5/1/199
WHYTEING, Alice, wid., Newton, 1595. A5/2/209
WHYTER, John, Cavendish, 1576. R2/37/180; W1/37/46; In. 3/1/60
Margaret, wid., Cavendish, 1553. W1/13/83
WHYTEWELL, George, Bury St. Edmunds, 1464. R2/2/82
William, Bury St. Edmunds, 1437. R2/1/230
WHYTFARE, Edmund, Bury St. Edmunds, 1506. R2/4/175
Edmund, baker, Bury St. Edmunds, 1506. R2/2/339
WHYTHAND, Thomas, labourer, Wattisfield, 1571. R2/35/313; W1/36/124; A5/1/220
WHYTHEDE, Margaret, Soham, 1451. R2/9/133
WHYTING, Henry, yeo., Mendlesham, 1634. R2/56/426; W1/90/211
Joan, wid., Wyverstone, 1572. R2/36/78; W1/31/58; A5/1/256
WHYTLEY, John, labourer, Sudbury, 1566, (N). R2/32/329; W1/28/60
WHYTLOCKE, Thomas, husb., Mildenhall, 1559. R2/28/385; W1/3/81
see also Wyttelok
WHYTNEY, Robert, parson, Ingham, 1556. R2/25/122; W1/16/189
WHYTT, Edmund, husb., Redgrave, 1588. R2/41/59; W1/45/50
John, Cavenham, 1540. R2/21/386; W1/38/72
WHYTTBY, Richard, yeo., Soham, 1585. R2/39/272; W1/42/301
WHYTWELL, John, husb., Worlington, 1592. R2/42/229; W1/49/48
WIARD, Henry, Great Horningsheath, 1663. R2/56/271; W1/90/36
WIAT, John, yeo., Newmarket, 1627. R2/54/61; W1/83/66
WIBOROWE, John, husb., Isleham, 1650. W7/53
WIBORROWE, Elisabeth, wid., Isleham, 1649. W7/49
Robert, yeo., Great Fakenham, 1685. R2/70/81; W1/139/73

WICKS, Edmund, Troston, 1587. R2/40/125; W1/44/8
Frances, wid., Fornham St. Genevieve, 1630. R2/55/55; W1/86/65
Harry, tailor, Hawstead, 1567. R2/32/380; W1/3/14
Jane, wid., Bury St. Edmunds, 1696. R2/73/54; W1/150/98
John, inn holder, Bury St. Edmunds, 1679. R2/67/219; W1/133/26
John, als. Mathew, Cavendish, 1687. A5/6/109, A4/27/22
John, bricklayer, Newmarket, 1693. R2/72/261; W1/147/146
John, Wordwell, 1663. A5/5/54
Marian, spinster, Bury St. Edmunds, 1685. R2/70/92; W1/139/83
Martin, shoe maker, Bury St. Edmunds, 1680. R2/67/695; W1/134/146; In. 3/20/205
Martin, Stowmarket, 1585. R2/39/242; W1/42/332
Miles, Newmarket, 1634. A5/4/33
Rebecca, wid., Badwell Ash, 1699. R2/73/470; W1/153/107; In. 3/26/17
Robert, butcher, Bury St. Edmunds, 1684. R2/69/188; W1/138/1; In. 3/22/2
Thomas, yeo., Barton, 1623. R2/52/711; W1/79/126
see also Wix, Wykes
WIDDOW, Nicholas, 1687. In. 11/5
WIET, Henry, yeo., Isleham, 1573. W7/37
WIFFEN, Dorothy, Haverhill, 1636. A5/4/43
Stephen, yeo., Whepstead, 1682. R2/68/466; W1/136/144; In. 3/21/57
Thomas, husb., Whepstead, 1597. R2/44/5; W1/56/7
William, baker, Rickinghall Superior, 1661. R2/62/316; W1/113/172, W1/114/15; In. 3/7/8
WIFFIN, John, husb., Lakenheath, 1648. R2/60/129; W1/105/154
Mary, spinster, Haverhill, 1649. R2/60/201; W1/106/44
Oliver, sen., husb., Whepstead, 1684. R2/69/323; W1/138/119
Richard, Withersfield, 1652. In. 3/4/42; A5/4/141
Robert, Hawstead, 1623. R2/52/715; W1/79/127
Robert, Rickinghall Inferior, 1662. In. 3/7/37; A5/5/27
Thomas, Great Bradley, 1582. R2/38/410; W1/41/26
Thomas, the elder, yeo., Horringer, 1669. R2/64/483; W1/121/75; In. 3/14/105
William, bricklayer, Bury St. Edmunds, 1661. R2/62/271; In. 3/6/233
William, yeo., Haverhill, 1630. R2/55/148; W1/86/166
see also Wefyn, Whiffen, Wyffen
WIGGEN, Robert, yeo., Stowupland, 1685. R2/70/110; W1/139/97
WIGHTE, John, Mildenhall, 1564. A5/1/155
WIGNALL, Ann, singlewoman, Great Horningsheath, 1599, (N). R2/44/208; W1/57/27
Elisabeth, Stoke by Nayland, 1587. R2/40/294
Elisabeth, Stoke by Nayland, 1592. A5/2/171
Michael, Stanningfield, 1610. A5/3/84
Robert, Stoke by Nayland, 1566. R2/32/305; W1/28/89
William, yeo., Stoke by Nayland, 1610. R2/47/141; W1/67/25
WIGNOLL, David, husb., Great Horningsheath, 1593. R2/42/450 & 473; W1/50/110
see also Wygenale, Wygnall
WIKES, Agnes, Assington, 1578. R2/37/370; W1/36/206
WILBEYE, John, Bury St. Edmunds, 1419. R2/1/147
Katherine, wid., Lavenham, 1591. R2/42/152; W1/48/91
WILBORE, Nicholas, linen draper, Stoke by Clare, 1644. R2/59/77; W1/101/3
WILBY, Robert, Wattisfield, 1588. A5/2/102
William, Oakley, 1640. A5/4/79
see also Wylby
WILCHEN, Anne, wid., Gislingham, 1625. R2/53/279; W1/81/59
WILCHINE, John, Gislingham, 1621. R2/52/267; W1/77/51
John, yeo., Stradishall, 1664. R2/63/136; W1/116/23; In. 3/9/54
see also Wylchyn
WILCOCK, Elisabeth, Great Waldingfield, 1571. R2/35/385
see also Willcock, Wylcoke
WILD, Thomas, Sapiston, 1644. A5/4/104
WILDBLUD, James, Long Melford, 1573. A5/1/256
WILDEN, Joan, wid., Bures, 1601. R2/44/346; W1/59/8
John, Pakenham, 1685. A5/6/89, A4/24/41
WILDING, Edward, Lavenham, 1673. A5/5/139, A4/10/54
Susan, wid. of David, Lavenham, 1667. R2/64/230; W1/119/84; In. 3/12/151

WILDON, Edward, tailor, Bures, 1593, (N). R2/42/428; W1/50/90
WILES, Edward, yeo., Hopton, 1662. In. 3/7/86; A5/5/30
John, bach., Braiseworth, 1682. A5/6/63, A4/19/88
William, the elder, clothier, Lavenham, 1667. R2/64/167; W1/119/2; In. 3/3/30
William, clothier, Lavenham, 1698. R2/73/324; W1/152/91
see also Whiles, Wyles
WILKENSON, Ann, Haverhill, 1610. A5/3/81
John, carpenter, Bury St. Edmunds, 1595. R2/43/82; W1/53/76
William, Lavenham, 1637. A5/4/53
WILKING(S), Ann, wid., Burwell, 1685. R2/70/203; W1/139/170
Elisabeth, wid., Burwell, 1683. R2/69/32; W1/137/26
WILKIN(S), Ann, Little Cornard, 1635. A5/4/40
John, weaver, Burwell, 1625. R2/53/417; W1/81/199
John, yeo., Burwell, 1641. R2/58/296; W1/98/81
John, yeo., Scroby, 1594. W1/51/136a
John, gent., Soham, 1673. R2/65/417; W1/125/39
Katherine, wife of Thomas, yeo., Soham, 1660. R2/62/112; W1/112/150
Robert, yeo., Kentford, 1675. R2/66/279; W1/127/147; In. 3/16/179
Simon, Burwell, 1630. A5/4/1
Simon, yeo., Burwell, 1681. R2/68/81; W1/135/61
Simon, Bury St. Edmunds, 1672. A5/5/134, A4/9/78
Simon, Bury St. Edmunds, 1691. A5/6/141, A4/33/35
Theodora, singlewoman, Great Thurlow, 1660. R2/62/94; W1/112/126; A4/3/67
Thomas, yeo., Soham, 1663. R2/63/51; W1/115/82; In. 3/8/97
William, Burwell, 1676. A5/5/160, A4/13/18
see also Wilkyng(s), Wilkyng, Wilkyn(s), Wylken, Wylkyn
WILKINSON, Benedict, Bury St. Edmunds, 1563. A5/1/149
Dorothy, wid., Bury St. Edmunds, 1596. R2/43/138; W1/54/16
John, yeo., Exning, 1695. R2/72/512; W1/149/64
John, als. Poplinton, husb., Stoke by Clare, 1549. R2/21/528; W1/8/80
Margaret, wid., Exning, 1696. R2/73/5; W1/150/29; In. 3/25/87
Nicholas, als. Poplington, Stoke by Nayland, 1573. A5/1/260
Richard, yeo., Fornham St. Martin, 1635. R2/56/510; W1/91/90
see also Wilkenson, Wilkynson, Wylkenson, Wylkynson
WILKYNG, Francis, gardener, Long Melford, 1626. R2/53/597; W1/82/125
WILKYN(S), Beatrice, Wicken, 1630. A5/4/7
John, metalman, Gislingham, 1623. R2/52/606; W1/79/55
Margaret, Burwell, 1688. A5/6/120, A4/29/51
Mark, Burwell, 1588. R2/41/97; W1/45/93
Martin, Soham, 1649. A5/4/126
Simon, bach., Great Livermere, 1685. A5/6/94, A4/24/104
William, the elder, Burwell, 1521. R2/15/143
WILKYNSON, Elisabeth, wid., Stoke by Clare, 1556. R2/25/4; W1/16/1
Patrick, Sudbury, 1567. A5/1/186
WILLCOCK, Thomas, clothier, Bures, 1615. R2/49/242; W1/72/29
WILLES, Nicholas, tailor, Mildenhall, (1536). R2/19/329
WILLESSONE, John, Bury St. Edmunds, 1458. R2/2/61
WILLET(T), Anthony, Brandon, 1641. A5/2/91
Edward, singleman, Bury St. Edmunds, 1636, (N). R2/57/62; W1/92/70
Edward, bach., Fornham, 1685. A5/6/89, A4/24/37
Henry, singleman, Eye, 1696. A5/6/189, A4/39/63
John, baker, Brandon, 1629. R2/54/380; W1/85/78
Mary, spinster, Thorndon, 1661. R2/62/225; W1/113/95; In. 3/6/121
Richard, husb., Timworth, 1627. R2/54/42; W1/83/48
Richard, Timworth, 1667, (N). R2/64/273; W1/119/136; A5/5/89, A4/5/84
Richard, Walsham le Willows, 1696. A5/6/189, A4/39/72
Robert, yeo., Westhorpe, 1606. R2/46/66; W1/64/80
Robert, gent., Westhorpe, 1650. R2/61/416; W1/107/123; In. 3/3/136
Rose, wid., West Stow, 1621, (N). R2/52/346; W1/77/126
Thomas, yeo., Little Saxham, 1623. R2/52/572; W1/79/31
see also Willitt, Wilott, Wyllett, Wyllott

WILLEYS, John, the younger, husb., Stoke by Nayland, 1521. R2/14/116
WILLIAM(S), David, Wickhambrook, 1565, (N). R2/32/238; W1/27/140
Grace, Freckenham, 1712. In. 10/41
Henry, blacksmith, Cockfield, 1684. R2/69/200; W1/138/11
John, Freckenham, 1693. W8/35; In. 10/35
John, Long Melford, 1630. A5/4/5
John, oatmeal maker, Redgrave, 1674. R2/66/6; W1/126/117
John, Stowmarket, 1642. A5/4/94
Margaret, wid., Exning, 1572. R2/36/56; W1/31/91
Richard, Saxham, 1699. A5/59/11, A4/41/9
Thomas, Exning, 1521. R2/15/151
William, Edwardstone, 1671. A5/5/126, A4/8/63
see also Williamys, Willyam, Wyllam, Wylloomes, Wyllyham, Wylyam
WILLIAMSON, Ann, wid., Wortham, 1611. A5/3/110
Christopher, Mildenhall, 1661. A5/5/21, A4/1/48
Ellen, wid., Burwell, 1629. R2/54/368; W1/85/66
John, husb., Burwell, 1628. R2/54/214; W1/84/77
John, Burwell, 1678. A5/6/7, A4/15/55
John, clerk, Fordham, 1592. A5/2/166
John, yeo., Sapiston, 1618. R2/51/228; W1/75/144
Laurence, husb., Sapiston, 1694. R2/72/282; W1/148/6
Lionel, miller, Hengrave, 1665. R2/63/360; W1/117/110; In. 3/10/150
Lionel, miller, Hengrave, 1684. R2/69/427; W1/138/204
Margaret, wid., Bury St. Edmunds, 1649. R2/60/248; W1/106/108
Margaret, wid., Sapiston, 1673. R2/65/450; W1/125/79
Mary, wid., Bury St. Edmunds, 1694. R2/72/412; W1/148/146
Richard, Knettishall, 1663. R2/63/104; W1/115/158
Robert, Sapiston, 1674. A5/5/148, A4/11/51
Thomas, Redgrave, 1580. A5/2/28
Thomas, Soham, 1594. A5/2/201
William, Bury St. Edmunds, 1679. A5/6/23, A4/16/79
William, Groton, 1593. A5/2/185
William, yeo., Hepworth, 1670. R2/65/127; W1/122/150; In. 3/15/198
William, Hepworth, 1685. R2/70/3; W1/139/3
William, husb., Worlington, 1614. R2/49/180; W1/71/122
see also Wylliyamson, Wyllyamsone, Taylor als. Wyllyamsone
WILLIAMYS, John, Bury St. Edmunds, 1471. R2/2/144
WILLINGHAM, Charles, Rede, 1685. A5/6/94, A4/24/98
Constance, wid., Hengrave, 1618. R2/51/129; W1/75/79
John, husb., Hengrave, 1613. R2/48/279; W1/70/52
Mary, wid., Brockley, 1680. R2/67/728; W1/134/167; In. 3/20/182
Thomas, Bury St. Edmunds, 1407. R2/1/118
Thomas, Rede, 1674. A5/5/150, A4/11/67
Thomas, West Stow, 1589. A5/2/118
see also Willyngham
WILLINS, Thomas, Exning, 1567, (N). R2/32/407; W1/19/84
WILLIS, Edmund, Little Whelnetham, 1665. R2/63/308; W1/117/39; In. 3/10/48
Edmund, Mildenhall, 1600. R2/45/86; W1/58/123
George, labourer, Exning, 1661. R2/62/288; W1/113/198; In. 3/6/243
George, yeo., Little Whelnetham, 1681. R2/68/121; W1/135/92
Henry, the elder, yeo., farmer, Bury St. Edmunds, 1680. R2/67/551; W1/134/35; In. 3/20/37
Joan, wid., Mildenhall, 1593. R2/42/359; W1/50/26
John, Preston, 1637. A5/4/53
Nicholas, Mildenhall, 1588. R2/41/13; W1/45/10
Richard, Knettishall, 1663. In. 3/8/207
Robert, joiner, Bury St. Edmunds, 1689. R2/71/259; W1/143/97
Samuel, yeo., Bury St. Edmunds, 1642. R2/58/352; W1/99/52
Thomas, husb., Acton, 1585. R2/39/346; W1/42/254
Thomas, singleman, Bury St. Edmunds, 1630. R2/55/92; W1/86/102
Thomas, Lavenham, 1648. A5/4/125
see also Willes, Willeys, Wills, Willys, Wylles, Wylleys, Wyllys
WILLISON, Alice, Redgrave, 1583. A5/2/50
Alice, Redgrave, 1584. A5/2/55
WILLITT, Edward, Timworth, 1610. R2/47/231; W1/67/111
Francis, yeo., Fornham All Saints, 1664. R2/63/224; W1/116/139; In. 3/9/170
Thomas, yeo., Brandon, 1681. R2/68/124; W1/135/95

WILLOUGHBY, Charles, gent., Bradfield St. George, 1639. R2/58/3; W1/94/3
WILLOWBYE, Edward, gent., Rougham, 1602, (N). R2/45/177; W1/60/100
William, Lavenham, 1590. A5/2/130
WILLOWS, Edward, yeo., Exning, 1576. R2/37/178; W1/37/44; In. 3/1/37
John, labourer, Burwell, 1616. R2/50/105; W1/73/113
John, Withersfield, 1675. In. 3/16/101; A5/5/153, A4/12/26
WILLS, Edward, Stoke by Nayland, 1579. A5/2/16
John, yeo., Sudbury, 1677. In. 3/18/135; A5/5/174, A4/14/68
Thomas, carpenter, Westhorpe, 1660. In. 3/5/26
Thomas, husb., Wortham, 1645. R2/59/211; W1/102/37
William, yeo., Wortham, 1661. R2/62/276; W1/113/182; In. 3/6/255
see also Willis
WILLSON, Edward, Isleham, 1614. R6/1
John, tailor, Burwell, 1619. R2/51/325; W1/132/41 a, b & c
John, yeo., Kirtling, 1648. R2/60/129; W1/105/153
Susan, wid., Stoke, 1684. R2/69/203; W1/138/15
Thomas, linen weaver, Rickinghall Inferior, 1670. In. 3/15/37
WILLY, John, shearman, Bury St. Edmunds, 1597. R2/43/326; W1/55/92
John, Stoke by Nayland, 1632. A5/4/22
WILLYAM, Anthony, sen., husb., Isleham, 1622. R6/33
WILLYNGHAM, John, Glemsford, 1476. R2/11/58
WILLYS, Robert, carpenter, Sudbury, 1629, (N). R2/54/344; W1/85/51
Thomas, maltster, Bury St. Edmunds, 1561. R2/8/360; W1/17/45
Thomas, bricklayer, Bury St. Edmunds, 1622. R2/52/408; W1/78/41
WILLYSON, Ellen, wid., Semer, 1568. W1/95/53
WILOTT, Isabel, wid., Bury St. Edmunds, 1512. R2/5/17
WILSHIRE, Seth, Haverhill, 1662. A5/5/32
Thomas, Haverhill, 1694. R2/72/362; W1/148/89
WILSON, Abraham, Nayland, 1582. A5/2/42
Anne, wid., Bury St. Edmunds, 1670. A5/5/115
Henry, inn holder, Bury St. Edmunds, 1643. R2/59/5; W1/100/8
James, shearman, Nayland, 1576. R2/37/21; In. 3/1/4
Joan, wid., Sudbury, 1593. R2/42/436; W1/50/97
John, husb., Burwell, 1575. R2/37/86; W1/34/7
John, Burwell, 1641. A5/4/88
John, comber, Bury St. Edmunds, 1663. In. 3/8/96; A5/5/47
John, Long Melford, 1559. R2/28/213; W1/22/195
John, husb., Mendlesham, 1660. In. 3/5/84; A5/5/4, A4/1/214
John, Soham, 1688. In. 3/23/62; A5/6/120, A4/29/49
Margaret, wid., Burwell, 1669. R2/64/476; W1/121/66; In. 3/14/116
Margaret, wid., Bury St. Edmunds, 1534. R2/7/19
Nicholas, miller, malt grinder, Bury St. Edmunds, 1688. R2/71/7; W1/142/5; In. 3/23/73
Richard, labourer, Brandon, 1678. R2/67/137; W1/130/122; In. 3/19/173
Richard, Knettishall, 1663. A5/5/51
Richard, rector, Rattlesden, 1614. R2/49/154; W1/71/103
Robert, Exning, 1586. A5/2/83
Stephen, labourer, Soham, 1683. R2/69/11; W1/137/12
Thomas, shepherd, Lakenheath, 1612. R2/48/137; W1/69/18
Thomas, linen weaver, Redgrave, 1670. R2/65/26; W1/122/28
Thomas, Soham, 1671, (N). R2/65/158; W1/123/21
Thomas, husb., Stuston, 1648. R2/60/96; W1/105/116
Thomas, Troston, 1652. A5/4/142
Valentine, inn holder, Bury St. Edmunds, 1689. R2/71/282; W1/143/117
William, dyer, Bury St. Edmunds, 1504. R2/4/155
William, Elmsett, 1586. A5/2/75
see also Willessone, Willison, Willson, Willyson, Wyllson, Wyllyson, Wylson
WILTON, John, Creeting St. Peter, 1607. A5/3/22
John, Isleham, 1567. W7/30
see also Wylton
WILTSHIRE, see Griggs, als. Wiltshire, Wilshire
WILYS, Richard, Creeting All Saints, 1668. In. 3/13/183; A5/5/96, A4/6/76
WIMARKE, John, Great Saxham, 1587. R2/40/263; W1/44/102

WINCH, Margaret, wid., Stoke by Clare, 1648. A5/4/120
Prudence, singlewoman, Stoke by Clare, 1648. A5/4/120
Richard, Long Melford, 1589. A5/2/113b
Thomas, blacksmith, Clare, 1620, (N). R2/52/69; W1/76/59
see also Wynch
WINCOL, Amy, gentlewoman, Denham, 1592. R2/42/280; W1/49/96
WINDE, John, Stowlangtoft, 1582. R2/38/425; W1/41/6
see also Wynde
WINDELL, Robert, bishop of Emly, co. Tipperary, Bury St. Edmunds, 1441. R2/1/253
WINDOUT, Elisabeth, wid., Bardwell, 1625. R2/53/257; W1/81/47
John, yeo., Bardwell, 1591. R2/42/51; W1/48/42
Robert, yeo., Bardwell, 1679. R2/67/213; W1/133/21
Rose, wid. of Robert, Bardwell, 1683. R2/69/76; W1/137/57
William, Bardwell, 1612. R2/48/125; W1/69/1
see also Wyndout, Pennall als. Windout
WING, Andrew, husb., Mildenhall, 1604, (N). R2/45/348
Andrew, victualler, Mildenhall, 1662. R2/62/430; W1/114/195
Isaac, Mildenhall, 1660. In. 3/5/72; A5/5/2, A4/1/228
James, husb., Mildenhall, 1662. R2/62/321; W1/114/22; In. 3/7/58
John, yeo., Icklingham, 1661. R2/62/290; W1/113/202; In. 3/6/279
John, singleman, Icklingham, 1663. In. 3/8/73; A5/5/46
John, singleman, husb., Mildenhall, 1667. R2/64/228; W1/119/81; In. 3/12/91
John, yeo., Mildenhall, 1678. R2/67/106; W1/130/90; In. 3/19/117
Margaret, wid., Little Barton, 1672. R2/65/355; W1/124/90; A5/5/127, A4/8/71 & 72
Margaret, Mildenhall, 1618. R2/51/233; W1/75/149
Richard, labourer, Little Barton, 1673. R2/65/452; W1/125/83
Richard, yeo., Mildenhall, 1610. R2/47/303; W1/67/194
Richard, Mildenhall, 1671. R2/65/178; W1/123/48
Simon, husb., Mildenhall, 1617. R2/50/308; W1/74/96
Thomas, singleman, Haverhill, 1619, (N). R2/51/473; W1/132/133
Thomas, Lakenheath, 1618. R2/51/10; W1/75/3
Thomas, Mildenhall, 1596. R2/43/182
Thomas, Mildenhall, 1672. R2/65/356; W1/124/91
Thomas, yeo., Mildenhall, 1683. R2/69/48; W1/137/37
Thomas, Mildenhall, 1694. R2/72/284; W1/148/8
see also Wyng
WINGFEILD, Thomas, Long Melford, 1700. A5/7/14, A4/41/83
WINGFELD, Thomas, gent., Layham, 1686. R2/70/465; W1/140/77; In. 3/22/54
WINGFIELD, John, gent., Ipswich, 1594. W1/51/259
see also Wyngfyld
WINIFFE, John, carpenter, Little Livermere, 1682. R2/68/327; W1/136/46; In. 3/21/121
WINKE, Roger, husb., Bacton, 1648. R2/60/48; W1/105/62
Thomas, linen weaver, Bradfield St. George, 1638. R2/57/396; W1/93/212
Thomas, the elder, cook, Haughley, 1669. In. 3/14/13; A5/5/104, A4/7/34
William, yeo., Brockford, 1696. R2/73/16; W1/150/14; In. 3/25/72
see also Wynck, Wynke
WINN, John, the elder, yeo., Alpheton, 1682. R2/68/422; W1/136/114; In. 3/21/112
Robert, yeo., Brundon, 1700. R2/74/50; W1/154/47
see also Wynne
WINNEY, George, Lindsey, 1681. R2/68/214; W1/135/157; A5/6/53, A4/18/119
see also Whinney, Wynney
WINNIFFE, Bland, tailor, Timworth, 1693. R2/72/120
John, Timworth, 1695. A5/6/178, A4/38/35
Nicholas, Coney Weston, 1570. A5/1/233
Richard, Timworth, 1693. A5/6/162, A4/35/36
Robert, the elder, yeo., Troston, 1621. R2/52/315; W1/77/93
see also Weneffe, Wenyffe, Winiffe, Wynefe, Wynnyff
WINNOW , John, yeo., Thurston, 1689. R2/71/239; W1/143/78
see also Wynnow

WINTER, Elisabeth, wid., Bury St. Edmunds, 1637. R2/57/192; W1/92/230
Elisabeth, wid., Hopton, 1661. In. 3/6/236; A5/5/23, A4/1/31
James, cordwainer, Barningham, 1676. In. 3/17/104; A5/5/163, A4/13/60
John, carpenter, Exning, 1627. R2/54/14; W1/83/17
John, husb., Thorndon, 1612. R2/48/227; W1/69/127
Margaret, spinster, Bury St. Edmunds, 1700. R2/74/33; W1/154/32
Morusco, spinster, Bury St. Edmunds, 1700. R2/74/63; W1/154/62
Nicholas, husb., Worlington, 1626. R2/53/468; W1/82/16
Oliver, ploughwright, Exning, 1642. W1/110/9
Ralph, clothworker, Bury St. Edmunds, 1636. R2/57/112; W1/92/135
Robert, Bardwell, 1691. A5/6/144, A4/33/68
Walter, yeo., Bradfield St. George, 1617. R2/50/378; W1/74/162
William, husb., Downham, 1602. R2/45/197; W1/60/125
William, yeo., Worlington, 1618. R2/51/39; W1/75/21
see also Wynter
WINTERBORNE, William, Wicken, 1682. In. 3/21/228; A5/6/56, A4/19/2
WISBITCH, Peter, wheelwright, Little Thurlow, 1612. W1/69/143
see also Wysbeche, Toftys als. Wysbeche
WINTERFLOD, Katherine, wid., Assington, 1629. R2/54/379; W1/85/77
WINTERFLOOD, John, Long Melford, 1648. A5/4/122
Thomas, tanner, Nayland, 1667. R2/64/222; W1/119/74; In. 3/12/99
WISBETCHE, William, wheelwright, Hundon, 1588. R2/41/16; W1/45/12
WISBICH, Michael, Mildenhall, 1589. A5/2/116
Nicholas, yeo., Little Thurlow, 1611. R2/47/315; W1/68/11
Peter, Little Thurlow, 1660. In. 3/5/191; A5/5/10
WISEMAN, Elisabeth, singlewoman, Long Melford, 1629. R2/54/376; W1/85/74
Henry, Wickham Skeith, 1642. A5/4/95
James, yeo., Wickhambrook, 1665. In. 3/10/128; A5/5/69, A4/3/65
Joanna, wid., Rede, (1479). R2/11/189
John, blacksmith, Brome, 1646. R2/59/364; W1/103/77
Martha, wid. of James, Wickhambrook, 1665. R2/63/388; W1/117/142; In. 3/10/170
Mary, Thurston, 1637. A5/4/52
Samuel, Bury St. Edmunds, 1691. A5/6/145, A4/33/76
Thomas, Great Finborough, 1606. A5/3/5
Thomas, Thurston, 1637. A5/4/50
see also Wyseman
WISKE, Robert, Shelland, 1555. A5/1/96
WITBEY, William, shepherd, Brandon, 1669. R2/64/428; W1/121/9; In. 3/14/47
WITE, Benedict, husb., Mendlesham, 1635. R2/56/472; W1/91/42
WITHAM, Edmund, Buxhall, 1687. A5/6/111, A4/27/46
Thomas, wid., clerk, Chilton, 1684. A5/6/80, A4/21/67
WITHEAT, Henry, cordwainer, Lavenham, 1696. In. 3/25/12; A5/6/186, A4/39/23
Isaac, collar maker, Lavenham, 1693. R2/72/218; W1/147/107
WITHERBIE, Thomas, yeo., Stowlangtoft, 1652. R2/61/592; W1/109/68; In. 3/4/86
WITHERBY, Agnes, wid., Shelland, 1637. A5/4/51
Joan, Haughley, 1608. A5/3/52
John, yeo., Stowlangtoft, 1671. R2/65/148; W1/128/7
Lawrence, yeo., Haughley, 1606. R2/46/19; W1/64/21
Margaret, wid., Haughley, 1651. R2/61/427
Thomas, singleman, Bury St. Edmunds, 1690. A5/6/136, A4/32/59
see also Wetherbie, Wytherby
WITHERELL, Margaret, wid., Thelnetham, 1693. A5/6/163, A4/35/25
see also Wythereld
WITHER(S), Elias, Burgate, 1678. In. 3/19/90; A5/6/6, A4/15/46
John, sen., yeo., Drinkstone, 1694. R2/72/282; W1/148/7
John, Honington, 1641. A5/4/88
Robert, lime burner, Stanton, 1619. R2/51/431; W1/132/103
Thomas, blacksmith, Woolpit, 1595. R2/43/118; W1/53/119
see also Wyther(s)

WITT(E), Thomas, yeo., Wortham, 1638. R2/57/318; W1/93/95
Thomas, yeo., Wortham, 1666. R2/64/138; W1/118/104; In. 3/11/133
see also Wytte
WITTIN, Steven, barber, Rickinghall Superior, 1677. R2/66/496; W1/129/76; In. 3/18/94
WITTINGAM, Ann, singlewoman, Great Cornard, 1665. R2/63/315; W1/117/49
WITWOODE, Thomas, the elder, saddler, Wortham, 1636. W1/110/6
WIX, Geoffrey, Great Cornard, 1665. In. 3/10/158; A5/5/70, A4/3/76
James, labourer, Mildenhall, 1617. R2/50/341; W1/74/124
John, linen weaver, Bury St. Edmunds, 1634, (N). R2/56/416; W1/90/200
John, Norton, 1608. A5/3/50
Martin, tailor, Bury St. Edmunds, 1602. R2/45/181; W1/60/107
Robert, Thelnetham, 1592. R2/42/329; W1/49/150
Robert, husb., Troston, 1588. R2/41/55; W1/45/48
William, Bury St. Edmunds, 1672. A5/5/128, A4/9/9
William, singleman, Bury St. Edmunds, 1687. R2/70/344; W1/141/81
William, Norton, 1684. A5/6/81
William, husb., Thelnetham, 1602. R2/45/203; W1/60/133
William, Troston, 1592. A5/2/168
see also Wicks, Wyxe
WODCROFTE, Robert, Bury St. Edmunds, 1579. A5/2/14
WODE, Eva, Bury St. Edmunds, 1412. R2/1/130
John, draper, Bury St. Edmunds, 1447. R2/2/21
John, Bury St. Edmunds, 1448. R2/2/26
John, Cowlinge, 1461. R2/9/282
Richard, Drinkstone, 1461. R2/9/272
Richard, Drinkstone, 1471. R2/10/429b
Richard, Stowmarket, 1585. A5/2/72
Simon, Mildenhall, 1526. R2/17/168; W1/23/65
Walter, Bury St. Edmunds, 1444. R2/2/9
WODEHYLL, John, Thrandeston, 1476. R2/11/61
WODELEFF, Thomas, cooper, Bury St. Edmunds, 1452. R2/2/37
see also Buntyng als. Wodeleff
WODEMAN, John, Sudbury, 1457. R2/9/191
WODENORTON, John, Bury St. Edmunds, 1361. R2/1/9
WODER, Margaret, wid., Lavenham, 1587. R2/40/221; W1/44/68
Thomas, Sudbury, 1592. A5/2/160
WODERIS, John, Mildenhall, 1504. R2/12/126
WODERYS, Robert, Mildenhall, 1452. R2/9/156
WODESEY, Stephen, Nayland, 1459. R2/9/268
Thomas, Stoke by Nayland, 1457. R2/9/190
WODEWARD, Robert, Lakenheath, 1482. R2/11/369
WODWARDE, Roger, Kersey, 1588. A5/2/99
WODSTOK, Thomas, Stoke by Nayland, 1478. R2/11/150
WODTHORPE, John, Lavenham, 1537. R2/20/36; W1/4/31
WODYE, Solomon, husb., Stowmarket, 1613. R2/48/249a; W1/70/22
WOLBETERE, Thomas, baker, Bury St. Edmunds, 1378. R2/1/45
see also Wollebetere
WOLBY, Thomas, Bury St. Edmunds, 1605. R2/45/437; W1/63/81
WOLDE, Edward, bowyer, Bury St. Edmunds, 1474. R2/2/189
WOLFE, Anne, wid., Bury St. Edmunds, 1584. R2/39/197; W1/42/130
Robert, Burwell, 1632. A5/4/18
see also Wulfe
WOLFHALE, Alexander, Bury St. Edmunds, 1404. R2/1/100
WOLLEBETERE, John, tailor, Bury St. Edmunds, 1428. R2/1/184
WOLLERT, William, Great Bradley, 1560. R2/29/28; W1/25/151
WOLLEMAN, Alice, wife of Geoffrey, Bury St. Edmunds, 1407. R2/1/114
WOLLEY, Edward, Bury St. Edmunds, 1566. A5/1/176
WOLLOK, John, Clare, 1440. R2/9/21
WOLLWARD, Bartholomew, tailor, Hartest, (1625). W1/111/68
WOLLYE, Edward, Bury St. Edmunds, 1628. R2/54/173; W1/84/48
WOLMAN, Agnes, wife of John, Bury St. Edmunds, 1406. R2/1/112
John, Bury St. Edmunds, 1406. R2/1/111
WOLNARD, Richard, tanner, Bury St. Edmunds, 1396. R2/1/83
WOLNAWE, Jane, wife of Lewis, Eye, 1567. A5/1/192

WOLNORTH, Margaret, Sapiston, 1525. R2/17/114; W1/21/110
WOLRYCH, Cary, gent., Cowlinge, 1675. R2/66/187; W1/127/61; In. 3/16/76
WOLSTON, Israel, Sudbury, 1644. A5/4/101
see also Woollarston, Wulston
WOLVERSTON, Gilbert, singleman, Timworth, 1603. R2/45/302; W1/61/112
WOLWARD, Edward, Stoke by Clare, 1582. A5/2/40
Robert, pail maker, Wickham Skeith, 1559. R2/28/78; W1/22/79
William, bottle maker, Bury St. Edmunds, 1556. R2/8/294; W1/18/23
WOMBE, John, Great Cornard, 1461. R2/9/278
WOOBY, Margaret, wid., Elveden, 1571. W1/36/117
WOOD, Alice, wid., Cotton, 1551. R2/23/83; W1/11/82
Alice, Great Waldingfield, 1590. A5/2/133
Alice, Lavenham, 1476. R2/11/68
Ann, wid., Bury St. Edmunds, 1525. R2/6/125
Ann, wid., Ixworth, 1638. A5/4/67
Anthony, tailor, Downham, 1604. R2/45/447; W1/63/93
Edward, bricklayer, Old Newton, 1665. R2/63/310; W1/117/42; In. 3/10/74
Etheldred, Soham, 1600, (N). W1/58/121
George, als. Davey, wheelwright, Bures, 1606. R2/46/56; W1/64/72
George, victualler, Bures, 1688. R2/70/308; W1/141/52
George, miller, Creeting All Saints, 1632. W1/89/6
Giles, clerk, Oakley, 1631. R2/56/100; W1/87/152
Henry, husb., Ixworth, 1611. R2/47/317; W1/68/14
Henry, Rickinghall, 1486. R2/11/321
Henry, Withersfield, 1572. A5/1/250
Hugh, wheelwright, Brent Eleigh, 1606. R2/46/4; W1/64/6
Isabel, wid. of John, Sudbury, 1477. R2/11/74
James, Combs, 1565. R2/32/237
Jeffery, yeo., Stoke by Nayland, 1624. R2/53/21; W1/80/32
Joan, wid., Bildeston, 1549. R2/21/517; W1/8/56
Joan, Glemsford, 1647. In. 3/2/124; A5/4/119
John, Bildeston, (1536). R2/18/168
John, shoe maker, Bury St. Edmunds, 1482. R2/2/338
John, miller, Buxhall, 1559. R2/28/371; W1/3/143
John, Combs, 1612. R2/48/153; W1/69/35
John, Elmswell, 1452. R2/9/109
John, Glemsford, 1542. R2/22/81; W1/6/40
John, Great Ashfield, 1562. R2/31/113
John, the elder, husb., Hitcham, 1542. R2/22/20; W1/6/76 & 79
John, the younger, Hitcham, 1593. R2/42/424; W1/50/85
John, Ixworth, 1553. R2/31/1
John, Lavenham, 1670. In. 3/15/116; A5/5/116
John, warden of the hospital, Long Melford, 1671. R2/65/237; W1/123/116
John, joiner, Stowmarket, 1564. R2/32/98; W1/27/47
John, yeo., Stradishall, 1649. R2/60/287; W1/106/159
Margaret, spinster, Bury St. Edmunds, 1593. A5/2/193
Margaret, Great Finborough, 1582. R2/38/358
Margery, Aspal, 1607. A5/3/38
Mary, als. Peters, Bures, 1687. A5/6/110, A4/27/33
Mary, wid., Fornham All Saints, 1639. A5/4/70
Matilda, Ixworth, 1461. R2/9/287
Nicholas, Great Thornham, 1453. R2/9/159
Peter, husb., Ixworth, 1577. R2/37/255
Ralph, Semer, 1599. R2/44/168; W1/57/2
Richard, Bury St. Edmunds, 1637. A5/4/53
Richard, Hitcham, 1559. R2/28/44; W1/22/47
Richard, the younger, singleman, Ixworth, 1582. R2/38/373; W1/41/68; A5/2/35
Richard, carpenter, Ixworth, 1600. R2/45/41; W1/58/59
Richard, butcher, Stowmarket, 1669. R2/64/441; W1/121/28
Richard, yeo., Stradishall, 1621. R2/52/216; W1/77/14
Robert, yeo., Aspal, 1621. R2/52/347; W1/77/127
Robert, the younger, Bildeston, 1546. R2/21/615; W1/28/147
Robert, yeo., Bildeston, 1563. R2/32/21
Robert, Brettenham, 1591. A5/2/149
Robert, shearman, Bury St. Edmunds, 1531. R2/7/1

WOOD continued
Robert, Combs, 1617. R2/50/253; W1/74/52
Robert, clothier, Glemsford, 1612. R2/48/226; W1/69/125
Robert, Hitcham, 1542, (N). R2/22/15; W1/6/6
Roland, gent., Fordham, 1690. R2/71/315; W1/144/15
Thomas, butcher, Bury St. Edmunds, 1597, (N). R2/43/347; W1/55/111
Thomas, clothier, Cavendish, 1666. R2/64/77; W1/118/53; In. 3/11/77
Thomas, Cheveley, 1591, (N). R2/42/29; W1/48/20
Thomas, yeo., Wetherden, 1686. R2/70/265; W1/140/33; In. 3/22/69; A5/6/101, A4/26/73a
Thomas, Withersfield, 1508. W1/9/23
see also Whode, Wode
WOODALL, Elisabeth, wid., Culford, 1652. R2/61/574; W1/109/47; In. 3/4/53
Josias, Brome, 1697. R2/73/160; W1/151/46
Prudence, wid., Little Stonham, 1697. R2/73/212; W1/151/98
Thomas, Brome, 1632. A5/4/18
William, vicar, Stoke by Nayland, 1565. A5/1/164
see also Wodehyll, Wudhall, Taylor als. Woodale
WOODARD, John, inn holder, Bury St. Edmunds, 1699. R2/73/405; W1/153/48
WOODBOURNE, John, husb., Brandon, 1576. R2/37/133; W1/37/4; In. 3/1/118
WOODBRIDGE, Agnes, Burwell, 1585. R2/39/256; W1/42/318
John, the elder, Burwell, 1675. R2/66/161; W1/127/36; In. 3/16/44
John, Burwell, 1694. A5/6/169, A4/37/37
Luke, the elder, yeo., Burwell, 1661. R2/62/292; W1/113/204; In. 3/6/280
Margaret, wid., Burwell, 1664. R2/63/123; W1/116/3; In. 3/9/32
Robert, Burwell, 1591. R2/42/32; W1/48/23
Thomas, husb., Burwell, 1625. R2/53/398; W1/81/179
WOODBURNE, Ann, wid., Bury St. Edmunds, 1700. R2/74/121; W1/154/117
George, Bury St. Edmunds, 1693. A5/6/160, A4/116/48
Henry, butcher, Soham, 1609. R2/47/14, W1/66/14
Henry, Soham, 1635. A5/4/41
James, apothecary, Bury St. Edmunds, 1611. R2/48/60; W1/68/83
James, gent., Bury St. Edmunds, 1623. R2/52/719; W1/79/132
James, tailor, Bury St. Edmunds, 1669. R2/64/546; W1/121/135; In. 3/14/130
Joan, wid., Soham, 1617. R2/50/353; W1/74/134
Simon, yeo., Brandon, 1559. R2/28/175; W1/22/159
see also Woodbourne
WOODCOCK, John, Onehouse, 1639. A5/4/71
Richard, Isleham, 1561. W7/24
Thomas, Walsham le Willows, 1611. A5/3/113
WOODCOKE, Elisabeth, wid., Newton, 1571. R2/35/251; W1/38/118
William, Newton, 1569. A5/1/210
WOODCRAFT, George, cooper, Wetherden, 1648. R2/60/138; W1/105/166
WOODCROFT, George, als. Thatcher, Haughley, 1602, (N). R2/45/142; W1/60/63
Michael, als. Thatcher, husb., Haughley, 1598. R2/44/38; W1/65/34
see also Wodcrofte
WOODER, John, Lavenham, 1577. A5/2/5
see also Woder, Berymell als. Woder
WOODFEN, Robert, Sudbury, 1584. R2/39/138; W1/42/189
WOODGATE, Andrew, Preston, 1674. A5/5/147, A4/11/21
Richard, yeo., Wattisham, 1693. R2/72/162
Thomas, Kersey, 1688. A5/6/119, A4/29/30
Thomas, cordwainer, Wetherden, 1696. R2/73/109; W1/150/125; A5/6/184, A4/39/3
William, wool comber, Lavenham, 1689. R2/71/174; W1/143/32
William, yeo., Rattlesden, 1603. R2/45/250; W1/61/51
WOODHOUSE, John, Eriswell, 1682. In. 3/21/215; A5/6/58, A4/19/27
WOODIE, James, husb., Stowupland, 1619. R2/51/355; W1/132/57

WOODMAN, William, als. Webbe, Eye, 1559. R2/28/229; W1/22/183
see also Wodeman
WOODROWE, John, yeo., Great Livermere, 1681. R2/68/217;
W1/135/159
WOODRYSE, Richard, Mildenhall, 1475. R2/11/111
see also Woderis, Wydrysse
WOODS, Elisabeth, wid., Bury St. Edmunds, 1642. R2/58/382;
W1/99/90
Elisabeth, wid., Great Ashfield, 1661. In. 3/6/71; A5/5/11, A4/1/150
Francis, Mildenhall, 1568. R2/33/7; W1/29/14
George, yeo., Creeting All Saints, 1669. In. 3/14/124;
A5/5/108, A4/7/52
Gregory, gent., Risby, 1668. In. 3/13/84
Henry, Withersfield, 1662. In. 3/7/18; A5/5/26
James, Stowmarket, 1662. A5/5/27
John, say maker, Cavendish, 1671. R2/65/198; W1/123/67
John, Euston, 1630. A5/4/6
John, yeo., Felsham, 1665. R2/63/307; W1/117/35; In. 3/10/85
John, Hepworth, 1688. In. 3/23/42; A5/6/119, A4/29/33
John, Little Cornard, 1634. A5/4/30
John, Mildenhall, 1606. A5/3/5
John, Mildenhall, 1624. R2/33/91; W1/80/99
John, wheelwright, Rickinghall Inferior, 1616. R2/50/143;
W1/73/146
John, Westhorpe, 1697. A5/7/1, A4/40/3
Joseph, linen weaver, Thrandeston, 1683. R2/69/96; W1/137/74
Richard, yeo., Ixworth, 1667. R2/64/273; W1/119/137;
In. 3/12/138
Richard, brick burner, Long Melford, 1686. In. 3/22/107;
A5/6/98, A4/26/103
Robert, the elder, Clare, 1674. R2/66/47; W1/126/73
Robert, inn holder, Clare, 1684. R2/69/389; W1/138/172
Robert, Old Newton, 1694. A5/6/169, A4/37/38
Samuel, carpenter, yeo., Brome, 1700. R2/74/101; W1/154/105;
In. 3/27/65
Simon, Mildenhall, 1628. R2/54/142; W1/84/12
Susan, wid., Icklingham, 1680. R2/67/718; W1/134/163;
In. 3/20/181
Susan, als. Cooke, Wetherden, 1686. R2/70/265; W1/140/32;
In. 3/22/69
Thomas, tailor, Icklingham, 1600. R2/45/36; W1/58/53
Thomas, cordwainer, Kentford, 1663. R2/63/114; W1/115/174;
In. 3/8/234
Thomas, labourer, Lakenheath, 1622. R2/52/487; W1/78/97
Thomas, Withersfield, 1670. In. 3/15/130; A5/5/115
Walter, Mellis, 1609. A5/3/78
William, the elder, Bury St. Edmunds, 1679. A5/6/26, A4/16/116
William, the elder, wool comber, Cavendish, 1662. R2/62/330;
W1/114/38; In. 3/7/39
William, the elder, say weaver, Cavendish, 1692. R2/72/96;
W1/146/88; In. 3/24/17
William, labourer, Isleham, 1616. R6/12
William, Mildenhall, 1637. A5/4/54
WOODSIDE, Robert, Sudbury, 1685. A5/6/90, A4/24/53
Thomas, baker, Sudbury, 1685. R2/70/63; W1/139/55
WOODWARD, Ann, singlewoman, Pakenham, 1625, (N). R2/53/307;
W1/81/92
Catherine, wid., Freckenham, 1631. R6/64
Edward, knacker, Bury St. Edmunds, 1680. In. 3/20/225; A5/6/42,
A4/17/117
Jeffery, Thorpe Morieux, 1635. A5/4/36
Joan, wid., Hengrave, 1628. R2/54/172; W1/84/47
John, Gislingham, 1634. A5/4/27
John, Mendlesham, 1639. A5/4/77
John, Mildenhall, 1660. In. 3/5/70; A5/5/2, A4/1/227
John, husb., Mildenhall, 1671. R2/65/190; W1/123/58
Richard, linen weaver, Mendlesham, 1589. R2/41/135; W1/46/142
Richard, husb., Mendlesham, 1629. R2/54/416; W1/85/104
Robert, baker, Eye, (1634). W1/111/46
Thomas, Flempton, 1681. R2/68/118; W1/135/90; A5/6/49,
A4/18/66

WOODWARD continued
Thomas, Fornham All Saints, 1699. A5/7/13, A4/41/47
Thomas, thatcher, Mendlesham, 1598. R2/44/48; W1/56/38
Thomas, Woolpit, 1607. A5/3/34
William, husb., Cavendish, 1556. R2/25/90; W1/16/118
William, collar maker, Fornham All Saints, 1663. R2/63/32; W1/115/51; In. 3/8/72
see also Wodeward
WOODY, Cicely, wid., Stowmarket, 1571. R2/35/165
Susan, wid., Wattisham, 1687. A5/6/115, A4/27/92
William, yeo., Naughton, 1681. R2/68/43; W1/135/36
see also Wodye, Woodie
WOOLLARSTON, Mary, spinster, Sudbury, 1686. A5/6/98, A4/26/105
WOOLLEY, Susan, wid., Bury St. Edmunds, 1628. R2/54/252; W1/84/113
see also Wolley, Wollye
WOOLMAN, Thomas, yeo., Barrow, 1642. R2/58/335; W1/99/28
see also Wolleman, Wolman, Parken als. Wolman, Parkin als. Wolman, Parkyn als. Wullman, Parkyn als. Wulman
WOOLNER, Simon, husb., Euston, 1625. R2/53/392; W1/81/171
WOOLNOUGH, William, Eye, 1687. A5/6/111, A4/27/49
see also Wolnawe, Wylnoth
WOOLWARD, John, Clare, 1608. A5/3/13
Mary, wid., Redgrave, 1650. A5/4/135
Richard, husb., Stradishall, 1666. R2/64/12; W1/118/12; In. 3/11/11
Roger, Redgrave, 1672. A5/5/133, A4/9/65
Thomas, Stoke by Nayland, 1635. A5/4/42
Thomas, Thurston, 1503. R2/13/145
see also Wollward, Wolward, Wulward
WOORD, John, Bury St. Edmunds, 1644. A5/4/103
WOORLICHE, William, Wickhambrook, 1593. R2/42/397; W1/50/63
WOORLYCHE, Peter, Felsham, 1573. A5/1/270
WORD, see Woord, Wurde, Ford als. Word, Gipps als. Worde
WORDALL, John, Bury St. Edmunds, 1610. A5/3/86
WORDLEY, George, Shimpling, 1594. A5/2/200
John, Hartest, 1639. A5/4/73
WORDLY, John, yeo., Hartest, 1684. R2/69/407; W1/138/187
Thomas, Felsham, 1579. R2/38/31; W1/39/45
William, maltster, Lavenham, 1685. R2/70/120; W1/139/107
WORDWELL, Edith, Bury St. Edmunds, 1585. A5/2/72
WORKEMAN, John, surgeon, Palgrave, 1590. R2/41/362; W1/47/58
WORLAND, Thomas, Boxford, 1550. R2/21/47; W1/10/184
WORLECHE, John, yeo., Wickhambrook, 1558. R2/27/499
WORLEDGE, Edward, the elder, tailor, Denston, 1668. R2/64/360; W1/120/72; In. 3/13/88
John, Mendlesham, 1680. A5/6/34, A4/17/37
John, Weston, 1660. In. 3/5/28; A5/5/2
Mary, Weston, 1660. A4/1/230
Richard, linen weaver, Thelnetham, 1640. R2/58/182; W1/96/101
William, maltster, Bury St. Edmunds, 1660. R2/62/52; W1/112/65; In. 3/5/45
William, tailor, Denston, 1622. R2/52/397; W1/78/31
William, Thelnetham, 1661. In. 3/6/89; A5/5/15, A4/1/104
WORLICH(E), Edward, sen., Denston, 1684. R2/69/316; W1/138/112
John, Flempton, 1596. R2/43/195; W1/55/82
Richard, als. Flecher, Mildenhall, 1468. R2/10/414
William, labourer, Denston, 1681. R2/68/255; W1/135/194
WORLIDGE, Helen, Thelnetham, 1639. R2/58/89; W1/94/150
Susanna, wid., Denston, 1678. In. 3/19/226; A5/6/14, A4/15/123
Thomas, singleman, Thelnetham, 1637. R2/57/138; W1/92/30
William, maltster, Bury St. Edmunds, 1686. R2/70/272; W1/140/37; In. 3/22/67
WORLYCH(E), Annice, Stanstead, 1494. R2/13/15
Joan, Ixworth, 1457. R2/9/187
see also Warlyche, Woorliche, Wyrlych, Brown als. Worlyche, Orage als. Worlidge, Orange als. Worlidge, Raynoldes als. Worlidge
WORMALL, Adam, the elder, Mildenhall, 1633. A5/4/27 & 38
Adam, the younger, Mildenhall, 1634. A5/4/31

WORNER, John, als. Fletcher, Wood Ditton, 1642. R2/58/366; W1/99/66
WORREN, John, husb., Wattisfield, 1688. R2/71/19; W1/142/17; In. 3/23/25
WORTH, Edward, labourer, Rattlesden, 1678. R2/67/130; W1/130/115; In. 3/19/161
Elisabeth, wid., Chelsworth, 1687. R2/70/284; W1/141/27
Francis, the elder, Chelsworth, 1678. In. 3/19/152; A5/6/10, A4/15/83
Francis, butcher, Chelsworth, 1682. R2/68/302; W1/136/30; In. 3/21/226
John, butcher, Hitcham, 1652. R2/61/604; W1/109/83; In. 3/4/100
John, Wattisham, 1642. A5/4/96
Richard, Rattlesden, 1645. A5/4/107
see also Grimwade als. Worth
WORTHAM, Ann, Boxford, 1585. A5/2/66
Robert, Stoke by Clare, 1561. R2/30/35; W1/28/224
Robert, singleman, Stoke by Clare, 1582. R2/38/395; W1/41/43
Robert, Stoke by Nayland, 1515. R2/13/218
Thomas, clothier, Boxford, 1571. R2/35/341; W1/36/130
Thomas, yeo., Clare, 1600. R2/45/29; W1/58/43
see also Wurtham
WORTON, John, innkeeper, Bury St. Edmunds, 1665. R2/63/309; W1/117/41; In. 3/10/75
Margaret, wid., Mildenhall, 1602. R2/45/207; W1/60/139
WORTS, John, Downham, 1672. A5/5/133, A4/9/69
WORWELL, James, Boxford, 1663. R2/63/87
WOTTON, Agnes, wid., Sudbury, 1590, (N). R2/41/419
Francis, inn holder, Rattlesden, 1686. R2/70/455; W1/140/66; In. 3/22/1
John, gent., Tuddenham, 1668. R2/64/397; W1/120/117; In. 3/13/164
Roger, gent., Hunston, 1672. R2/65/306; W1/124/28
Thomas, Oxford, 1474. R2/2/193
WRAGG(E), Francis, inn holder, Bury St. Edmunds, 1679. R2/67/287; W1/133/72
Richard, Bury St. Edmunds, 1608. A5/3/40
Richard, Soham, 1600. R2/45/13; W1/58/21
WRANGYLL, Katherine, wife of William, Thrandeston, 1448. R2/9/94
WRATTAM, William, Stanningfield, 1563. A5/1/147
WRAW, Hugh, butcher, Bury St. Edmunds, 1419. R2/1/148
WRECHE, Walter, Long Melford, 1462. R2/9/291
WREN(N), Agnes, wife of John, Drinkstone, 1558. R2/27/135
Elisabeth, wid., Drinkstone, 1540. R2/21/362; W1/38/82
John, Drinkstone, 1563. R2/31/168; W1/26/49
John, gent., Drinkstone, 1568. R2/33/58; W1/29/78
Lionel, Great Thornham, 1630. A5/4/2
Robert, Thwaite, 1560. R2/29/147; W1/25/28
WRENCH, Ann, Boxford, 1596. A5/2/222
Henry, husb., Soham, 1586. R2/40/13; W1/43/11
Joan, wid., Soham, 1586. R2/40/65; W1/43/52
John, husb., Soham, 1593. R2/42/455; W1/50/113
WRETHAM, Robert, chirurgeon, Bury St. Edmunds, 1609. R2/47/100; W1/66/118
WRETHE, Thomas, Soham, 1461. R2/9/295
Thomas, Thurston, 1512. R2/13/206
WREYGHT, William, Polstead, 1476. W1/24/118a
WRIGHT, Abraham, yeo., Cowlinge, 1689. R2/71/253; W1/143/92
Abraham, Lawshall, 1638. R2/57/375; W1/93/179
Abraham, Lawshall, 1651. A5/4/138
Adam, Stanstead, 1686. In. 3/22/127; A5/6/105, A4/26/25
Agnes, als. Corner, wid., Stradbroke, 1574. W1/51/232
Alice, spinster, Aspal, 1661. R2/62/221; W1/113/87; In. 3/6/117
Alice, Fornham St. Martin, 1523. R2/14/72
Alice, als. Hardy, wid., Lawshall, 1680. A5/6/39, A4/17/83
Alice, Thorndon, 1641. A5/4/90
Alice, wid., 1565. R2/32/157; W1/27/98
Ambrose, Cowlinge, 1678. In. 3/19/179; A5/6/11, A4/15/98
Ambrose, yeo., Lawshall, 1679. R2/67/417; W1/133/154

WRIGHT continued
Ambrose, cordwainer, Lawshall, 1689. R2/71/218; W1/143/62
Andrew, yeo., Thurston, 1631. R2/56/2; W1/87/3
Ann, wid., Little Thurlow, 1691. R2/71/468; A5/6/141, A4/31/37
Ann, wid., Stanton, 1682. In. 3/21/157; A5/6/61, A4/19/60
Anne, wife of Ambrose, Clare, 1635, (N). R2/56/502; W1/91/78
Anthony, yeo., Bradfield St. George, 1676. R2/66/335; W1/128/40; In. 3/17/32
Barnaby, yeo., Bradfield St. George, 1687. R2/70/356; W1/141/89
Benjamin, yeo., Shimpling, 1664. R2/63/163; W1/116/61; In. 3/9/1
Bennett, yeo., Thurston, 1631. R2/56/67; W1/87/98
Cornelius, tailor, Ixworth, 1638. R2/57/363; W1/93/161
Daniel, singleman, Cavendish, 1646. R2/59/290; W1/103/4
Daniel, yeo., Newton, 1694. R2/72/320; W1/148/48
Dorothy, Lawshall, 1644. A5/4/104
Edmund, yeo., Layham, 1644. R2/59/160; W1/101/86
Edmund, yeo., Mildenhall, 1614. R2/49/32; W1/71/27
Edmund, husb., Soham, 1620. R2/52/126; W1/76/110
Edward, Pakenham, 1647, (N). R2/59/464; W1/104/97
Edward, yeo., Tostock, 1660. R2/62/78; W1/112/100; In. 3/5/111
Edward, gent., Tostock, 1665. R2/63/383; W1/117/136; In. 3/10/162
Edward, Tostock, 1675, (N). R2/66/195; W1/127/72; In. 3/16/87; A5/5/155, A4/12/36
Elisabeth, wid., Bury St. Edmunds, 1577. R2/37/252
Elisabeth, Bury St. Edmunds, 1630. A5/4/3
Elisabeth, als. Mower, wid., Coney Weston, (1598), (N). R2/44/12; W1/56/12
Elisabeth, als. Reve, gentlewoman, Cotton, 1589. R2/41/275; W1/46/33
Elisabeth, wid., Mildenhall, 1622. R2/52/488; W1/78/98
Elisabeth, wid., Polstead, 1666. R2/64/6; W1/118/7; In. 3/11/44
Emma, wid., Hessett, 1592. R2/42/214; W1/49/31
Francis, husb., Icklingham, 1617. R2/50/326; W1/74/113
Francis, blacksmith, Lawshall, 1683. R2/69/44; W1/137/35
Francis, shoe maker, Walsham le Willows, 1632. R2/56/195; W1/89/107
George, smith, Acton, 1625. R2/53/218; W1/81/19
George, yeo., Bradfield St. George, 1681. R2/68/89; W1/135/67
George, yeo., Clare, 1637. R2/57/158; W1/92/197
George, Redlingfield, 1682. In. 3/21/235; A5/6/65, A4/19/115
George, Rougham, 1638. A5/4/62
Giles, husb., Acton, 1553. R2/31/166; W1/13/110
Grizel, wid., Tostock, 1677. R2/66/436; W1/129/9
Grizel, wid., Tostock, 1680. A5/6/42, A4/17/127
Helen, wid., Great Wratting, 1569. A5/1/206
Henry, Brandon, 1670. In. 3/15/166; A5/5/115
Henry, husb., Lawshall, 1637. R2/57/231; W1/92/281
Henry, yeo., Lawshall, 1649. R2/60/235; W1/106/89
Hester, spinster, Sudbury, 1695. A5/6/176, A4/38/4
Hugh, yeo., Bildeston, 1600. R2/45/75; W1/58/107
Hugh, Brandon, 1634. A5/4/32
Hugh, Lindsey, 1593. A5/2/191
Hugh, yeo., Wattisham, 1591. R2/42/9; W1/48/6
Isabel, Haverhill, 1692. R2/72/88; W1/146/82; In. 3/24/14
James, gent., Bury St. Edmunds, 1592. R2/42/273; W1/49/93
James, sen., husb., Lavenham, 1660. R2/62/105; W1/112/138; In. 3/5/148
Joan, wid., Lawshall, 1573, (N). R2/36/197; W1/32/124; A5/1/267
Joan, wid., Little Waldingfield, 1612. W1/95/110
John, husb., Bradfield St. George, 1575. R2/37/117; W1/34/58
John, yeo., Bradfield St. George, 1610. R2/47/203; W1/67/83
John, yeo., Bradfield St. George, 1618. R2/51/122; W1/72/76
John, yeo., Bradfield St. George, 1666. R2/64/70; W1/118/49; In. 3/11/76

WRIGHT continued
John, yeo., Bradfield St. George, 1670. R2/65/62; W1/122/75; In. 3/15/91
John, sen., yeo., Bradfield St. George, 1687. R2/70/358; W1/141/90
John, yeo., Bradfield St. George, 1694. R2/72/304; W1/148/32
John, inn holder, Brandon, 1664. R2/63/238; W1/116/159; In. 3/9/234
John, yeo., Brettenham, 1670. R2/65/35; W1/122/40; In. 3/15/43
John, tanner, Bury St. Edmunds, 1606. R2/46/43; W1/64/58
John, Bury St. Edmunds, 1607. A5/3/31
John, yeo., Chevington, 1677. R2/66/485; W1/129/66; In. 3/18/82
John, clothmaker, Clare, 1524. R2/17/41; W1/21/46
John, clothmaker, Clare, 1533. R2/19/173 & 204; W1/2/71
John, yeo., Cockfield, 1672. R2/65/316; W1/124/39
John, yeo., Hartest, 1599. R2/44/214; W1/57/34
John, als. Campion, husb., Hunston, 1575. R2/37/119; W1/34/61
John, Ingham, 1569. A5/1/209
John, yeo., Ixworth Thorpe, 1674. R2/66/106; W1/126/13
John, Lavenham, 1682. In. 3/21/129; A5/6/62, A4/19/85
John, husb., Lawshall, 1578. R2/37/348
John, Lawshall, 1634. A5/4/31
John, Lawshall, 1642. A5/4/93
John, the elder, yeo., Lawshall, 1673. R2/65/438; W1/125/66
John, yeo., Lawshall, 1685. R2/70/130; W1/139/115
John, Lidgate, 1680. A5/6/40, A4/17/100
John, Long Melford, 1586. A5/2/77
John, Mildenhall, 1595. A5/2/206
John, Nayland, 1684. A5/6/74, A4/17/1
John, Newmarket, 1604. R2/45/340; W1/62/56
John, the elder, bricklayer, Ousden, 1667. In. 3/12/166; A5/5/89, A4/5/85
John, blacksmith, Rede, 1618. R2/51/61; W1/75/36
John, carpenter, Soham, 1678. R2/67/169; W1/130/149; In. 3/19/199b; A5/6/63
John, bach., Soham, 1682. A5/6/63, A4/19/96
John, locksmith, Stowmarket, 1660. R2/62/114; W1/112/152; In. 3/5/175
John, yeo., bricklayer, Stowmarket, 1686. R2/70/445; W1/140/59; In. 3/22/34
John, als. Camplyon, yeo., Stowupland, 1592. R2/42/204; W1/49/27
John, sen., Stowupland, 1641. A5/4/91
John, wheelwright, Sudbury, 1635. R2/56/532; W1/91/114
John, Sudbury, 1662. A5/5/28
John, husb., Tuddenham, 1625. R2/53/202; W1/81/5
Joseph, Bury St. Edmunds, 1675. In. 3/16/124; A5/5/157, A4/12/53
Joseph, Lawshall, 1609. A5/3/65
Josias, Horningsheath, 1683. A5/6/71, A4/20/83
Katherine, wid., Great Barton, (1664). W1/312/17
Katherine, wid., Great Barton, 1695. R2/72/454; W1/149/9
Katherine, wid., Norton, 1600. R2/45/85; W1/58/122 & 127
Lawrence, gent., Drinkstone, 1680. A5/6/38, A4/17/78
Lawrence, the elder, yeo., Tostock, 1661. R2/62/236; W1/113/109; In. 3/6/138
Lawrence, yeo., Tostock, 1666. R2/63/94; W1/118/68; In. 3/11/142
Lydia, Bury St. Edmunds, 1690. A5/6/132, A4/32/14
Lydia, Rattlesden, 1670. A5/5/119
Mabel, wid., Lawshall, 1591. R2/42/117; W1/48/116b
Mark, bach., Soham, 1682. A5/6/63, A4/19/95
Martin, als. Mower, husb., Coney Weston, 1592. R2/42/190; W1/49/14
Mary, wid., Lawshall, 1652. R2/61/606; W1/109/86
Nicholas, East Dereham, (1537). W1/51/64
Ralph, husb., Lawshall, 1603. R2/45/261; W1/61/69
Ralph, husb., Lawshall, 1649. R2/60/233; W1/106/87
Ralph, yeo., Lindsey, 1600. R2/45/35; W1/58/52
Reginald, husb., Mildenhall, 1585. R2/39/264; W1/42/308

WRIGHT continued
Richard, yeo., Badwell Ash, 1552. R2/31/53; W1/13/41
Richard, Bradfield Combust, 1587. A5/2/90
Richard, yeo., Combs, 1680. R2/67/619; W1/134/85; In. 3/20/94
Richard, miller, Kedington, 1680. R2/67/697; W1/134/148; In. 3/20/168
Richard, Lakenheath, 1584. A5/2/60
Richard, Nayland, 1565. A5/1/169
Richard, bricklayer, Wickhambrook, 1651. R2/61/445
Richard, glover, Woolpit, 1638. R2/57/415; W1/93/238
Robert, bricklayer, Barnardiston, 1676, (N). R2/66/364; W1/128/75; In. 3/17/85
Robert, Bradfield Combust, 1536. R2/19/239
Robert, Bradfield St. George, 1582. A5/2/40
Robert, yeo., Bradfield St. George, 1693. R2/72/257; W1/147/144
Robert, Gazeley, 1648. A5/4/125
Robert, Hessett, 1577. R2/37/302
Robert, joiner, Stowmarket, 1633. R2/56/268; W1/90/33
Robert, Wattisham, 1589. A5/2/127
Samuel, yeo., Bradfield St. George, 1670. R2/65/135; W1/122/163; In. 3/15/207
Silvester, Fordham, 1525. R2/12/132
Simon, mercer, Bury St. Edmunds, 1553. R2/8/59; W1/21/194
Simon, Chevington, 1696. A5/6/190, A4/39/83
Simon, maltster, Mildenhall, 1599. R2/44/322; W1/57/113
Susan, wid., Lidgate, 1684. R2/69/395; W1/138/178
Thomas, yeo., Bildeston, 1626. R2/53/664; W1/82/190
Thomas, Bradfield St. George, 1681. A5/6/54, A4/18/123
Thomas, wool comber, Brandon, 1684. R2/69/314b; W1/138/110
Thomas, smith, Brent Eleigh, 1561. R2/30/81; W1/28/271
Thomas, butcher, Bury St. Edmunds, 1625. R2/53/330; W1/81/114
Thomas, cooper, Bury St. Edmunds, 1643. R2/59/65; W1/100/73
Thomas, carpenter, inn holder, Bury St. Edmunds, 1687. R2/70/566; W1/141/5; In. 3/23/57
Thomas, Bury St. Edmunds, 1690. A5/6/132, A4/32/13
Thomas, Exning, 1635. A5/4/38
Thomas, gent., Hartest, 1648. R2/60/57; W1/105/75
Thomas, gent., Hawkedon, 1662. R2/62/362; W1/114/90; In. 3/7/113
Thomas, shepherd, Icklingham, 1625. R2/53/361; W1/81/140
Thomas, yeo., Lawshall, 1622. R2/52/472; W1/78/86
Thomas, yeo., Lindsey, 1572. R2/36/42; W1/31/96
Thomas, Little Waldingfield, 1560. A5/1/104
Thomas, husb., Mildenhall, 1605. R2/45/426; W1/63/71
Thomas, husb., Mildenhall, 1679. R2/67/420; W1/133/156
Thomas, Soham, 1544. R2/21/598
Thomas, maltster, Stoke by Clare, 1617. R2/50/243; W1/74/42
Thomas, 1585. R2/39/264; W1/42/309
Walter, carpenter, Barnardiston, 1648, (N). R2/60/81; W1/105/98
Walter, Brettenham, 1560. R2/29/164; W1/25/11
William, yeo., Bildeston, 1698. R2/73/317; W1/152/84
William, Bradfield, 1589. W1/46/47 (inventory only)
William, Bradfield St. George, 1644. A5/4/102
William, yeo., Clare, 1605. R2/45/383; W1/63/11
William, Hartest, 1612. R2/48/185; W1/69/67
William, locksmith, Haughley, 1679. R2/67/227; W1/133/37
William, Hundon, 1642. R2/58/332; W1/99/23
William, yeo., Kettlebaston, 1681. R2/68/112; W1/135/86
William, Kirtling, 1663. A5/5/48
William, Langham, 1667. In. 3/12/12; A5/5/82, A4/5/23
William, tailor, Langham, 1693. R2/72/145
William, yeo., Lawshall, 1649. R2/60/195; W1/106/38
William, butcher, Lidgate, 1671. R2/65/156; W1/123/18
William, labourer, Mildenhall, 1627. R2/54/129; W1/83/129
William, glover, Pakenham, 1608. R2/46/216; W1/65/116
William, carpenter, Pakenham, 1674. R2/66/94; W1/126/27
William, labourer, Rougham, 1591. R2/42/113; W1/48/120
William, labourer, Wattisfield, 1694. R2/72/286; W1/148/11

WRIGHT continued
see also Right, Write, Wryght, Wyrythe, Camplion als. Wright, Camplyn als. Wright, Camplyn als. Wryght, Camplyon als. Wryght, Myller als. Wright, Myller als. Wryght, Scott als. Wright
WRINCH, John, Boxford, 1610. A5/3/97
WRITE, Henry, yeo., Bradfield St. George, 1638. R2/57/357; W1/93/152
Hugh, Bildeston, 1557. R2/26/153; W1/20/101
John, maltster, Lidgate, 1699. R2/73/434; W1/153/73
William, yeo., Stowupland, 1682. R2/68/352; W1/136/65; In. 3/21/163
WRITTE, Thomas, husb., Lindsey, (1610). R2/47/260; W1/67/142
WROE, Dorcas, spinster, Little Thornham, 1675. R2/66/214
Henry, husb., Little Thornham, 1661. R2/62/246; W1/113/127; In. 3/6/193
Thomas, linen weaver, Little Thornham, 1634. R2/56/323; W1/90/89
WROKTON, Agnes, wid., Bury St. Edmunds, 1445. R2/2/15
WROO, Elise, Haughley, 1526. R2/17/200; W1/23/32
Henry, Rickinghall Superior, 1461. R2/9/273
Joan, Eye, 1475. R2/11/97
John, husb., Yaxley, 1540. R2/20/163; W1/4/139
Robert, Yaxley, 1609. R2/47/19; W1/66/21
Thomas, husb., Yaxley, 1574. R2/37/32; W1/33/57
WROTH, Anthony, gent., Cotton, 1698. R2/73/298; W1/152/69
WROTHAM, Edward, Bury St. Edmunds, 1361. R2/1/16
Edward, draper, Bury St. Edmunds, 1456. R2/2/28
Henry, Bury St. Edmunds, 1396. R2/1/83
Marion, Bury St. Edmunds, 1399. R2/1/88
WRYGH, Agnes, Brome, 1454. R2/9/230
Beatrice, wid. of John, sen., Wortham, 1462. R2/9/291
Richard, Glemsford, 1458. R2/9/201
Robert, Sudbury, 1451. R2/9/137
WRYGHT, Andrew, Bradfield St. George, 1547. R2/21/297; W1/7/123
Helen, Great Wratting, 1559. R2/28/213; W1/22/196
Helen, Great Wratting, 1565. A5/1/165
Hugh, Little Finborough, 1503. R2/12/64
James, cordwainer, Bury St. Edmunds, 1597. R2/43/269 & 320; W1/55/46
James, Lindsey, 1579. R2/38/49; W1/39/39
Joan, singlewoman, Lawshall, 1575. W1/95/11
Joan, wid., Lawshall, 1590. R2/41/376; W1/47/70
John, Barway, 1442. R2/9/48
John, Chilton, 1474. R2/11/18
John, the elder, Lawshall, 1537. R2/20/35
John, the elder, Lawshall, 1540. R2/20/154 & 156; W1/4/28 & 131, W1/36/25
John, husb., Lawshall, 1559. R2/28/331; W1/22/290
John, oatmeal maker, Lawshall, 1565. R2/32/232; W1/27/147
John, Mildenhall, 1537. R2/20/7; W1/4/6
John, Soham, 1471. R2/10/481
John, als. Camplyon, Stowmarket, 1558. R2/27/15; W1/31/5
John, Wickham, 1458. R2/9/239; W1/24/127
Katherine, wid., Badwell Ash, 1559. R2/28/290; W1/22/254
Katherine, Bury St. Edmunds, 1531. R2/7/2
Nicholas, Little Saxham, 1573. R2/36/212; W1/32/140
Richard, Bures, 1462. R2/10/327
Richard, saddler, Bury St. Edmunds, 1439. R2/1/239
Richard, Hitcham, 1440. R2/9/28
Richard, Hitcham, 1503. R2/12/64
Richard, yeo., Kersey, 1540. R2/20/293; W1/4/221
Richard, labourer, Shimpling, 1558. R2/27/267
Robert, ash burner, Boxford, 1565. R2/32/264
Robert, Brettenham, 1484. R2/11/289
Robert, glazier, Bury St. Edmunds, 1550. R2/8/48
Robert, yeo., Lindsey, 1603. R2/45/236; W1/61/29
Robert, Soham, 1475. R2/11/91
Roger, Thrandeston, 1481. R2/11/225
Simon, Bury St. Edmunds, 1403. R2/1/97
Simon, Cotton, 1446. R2/9/89
Simon, Stanstead, 1503. R2/13/144
Stephen, Bury St. Edmunds, 1413. R2/1/132

WRYGHT continued
Thomas, Great Ashfield, 1498. R2/13/110
Thomas, Groton, 1504. R2/12/28
Thomas, labourer, Kirtling, 1536. R2/18/109
Thomas, husb., Lakenheath, 1553. R2/31/196; W1/21/215
William, the elder, Bradfield St. George, 1557. R2/26/322; W1/20/243
William, Bury St. Edmunds, 1573. A5/1/259
William, oatmeal maker, Nowton, 1587. R2/40/121; W1/44/3b; A5/2/97
William, Soham, 1540. R2/20/266; W1/4/200
William, Soham, 1592. R2/42/188; W1/49/10
WRYGTH, John, Groton, 1502. R2/11/231
Robert, Bury St. Edmunds, 1367. R2/1/20
Roger, Thrandeston, 1487. R2/11/404
Simon, Bury St. Edmunds, 1396. R2/1/76
Thomas, Bury St. Edmunds, 1396. R2/1/80
Thomas, Stuston, 1464. R2/10/359
WRYHT, John, Wickham Skeith, 1464. R2/10/372
WRYTE, Robert, Long Melford, 1484. R2/11/366
William, Bradfield St. George, 1573. R2/36/182
WRYTH, John, Lindsey, 1506. R2/13/168
Richard, barber, Bury St. Edmunds, 1497. R2/4/60
William, Great Bradley, 1450. R2/9/122
WRYTTE, Alice, Groton, (1504). W1/7/20
WUDHALL, William, parson, Knettishall, 1540. R2/20/198
WULFE, John, yeo., Bury St. Edmunds, 1564. R2/8/391; W1/17/11
Ralph, gent., Thurton, 1535. W1/51/31
WULSTON, Henry, Great Cornard, 1558. R2/27/193
WULWARD, Alice, wid., Sudbury, (1508). R2/13/199
Thomas, Bildeston, (1497). R2/13/65; W1/24/146
WURDE, Thomas, als. Fourde, woollen draper, Bury St. Edmunds, 1563. R2/8/380; W1/17/26
---, wid., Bury St. Edmunds, 1582. W1/41/14
WURTHAM, Margaret, wife of Thomas, Sudbury, 1480. R2/12/7
Thomas, Sudbury, 1482. R2/11/250
WYAND, John, Kirtling, 1693. A5/6/156, A4/35/81
WYARD, Elisabeth, wid., Horningsheath, 1675. R2/66/192; W1/127/68
Henry, yeo., Great Horningsheath, 1689. R2/71/187; W1/143/42
William, Horningsheath, 1694. In. 3/26/59; A5/6/169, A4/37/39
see also Wiard
WYATT, Allan, glazier, Newmarket, 1675. R2/66/180; W1/127/54; In. 3/16/62
Isaac, carpenter, Sudbury, 1700. R2/74/60; W1/154/58
John, Isleham, 1556. W7/6
Martha, Newmarket, 1682. R2/68/424; W1/136/116; In. 3/21/106
Richard, Stanningfield, 1589. A5/2/117a
Thomas, yeo., Kedington, 1629. R2/54/335; W1/85/42
William, Preston, 1464. R2/10/366
see also Wiat, Wiet, Wyett, Wyot
WYBARD, John, chaplain, Westhorpe, 1361. R2/1/10
WYBEROWE, William, Denston, 1540. R2/21/358; W1/38/84
WYBOROWE, Edward, labourer, Isleham, 1630. R6/58
Joan, wid., Isleham, 1620. R6/21
John, Isleham, 1650. A4/1/3
John, husb., Withersfield, 1638, (N). R2/57/371; W1/93/173
Robert, Milden, 1649. A5/4/127
William, Isleham, 1556. W7/1
William, Isleham, 1625. R6/38
William, yeo., Isleham, 1626. R6/40
WYBROUGH, Robert, maltster, Great Fakenham, 1682. R2/68/391; W1/136/92; In. 3/21/86
WYBROW, William, yeo., Isleham, 1697. W7/131; In. 9/99
WYBURGH, John, cordwainer, Bury St. Edmunds, 1470. R2/2/136
William, Denston, 1473. R2/10/579
see also Wiborowe
WYCKES, Clement, Great Livermere, 1545. R2/19/514; W1/7/34
Elisabeth, wid., Stowmarket, 1601. R2/44/411; W1/59/86
Joan, wid. of Robert, Snailwell, 1559. R2/28/271

WYCKES continued
John, labourer, Ingham, 1590. R2/41/433; W1/47/116
Margaret, wid., Ingham, 1591. R2/42/41; W1/48/33
Robert, Snailwell, 1558. R2/27/33; W1/31/23
WYDER, Alice, Elmswell, (1521). R2/14/43
WYDHAM, Nicholas, Bury St. Edmunds, 1445. R2/2/15
WYDRYSSE, Thomas, Mildenhall, 1554. R2/24/92; W1/14/71
WYDYE, John, Chippenham, 1554, (N). R2/24/120; W1/14/92
WYETT, James, Clare, 1667. In. 3/12/26; A5/5/82, A4/5/13
John, Stuston, 1595. R2/43/14; W1/53/14
Thomas, Burwell, 1635. A5/4/35
Thomas, Isleham, 1560. W7/16
Thomas, Redgrave, 1626. R2/53/547; W1/82/72
William, Brandon, 1544. A5/1/52
William, Burwell, 1544. R2/19/443
WYFF, John, Cockfield, 1451. R2/9/105
WYFFEN, John, Great Wratting, 1544. R2/21/602
John, Hundon, 1590. R2/41/362; W1/47/59
Richard, Timworth, 1549. R2/21/142 & 625; W1/9/73, W1/28/136
Simon, Lawshall, 1568. A5/1/201
William, Stoke by Clare, 1558. R2/27/169
William, yeo., Whepstead, 1623. R2/52/617; W1/79/62b
WYFFYN, Edony, wife of William, Hawstead, 1522. R2/14/61
Giles, husb., Hawstead, 1544. R2/19/469
John, the elder, husb., Great Wratting, 1542. R2/22/87; W1/6/35
Margaret, wid., Bury St. Edmunds, 1597. R2/43/264; W1/55/43
Margaret, wid., Great Thurlow, 1565. R2/32/242; W1/27/137
Richard, Kedington, 1579. A5/2/16
William, the elder, Bury St. Edmunds, 1557. R2/8/299; W1/18/28
William, Hawstead, 1467. W1/23/107
William, the elder, Hawstead, 1506. R2/13/171
William, husb., Hawstead, 1528. R2/15/217; W1/19/30
William, als. Badson, Stowmarket, 1557. R2/26/35; W1/20/15
WYGENALE, John, Boxford, 1496. R2/13/32
Roger, Boxford, 1441. R2/9/22
WYGENHALE, Marion, Bury St. Edmunds, 1431. R2/1/197
WYGER, John, chaplain, Bury St. Edmunds, 1462. R2/2/71
WYGNALL, Richard, husb., Polstead, 1552. R2/31/33; W1/13/22
William, Stoke by Nayland, 1569. R2/33/106
WYKES, Agnes, Troston, 1557. R2/26/276; W1/20/194
Joan, wid., Troston, 1557. R2/26/272; W1/20/189
John, the younger, Great Livermere, 1542. R2/22/63; W1/6/52
John, husb., Great Livermere, 1543. R2/19/372
Matthew, labourer, Little Cornard, 1553. R2/31/14; W1/13/9
Ralph, als. Mone, baker, Bury St. Edmunds, 1492. R2/4/4
Robert, husb., Timworth, 1569. R2/33/117; W1/28/182
William, Redgrave, (1504). W1/7/16
William, Troston, 1543. R2/22/48; W1/6/169
see also Wicks, Wikes, Wyckes, Wykys
WYKHAM, John, Great Horningsheath, 1453. R2/9/151
John, Wickhambrook, 1461. R2/9/292
WYKYS, John, Fordham, 1484. R2/11/346
WYLBY, William, Thorndon, 1473. R2/11/5
WYLCHYN, Thomas, brick maker, Gislingham, 1559. R2/28/273; W1/22/215
William, Gislingham, 1458. R2/9/196
WYLCOKE, Richard, cordwainer, Sudbury, 1558. R2/27/43; W1/21/159
WYLES, Cicely, wid., Combs, 1624. R2/53/37; W1/80/53
Fortune, wid., Hopton, 1667. In. 3/12/198; A5/5/84, A4/5/36
Richard, yeo., Whatfield, 1640. R2/58/179; W1/96/97
Thomas, husb., Stoke by Nayland, 1522. R2/15/42
William, Combs, 1561. A5/1/110
William, husb., Combs, 1613. R2/48/255; W1/70/28
see also Wiles
WYLKEN, Edward, thatcher, Soham, 1589. R2/41/227; W1/46/63
WYLKENSON, John, Bury St. Edmunds, 1595. A5/2/205

WYLKYN, John, Burwell, 1452. R2/9/147
John, the elder, Burwell, (1480). R2/11/221
John, Burwell, 1530. R2/19/23
Laurence, reeder, Bury St. Edmunds, 1421. R2/1/156
Margaret, wid., Burwell, 1476. R2/11/56
Robert, Burwell, 1458. R2/9/212
Thomas, yeo., Pakenham, 1586. R2/40/23; W1/43/16
William, Burwell, 1474. R2/10/513
WYLKYNSON, John, Stoke, 1504. W1/7/13
WYLLAM, Thomas, Exning, 1569. A5/1/209
WYLLES, John, Acton, 1580. A5/2/22
WYLLETT, John, Great Thornham, 1559. R2/28/193; W1/22/171
John, Stradishall, 1511. W1/9/36
Thomas, Wyverstone, 1552. R2/23/174; W1/12/10
WYLLEYS, Alice, Mildenhall, 1545. A5/1/62
WYLLING, Agnes, als. Senyhall, Bury St. Edmunds, (1559) W1/17/53
WYLLINGTON, John, Brandon, 1525. W1/21/120b
William, Brandon, 1525. R2/17/124
WYLLIYAMSON, Margery, Redgrave, 1559. R2/28/237
WYLLOOMES, Margery, Exning, 1587. R2/40/124; W1/44/7
WYLLOTT, Robert, Euston, 1561. A5/1/118
WYLLSON, Christopher, labourer, Icklingham, 1567. R2/32/409; W1/19/114
John, mariner, Dunwich, 1574. W1/51/193
John, husb., Lakenheath, 1572. R2/36/45; W1/31/99
WYLLYAMSONE, William, woollen draper, Soham, 1557. R2/26/246; W1/20/161
WYLLYHAM, Beatrice, Brandon, 1442. R2/9/18
WYLLYMOT, John, fuller, Lavenham, 1477. R2/11/86
Thomas, Lavenham, 1460. R2/9/304
WYLLYS, Isabel, Acton, 1571. R2/35/69; W1/36/62
Thomas, jun., Bury St. Edmunds, 1560. R2/8/353; W1/17/52
WYLLYSON, Helen, wid., Semer, 1568. A5/1/201
John, Semer, 1561. A5/1/111
WYLNOTH, Ralph, Sapiston, 1477. R2/11/100
WYLSON, John, yeo., Icklingham, 1558. R2/27/519
John, Mendlesham, 1499. W1/24/194
Margaret, wid., Brandon, (1507). R2/13/196
Thomas, Brandon, 1558. W1/7/124
Thomas, als. Andrew, husb., Wyverstone, 1565. R2/32/348; W1/27/170
WYLTON, Roger, labourer, Chelsworth, 1561. R2/42/111; W1/28/261
Thomas, Hessett, 1523. R2/14/80
WYLTOON, Walter, husb., Beyton, 1504. R2/13/155
WYLYAM, William, Exning, 1505. R2/13/163
WYMAN, Henry, Burwell, 1698. A5/7/8
WYMARK(E), Ann, wid., Dalham, 1637. A5/4/55
Ann, wid., Dalham, 1683. A5/6/71, A4/20/76
Christopher, yeo., Cheveley, 1604. R2/45/368; W1/62/96
Christopher, Kirtling, 1693. A5/6/158, A4/35/70
Edward, draper, Bury St. Edmunds, 1521. R2/6/85
Edward, yeo., Dalham, 1600. R2/45/56; W1/58/79
Edward, blacksmith, Lakenheath, 1631. R2/56/58; W1/87/83
George, yeo., Long Melford, 1691. R2/71/500; W1/145/62
James, yeo., Cheveley, 1635. R2/56/529; W1/91/112
John, Assington, 1681. A5/6/47, A4/18/44
John, Bury St. Edmunds, 1428. R2/1/187
John, Bury St. Edmunds, 1482. R2/2/331
John, Cheveley, 1582. R2/38/287; W1/40/33
John, husb., Chevington, 1559. R2/28/93; W1/22/92
John, collar maker, Chevington, 1660. R2/62/90; W1/112/119; In. 3/5/138
John, yeo., Dalham, 1628. R2/54/216; W1/84/80
John, yeo., Little Saxham, 1652. R2/61/535; W1/109/20
Ralph, yeo., Cheveley, 1609. R2/47/114; W1/66/130
Thomas, yeo., Denham, 1631, (N). R2/56/73; W1/87/110
William, yeo., Chevington, 1598. R2/44/136; W1/56/98
William, the elder, Kirtling, 1648, (N). R2/60/66; W1/105/83
see also Whymercke, Wimarke

WYMBYLL, Bartholomew, Langham, 1494. R2/13/72
Isabel, wid., Pakenham, 1527. R2/12/148
Joan, Hunston, 1459. R2/9/242
Richard, husb., Pakenham, 1525. R2/12/134, R2/17/125; W1/21/121
WYMBYSCH, Henry, Kentford, 1503. R2/13/136
John, Cowlinge, 1561. R2/30/94; W1/28/266
John, sen., Kentford, 1443. R2/9/51
Margery, wid., Kentford, 1457. R2/9/222
WYMBYSH, Alice, Buxhall, 1494. R2/11/448
Henry, Kentford, 1473. R2/11/13
Stephen, Buxhall, 1470. R2/10/432
William, Kentford, 1439. R2/9/7; W1/24/118b
WYMER, Agnes, wid., Honington, 1565. R2/32/225
Barbara, wid., Honington, 1620. R2/52/34; W1/76/31
Davy, Honington, 1450. W1/24/68
John, Honington, 1459. R2/9/257
Katherine, wid., Honington, 1476. R2/11/96
Margery, Honington, 1451. R2/9/113
Michael, Honington, 1473. R2/11/16
Rose, Honington, 1458. R2/9/196
William, Honington, 1557. R2/25/162; W1/16/152
WYMNUNDHAM, Richard, chaplain, 1473. R2/11/4
see also Wyndym
WYNCH, John, Long Melford, 1593. A5/2/184
John, the elder, Stanstead, 1547. R2/21/343
Thomas, blacksmith, Stoke by Clare, 1636. R2/57/8; W1/92/12
WYNCHESTER, Thomas, Bury St. Edmunds, 1476. R2/2/228
William, Bury St. Edmunds, 1468. R2/2/120
WYNCHESTRE, Thomas, knight, Mendlesham, 1393. R2/1/62
WYNCHESTYR, Edmund, priest, Bury St. Edmunds, 1500. R2/4/103
WYNCK, Margaret, Old Newton, 1595. A5/2/206
WYNCOLL, John, gent., Little Waldingfield, 1576. R2/37/222; W1/37/82
see also Wincol
WYNDE, John, Honington, 1482. R2/11/270; W1/24/114
Margaret, wife of John, Pakenham, 1461. R2/9/295
Margaret, wife of Walter, Rickinghall Superior, 1494. R2/13/29
Roger, Ingham, 1578. A5/2/8
WYNDOUT, Andrew, Mildenhall, 1639. A5/4/72
Stephen, yeo., Bardwell, 1624. R2/53/171; W1/80/149
Stephen, cordwainer, Bardwell, 1629. R2/54/389; W1/85/83
WYNDOWGHT, Christian, wid., Bardwell, 1560. R2/29/2
WYNDOWTE, Thomas, Bardwell, 1503. R2/12/51
WYNDYM, William, Stansfield, 1529. W1/311/1
WYNEFE, Mary, wid., Brettenham, 1620. R2/52/174; W1/76/156
WYNEVE, John, Troston, 1478. R2/11/180
WYNEYEVE, Elisabeth, Troston, 1469. R2/10/429a
WYNYEVE, William, Troston, 1494. R2/13/28
WYNG, Francis, the elder, husb., Mildenhall, 1578. R2/37/336; W1/36/238
Francis, Mildenhall, 1595. A5/2/208
Francis, the elder, Mildenhall, 1619. R2/51/260; W1/132/5
John, the elder, Mildenhall, 1610. R2/47/282; W1/67/168
John, Mildenhall, 1640. R2/58/161; W1/96/69
Richard, singleman, Mildenhall, 1625. R2/53/261; W1/81/51
Thomas, husb., Mildenhall, 1586. R2/40/41; W1/43/29
William, Layham, 1598. R2/44/34; W1/56/36
WYNGFYLD, Thomas, Stalham, 1575. W1/51/219
WYNKE, Thomas, Old Newton, 1592. R2/42/182
William, husb., Bacton, 1610. R2/47/122; W1/67/7
WYNNE, Henry, weaver, Sudbury, 1587. R2/40/284; W1/44/114
see also Whin, Winn
WYNNEY, John, yeo., Troston, 1584. R2/39/170; W1/42/142
WYNNOW, Elinor, wid., Coney Weston, 1571. R2/35/245; W1/38/150
Robert, yeo., Coney Weston, 1617. R2/50/314; W1/74/102
WYNNYFF, Roger, Hitcham, 1565. R2/32/173; W1/27/111
Thomas, Brettenham, 1479. R2/11/163

WYNTER, Adam, Bury St. Edmunds, 1471. R2/2/148
Elisabeth, wid., Downham, 1610. R2/47/156; W1/67/37
Elisabeth, Rushbrook, 1611. A5/3/109
George, Worlington, 1559. R2/28/96; W1/22/94
John, Bury St. Edmunds, 1638. A5/4/64
John, yeo., Rushbrook, 1611. R2/47/316; W1/68/13
Nicholas, tanner, Bury St. Edmunds, 1579. R2/38/68; W1/39/14
Richard, husb., Little Bradley, 1545. R2/19/550; W1/7/72
Robert, Herringswell, 1543. R2/19/355; W1/6/164
Thomas, Bury St. Edmunds, 1632, (N). R2/56/204; W1/89/120
Thomas, Sudbury, 1608. A5/3/42
Walter, Wood Ditton, 1526. R2/12/141, R2/17/166; W1/23/67
WYNTOR, John, Bury St. Edmunds, 1500. R2/4/108
WYNTUR, William, Westhorpe, 1537. R2/18/152
WYNTYR, Nicholas, Chedburgh, 1494. R2/13/17
Richard, Soham, 1471. R2/10/481
WYOT, Alice, Burwell, 1560. R2/29/149; W1/25/25
John, Burwell, 1444. R2/9/45
John, yeo., Burwell, 1557. R2/26/311; W1/20/233
Margaret, wid. of Thomas, Burwell, 1520. R2/15/77
Robert, Burwell, 1476. R2/11/120
Robert, Bury St. Edmunds, 1466. R2/2/93
Robert, Exning, 1444. R2/9/52
Thomas, Burwell, 1506. R2/13/177
WYRLYNGWORTH, Robert, parson, Coney Weston, 1396. R2/1/83
WYRLYCH, John, Bury St. Edmunds, 1500. R2/4/99
WYRYTHE, Thomas, rough mason, Elmswell, 1545. W1/7/114
WYSBECHE, William, glasswright, Bury St. Edmunds, 1466. R2/2/94
WYSBISHE, Henry, wheelwright, Barnardiston, 1590. R2/41/381; W1/47/74
WYSBYCHE, John, Brandon, 1461. R2/9/293
WYSCHE, Joan, wid., Bury St. Edmunds, 1553. R2/31/206
WYSEMAN, Nicholas, Great Livermere, 1476. R2/11/75
Richard, wid., Wickhambrook, 1684. A5/6/75, A4/21/20
Robert, Brockford, 1531. R2/19/85
Simon, Rickinghall Superior, 1487. R2/13/30
William, parson, gent., Great Thornham, 1558. R2/27/285
William, husb., Rede, 1580. R2/38/194; W1/39/113
WYSKYN, Thomas, Hundon, 1457. R2/9/192
WYSSHE, Henry, smith, Bury St. Edmunds, 1538. R2/7/48
WYSTOWES, Jasper, Sudbury, 1562. A5/1/136
WYTEHAND, John, jun., Eriswell, ----. W1/24/25
WYTH, Thomas, mercer, Bury St. Edmunds, 1643. R2/59/32; W1/100/43
Thomas, Haughley, 1536. R2/19/258
Robert, chaplain, Colkirk, 1361. R2/1/8
Robert, Creeting, 1476. R2/11/54
WYTHCHERCH, Nicholas, Wicken, 1470. R2/10/445
WYTHERBY, John, the elder, yeo., Haughley, 1600. R2/45/6; W1/58/9
WYTHERELD, William, Brockford, 1475. R2/11/69
WYTHER(S), Edmund, haberdasher, Bury St. Edmunds, 1589. R2/41/137; W1/46/140
John, shepherd, Rushbrook, 1592, (N). R2/42/253; W1/49/71
John, yeo., Stowlangtoft, 1600. R2/45/57; W1/58/80
Samuel, cooper, Brockford, 1664. R2/63/242; W1/116/164; In. 3/9/240
Thomas, yeo., Norton, 1640. R2/58/217; W1/96/154
Thomas, draper, Rickinghall Inferior, 1558. R2/27/67
WYTHERSBEY, Elisabeth, als. Clopton, wid. of Robert, gent., Sudbury, 1564. R2/32/79; W1/27/31
WYTMAN, Simon, Combs, 1552. R2/23/225, R2/32/444; W1/12/43, W1/19/60b
WYTTE, John, husb., Wortham, 1591. R2/42/123; W1/48/114
WYTTELOK, Cecily, wid., Norton, 1477. R2/11/123
WYTTEWYLL, Thomas, Mildenhall, 1510. W1/9/31
Thomas, Mildenhall, 1520. R2/15/68
WYTTYNGHAM, Margaret, wid., 1529. R2/18/18
WYXE, Henry, Troston, 1550. R2/21/84
John, sen., yeo., Troston, 1587. R2/40/167; W1/44/40
William, Soham, 1563. A5/1/145

Y

YAKESLEY, Richard, Soham, 1460. R2/9/270
YARDLEY, John, Lidgate, 1462. R2/9/301
YARDLIE, Andrew, Fordham, 1590. A5/2/139
see also Yerdlie
YARROW, Philip, Soham, 1690. A5/6/132, A4/32/16
YATES, James, Bury St. Edmunds, 1584. A5/2/54
see also Yeates
YAXLEE, Richard, husb., Soham, 1555. R2/24/143; W1/15/96
YAXLEY, Harry, the elder, Soham, (1547). R2/21/136; W1/9/72
Henry, husb., Soham, 1591. R2/42/49; W1/48/41
Henry, singleman, shoe maker, Soham, 1606. R2/46/52; W1/64/67
Margaret, wid., Soham, 1552. R2/23/211; W1/12/37
Richard, Soham, 1535. R2/19/579 & 581
Robert, husb., Soham, 1554. R2/24/126; W1/14/100
Rose, Soham, 1649. A5/4/128
Thomas, Soham, 1524. R2/23/68; W1/21/24
William, yeo., Lavenham, 1625. R2/53/393; W1/81/174
William, Soham, (1528). R2/15/212, R2/17/285
YAXLIE, Henry, the elder, yeo., Soham, 1579. R2/38/70; W1/39/12
YAXLY, Anthony, Mellis, 1581. A5/2/31
Henry, Soham, 1558. R2/27/157; W1/7/126
Margaret, wid., Soham, 1605. R2/45/419; W1/63/65
see also Yakesley
YDEYNE, Cicely, Burwell, 1435. R2/9/277
Cicely, Burwell, 1460. R2/9/302
YEATES, John, clerk, Worlington, 1597. R2/43/363; W1/55/126
YEBYSWYCHE, George, Burgate, 1503. R2/12/58
YELDHAM, John, Bury St. Edmunds, 1449. R2/2/31
Thomas, lister, Bury St. Edmunds, 1421. R2/1/153
YELLOPP, Esther, spinster, Haughley, 1662. R2/62/311; W1/114/7
YEMAN, William, Gazeley, 1558. R2/27/451
YEMAYN, Alice, wid., Gazeley, 1523. R2/17/35; W1/21/51
YENGS, Grace, wid., Horningsheath, 1688. R2/71/122; W1/142/110
YEOMAN, John, weaver, Boxford, 1598. R2/44/33; W1/56/32
see also Yeman, Yoman
YEOMANSON, Henry, yeo., Stanningfield, 1631. R2/56/80; W1/87/121
YERDLIE, George, Fordham, 1571. R2/35/131; W1/36/83
YERDLY, John, Fordham, 1576. R2/37/177; W1/37/43; In. 3/1/62
YERMOUTH, Amy, wife of William, Norwich, (1516). W1/51/59
YESTAS, Catherine, Mendlesham, 1475. R2/11/111
Edward, Thrandeston, 1560. R2/29/78
Edward, husb., Wickham Skeith, 1582. R2/38/416; W1/41/19
Edward, husb., Wickham Skeith, 1635. R2/56/500; W1/91/77
John, Eye, 1475. R2/11/97
John, Thorndon, 1462. R2/10/326
John, ploughwright, Thrandeston, 1638. R2/57/313; W1/93/89
Mary, wife of Edward, Wickham Skeith, 1612, (N). R2/48/189; W1/69/74; A5/3/118
Robert, Mendlesham, 1471. R2/10/574
William, yeo., Stuston, 1661. R2/62/226; W1/113/96
YEWNGE, Thomas, Downham, 1535. R2/18/138
YLONDE, Richard, Boxted, 1505. R2/13/158
YMMINSON, William, 1631, (N). R2/56/80; W1/87/120
YNGERAM, William, Stoke by Nayland, 1450. R2/9/117
YNGHAM, John, shoe maker, Mellis, (1544). R2/21/600; A5/1/13
YNGOME, Robert, thatcher, Ashfield, 1573. R2/36/137; W1/32/42
YNNEN, Robert, Gazeley, 1571. A5/1/241
YOLE, John, Bury St. Edmunds, 1535. R2/7/27

YOMAN, Elisabeth, Boxford, 1604. R2/45/339; W1/62/54
YON, John, Lawshall, 1453. R2/9/147
YONGE, Henry, yeo., Elmswell, 1617. R2/50/290; W1/74/84
Henry, labourer, Mildenhall, 1592. R2/42/197; W1/49/22
John, cooper, Bury St. Edmunds, 1477. R2/2/233
John, Bury St. Edmunds, 1479. R2/2/281
John, Rickinghall Superior, 1471. R2/10/475
John, Rickinghall Superior, 1570. R5/1/219
Richard, mercer, Bury St. Edmunds, 1635. R2/56/440; W1/91/4
Robert, Bury St. Edmunds, 1473. R2/2/169
Simon, Rickinghall Superior, 1450. R2/9/124; W1/24/129
Simon, Rickinghall Superior, 1505. R2/12/39
William, baker, Bury St. Edmunds, 1466. R2/2/91
YONGEMAN, Agnes, wid., Bury St. Edmunds, 1456. R2/2/54
YONGMAN, Thomas, currier, Bury St. Edmunds, 1452. R2/2/35
YONGS, Joan, wid., Rickinghall, 1591. R2/42/112; W1/48/121
John, the elder, husb., Lakenheath, 1624. R2/53/128; W1/80/124
John, Mellis, 1608. R2/46/194; W1/65/63
John, husb., Redgrave, 1586. R2/40/85; W1/43/65
John, sen., Rickinghall Superior, 1559. R2/28/309; W1/22/281
John, Rickinghall Superior, 1570. R2/34/3; W1/30/2
Robert, Haughley, 1612. A5/3/116
Rose, wid., Rickinghall Superior, 1557. R2/26/116; W1/20/68
Stephen, Stanton, 1590. A5/2/134
Thomas, yeo., Haughley, 1606. R2/46/16; W1/64/19
Thomas, Rickinghall Superior, 1566. A5/1/183
Thomas, Stowmarket, 1588. A5/2/105b
William, husb., Lakenheath, 1612. R2/48/137; W1/69/19
YONGYS, Richard, Wetheringsett, 1542. R2/22/61 & 71; W1/6/53
YOOLE, Richard, the elder, Bury St. Edmunds, 1514. R2/6/7
YORKE, John, cordwainer, Bury St. Edmunds, 1399. R2/1/86
Kathleen, wid., Chevington, 1546. R2/21/631; W1/28/130
William, Wetherden, 1632. A5/4/20
YOUNG, Arthur, gent., Bradfield St. George, 1694. R2/72/306; W1/148/33
Audrey, wid., Mildenhall, 1630, (N). R2/55/38; W1/86/43
Francis, Stansfield, 1665. A5/5/66, A4/3/23
Henry, grocer, Stowmarket, 1680. R2/67/731; W1/134/172; In. 3/20/185
James, husb., Polstead, 1568. R2/33/46; W1/29/58
John, Downham, 1445. R2/9/92
John, clerk, Great Saxham, 1675. R2/66/260; W1/127/128; In. 3/16/165
Richard, Bury St. Edmunds, 1633. A5/4/23
Robert, husb., Barnham, 1665. R2/63/279; W1/117/6; In. 3/10/56
Roger, clerk, Lavenham, 1688. A5/6/118, A4/29/21
Thomas, gent., Barningham, 1688. R2/71/57; W1/142/51
Thomas, gent., Brandon, 1691. R2/71/536; W1/145/93
Thomas, Bury St. Edmunds, 1569. A5/1/214
William, Haughley, 1545. A5/1/57
see also Yewynge, Yonge, Yownge
YOUNGMAN, Adam, miller, Hopton, 1682. R2/68/274; W1/136/12; In. 3/21/222
Charles, Walsham le Willows, 1691. A5/6/145, A4/33/81
John, Botesdale, 1682. A5/6/58, A4/19/30
Jonathan, yeo., Hepworth, 1699. R2/73/400; W1/153/44
see also Yongeman, Yungman
YOUNGS, Edmund, tailor, Bury St. Edmunds, 1556. W1/18/9
Elisabeth, wid., Barnham, 1682. In. 3/21/10; A5/6/65, A4/19/107
Elisabeth, spinster, Hepworth, 1672. A5/5/129, A4/9/13
John, husb., Mildenhall, 1637. R2/57/202; W1/92/241
John, Stanton, 1573. A5/1/257
Richard, shepherd, Barnham, 1661. In. 3/6/26; A5/5/12, A4/1/131

YOUNGS continued
Richard, shepherd, Eriswell, 1680. R2/67/763; W1/134/195; In. 3/20/214
Simon, shepherd, Barnham, 1675. R2/66/234; W1/127/106; In. 3/16/137
see also Yengs, Yongs
YOWLE, Martin, weaver, Drinkstone, 1600. R2/45/61; W1/58/85
YOWDE, John, sen., Haverhill, 1472. R2/10/541
YOWNGE, John, the elder, Mildenhall, 1555. R2/24/188; W1/15/23
YOXFORD, John, chaplain, Bury St. Edmunds, 1394. R2/1/63
Thomas, Bury St. Edmunds, 1390. R2/1/54
YUNGMAN, Nicholas, Hopton, 1452. R2/9/134
YVE, Henry, Little Waldingfield, 1460. R2/9/304
Robert, Troston, 1539. R2/19/295 & 601; W1/5/75
Thomas, Honington, 1503. R2/12/71

INDEX OF PLACE NAMES

An asterisk indicates that more than one reference occurs on a page, unless such multiple entries occur in sequence.

The term passim is used when references occur on all, or nearly all pages.

BERKSHIRE

CAMBRIDGESHIRE

WEST MIDLANDS

INDEX OF TRADES AND CONDITIONS

An asterisk indicates that more than one reference occurs on a page, unless such multiple entries occur in sequence.

The term passim is used when references occur on all, or nearly all pages.